SOFTWARE ENGINEERING ·
A Practitioner's Approach

McGraw-Hill Series in Computer Science

SENIOR CONSULTING EDITOR
C.L. Liu, *University of Illinois at Urbana-Champaign*

CONSULTING EDITOR
Allen B. Tucker, *Bowdoin College*

Fundamentals of Computing and Programming
Computer Organization and Architecture
Computers in Society/Ethics
Systems and Languages
Theoretical Foundations
Software Engineering and Database
Artificial Intelligence
Networks, Parallel and Distributed Computing
Graphics and Visualization
The MIT Electrical and Computer Science Series

Software Engineering and Database

Ceri and Palagatti: Distributed Databases: Principles and Systems
Cohen: Ada as a Second Language
Fairley: Software Engineering Concepts
Jones: Programming Productivity
Korth and Silberschatz: Database System Concepts
Musa, Iannino, and Okumoto: Software Reliability
Pressman: Software Engineering: A Beginner's Guide
Pressman: Software Engineering: A Practitioner's Approach
Wiederhold: Database Design

SOFTWARE ENGINEERING

A PRACTITIONER'S APPROACH

FOURTH EDITION

Roger S. Pressman, Ph.D.

The McGraw-Hill Companies, Inc.
New York   St. Louis   San Francisco   Auckland   Bogotá
Caracas   Lisbon   London   Madrid   Mexico City   Milan
Montreal   New Delhi   San Juan   Singapore
Sydney   Tokyo   Toronto

McGraw-Hill
A Division of The **McGraw·Hill** Companies

To my parents

SOFTWARE ENGINEERING:
A PRACTITIONER'S APPROACH

4 5 6 7 8 9 0   FGR FGR 9 0 9 8

ISBN 0-07-052182-4

This book was set in New Century Schoolbook by York Graphic Services, Inc.
The editor was Eric M. Munson;
The production supervisor was Annette Mayeski.
Cover illustration and design by Joseph Gillians
New drawings were done by York Production Services.
Project supervision was done by York Production Services.
Quebecor Printing/Fairfield was printer and binder.
Library of Congress Cataloging-in-Publication Data is available.
LC Card #96-77396

International Edition
Copyright 1997. Exclusive rights by The McGraw-Hill Companies, Inc. for manufacture and export. This book cannot be re-exported from the country to which it is consigned by McGraw-Hill. The International Edition is not available in North America.
When ordering this title, use ISBN 0-07-114603-2.

Roger S. Pressman is an internationally recognized consultant and author in software engineering. He received a B.S.E. (cum laude) from the University of Connecticut, an M.S. from the University of Bridgeport and a Ph.D. in engineering from the University of Connecticut, and has over 25 years of industry experience, holding both technical and management positions with responsibility for the development of software for engineered products and systems.

As an industry practitioner and manager, Dr. Pressman worked on the development of CAD/CAM systems for advanced engineering and manufacturing in aerospace applications. He has also held positions with responsibility for scientific and systems programming.

In addition to his industry experience, Dr. Pressman was Bullard Associate Professor of Computer Engineering at the University of Bridgeport and Director of the University's Computer-Aided Design and Manufacturing Center.

Dr. Pressman is President of R.S. Pressman & Associates, Inc., a consulting firm specializing in software engineering methods and training. He serves as principal consultant, specializing in helping companies establish effective software engineering practices. He developed the RSP&A software engineering assessment method, a unique blend of quantitative and qualitative analysis that helps clients assess their current state of software engineering practice.

In addition to consulting services rendered to many Fortune 500 clients, R.S. Pressman & Associates, Inc. markets a wide variety of software engineering training products and process improvement services. The company has developed a state-of-the-art video curriculum, *Essential Software Engineering*, which is among the industry's most comprehensive treatments of the subject.

Another product, *Process Advisor,* is a self-directed system for software process improvement.

Dr. Pressman is author of many technical papers, is a regular contributor to industry periodicals, and is author of six books. In addition to *Software Engineering: A Practitioner's Approach,* he has written *Making Software Engineering Happen* (Prentice Hall), the first book to address the critical management problems associated with software engineering process improvement, *Software Shock* (Dorset House), a treatment of software and its impact on business and society, and *A Manager's Guide to Software Engineering* (McGraw-Hill), a book that uses a unique Q&A format to present management guidelines for instituting and understanding the technology. Dr. Pressman is on the editorial boards of *American Programmer* and *IEEE Software,* and is editor of the "Manager" column in *IEEE Software*. He is a member of the ACM, IEEE, and Tau Beta Pi, Phi Kappa Phi, Eta Kappa Nu, and Pi Tau Sigma.

CONTENTS AT A GLANCE

TABLE OF CONTENTS

PREFACE

As software engineering moves into its fourth decade of existence, it suffers from many of the strengths and some of the frailties that are experienced by humans of the same age. The innocence and enthusiasm of its early years have been replaced by more reasonable expectations (and even a healthy cynicism) fostered by years of experience. Software engineering approaches its midlife with many accomplishments, but with significant work yet to do. Today, it is recognized as a legitimate discipline, one worthy of serious research, conscientious study, and tumultuous debate. Throughout the industry, "software engineer" has replaced "programmer" as the job title of preference. Software process models, software engineering methods, and software tools have been adopted successfully across a broad spectrum of industry applications. Managers and practitioners alike recognize the need for a more disciplined approach to software.

But many of the problems discussed in earlier editions of this book remain with us. Many individuals and companies still develop software haphazardly. Many professionals and students are unaware of modern methods. And as a result, the quality of the software that we produce suffers. In addition, debate and controversy about the true nature of the software engineering approach continue. The status of software engineering is a study in contrasts. Attitudes have changed, progress has been made, but much remains to be done before the discipline reaches full maturity.

The fourth edition of *Software Engineering: A Practitioner's Approach* is intended to serve as a guide to a maturing engineering discipline. The fourth edition, like the three editions that have preceded it, is intended for both students and practitioners, and maintains the same format and style of its predecessors. The book retains its appeal as a guide to the industry professional and a comprehensive introduction to the student at the upper level undergraduate or first year graduate level.

The fourth edition is considerably more than a simple update. The book has been completely restructured to accommodate the dramatic growth in the field and to emphasize new and important software engineering methods. Chapters that have been retained from earlier editions have been revised and updated. Twelve new chapters have been added to provide more complete treatment of contemporary trends and techniques. Many new examples, problems and points to ponder have been included. The *Further Readings and Other Information Sources* sections (one of the more popular tidbits in earlier editions) have been expanded for every chapter. Hundreds of new published sources and over 160 sources from the World Wide Web[1] have been included.

The 30 chapters of the fourth edition have been organized into five parts. This has been done to compartmentalize topics and assist instructors who may not have the time to complete the entire book in one term. Part One, *The Product and the Process,* presents an introduction to the software engineering milieu. It is intended to introduce the subject matter and, more importantly, to present concepts that will be necessary for later chapters. Part Two, *Managing Software Projects,* presents topics that are relevant to those who plan, manage, and control a software development project. Part Three, *Conventional Methods for Software Engineering,* presents the analysis, design, and testing methods that some view as the "conventional" school of software engineering. Part Four, *Object-Oriented Software Engineering,* presents object-oriented methods across the entire software engineering process, including analysis, design, and testing. Part Five, *Advanced Software Engineering Topics,* presents dedicated chapters that address formal methods, cleanroom software engineering, reuse, reengineering, client/server software engineering, and CASE.

It is important to note that the fourth edition has a much greater emphasis on metrics and measurement than earlier editions. Three separate chapters on software metrics address measurement of the software process, technical metrics for analysis, design, and testing using conventional methods, and technical metrics for object-oriented software engineering.

The five-part organization of the fourth edition enables an instructor to cluster topics based on available time and student need. An entire one-term course can be built around one or more of the five parts. For example, a "design course" might emphasize only Part III or Part IV; a "methods course" might present selected chapters in Parts III, IV, and V. A "management course" would stress Parts I and II. By organizing the fourth edition in this way, I have attempted to provide an instructor with a number of teaching options.

---

[1]Because World Wide Web addresses change frequently, only those that are likely to persist have been noted in *Further Readings and Other Information Sources.* However, even these may become invalid as time passes. An up-to-date "hot list" of the URLs presented in this book can be found at **http://www.rspa.com.**

Like the first three editions, an *Instructor's Guide* for *Software Engineering: A Practitioner's Approach* is available from McGraw-Hill. The *Instructor's Guide* presents suggestions for conducting various types of software engineering courses, recommendations for a variety of software projects to be conducted in conjunction with a course, solutions to selected problems, and transparency masters to aid in teaching selected topics. In addition, a comprehensive video curriculum, *Essential Software Engineering,* is available to complement this book. The video curriculum has been designed for industry training and has been modularized to enable individual software engineering topics to be presented on an as-needed, when-needed basis. Further information on the video can be obtained by mailing the request card at the back of this book.[2]

My work on the four editions of *Software Engineering: A Practitioner's Approach* has been the longest continuing technical project of my life. Even when the writing stops, information extracted from the technical literature continues to be assimilated and organized. For this reason, my thanks to the many authors of books, papers, and articles as well as a new generation of contributors to electronic media (newsgroups and the World Wide Web) who have provided me with additional insight, ideas, and commentary over the past 15 years. Many have been referenced within the pages of each chapter. All deserve credit for their contribution to this rapidly evolving field. I also wish to thank the reviewers of the fourth edition: Frank H. Westervelt, Wayne State University; Steven A. Demurjian, The University of Connecticut; Chung Lee, California State Polytechnic University; Alan Davis, University of Colorado; Michael C. Mah, QSM Associates; Richard N. Taylor, University of California–Irvine; Osman Balci, Virginia Tech; James H. Cross, Auburn University; Warren Harrison, Portland State University; Mieczyslaw M. Kokar, Northeastern University. Their comments and criticism have been invaluable.

The content of the fourth edition of *Software Engineering: A Practitioner's Approach* has been shaped by industry professionals, university professors, and students who have used earlier editions of the book and have taken the time to communicate their suggestions, criticisms, and ideas. My thanks to each of you. In addition, my personal thanks go to our many industry clients throughout North America and Europe, who certainly teach me as much as or more than I can teach them.

As the editions of this book have evolved, my sons, Mathew and Michael, have grown from boys to men. Their maturity and character have been an inspiration to me. Nothing has filled me with more pride. And finally, to Barbara, my love and thanks for tolerating my travel schedule, understanding the evenings at the office, and encouraging still another edition of "the book."

Roger S. Pressman

---

[2]Instructors at accredited universities should see their *Instructor's Guide* for special options associated with the video curriculum. If the reply card is missing, please e-mail a request for information to **ESEinfo@rspa.com** or fax a request to R.S. Pressman & Associates, Inc. at (203) 799-1023.

PART ONE

THE PRODUCT AND THE PROCESS

In this part of *Software Engineering: A Practitioner's Approach* we consider the product that is to be engineered and the process that provides a framework for the engineering technology. In the chapters that follow, we address the following questions:

- What is computer software . . . really?
- Why do we struggle to build high quality computer-based systems?
- How can we categorize application domains for computer software?
- What myths about software still exist?
- What is a 'software process'?
- Is there a generic way to assess the quality of a process?
- What process models can be applied to software development?
- How do linear and iterative process models differ?
- What are their strengths and weaknesses?
- What advanced process models have been proposed for software engineering work?

Once these questions are answered, you'll be better prepared to understand the management and technical aspects of the engineering discipline to which the remainder of this book is dedicated.

CHAPTER 1

THE PRODUCT

Just after the first edition of this book was published in the early 1980s, a front page story in *Business Week* magazine trumpeted the following headline: "Software: The New Driving Force." The editors had absolutely no idea how right they would be. At that time, software was still an unknown to most of the general public. Mega-software companies like Microsoft didn't exist; computer superstores with 15,000 square feet dedicated to shrink-wrapped software products were unknown; the idea of 60-second TV commercials advertising computer operating systems would have been laughable; and the Internet was known to only a few researchers and academics. But in less than two decades, changes that have led to all of this (and much more) have come to pass.

Computer software has become a driving force. It is the engine that drives business decision making. It serves as the basis for modern scientific investigation and engineering problem solving. It is a key factor that differentiates modern products and services. It is embedded in systems of all kinds: transportation, medical, telecommunications, military, industrial processes, entertainment, office products, . . . the list is almost endless. Software is virtually inescapable in a modern world. And as we move into the twenty-first century, it will become the driver for new advances in everything from elementary education to genetic engineering.

All of this has changed the public perception of software. Computer programs are ubiquitous, and the public views them as a technological fact of life. In many instances, people bet their jobs, their comforts, their safety, their entertainment, their decisions, and their very lives on computer software. It better be right.

This book presents the technology that should be used by those who build computer software—people who must get it right. The technology encompasses a process, a set of methods, and an array of tools that we call *software engineering*.

1.1 THE EVOLVING ROLE OF SOFTWARE

Today, software takes on a dual role. It is a product, and at the same time, the vehicle for delivering a product. As a product, it delivers the computing potential embodied by computer hardware. Whether it resides within a cellular phone or operates inside a mainframe computer, software is an information transformer—producing, managing, acquiring, modifying, displaying, or transmitting information that can be as simple as a single bit or as complex as a multimedia simulation. As the vehicle used to deliver the product, software acts as the basis for the control of the computer (operating systems), the communication of information (networks), and the creation and control of other programs (software tools and environments).

Software delivers what many believe will be the most important product of the twenty-first century—information. Software transforms personal data (e.g., an individual's financial transactions) so that the data can be more useful in a local context; it manages business information to enhance competitiveness; it provides a gateway to worldwide information networks (e.g., the Internet); and it provides the means for acquiring information in all of its forms.

The role of computer software has undergone significant change through the second half of the twentieth century. Dramatic improvements in hardware performance, profound changes in computing architectures, vast increases in memory and storage capacity, and a wide variety of exotic input and output options have all precipitated more sophisticated and complex computer-based systems. Sophistication and complexity can produce dazzling results when a system succeeds, but they can also pose huge problems for those who must build complex systems.

Popular books published during the 1970s and 1980s provide useful historical insight into the changing perception of computers and software and their impact on our culture. Osborne [OSB79] characterized a "new industrial revolution." Toffler [TOF80] called the advent of microelectronics part of "the third wave of change" in human history, and Naisbitt [NAI82] predicted the transformation from an industrial society to an "information society." Feigenbaum and McCorduck [FEI83] suggested that information and knowledge (controlled by computers) would be the focal point for power in the twenty-first century, and Stoll [STO89] argued that the "electronic community" created by networks and software was the key to knowledge interchange throughout the world.

As the 1990s began, Toffler [TOF90] described a "power shift" in which old power structures (governmental, educational, industrial, economic, and military) disintegrate as computers and software lead to a "democratization of knowledge." Yourdon [YOU92] worried that U.S. companies might lose their competitive edge in software-related businesses and predicted "the decline and fall of the American programmer." Hammer and Champy [HAM93] argued that information technologies were to play a pivotal role in the "reengineering of the corporation." During the mid-1990s, the pervasiveness of computers and software spawned a rash of books by "neo-Luddites" (e.g., *Resisting the Virtual Life,* edited by James Brook and Iain Boal, and *The Future Does Not Compute* by Stephen Talbot). These authors demonize the computer, emphasizing legitimate concerns but ignoring the profound benefits that have already been realized [LEV95].

During the early years of the computer era, software was viewed by many an afterthought. Computer programming was a "seat-of-the-pants" art for which few systematic methods existed. Software development was virtually unmanaged—until schedules slipped or costs began to escalate. Then programmers scrambled to make things right, and with heroic effort, they often succeeded.

During the early years general-purpose hardware became commonplace. Software, on the other hand, was custom-designed for each application and had a relatively limited distribution. Product software (i.e., programs developed to be sold to one or more customers) was in its infancy. Most software was developed and ultimately used by the same person or organization. You wrote it, you got it running, and if it failed, you fixed it. Because job mobility was low, managers could rest assured that you'd be there when bugs were encountered. Because of this personalized software environment, design was an implicit process performed in one's head, and documentation was often nonexistent.

During the early years we learned much about the implementation of computer-based systems, but relatively little about computer system engineering. In fairness, however, we must acknowledge the many outstanding computer-based systems that were developed during this era. Some of these remain in use today and provide landmark achievements that continue to justify admiration.

The second era of computer system evolution spanned the decade from the mid-1960s to the late 1970s (Figure 1.1). Multiprogramming, multiuser systems introduced new concepts of human–machine interaction. Interactive techniques opened a new world of applications and new levels of hardware and software sophistication. Real-time systems could collect, analyze, and transform data from multiple sources, thereby controlling processes and producing output in milliseconds rather than minutes. Advances in on-line storage led to the first generation of database management systems.

The second era was also characterized by the use of product software and the advent of "software houses." Software was developed for widespread distri-

The early years	The second era	The third era	The fourth era
• Batch orientation	• Multiuser	• Distributed systems	• Powerful desk-top systems
• Limited distribution	• Real-time	• Embedded "intelligence"	• Object-oriented technologies
• Custom software	• Database	• Low cost hardware	• Expert systems
	• Product software	• Consumer impact	• Artificial neural networks
			• Parallel computing
			• Network computers

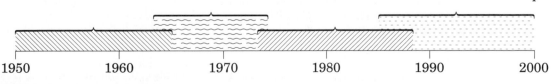

1950   1960   1970   1980   1990   2000

FIGURE 1.1. Evolution of software.

bution in a multidisciplinary market. Programs for mainframes and minicomputers were distributed to hundreds and sometimes thousands of users. Entrepreneurs from industry, government, and academia broke away to develop the ultimate software package and earn a bundle of money.

As the number of computer-based systems grew, libraries of computer software began to expand. In-house developed projects produced tens of thousands of program source statements. Software products purchased from the outside added hundreds of thousands of new statements. A dark cloud appeared on the horizon. All of these programs—all of these source statements—had to be corrected when faults were detected, modified as user requirements changed, or adapted to new hardware that was purchased. These activities were collectively called *software maintenance*. Effort spent on software maintenance began to absorb resources at an alarming rate.

Worse yet, the personalized nature of many programs made them virtually unmaintainable. A "software crisis" loomed on the horizon.

The third era of computer system evolution began in the mid-1970s and spanned more than a full decade. The distributed system—multiple computers, each performing functions concurrently and communicating with one another—greatly increased the complexity of computer-based systems. Global and local area networks, high-bandwidth digital communications and increasing demands for "instantaneous" data access put heavy demands on software developers. Yet, software and the systems that it enabled continued to reside within industry and academia. Personal use was rare.

The conclusion of the third era was characterized by the advent and widespread use of microprocessors. The microprocessor has spawned a wide array of intelligent products—from automobiles to microwave ovens, from industrial robots to blood serum diagnostic equipment—but none has been more important than the personal computer. In less than a decade, computers became readily accessible to the public at large.[1]

The fourth era of computer system evolution moves us away from individual computers and computer programs and toward the collective impact of computers and software. Powerful desk-top machines controlled by sophisticated operating systems, networked locally and globally, and coupled with advanced software applications have become the norm. Computing architectures are rapidly changing from centralized mainframe environments to decentralized client/server environments. Worldwide information networks provide an infrastructure that causes pundits and politicians alike to muse about an "information superhighway" and "cyberspace connectivity." In fact, the Internet can be viewed as "software" that can be accessed by individual users.

The software industry is no longer a niche in the world economy. The decisions made by industry giants such as Microsoft put billions of dollars at risk. As the fourth era progresses, new technologies have begun to emerge. Object-oriented technologies (Part Four of this book) are rapidly displacing more conventional software development approaches in many application areas. Although predictions of "fifth generation" computers ([FEI83] and [ALL89]), continue to elude us, "fourth generation techniques" for software development

---

[1]It is currently estimated that 40 percent of all households in the United States have personal computers.

are changing the manner in which the software community builds computer programs. Expert systems and artificial intelligence software have finally moved from the laboratory into practical application for wide-ranging problems in the real world. Artificial neural network software coupled with the application of fuzzy logic has opened exciting possibilities for pattern recognition and human-like information processing abilities. Virtual reality programming and multimedia systems offer radically different ways of communicating information to end-users. "Genetic algorithms" [BEG95] offer the potential for software that resides within massively parallel biological computers.

Yet, a set of software-related problems has persisted throughout the evolution of computer-based systems, and these problems continue to intensify.

1. Hardware advances continue to outpace our ability to build software to tap hardware's potential.
2. Our ability to build new programs cannot keep pace with the demand for new programs, nor can we build programs rapidly enough to meet business and market needs.
3. The widespread use of computers has made society increasingly dependent on reliable operation of software. Enormous economic damage and potential human suffering can occur when software fails.
4. We struggle to build computer software that has high reliability and quality.
5. Our ability to support and enhance existing programs is threatened by poor design and inadequate resources.

In response to these problems, software engineering practices are being adopted throughout the industry.

1.1.1　An Industry Perspective

In the early days of computing, computer-based systems were developed using hardware-oriented management. Project managers focused on hardware because it was the single largest budget item for system development. To control hardware costs, managers instituted formal controls and technical standards. They demanded thorough analysis and design before something was built. They measured the process to determine where improvement could be made. They insisted on quality control and quality assurance. They instituted procedures to manage change. Stated simply, they applied the controls, methods, and tools that we recognize as hardware engineering. Sadly, software was often little more than an afterthought.

In the early days, programming was viewed as an "art form." Few formal methods existed and fewer people used them. The programmer often learned his or her craft by trial and error. The jargon and challenges of building computer software created a mystique that few managers cared to penetrate. The software world was virtually undisciplined—and many practitioners of the day loved it!

Today, the distribution of costs for the development of computer-based systems has changed dramatically. Software, rather than hardware, is the largest single cost item. For almost two decades managers and many technical practitioners have asked the following questions:

- Why does it take so long to get programs finished?
- Why are costs so high?
- Why can't we find all errors before we give the software to our customers?
- Why do we have difficulty in measuring progress as software is being developed.

These, and many other questions, are a manifestation of the concern about software and the manner in which it is developed—a concern that has lead to the adoption of software engineering practice.

1.1.2 An Aging Software Plant[2]

In the 1950s and 1960s many commentators criticized the steel industry in the United States for lack of investment in its physical plant. Factories had begun to deteriorate, modern methods were rarely applied, the quality and cost of the end product suffered, and competition began to win substantial market share. Management in these industries decided against making the capital investment that was required to remain competitive in their core business. Over time, the steel industry suffered, losing significant market share to foreign competition—competition that had newer plants, used more modern technology, and was provided with government subsidies to make them extremely cost competitive.

During that period, many of us in the fledgling computer industry looked at the steel industry with contempt. "If they're unwilling to invest in their own business," we said, "they deserve to lose market share." Those words may come back to haunt us.

At the risk of sounding melodramatic, the software industry today is in a position that is quite similar to that of the steel industry of the 1950s and 1960s. Across companies large and small, we have an aging "software plant"—there are thousands of critical software-based applications that are in dramatic need of refurbishing:

- Information system applications written twenty years ago that have undergone 40 generations of changes and are now virtually unmaintainable. Even the smallest modification can cause the entire system to fail.

- Engineering applications that are used to produce critical design data, and yet, because of their age and state of repair, no one really understands their internal structure.

- Embedded systems (used to control power plants, air traffic, and factories, among thousand of applications) that exhibit strange and sometimes unexplained behavior, but that cannot be taken out of service because there's nothing available to replace them.

---

[2]This section has been adapted from the introductory chapter of the book *Software Shock* by Pressman and Herron [PRE91].

It will not be enough to "patch" what is broken and give these applications a modern look. Many components of the software plant require significant reengineering, or they will no longer be competitive. Unfortunately, many business managers are unwilling to commit the resources to undertake this reengineering effort. "The applications still work," they say, "and it is 'uneconomic' to commit the resources to make them better."

1.1.3 Software Competitiveness

For many years, software developers employed by large and small companies were the only show in town. And they often acted like it. Because every computer program was custom-built, these in-house software people dictated costs, schedule, and quality. Today, all of this has changed.

Software is now an extremely competitive business. Software that was once built internally can now be purchased off-the-shelf. Many companies that once paid legions of programmers to create specialized applications have now outsourced much of their software work to a third party [MIN95].

Cost, timeliness, and quality are primary drivers that will lead to intense competition for software work over the next few decades. The United States and Western Europe have well-established software industries. But countries in the Far East (e.g., Korea, Singapore), in Asia (e.g., India, China), and in Eastern Europe all offer a large pool of highly motivated, competently educated and relatively low-cost professionals [ECO94]. This work force is moving rapidly to adopt modern software engineering practices and has become a force to be reckoned with as a worldwide pool of software professionals chase a finite number of development dollars.

In their book on the impact of information services on the United States and the world, Feigenbaum and McCorduck [FEI83] state the following:

> Knowledge is power, and the computer is an amplifier of that power. . . . The American computer industry has been innovative, vital, successful. It is, in a way, the ideal industry. It creates value by transforming the brainpower of knowledge workers, with little consumption of energy and raw materials. Today, we dominate the world's ideas and markets in this most important of all modern technologies. But what about tomorrow?

Indeed, what about tomorrow? Computer hardware has become a commodity, available from many sources. But software remains an industry where the United States has been "innovative, vital, [and] successful." But will we maintain our place at the top? At least part of the answer lies in the approach we take to the construction of software for the next generation of computer-based systems.

1.2   SOFTWARE

In 1970, less than 1 percent of the public could have intelligently described what "computer software" meant. Today, most professionals and many members of the public at large feel that they understand software. But do they?

A textbook description of software might take the following form: *Software is (1) instructions (computer programs) that when executed provide desired function and performance, (2) data structures that enable the programs to adequately manipulate information, and (3) documents that describe the operation and use of the programs.* There is no question that other, more complete definitions could be offered. But we need more than a formal definition.

1.2.1 Software Characteristics

To gain an understanding of software (and ultimately an understanding of software engineering), it is important to examine the characteristics of software that make it different from other things that human beings build. When hardware is built, the human creative process (analysis, design, construction, testing) is ultimately translated into a physical form. If we build a new computer, our initial sketches, formal design drawings, and breadboarded prototypes evolve into a physical product (VLSI chips, circuit boards, power supplies, etc.).

Software is a logical rather than a physical system element. Therefore, software has characteristics that differ considerably from those of hardware:

1. *Software is developed or engineered, it is not manufactured in the classical sense.*

Although some similarities exist between software development and hardware manufacture, the two activities are fundamentally different. In both activities, high quality is achieved through good design, but the manufacturing phase for hardware can introduce quality problems that are nonexistent (or easily corrected) for software. Both activities depend on people, but the relationship between people applied and work accomplished is entirely different (see Chapter 3). Both activities require the construction of a "product," but the approaches are different.

Software costs are concentrated in engineering. This means that software projects cannot be managed as if they were manufacturing projects.

In the mid-1980s, the concept of the "software factory" was introduced in the literature (e.g., [MAN84], [TAJ84]). It is important to note that this term does not imply that hardware manufacturing and software development are equivalent. Rather, the software factory concept recommends the use of automated tools (see Part Five) for software development.

2. *Software doesn't "wear out."*

Figure 1.2 depicts failure rate as a function of time for hardware. The relationship, often called the "bathtub curve," indicates that hardware exhibits relatively high failure rates early in its life (these failures are often attributable to design or manufacturing defects); defects are corrected, and the failure rate drops to a steady-state level (hopefully, quite low) for some period of time. As time passes, however, the failure rate rises again as hardware components suffer from the cumulative affects of dust, vibration, abuse, temperature extremes, and many other environmental maladies. Stated simply, the hardware begins to wear out.

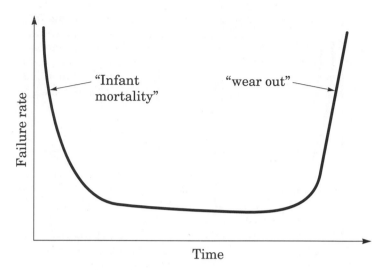

FIGURE 1.2.
Failure curve for
hardware.

Software is not susceptible to the environmental maladies that cause hardware to wear out. In theory, therefore, the failure rate curve for software should take the form shown in Figure 1.3. Undiscovered defects will cause high failure rates early in the life of a program. However, these are corrected (hopefully without introducing other errors) and the curve flattens as shown. Figure 1.3 is a gross oversimplification of actual failure models (see Chapter 8 for more information) for software. However, the implication is clear—software doesn't wear out. But it does deteriorate!

This seeming contradiction can best be explained by considering Figure 1.4. During its life, software will undergo change (maintenance). As changes are made, it is likely that some new defects will be introduced, causing the failure

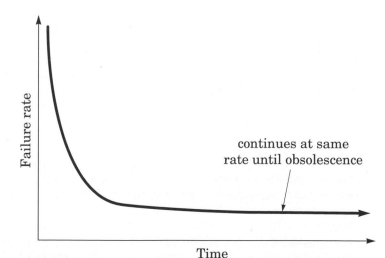

FIGURE 1.3.
Failure curve for
software (idealized).

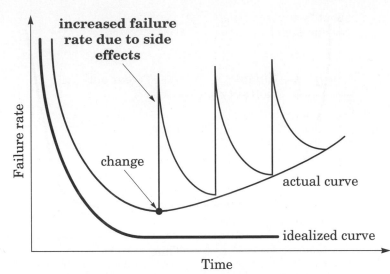

FIGURE 1.4.
Actual failure curve
for software.

rate curve to spike as shown in Figure 1.4. Before the curve can return to the original steady-state failure rate, another change is requested, causing the curve to spike again. Slowly, the minimum failure rate level begins to rise—the software is deteriorating due to change.

Another aspect of wear illustrates the difference between hardware and software. When a hardware component wears out, it is replaced by a spare part. There are no software spare parts. Every software failure indicates an error in design or in the process through which design was translated into machine executable code. Therefore, software maintenance involves considerably more complexity than hardware maintenance.

3. *Most software is custom-built, rather than being assembled from existing components.*

Consider the manner in which the control hardware for a microprocessor-based product is designed and built. The design engineer draws a simple schematic of the digital circuitry, does some fundamental analysis to ensure that proper function will be achieved, and then refers to a catalog of digital components. Each integrated circuit (often called an "IC" or a "chip") has a part number, a defined and validated function, a well-defined interface, and a standard set of integration guidelines. After each component is selected, it can be ordered off-the-shelf.

Sadly, software designers are not afforded the luxury described above. With few exceptions, there are no catalogs of software components. It is possible to order off-the-shelf software, but only as a complete unit, not as components that can be reassembled into new programs.[3] Although much has been written

---

[3]This situation is changing rapidly. The widespread use of object-oriented technology has resulted in the creation of *software components*. These are discussed in Chapters 19 and 26.

about "software reusability" (e.g., [TRA88], [MEY95]), we are only beginning to see successful implementations of the concept.

1.2.2 Software Components

As an engineering discipline evolves, a collection of standard design components is created. Standard screws and off-the-shelf integrated circuits are only two of thousands of standard components that are used by mechanical and electrical engineers as they design new systems. The reusable components have been created so that the engineer can concentrate on the truly innovative elements of a design (i.e., the parts of the design that represent something new). In the hardware world, component reuse is a natural part of the engineering process. In the software world, it is something that has yet to be achieved on a broad scale.

Reusability is an important characteristic of a high-quality software component (see Chapter 26 for additional information). A software component should be designed and implemented so that it can be reused in many different programs. In the 1960s, we built scientific subroutine libraries that were reusable in a broad array of engineering and scientific applications. These subroutine libraries reused well-defined algorithms in an effective manner, but had a limited domain of application. Today, we have extended our view of reuse to encompass not only algorithms, but also data structures. Modern reusable components encapsulate both data and the processing that is applied to the data, enabling the software engineer to create new applications from reusable parts.[4] For example, today's interactive interfaces are built using reusable components that enable the creation of graphics windows, pull-down menus and a wide variety of interaction mechanisms. The data structures and processing detail required to build the interface are contained within a library of reusable components for interface construction.

Software components are built using a programming language that has a limited vocabulary, an explicitly defined grammar, and well formed rules of syntax and semantics. At the lowest level, the language mirrors the instruction set of the hardware. At mid-level, programming languages such as Ada 95, C, or Smalltalk are used to create a procedural description of the program. At the highest level, the language uses graphical icons or other symbology to represent the requirements for a solution. Executable instructions are automatically generated.

Machine-level language is a symbolic representation of the CPU instruction set. When a good software developer produces a maintainable, well-documented program, machine-level language can make extremely efficient use of memory and "optimize" program execution speed. When a program is poorly designed and has little documentation, machine language is a nightmare.

Mid-level languages allow the software developer and the program to be machine-independent. When a more sophisticated translator is used, the vo-

---

[4]In Part Four of this book we examine the use of object-oriented technologies and their impact on component reuse.

cabulary, grammar, syntax, and semantics of a mid-level language can be much more sophisticated than machine-level languages. In fact, mid-level language compilers and interpreters produce machine-level language as output.

Although hundreds of programming languages are in use today, fewer than ten mid-level programming languages are widely used in the industry. Languages such as COBOL and FORTRAN remain in widespread use more than 30 years after their introduction. More modern programming languages such as Ada95, C, C++ Eiffel, Java, and Smalltalk have each gained an enthusiastic following.

Machine code, assembly (machine-level) languages, and mid-level programming languages are often referred to as the first three generations of computer languages. With any of these languages, the programmer must be concerned both with the specification of the information structure and the control of the program itself. Hence, languages in the first three generations are termed procedural languages.

Fourth generation languages, also called *nonprocedural* languages, move the software developer even further from the computer hardware. Rather than requiring the developer to specify procedural detail, the nonprocedural language implies a program by "specifying the desired result, rather than specifying action required to achieve that result" [COB85]. Support software translates the specification of result into a machine executable program.

1.2.3 Software Applications

Software may be applied in any situation for which a prespecified set of procedural steps (i.e., an algorithm) has been defined (notable exceptions to this rule are expert systems and artificial neural network software). Information content and determinacy are important factors in determining the nature of a software application. *Content* refers to the meaning and form of incoming and outgoing information. For example, many business applications make use of highly structured input data (a database) and produce formatted "reports." Software that controls an automated machine (e.g., a numerical control) accepts discrete data items with limited structure and produces individual machine commands in rapid succession.

Information determinacy refers to the predictability of the order and timing of information. An engineering analysis program accepts data that have a predefined order, executes the analysis algorithm(s) without interruption, and produces resultant data in report or graphical format. Such applications are determinate. A multiuser operating system, on the other hand, accepts inputs that have varied content and arbitrary timing, executes algorithms that can be interrupted by external conditions, and produces output that varies as a function of environment and time. Applications with these characteristics are indeterminate.

It is somewhat difficult to develop meaningful generic categories for software applications. As software complexity grows, neat compartmentalization disappears. The following software areas indicate the breadth of potential applications:

System Software   System software is a collection of programs written to service other programs. Some system software (e.g., compilers, editors, and file management utilities) processes complex, but determinate, information structures. Other systems applications (e.g., operating system components, drivers, telecommunications processors) process largely indeterminate data. In either case, the systems software area is characterized by heavy interaction with computer hardware; heavy usage by multiple users; concurrent operation that requires scheduling, resource sharing, and sophisticated process management; complex data structures; and multiple external interfaces.

Real-Time Software   Programs that monitor/analyze/control real world events as they occur are called real-time software. Elements of real-time software include a data gathering component that collects and formats information from an external environment, an analysis component that transforms information as required by the application, a control/output component that responds to the external environment, and a monitoring component that coordinates all other components so that real-time response (typically ranging from 1 millisecond to 1 minute) can be maintained. It should be noted that the term "real-time" differs from "interactive" or "timesharing." A real-time system must respond within strict time constraints. The response time of an interactive (or time-sharing) system can normally be exceeded without disastrous results.

Business Software   Business information processing is the largest single software application area. Discrete "systems" (e.g., payroll, accounts receivable/payable, inventory, etc.) have evolved into management information system (MIS) software that accesses one or more large databases containing business information. Applications in this area restructure existing data in a way that facilitates business operations or management decision making. In addition to conventional data processing applications, business software applications also encompass interactive and client/server computing (e.g., point-of-sale transaction processing).

Engineering and Scientific Software   Engineering and scientific software has been characterized by "number crunching" algorithms. Applications range from astronomy to volcanology, from automotive stress analysis to space shuttle orbital dynamics, and from molecular biology to automated manufacturing. However, new applications within the engineering/scientific area are moving away from conventional numerical algorithms. Computer-aided design, system simulation, and other interactive applications have begun to take on real-time and even system software characteristics.

Embedded Software   Intelligent products have become commonplace in nearly every consumer and industrial market. Embedded software resides in read-only memory and is used to control products and systems for the consumer and industrial markets. Embedded software can perform very limited and esoteric functions (e.g., key pad control for a microwave oven) or provide significant function and control capability (e.g., digital functions in an automobile such as fuel control, dashboard displays, braking systems, etc.).

Personal Computer Software   The personal computer software market has burgeoned over the past decade. Word processing, spreadsheets, computer graphics, multimedia, entertainment, database management, personal and business financial applications, and external network or database access are only a few of hundreds of applications.

Artificial Intelligence Software   Artificial intelligence (AI) software makes use of nonnumerical algorithms to solve complex problems that are not amenable to computation or straightforward analysis. An active AI area is expert systems, also called knowledge-based systems. However, other application areas for AI software are pattern recognition (image and voice), theorem proving, and game playing. In recent years, a new branch of AI software, called *artificial neural networks,* has evolved. A neural network simulates the structure of brain processes (the functions of the biological neuron) and may ultimately lead to a new class of software that can recognize complex patterns and learn from past experience.

1.3   SOFTWARE: A CRISIS ON THE HORIZON

Many industry observers (including this author in earlier editions of this book) have characterized the problems associated with software development as a "crisis." Yet, what we really have may be something rather different.

The word "crisis" is defined in *Webster's Dictionary* as "a turning point in the course of anything; decisive or crucial time, stage or event." Yet, for software there has been no "turning point," no "decisive time," only slow, evolutionary change. In the software industry, we have had a "crisis" that has been with us for close to 30 years, and that is a contradiction in terms.

Anyone who looks up the word "crisis" in the dictionary will find another definition: "the turning point in the course of a disease, when it becomes clear whether the patient will live or die." This definition may give us a clue about the real nature of the problems that have plagued software development.

We have yet to reach the stage of crisis in computer software. What we really have is a *chronic affliction.*[5] The word "affliction" is defined as "anything causing pain or distress." But it is the definition of the adjective "chronic" that is the key to our argument: "lasting a long time or recurring often; continuing indefinitely." It is far more accurate to describe what we have endured for the past three decades as a chronic affliction, rather than a crisis. There are no miracle cures, but there are many ways that we can reduce the pain as we strive to discover a cure.

Whether we call it a software crisis or a software affliction, the term alludes to a set of problems that are encountered in the development of computer software. The problems are not limited to software that "doesn't function properly." Rather, the affliction encompasses problems associated with how we develop software, how we maintain a growing volume of existing software, and how we can expect to keep pace with a growing demand for more software.

---

[5]This terminology was suggested by Professor Daniel Tiechrow of the University of Michigan in a talk presented in Geneva, Switzerland, April, 1989.

Although reference to a crisis or even an affliction can be criticized for being melodramatic, the phrases do serve a useful purpose by denoting real problems that are encountered in all areas of software development.

1.4   SOFTWARE MYTHS

Many causes of a software affliction can be traced to a mythology that arose during the early history of software development. Unlike ancient myths, which often provided human lessons that are well worth heeding, software myths propagated misinformation and confusion. Software myths had a number of attributes that made them insidious: For instance, they appeared to be reasonable statements of fact (sometimes containing elements of truth), they had an intuitive feel, and they were often promulgated by experienced practitioners who "knew the score."

Today, most knowledgeable professionals recognize myths for what they are—misleading attitudes that have caused serious problems for managers and technical people alike. However, old attitudes and habits are difficult to modify, and remnants of software myths are still believed.

Management Myths   Managers with software responsibility, like managers in most disciplines, are often under pressure to maintain budgets, keep schedules from slipping, and improve quality. Like a drowning person who grasps at a straw, a software manager often grasps at belief in a software myth, if that belief will lessen the pressure (even temporarily).

> *Myth:*   We already have a book that's full of standards and procedures for building software. Won't that provide my people with everything they need to know?
>
> *Reality:*   The book of standards may very well exist, but is it used? Are software practitioners aware of its existence? Does it reflect modern software development practice? Is it complete? In many cases, the answer to all of these questions is "no."
>
> *Myth:*   My people do have state-of-the-art software development tools. After all, we buy them the newest computers.
>
> *Reality:*   It takes much more that the latest model mainframe, workstation or PC to do high-quality software development. Computer-aided software engineering (CASE) tools are more important than hardware for achieving good quality and productivity, yet the majority of software developers still do not use them.
>
> *Myth:*   If we get behind schedule, we can add more programmers and catch up (sometimes called the "Mongolian horde concept").
>
> *Reality:*   Software development is not a mechanistic process like manufacturing. In the words of Brooks [BRO75], "adding people to a late software project makes it later." At first, this statement may seem counterintuitive. However, as new people are added, people who were working must spend time educating the newcomers, thereby reducing the amount of time spent on productive development effort. People can be added, but only in a planned and well-coordinated manner.

Customer Myths   A customer who requests computer software may be a person at the next desk, a technical group down the hall, the marketing/sales department, or an outside company that has requested software under contract. In many cases, the customer believes myths about software because software responsible managers and practitioners do little to correct misinformation. Myths lead to false expectations (by the customer) and ultimately, dissatisfaction with the developer.

Myth: A general statement of objectives is sufficient to begin writing programs—we can fill in the details later.

Reality: Poor up-front definition is the major cause of failed software efforts. A formal and detailed description of information domain, function, performance, interfaces, design constraints, and validation criteria is essential. These characteristics can be determined only after thorough communication between customer and developer.

Myth: Project requirements continually change, but change can be easily accommodated because software is flexible.

Reality: It is true that software requirements do change, but the impact of change varies with the time at which it is introduced. Figure 1.5 illustrates the impact of change. If serious attention is given to up-front definition, early requests for change can be accommodated easily. The customer can review requirements and recommend modifications with relatively little impact on cost. When changes are requested during software design, cost impact grows rapidly. Resources have been committed and a design framework has been established. Change can cause upheaval that requires additional resources and major design modification, i.e., additional cost. Changes in function, performance, interfaces or other characteristics during implementation (code and test) have a severe impact on cost. Change, when requested after software is in production use, can be more than an order of magnitude more expensive than the same change requested earlier.

Practitioner's Myths   Myths that are still believed by software practitioners have been fostered by decades of programming culture. As we noted earlier in this chapter, during the early days of software, programming was viewed as an art form. Old ways and attitudes die hard.

Myth: Once we write the program and get it to work, our job is done.

Reality: Someone once said that "the sooner you begin 'writing code', the longer it'll take you to get done." Industry data [LIE80] indicate that between 50 and 70 percent of all effort expended on a program will be expended after it is delivered to the customer for the first time.

Myth: Until I get the program "running," I really have no way of assessing its quality.

Reality: One of the most effective software quality assurance mechanisms can be applied from the inception of a project—the *formal technical review*. Software reviews (described in Chapter 8) are a "quality filter" that has been found to be more effective than testing for finding certain classes of software errors.

Myth: The only deliverable for a successful project is the working program.

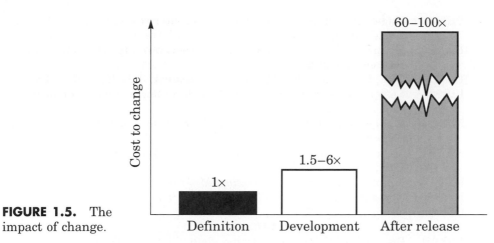

FIGURE 1.5. The impact of change.

> ***Reality:*** A working program is only one part of a *software configuration* that includes programs, documents, and data. Documentation forms the foundation for successful development and, more important, provides guidance for the software maintenance task.

Many software professionals recognize the fallacy of the myths described above. Regrettably, habitual attitudes and methods foster poor management and technical practices even when reality dictates a better approach. Recognition of software realities is the first step toward formulation of practical solutions for software development.

1.5   SUMMARY

Software has become the key element in the evolution of computer based systems and products. Over the past four decades, software has evolved from a specialized problem-solving and information analysis tool to an industry in itself. But early "programming" culture and history have created a set of problems that persist today. Software has become a limiting factor in the evolution of computer-based systems. Software is composed of programs, data, and documents. Each of these items comprises a configuration that is created as part of the software engineering process. The intent of software engineering is to provide a framework for building software with higher quality.

REFERENCES

[ALL89]   Allman, W.F., *Apprentices of Wonder,* Bantam, 1989.
[BEG95]   Begley, S., "Software au Naturel," *Newsweek,* May 8, 1995, pp. 70–71.
[BRO75]   Brooks, F., *The Mythical Man-Month,* Addison-Wesley, 1975.
[COB85]   Cobb, R.H., "In Praise of 4GLs," *Datamation,* July 15, 1985, p. 92.
[ECO94]   "How Much is that Ant in the Window," *Economist,* vol. 331, no. 7923, July 1994, p. 63.

[FEI83]   Feigenbaum, E.A., and P. McCorduck, *The Fifth Generation,* Addison-Wesley, 1983.

[HAM93]   Hammer, M., and J. Champy, *Reengineering the Corporation,* HarperCollins, 1993.

[LEV95]   Levy, S., "The Luddites Are Back," *Newsweek,* July 12, 1995, p. 55.

[LIE80]   Lientz, B., and E. Swanson, *Software Maintenance Management,* Addison-Wesley, 1980.

[MAN84]   Manley, J.H., "CASE: Foundation for Software Factories," *COMPCON Proceedings,* IEEE, September 1984, pp. 84–91.

[MEY95]   Meyer, B., *Reusable Software: The Base Object-Oriented Component Libraries,* Prentice-Hall, 1995.

[MIN95]   Minoli, D, *Analyzing Outsourcing,* McGraw-Hill, 1995.

[NAI82]   Naisbitt, J. *Megatrends,* Warner Books, 1982.

[OSB79]   Osborne, A., *Running Wild—The Next Industrial Revolution,* Osborne/McGraw-Hill, 1979.

[PRE91]   Pressman, R.S., and S.R. Herron, *Software Shock,* Dorset House, 1991.

[STO89]   Stoll, C., *The Cuckoo's Egg,* Doubleday, 1989.

[TAJ84]   Tajima, D., and T. Matsubara, "Inside the Japanese Software Factory," *Computer,* vol. 17, no. 3, March 1984, pp. 34–43.

[TOF80]   Toffler, A., *The Third Wave,* Morrow, 1980.

[TOF90]   Toffler, A., *Powershift,* Bantam, 1990.

[TRA88]   Tracz, W., *Software Reuse: Emerging Technology,* IEEE Computer Society Press, 1988.

[YOU92]   Yourdon, E., *The Decline and Fall of the American Programmer,* Yourdon Press, 1992.

PROBLEMS AND POINTS TO PONDER

1.1. Software is the differentiating characteristic in many computer-based products and systems. Provide examples of two or three products and at least one system in which software, not hardware, is the differentiating element.

1.2. In the 1950s and 1960s computer programming was an art form learned in an apprentice-like environment. How have the early days affected software development practices today?

1.3. Many authors have discussed the impact of the "information era." Provide a number of examples (both positive and negative) that indicate the impact of software on our society. Review one of the pre-1990 references in Section 1.1 and indicate where the author's predictions were right and where he was wrong.

1.4. Choose a specific application and indicate (a) the software application category (Section 1.2.3) into which it fits; (b) the data content associated with the application; (c) the information determinacy of the application.

1.5. As software become more pervasive, risks to the public (due to faulty programs) become an increasingly significant concern. Develop a realistic doomsday scenario where the failure of a computer program could do great harm (either economic or human).

1.6. Peruse the Internet newsgroup **comp.risks** and prepare a summary of risks to the public that have recently been discussed. [Alternate source: *Software Engineering Notes,* published by the Association of Computing Machinery (ACM).]

1.7. Write a paper summarizing recent advances in one of the leading-edge software application areas. Potential choices include artificial intelligence, virtual reality, artificial neural networks, advanced human interfaces, and intelligent agents.

1.8. The "myths" noted in Section 1.4 are slowly fading as the years pass, but others are taking their place. Attempt to add one or two "new" myths to each category.

FURTHER READINGS AND INFORMATION SOURCES[6]

There are literally thousands of books written about computer software. The vast majority discuss programming languages or software applications, but a few discuss software itself. An informal treatment of the subject can be found in [PRE91]. Negroponte's (*Being Digital,* Alfred A. Knopf, Inc., 1995) bestselling book provides a view of computing and its overall impact in the twenty-first century. DeMarco (*Why Does Software Cost So Much?* Dorset House, 1995) has produced a collection of amusing and insightful essays on software and the process through which it is developed.

The basis for a solid understanding of computer software and software engineering lies in computer science, a broad collection of topics that are far beyond the scope of this book. The *Computer Science Bibliography Collection* is a collection of close to 600 bibliographies in the field of computer science. Nearly every topic that is relevant to software engineering is considered in its 300,000 references:

http://www.pilgrim.umass.edu/pub/misc/bibliographies/index.html

The World Guide to Computer Science contains pointers to many university research organizations with programs in computing:

http://www.worldwidenews.net/subjects/htm

A voluminous glossary of software terms, including many common acronyms can be found at:

http://dxsting.cern.ch/sting/glossary.html

Internet Connections for Engineering provides a searchable index for engineering programs throughout the world:

http://www.englib.cornell.edu/ice/ice-index.html

---

[6]The "Further Reading and Information Sources" section presented at the conclusion of each chapter presents print and electronic information sources that can help to expand your understanding of the major topics presented in the chapter. World Wide Web addresses change frequently. Therefore, some of the uniform resource locators (URLs) noted in this book may have changed by the time you need them. For an up-to-date set of software engineering resources, visit the R.S. Pressman & Associates, Inc., Web site at **http://www.rspa.com.**

THE PROCESS

The software process has been the focus of considerable attention over the last decade. But what exactly is a software process? Within the context of this book, we define a software process as a framework for the tasks that are required to build high-quality software. Is "process" synonymous with software engineering? The answer is "yes and no." A software process defines the approach that is taken as software is engineered, but software engineering also encompasses technologies that populate the process—technical methods and automated tools.

More important, software engineering is performed by creative, knowledgeable people who should work within a defined and mature software process. The intent of this chapter is to provide a survey of the current state of the software process and to provide pointers to more detailed discussion of management and technical topics presented later in this book.

2.1   SOFTWARE ENGINEERING—A LAYERED TECHNOLOGY

Although hundreds of authors have developed personal definitions of software engineering, a definition proposed by Fritz Bauer [NAU69] at the seminal conference on the subject still serves as a basis for discussion:

> [Software engineering is] the establishment and use of sound engineering principles in order to obtain economically software that is reliable and works efficiently on real machines.

Almost every reader will be tempted to add to this definition. It says little about the technical aspects of software quality; it does not directly address the need for customer satisfaction or timely product delivery; it omits mention of the importance of measurement and metrics; it does not state the importance of a mature process. And yet, Bauer's definition provides us with a baseline. What are the "sound engineering principles" that can be applied to computer software development? How do we "economically" build software so that it is "reliable"? What is required to create computer programs that work "efficiently" on not one but many different "real machines"? These are the questions that continue to challenge software engineers.

The IEEE [IEE93] has developed a more comprehensive definition when it states:

> Software Engineering: (1) The application of a systematic, disciplined, quantifiable approach to the development, operation, and maintenance of software; that is, the application of engineering to software. (2) The study of approaches as in (1).

2.1.1 Process, Methods, and Tools

Software engineering is a layered technology (Figure 2.1). Any engineering approach (including software engineering) must rest on an organizational commitment to quality. Total quality management and similar philosophies foster a continuous process improvement culture, and it is this culture that ultimately leads to the development of increasingly more mature approaches to software engineering. The bedrock that supports software engineering is a focus on quality.

The foundation for software engineering is the *process* layer. Software engineering process is the glue that holds the technology layers together and enables rational and timely development of computer software. Process defines a framework for a set of *key process areas (KPAs)* [PAU93] that must be established for effective delivery of software engineering technology. The key process areas form the basis for management control of software projects and establish the context in which technical methods are applied, work products (models, documents, data, reports, forms, etc.) are produced, milestones are established, quality is ensured, and change is properly managed.

Software engineering *methods* provide the technical "how to's" for building software. Methods encompass a broad array of tasks that include requirements analysis, design, program construction, testing, and maintenance. Software en-

FIGURE 2.1.
Software engineering layers.

gineering methods rely on a set of basic principles that govern each area of the technology and include modeling activities and other descriptive techniques.

Software engineering *tools* provide automated or semi-automated support for the process and the methods. When tools are integrated so that information created by one tool can be used by another, a system for the support of software development, called *computer-aided software engineering* (CASE), is established. CASE combines software, hardware, and a software engineering database (a repository containing important information about analysis, design, program construction, and testing) to create a software engineering environment that is analogous to CAD/CAE (computer-aided design/engineering) for hardware.

2.1.2 A Generic View of Software Engineering

Engineering is the analysis, design, construction, verification, and management of technical (or social) entities. Regardless of the entity that is to be engineered, the following questions must be asked and answered:

- What is the problem to be solved?
- What are the characteristics of the entity that is used to solve the problem?
- How will the entity (and the solution) be realized?
- How will the entity be constructed?
- What approach will be used to uncover errors that were made in the design and construction of the entity?
- How will the entity be supported over the long term, when corrections, adaptations, and enhancements are requested by users of the entity?

Throughout this book we focus on a single entity—computer software. To engineer software adequately, a software development process must be defined. In this section the generic characteristics of the software process are considered. Later in this chapter, specific process models are addressed.

The work that is associated with software engineering can be categorized into three generic phases, regardless of application area, project size, or complexity. Each phase addresses one or more of the questions noted above.

The *definition phase* focuses on *what*. That is, during definition, the software developer attempts to identify what information is to be processed, what function and performance are desired, what system behavior can be expected, what interfaces are to be established, what design constraints exist, and what validation criteria are required to define a successful system. The key requirements of the system and the software are identified. Although the methods applied during the definition phase will vary depending upon the software engineering paradigm (or combination of paradigms) that is applied, three major tasks will occur in some form: system or information engineering (Chapter 10), software project planning (Chapters 3 through 7), and requirements analysis (Chapters 11, 12, and 20).

The *development phase* focuses on *how*. That is, during development a software engineer attempts to define how data are to be structured, how function is to be implemented as a software architecture, how procedural details are to be implemented, how interfaces are to be characterized, how the design will be translated into a programming language (or nonprocedural language), and how testing will be performed. The methods applied during the development phase will vary, but three specific technical tasks should always occur: software design (Chapters 14, 15, and 21), code generation, and software testing (Chapters 16, 17, and 22).

The *maintenance phase* focuses on *change* that is associated with error correction, adaptations required as the software's environment evolves, and changes due to enhancements brought about by changing customer requirements. The maintenance phase reapplies the steps of the definition and development phases, but does so in the context of existing software. Four types of change are encountered during the maintenance phase:

Correction   Even with the best quality assurance activities, it is likely that the customer will uncover defects in the software. *Corrective maintenance* changes the software to correct defects.

Adaptation   Over time, the original environment (e.g., CPU, operating system, business rules, external product characteristics) for which the software was developed is likely to change. *Adaptive maintenance* results in modification to the software to accommodate changes to its external environment.

Enhancement   As software is used, the customer/user will recognize additional functions that will provide benefit. *Perfective maintenance* extends the software beyond its original functional requirements.

Prevention   Computer software deteriorates due to change, and because of this, *preventive maintenance,* often called *software reengineering,* must be conducted to enable the software to serve the needs of its end users. In essence, preventive maintenance makes changes to computer programs so that they can be more easily corrected, adapted, and enhanced.

Today, the "aging software plant" (Section 1.1.2) is forcing many companies to pursue software reengineering strategies (Chapter 27). In a global sense, software reengineering is often considered as part of business process reengineering [STR95].

The phases and related steps described in our generic view of software engineering are complemented by a number of *umbrella activities.* Typical activities in this category include:

- Software project tracking and control
- Formal technical reviews
- Software quality assurance
- Software configuration management
- Document preparation and production
- Reusability management
- Measurement
- Risk management

Umbrella activities are applied throughout the software process and are discussed in Parts Two and Five of this book.

2.2   THE SOFTWARE PROCESS

A software process can be characterized as shown in Figure 2.2. A *common process framework* is established by defining a small number of *framework activities* that are applicable to all software projects, regardless of their size or complexity. A number of *task sets*—each a collection of software engineering work tasks, project milestones, software work products and deliverables, and quality assurance points—enable the framework activities to be adapted to the characteristics of the software project and the requirements of the project team. Finally, umbrella activities—such as software quality assurance, software configuration management, and measurement[1]—overlay the process model. Umbrella activities are independent of any one framework activity and occur throughout the process.

In recent years, there has been a significant emphasis on "process maturity" [PAU93]. The Software Engineering Institute (SEI) has developed a comprehensive model that is predicated on a set of software engineering capabilities that should be present as organizations reach different levels of process maturity. To determine an organization's current state of process maturity, the SEI uses an assessment questionnaire and a five-point grading scheme. The grading scheme determines compliance with a *capability maturity model* [PAU93] that defines key activities required at different levels of process ma-

---

[1]These topics are discussed in detail in later chapters.

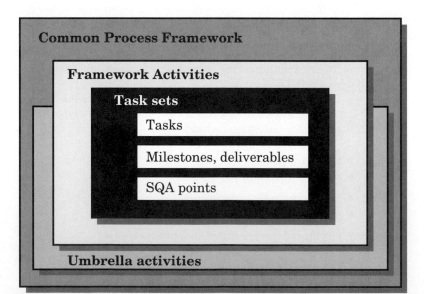

FIGURE 2.2. The software process.

turity. The SEI approach provides a measure of the global effectiveness of a company's software engineering practices and establishes five process maturity levels, which are defined in the following manner:

Level 1: **Initial**—The software process is characterized as ad hoc, and occasionally even chaotic. Few processes are defined, and success depends on individual effort.

Level 2: **Repeatable**—Basic project management processes are established to track cost, schedule, and functionality. The necessary process discipline is in place to repeat earlier successes on projects with similar applications.

Level 3: **Defined**—The software process for both management and engineering activities is documented, standardized, and integrated into an organization-wide software process. All projects use a documented and approved version of the organization's process for developing and maintaining software. This level includes all characteristics defined for level 3.

Level 4: **Managed**—Detailed measures of the software process and product quality are collected. Both the software process and products are quantitatively understood and controlled using detailed measures. This level includes all characteristics defined for level 3.

Level 5: **Optimizing**—Continuous process improvement is enabled by quantitative feedback from the process and from testing innovative ideas and technologies. This level includes all characteristics defined for level 4.

The five levels defined by the SEI are derived as a consequence of evaluating responses to the SEI assessment questionnaire that is based on the CMM. The results of the questionnaire are distilled to a single numerical grade that provides an indication of an organization's process maturity.

The SEI has associated key process areas with each of the maturity levels. The KPAs describe those software engineering functions (e.g., software project planning, requirements management) that must be present to satisfy good practice at a particular level. Each KPA is described by identifying the following characteristics:

- *goals*—the overall objectives that the KPA must achieve
- *commitments*—requirements (imposed on the organization) that must be met to achieve the goals, and that provide proof of intent to comply with the goals
- *abilities*—those things that must be in place (organizationally and technically) that will enable the organization to meet the commitments
- *activities*—the specific tasks that are required to achieve the KPA function
- *methods for monitoring implementation*—the manner in which the activities are monitored as they are put into place
- *methods for verifying implementation*—the manner in which proper practice for the KPA can be verified. Eighteen KPAs (each described using the structure noted above) are defined across the maturity model and are mapped into

different levels of process maturity. The following KPAs should be achieved at each process maturity level:[2]

> *Process Maturity Level 2*
>
> Software configuration management
>
> Software quality assurance
>
> Software subcontract management
>
> Software project tracking and oversight
>
> Software project planning
>
> Requirements management
>
> *Process Maturity Level 3*
>
> Peer reviews
>
> Intergroup coordination
>
> Software product engineering
>
> Integrated software management
>
> Training program
>
> Organization process definition
>
> Organization process focus
>
> *Process Maturity Level 4*
>
> Software quality management
>
> Quantitative process management
>
> *Process Maturity Level 5*
>
> Process change management
>
> Technology change management
>
> Defect prevention

Each of the KPAs is defined by a set of *key practices* that contribute to satisfying its goals. The key practices are policies, procedures, and activities that must occur before a key process area has been fully instituted. The SEI defines *key indicators* as "those key practices or components of key practices that offer the greatest insight into whether the goals of a key process area have been achieved." Assessment questions are designed to probe for the existence (or lack thereof) of a key indicator.

2.3   SOFTWARE PROCESS MODELS

To solve actual problems in an industry setting, a software engineer or a team of engineers must incorporate a development strategy that encompasses the process, methods, and tools layers described in Section 2.1.1 and the generic phases discussed in Section 2.1.2. This strategy is often referred to as a *process model* or a

---

[2]Note that the KPAs are additive. For example, process maturity level 3 contains all level 2 KPAs plus those noted for level 2.

software engineering paradigm. A process model for software engineering is chosen based on the nature of the project and application, the methods and tools to be used, and the controls and deliverables that are required. In an intriguing paper on the nature of the software process, L.B.S. Raccoon [RAC95] uses fractals as the basis for a discussion of the true nature of the software process.

All software development can be characterized as a problem solving loop (Figure 2.3a) in which four distinct stages are encountered: status quo, problem definition, technical development, and solution integration. Status quo "represents the current state of affairs" [RAC95]; problem definition identifies the specific problem to be solved; technical development solves the problem through the application of some technology, and solution integration delivers the results (e.g., documents, programs, data, new business function, new product) to those who requested the solution in the first place. The generic software engineering phases and steps defined in Section 2.1.2 easily map into these stages.

The problem solving loop described above applies to software engineering work at many different levels of resolution. It can be used at the macro level when the entire application is considered; at a middle level when program components are being engineered, and even at the line of code level. Therefore, a fractal[3] representation can be used to provide an idealized view of process. In Figure 2.3b, each stage in the problem solving loop contains an identical problem solving loop, which contains still another problem solving loop (this continues to some rational boundary; for software, a line of code).

Realistically, it is difficult to compartmentalize activities as neatly as Figure 2.3b implies because cross-talk occurs within and across stages, yet this simplified view leads to a very important idea: Regardless of the process model that is chosen for a software project, all of the stages—status quo, problem definition, technical development, and solution integration—coexist simultaneously at some level of detail. Given the recursive nature Figure 2.3b, the four stages discussed above apply equally to the analysis of a complete application and to the generation of a small segment of code.

Raccoon [RAC95] suggests a "Chaos model" that describes "software development [as] a continuum from the user to the developer to the technology." As work progresses toward a complete system, the stages described above are applied recursively to user needs and the developer's technical specification of the software.

In the sections that follow, a variety of different process models for software engineering are discussed. Each represents an attempt to bring order to an inherently chaotic activity. It is important to remember that each of the models has been characterized in a way that (hopefully) assists in the control and coordination of a real software project. And yet, at their core, all of the models exhibit characteristics of the Chaos model.

2.4   THE LINEAR SEQUENTIAL MODEL

Figure 2.4 illustrates the *linear sequential* model for software engineering. Sometimes called the "classic life cycle" or the "waterfall model," the linear se-

---

[3]Fractals were originally proposed for geometric representations. A pattern is defined and then applied recursively at successively smaller scales; patterns fall inside patterns.

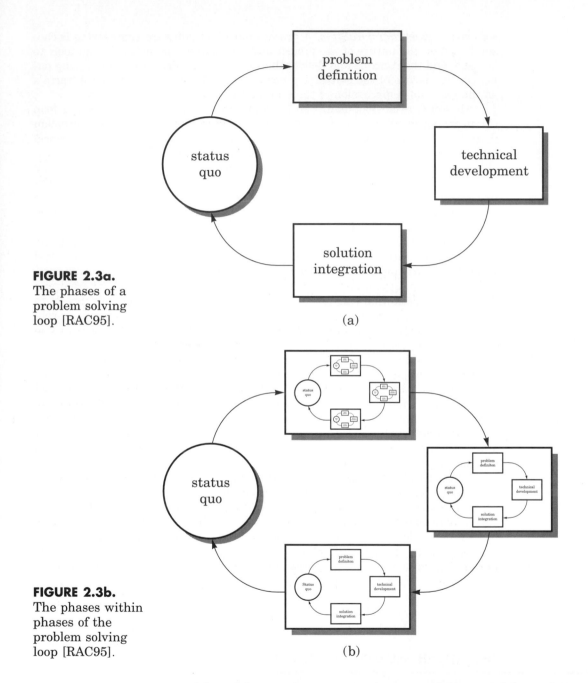

FIGURE 2.3a.
The phases of a
problem solving
loop [RAC95].

(a)

FIGURE 2.3b.
The phases within
phases of the
problem solving
loop [RAC95].

(b)

quential model suggests a systematic, sequential approach[4] to software development that begins at the system level and progresses through analysis, de-

---

[4]Although the original waterfall model proposed by Winston Royce [ROY70] made provision
for feedback loops, the vast majority of organizations that apply this process model treat it as
if it were strictly linear.

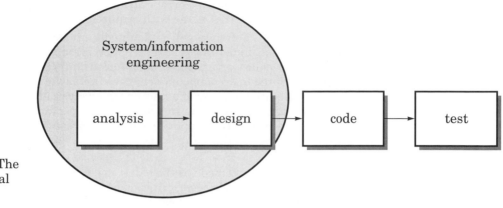

FIGURE 2.4. The linear sequential model.

sign, coding, testing, and maintenance. Modeled after the conventional engineering cycle, the linear sequential model encompasses the following activities:

System/information engineering and modeling. Because software is always part of a larger system (or business), work begins by establishing requirements for all system elements and then allocating some subset of these requirements to software. This system view is essential when software must interface with other elements such as hardware, people, and databases. System engineering and analysis encompasses requirements gathering at the system level with a small amount of top-level analysis and design. Information engineering encompasses requirements gathering at the strategic business level and at the business area level.

Software requirements analysis. The requirements gathering process is intensified and focused specifically on software. To understand the nature of the program(s) to be built, the software engineer ("analyst") must understand the information domain (described in Chapter 11) for the software, as well as required function, behavior, performance, and interfacing. Requirements for both the system and the software are documented and reviewed with the customer.

Design. Software design is actually a multistep process that focuses on four distinct attributes of a program: data structure, software architecture, interface representations, and procedural (algorithmic) detail. The design process translates requirements into a representation of the software that can be assessed for quality before code generation begins. Like requirements, the design is documented and becomes part of the software configuration.

Code generation. The design must be translated into a machine readable form. The code generation step performs this task. If design is performed in a detailed manner, code generation can be accomplished mechanistically.

Testing. Once code has been generated, program testing begins. The testing process focuses on the logical internals of the software, assuring that all statements have been tested, and on the functional externals—that is, conducting tests to uncover errors and ensure that defined input will produce actual results that agree with required results.

Maintenance. Software will undoubtedly undergo change after it is delivered to the customer (a possible exception is embedded software). Change will occur because errors have been encountered, because the software must be adapted to accommodate changes in its external environment (e.g., a change required because of a new operating system or peripheral device), or because the customer requires functional or performance enhancements. Software maintenance reapplies each of the preceding phases to an existing program rather than a new one.

The linear sequential model is the oldest and the most widely used paradigm for software engineering. However, criticism of the paradigm has caused even active supporters to question its efficacy [HAN95]. Among the problems that are sometimes encountered when the linear sequential model is applied are:

1. Real projects rarely follow the sequential flow that the model proposes. Although the linear model can accommodate iteration, it does so indirectly. As a result, changes can cause confusion as the project team proceeds.

2. It is often difficult for the customer to state all requirements explicitly. The linear sequential model requires this and has difficulty accommodating the natural uncertainty that exists at the beginning of many projects.

3. The customer must have patience. A working version of the program(s) will not be available until late in the project time-span. A major blunder, if undetected until the working program is reviewed, can be disastrous.

4. Developers are often delayed unnecessarily. In an interesting analysis of actual projects, Bradac [BRA94] found that the linear nature of the classic life cycle leads to "blocking states" in which some project team members must wait for other members of the team to complete dependent tasks. In fact, the time spent waiting can exceed the time spent on productive work! The blocking states tend to be more prevalent at the beginning and end of a linear sequential process.

Each of these problems is real. However, the classic life cycle paradigm has a definite and important place in software engineering work. It provides a template into which methods for analysis, design, coding, testing, and maintenance can be placed. The classic life cycle remains the most widely used process model for software engineering. While it does have weaknesses, it is significantly better than a haphazard approach to software development.

2.5   THE PROTOTYPING MODEL

Often, a customer defines a set of general objectives for software but does not identify detailed input, processing, or output requirements. In other cases, the developer may be unsure of the efficiency of an algorithm, the adaptability of an operating system, or the form that human-machine interaction should take.

In these and many other situations, a *prototyping paradigm* may offer the best approach.

The prototyping paradigm (Figure 2.5) begins with requirements gathering. Developer and customer meet and define the overall objectives for the software, identify whatever requirements are known, and outline areas where further definition is mandatory. A "quick design" then occurs. The quick design focuses on a representation of those aspects of the software that will be visible to the customer/user (e.g., input approaches and output formats). The quick design leads to the construction of a prototype. The prototype is evaluated by the customer/user and is used to refine requirements for the software to be developed. Iteration occurs as the prototype is tuned to satisfy the needs of the customer, at the same time enabling the developer to better understand what needs to be done.

Ideally, the prototype serves as a mechanism for identifying software requirements. If a working prototype is built, the developer attempts to make use of existing program fragments or applies tools (e.g., report generators, window managers, etc.) that enable working programs to be generated quickly.

But what do we do with the prototype when it has served the purpose described above? Brooks [BRO75] provides an answer:

> In most projects, the first system built is barely usable. It may be too slow, too big, awkward in use or all three. There is no alternative but to start again, smarting but smarter, and build a redesigned version in which these problems are solved. . . . When a new system concept or new technology is used, one has to build a system to throw away, for even the best planning is not so omniscient as to get it right the first time. The management question, therefore, is not

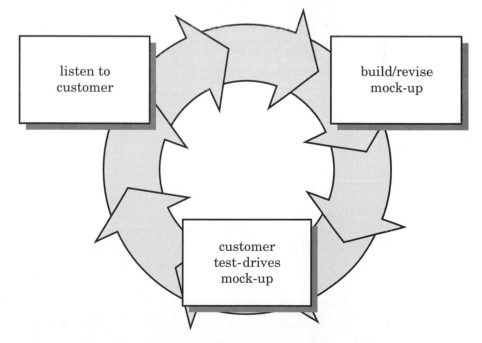

FIGURE 2.5. The prototyping paradigm.

whether to build a pilot system and throw it away. You will do that. The only question is whether to plan in advance to build a throwaway, or to promise to deliver the throwaway to customers. . . .

The prototype can serve as "the first system." The one that Brooks recommends we throw away. But this may be an idealized view. It is true that both customers and developers like the prototyping paradigm. Users get a feel for the actual system and developers get to build something immediately. Yet, prototyping can also be problematic for the following reasons:

1. The customer sees what appears to be a working version of the software, unaware that the prototype is held together "with chewing gum and baling wire," unaware that in the rush to get it working we haven't considered overall software quality or long-term maintainability. When informed that the product must be rebuilt so that high levels of quality can be maintained, the customer cries foul and demands that "a few fixes" be applied to make the prototype a working product. Too often, software development management relents.

2. The developer often makes implementation compromises in order to get a prototype working quickly. An inappropriate operating system or programming language may be used simply because it is available and known; an inefficient algorithm may be implemented simply to demonstrate capability. After a time, the developer may become familiar with these choices and forget all the reasons why they were inappropriate. The less-than-ideal choice has now become an integral part of the system.

Although problems can occur, prototyping can be an effective paradigm for software engineering. The key is to define the rules of the game at the beginning; that is, the customer and developer must both agree that the prototype is built to serve as a mechanism for defining requirements. It is then discarded (at least in part), and the actual software is engineered with an eye toward quality and maintainability.

2.6   THE RAD MODEL

Rapid Application Development (RAD) is a linear sequential software development process model that emphasizes an extremely short development cycle. The RAD model is a "high-speed" adaptation of the linear sequential model in which rapid development is achieved by using a component-based construction approach. If requirements are well understood and project scope is constrained,[5] the RAD process enables a development team to create a "fully functional sys-

---

[5]These conditions are by no means guaranteed. In fact, many software projects have poorly defined requirements at the start. In such cases prototyping (Section 2.5) or evolutionary approaches (Section 2.7) are much better process options. See [REI95].

tem" within very short time periods (e.g., 60 to 90 days) [MAR91]. Used primarily for information systems applications, the RAD approach encompasses the following phases [KER94]:

Business modeling.   The information flow among business functions is modeled in a way that answers the following questions: What information drives the business process? What information is generated? Who generates it? Where does the information go? Who processes it? Business modeling is described in more detail in Chapter 10.

Data modeling.   The information flow defined as part of the business modeling phase is refined into a set of data objects that are needed to support the business. The characteristics (called attributes) of each object are identified and the relationships between these objects are defined. Data modeling is considered in Chapter 12.

Process modeling.   The data objects defined in the data modeling phase are transformed to achieve the information flow necessary to implement a business function. Processing descriptions are created for adding, modifying, deleting, or retrieving a data object.

Application generation.   RAD assumes the use of fourth generation techniques (Section 2.9). Rather than creating software using conventional third generation programming languages, the RAD process works to reuse existing program components (when possible) or create reusable components (when necessary). In all cases, automated tools are used to facilitate construction of the software.

Testing and turnover.   Since the RAD process emphasizes reuse, many of the program components have already been testing. This reduces overall testing time. However, new components must be tested and all interfaces must be fully exercised.

The RAD process model is illustrated in Figure 2.6. Obviously, the time constraints imposed on a RAD project demand "scalable scope" [KER94]. If a business application can be modularized in a way that enables each major function to be completed in less than three months (using the approach described above), it is a candidate for RAD. Each major function can be addressed by a separate RAD team and then integrated to form a whole.

Like all process models, the RAD approach has drawbacks [BUT94]:

- For large, but scalable projects, RAD requires sufficient human resources to create the right number of RAD teams.
- RAD requires developers and customers who are committed to the rapid-fire activities necessary to complete a system in a much abbreviated time frame. If commitment is lacking from either constituency, RAD projects will fail.

Not all types of applications are appropriate for RAD. If a system cannot be properly modularized, building the components necessary for RAD will be problematic. If high performance is an issue, and performance is to be achieved through tuning the interfaces to system components, the RAD approach may not work.

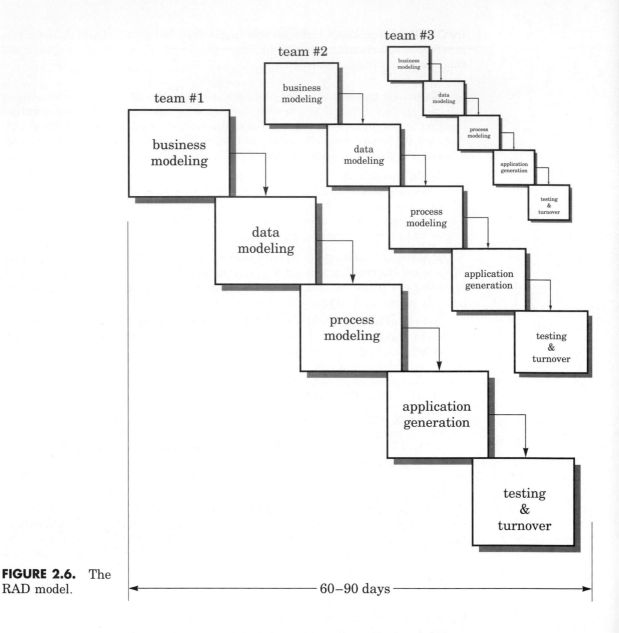

FIGURE 2.6. The RAD model.

RAD is not appropriate when technical risks are high. This occurs when a new application makes heavy use of new technology or when the new software requires a high degree of interoperability with existing computer programs.

RAD emphasizes the development of reusable program components. Reusability (see Chapter 26) is the cornerstone of object technologies (Part Four of this book), and is encountered in the component assembly process model discussed in Section 2.7.3.

2.7 **EVOLUTIONARY SOFTWARE PROCESS MODELS**

There is growing recognition that software, like all complex systems, evolves over a period of time [GIL88]. Business and product requirements often change as development proceeds, making a straight line path to an end product unrealistic; tight market deadlines make completion of a comprehensive software product impossible, but a limited version must be introduced to meet competitive or business pressure; a set of core product or system requirements is well understood, but the details of product or system extensions have yet to be defined. In these and similar situations, software engineers need a process model that has been explicitly designed to accommodate a product that evolves over time.

The linear sequential model (Section 2.4) is designed for straight line development. In essence, this waterfall approach assumes that a complete system will be delivered after the linear sequence is completed. The prototyping model (Section 2.5) is designed to assist the customer (or developer) in understanding requirements. In general, it is not designed to deliver a production system. The evolutionary nature of software is not considered in either of these classic software engineering paradigms.

Evolutionary models are iterative. They are characterized in a manner that enables software engineers to develop increasingly more complete versions of the software.

2.7.1 The Incremental Model

The incremental model combines elements of the linear sequential model (applied repetitively) with the iterative philosophy of prototyping. As Figure 2.7 shows, the incremental model applies linear sequences in a staggered fashion as calendar time progresses. Each linear sequence produces a deliverable "increment" of the software [McDE93]. For example, word-processing software developed using the incremental paradigm might deliver basic file management, editing, and document production functions in the first increment; more sophisticated editing and document production capabilities in the second increment; spelling and grammar checking in the third increment; and advanced page layout capability in the fourth increment. It should be noted that the process flow for any increment can incorporate the prototyping paradigm.

When an incremental model is used, the first increment is often a *core product*. That is, basic requirements are addressed, but many supplementary features (some known, others unknown) remain undelivered. The core product is used by the customer (or undergoes detailed review). As a result of use and/or evaluation, a plan is developed for the next increment. The plan addresses the modification of the core product to better meet the needs of the customer and the delivery of additional features and functionality. This process is repeated following the delivery of each increment, until the complete product is produced.

The incremental process model, like prototyping (Section 2.5) and other evolutionary approaches, is iterative in nature. But unlike prototyping, the in-

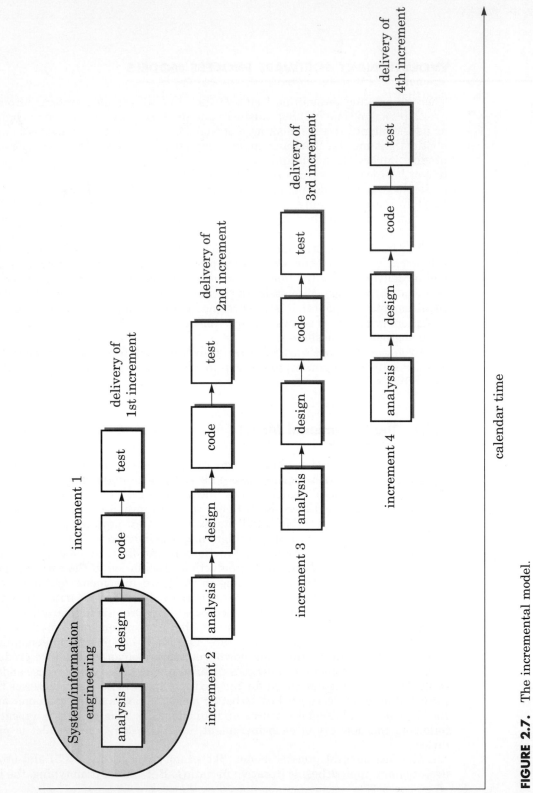

FIGURE 2.7. The incremental model.

cremental model focuses on the delivery of a operational product with each increment. Early increments are "stripped down" versions of the final product, but they do provide capability that serves the user and also provide a platform for evaluation by the user.

Incremental development is particularly useful when staffing is unavailable for a complete implementation by the business deadline that has been established for the project. Early increments can be implemented with fewer people. If the core product is well received, then additional staff (if required) can be added to implement the next increment. In addition, increments can be planned to manage technical risks. For example, a major system might require the availability of new hardware that is under development and whose delivery date is uncertain. It might be possible to plan early increments in a way that avoids the use of this hardware, thereby enabling partial functionality to be delivered to end users without inordinate delay.

2.7.2 The Spiral Model

The *spiral model,* originally proposed by Boehm [BOE88], is an evolutionary software process model that couples the iterative nature of prototyping with the controlled and systematic aspects of the linear sequential model. It provides the potential for rapid development of incremental versions of the software. In the spiral model, software is developed in a series of incremental releases. During early iterations, the incremental release might be a paper model or prototype. During later iterations, increasingly more complete versions of the engineered system are produced.

The spiral model is divided into a number of *framework activities,* also called *task regions.*[6] Typically, there are between three and six task regions. Figure 2.8 depicts a spiral model that contains six task regions:

- **customer communication**—tasks required to establish effective communication between developer and customer
- **planning**—tasks required to define resources, timelines, and other project related information
- **risk analysis**—tasks required to assess both technical and management risks
- **engineering**—tasks required to build one or more representations of the application
- **construction & release**—tasks required to construct, test, install and provide user support (e.g., documentation and training)
- **customer evaluation**—tasks required to obtain customer feedback based on evaluation of the software representations created during the engineering stage and implemented during the installation stage.

---

[6]The spiral model discussed in this section is a variation on the model proposed by Boehm. For further information on the original spiral model, see [BOE88].

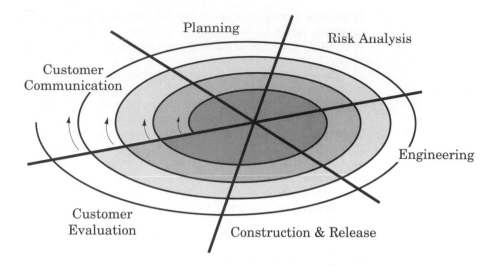

FIGURE 2.8. A typical spiral model.

Each of the regions is populated by a series of work tasks that are adapted to the characteristics of the project to be undertaken. For small projects, the number of work tasks and their formality is low. For larger, more critical projects, each task region contains more work tasks that are defined to achieve a higher level of formality. In all cases, the umbrella activities (e.g., software configuration management and software quality assurance) noted in Section 2.2 are applied.

As this evolutionary process begins, the software engineering team moves around the spiral in a clockwise direction, beginning at the core. The first circuit around the spiral might result in the development of a product specification; subsequent passes around the spiral might be used to develop a prototype and then progressively more sophisticated versions of the software. Each pass through the planning region results in adjustments to the project plan. Cost and schedule are adjusted based on feedback derived from customer evaluation. In addition, the project manager adjusts the planned number of iterations required to complete the software.

Unlike classical process models that end when software is delivered, the spiral model can be adapted to apply throughout the life of the computer software. A *project entry point* axis is defined in Figure 2.9. Each cube placed along the axis represents the starting point for a different type of project. A **concept development project** starts at the core of the spiral and will continue (multiple iterations occur along the spiral path that bounds the central shaded region) until concept development is complete. If the concept is to be developed into an actual product, the process proceeds through the next cube (**new product development project** entry point) and a new development project is initiated. The new product will evolve through a number of iterations around the spiral following the path that bounds the region that has somewhat lighter shading than the core. A similar process flow occurs for other types of projects.

In essence, the spiral, when characterized in this way, remains operative until the software is retired. There are times when the process is dormant, but whenever a change is initiated, the process starts at the appropriate entry point (e.g., product enhancement).

The spiral model is a realistic approach to the development of large scale systems and software. Because software evolves as the process progresses, the developer and customer better understand and react to risks at each evolutionary level. The spiral model uses prototyping as a risk reduction mechanism, but more important, enables the developer to apply the prototyping approach at any stage in the evolution of the product. It maintains the systematic stepwise approach suggested by the classic life cycle, but incorporates it into an iterative framework that more realistically reflects the real word. The spiral model demands a direct consideration of technical risks at all stages of the project, and if properly applied, should reduce risks before they become problematic.

But like other paradigms, the spiral model is not a panacea. It may be difficult to convince customers (particularly in contract situations) that the evolutionary approach is controllable. It demands considerable risk assessment expertise, and relies on this expertise for success. If a major risk is not uncovered and managed, problems will undoubtedly occur. Finally, the model itself is relatively new and has not been used as widely as the linear sequential or prototyping paradigms. It will take a number of years before the efficacy of this important new paradigm can be determined with absolute certainty.

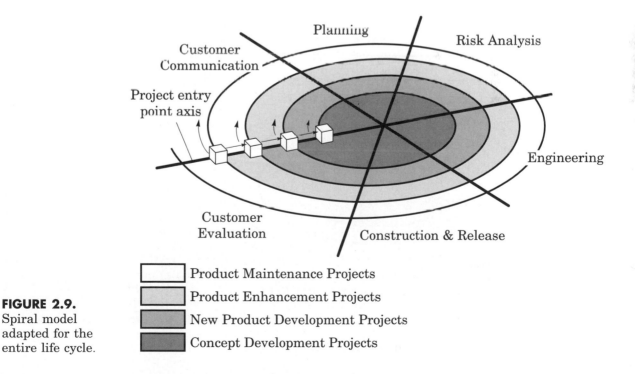

FIGURE 2.9.
Spiral model adapted for the entire life cycle.

2.7.3 The Component Assembly Model

Object technologies (Chapter 19) provide the technical framework for a component-based process model for software engineering. The object-oriented paradigm emphasizes the creation of classes that encapsulate both data and the algorithms that are used to manipulate the data. If properly designed and implemented, object-oriented classes are reusable across different applications and computer-based system architectures.

The component assembly model (Figure 2.10) incorporates many of the characteristics of the spiral model. It is evolutionary in nature [NIE92], demanding an iterative approach to the creation of software. However, the component assembly model composes applications from prepackaged software components (sometimes called "classes").

The engineering activity begins with the identification of candidate classes. This is accomplished by examining the data that are to be manipulated by the application and the algorithms that will be applied to accomplish the manipulation.[7] Corresponding data and algorithms are packaged into a class.

---

[7]This is a simplified description of class definition. For a more detailed discussion, see Chapter 19.

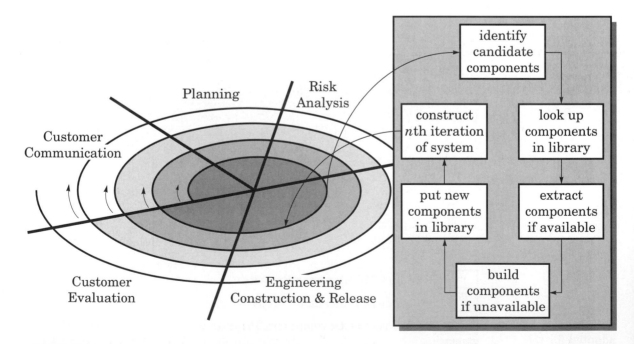

FIGURE 2.10. The component assembly model.

Classes (called components in Figure 2.10) created in past software engineering projects are stored in a *class library* or repository (Chapter 29). Once candidate classes are identified, the class library is searched to determine if these classes already exist. If they do, they are extracted from the library and reused. If a candidate class does not reside in the library, it is engineered using object-oriented methods (Chapters 20–22). The first iteration of the application to be built is then composed, using classes extracted from the library and any new classes built to meet the unique needs of the application. Process flow then returns to the spiral and will ultimately reenter the component assembly iteration during subsequent passes through the engineering activity.

The component assembly model leads to software reuse, and reusability provides software engineers with a number of measurable benefits. Based on studies of reusability, QSM Associates, Inc. reports component assembly leads to a 70% reduction in development cycle time, an 84% reduction in project cost, and a productivity index of 26.2, compared to an industry norm of 16.9 [YOU94]. Although these results are a function of the robustness of the component library, there is little question that the component assembly model provides significant advantages for software engineers.

2.7.4 The Concurrent Development Model

The *concurrent development model,* sometimes called *concurrent engineering,* has been described in the following manner by Davis and Sitaram [DAV94]:

> Project managers who track project status in terms of the major phases [of the classic life cycle] have no idea of the status of their projects. These are examples of trying to track extremely complex sets of activities using overly simple models. Note that although [a large] project is in the coding phase, there are personnel on the project involved in activities typically associated with many phases of development simultaneously. For example, . . . personnel are writing requirements, designing, coding, testing, and integration testing [all at the same time]. Software engineering process models by Humphrey and Kellner [HUM89, KEL89] have shown the concurrency that exists for activities occurring during any one phase. Kellner's more recent work [KEL91] uses state-charts [a notation that represents the states of a process, see Chapter 15] to represent the concurrent relationship existent among activities associated with a specific event (e.g., a requirements change during late development), but fails to capture the richness of concurrency that exists across all software development and management activities in a project. . . . Most software development process models are driven by time; the later it is, the later in the development process you are. [A concurrent process model] is driven by user needs, management decisions, and review results.

The concurrent process model can be represented schematically as a series of major technical activities, tasks, and their associated states. For example, the *engineering* activity defined for the spiral model (Section 2.7.2), is accomplished

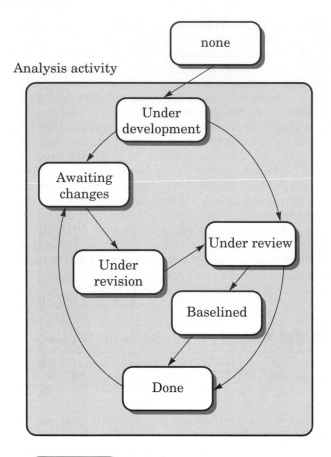

Analysis activity

FIGURE 2.11.
One element of
the concurrent
process model.

represents a state of a
software engineered activity

by invoking the following tasks: prototyping and/or analysis modeling, requirements specification, and design.[8]

Figure 2.11 provides a schematic representation of one activity within the concurrent process model. The activity—*analysis*—may be in any one of the states[9] noted at any given time. Similarly, other activities (e.g., design or customer communication) can be represented in an analogous manner. All activities exist concurrently but reside in different states. For example, early in a project the *customer communication* activity (not shown in the figure) has completed its first iteration and exists in the **awaiting changes** state. The *analy-*

---

[8]It should be noted that analysis and design are complex tasks that require substantial discussion. Parts Three and Four of this book consider these topics in detail.

[9]A state is some externally observable mode of behavior.

sis activity (which existed in the **none** state while initial customer communication was completed) now makes a transition into the **under development** state. If, however, the customer indicates that changes in requirements must be made, the *analysis* activity moves from the **under development** state into the **awaiting changes** state.

The concurrent process model defines a series of events that will trigger transitions from state to state for each of the software engineering activities. For example, during early stages of design, an inconsistency in the analysis model is uncovered. This generates the event *analysis model correction,* which will trigger the analysis activity from the **done** state into the **awaiting changes** state.

The concurrent process model is often used as the paradigm for the development of client/server[10] applications (Chapter 28). A client/server system is composed of a set of functional components. When applied to client/server, the concurrent process model defines activities in two dimensions [SHE94]: a *system dimension* and a *component dimension*. System level issues are addressed using three activities: *design, assembly,* and *use.* The component dimension is addressed with two activities: *design* and *realization.* Concurrency is achieved in two ways: (1) system and component activities occur simultaneously and can be modeling using the state-oriented approach described above; (2) a typical client/server application is implemented with many components, each of which can be designed and realized concurrently.

In reality, the concurrent process model is applicable to all types of software development and provides an accurate picture of the current state of a project. Rather than confining software engineering activities to a sequence of events, it defines a network of activities. Each activity on the network exists simultaneously with other activities. Events generated within a given activity or at some other place in the activity network trigger transitions among the states of an activity.

2.8   THE FORMAL METHODS MODEL

The formal methods model encompasses a set of activities that lead to mathematical specification of computer software. Formal methods enable a software engineer to specify, develop, and verify a computer-based system by applying a rigorous, mathematical notation. A variation on this approach, called *cleanroom software engineering* [MIL87, DYE92], is currently applied by some software development organizations.

When formal methods (Chapters 24 and 25) are used during development, they provide a mechanism for eliminating many of the problems that are difficult to overcome using other software engineering paradigms. Ambiguity, incompleteness, and inconsistency can be discovered and corrected more easily— not through ad hoc review, but through the application of mathematical analysis. When formal methods are used during design, they serve as a basis for pro-

---

[10]In client/server applications, software functionality is divided between clients (normally PCs) and a server (a more powerful computer) that typically maintains a centralized database.

gram verification and therefore enable the software engineer to discover and correct errors that might otherwise go undetected.

Although not yet a mainstream approach, the formal methods model offers the promise of defect-free software. Yet, concern about its applicability in a business environment has been voiced:

1. The development of formal models is currently quite time-consuming and expensive.
2. Because few software developers have the necessary background to apply formal methods, extensive training is required.
3. It is difficult to use the models as a communication mechanism for technically unsophisticated customers.

These concerns notwithstanding, it is likely that the formal methods approach will gain adherents among software developers that must build safety-critical software (e.g., developers of aircraft avionics and medical devices) and among developers that would suffer severe economic hardship should software errors occur.

2.9   FOURTH GENERATION TECHNIQUES

The term "fourth generation techniques" (4GT) encompasses a broad array of software tools that have one thing in common: Each enables the software engineer to specify some characteristic of software at a high level. The tool then automatically generates source code based on the developer's specification. There is little debate that the higher the level at which software can be specified to a machine, the faster a program can be built. The 4GT paradigm for software engineering focuses on the ability to specify software using specialized language forms or a graphic notation that describes the problem to be solved in terms that the customer can understand.

Currently, a software development environment that supports the 4GT paradigm includes some or all of the following tools: nonprocedural languages for database query, report generation, data manipulation, screen interaction and definition, and code generation; high-level graphics capability; and spreadsheet capability. Initially, many of the tools noted above were available only for very specific application domains, but today 4GT environments have been extended to address most software application categories.

Like other paradigms, 4GT begins with a requirements gathering step. Ideally, the customer would describe requirements and these would be directly translated into an operational prototype. But this is unworkable. The customer may be unsure of what is required, may be ambiguous in specifying facts that are known, and may be unable or unwilling to specify information in a manner that a 4GT tool can consume. For this reason, the customer-developer dialog described for other process models remains an essential part of the 4GT approach.

For small applications, it may be possible to move directly from the requirements gathering step to implementation using a nonprocedural *fourth generation language* (4GL). However, for larger efforts, it is necessary to develop a design strategy for the system, even if a 4GL is to be used. The use of 4GT without design (for large projects) will cause the same difficulties (poor quality, poor maintainability, poor customer acceptance) that we have encountered when developing software using ad hoc approaches.

Implementation using a 4GL enables the software developer to represent desired output in a manner that results in automatic generation of code to generate the output. Obviously, a data structure with relevant information must exist and be readily accessible by the 4GL.

To transform a 4GT implementation into a product, the developer must conduct thorough testing, develop meaningful documentation, and perform all other solution integration activities that are required in other software engineering paradigms. In addition, the 4GT-developed software must be built in a manner that enables maintenance to be performed expeditiously.

Like all software engineering paradigms, the 4GT model has advantages and disadvantages. Proponents claim dramatic reduction in software development time and greatly improved productivity for people who build software. Opponents claim that current 4GT tools are not all that much easier to use than programming languages, that the resultant source code produced by such tools is "inefficient," and that the maintainability of large software systems developed using 4GT is open to question.

There is some merit in the claims of both sides and it is possible to summarize the current state of 4GT approaches:

1. The use of 4GT has broadened considerably over the past decade and is now a viable approach for many different application areas. Coupled with *computer-aided software engineering* (CASE) tools and code generators, 4GT offers a credible solution to many software problems.

2. Data collected from companies who are using 4GT indicates that the time required to produce software is greatly reduced for small and intermediate applications and that the amount of design and analysis for small applications is also reduced.

3. However, the use of 4GT for large software development efforts demands as much or more analysis, design, and testing (software engineering activities) to obtain the substantial time saving that can be achieved through the elimination of coding.

To summarize, fourth generation techniques have already become an important part of software development. When coupled with component assembly approaches (Section 2.7.3), the 4GT paradigm may become the dominant approach to software development.

2.10   PROCESS TECHNOLOGY

The process models discussed in the preceding sections must be adapted for use by a software project team. To accomplish this, *process technology* tools have been developed to help software organizations analyze their current process, organize work tasks, control and monitor progress, and manage technical quality [BAN95].

Process technology tools allow a software organization to build an automated model of the common process framework, task sets, and umbrella activities discussed in Section 2.3. The model, normally represented as a network, can then be analyzed to determine typical workflow and examine alternative process structures that might lead to reduced development time or cost.

Once an acceptable process has been created, other process technology tools can be used to allocate, monitor, and even control all software engineering tasks defined as part of the process model. Each member of a software project team can use such tools to develop a checklist of work tasks to be performed, work products to be produced, and quality assurance activities to be conducted. The process technology tool can also be used to coordinate the use of other computer-aided software engineering tools (Chapter 29) that are appropriate for a particular work task.

2.11   PRODUCT AND PROCESS

If the process is weak, the end product will undoubtedly suffer. But an obsessive over-reliance on process is also dangerous. In a brief essay, Margaret Davis [DAV95] comments on the duality of product and process:

> About every ten years give or take five, the software community redefines "the problem" by shifting its focus from product issues to process issues. Thus, we have embraced structured programming languages (product) followed by structured analysis methods (process) followed by data encapsulation (product) followed by the current emphasis on the Software Engineering Institute's Software Development Capability Maturity Model (process).
>
> While the natural tendency of a pendulum is to come to rest at a point midway between two extremes, the software community's focus constantly shifts because new force is applied when the last swing fails. These swings are harmful in and of themselves because they confuse the average software practitioner by radically changing what it means to perform the job, let alone perform it well. The swings also do not solve "the problem," for they are doomed to fail as long as product and process are treated as forming a dichotomy instead of a duality.
>
> There is precedence in the scientific community to advance notions of duality when contradictions in observations cannot be fully explained by one competing theory or another. The dual nature of light, which seems to be simultaneously particle and wave, has been accepted since the 1920s when Louis de Broglie proposed it. I believe that the observations we can make on the artifacts of software and its development demonstrate a fundamental duality between product and process. You can never derive or understand the full artifact, its context, use, meaning, and worth if you view it as only a process or only a product. . . .
>
> All of human activity may be a process, but each of us derives a sense of self-worth from those activities that result in a representation or instance that can be used or appreciated either by more than one person, used over and over, or used in some other context not considered. That is, we derive feelings of satisfaction from reuse of our products by ourselves or others.

Thus, while the rapid assimilation of reuse goals into software development potentially increases the satisfaction software practitioners derive from their work, it also increases the urgency for acceptance of the duality of product and process. Thinking of a reusable artifact as only product or only process either obscures the context and ways to use it or obscures the fact that each use results in product that will, in turn, be used as input to some other software development activity. Taking one view over the other dramatically reduces the opportunities for reuse and, hence, loses the opportunity for increasing job satisfaction.

People derive as much (or more) satisfaction from the creative process as they do from the end product. An artist enjoys the brush strokes as much as she enjoys the framed result. A writer enjoys the search for the proper metaphor as much as the finished book. A creative software professional should also derive as much satisfaction from the process as the end product.

The work of software people will change in the years ahead. The duality of product and process is one important element in keeping creative people engaged as the transition from programming to software engineering is finalized.

2.12   SUMMARY

Software engineering is a discipline that integrates process, methods, and tools for the development of computer software. A number of different process models for software engineering have been proposed, each exhibiting strengths and weaknesses, but all having a series of generic phases in common. The principles, concepts, and methods that enable us to perform the process that we call software engineering are considered throughout the remainder of this book.

REFERENCES

[BAN95]   Bandinelli, S. et al., "Modeling and Improving an Industrial Software Process," *IEEE Trans. Software Engineering,* vol. 21, no. 5, May 1995, pp. 440–454.

[BOE88]   Boehm, B., "A Spiral Model for Software Development and Enhancement," *Computer,* vol. 21, no. 5, May 1988, pp. 61–72.

[BRA94]   Bradac, M., D. Perry, and L. Votta, "Prototyping a Process Monitoring Experiment," *IEEE Trans. Software Engineering,* vol. 20, no. 10, October 1994, pp. 774–784.

[BRO75]   Brooks, F., *The Mythical Man-Month,* Addison-Wesley, 1975.

[BUT94]   Butler, J., "Rapid Application Development in Action," *Managing System Development,* Applied Computer Research, vol. 14, no. 5, May 1994, pp. 6–8.

[DAV94]   Davis, A., and P. Sitaram, "A Concurrent Process Model for Software Development, *Software Engineering Notes,* ACM Press, vol. 19, no. 2, April 1994, pp. 38–51.

[DAV95]   Davis, M.J., "Process and Product: Dichotomy or Duality," *Software Engineering Notes,* ACM Press, vol. 20, no. 2, April 1995, pp. 17–18.

[DYE92]   Dyer, M., *The Cleanroom Approach to Quality Software Development,* Wiley, 1992.

[GIL88]   Gilb, T., *Principles of Software Engineering Management,* Addison-Wesley, 1988.

[HAN95]   Hanna, M., "Farewell to Waterfalls," *Software Magazine,* May 1995, pp. 38–46.

[HUM89]   Humphrey, W., and M. Kellner, "Software Process Modeling: Principles of Entity Process Models," *Proc. 11th Intl. Conf. on Software Engineering,* IEEE Computer Society Press, pp. 331–342.

[IEE93]   *IEEE Standards Collection: Software Engineering,* IEEE Standard 610.12-1990, IEEE, 1993.

[KEL89]   Kellner, M., *Software Process Modeling: Value and Experience,* SEI Technical Review—1989, SEI, Pittsburgh, PA, 1989.

[KEL91]   Kellner, M., "Software Process Modeling Support for Management Planning and Control," *Proc. 1st Intl. Conf. on the Software Process,* IEEE Computer Society Press, 1991, pp. 8–28.

[KER94]   Kerr, J., and R. Hunter, *Inside RAD,* McGraw-Hill, 1994.

[MAR91]   Martin, J., *Rapid Application Development,* Prentice-Hall, 1991.

[McDE93]   McDermid, J., and P. Rook, "Software Development Process Models," in *Software Engineer's Reference Book,* CRC Press, 1993, pp. 15/26–15/28.

[MIL87]   Mills, H.D., M. Dyer, and R. Linger, "Cleanroom Software Engineering," *IEEE Software,* September 1987, pp. 19–25.

[NAU69]   Naur, P., and B. Randall (eds.), *Software Engineering: A Report on a Conference Sponsored by the NATO Science Committee,* NATO, 1969.

[NIE92]   Nierstrasz, "Component-Oriented Software Development, *CACM,* vol. 35, no. 9, September, 1992, pp. 160–165.

[PAU93]   Paulk, M. et al., *Capability Maturity Model for Software,* Software Engineering Institute, Carnegie Mellon University, Pittsburgh, PA, 1993.

[RAC95]   Raccoon, L.B.S., "The Chaos Model and the Chaos Life Cycle," *ACM Software Engineering Notes,* vol. 20., no. 1, January, 1995, pp. 55–66.

[REI95]   Reilly, J.P., "Does RAD Live Up to the Hype?" *IEEE Software,* September, 1995, pp. 24–26.

[ROY70]   Royce, W.W., "Managing the Development of Large Software Systems: Concepts and Techniques," *Proc. WESCON,* August 1970.

[SHE94]   Sheleg, W., "Concurrent Engineering: A New Paradigm for C/S Development," *Application Development Trends,* vol. 1, no. 6, June 1994, pp. 28–33.

[STR95]   Strassman, P., "The Roots of Business Process Reengineering, *American Programmer,* vol. 8, no. 6, June 1995, pp. 3–7.

[YOU94]   Yourdon, E., "Software Reuse," *Application Development Strategies,* vol. VI, no. 12, December 1994, p. 1–16.

PROBLEMS AND POINTS TO PONDER

2.1. Figure 2.1 places the three software engineering layers on top of a layer entitled "a quality focus." This implies a quality program such as *Total Quality*

Management. Do a bit of research and develop an outline of the key tenets of a Total Quality Management program.

2.2. Is there ever a case when the generic phases of the software engineering process don't apply? If so, describe it.

2.3. The SEI's *Capability Maturity Model* is an evolving document. Do some research and determine if any new KPAs have been added since the publication of this book.

2.4. The Chaos model suggests that a problem solving loop can be applied at any degree of resolution. Discuss the way in which you would apply the loop to (1) understand requirements for a new word-processing product; (2) develop a advanced spelling/grammar checking component for the word processor; (3) generate code for a program module that determines the subject, predicate, and object in an English language sentence.

2.5. Which of the software engineering paradigms presented in this chapter do you think would be most effective? Why?

2.6. Provide five examples of software development projects that would be amenable to prototyping. Name two or three applications that would be more difficult to prototype.

2.7. The RAD model is often tied to CASE tools. Research the literature and provide a summary of a typical CASE tool that supports RAD.

2.8. Propose a specific software project that would be amenable to the incremental model. Present a scenario for applying the model to the software.

2.9. As you move outward along the process flow path of the spiral model, what can you say about the software that is being developed or maintained?

2.10. Many people believe that the only way in which order of magnitude improvements in software quality and productivity will be achieved is through component assembly. Find three or four recent papers on the subject and summarize them for the class.

2.11. Describe the concurrent development model in your own words.

2.12. Provide three examples of fourth generation techniques.

2.13. Which is more important—the product or the process?

FURTHER READINGS AND OTHER INFORMATION SOURCES

The current state of the art in software engineering can best be determined from monthly publications such as *IEEE Software, Computer,* and the *IEEE Transactions on Software Engineering.* Industry periodicals such as *Application Development Trends* and *Software Development* often contain articles on software engineering topics. The discipline is "summarized" every year in the *Proceedings of the International Conference on Software Engineering* (sponsored by the IEEE and ACM) and is discussed in depth in journals such as *ACM Transactions on Software Engineering and Methodology, ACM Software Engineering Notes,* and *Annals of Software Engineering.*

Many software engineering books have been published in recent years. Some present an overview of the entire process while others delve into a few important topics to the exclusion of others. Three anthologies that cover a wide range of software engineering topics are:

Keyes, J. (ed.), *Software Engineering Productivity Handbook,* McGraw-Hill, 1993.

Marchiniak, J.J. (ed.), *Encyclopedia of Software Engineering,* Wiley, 1994.

McDermid, J. (ed.), *Software Engineer's Reference Book,* CRC Press, 1993.

Gautier (*Distributed Engineering of Software,* Prentice-Hall, 1996) provides suggestions and guidelines for organizations that must develop software across geographically dispersed locations.

On the lighter side, a book by Robert Glass (*Software Conflict,* Yourdon Press, 1991) presents amusing and controversial essays on software and the software engineering process. Pressman and Herron (*Software Shock,* Dorset House, 1991) consider software and its impact on individuals, businesses, and government.

The *Software Engineering Institute* (SEI is located at Carnegie-Mellon University) has been chartered with the responsibility of sponsoring a software engineering monograph series. Practitioners from industry, government, and academia are contributing important new work. Additional software engineering publications are produced regularly by the *Software Productivity Consortium.*

A wide variety of software engineering standards and procedures have been published over the past decade. The IEEE *Software Engineering Standards* contains many different standards that cover almost every important aspect of the technology. ISO 9000-3 guidelines provides guidance for software organizations that require registration to the ISO 9001 quality standard. Other software engineering standards can be obtained from the Department of Defense, the FAA, and other government and not-for-profit agencies. Fairclough (*Software Engineering Guides,* Prentice-Hall, 1996) provides a detailed reference to software engineering standards produced by the European Space Agency (ESA).

A wide variety of information sources on software engineering and the software process are available on the Internet. Further information on software engineering can be obtained from technical societies and organizations:

ACM	**http://www.acm.org**
European SPI Initiative	**http://www.sea.uni-linz.ac.at/espiti/home.html**
IEEE	**http://www.computer.org**
NASA Software Engineering Lab	**http://fdd.gsfc.nasa.gov/seltext.html**
Research Access Clearing House	**http://www.rai.com/HomePage.html**
Software Engineering Institute	**http://www.sei.cmu.edu/**
Software Engineering Lab, EPFL	**http://lglwww.epfl.ch/**
Software Engineering Web Sites	**http://wwwsel.iit.nrc.ca/favourites.html**
Software Productivity Center, Canada	**http://www.spc.ca/spc/**
Software Productivity Consortium	**http://software.software.org/vcoe/Home.html**

A useful source of software engineering information, including a quarterly newsletter, can be found at:

http://www.tcse.org

The Software Engineering Research Center (SERC) has an ongoing technical report series describing research results. These can be found at:

http://www.cs.purdue.edu/tech-reports/serc-orders.html

A compendium of frequently asked questions (FAQ) that have been posed to the Internet newsgroup **comp.software-eng** are available at:

http://www.qucis.queensu.ca/Software-Engineering/reading.html

An up-to-date list of World Wide Web references that are relevant to the software process can be found at: **http://www.rspa.com**

MANAGING SOFTWARE PROJECTS

In this part of *Software Engineering: A Practitioner's Approach* we consider the management techniques required to plan, organize, monitor, and control software projects. In the chapters that follow, we address the following questions:

- How must people, process, and problem be managed during a software project?
- What are software metrics and how can they be used to manage the software process and the project conducted as part of the process?
- What metrics assist a manager is assessing the quality of the products that are produced and the effectiveness of the process that is applied?
- How does a software team generate reliable estimates of effort, cost, and project duration?
- When should an organization build computer software; when should it acquire software, and when should it outsource?
- What techniques can be used to formally assess the risks that can have an impact on project success?
- How does a software project manager select the set of software engineering work tasks that are appropriate for a particular project?
- How is a project schedule created?
- How is quality defined in a manner that allows a software project team to control it?
- What is software quality assurance and how is it used as a project control mechanism?
- Why are formal technical reviews so important?
- How is change managed during the development of computer software and after it is delivered to the customer?

Once these questions are answered, you'll be better prepared to manage software projects in a way that will lead to timely delivery of a high quality product.

PROJECT MANAGEMENT CONCEPTS

In the preface to his book on software project management, Meiler Page-Jones [PAG85] makes a statement that can be echoed by many software engineering consultants:

> I've visited dozens of commercial shops, both good and bad, and I've observed scores of data processing managers, again, both good and bad. Too often, I've watched in horror as these managers futilely struggled through nightmarish projects, squirmed under impossible deadlines, or delivered systems that outraged their users and went on to devour huge chunks of maintenance time.

What Page-Jones describes are symptoms that result from an array of management and technical problems. However, if a postmortem were to be conducted for every project, it is very likely that a consistent theme would be encountered: project management was weak.

In this chapter and the six that follow we will consider the key concepts that lead to effective software project management. This chapter considers basic software project management concepts and principles. Chapter 4 presents process and project metrics, the basis for effective management decision making. The techniques that are used to estimate cost and resource requirements and establish an effective project plan are discussed in Chapter 5. The management activities that lead to effective risk monitoring, mitigation, and management are presented in Chapter 6. Chapter 7 discusses the activities that are required to define project tasks and establish a workable project schedule. Finally, Chapters 8 and 9 consider techniques for ensuring quality as a project is conducted and controlling changes throughout the life of an application.

3.1   THE MANAGEMENT SPECTRUM

Effective software project management focuses on the three P's: *people, problem,* and *process.* The order is not arbitrary. The manager who forgets that software engineering work is an intensely human endeavor will never have success in project management. A manager who fails to encourage comprehensive customer communication early in the evolution of a project risks building an elegant solution for the wrong problem. Finally, the manager who pays little attention to the process runs the risk of inserting competent technical methods and tools into a vacuum.

3.1.1   People

The cultivation of motivated, highly skilled software people has been discussed since the 1960s (e.g., [COU80, DeM87, WIT94]. In fact, the "people factor" is so important that the Software Engineering Institute has developed a *people management capability maturity model* (PM-CMM) "to enhance the readiness of software organizations to undertake increasingly complex applications by helping to attract, grow, motivate, deploy, and retain the talent needed to improve their software development capability" [CUR94].

The people management maturity model defines the following key practice areas for software people: recruiting, selection, performance management, training, compensation, career development, organization and work design, and team/culture development. Organizations that achieve high levels of maturity in the people management area have a higher likelihood of implementing effective software engineering practices.

The PM-CMM is a companion to the software capability maturity model (Chapter 2), which guides organizations in the creation of a mature software process. Issues associated with people management and structure for software projects are considered later in this chapter.

3.1.2   The Problem

Before a project can be planned, its objectives and scope should be established, alternative solutions should be considered, and technical and management constraints should be identified. Without this information, it is impossible to define reasonable (and accurate) estimates of the cost; an effective assessment of risk; a realistic breakdown of project tasks; or a manageable project schedule that provides a meaningful indication of progress.

The software developer and customer must meet to define project objectives and scope. In many cases, this activity begins as part of the system engineering process (Chapter 10) and continues as the first step in software requirements analysis (Chapter 11). Objectives identify the overall goals of the project without considering how these goals will be achieved. Scope identifies the primary data, functions, and behaviors that characterize the problem, and more important, attempts to *bound* these characteristics in a quantitative manner.

Once the project objectives and scope are understood, alternative solutions are considered. Although very little detail is discussed, the alternatives enable managers and practitioners to select a "best" approach, given the constraints imposed by delivery deadlines, budgetary restrictions, personnel availability, technical interfaces, and myriad other factors.

3.1.3 The Process

A software process (Chapter 2) provides the framework from which a comprehensive plan for software development can be established. A small number of *framework activities* are applicable to all software projects, regardless of their size or complexity. A number of different *task sets*—tasks, milestones, deliverables, and quality assurance points—enable the framework activities to be adapted to the characteristics of the software project and the requirements of the project team. Finally, umbrella activities—such as software quality assurance, software configuration management, and measurement—overlay the process model. Umbrella activities are independent of any one framework activity and occur throughout the process.

3.2   PEOPLE

In a study published by the IEEE [CUR88] the engineering vice presidents of three major technology companies were asked the most important contributor to a successful software project. They answered in the following way:

VP 1:   I guess if you had to pick one thing out that is most important in our environment, I'd say it's not the tools that we use, it's the people.

VP 2:   The most important ingredient that was successful on this project was having smart people . . . very little else matters in my opinion... The most important thing you do for a project is selecting the staff... The success of the software development organization is very, very much associated with the ability to recruit good people.

VP 3:   The only rule I have in management is to ensure I have good people—real good people—and that I grow good people—and that I provide an environment in which good people can produce.

Indeed, this is a compelling testimonial on the importance of people in the software engineering process. And yet, all of us, from senior engineering vice presidents to the lowliest practitioner, often take people for granted. Managers argue (as the group above had done) that people are primary, but their actions sometimes belie their words. In this section we examine the players who participate in the software process and the manner in which they are organized to perform effective software engineering.

3.2.1 The Players

The software process (and every software project) is populated by players who can be categorized into one of five constituencies:

1. *Senior managers,* who define the business issues that often have significant influence on the project.
2. *Project (technical) managers,* who must plan, motivate, organize, and control the practitioners who do software work.
3. *Practitioners,* who deliver the technical skills that are necessary to engineer a product or application.
4. *Customers,* who specify the requirements for the software to be engineered.
5. *End users,* who interact with the software once it is released for production use.

Every software project is populated by the players noted above. To be effective, the project team must be organized in a way that maximizes each person's skills and abilities. That's the job of the team leader.

3.2.2 Team Leaders

Project management is a people-intensive activity, and for this reason, competent practitioners often make poor team leaders. They simply don't have the right mix of people skills. And yet, as Edgemon states: "Unfortunately and all too frequently it seems, individuals just fall into a project manager role and become accidental project managers" [EDG95].

What do we look for when we select someone to lead a software project? In an excellent book of technical leadership, Jerry Weinberg [WEI86] attempts to answer this question by suggesting the MOI Model of leadership:

Motivation.   The ability to encourage (by "push or pull") technical people to produce to their best ability.

Organization.   The ability to mold existing processes (or invent new ones) that will enable the initial concept to be translated into a final product.

Ideas or innovation.   The ability to encourage people to create and feel creative even when they must work within bounds established for a particular software product or application.

Weinberg suggests that successful project leaders apply a problem solving management style. That is, a software project manager should concentrate on understanding the problem to be solved, managing the flow of ideas, and at the same time, letting everyone on the team know (by words, and far more important, by actions) that quality counts and that it will not be compromised.

Another view [EDG95] of the characteristics that define an effective project manager emphasizes four key traits:

Problem solving. An effective software project manager can diagnose the technical and organizational issues that are most relevant, systematically structure a solution or properly motivate other practitioners to develop the solution, apply lessons learned from past projects to new situations, and remain flexible enough to change direction if initial attempts at problem solution are fruitless.

Managerial identity. A good project manager must take charge of the project. She must have the confidence to assume control when necessary and the assurance to allow good technical people to follow their instincts.

Achievement. To optimize the productivity of a project team, a manager must reward initiative and accomplishment, and demonstrate through his own actions that controlled risk taking will not be punished.

Influence and team building. An effective project manager must be able to "read" people; she must be able to understand verbal and nonverbal signals and react to the needs of the people sending these signals. The manager must remain under control in high-stress situations.

3.2.3 The Software Team

There are almost as many human organizational structures for software development as there are organizations that develop software. For better or worse, organizational structure cannot be easily modified. Concern with the practical and political consequences of organizational change is not within the software project manager's scope of responsibilities. However, the organization of the people directly involved in a new software project is within the project manager's purview.

The following options are available for applying human resources to a project that will require n people working for k years:

1. n individuals are assigned to m different functional tasks, relatively little combined work occurs; coordination is the responsibility of a software manager who may have six other projects to be concerned with;

2. n individuals are assigned to m different functional tasks ($m < n$) so that informal "teams" are established; an ad hoc team leader may be appointed; coordination among teams is the responsibility of a software manager;

3. n individuals are organized into t teams; each team is assigned one or more functional tasks; each team has a specific structure that is defined for all teams working on a project; coordination is controlled by both the team and a software project manager.

Although it is possible to voice pro and con arguments for each of the above approaches, there is a growing body of evidence that indicates that a formal team organization (option 3) is most productive.

The "best" team structure depends on the management style of an organization, the number of people who will populate the team and their skill levels, and the overall problem difficulty. Mantei [MAN81] suggests three generic team organizations:

Democratic decentralized (DD). This software engineering team has no permanent leader. Rather, "task coordinators are appointed for short durations and then replaced by others who may coordinate different tasks." Decisions on problems and approach are made by group consensus. Communication among team members is horizontal.

Controlled decentralized (CD). This software engineering team has a defined leader who coordinates specific tasks and secondary leaders that have responsibility for subtasks. Problem solving remains a group activity, but implementation of solutions is partitioned among subgroups by the team leader. Communication among subgroups and individuals is horizontal. Vertical communication along the control hierarchy also occurs.

Controlled Centralized (CC). Top-level problem solving and internal team coordination are managed by a team leader. Communication between the leader and team members is vertical.

Mantei also describes seven project factors that should be considered when planning the structure of software engineering teams:

- the difficulty of the problem to be solved
- the size of the resultant program(s) in lines of code or function points
- the time the team will stay together (team lifetime)
- the degree to which the problem can be modularized
- the required quality and reliability of the system to be built
- the rigidity of the delivery date
- the degree of sociability (communication) required for the project

Table 3.1 [MAN81] summarizes the impact of project characteristics on team organization. Because a centralized structure completes tasks faster, it is the most adept at handling simple problems. Decentralized teams generate more and better solutions than individuals. Therefore such teams have a greater probability of success when working on difficult problems. Since the CD team is centralized for problem solving, either the CD or the CC team structure can be successfully applied to simple problems. A DD structure is best for difficult problems.

Because the performance of a team is inversely proportional to the amount of communication that must be conducted, very large projects are best addressed by teams with a CC or CD structure when subgrouping can be easily accommodated.

TABLE 3.1

THE IMPACT OF PROJECT CHARACTERISTICS ON TEAM STRUCTURE [MAN81]

Team type:	DD	CD	CC
Difficulty			
high	x		
low		x	x
Size			
large		x	x
small	x		
Team lifetime			
short		x	x
long	x		
Modularity			
high		x	x
low	x		
Reliability			
high	x	x	
low			x
Delivery date			
strict			x
lax	x	x	
Sociability			
high	x		
low		x	x

The length of time the team will "live together" affects team morale. It has been found that DD team structures result in high morale and job satisfaction and are therefore good for long lifetime teams.

The DD team structure is best applied to problems with relatively low modularity because of the higher volume of communication that is needed. When high modularity is possible (and people can do their own thing), the CC or CD structure will work well.

CC and CD teams have been found to produce fewer defects than DD teams, but these data have much to do with the specific quality assurance activities that are applied by the team. Decentralized teams generally require more time to complete a project than a centralized structure and at the same time are best when high sociability is required.

Constantine [CON93] suggests four "organizational paradigms" for software engineering teams:

1. A *closed paradigm* structures a team along a traditional hierarchy of authority (similar to a CC team). Such teams can work well when producing

software that is quite similar to past efforts, but they will be less likely to be innovative when working within the closed paradigm.

2. The *random paradigm* structures a team loosely and depends on individual initiative of the team members. When innovation or technological breakthrough is required, teams following the random paradigm will excel. But such teams may struggle when "orderly performance" is required.

3. The *open paradigm* attempts to structure a team in a manner that achieves some of the controls associated with the closed paradigm but also much of the innovation that occurs when using the random paradigm. Work is performed collaboratively with heavy communication and consensus-based decision making. Open paradigm team structures are well suited to the solution of complex problems, but may not perform as efficiently as other teams.

4. The *synchronous paradigm* relies on the natural compartmentalization of a problem and organizes team members to work on pieces of the problem with little active communication among themselves.

As an historical footnote, the earliest software team organization was a controlled centralized (CD) structure originally called the *chief programmer team.* This structure was first proposed by Harlan Mills and described by Baker [BAK72]. The nucleus of the team is composed of a *senior engineer* ("the chief programmer") who plans, coordinates, and reviews all technical activities of the team; *technical staff* (normally two to five people) who conduct analysis and development activities, and a *backup engineer* who supports the senior engineer in his or her activities and can replace the senior engineer with minimum loss in project continuity.

The chief programmer may be served by one or more specialists (e.g., telecommunications expert, database designer), support staff (e.g., technical writers, clerical personnel) and a *software librarian.* The librarian serves many teams and performs the following functions: maintains and controls all elements of the software configuration (i.e., documentation, source listings, data, magnetic media); helps collect and format software productivity data; catalogs and indexes reusable software modules; and assists the teams in research, evaluation, and document preparation. The importance of a librarian cannot be overemphasized. The librarian acts as a controller, coordinator, and potentially, an evaluator of the software configuration.

Regardless of team organization, the objective for every project manager is to help create a team that exhibits cohesiveness. In their book, *Peopleware,* DeMarco and Lister [DeM87] discuss this issue:

> We tend to use the word *team* fairly loosely in the business world, calling any group of people assigned to work together a "team." But many of these groups just don't seem like teams. They don't have a common definition of success or any identifiable team spirit. What is missing is a phenomenon that we call *jell.*
>
> A jelled team is a group of people so strongly knit that the whole is greater than the sum of the parts...
>
> Once a team begins to jell, the probability of success goes way up. The team can become unstoppable, a juggernaut for success... They don't need to be man-

aged in the traditional way, and they certainly don't need to be motivated. They've got *momentum*.

DeMarco and Lister contend that members of jelled teams are significantly more productive and more motivated than average. They share a common goal, a common culture, and in many cases, a "sense of eliteness" that makes them unique.

3.2.4 Coordination and Communication Issues

There are many reasons that software projects get into trouble. The *scale* of many development efforts is large, leading to complexity, confusion, and significant difficulties in coordinating team members. *Uncertainty* is common, resulting in a continuing stream of changes that ratchets the project team. *Interoperability* has become a key characteristic of many systems. New software must communicate with existing software and conform to predefined constraints imposed by the system or product.

These characteristics of modern software—scale, uncertainty, and interoperability—are facts of life. To deal with them effectively, a software engineering team must establish effective methods for coordinating the people who do the work. To accomplish this, mechanisms for formal and informal communication among team members and between multiple teams must be established. Formal communication is accomplished through "writing, structured meetings, and other relatively non-interactive and impersonal communication channels" [KRA95]. Informal communication is more personal. Members of a software engineering team share ideas on an ad hoc basis, ask for help as problems arise, and interact with one another daily.

Kraul and Streeter [KRA95] examine a collection of project coordination techniques that are categorized in the following manner:

Formal, impersonal approaches. Include software engineering documents and deliverables (e.g. source code), technical memos, project milestones, schedules and project control tools (Chapter 7), changes requests and related documentation (Chapter 9), error tracking reports, and repository data (see Chapter 29).

Formal, interpersonal procedures. Focus on quality assurance activities (Chapter 8) applied to software engineering work products. These include status review meetings and design and code inspections.

Informal, interpersonal procedures. Include group meetings for information dissemination and problem solving and "collocation of requirements and development staff."

Electronic communication. Encompasses electronic mail, electronic bulletin boards, Web sites, and by extension, video-based conferencing systems.

Interpersonal network. Informal discussions with those outside the project who may have experience or insight that can assist team members.

To assess the efficacy of these techniques for project coordination, Kraul and Streeter studied 65 software projects involving hundreds of technical staff. Figure 3.1 (adapted from [KRA95]) expresses the value and use of the coordination techniques noted above. In the figure the perceived value (rated on a seven-point scale) of various coordination and communication techniques is plotted against their frequency of use on a project. Techniques that fall above the regression line were "judged to be relatively valuable, given the amount that they were used" [KRA95]. Techniques that fall below the line were perceived to have less value. It is interesting to note that interpersonal networking (discussion with peers) was rated the technique with highest coordination and communication value. It is also important to note that early software quality assurance mechanisms (requirements and design reviews) were perceived to have more value than later evaluations of source code (code inspections).

3.3   THE PROBLEM

A software project manager is confronted with a dilemma at the very beginning of a software engineering project. Quantitative estimates and an organized plan are required, but solid information is unavailable. A detailed analysis of software requirements would provide necessary information for estimates, but analysis often takes weeks or months to complete. Worse, requirements may be fluid, changing regularly as the project proceeds. Yet, a plan is needed "now!"

Therefore, we must examine the problem at the very beginning of the project. At a minimum, the scope of the problem must be established and bounded.

3.3.1   Software Scope

The first software project management activity is the determination of *software scope*. Scope is defined by answering the following questions:

Context. How does the software to be built fit into a larger system, product, or business context, and what constraints are imposed as a result of the context?

Information objectives. What customer-visible data objects (Chapter 11) are produced as output from the software? What data objects are required for input?

Function and performance. What function does the software perform to transform input data into output? Are any special performance characteristics to be addressed?

Software project scope must be unambiguous and understandable at management and technical levels. A statement of software scope must be *bounded*. That is, quantitative data (e.g., number of simultaneous users, size of mailing

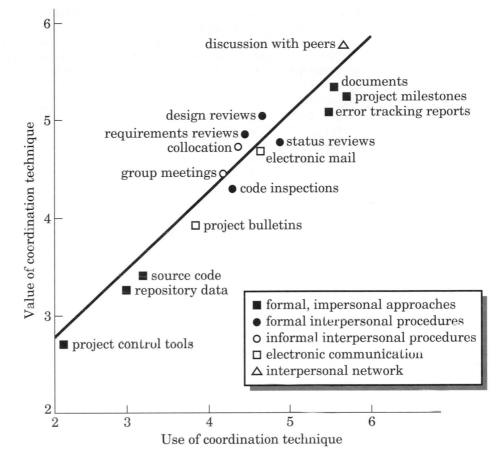

FIGURE 3.1.
Value and use of coordination and communication techniques [KRA95].

list, maximum allowable response time) are stated explicitly; constraints and/or limitations (e.g., product cost restricts memory size) are noted, and mitigating factors (e.g., desired algorithms are well understood and available in C++) are described.

3.3.2 Problem Decomposition

Problem decomposition, sometimes called *partitioning*, is an activity that sits at the core of software requirements analysis (Chapter 11). During the scoping activity there is no attempt to fully decompose the problem. Rather, decomposition is applied in two major areas: (1) the functionality that must be delivered and (2) the process that will be used to deliver it.

Human beings tend to apply a divide and conquer strategy when they are confronted with a complex problem. Stated simply, a complex problem is partitioned into smaller problems that are more manageable. This is the strategy that is applied as project planning begins. Software functions, described in the statement of scope, are evaluated and refined to provide more detail prior to the beginning of estimation (Chapter 5). Because both cost and schedule estimates are functionally oriented, some degree of decomposition is often useful.

As an example, consider a project that will build a new word processing product. Among the unique features of the product are continuous voice as well as keyboard input; extremely sophisticated "automatic copy edit" features; page layout capability; automatic indexing and table of contents; and others. The project manager must first establish a statement of scope that bounds these features (as well as other more mundane functions such as editing, file management, document production, and the like). For example, will continuous voice input require that the product be "trained" by the user? Specifically what capabilities will the copy edit feature provide? Just how sophisticated will the page layout capability be?

As the statement of scope evolves, a first level of partitioning naturally occurs. The project team learns that the marketing department has talked with potential customers and found that the following functions should be part of automatic copy editing:

- spell checking
- sentence grammar checking
- reference checking for large documents (e.g., is a reference to a bibliography entry found in the list of entries in the bibliography?)
- section and chapter reference validation for large documents

Each of these features represents a subfunction to be implemented in software. Each in turn can be further refined if the decomposition will make planning easier.

3.4   THE PROCESS

The generic phases that characterize the software process—definition, development, and maintenance—are applicable to all software. The problem is to select the process model that is appropriate for the software to be engineered by a project team. In Chapter 2, a wide array of software engineering paradigms were discussed:

- the linear sequential model
- the prototyping model
- the RAD model
- the incremental model
- the spiral model
- the component assembly model
- the concurrent development model
- the formal methods model
- the fourth generation techniques model

The project manager must decide which process model is most appropriate for the project, then define a preliminary plan based on the set of common process framework activities. Once the preliminary plan is established, process decomposition begins. That is, a complete plan reflecting the work tasks required to populate the framework activities must be created. We explore these activities briefly in the sections that follow and present a more detailed view in Chapter 7.

3.4.1 Melding the Problem and the Process

Project planning begins with the melding of the problem and the process. Each function to be engineered by the software team must pass through the set of framework activities that have been defined for a software organization. Assume that the organization has adopted the following set of framework activities (Chapter 2):

- *customer communication*—tasks required to establish effective communication between developer and customer
- *planning*—tasks required to define resources, timelines, and other project related information
- *risk analysis*—tasks required to assess both technical and management risks
- *engineering*—tasks required to build one or more representations of the application
- *construction and release*—tasks required to construct, test, install, and provide user support (e.g., documentation and training)
- *customer evaluation*—tasks required to obtain customer feedback based on evaluation of the software representations created during the engineering stage and implemented during the installation stage

The team members who work on each function will apply each of the framework activities to it. In essence, a matrix similar to the one shown in Figure 3.2 is created. Each major problem function (the figure notes functions for the word-processing software discussed earlier) is listed in the left hand column. Framework activities are listed in the top row. Software engineering work tasks (for each framework activity) would be entered in the following row.[1] The job of the project manager (and other team members) is to estimate resource requirements for each matrix cell, start and end dates for the tasks associated with each cell, and work products to be produced as a consequence of each cell. These issues are considered in Chapters 5 and 7.

---

[1] It should be noted that work tasks must be adapted to the specific needs of a project. Framework activities always remain the same, but work tasks will be selected based on a number of adaptation criteria. For a detailed discussion, see Chapter 7.

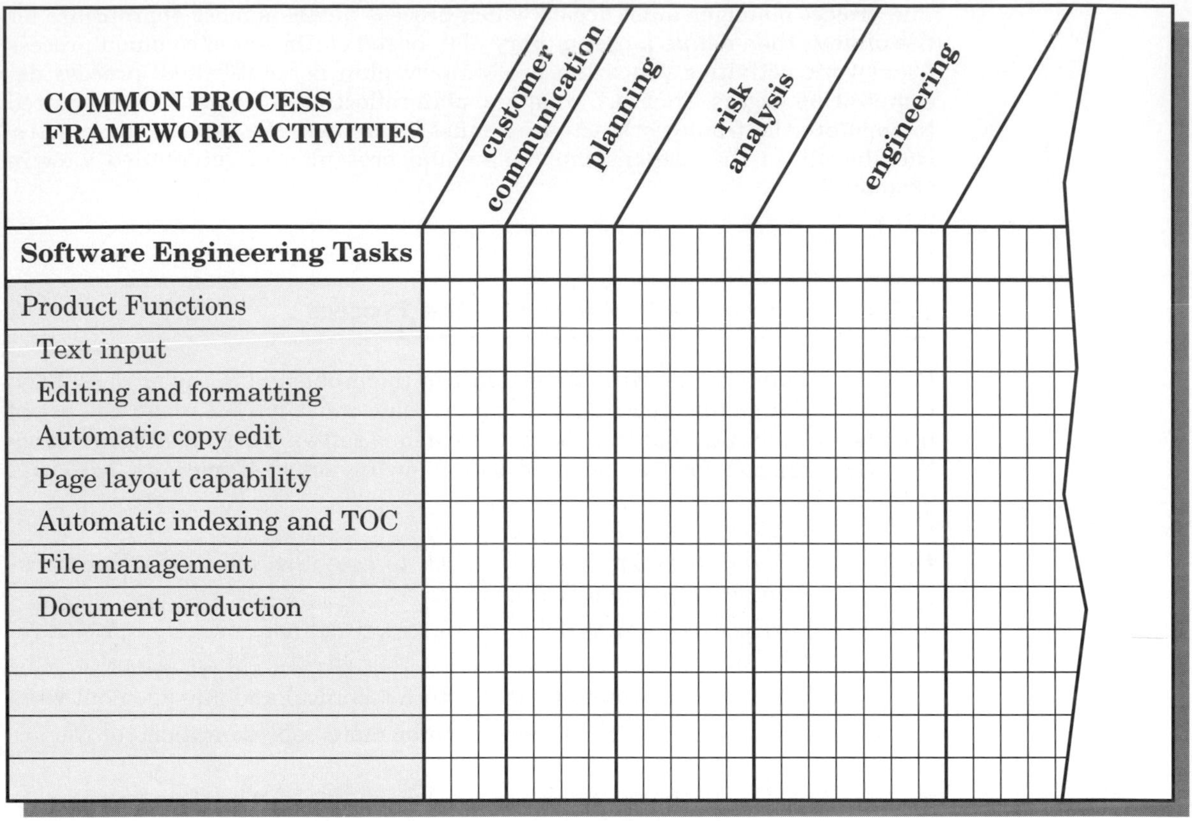

COMMON PROCESS FRAMEWORK ACTIVITIES	customer communication	planning	risk analysis	engineering	
Software Engineering Tasks					
Product Functions					
Text input					
Editing and formatting					
Automatic copy edit					
Page layout capability					
Automatic indexing and TOC					
File management					
Document production					

FIGURE 3.2.   Melding the problem and the process.

3.4.2   Process Decomposition

A software team should have a significant degree of flexibility in choosing the software engineering paradigm that is best for the project and the software engineering tasks that populate the process model once it is chosen. A relatively small project that is similar to past efforts might be best accomplished using the linear sequential approach. If very tight time constraints are imposed and the problem can be heavily compartmentalized, the RAD model is probably the right option. If the deadline is so tight that full functionality cannot reasonably be delivered, an incremental strategy might be best. Similarly, projects with other characteristics (e.g., uncertain requirements, breakthrough technology, difficult customers, significant reuse potential) will lead to the selection of other process models.[2]

---

[2]Recall that project characteristics also have a strong bearing on the structure of the team that is to do the work. See Section 3.2.3.

Once the process model has been chosen, the common process framework (CPF) is adapted to it. In every case, the CPF discussed earlier in this chapter—customer communication, planning, risk analysis, engineering, construction and release, customer evaluation—can be fitted to the paradigm. It will work for linear models, for iterative and incremental models, for evolution models, and even for concurrent or component assembly models. The CPF is invariant and serves as the basis for all software work performed by a software organization.

But actual work tasks do vary. Process decomposition commences when the project manager asks: "How do we accomplish this CPF activity?" For example, a small, relatively simple project might require the following work tasks for the *customer communication* activity:

1. Develop list of clarification issues.
2. Meet with customer to address clarification issues.
3. Jointly develop a statement of scope.
4. Review the state of scope with all concerned.
5. Modify the statement of scope as required.

These events might occur over a period of less than 48 hours. They represent a process decomposition that is appropriate for the small, relatively simple project.

Now, we consider a more complex project that has a broader scope and more significant business impact. Such a project might require the following work tasks for the *customer communication* activity:

1. Review the customer request.
2. Plan and schedule a formal, facilitated meeting with the customer.
3. Conduct research to define proposed solutions and existing approaches.
4. Prepare a "working document" and an agenda for the formal meeting.
5. Conduct the meeting.
6. Jointly develop mini-specs that reflect data, function, and behavioral features of the software.
7. Review each mini-spec for correctness, consistency, and lack of ambiguity.
8. Assemble the mini-specs into a scoping document.
9. Review the scoping document with all concerned.
10. Modify the scoping document as required.

Both projects perform the framework activity that we call customer communication, but the first project team performs half as many software engineering work tasks as the second.

3.5 THE PROJECT

Jaded industry professionals often refer to the *90-90 rule* when discussing particularly difficult software projects: *The first 90 percent of a system absorbs 90 percent of the allotted effort and time. The last 10 percent takes the other 90 percent of the allotted effort and time* [ZAH94]. This statement tells us much about the state of a project that gets into trouble:

- The manner in which progress is assessed is flawed. (Obviously, if the 90-90 rule is true, 90 percent complete is *not* an accurate indicator!)
- There is no way to calibrate progress because quantitative metrics are unavailable.
- The project plan has not been designed to accommodate resources required at the end of a project.
- Risks have not been considered explicitly, and a plan for mitigating, monitoring, and managing them has not been created.
- The schedule is (1) unrealistic or (2) flawed.

To overcome these problems, time must be spent at the beginning of a project to establish a realistic plan, during the project to monitor the plan, and throughout the project to control quality and change. The activities that absorb this time are discussed in detail in the chapters that follow.

3.6   SUMMARY

Software project management is an umbrella activity within software engineering. It begins before any technical activity is initiated and continues throughout the definition, development, and maintenance of computer software.

Three P's have a substantial influence on software project management—people, problem, and process. People must be organized into effective teams, motivated to do high-quality software work, and coordinated to achieve effective communication. The problem must be communicated from customer to developer, partitioned (decomposed) into its constituent parts, and positioned for work by the software team. The process must be adapted to the people and the problem. A common process framework is selected, an appropriate software engineering paradigm is applied, and a set of work tasks is chosen to get the job done.

The pivotal element in all software projects is people. Software engineers can be organized in a number of different team structures that range from traditional control hierarchies to "open paradigm" teams. A variety of coordination and communication techniques can be applied to support the work of the team. In general, formal reviews and informal person-to-person communication have the most value for practitioners.

The project management activity encompasses measurement and metrics, estimation, risk analysis, schedules, tracking, and control. Each of these topics is considered in the chapters that follow.

REFERENCES

[BAK72]   Baker, F.T., "Chief Programmer Team Management of Production Programming," *IBM Systems Journal,* vol. 11, no. 1, 1972, pp. 56–73.

[CON93]   Constantine, L., "Work Organization: Paradigms for Project Management and Organization, *CACM,* vol. 36, no. 10, October 1993, pp. 34–43.

[COU80]   Cougar, J., and R. Zawacki, *Managing and Motivating Computer Personnel,* Wiley, 1980.

[CUR88]   Curtis, B. et al., "A Field Study of the Software Design Process for Large Systems," *IEEE Trans. Software Engineering,* vol. 31, no. 11, November 1988, pp. 1268–1287.

[CUR94]   Curtis, B., et al., *People Management Capability Maturity Model,* Software Engineering Institute, Pittsburgh, PA, 1994.

[DeM87]   DeMarco, T., and T. Lister, *Peopleware,* Dorset House, 1987.

[EDG95]   Edgemon, J., "Right Stuff: How to Recognize It When Selecting a Project Manager," *Application Development Trends,* vol. 2, no. 5, May 1995, pp. 37–42.

[KRA95]   Kraul, R., and L. Streeter, "Coordination in Software Development," *CACM,* vol. 38, no. 3, March 1995, pp. 69–81.

[MAN81]   Mantei, M., "The Effect of Programming Team Structures on Programming Tasks," *CACM,* vol. 24, no. 3, March 1981, pp. 106–113.

[PAG85]   Page-Jones, M., *Practical Project Management,* Dorset House, 1985, p. vii.

[WEI86]   Weinberg, G., *On Becoming a Technical Leader,* Dorset House, 1986.

[WIT94]   Whitaker, K., *Managing Software Maniacs,* Wiley, 1994.

[ZAH94]   Zahniser, R., "Timeboxing for Top Team Performance," *Software Development,* March 1994, pp. 35–38.

PROBLEMS AND POINTS TO PONDER

3.1. Based on information contained in this chapter and your own experience, develop a "ten commandments" for empowering software engineers. That is, make a list of 10 guidelines that will lead to software people who work to their full potential.

3.2. The Software Engineering Institute's *People Management Capability Maturity Model (PM-CMM)* takes an organized look at "key practice areas" that cultivate good software people. Your instructor will assign you one KPA for analysis and summary.

3.3. Describe three real-life situations in which the customer and the end user are one and the same. Describe three situations in which they are different people.

3.4. The decisions made by senior management can have a significant impact on the effectiveness of a software engineering team. Provide five examples to illustrate that this is true.

3.5. Review a copy of Weinberg's book [WEI86] and write a two- or three-page summary of the issues that should be considered in applying the MOI model.

3.6. You have been appointed a project manager within an information systems organization. Your job is to build an application that is quite similar to others that your team has built, although this one is larger and more complex. Requirements have been thoroughly documented by the customer. What team structure would you choose and why? What software process model(s) would you choose and why?

3.7. You have been appointed a project manager for a small software products company. Your job is to build a breakthrough product that combines virtual reality hardware with state-of-the art software. Because competition for the home entertainment market is intense, there is significant pressure to get the job done. What team structure would you choose and why? What software process model(s) would you choose and why?

3.8. You have been appointed a project manager for a major software products company. Your job is to manage the development of the next generation version of its widely used word-processing software. Because competition is intense, tight deadlines have been established and announced. What team structure would you choose and why? What software process model(s) would you choose and why?

3.9. You have been appointed a software project manager for a company that services the genetic engineering world. Your job is to manage the development of a new software product that will accelerate the pace of gene typing. The work is R&D oriented, but the goal is to produce a product within the next year. What team structure would you choose and why? What software process model(s) would you choose and why?

3.10. Based on the results of the study referred to in Figure 3.1, documents are perceived to have more use than value. Why do you think this occurred and what can be done to move the "documents" data point above the regression line in the graph? That is, what can be done to improve the perceived value of documents?

3.11. You have been asked to develop a small application that analyzes each course offered by a university and reports the average grade obtained in the course (for a given term). Write a statement of scope that bounds this problem.

3.12. Do a first-level functional decomposition of the page layout function discussed briefly in Section 3.3.2.

FURTHER READINGS AND OTHER INFORMATION SOURCES

An excellent three volume series written by Weinberg (*Quality Software Management,* Dorset House, 1992, 1993, 1994) introduces basic of systems thinking and management concepts, explains how to use measurements effectively, and addresses "congruent action," the ability to establish "fit" between the manager's needs, the needs of technical staff, and the needs of the business. It will provide both new and experienced managers with useful information. Brooks (*The Mythical Man-Month,* Anniversary Edition, Addison-Wesley, 1995) has updated his classic book to provide new insight into software project and management issues. Purba and Shah (*How to Manage a Successful Software Project,* Wiley, 1995) present a number of case studies that indicate why some projects succeed and others fail. Bennatan (*Software Project Management in a Client/Server Environment,* Wiley, 1995) discusses special management issues associated with the development of client/server systems.

Another excellent book by Weinberg [WEI86] is must reading for every project manager and every team leader. It will give you insight and guidance in ways to do your job more effectively. House (*The Human Side of Project Management,* Addison-Wesley, 1988) and Crosby (*Running Things: The Art of Making Things Happen,* McGraw-Hill, 1989) provide practical advice for managers who must deal with human as well as technical problems. Books by

DeMarco and Lister [DeM87] and Weinberg (*Understanding the Professional Programmer,* Dorset House, 1988) provide useful insight into software people and the way in which they should be managed.

Pragmatic guidance on project management is presented by Wysocki et al. (*Effective Project Management,* Wiley, 1996), Metzger and Boddie (*Managing a Programming Project: Processes and People,* 3rd edition, Prentice-Hall, 1995), and O'Connell (*How To Run Successful Projects,* Prentice-Hall, 1994). Still another take on project management in the software world is provided by Constantine (*Constantine on Peopleware,* Prentice-Hall, 1995). McCarthy (*Dynamics of Software Development,* Microsoft Press, 1995) has written an amusing and insightful book of rules for shipping "great software" on schedule.

An excellent project management resource, containing useful information and copious references to books, tools, and training can be found at:

http://www.cis.ohio-state.edu/hypertext/faq/usenet/proj-plan-faq/faq.html

Project 2000 (PS 2000) is a European research and development program in project management. A wide variety of useful information and pointers can be obtained at:

http://www.ntnu.no/ps2000/welcome.html

The Project Management Institute Web site contains useful information on project management education programs, publications, special interest groups, and tools:

http://www.pmi.org/

An up-to-date list of World Wide Web references for software project management can be found at **http://www.rspa.com**

SOFTWARE PROCESS AND PROJECT METRICS

Measurement is fundamental to any engineering discipline, and software engineering is no exception. Lord Kelvin once said:

> When you can measure what you are speaking about and express it in numbers, you know something about it; but when you cannot measure, when you cannot express it in numbers, your knowledge is of a meager and unsatisfactory kind: it may be the beginning of knowledge, but you have scarcely, in your thoughts, advanced to the stage of a science.

Over the past decade, the software engineering community has finally begun to take Lord Kelvin's words to heart. But not without frustration and more than a little controversy!

Software metrics refers to a broad range of measurements for computer software. Measurement can be applied to the software process with the intent of improving it on a continuous basis. Measurement can be used throughout a software project to assist in estimation, quality control, productivity assessment, and project control. Finally, measurement can be used by software engineers to help assess the quality of technical work products and to assist in tactical decision making as a project proceeds.

Within the context of software project management, we are concerned primarily with productivity and quality metrics—measures of software development "output" as a function of effort and time applied and measures of the "fitness for use" of the work products that are produced. For planning and estimating purposes, our interest is historical. What was software development productivity on past projects? What was the quality of the software that was produced? How can past productivity and quality data be extrapolated to the present? How can the past help us plan and estimate more accurately?

In this chapter we consider software metrics that are used at the process and project level. In later chapters, we present metrics that are applied by software engineers in a technical setting.

4.1   MEASURES, METRICS, AND INDICATORS

Although the terms "measure," "measurement," and "metrics" are often used interchangeably, it is important to note the subtle differences between them. Because "measure" and "measurement" can be used either as a noun or a verb, definitions of the terms can become confusing. Within the software engineering context, a *measure* provides a quantitative indication of the extent, amount, dimensions, capacity, or size of some attribute of a product or process. *Measurement* is the act of determining a measure. The *IEEE Standard Glossary of Software Engineering Terms* [IEE93] defines *metric* as "a quantitative measure of the degree to which a system, component, or process possesses a given attribute."

When a single data point has been collected (e.g., the number of errors uncovered in the review of a single module), a measure has been established. Measurement occurs as the result of the collection of one or more data points (e.g., a number of module reviews are investigated to collect measures of the number of errors found during each review). A software metric relates the individual measures in some way (e.g., the average number of errors found per review or the average number of errors found per person-hour expended on reviews[1]).

A software engineer collects measures and develops metrics so that indicators will be obtained. An *indicator* is a metric or combination of metrics that provide insight into the software process, a software project, or the product itself [RAG95]. An indicator provides insight that enables the project manager or software engineers to adjust the process, the project, or the product to make things better.

For example, four software teams are working on a large software project. Each team must conduct design reviews, but is allowed to select the type of review that it will use. Upon examination of the metric, *errors found per person-hour expended,* the project manager notices that the two teams using more formal review methods exhibit an *errors found per person-hour expended* that is 40 percent higher than the other teams. Assuming all other parameters equal, this provides the project manager with an indicator that formal review methods may provide a higher return on time investment that other review approaches. She may decide to suggest that all teams use the more formal approach. The metric provides the manager with insight. And insight leads to informed decision making.

4.2   METRICS IN THE PROCESS AND PROJECT DOMAINS

Measurement is commonplace in the engineering world. We measure power consumption, weight, physical dimensions, temperature, voltage, signal-to-

---

[1]This assumes that another measure, person-hours expended, is collected for each review.

noise ratio . . . the list is almost endless. Unfortunately, measurement is far less common in the software engineering world. We have trouble agreeing on what to measure and trouble evaluating metrics that are collected.

Metrics should be collected so that process and product indicators can be ascertained. *Process indicators* enable a software engineering organization to gain insight into the efficacy of an existing process (i.e., the paradigm, software engineering tasks, work products, and milestones). They enable managers and practitioners to assess what works and what doesn't. Process metrics are collected across all projects and over long periods of time. Their intent is to provide indicators that lead to long-term software process improvement.

Project indicators enable a software project manager to (1) assess the status of an ongoing project; (2) track potential risks; (3) uncover problem areas before they "go critical"; (4) adjust work flow or tasks; and (5) evaluate the project team's ability to control quality of software engineering work products.

In some cases, the same software metrics can be used to determine both project and then process indicators. In fact, measures that are collected by a project team and converted into metrics for use during a project can also be transmitted to those with responsibility for software process improvement. For this reason, many of the same metrics are used in both the process and project domain.

4.2.1   Process Metrics and Software Process Improvement

The only rational way to improve any process is to measure specific attributes of the process, develop a set of meaningful metrics based on these attributes, and then use the metrics to provide indicators that will lead to a strategy for improvement. But before we discuss software metrics and their impact on software process improvement, it is important to note that process is only one of a number of "controllable factors in improving software quality and organizational performance" [PAU94].

In Figure 4.1, process sits at the center of a triangle connecting three factors that have a profound influence on software quality and organizational performance. The skill and motivation of people has been shown [BOE81] to be the single most influential factor in quality and performance. The complexity of the product can have a substantial impact on quality and team performance. The technology (i.e., the software engineering methods) that populates the process also has an impact. In addition, the process triangle exists within a circle of environmental conditions that include the development environment (e.g., CASE tools), business conditions (e.g., deadlines, business rules), and customer characteristics (e.g., ease of communication).

We measure the efficacy of a software process indirectly. That is, we derive a set of metrics based on the outcomes that can be derived from the process. Outcomes include measures of errors uncovered before release of the software, defects delivered to and reported by end users, work products delivered, human effort expended, calendar time expended, schedule conformance, and other measures. We also derive process metrics by measuring the characteristics of specific software engineering tasks. For example, we might measure the effort and time spent performing the umbrella activities and the generic software engineering activities described in Chapter 2.

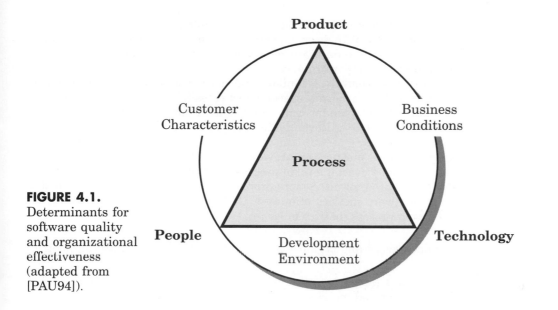

FIGURE 4.1.
Determinants for
software quality
and organizational
effectiveness
(adapted from
[PAU94]).

Grady [GRA92] argues that there are "private and public" uses for different types of process data. Because it is natural that individual software engineers might be sensitive to the use of metrics collected on an individual basis,
these data should be *private* to the individual and serve as an indicator for the
individual only. Examples of metrics that are private to the individual include:

- defect rates (by individual)
- defect rates (by module)
- errors found during development

The "private process data" philosophy conforms well with the *personal software
process* approach proposed by Humphrey [HUM95]. Humphrey describes the
approach in the following manner:

> The personal software process (PSP) is a structured set of process descriptions,
> measurements, and methods that can help engineers to improve their personal
> performance. It provides the forms, scripts, and standards that help them esti-
> mate and plan their work. It shows them how to define processes and how to
> measure their quality and productivity. A fundamental PSP principle is that
> everyone is different and that a method that is effective for one engineer may
> not be suitable for another. The PSP thus helps engineers to measure and track
> their own work so they can find the methods that are best for them.

Humphrey recognizes that software process improvement can and should begin at the individual level. Private process data can serve as an important driver as the individual software engineer works to improve.

Some process metrics are private to the software project team but *public*
to all team members. Examples include defects reported for major software

functions (that have been developed by a number of practitioners), errors found during formal technical reviews, and lines of code or function points per module and function.[2] These data are reviewed by the team to uncover indicators that can improve team performance.

Public metrics generally assimilate information that originally was private to individuals and teams. Project-level defect rates (absolutely *not* attributed to an individual), effort, calendar times, and related data are collected and evaluated in an attempt to uncover indicators that can improve organizational process performance.

Software process metrics can provide significant benefit as an organization works to improve its overall level of process maturity. However, like all metrics, these can be misused, creating more problems than they solve. Grady [GRA92] suggests a "software metrics etiquette" that is appropriate for managers as they institute a process metrics program:

- Use common sense and organizational sensitivity when interpreting metrics data.
- Provide regular feedback to the individuals and teams who have worked to collect measures and metrics.
- Don't use metrics to appraise individuals.
- Work with practitioners and teams to set clear goals and metrics that will be used to achieve them.
- Never use metrics to threaten individuals or teams.
- Metrics data that indicate a problem area should not be considered "negative." These data are merely an indicator for process improvement.
- Don't obsess on a single metric to the exclusion of other important metrics.

As an organization becomes more comfortable with the collection and use of process metrics, the derivation of simple indicators gives way to a more rigorous approach called *statistical software process improvement (SSPI)*. In essence, SSPI uses software failure analysis to collect information about all errors and defects[3] encountered as an application, system, or product is developed and used. Failure analysis works in the following manner:

1. All errors and defects are categorized by origin (e.g., flaw in specification, flaw in logic, nonconformance to standards).
2. The cost to correct each error and defect is recorded.
3. The number of errors and defects in each category are counted and ordered in descending order.

---

[2]See Sections 4.3.1 and 4.3.2 for detailed discussions of LOC and function point metrics.

[3]As we discuss in Chapter 8, an *error* is some flaw in a software engineering work product or deliverable that is uncovered by software engineers before the software is delivered to the end user. A *defect* is a flaw that is uncovered after delivery to the end user.

4. The overall cost of errors and defects in each category is computed.
5. Resultant data are analyzed to uncover the categories that result in highest cost to the organization.
6. Plans are developed to modify the process with the intent of eliminating (or reducing the frequency of occurrence of) the class of errors and defects that is most costly.

Following steps 1 and 2 above, a simple defect distribution can be developed (Figure 4.2) [GRA94]. For the pie chart noted in the figure, eight causes of defects and their origin (indicated by shading) are shown. Grady suggests the development of a *fishbone diagram* [GRA92] to help in diagnosing the data represented in the frequency diagram. In Figure 4.3 the spine of the diagram (the central line) represents the quality factor that is under consideration (in this case *specification defects* that account for 25 percent of the total). Each of the ribs (diagonal lines) connected to the spine indicates a potential cause for the quality problem (e.g., missing requirements, ambiguous specification, incorrect requirements, changed requirements). The spine and ribs notation is then added to each of the major ribs of the diagram to expand upon the cause noted. Expansion is shown only for the "incorrect" cause in Figure 4.3.

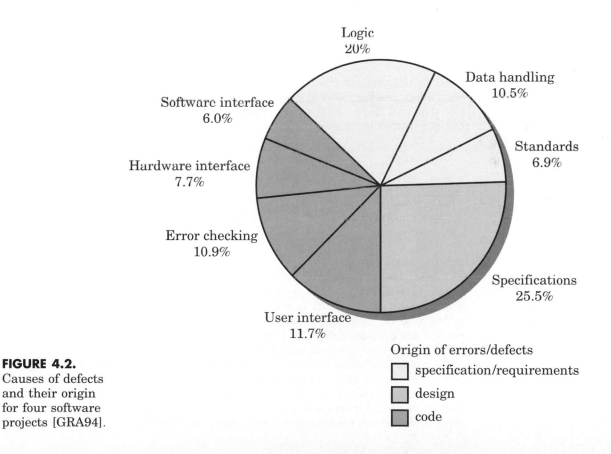

FIGURE 4.2.
Causes of defects and their origin for four software projects [GRA94].

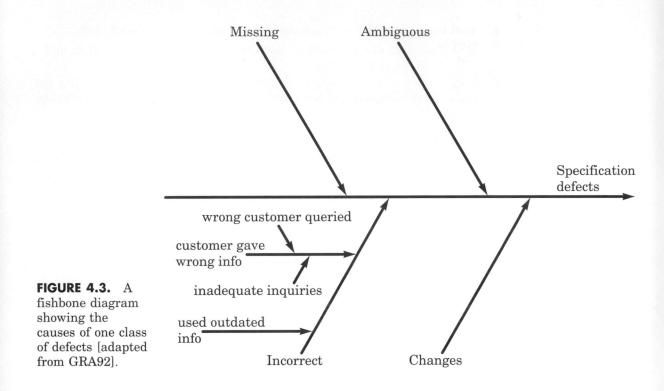

FIGURE 4.3. A fishbone diagram showing the causes of one class of defects [adapted from GRA92].

The collection of process metrics is the driver for the creation of the fishbone diagram. A completed fishbone diagram can be analyzed to derive indicators that will enable a software organization to modify its process to reduce the frequency of errors and defects.

4.2.2 Project Metrics

Software process metrics are used for strategic purposes. Software project measures are tactical. That is, project metrics and the indicators derived from them are used by a project manager and a software team to adapt project work flow and technical activities.

The first application of project metrics on most software projects occurs during estimation (Chapter 5). Metrics collected from past projects are used as a basis from which effort and time duration estimates are made for current software work. As a project proceeds, measures of effort and calendar time expended are compared to original estimates (and the project schedule). The project manager uses these data to monitor and control progress.

As technical work commences, other project metrics begin to have significance. Production rates represented in terms of pages of documentation, review hours, function points, and delivered source lines are measured. In addition, errors uncovered during each software engineering task are tracked. As the software evolves from specification into design, technical metrics (Chapter 18) are collected to assess design quality and to provide indicators that will influence the approach taken to code generation and module and integration testing.

The intent of project metrics is twofold. First, these metrics are used to minimize the development schedule by guiding the adjustments necessary to avoid delays and mitigate potential problems and risks. Second, project metrics are used to assess product quality on an ongoing basis and when necessary, modify the technical approach to improve quality.

As quality improves, errors are minimized, and as the errors count goes down, the amount of rework required during the project is also reduced. This leads to a reduction in overall project cost.

Another model of software project metrics [HET93] suggests that every project should measure:

- inputs—measures of the resources (e.g., people, environment) required to do the work,
- outputs—measures of the deliverables or work products created during the software engineering process,
- results—measures that indicate the effectiveness of the deliverables

In actuality, this model can be applied to both process and project. In the project context, the model can be applied recursively as each framework activity occurs. Therefore the outputs from one activity become inputs to the next. Results metrics can be used to provide an indication of the usefulness of work products as they flow from one framework activity (or task) to the next.

4.3   SOFTWARE MEASUREMENT

Measurements in the physical world can be categorized in two ways: *direct measures* (e.g., the length of a bolt) and *indirect measures* (e.g., the "quality" of bolts produced, measured by counting rejects). Software metrics can be categorized similarly.

Direct measures of the software engineering process include cost and effort applied. Direct measures of the product include lines of code (LOC) produced, execution speed, memory size, and defects reported over some set period of time. Indirect measures of the product include functionality, quality, complexity, efficiency, reliability, maintainability, and many other "abilities" that are discussed in Chapter 18.

We have already partitioned the software metrics domain into process, project, and product metrics. We have also noted that product metrics that are private to an individual are often combined to develop project metrics that are public to a software team. Project metrics are then consolidated to create process metrics that are public to the software organization as a whole. But how does an organization combine metrics that come from different individuals or projects?

To illustrate, we consider a simple example. Individuals on two different project teams record and categorize all errors that they find during the software engineering process. Individual measures are then combined to develop team measures. Team A found 342 errors during the software engineering process prior to release. Team B found 184 errors. All other things being equal, which team is more effective in uncovering errors throughout the process? Because we do not know the size or complexity of the projects, we cannot answer this question. However, if the measures are normalized, it is possible to create software metrics that enable comparison to broader organizational averages.

4.3.1 Size-Oriented Metrics

Size-oriented software metrics are derived by normalizing quality and/or productivity measures by considering the "size" of the software that has been produced. If a software organization maintains simple records, a table of size-oriented measures, such as the one shown in Figure 4.4, can be created. The table lists each software development project that has been completed over the past few years and corresponding measures for that project. Referring to the table entry (Figure 4.4) for project *alpha:* 12,100 lines of code (LOC) were developed with 24 person-months of effort at a cost of $168,000. It should be noted that the effort and cost recorded in the table represent all software engineering activities (analysis, design, coding, and testing), not just coding. Further information for project alpha indicates that 365 pages of documentation were developed, 134 errors were recorded before the software was released, and 29 defects were encountered after release to the customer within the first year of operation. Three people worked on the development of software for project alpha.

In order to develop metrics that can be assimilated with similar metrics from other projects, we choose lines of code as our normalization value. From

Project	LOC	Effort	$(000)	pp. doc.	Errors	Defects	People
alpha	12,100	24	168	365	134	29	3
beta	27,200	62	440	1224	321	86	5
gamma	20,200	43	314	1050	256	64	6

FIGURE 4.4.
Size-oriented metrics.

the rudimentary data contained in the table, a set of simple size-oriented metrics can be developed for each project:

- errors per KLOC (thousand lines of code)
- defects per KLOC
- $ per LOC
- pages of documentation per KLOC

In addition, other interesting metrics can be computed:

- errors/person-month
- LOC per person-month
- $/page of documentation

Size-oriented metrics are not universally accepted as the best way to measure the process of software development [JON86]. Most of the controversy swirls around the use of lines of code (LOC) as a key measure. Proponents of the LOC measure claim that LOC is an "artifact" of all software development projects and can be easily counted; that many existing software estimation models use LOC or KLOC as a key input, and that a large body of literature and data predicated on LOC already exists. On the other hand, opponents claim that LOC measures are programming language dependent; that they penalize well-designed but shorter programs; that they cannot easily accommodate non-procedural languages, and that their use in estimation requires a level of detail that may be difficult to achieve (i.e., the planner must estimate the LOC to be produced long before analysis and design have been completed).

4.3.2 Function-Oriented Metrics

Function-oriented software metrics use a measure of the functionality delivered by the application as a normalization value. Since "functionality" cannot be measured directly, it must be derived indirectly using other direct measures. Function-oriented metrics were first proposed by Albrecht [ALB79], who suggested a measure called the *function point*. Function points are derived using an empirical relationship based on countable (direct) measures of software's information domain and assessments of software complexity.

Function points are computed by completing the table shown in Figure 4.5. Five information domain characteristics are determined, and counts are provided in the appropriate table location. Information domain values are defined in the following manner[4]:

---

[4]In actuality, the definition of information domain values and the manner in which they are counted are a bit more complex. The interested reader should see [IFP94] for details.

Weighting Factor

measurement parameter	count		simple	average	complex		
number of user inputs	☐	×	3	4	6	=	☐
number of user outputs	☐	×	4	5	7	=	☐
number of user inquiries	☐	×	3	4	6	=	☐
number of files	☐	×	7	10	15	=	☐
number of external interfaces	☐	×	5	7	10	=	☐
count = total							☐

FIGURE 4.5. Computing function point metrics.

Number of user inputs. Each user input that provides distinct application-oriented data to the software is counted. Inputs should be distinguished from inquiries, which are counted separately.

Number of user outputs. Each user output that provides application-oriented information to the user is counted. In this context output refers to reports, screens, error messages, and so on. Individual data items within a report are not counted separately.

Number of user inquiries. An inquiry is defined as an on-line input that results in the generation of some immediate software response in the form of an on-line output. Each distinct inquiry is counted.

Number of files. Each logical master file (i.e., a logical grouping of data that may be one part of a large database or a separate file), is counted.

Number of external interfaces. All machine readable interfaces (e.g., data files on tape or disk) that are used to transmit information to another system are counted.

Once the above data have been collected, a complexity value is associated with each count. Organizations that use function point methods develop criteria for determining whether a particular entry is simple, average, or complex. Nonetheless, the determination of complexity is somewhat subjective.

To compute function points (FP), the following relationship is used:

$$FP = \text{count-total} \times [0.65 + 0.01 \times \Sigma \ F_i] \tag{4.1}$$

where count-total is the sum of all entries obtained from Figure 4.5.

The F_i ($i = 1$ to 14) are "complexity adjustment values" based on responses to questions [ART85] noted in Table 4.1. The constant values in the equation

---

TABLE 4.1

COMPUTING FUNCTION POINTS

Rate each factor on a scale of 0 to 5:

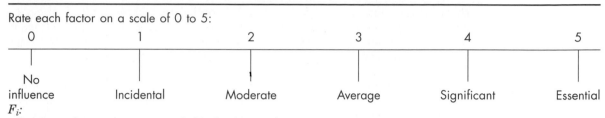

| 0 | 1 | 2 | 3 | 4 | 5 |
| No influence | Incidental | Moderate | Average | Significant | Essential |

F_i:
1. Does the system require reliable backup and recovery?
2. Are data communications required?
3. Are there distributed processing functions?
4. Is performance critical?
5. Will the system run in an existing, heavily utilized operational environment?
6. Does the system require on-line data entry?
7. Does the on-line data entry require the input transaction to be built over multiple screens or operations?
8. Are the master files updated on-line?
9. Are the inputs, outputs, files, or inquiries complex?
10. Is the internal processing complex?
11. Is the code designed to be reusable?
12. Are conversion and installation included in the design?
13. Is the system designed for multiple installations in different organizations?
14. Is the application designed to facilitate change and ease of use by the user?

and the weighting factors that are applied to information domain counts are determined empirically.

Once function points have been calculated, they are used in a manner analogous to LOC to normalize measures of software productivity, quality, and other attributes:

- errors per FP
- defects per FP
- $ per FP
- page of documentation per FP
- FP per person-month

4.3.3 Extended Function Point Metrics

The function point metric was originally designed to be applied to business information systems applications. To accommodate these applications, the data dimension (the information domain values discussed above) was emphasized to the exclusion of the functional and behavioral (control) dimensions. For this reason, the function point measure was inadequate for many engineering and embedded systems (which emphasize function and control). A number of extensions to the basic function point measure have been proposed to remedy this situation.

A function point extension called *feature points* [JON91], is a superset of the function point measure that can be applied to systems and engineering software applications. The feature point measure accommodates applications in which algorithmic complexity is high. Real-time, process control, and embedded software applications tend to have high algorithmic complexity and are therefore amenable to the feature point.

To compute the feature point, information domain values are again counted and weighted as described in Section 4.3.2. In addition, the feature point metric counts a new software characteristic, *algorithms*. An algorithm is defined as "a bounded computational problem that is included within a specific computer program" [JON91]. Inverting a matrix, decoding a bit string, or handling an interrupt are all examples of algorithms.

Another function point extension for real-time systems and engineered products has been developed by Boeing. The Boeing approach integrates the data dimension of software with the functional and control dimensions to provide a function oriented measure, called the *3D Function Point* [WHI95], that is amenable to applications that emphasize function and control capabilities. Characteristics of all three software dimensions are "counted, quantified, and transformed" into a measure that provides an indication of the functionality delivered by the software.

The *data dimension* is evaluated in much the same way as described in Section 4.3.2. Counts of retained data (the internal program data structure, e.g., files) and external data (inputs, outputs, inquiries, and external references) are used along with measures of complexity to derive a data dimension count.

The *functional dimension* is measured by considering "the number of internal operations required to transform input to output data" [WHI95]. For the purposes of 3D function point computation, a "transformation" is viewed as a series of processing steps that are constrained by a set of semantic statements. As a general rule, a transformation is accomplished with an algorithm that results in a fundamental change to input data as it is processed to become output data. Processing steps that acquire data from a file and simply place that data into program memory would not be considered a transformation. The data itself has not been changed in any fundamental way.

The level of complexity assigned to each transformation is a function of the number of processing steps and the number of semantic statements that control the processing steps. Figure 4.6 provides guidelines for assigning complexity in the functional dimension.

The *control dimension* is measured by counting the number of transitions between states.[5] A state represents some externally observable mode of behavior, and a transition occurs as a result of some event that causes the software or system to change its mode of behavior (i.e., to change state). For example, a cel-

---

[5] A detailed discussion of the behavioral dimension, including states and state transitions, is presented in Chapter 12.

Processing Steps \ Semantic Statements	1–5	6–10	11+
1–10	low	low	average
11–20	low	average	high
21+	average	high	high

FIGURE 4.6.
Determining the complexity of a transformation for 3D function points [WHI95].

lular phone contains software that supports auto dial functions. To enter the **auto-dial** state from a **resting** state, the user presses an *Auto* key on the key pad. This event causes an LCD display to prompt for a code that will indicate the party to be called. Upon entry of the code and touching the *Dial* key (another event), the cellular phone software makes a transition to the **dialing** state. When computing 3D function points, transitions are not assigned a complexity value.

To compute 3D function points, the following relationship is used:

$$\text{index} = I + O + Q + F + E + T + R \qquad (4.2)$$

where I, O, Q, F, E, T, and R represent complexity weighted values for the elements discussed above: inputs, outputs, inquiries, internal data structures, external files, transformations, and transitions, respectively. Each complexity weighted value is computed using the following relationship:

$$\text{complexity weighted value} = N_{il}W_{il} + N_{ia}W_{ia} + N_{ih}W_{ih} \qquad (4.3)$$

where N_{il}, N_{ia}, and N_{ih} represent the number of occurrences of element i (e.g., outputs) for each level of complexity (low, average, high), and W_{il}, W_{ia}, and W_{ih} are the corresponding weights. The overall computation for 3D function points is shown in Figure 4.7.

It should be noted that function points, feature points, and 3D function points represent the same thing—"functionality" or "utility" delivered by software. In fact, each of these measures results in the same value if only the data dimension of an application is considered. For more complex real-time systems, the feature point count is often between 20 and 35 percent higher than the count determined using function points alone.

The function point (and its extensions), like the LOC measure, is controversial. Proponents claim that FP is programming language independent, making it ideal for applications using conventional and nonprocedural languages, and that it is based on data that are more likely to be known early in the evolution of a project, making FP more attractive as an estimation approach.

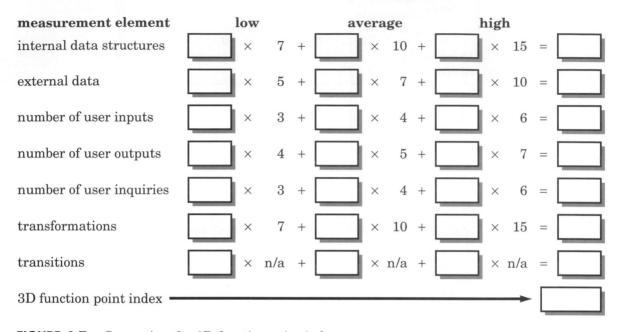

Complexity Weighting

measurement element	low			average			high			=	
internal data structures		× 7	+		× 10	+		× 15	=		
external data		× 5	+		× 7	+		× 10	=		
number of user inputs		× 3	+		× 4	+		× 6	=		
number of user outputs		× 4	+		× 5	+		× 7	=		
number of user inquiries		× 3	+		× 4	+		× 6	=		
transformations		× 7	+		× 10	+		× 15	=		
transitions		× n/a	+		× n/a	+		× n/a	=		

3D function point index ⟶ ☐

FIGURE 4.7. Computing the 3D function point index.

Opponents claim that the method requires some "sleight of hand" in that computation is based on subjective, rather than objective, data; that counts of the information domain (and other dimensions) can be difficult to collect after-the-fact; and that FP has no direct physical meaning—it's just a number.

4.4   RECONCILING DIFFERENT METRICS APPROACHES

The relationship between lines of code and function points depends upon the programming language that is used to implement the software and the quality of the design. A number of studies have attempted to relate FP and LOC measures. To quote Albrecht and Gaffney [ALB83]:

The thesis of this work is that the amount of function to be provided by the application (program) can be estimated from the itemization of the major components[6] of data to be used or provided by it. Furthermore, this estimate of func-

---

[6]It is important to note that "the itemization of major components" can be interpreted in a variety of ways. Some software engineers who work in an object-oriented development environment use the number of classes or objects as the dominant size metric (see Chapter 23 for additional discussion). A maintenance organization might view project size in terms of the number of engineering change orders (Chapter 9). An information systems organization might view the number of business processes impacted by an application.

tion should be correlated to both the amount of LOC to be developed and the development effort needed.

The following table [ALB83, JON91] provides rough estimates of the average number of lines of code required to build one function point in various programming languages:

Programming Language	LOC/FP (average)
assembly language	320
C	128
Cobol	105
Fortran	105
Pascal	90
Ada	70
object-oriented languages	30
fourth generation languages (4GLs)	20
code generators	15
spreadsheets	6
graphical languages (icons)	4

A review of the above data indicates that one LOC of Ada provides approximately 1.4 times as much "functionality" (on average) as one LOC of Fortran. Furthermore, one LOC of a 4GL provides between three and five times the functionality of a LOC for a conventional programming language. More detailed data on the relationship between FP and LOC are presented in [JON91] and can be used to "backfire" (i.e., to compute the number of function points when the number of delivered LOC are known) existing programs to determine the FP measure for each.

LOC and FP measures are often used to derive productivity metrics. This invariably leads to a debate about the use of such data. Should the LOC/person-month (or FP/person-month) of one group be compared to similar data from another? Should managers appraise the performance of individuals by using these metrics? The answers to these questions is an emphatic NO! The reason for this response is that many factors influence productivity, making for "apples and oranges" comparisons that can be easily misinterpreted.

Basili and Zelkowitz [BAS78] define five important factors that influence software productivity:

People factors. The size and expertise of the development organization.

Problem factors. The complexity of the problem to be solved and the number of changes in design constraints or requirements.

Process factors. Analysis and design techniques that are used, languages and CASE tools available, and review techniques.

Product factors. Reliability and performance of the computer-based system.

Resource factors. Availability of CASE tools and hardware and software resources.

If one of the productivity factors is above average (highly favorable) for a given project, software development productivity will be significantly higher than if the same factor is below average (unfavorable).

4.5   METRICS FOR SOFTWARE QUALITY

The overriding goal of software engineering is to produce a high-quality system, application, or product. To achieve this goal, software engineers must apply effective methods coupled with modern tools within the context of a mature software process. In addition, a good software engineer (and good software engineering managers) must measure if high quality is to be realized.

The quality of a system, application, or product is only as good as the requirements that describe the problem, the design that models the solution, the code that leads to an executable program, and the tests that exercise the software to uncover errors. A good software engineer uses measurement to assess the quality of the analysis and design models, the source code, and the test cases that have been created as the software is engineered. To accomplish this real-time quality assessment, the engineer must use *technical measures* (Chapters 18 and 23) to evaluate quality in objective, rather than subjective, ways.

The project manager must also evaluate quality as the project progresses. Private metrics collected by individual software engineers are assimilated to provide project-level results. Although many quality measures can be collected, the primary thrust at the project level is to measure errors and defects. Metrics derived from these measures provide an indication of the effectiveness of individual and group software quality assurance and control activities.

Errors uncovered per review hour and errors uncovered per testing hour provide insight into the efficacy of each of the activities implied by the metric. Error data can also be used to compute the *defect removal efficiency (DRE)*[7] for each process framework activity. DRE is discussed in Section 4.5.3.

4.5.1   An Overview of Factors that Affect Quality

Over two decades ago, McCall and Cavano [MCC78] defined a set of quality factors that were a first step toward the development of metrics for software quality. These factors assess software from three distinct points of view: (1) product operation (using it), (2) product revision (changing it), and (3) product transition (modifying it to work in a different environment, i.e., "porting" it). In their work, the authors describe the relationship between these quality factors (what they call a "framework") and other aspects of the software engineering process:

First, the framework provides a mechanism for the project manager to identify what qualities are important. These qualities are attributes of the software, in

---

[7]Defect removal efficiency can also be used to assess the impact of quality assurance activities across the entire process. This topic is considered in Chapter 8.

addition to its functional correctness and performance, which have life cycle implications. Such factors as maintainability and portability have been shown in recent years to have significant life cycle cost impact . . .

Secondly, the framework provides a means for quantitatively assessing how well the development is progressing relative to the quality goals established. . . .

Thirdly, the framework provides for more interaction of QA personnel throughout the development effort. . . .

Lastly, ... quality assurance personnel can use indications of poor quality to help identify [better] standards to be enforced in the future.

A detailed discussion of McCall and Cavano's framework, as well as other quality factors, is presented in Chapter 18. It is interesting to note that nearly every aspect of computing has undergone radical change as the years have passed since McCall and Cavano did their seminal work in 1978. But the attributes that provide an indication of software quality remain the same.

What does this mean? If a software organization adopts a set of quality factors as a "checklist" for assessing software quality, it is likely that software built today will still exhibit quality well into the first few decades of the twenty-first century. Even as computing architectures undergo radical change (as they surely will), software that exhibits high quality in operation, transition, and revision will continue to serve its users well.

4.5.2 Measuring Quality

Although there are many measures of software quality, *correctness, maintainability, integrity,* and *usability* provide useful indicators for the project team. Gilb [GIL88] suggests definitions and measures for each.

Correctness.   A program must operate correctly or it provides little value to its users. Correctness is the degree to which the software performs its required function. The most common measure for correctness is *defects per KLOC,* where a defect is defined as a verified lack of conformance to requirements.

Maintainability.   Software maintenance accounts for more effort than any other software engineering activity. Maintainability is the ease with which a program can be corrected if an error is encountered, adapted if its environment changes, or enhanced if the customer desires a change in requirements. There is no way to measure maintainability directly; therefore, we must use indirect measures. A simple time-oriented metric is mean-time-to-change (MTTC), the time it takes to analyze the change request, design an appropriate modification, implement the change, test it, and distribute the change to all users. On average, programs that are maintainable will have a lower MTTC (for equivalent types of changes) than programs that are not maintainable.

Hitachi [TAJ81] has used a cost-oriented metric for maintainability called "spoilage"—the cost to correct defects encountered after the software has been released to its end users. When the ratio of spoilage to overall project cost (for many projects) is plotted as a function of time, a manager can determine whether the overall maintainability of software produced by a software development organization is improving. Actions can then be taken in response to the insight gained from this information.

Integrity.   Software integrity has become increasingly important in the age of hackers and viruses. This attribute measures a system's ability to withstand attacks (both accidental and intentional) on its security. Attacks can be made on all three components of software: programs, data, and documents.

To measure integrity, two additional attributes must be defined: threat and security. *Threat* is the probability (which can be estimated or derived from empirical evidence) that an attack of a specific type will occur within a given time. *Security* is the probability (which can be estimated or derived from empirical evidence) that the attack of a specific type will be repelled. The integrity of a system can then be defined as:

$$\text{integrity} = \sum \, [1 - \text{threat} \times (1 - \text{security})]$$

where threat and security are summed over each type of attack.

Usability.   The catch-phrase "user friendliness" has become ubiquitous in discussions of software products. If a program is not "user friendly," it is often doomed to failure, even if the functions that it performs are valuable. Usability is an attempt to quantify "user friendliness" and can be measured in terms of four characteristics: (1) the physical and/or intellectual skill required to learn the system; (2) the time required to become moderately efficient in the use of the system; (3) the net increase in productivity (over the approach that the system replaces) measured when the system is used by someone who is moderately efficient, and (4) a subjective assessment (sometimes obtained through a questionnaire) of users attitudes toward the system. Further discussion of this topic is contained in Chapter 14.

The four factors described above are only a sampling of those that have been proposed as measures for software quality. Chapter 18 considers this topic in additional detail.

4.5.3   Defect Removal Efficiency

A quality metric that provides benefit at both the project and process level is defect removal efficiency (DRE). In essence, DRE is a measure of the filtering ability of quality assurance and control activities as they are applied throughout all process framework activities.

When considered for a project as a whole, DRE is defined in the following manner:

$$\text{DRE} = E/(E + D) \qquad\qquad (4.4)$$

where E = number of errors found before delivery of the software to
the end user

D = number of defects found after delivery

The ideal value for DRE is 1. That is, no defects are found in the software. Realistically, D will be greater than zero, but the value of DRE can still approach 1 as E increases. In fact, as E increases, it is likely that the final value of D will decrease (errors are filtered out before they become defects). If used as a metric that provides an indicator of the filtering ability of quality control and assurance activities, DRE encourages a software project team to institute techniques for finding as many errors as possible before delivery.

DRE can also be used within the project to assess a team's ability to find errors before they are passed to the next framework activity or software engineering task. For example, the requirements analysis task produces an analysis model that can be reviewed to find and correct errors. Those errors that are not found during the review of the analysis model are passed on to the design task (where they may or may not be found). When used in this context, we redefine DRE as:

$$\text{DRE}_i = E_i/(E_i + E_{i+1}) \qquad\qquad (4.5)$$

where E_i = number of errors found during software engineering activity i

E_{i+1} = number of errors found during software engineering activity $i + 1$ that are traceable to errors that were not discovered in software engineering activity i

A quality objective for a software team (or an individual software engineer) is to achieve DRE_i that approaches 1. That is, errors should be filtered out before they are passed on to the next activity.

4.6   **INTEGRATING METRICS WITHIN THE SOFTWARE PROCESS**

The majority of software developers still do not measure, and sadly, most have little desire to begin. As we noted earlier in this chapter, the problem is cultural. Attempting to collect measures where none had been collected in the past often precipitates resistance. "Why do we need to do this?" asks a harried project manager. "I don't see the point," complains an overworked practitioner.

Why is it so important to measure the process of software engineering and the product (software) that it produces? The answer is relatively obvious. If we do not measure, there is no real way of determining whether we are improving. And if we are not improving, we are lost.

Measurement is one of a number of "medications" that may help cure the "software affliction" described in Chapter 1. It provides benefits at the strategic level, at the project level, and at the technical level.

By requesting and evaluating productivity and quality measures, senior management can establish meaningful goals for improvement of the software engineering process. In Chapter 1 we noted that software is a strategic business issue for many companies. If the process through which it is developed can be improved, a direct impact on the bottom line can result. But to establish goals for improvement, the current status of software development must be understood. Hence, measurement is used to establish a process baseline from which improvements can be assessed.

The day-to-day rigors of software project work leave little time for strategic thinking. Software project managers are concerned with more mundane (but equally important) issues: developing meaningful project estimates; producing higher-quality systems; getting product out the door on time. By using measurement to establish a project baseline, each of these issues becomes more manageable. We have already noted that the baseline serves as a basis for estimation. Additionally, the collection of quality metrics enables an organization to "tune" its software engineering process to remove the "vital few" causes of defects that have the greatest impact on software development.[8]

At the project and technical level (in the trenches), software metrics provide immediate benefit. As the software design is completed, most developers would be anxious to obtain answers to the questions such as:

- Which user requirements are most likely to change?
- Which modules in this system are most error prone?
- How much testing should be planned for each module?
- How many errors (of specific types) can I expect when testing commences?

Answers to these questions can be determined if metrics have been collected and used as a technical guide. In later chapters we will examine how this is done.

The process for establishing a baseline[9] is illustrated in Figure 4.8. Ideally, data needed to establish a baseline has been collected in an ongoing manner. Sadly, this is rarely the case. Therefore, *data collection* requires an historical investigation of past projects to reconstruct required data. Once measures have been collected (unquestionably the most difficult step), *metrics computation* is possible. Depending on the breadth of measures collected, metrics can span a broad range of LOC or FP metrics as well as other quality and project-oriented metrics. Finally, metrics must be evaluated and applied during estimation, technical work, project control, and process improvement. *Metrics evaluation* focuses on the underlying reasons for the results obtained and produces a set of indicators that guide the project or process.

---

[8]These ideas have been formalized into an approach called *statistical software quality assurance* and are discussed in detail in Chapter 8.

[9]The metrics baseline consists of data collected from past software development projects and can be as simple as the table presented in Figure 4.4 or as complex as a comprehensive database containing dozens of project measures and the metrics derived from them.

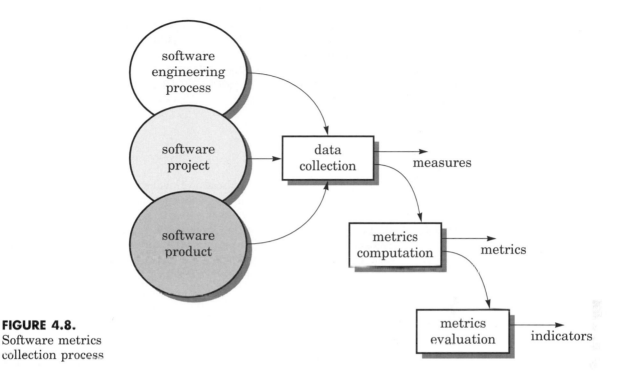

FIGURE 4.8.
Software metrics
collection process

4.7   SUMMARY

Measurement enables managers and practitioners to improve the software process; assist in the planning, tracking, and control of a software project; and assess the quality of the product (software) that is produced. Measures of specific attributes of the process, project, and product are used to compute software metrics. These metrics can be analyzed to provide indicators that guide management and technical actions.

Process metrics enable an organization to take a strategic view by providing insight into the effectiveness of a software process. Project metrics are tactical. They enable a project manager to adapt project work flow and technical approach in a real-time manner.

Both size- and function-oriented metrics are used throughout the industry. Size-oriented metrics make use of the line of code as a normalizing factor for other measures such as person-months or defects. The function point is derived from measures of the information domain and a subjective assessment of problem complexity.

Software quality metrics, like productivity metrics, focus on the process, the project, and the product. By developing and analyzing a metrics baseline for quality, an organization can act to correct those areas of the software process that are the cause of software defects. In this chapter, four quality metrics—correctness, maintainability, integrity, and usability—are discussed. Additional quality metrics are described later in this book.

Measurement results in cultural change. Data collection, metrics computation, and metrics evaluation are the three steps that must be implemented to begin a metrics program. By creating a metrics baseline—a database containing process and product measurements—software engineers and their managers can gain better insight into the work that they do and the product that they produce.

REFERENCES

[ALB79]   Albrecht, A.J., "Measuring Application Development Productivity," *Proc. IBM Application Development Symposium,* Monterey, CA, October 1979, pp. 83–92.

[ALB83]   Albrecht, A.J., and J.E. Gaffney, "Software Function, Source Lines of Code and Development Effort Prediction: A Software Science Validation," *IEEE Trans. Software Engineering,* November 1983, pp. 639–648.

[ART85]   Arthur, L.J., *Measuring Programmer Productivity and Software Quality,* Wiley-Interscience, 1985.

[BAS78]   Basili, V., and M. Zelkowitz, "Analyzing Medium Scale Software Development," *Proc. 3rd Intl. Conf. Software Engineering,* IEEE, 1978, pp. 116–123.

[BOE81]   Boehm, B., *Software Engineering Economics,* Prentice-Hall, 1981.

[GIL88]   Gilb, T., *Principles of Software Project Management,* Addison-Wesley, 1988.

[GRA87]   Grady, R.B. and Caswell, D.L., *Software Metrics: Establishing a Company-Wide Program,* Prentice-Hall, 1987.

[GRA92]   Grady, R.B., *Practical Software Metrics for Project Management and Process Improvement,* Prentice-Hall, 1992.

[GRA94]   Grady, R.B., "Successfully Applying Software Metrics," *Computer,* vol. 27, no. 9, September 1994, pp. 18–25.

[HET93]   Hetzel, W., *Making Software Measurement Work,* QED Publishing Group, 1993.

[HUM95]   Humphrey, W., *A Discipline for Software Engineering,* Addison-Wesley, 1995.

[IEE93]   *IEEE Software Engineering Standards,* Std. 610.12-1990, pp. 47–48.

[IFP94]   *Function Point Counting Practices Manual,* Release 4.0, International Function Point Users Group (IFPUG), 1994.

[JON86]   Jones, C., *Programming Productivity,* McGraw-Hill, 1986.

[JON91]   Jones, C., *Applied Software Measurement,* McGraw-Hill, 1991.

[MCC78]   McCall, J.A., and J.P. Cavano, "A Framework for the Measurement of Software Quality," *ACM Software Quality Assurance Workshop*. November 1978.

[PAU94]   Paulish, D., and A. Carleton, "Case Studies of Software Process Improvement Measurement," *Computer,* vol. 27, no. 9, September 1994, pp. 50–57.

[RAG95]   Ragland, B., "Measure, Metric or Indicator: What's the Difference?" *Crosstalk,* vol. 8, no. 3, March 1995, pp. 29–30.

[TAJ81]   Tajima, D., and T. Matsubara, "The Computer Software Industry in Japan," *Computer,* May 1981, p. 96.

[WHI95] Whitmire, S.A., "An Introduction to 3D Function Points, *Software Development,* April 1995, pp. 43–53.

PROBLEMS AND POINTS TO PONDER

4.1. Suggest three measures, three metrics, and corresponding indicators that might be used to assess an automobile.

4.2. Suggest three measures, three metrics, and corresponding indicators that might be used to assess the service department of an automobile dealership.

4.3. Describe the difference between process and project metrics in your own words.

4.4. Why should some software metrics be kept "private"? Provide examples of three metrics that should be private. Provide examples of three metrics that should be public.

4.5. Obtain a copy of [HUM95] and write a one- or two-page summary that outlines the PSP approach.

4.6. Grady suggests an etiquette for software metrics. Can you add three more rules to those noted in Section 4.2.1?

4.7. Attempt to complete the fishbone diagram shown in Figure 4.3. That is, following the approach used for "Incorrect" specifications, provide analogous information for "Missing," "Ambiguous," and "Changes."

4.8. What is an indirect measure and why are such measures common in software metrics work?

4.9. Team A found 342 errors during the software engineering process prior to release. Team B found 184 errors. What additional measures would have to be made for projects A and B to determine which of the teams eliminated errors more efficiently? What metrics would you propose to help make the determination? What historical data might be useful?

4.10. Present an argument against lines of code as a measure for software productivity. Will your case hold up when dozens or hundreds of projects are considered?

4.11. Compute the function point value for a project with the following information domain characteristics:

Number of user inputs: 32

Number of user outputs: 60

Number of user inquiries: 24

Number of files: 8

Number of external interfaces: 2

Assume that all complexity adjustment values are average. Assume that 14 algorithms have been counted. Compute the feature point value under the same conditions.

4.12. Compute the 3D function point value for an embedded system with the following characteristics:

Internal data structures: 6

External data structures: 3

Number of user inputs: 12

Number of user outputs: 60

Number of user inquiries: 9

Number of external interfaces: 3

Transformations: 36

Transitions: 24

Assume that the complexity of the above counts is evenly divided among low, average, and high.

4.13. The software used to control an advanced photocopier requires 32,000 lines of C and 4200 lines of a 4GL-like specialized language. Estimate the number of function points for the software inside the photocopier.

4.14. McCall and Cavano (Section 4.5.1) define a "framework" for software quality. Using information contained in this and other books, expand each of the three major "points of view" into a set of quality factors and metrics.

4.15. Develop your own metrics (do not use those presented in this chapter) for correctness, maintainability, integrity, and usability. Be sure that they can be translated into quantitative values.

4.16. Is it possible for spoilage to increase while defects/KLOC decreases? Explain.

4.17. Does the LOC measure make any sense when fourth generation languages are used? Explain.

4.18. Write a paper outlining the results of software productivity studies (see Further Readings). Is there commonality among the results?

4.19. Collect software metrics for 2 to 5 projects on which you have worked. Basic information should include cost (if applicable), LOC or function points, effort (person-months), a complexity indicator (scale 1 to 10), and chronological time to completion. Combine your data with information from other students/colleagues and check a class metrics baseline.

4.20. Put together a presentation that could be used to convince management that measurement would be a worthwhile activity. Be sure to use a quantitative argument. Present it to your class.

FURTHER READINGS AND OTHER INFORMATION SOURCES

Software process improvement has received a significant amount of attention in recent years. Books by Humphrey [HUM95], Yeh (*Software Process Control,* McGraw-Hill, 1993), Hetzel [HET93], and Grady [GRA92] discuss how software metrics can be used to provide the indicators necessary to improve the software process. Putnam and Myers (*Executive Briefing: Controlling Software Development,* IEEE Computer Society, 1996) and Pulford and his colleagues (*A Quantitative Approach to Software Management,* Addison-Wesley, 1996) discuss process metrics and their use from a management point of view.

Weinberg (*Quality Software Management, Volume 2: First Order Measurement,* Dorset House, 1993) presents a useful model for observing software projects, ascertaining the meaning of the observation, and determining its significance for tactical and strategic decisions. Garmus and Herron (*Measuring the Software Process,* Prentice-Hall, 1996) discuss process metrics with an emphasis on function point analysis. The Software Productivity Consortium, (*The Software Measurement Guidebook,* Thomson Computer Press, 1995) provides useful suggestions for instituting an effective metrics approach.

Many industry reports and metrics guidebooks, published by the Department of Defense and government/industry research centers, have emerged over the past decade. A sampling includes:

Andres, D., *Software Project Management Using Effective Process Metrics: The CCPDS-R Experience,* TRW-TS-89-01, TRW Systems Engineering & Development Division, November 1989.

Carleton, A.D. et al., *Software Measurement for DoD Systems: Recommendations for Initial Core Measures,* CUM/SEI-92-TR-19, Carnegie-Mellon University, Software Engineering Institute, September 1992.

Florac, W.A., Software Quality Measurement: A Framework for Counting Problems and Defects, CMU/SEI-92-TR-22, Carnegie-Mellon University, Software Engineering Institute, September 1992.

Metrics Reporting Guidebook, Version 1.1, Defense Information Systems Agency, prepared by Mitre Corp., May 1994.

Metrics Starter Kit and Guidelines, Software Technology Support Center, Hill AFB, UT, 1994.

On the Internet, research reports and pointers to information on software metrics are available at the Software Engineering Laboratory:

http://fdd.gsfc.nasa.gov/seltext.html

The U.S. Army software Metric System Web site contains a variety of useful information on process metrics:

http://www.army.mil/optec-pg/homepage.htm

A comprehensive listing of textbooks and papers on process metrics can be obtained at:

http://www.rai.com/soft_eng/sme.html

A Listserv mailing list that addresses function point metrics has been established. To subscribe, send mail to: cim **@crim.ca**

SUBJECT: "none" (this field must be empty)
CONTENT: SUB FUNCTION.POINT.LIST "Your name"

An up-to-date list of World Wide Web references for software process metrics can be found at: **http://www.rspa.com**

SOFTWARE PROJECT PLANNING

The software project management process begins with a set of activities that are collectively called *project planning*. The first of these activities is *estimation*. Whenever estimates are made, we look into the future and accept some degree of uncertainty as a matter of course. To quote Frederick Brooks [BRO75]:

> [O]ur techniques of estimating are poorly developed. More seriously, they reflect an unvoiced assumption that is quite untrue, i.e., that all will go well . . . [B]ecause we are uncertain of our estimates, software managers often lack the courteous stubbornness to make people wait for a good product.

Although estimating is as much art as it is science, this important activity need not be conducted in a haphazard manner. Useful techniques for time and effort estimation do exist. And because estimation lays a foundation for all other project planning activities, and project planning provides the road map for successful software engineering, we would be ill-advised to embark without it.

5.1 OBSERVATIONS ON ESTIMATING

A leading executive was once asked what single characteristic was most important when selecting a project manager. His response: "a person with the ability to know what will go wrong before it actually does." We might add: "and the courage to estimate when the future is cloudy."

Estimation of resources, cost, and schedule for a software development effort requires experience, access to good historical information, and the courage to commit to quantitative measures when qualitative data are all that exist. Estimation carries inherent risk[1] and it is this risk that leads to uncertainty.

Project complexity has a strong effect on uncertainty that is inherent in planning. Complexity, however, is a relative measure that is affected by familiarity with past effort. A real-time application might be perceived as "exceedingly complex" to a software group that has previously developed only batch applications. The same real-time application might be perceived as "run-of-the-mill" for a software group that has been heavily involved in high speed process control. A number of quantitative software complexity measures have been proposed (Chapters 18 and 23). Such measures are applied at the design or code level and are therefore difficult to use during software planning (before a design and code exist). However, other, more subjective assessments of complexity (e.g., the function point complexity adjustment factors described in Chapter 4) can be established early in the planning process.

Project size is another important factor that can affect the accuracy of estimates. As size increases, the interdependency among various elements of the software grows rapidly.[2] Problem decomposition, an important approach to estimating, becomes more difficult because decomposed elements may still be formidable. To paraphrase Murphy's law: "what can go wrong will go wrong"—and if there are more things that can fail, more things will fail.

The degree of *structural uncertainty* also has an effect on estimation risk. In this context, structure refers to the degree to which requirements have been solidified, the ease with which functions can be compartmentalized, and the hierarchical nature of information that must be processed.

The availability of historical information also determines estimation risk. Santayana once said, "Those who cannot remember the past are condemned to repeat it." By looking back, we can emulate things that worked and avoid areas where problems arose. When comprehensive software metrics (Chapter 4) are available for past projects, estimates can be made with greater assurance; schedules can be established to avoid past difficulties, and overall risk is reduced.

Risk is measured by the degree of uncertainty in the quantitative estimates established for resources, cost, and schedule. If project scope is poorly understood or project requirements are subject to change, uncertainty and risk become dangerously high. The software planner should demand completeness of function, performance, and interface definitions (contained in a *system specification*). The planner, and more important the customer, should recognize that variability in software requirements means instability in cost and schedule.

As a final observation on estimating, we consider the words of Aristotle (330 B.C.):

> [I]t is the mark of an instructed mind to rest satisfied with the degree of precision which the nature of a subject admits, and not to seek exactness when only an approximation of the truth is possible. . . .

---

[1]Systematic techniques for risk analysis are presented in Chapter 6.

[2]Size often increases due to the "scope creep" that occurs when the customer changes requirements. Increases in project size can have a geometric impact on project cost and schedule [MAH96].

A project manager should not become obsessive about estimation. Modern software engineering approaches (e.g., evolutionary process models) take an iterative view of development. In such approaches, it is possible[3] to revisit the estimate (as more information is known) and revise it when the customer makes changes to requirements.

5.2   PROJECT PLANNING OBJECTIVES

The objective of software project planning is to provide a framework that enables the manager to make reasonable estimates of resources, cost, and schedule. These estimates are made within a limited time frame at the beginning of a software project and should be updated regularly as the project progresses. In addition, estimates should attempt to define "best case" and "worst case" scenarios so that project outcomes can be bounded.

The planning objective is achieved through a process of information discovery that leads to reasonable estimates. In the following sections, each of the activities associated with software project planning is discussed.

5.3   SOFTWARE SCOPE

The first activity in software project planning is the determination of *software scope*. Function and performance allocated to software during system engineering (Chapter 10) should be assessed to establish a project scope that is unambiguous and understandable at management and technical levels.

Software scope describes function, performance, constraints, interfaces, and reliability. *Functions* described in the statement of scope are evaluated and in some cases refined to provide more detail prior to the beginning of estimation. Because both cost and schedule estimates are functionally oriented, some degree of decomposition is often useful. *Performance* considerations encompass processing and response time requirements. *Constraints* identify limits placed on the software by external hardware, available memory or other existing systems.

5.3.1   Obtaining Information Necessary for Scope

Things are always somewhat hazy at the beginning of a software project. A need has been defined and basic goals and objectives have been enunciated, but the information necessary to define scope (a prerequisite for estimation) has not yet been defined.

The most commonly used technique to bridge the communication gap between the customer and developer and to get the communication process started

---

[3]This is not meant to imply that it is always politically acceptable to modify initial estimates. A mature software organization and its managers recognize that change is *not* free. And yet, many customers demand (incorrectly) that an estimate once made must be maintained regardless of changing circumstances.

is to conduct a preliminary meeting or interview. The first meeting between a software engineer (the analyst) and the customer can be likened to the awkwardness of a first date between two adolescents. Neither person knows what to say or ask; both are worried that what they do say will be misinterpreted; both are thinking about where it might lead (both likely have radically different expectations here); both want to get the thing over with; but at the same time, both want it to be a success.

Yet, communication must be initiated. Gause and Weinberg [GAU89] suggest that the analyst start by asking *context free questions*. That is, a set of questions that will lead to a basic understanding of the problem, the people who want a solution, the nature of the solution that is desired, and the effectiveness of the first encounter itself.

The first set of context free questions focus on the customer, the overall goals, and the benefits. For example, the analyst might ask:

- Who is behind the request for this work?
- Who will use the solution?
- What will be the economic benefit of a successful solution?
- Is there another source for the solution?

The next set of questions enable the analyst to gain a better understanding of the problem and the customer to voice his or her perceptions about a solution:

- How would you [the customer] characterize "good" output that would be generated by a successful solution?
- What problem(s) will this solution address?
- Can you show me (or describe) the environment in which the solution will be used?
- Are there special performance issues or constraints that will affect the way the solution is approached?

The final set of questions focus on the effectiveness of the meeting. Gause and Weinberg call these "meta-questions" and propose the following (abbreviated) list:

- Are you the right person to answer these questions? Are your answers "official?"
- Are my questions relevant to the problem that you have?
- Am I asking too many questions?
- Is there anyone else who can provide additional information?
- Is there anything else that I should be asking you?

These questions (and others) will help to "break the ice" and initiate the communication that is essential to establish the scope of the project. But a question and answer meeting format is not an approach that has been overwhelmingly successful. In fact, the Q&A session should be used for the first encounter only and then be replaced by a meeting format that combines elements of problem solving, negotiation, and specification.

A number of independent investigators have developed a team-oriented approach to requirements gathering that can be applied to help establish the scope of a project.[4] Called *facilitated application specification techniques (FAST),* this approach encourages the creation of a joint team of customers and developers who work together to identify the problem, propose elements of the solution, negotiate different approaches, and specify a preliminary set of requirements.

5.3.2 A Scoping Example

Communication with the customer leads to a definition of the data, functions, and behavior that must be implemented, the performance and constraints that bound the system, and related information. As an example, consider software that must be developed to drive a conveyor line sorting system (CLSS). The statement of scope for the CLSS follows:

> The conveyor line sorting system (CLSS) sorts boxes moving along a conveyor line. Each box is identified by a bar code that contains a part number and is sorted into one of six bins at the end of the line. The boxes pass by a sorting station that contains a bar code reader and a PC. The sorting station PC is connected to a shunting mechanism that sorts the boxes into the bins. Boxes pass in random order and are evenly spaced. The line is moving at five feet per minute. A CLSS is depicted schematically in Figure 5.1.
>
> CLSS software receives input information from a bar code reader at time intervals that conform to the conveyor line speed. Bar code data will be decoded into box identification format. The software will do a look-up in a part number data base containing a maximum of 1000 entries to determine proper bin location for the box currently at the reader (sorting station). The proper bin location is passed to a sorting shunt that will position boxes in the appropriate bin. A record of the bin destination for each box will be maintained for later recovery and reporting. CLSS software will also receive input from a pulse tachometer that will be used to synchronize the control signal to the shunting mechanism. Based on the number of pulses that will be generated between the sorting station and the shunt, the software will produce a control signal to the shunt to properly position the box.

The project planner examines the statement of scope and extracts all important software functions. This process, called *decomposition,* is was discussed in Chapter 3 and results in the following functions:[5]

---

[4]It should be noted that these techniques are often viewed as a first step in requirements analysis and are discussed in more detail in Chapter 11.

[5]In reality, the functional decomposition is performed during system engineering (Chapter 10). The planner uses information derived from the system specification to define software functions.

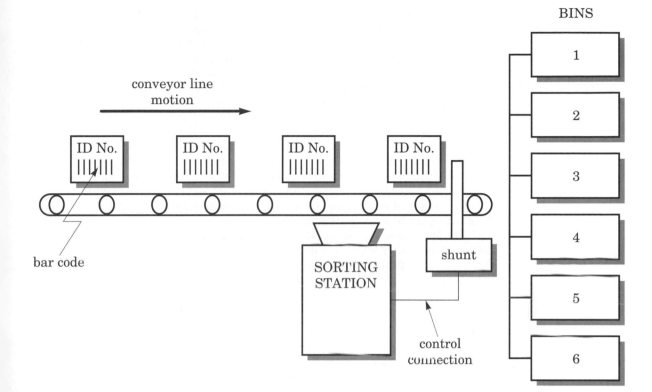

FIGURE 5.1. A conveyor line sorting system.

- read bar code input
- read pulse tachometer
- decode part code data
- do database look-up
- determine bin location
- produce control signal for shunt
- maintain record of box destinations

In this case, performance is dictated by conveyor line speed. Processing for each box must be completed before the next box arrives at the bar code reader. The CLSS software is constrained by the hardware it must access (the bar code reader, the shunt, the PC), the available memory, and the overall conveyor line configuration (evenly spaced boxes).

Function, performance, and constraints must be evaluated together. The same function can precipitate an order of magnitude difference in development effort when considered in the context of different performance bounds. The effort and cost required to develop CLSS software would be dramatically different if function remains the same (i.e., put boxes into bins) but performance varies. For instance, if conveyor line average speed increases by a factor of 10 (performance) and boxes are no longer spaced evenly (a constraint), software would become considerably more complex and thereby require more effort. Function, performance, and constraint are intimately connected.

Software interacts with other elements of a computer-based system. The planner considers the nature and complexity of each interface to determine any affect on development resources, cost, and schedule. The concept of an interface is interpreted to mean (1) hardware (e.g., processor, peripherals) that executes the software and devices (e.g., machines, displays) that are indirectly controlled by the software; (2) software that already exists (e.g., database access routines, reusable software components, operating system) and must be linked to the new software; (3) people who make use of the software via keyboard or other I/O devices; and (4) procedures that precede or succeed the software as a sequential series of operations. In each case the information transfer across the interface must be clearly understood.

The least precise aspect of software scope is a discussion of reliability. Software reliability measures do exist (Chapter 8), but they are rarely used at this stage of a project. Classic hardware reliability characteristics like mean-time-between-failure (MTBF) can be difficult to translate to the software domain. However, the general nature of the software may dictate special considerations to ensure "reliability." For example, software for an air traffic control system or the Space Shuttle (both human-rated systems) must not fail or human life may be lost. An inventory control system or word-processing software should not fail, but the impact of failure is considerably less dramatic. Although it may not be possible to quantify software reliability as precisely as we would like in the statement of scope, we can use the nature of the project to aid in formulating estimates of effort and cost to assure reliability.

If a system specification (see Chapter 10) has been properly developed, nearly all information required for a description of software scope is available and documented before software project planning begins. In cases where a specification has not been developed, the planner must take on the role of system analyst to determine attributes and bounds that will influence estimation tasks.

5.4   RESOURCES

The second task of software planning is estimation of resources required to accomplish the software development effort. Figure 5.2 illustrates development resources as a pyramid. The *development environment*—hardware and software tools—sits at the foundation of the resources pyramid and provides the infrastructure to support the development effort. At a higher level we encounter *reusable software components*—software building blocks that can dramatically reduce development costs and accelerate delivery. At the top of the pyramid is the primary resource—*people*. Each resource is specified with four characteristics: description of the resource, a statement of availability, chronological time that the resource will be required, and duration of time that the resource will be applied. The last two characteristics can be viewed as a *time window*. Availability of the resource for a specified window must be established at the earliest practical time.

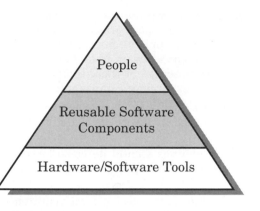

FIGURE 5.2.
Resources.

5.4.1 Human Resources

The planner begins by evaluating scope and selecting the skills required to complete development. Both organizational position (e.g., manager, senior software engineer, etc.) and specialty (e.g., telecommunications, database, client/server) are specified. For relatively small projects (six person-months or less) a single individual may perform all software engineering steps, consulting with specialists as required.

The number of people required for a software project can be determined only after an estimate of development effort (e.g., person-months or person-years) is made. Techniques for estimating effort are discussed later in the chapter.

5.4.2 Reusable Software Resources

Any discussion of the software resource would be incomplete without recognition of *reusability*—that is, the creation and reuse of software building blocks [HOO91]. Such building blocks must be catalogued for easy reference, standardized for easy application, and validated for easy integration.

Bennatan [BEN92] suggests four software resource categories that should be considered as planning proceeds:

Off-the-shelf components. Existing software that can be acquired from a third party or that has been developed internally for a past project. These components are ready for use on the current project and have been fully validated.

Full-experience components. Existing specifications, designs, code, or test data developed for past projects that are similar to the software to be built for the current project. Members of the current software team have had full experience in the application area represented by these components. Therefore, modifications required for full-experience components will be relatively low-risk.

Partial-experience components.   Existing specifications, designs, code, or test data developed for past projects that are related to the software to be built for the current project, but will require substantial modification. Members of the current software team have only limited experience in the application area represented by these components. Therefore, modifications required for partial-experience components have a fair degree of risk.

New components.   Software components that must be built by the software team specifically for the needs of the current project.

The following guidelines should be considered by the software planner when reusable components are specified as a resource:

1. If off-the-shelf components meet project requirements, acquire them. The cost for acquisition and integration of off-the-shelf components will almost always be less than the cost to develop equivalent software.[6] In addition, risk is relatively low.

2. If full-experience components are available, the risks associated with modification and integration are generally acceptable. The project plan should reflect the use of these components.

3. If partial-experience components are available, their use for the current project must be analyzed in detail. If extensive modification is required before the components can be properly integrated with other elements of the software, proceed carefully. The cost to modify partial-experience components can sometimes be greater than the cost to develop new components.

Ironically, the use of reusable software components is often neglected during planning, only to become a paramount concern during the development phase of the software process. It is far better to specify software resource requirements early. In this way technical evaluation of alternatives can be conducted and timely acquisition can occur.

5.4.3 Environmental Resources

The environment that supports the software project, often called a *software engineering environment (SEE),* incorporates hardware and software. Hardware provides a platform that supports the tools (software) required to produce the work products that are an outcome of good software engineering practice.[7] Because most software organizations have multiple constituencies that require access to the SEE, a project planner must prescribe the time window required for hardware and software and verify that these resources will be available.

---

[6]When existing software components are used during a project, the overall cost reduction can be dramatic. In fact, industry data indicate that cost, time to market, and the number of defects delivered to the field all are reduced [MAH96].

[7]Other hardware—the *target environment*—is the computer on which the software will execute when it has been released to the end user.

When a computer-based system (incorporating specialized hardware and software) is to be engineered, the software team may require access to hardware elements being developed by other engineering teams. For example, software for a numerical control (NC) used on a class of machine tools may require a specific machine tool (e.g., a NC lathe) as part of the validation test step; a software project for automated typesetting may need a photo-typesetter at some point during development. Each hardware element must be specified by the software project planner.

5.5   SOFTWARE PROJECT ESTIMATION

In the early days of computing, software costs comprised a small percentage of overall computer-based system cost. An order of magnitude error in estimates of software cost had relatively little impact. Today, software is the most expensive element in most computer-based systems. A large cost estimation error can make the difference between profit and loss. Cost overrun can be disastrous for the developer.

Software cost and effort estimation will never be an exact science. Too many variables—human, technical, environmental, political—can affect the ultimate cost of software and effort applied to develop it. However, software project estimation can be transformed from a mysterious art to a series of systematic steps that provide estimates with acceptable risk.

To achieve reliable cost and effort estimates, a number of options arise:

1. Delay estimation until late in the project (obviously, we can achieve 100% accurate estimates after the project is complete!).
2. Base estimates on similar projects that have already been completed.
3. Use relatively simple "decomposition techniques" to generate project cost and effort estimates.
4. Use one or more empirical models for software cost and effort estimation.

Unfortunately, the first option, however attractive, is not practical. Cost estimates must be provided "up-front." However, we should recognize that the longer we wait, the more we know, and the more we know, the less likely we are to make serious errors in our estimates.

The second option can work reasonably well if the current project is quite similar to past efforts and other project influences (e.g., the customer, business conditions, the SEE, deadlines) are equivalent. Unfortunately, past experience has not always been a good indicator of future results.

The remaining options are viable approaches to software project estimation. Ideally, the techniques noted for each option should be applied in tandem, each used as a cross-check for the other. *Decomposition techniques* take a "divide and conquer" approach to software project estimation. By decomposing a project into major functions and related software engineering activities, cost and effort estimation can be performed in a stepwise fashion. *Empirical estimation models* can be used to complement decomposition techniques and offer a potentially valuable estimation approach in their own right. A model is based on experience (historical data) and takes the form:

$$d = f(v_i)$$

where d is one of a number of estimated values (e.g., effort, cost, project duration) and v_i are selected independent parameters (e.g., estimated LOC or FP).

Automated estimation tools implement one or more decomposition techniques or empirical models. When combined with an interactive human–machine interface, automated tools provide an attractive option for estimating. In such systems, the characteristics of the development organization (e.g., experience, environment) and the software to be developed are described. Cost and effort estimates are derived from these data.

Each of the viable software cost estimation options is only as good as the historical data used to seed the estimate. If no historical data exist, costing rests on a very shaky foundation. In Chapter 4, we examined the characteristics of some of the software metrics that provide the basis for historical estimation data.

5.6   DECOMPOSITION TECHNIQUES

Software project estimation is a form of problem solving, and in most cases, the problem to be solved (i.e., developing a cost and effort estimate for a software project) is too complex to be considered in one piece. For this reason, we decompose the problem, recharacterizing it as a set of smaller (and hopefully more manageable) problems.

In Chapter 3, the decomposition approach was discussed from two different points of view: decomposition of the problem and decomposition of the process. Estimation makes use of one or both of these forms of partitioning. But before an estimate can be made, the project planner must understand the scope of the software to be built and generate an estimate of its "size."

5.6.1 Software Sizing

The accuracy of a software project estimate is predicated on a number of things: (1) the degree to which the planner has properly estimated the size of the product to be built; (2) the ability to translate the size estimate into human effort, calendar time, and dollars (a function of the availability of reliable software metrics from past projects); (3) the degree to which the project plan reflects the abilities of the software team; and (4) the stability of product requirements and the environment that supports the software engineering effort.

In this section, we consider the *software sizing* problem. Because a project estimate is only as good as the estimate of the size of the work to be accomplished, sizing represents the project planner's first major challenge. In the context of project planning, size refers to a quantifiable outcome of the software project. If a direct approach is taken, size can be measured in LOC. If an indirect approach is chosen, size is represented as FP.

Putnam and Myers [PUT92] suggest four different approaches to the sizing problem:

"Fuzzy-logic" sizing. This approach uses the approximate reasoning techniques that are the cornerstone of fuzzy logic. To apply this approach, the planner must identify the type of application, establish its magnitude on a qualitative scale, and then refine the magnitude within the original range. Although personal experience can be used, the planner should also have access to an historical database of projects[8] so that estimates can be compared to actual experience.

Function point sizing. The planner develops estimates of the information domain characteristics discussed in Chapter 4.

Standard component sizing. Software is composed of a number of different "standard components" that are generic to a particular application area. For example, the standard components for an information system are subsystems, modules, screens, reports, interactive programs, batch programs, files, LOC, and object-level instructions. The project planner estimates the number of occurrences of each standard component and then uses historical project data to determine the delivered size per standard component. To illustrate, consider an information systems application. The planner estimates that 18 reports will be generated. Historical data indicates that 967 lines of Cobol [PUT92] are required per report. This enables the planner to estimate that 17,000 LOC will be required for the reports component. Similar estimates and calculations are made for other standard components, and a combined size value (adjusted statistically) results.

Change sizing. This approach is used when a project encompasses the use of existing software that must be modified in some way as part of a project. The planner estimates the number and type (e.g., reuse, adding code, changing code, deleting code) of modifications that must be accomplished. Using an "effort ratio" [PUT92] for each type of change, the size of the change may be estimated.

Putnam and Myers suggest that the results of each of the sizing approaches noted above be combined statistically to create a *three-point* or *expected value* estimate. This is accomplished by developing optimistic (low), most likely, and pessimistic (high) values for size and combining them using equations (5.1) described in the next section.

5.6.2 Problem-Based Estimation

In Chapter 4, lines of code (LOC) and function points (FP) were described as basic measures from which productivity metrics can be computed. LOC and FP data are used in two ways during software project estimation: (1) as an *estimation variable* that is used to "size" each element of the software, and (2) as *baseline metrics* collected from past projects and used in conjunction with estimation variables to develop cost and effort projections.

---

[8]See Section 5.9 for a brief discussion of tools that support fuzzy-logic sizing and the other techniques discussed in this section.

LOC and FP estimation are distinct estimation techniques, yet both have a number of characteristics in common. The project planner begins with a bounded statement of software scope and from this statement attempts to decompose software into problem functions that can each be estimated individually. LOC or FP (the estimation variable) is then estimated for each function. Alternatively, the planner may choose another component for sizing such as classes or objects, changes, or business processes impacted.

Baseline productivity metrics (e.g., LOC/pm or FP/pm[9]) are then applied to the appropriate estimation variable and cost or effort for the function is derived. Function estimates are combined to produce an overall estimate for the entire project.

It is important to note, however, that there is often substantial scatter in productivity metrics for an organization, making the use of a single baseline productivity metric suspect. In general, LOC/pm or FP/pm averages should be computed by project domain. That is, projects should be grouped by team size, application area, complexity, and other relevant parameters. Local domain averages should then be computed. When a new project is estimated, it should first be allocated to a domain, and then the appropriate domain average for productivity should be used in generating the estimate.

The LOC and FP estimation techniques differ in the level of detail required for decomposition and the target of the partitioning. When LOC is used as the estimation variable, decomposition[10] is absolutely essential and is often taken to considerable levels of detail. The greater the degree of partitioning, the more likely that reasonably accurate estimates of LOC can be developed.

For FP estimates, decomposition works differently. Rather than focusing on function, each of the information domain characteristics—inputs, outputs, data files, inquiries, and external interfaces—and the fourteen *complexity adjustment values* discussed in Chapter 4 are estimated. The resultant estimates are used to derive a FP value that can be tied to past data and used to generate an estimate.

Regardless of the estimation variable that is used, the project planner begins by estimating a range of values for each function or information domain value. Using historical data or (when all else fails) intuition, the planner estimates an optimistic, most likely, and pessimistic size value for each function or count for each information domain value. An implicit indication of the degree of uncertainty is provided when a range of values is specified.

A *three-point* or *expected value* is then computed. The expected value for the estimation variable (size), *EV,* can be computed as a weighted average of the optimistic (s_{opt}), most likely (s_m), and pessimistic (s_{pess}) estimates. For example,

$$EV = (s_{opt} + 4s_m + s_{pess})/6 \tag{5.1}$$

gives heaviest credence to the "most likely" estimate and follows a beta probability distribution.

---

[9]The acronym pm stands for person-month.

[10]In general, problem functions are decomposed. However, a list of standard components (Section 5.6.1) may be used instead.

We assume that there is a very small probability that the actual size result will fall outside the optimistic or pessimistic values. Using standard statistical techniques, we can compute the deviation of the estimates. However, it should be noted that a deviation based on uncertain (estimated) data must be used judiciously.

Once the expected value for the estimation variable has been determined, historical LOC or FP productivity data are applied. Are the estimates correct? The only reasonable answer to this question is: "We can't be sure." Any estimation technique, no matter how sophisticated, must be cross-checked with another approach. Even then, common sense and experience must prevail.

5.6.3   An Example of LOC-Based Estimation

As an example of LOC and FP estimation techniques, let us consider a software package to be developed for a computer-aided design (CAD) application for mechanical components. A review of the system specification indicates that the software is to execute on an engineering workstation and must interface with various computer graphics peripherals including a mouse, digitizer, high-resolution color display, and laser printer.

Using a system specification as a guide, a preliminary statement of software scope can be developed:

> The CAD software will accept two- and three-dimensional geometric data from an engineer. The engineer will interact and control the CAD system through a user interface that will exhibit characteristics of good human-machine interface design. All geometric data and other supporting information will be maintained in a CAD database. Design analysis modules will be developed to produce required output which will be displayed on a variety of graphics devices. The software will be designed to control and interact with peripheral devices that include a mouse, digitizer, and laser printer.

The above statement of scope is preliminary—it is *not* bounded. Every sentence would have to be expanded to provide concrete detail and quantitative bounding. For example, before estimation can begin the planner must determine what "characteristics of good human-machine interface design" means or what the size and sophistication of the "CAD database" is to be.

For our purposes, we assume that further refinement has occurred and that the following major software functions are identified:

- user interface and control facilities (UICF)
- two-dimensional geometric analysis (2DGA)
- three-dimensional geometric analysis (3DGA)
- database management (DBM)
- computer graphics display facilities (CGDF)
- peripheral control (PC)
- design analysis modules (DAM)

Function	Estimated LOC
user interface and control facilities (UICF)	2,300
two-dimensional geometric analysis (2DGA)	5,300
three-dimensional geometric analysis (3DGA)	6,800
database management (DBM)	3,350
computer graphics display facilities (CGDF)	4,950
peripheral control (PC)	2,100
design analysis modules (DAM)	8,400
estimated lines of code	33,200

FIGURE 5.3.
Estimation table
for LOC method.

Following the three-point estimation technique for LOC, the table shown in Figure 5.3 is developed. For example, the range of LOC estimates for the 3D geometric analysis function is:

    optimistic: 4600
    most likely: 6900
    pessimistic: 8600

Applying equation (5.1), the expected value for the 3D geometric analysis function is 6800 LOC. This number is entered in the table. Other estimates are derived in a similar fashion. By summing vertically in the *estimated LOC* column, an estimate of 33,200 lines of code is established for the CAD system.

A review of historical data indicates that the organizational average productivity for systems of this type is 620 LOC/pm. Based on a burdened labor rate of $8000 per month, the cost per line of code is approximately $13.00. Based on the LOC estimate and the historical productivity data, the total estimated project cost is $431,000 and the estimated effort is 54 person-months.[11]

5.6.4 An Example of FP-Based Estimation

Decomposition for FP-based estimation focuses on information domain values, rather than software functions. Recalling the function point calculation table presented in Figure 4.5, the project planner estimates inputs, outputs, inquiries, files, and external interfaces for the CAD software. For the purposes of this estimate, the complexity weighting factor is assumed to be average. Figure 5.4 presents the results of this estimate.

---

[11]Estimates are rounded off to the nearest $1000 and person-month. Arithmetic precision to the nearest dollar or tenth of a month is unrealistic.

Information Domain Value	opt.	likely	pess.	est. count	weight	FP-count
number of inputs	20	24	30	24	4	96
number of outputs	12	15	22	16	5	80
number of inquiries	16	22	28	22	4	88
number of files	4	4	5	4	10	40
number of external interfaces	2	2	3	2	7	14
count-total						**318**

FIGURE 5.4. Estimating information domain values.

Each of the complexity weighting factors is estimated and the complexity adjustment factor is computed as described in Chapter 4:

Factor	Value
Backup and recovery	4
Data communications	2
Distributed processing	0
Performance critical	4
Existing operating environment	3
On-line data entry	4
Input transaction over multiple screens	5
Master files updated on-line	3
Information domain values complex	5
Internal processing complex	5
Code designed for reuse	4
Conversion/installation in design	3
Multiple installations	5
Application designed for change	5
Complexity adjustment factor	1.17

Finally, the estimated number of FP is derived:

$$FP_{estimated} = \text{count-total} \times [0.65 + 0.01 \times \Sigma F_i]$$

$$FP_{estimated} = 372$$

Historical data normalized using function points indicate that the organizational average productivity for systems of this type is 6.5 FP/pm. Based on a burdened labor rate of $8000 per month, the cost per FP is approximately $1230. Based on the LOC estimate and the historical productivity data, the total estimated project cost is $457,000 and the estimated effort is 58 person-months.

5.6.5   Process-Based Estimation

The most common technique for estimating a project is to base the estimate on the process that will be used. That is, the process is decomposed into a relatively small set of activities or tasks and the effort required to accomplish each task is estimated.

Like the problem-based techniques, process-based estimation begins with a delineation of software functions obtained from the project scope. A series of software process activities must be performed for each function. Functions and related software process activities may be represented as part of a table similar to the one presented in Figure 3.2.

Once problem functions and process activities are melded, the planner estimates the effort (e.g., person-months) that will be required to accomplish each software process activity for each software function. These data comprise the central matrix of the table in Figure 3.2. Average labor rates (i.e., cost/unit effort) are then applied to the effort estimated for each process activity. It is very likely the labor rate will vary for each task. Senior staff are heavily involved in early activities and are generally more expensive than junior staff, who are involved in later design tasks, coding, and early testing.

Costs and effort for each function and software process activity are computed as the last step. If process-based estimation is performed independently of LOC or FP estimation, we now have two or three estimates for cost and effort that may be compared and reconciled. If both sets of estimates show reasonable agreement, there is good reason to believe that the estimates are reliable. If, on the other hand, the results of these decomposition techniques show little agreement, further investigation and analysis must be conducted.

5.6.6   An Example of Process-Based Estimation

To illustrate the use of process-based estimation, we again consider the CAD software introduced in Section 5.6.3. The system configuration and all software functions remain unchanged and are indicated by project scope.

The completed process-based table in Figure 5.5 shows estimates of effort (in person-months) for each software engineering activity provided for each CAD software function (abbreviated for brevity). The *engineering* and *construction/release* activities are subdivided into the major software engineering tasks shown. Gross estimates of effort are provided for *customer communication, planning,* and *risk analysis.* These are noted in the "Total" row at the bottom of the table. Horizontal and vertical totals provide an indication of estimated effort required for analysis, design, coding, and testing. It should be noted that 53 percent of all effort is expended on "front-end" engineering tasks (requirements analysis and design) indicating the relative importance of this work.

Activity →	Customer Communication	Planning	Risk Analysis	Engineering		Construction		Customer Evaluation	Totals
						Release			
Task →				Analysis	Design	Code	Test		
Function									
UICF				0.50	2.50	0.40	5.00	n/a	8.40
2DGA				0.75	4.00	0.60	2.00	n/a	7.35
3DGA				0.50	4.00	1.00	3.00	n/a	8.50
DSM				0.50	3.00	1.00	1.50	n/a	6.00
CGDF				0.50	3.00	0.75	1.50	n/a	5.75
PCF				0.25	2.00	0.50	1.50	n/a	4.25
DAM				0.50	2.00	0.50	2.00	n/a	5.00
Total	0.25	0.25	0.25	3.50	20.50	4.75	16.50		46.00
% effort	1%	1%	1%	8%	45%	10%	36%		

FIGURE 5.5. Process-based estimation table.

Based on an average burdened labor rate of $8000 per month, the total estimated project cost is $368,000 and the estimated effort is 46 person-months. If desired, different labor rates could associated with each software process activity.

Total estimated effort for the CAD software ranges from a low of 46 person-months (derived using a process-based estimation approach) to a high of 58 person-months (derived using a FP estimation approach). The average estimate (using all three approaches) is 53 person-months. The maximum variation from the average estimate is approximately 13 percent.

What happens when agreement between estimates is poor? The answer to this question requires a re-evaluation of information used to make the estimates. Widely divergent estimates can often be traced to one of two causes:

1. The scope of the project is not adequately understood or has been misinterpreted by the planner.

2. Productivity data used for problem-based estimation techniques is inappropriate for the application, is obsolete (in that it no longer accurately reflects the software engineering organization), or has been misapplied.

The planner must determine the cause of divergence and reconcile the estimates.

5.7   EMPIRICAL ESTIMATION MODELS

An *estimation model* for computer software uses empirically derived formulas to predict effort as a function of LOC or FP. Values for LOC or FP are estimated using the approach described in Sections 5.6.2 and 5.6.3. But instead of using the tables described in those sections, the resultant values for LOC or FP are plugged into the estimation model.

The empirical data that support most estimation models is derived from a limited sample of projects. For this reason, no estimation model is appropriate for all classes of software and in all development environments. Therefore, the results obtained from such models must be used judiciously.[12]

5.7.1 The Structure of Estimation Models

A typical estimation model is derived using regression analysis on data collected from past software projects. The overall structure of such models takes the form [MAT94]:

$$E = A + B \times (ev)^C \tag{5.2}$$

---

[12]In general, an estimation model should be calibrated for local conditions. The model should be run using the results of completed projects. Data predicted by the model should be compared to actual results, and the efficacy of the model (for local conditions) should be assessed. If agreement is not good, model coefficients and exponents must be recomputed using local data.

where A, B, and C are empirically derived constants, E is effort in person months, and ev is the estimation variable (either LOC or FP). In addition to the relationship noted in equation (5.2), the majority of estimation models have some form of project adjustment component that enables E to be adjusted by on other project characteristics (e.g., problem complexity, staff experience, development environment).

Among the many LOC-oriented estimation models proposed in the literature are:

$$E = 5.2 \times (KLOC)^{0.91}$$ Walston-Felix Model

$$E = 5.5 + 0.73 \times (KLOC)^{1.16}$$ Bailey-Basili Model

$$E = 3.2 \times (KLOC)^{1.05}$$ Boehm simple model

$$E = 5.288 \times (KLOC)^{1.047}$$ Doty Model for KLOC > 9

FP-oriented models have also been proposed. These include:

$$E = -13.39 + 0.0545 \text{ FP}$$ Albrecht and Gaffney Model

$$E = 60.62 \times 7.728 \times 10^{-8} \text{ FP}^3$$ Kemerer Model

$$E = 585.7 + 15.12 \text{ FP}$$ Matson, Barnett, and Mellichamp Model

A quick examination of the models listed above indicates that each will yield a different result[13] for the same value of LOC or FP. The implication is clear. Estimation models must be calibrated for local needs!

5.7.2 The COCOMO Model

In his classic book on "software engineering economics," Barry Boehm [BOE81] introduces a hierarchy of software estimation models bearing the name CO-COMO, for *COnstructive COst MOdel.* Boehm's hierarchy of models takes the following form:

Model 1. The Basic COCOMO model computes software development effort (and cost) as a function of program size expressed in estimated lines of code.

Model 2. The Intermediate COCOMO model computes software development effort as a function of program size and a set of "cost drivers" that include subjective assessments of product, hardware, personnel, and project attributes.

Model 3. The Advanced COCOMO model incorporates all characteristics of the intermediate version with an assessment of the cost driver's impact on each step (analysis, design, etc.) of the software engineering process.

---

[13]Part of the reason is that these models are often derived from relatively small populations of projects in only a few application domains.

TABLE 5.1

BASIC COCOMO MODEL

Software Project	a_b	b_b	c_b	d_b
organic	2.4	1.05	2.5	0.38
semi-detached	3.0	1.12	2.5	0.35
embedded	3.6	1.20	2.5	0.32

To illustrate the COCOMO model, we present an overview of the Basic and Intermediate versions. For a more detailed discussion, the reader is urged to study [BOE81].[14]

The COCOMO models are defined for three classes of software projects. Using Boehm's terminology these are (1) *organic mode*—relatively small, simple software projects in which small teams with good application experience work to a set of less than rigid requirements (e.g., a thermal analysis program developed for a heat transfer group); (2) *semi-detached mode*—an intermediate (in size and complexity) software project in which teams with mixed experience levels must meet a mix of rigid and less than rigid requirements (e.g., a transaction processing system with fixed requirements for terminal hardware and database software); (3) *embedded mode*—a software project that must be developed within a set of tight hardware, software and operational constraints (e.g., flight control software for aircraft).

The Basic COCOMO equations take the form:

$$E = a_b \text{KLOC}^{b_b}$$

$$D = c_b E^{d_b}$$

where E is the effort applied in person-months, D is the development time in chronological months, and KLOC is the estimated number of delivered lines of code for the project (express in thousands). The coefficients a_b and c_b and the exponents b_b and d_b are given in Table 5.1.

The basic model is extended to consider a set of "cost driver attributes" [BOE81] that can be grouped into four major categories: product attributes, hardware attributes, personnel attributes, and project attributes. Each of the 15 attributes in these categories is rated on a six-point scale that ranges from "very low" to "extra high" (in importance or value). Based on the rating, an effort multiplier is determined from tables published by Boehm [BOE81], and the product of all effort multipliers results is an *effort adjustment factor* (EAF). Typical values for EAF range from 0.9 to 1.4.

The intermediate COCOMO model takes the form:

$$E = a_i \text{KLOC}^{b_i} \times \text{EAF}$$

---

[14]The COCOMO model is undergoing revision at the time of this writing. The model will likely be extended to accommodate FP measures and will be refined based on a larger population of projects.

Software Project	a_i	b_i
TABLE 5.2 INTERMEDIATE COCOMO MODEL		
organic	3.2	1.05
semi-detached	3.0	1.12
embedded	2.8	1.20

where E is the effort applied in person-months and KLOC is the estimated number of delivered lines of code for the project. The coefficient a_i and the exponent b_i are given in Table 5.2.

COCOMO represents a comprehensive empirical model for software estimation. However, Boehm's own comments [BOE81] about COCOMO (and by extension all models) should be heeded:

> Today, a software cost estimation model is doing well if it can estimate software development costs within 20% of actual costs, 70% of the time, and on its own turf (that is, within the class of projects to which it has been calibrated). . . . This is not as precise as we might like, but it is accurate enough to provide a good deal of help in software engineering economic analysis and decision making.

To illustrate the use of the COCOMO model, we apply the basic model to the CAD software example described earlier in this chapter. Using the LOC estimate developed in Figure 5.3 and the coefficients noted in Table 5.1, we use the basic model to get:

$$E = 2.4(\text{KLOC})^{1.05}$$

$$= 2.4(33.2)^{1.05}$$

$$= 95 \text{ person-months}$$

This value is considerably higher than the estimates derived in Section 5.6. Because the COCOMO model assumes considerably lower LOC/pm levels than those noted in Section 5.6, the results are not surprising. To be useful in the context of the example problem, the COCOMO model would have to be recalibrated to the local environment.

To compute project duration, we use the effort estimate described above:

$$D = 2.5E^{0.35}$$

$$= 2.5(95)^{0.35}$$

$$= 12.3 \text{ months}$$

The value for project duration enables the planner to determine a recommended number of people, N, for the project:

$$N = E/D$$

$$= 95/12.3$$

$$\sim 8 \text{ people}$$

In reality, the planner may decide to use only four people and extend the project duration accordingly.[15]

5.7.3 The Software Equation

The *software equation* [PUT92] is a multivariable model that assumes a specific distribution of effort over the life of a software development project. The model has been derived from productivity data collected for over 4000 contemporary software projects. Based on these data, an estimation model of the form:

$$E = [\text{LOC} \times B^{0.333}/P]^3 \times (1/t^4) \tag{5.3}$$

where E = effort in person-months or person-years

t = project duration in months or years

B = "special skills factor" that increases slowly as "the need for integration, testing, quality assurance, documentation, and management skills grow" [PUT92]. For small programs (KLOC = 5 to 15), $B = 0.16$. For programs greater than 70 KLOC, $B = 0.39$.

P = "productivity parameter" that reflects:

- overall process maturity and management practices
- the extent to which good software engineering practices are used
- the level of programming languages used
- the state of the software environment
- the skills and experience of the software team
- the complexity of the application

Typical values might be $P = 2000$ for development of real-time embedded software; $P = 10,000$ for telecommunication and systems software; and $P = 28,000$ for business systems applications. The productivity parameter can be derived for local conditions using historical data collected from past development efforts.

It is important to note that the software equation has two independent parameters: (1) an estimate of size (in LOC) and (2) an indication of project duration in calendar months or years.

To simplify the estimation process and use a more common form for their

---

[15]It is important to note that the relationship between effort and time is not linear. Therefore, reducing the number of people to four would *not* necessarily cause the project to require twice as much calendar time. See [PUT92] for additional discussion.

estimation model, Putnam and Myers [PUT92] suggest a set of equations derived from the software equation. Minimum development time is defined as:

$$t_{min} = 8.14(LOC/PP)^{0.43} \text{ in months for } t_{min} > 6 \text{ months} \qquad (5.4a)$$

$$E = 180Bt^3 \text{ in person-months for } E \geq 20 \text{ person-months} \qquad (5.4b)$$

Note that t in equation (5.4b) is represented in years.

Using equations (5.4) with $P = 12,000$ (recommended value for scientific software) for the CAD software discussed earlier in this chapter,

$$t_{min} = 8.14 \, (33,200/12,000)^{0.43}$$

$$t_{min} = 12.6 \text{ calendar months}$$

$$E = 180 \times 0.28 \times (1.05)^3$$

$$E = 58 \text{ person-months}$$

The results of the software equation correspond favorably with the estimates developed in Section 5.6.

5.8 THE MAKE–BUY DECISION

In many software application areas, it is often more cost effective to acquire, rather than develop, computer software. Software engineering managers are faced with a *make–buy decision* that can be further complicated by a number of acquisition options: (1) software may be purchased (or licensed) *off-the-shelf;* (2) "full-experience" or "partial-experience" software components (see Section 5.4.2) may be acquired and then modified and integrated to meet specific needs, or (3) software may be custom-built by an outside contractor to meet the purchaser's specifications.

The steps involved in the acquisition of software are defined by the criticality of the software to be purchased and the end cost. In some cases (e.g., low-cost PC software), it is less expensive to purchase and experiment than to conduct a lengthy evaluation of potential software packages. For more expensive software products, the following guidelines can be applied:

1. Develop a specification for function and performance of the desired software. Define measurable characteristics whenever possible.

2. Estimate the internal cost to develop and the delivery date.

3a. Select three or four candidate applications that best meet your specification.

3b. Select reusable software components that will assist in constructing the required application.

4. Develop a comparison matrix that presents a head-to-head comparison of key functions. Alternatively, conduct benchmark tests to compare candidate software.

5. Evaluate each software package or component based on past product quality, vendor support, product direction, reputation, and so on.

6. Contact other users of the software and ask for opinions.

In the final analysis, the make–buy decision is made based on the following conditions: (1) Will the delivery date of the software product be sooner than that for internally developed software? (2) Will the cost of acquisition plus the cost of customization be less than the cost of developing the software internally? (3) Will the cost of outside support (e.g., a maintenance contract) be less than the cost of internal support? These conditions apply for each of the acquisition options noted above.

5.8.1 Creating a Decision Tree

The steps described above can be augmented using statistical techniques such as *decision tree analysis* [BOE89]. For example, Figure 5.6 depicts a decision tree for a software-based system, X. In this case, the software engineering organization can (1) build system X from scratch; (2) reuse existing "partial experience" components to construct the system; (3) buy an available software product and modify it to meet local needs; or (4) contract the software development to an outside vendor.

If the system is to be built from scratch, there is a 70 percent probability that the job will be difficult. Using the estimation techniques discussed earlier in this chapter, the project planner projects that a difficult development effort will cost $450,000. A "simple" development effort is estimated to cost $380,000. The expected value for cost, computed along any branch of the decision tree, is:

$$\text{expected cost} = \sum (\text{path probability})_i \times (\text{estimated path cost})_i$$

where i is the decision tree path. For the *build* path,

$$\text{expected cost}_{\text{build}} = 0.30\ (\$380K) + 0.70\ (\$450K) = \$429K$$

Following other paths of the decision tree, the projected costs for *reuse, purchase,* and *contract,* under a variety of circumstances, are also shown. The expected costs for these paths are:

$$\text{expected cost}_{\text{reuse}} = 0.40\ (\$275K) + 0.60\ [0.20\ (\$310K) + 0.80\ (\$490K)] = \$382K$$

$$\text{expected cost}_{\text{buy}} = 0.70\ (\$210K) + 0.30\ (\$400K)] = \$267K$$

$$\text{expected cost}_{\text{contract}} = 0.60\ (\$350K) + 0.40\ (\$500K)] = \$410K$$

Based on the probability and projected costs that have been noted in Figure 5.6, the lowest expected cost is the *buy* option.

It is important to note, however, that many criteria—not just cost—must be considered during the decision making process. Availability, experience of the developer/vendor/contractor, conformance to requirements, local "politics," and the likelihood of change are but a few of the criteria that may affect the ultimate decision to build, reuse, buy or contract.

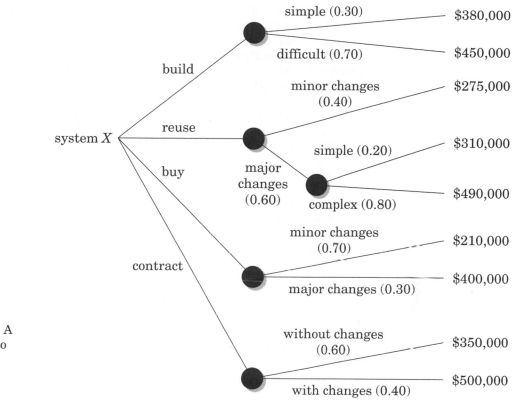

FIGURE 5.6. A decision tree to support the make–buy decision.

5.8.2 Outsourcing

Sooner or later, every company that develops computer software asks a fundamental question: "Is there a way that we can get the software and systems that we need at a lower price?" The answer to this question is not a simple one, and the emotional discussions that occur in response to the question always lead to a single word: "outsourcing."

In concept, outsourcing is extremely simple. Software engineering activities are contracted to a third party who does the work at lower cost, and hopefully, higher quality. Software work conducted within a company is reduced to a contract management activity.

Edward Yourdon [YOU92] discusses the broader implications of the growing trend toward outsourcing when he states:

> If you have been brought up in a culture that glorifies the American software industry as a world leader, I ask simply that you remember that it was only a few years ago that we had the same opinion of our automobile industry. . . . [S]oftware development may well move out of the U.S. into software factories in a dozen countries whose people are well educated, less expensive, and more passionately devoted to quality and productivity.

A strong statement! But one that is already becoming a reality.

The decision to outsource can be either strategic or tactical. At the strategic level, business managers consider whether a significant portion of all software work can be contracted to others. At the tactical level, a project manager determines whether part or all of a project can be best accomplished by subcontracting some portion of the software work.

Regardless of the breadth of focus, the outsourcing decision is often a financial one. A detailed discussion of the financial analysis of outsourcing is beyond the scope of this book and is best left to others (e.g., [MIN95]). However, a brief review of the pros and cons of the decision is worthwhile.

On the positive side, cost savings can usually be achieved by reducing the number of software people and the facilities (e.g., computers, infrastructure) that support them. On the negative side, a company loses some control over the software that it needs. Since software is a technology that differentiates its systems, services, and products, a company runs the risk of putting the fate of its competitiveness into the hands of a third party.

The trend toward outsourcing will undoubtedly continue. The only way to blunt the trend is to recognize that software work in the twenty-first century will be extremely competitive at all levels. The only way to survive is to become as competitive as the outsourcing vendors themselves.

5.9 AUTOMATED ESTIMATION TOOLS

The decomposition techniques and empirical estimation models described in the preceding sections are available as part of a wide variety of software tools. These automated estimation tools allow the planner to estimate cost and effort and to perform "what if" analyses for important project variables such as delivery date or staffing. Although many automated estimation tools exist, all exhibit the same general characteristics and all require one or more of the following data categories:

1. A quantitative estimate of project size (e.g., LOC) or functionality (function point data)
2. Qualitative project characteristics such as complexity, required reliability, or business criticality
3. Some description of the development staff and/or development environment

From these data, the model implemented by the automated estimation tool provides estimates of effort required to complete the project, costs, staff loading, time duration, and in some cases, development schedule and associated risk.

An interesting comparison of automated estimation tools has been done by Martin [MAR88]. A number of different tools were applied to the same project. It was not surprising that a relatively large variation in estimated results was encountered. More important, the predicted values sometimes were significantly different than actual values. This reinforces the notion that the output of estimation tools should be used as one "data point" from which estimates are derived—not as the only source for an estimate.

5.10   **SUMMARY**

The software project planner must estimate three things before a project begins: how long it will take, how much effort will be required, and how many people will be involved. In addition, the planner must predict the resources (hardware and software) that will be required and the risk involved.

The statement of scope helps the planner to develop estimates using one or more techniques that fall into two broad categories: decomposition and empirical modeling. Decomposition techniques require a delineation of major software functions, followed by estimates of either the size or the number of person-months required to implement each function. Empirical techniques use empirically derived expressions for effort and time to predict these project quantities. Automated tools can be used to implement a specific empirical model.

Accurate project estimates generally make use of at least two of the three techniques noted above. By comparing and reconciling estimates derived using different techniques, the planner is more likely to derive an accurate estimate. Software project estimation can never be an exact science, but a combination of good historical data and systematic techniques can improve estimation accuracy.

REFERENCES

[BEN92]   Bennatan, E.M., *Software Project Management: A Practitioner's Approach,* McGraw-Hill, 1992.

[BOE81]   Boehm, B., *Software Engineering Economics,* Prentice-Hall, 1981.

[BOE89]   Boehm, B., *Risk Management,* IEEE Computer Society Press, 1989.

[BRO75]   Brooks, F., *The Mythical Man-Month,* Addison-Wesley, 1975.

[GAU89]   Gause, D.C., and G.M. Weinberg, *Exploring Requirements: Quality Before Design,* Dorset House, 1989.

[HOO91]   Hooper, J.W.E., and R.O. Chester, *Software Reuse: Guidelines and Methods,* Plenum Press, 1991.

[MAH96]   Mah, M., Quantitative Software Management, Inc., private communication.

[MAR88]   Martin, R., "Evaluation of Current Software Costing Tools," *ACM Sigsoft Notes,* vol. 13, no. 3, July 1988, pp. 49–51.

[MAT94]   Matson, J., B. Barrett, and J. Mellichamp, "Software Development Cost Estimation Using Function Points," *IEEE Trans. Software Engineering,* vol. 20, no. 4, April 1994, pp. 275–287.

[MIN95]   Minoli, D., *Analyzing Outsourcing,* McGraw-Hill, 1995.

[PUT92]   Putnam, L., and W. Myers, *Measures for Excellence,* Yourdon Press, 1992.

[YOU92]   Yourdon, E., *The Decline and Fall of the American Programmer,* Yourdon Press, 1992.

PROBLEMS AND POINTS TO PONDER

5.1.   Assume that you are the project manager for a company that builds software for consumer products. You have been contracted to build the software for a home security system. Write a statement of scope that describes the software.

Be sure your statement of scope is bounded. If you're unfamiliar with home security systems, do a bit of research before you begin writing. Alternate: Replace the home security system with another problem that is of interest to you.

5.2. Software project complexity is discussed briefly in Section 5.1. Develop a list of software characteristics (e.g., concurrent operation, graphical output, etc.) that affect the complexity of a project. Prioritize the list.

5.3. Performance is an important consideration during planning. Discuss how performance can be interpreted differently depending upon the software application area.

5.4. Do a functional decomposition of the home security system software you described in problem 5.1. Estimate the size of each function in LOC. Assuming that your organization produces 450 LOC/pm with a burdened labor rate of $7000 per person-month, estimate the effort and cost required to build the software using the LOC-based estimation technique described in Section 5.6.3.

5.5. Using the 3D function point measure described in Chapter 4, compute the number of FP for the home security system software and derive effort and cost estimates using the FP-based estimation technique described in Section 5.6.4.

5.6. Use the COCOMO model to estimate the home security system software. Assume that the basic model is applicable.

5.7. Use the "software equation" to estimate the home security system software. Assume that equations (5.4) are applicable and that $P = 8000$.

5.8. Compare the effort estimates derived in problems 5.4 through 5.7. Develop a single estimate for the project using a three-point estimate. What is the standard deviation, and how does it affect your degree of certainty about the estimate?

5.9. Using the results obtained in problem 5.8, determine whether it's reasonable to expect that the software can be built within the next 6 months and how many people would have to be used to get the job done.

5.10. Develop a spreadsheet model that implements one or more of the estimation techniques described in this chapter.

5.11. For a project team: Develop a software tool that implements each of the estimation techniques developed in this chapter.

5.12. It seems odd that cost and schedule estimates are developed during software project planning—before detailed software requirements analysis or design has been conducted. Why do you think this is done? Are there circumstances when it should not be done?

5.13. Recompute the expected values noted for the decision tree in Figure 5.6 assuming that every branch has a 50-50 probability. Would this change your final decision?

5.14. Research the trade literature (e.g., *Computerworld, Software Magazine*) for recent articles on outsourcing. Write a two- or three-page paper describing what you've learned.

FURTHER READINGS AND OTHER INFORMATION SOURCES

Books by Bennatan [BEN92], Wellman (*Software Costing,* Prentice-Hall, 1992), and Londeix (*Cost Estimation for Software Development,* Addison-Wesley, 1987) contain useful information on software project planning and estimation. Lederer and Prasad ("Nine Management Guidelines for Better Cost Estimating," *Communications of the ACM,* February 1992) provide a collection of useful statistics that can serve as a guide for better cost estimating.

Putnam and Myer's detailed treatment of software cost estimating [PUT92] and Boehm's book on software engineering economics [BOE81] describe empirical software estimation models. Both books provide detailed analysis of data derived form hundreds of software projects. An excellent book by DeMarco (*Controlling Software Projects,* Yourdon Press, 1982) provides valuable insight into the management, measurement, and estimation of software projects. Sneed (*Software Engineering Management,* Wiley, 1989) and Macro (*Software Engineering: Concepts and Management,* Prentice-Hall, 1990) consider software project estimation in considerable detail.

Lines-of-code cost estimation is the most commonly used approach in the industry. However, the impact of the object-oriented paradigm (see Part Four) may invalidate some estimation models. Lorenz and Kidd (*Object-Oriented Software Metrics,* Prentice-Hall, 1994) consider estimation for object-oriented systems.

A new version of the COCOMO model, updated for the 1990s, can be obtained at:

http://sunset.usc.edu/COCOMO2.0/Cocomo.html

Frequently asked questions (FAQ) and a glossary of project management terms are addressed at the following sites:

http://www.wst.com/projplan/proj-plan.FAQ.html
http://smurfland.cit.buffalo.edu/NetMan/FAQs/proj-plan.FAQ.html
http://www.wst.com/projplan/proj-plan.glossary.html

A review of software project management tools can be obtained at:

http://www.wst.com/projplan/proj-plan.reviews.html

A listing of project management resources can be obtained at:

http://www.pmi.org/pmi/mem_prod/pmmisc.htm

A detailed paper and many references for project cost analysis can be acquired from:

http://mijuno.larc.nasa.gov/dfc/pca.html

An up-to-date list of World Wide Web references for software project estimation can be found at: **http://www.rspa.com**

RISK MANAGEMENT

In his book on risk analysis and management, Robert Charette [CHA89] presents the following conceptual definition of risk:

> First, risk concerns future happenings. Today and yesterday are beyond active concern, as we are already reaping what was previously sowed by our past actions. The question is, can we, therefore, by changing our actions today, create an opportunity for a different and hopefully better situation for ourselves tomorrow. This means, second, that risk involves change, such as in changes of mind, opinion, actions, or places. . . . [Third,] risk involves choice, and the uncertainty that choice itself entails. Thus paradoxically, risk, like death and taxes, is one of the few certainties of life.

When risk is considered in the context of software engineering, Charette's three conceptual underpinnings are always in evidence. The future is our concern—what risks might cause the software project to go awry? Change is our concern—how will changes in customer requirements, development technologies, target computers, and all other entities connected to the project affect timeliness and overall success? Last, we must grapple with choices—what methods and tools should we use, how many people should be involved, how much emphasis on quality is "enough?"

Peter Drucker [DRU75] once said, "While it is futile to try to eliminate risk, and questionable to try to minimize it, it is essential that the risks taken be the right risks." Before we can identify the "right risks" to be taken during a software project, it is important to identify all risks that are obvious to both managers and practitioners.

6.1   REACTIVE VS. PROACTIVE RISK STRATEGIES

Reactive risk strategies have been laughingly called the "Indiana Jones school of risk management" [THO92]. In the movies that carried his name, Indiana Jones, when faced with overwhelming difficulty, would invariably say, "Don't worry, I'll think of something!" Never worrying about problems until they happened, Indy would react in some heroic way.

Sadly, the average software project manager is not Indiana Jones and the members of the software project team are not his trusty sidekicks. Yet, the majority of software teams rely solely on reactive risk strategies. At best, a reactive strategy monitors the project for likely risks. Resources are set aside to deal with them, should they become actual problems. More commonly, the software team does nothing about risks until something goes wrong. Then, the team flies into action in an attempt to correct the problem rapidly. This is often called "fire fighting mode." When this fails, "crisis management" [CHA92] takes over and the project is in real jeopardy.

A considerably more intelligent strategy for risk management is to be proactive. A proactive strategy begins long before technical work is initiated. Potential risks are identified, their probability and impact are assessed, and they are prioritized by importance. Then, the software team establishes a plan for managing risk. The primary objective is to avoid risk, but because not all risks can be avoided, the team works to develop a contingency plan that will enable it to respond in a controlled and effective manner. Throughout the remainder of this chapter, we discuss a proactive strategy for risk management.

6.2   SOFTWARE RISKS

Although there has been considerable debate about the proper definition for software risk, there is general agreement that risk always involves two characteristics [HIG95]:

- *uncertainty*—The event that characterizes the risk may or may not happen; i.e., there are no 100% probable risks.[1]
- *loss*—If the risk becomes a reality, unwanted consequences or losses will occur.

When risks are analyzed, it is important to quantify the level of uncertainty and the degree of loss associated with each risk. To accomplish this, different categories of risks are considered.

Project risks threaten the project plan. That is, if project risks become real, it is likely that the project schedule will slip and that costs will increase. Project risks identify potential budgetary, schedule, personnel (staffing and organization), resource, customer, and requirements problems and their impact on a soft-

---

[1]A risk that is 100% probable is a constraint on the software project.

ware project. In Chapter 5, project complexity, size, and the degree of structural uncertainty were also defined as project (and estimation) risk factors.

Technical risks threaten the quality and timeliness of the software to be produced. If a technical risk becomes a reality, implementation may become difficult or impossible. Technical risks identify potential design, implementation, interfacing, verification, and maintenance problems. In addition, specification ambiguity, technical uncertainty, technical obsolescence, and "leading-edge" technology are also risk factors. Technical risks occur because the problem is harder to solve than we thought it would be.

Business risks threaten the viability of the software to be built. Business risks often jeopardize the project or the product. Candidates for the top five business risks are (1) building an excellent product or system that no one really wants (market risk); (2) building a product that no longer fits into the overall business strategy for the company (strategic risk); (3) building a product that the sales force doesn't understand how to sell; (4) losing the support of senior management due to a change in focus or a change in people (management risk); and (5) losing budgetary or personnel commitment (budget risks). It is extremely important to note that simple categorization won't always work. Some risks are simply unpredictable in advance.

Another general categorization of risks has been proposed by Charette [CHA89]. *Known risks* are those that can be uncovered after careful evaluation of the project plan, the business and technical environment in which the project is being developed, and other reliable information sources (e.g., unrealistic delivery date, lack of documented requirements or software scope, poor development environment). *Predictable risks* are extrapolated from past project experience (e.g., staff turnover, poor communication with the customer, dilution of staff effort as ongoing maintenance requests are serviced). *Unpredictable risks* are the joker in the deck. They can and do occur, but they are extremely difficult to identify in advance.

6.3   RISK IDENTIFICATION

Risk identification is a systematic attempt to specify threats to the project plan (estimates, schedule, resource loading, etc.). By identifying known and predictable risks, the project manager takes a first step toward avoiding them when possible and controlling them when necessary.

There are two distinct types of risks for each of the categories that have been presented in Section 6.2: generic risks and product-specific risks. Generic risks are a potential threat to every software project. Product-specific risks can only be identified by those with a clear understanding of the technology, the people, and the environment that is specific to the project at hand. To identify product-specific risks, the project plan and the software statement of scope are examined and an answer to the following question is developed: "What special characteristics of this product may threaten our project plan?"

Both generic and product-specific risks should be identified systematically. Tom Gilb [GIL88] drives this point home when he states: "If you don't actively attack the risks, they will actively attack you."

One method for identifying risks is to create a *risk item checklist*. The checklist can be used for risk identification and focuses on some subset of known and predictable risks in the following generic subcategories:

- *Product size*—risks associated with the overall size of the software to be built or modified
- *Business impact*—risks associated with constraints imposed by management or the marketplace
- *Customer characteristics*—risks associated with the sophistication of the customer and the developer's ability to communicate with the customer in a timely manner
- *Process definition*—risks associated with the degree to which the software process has been defined and is followed by the development organization
- *Development environment*—risks associated with the availability and quality of the tools to be used to build the product
- *Technology to be built*—risks associated with the complexity of the system to be built and the "newness" of the technology that is packaged by the system
- *Staff size and experience*—risks associated with the overall technical and project experience of the software engineers who will do the work.

The risk item checklist can be organized in different ways. Questions relevant to each of the topics noted above can be answered for each software project. The answers to these questions allow the planner to estimate the impact of risk. A different risk item checklist format simply lists characteristics that are relevant to each generic subcategory. Finally, a set of "risk components and drivers" [AFC88] are listed along with their probability of occurrence. Drivers for performance, support, cost, and schedule are discussed in answer to later questions.

6.3.1 Product Size Risks

Few experienced managers would debate the following statement: *Project risk is directly proportional to product size*. The following risk item checklist identifies generic risks associated with product (software) size:

- Estimated size of the product in LOC or FP?
- Degree of confidence in estimated size estimate?
- Estimated size of product in number of programs, files, transactions?
- Percentage deviation in size of product from average for previous products?
- Size of database created or used by the product?
- Number of users of the product?
- Number of projected changes to the requirements for the product? before delivery? after delivery?
- Amount of reused software?

In each case, the information for the product to be developed must be compared to past experience. If a large percentage deviation occurs or if numbers are similar, but past results were considerably less than satisfactory, risk is high.

6.3.2 Business Impact Risks

An engineering manager at a major software company placed the following framed plaque on his wall: "God grant me brains to be a good project manager and the common sense to run like hell whenever marketing sets project deadlines!" The marketing department is driven by business considerations, and business considerations sometimes come into direct conflict with technical realities. The following risk item checklist identifies generic risks associated with business impact:

- Effect of this product on company revenue?
- Visibility of this product to senior management?
- Reasonableness of delivery deadline?
- Number of customers who will use this product and the consistency of their needs relative to the product?
- Number of other products/systems with which this product must be interoperable?
- Sophistication of end users?
- Amount and quality of product documentation that must be produced and delivered to the customer?
- Governmental constraints on the construction of the product?
- Costs associated with late delivery?
- Costs associated with a defective product?

Each response for the product to be developed must be compared to past experience. If a large percentage deviation occurs or if numbers are similar, but past results were considerably less than satisfactory, risk is high.

6.3.3 Customer Related Risks

All customers are not created equal. Pressman and Herron [PRE91] discuss this issue when they state:

> *Customers have different needs.* Some know what they want; others know what they don't want. Some customers are willing to sweat the details, while others are satisfied with a vague promises.

> *Customers have different personalities.* Some enjoy being customers—the tension, the negotiation, the psychological rewards of a good product. Others

would prefer not to be customers at all. Some will happily accept almost anything that is delivered and make the very best of a poor product. Others will complain bitterly when quality is lacking; some will show their appreciation when quality is good; a few will complain no matter what.

Customers also have varied associations with their suppliers. Some know the product and producer well; others may be faceless, communicating with the producer only by written correspondence and a few hurried telephone calls.

Customers are often contradictory. They want everything yesterday for free. Often, the producer is caught among the customers' own contradictions.

A "bad" customer can have a profound impact on a software team's ability to complete a project on time and within budget. A bad customer represents a significant threat to the project plan and a substantial risk for the project manager. The following risk item checklist identifies generic risks associated with different customers:

- Have you worked with the customer in the past?
- Does the customer have a solid idea of what is required? Has the customer spent the time to write it down?
- Will the customer agree to spend time in formal requirements gathering meetings (Chapter 11) to identify project scope?
- Is the customer willing to establish rapid communication links with the developer?
- Is the customer willing to participate in reviews?
- Is the customer technically sophisticated in the product area?
- Is the customer willing to let your people do their job—that is, will the customer resist looking over your shoulder during technically detailed work?
- Does the customer understand the software process?

If the answer to any of these questions is "no," further investigation should be undertaken to assess risk potential.

6.3.4 Process Risks

If the software process (Chapter 2) is ill-defined; if analysis, design, and testing are conducted in an ad hoc fashion; if quality is a concept that everyone agrees is important, but no one acts to achieve in any tangible way, then the project is at risk. The following questions are extracted from a workshop on the assessment of software engineering practice developed by R.S. Pressman & Associates, Inc. [PRE95]. The questions themselves have been adapted from the Software Engineering Institute (SEI) software process assessment questionnaire.

Process Issues

- Does your senior management support a written policy statement that emphasizes the importance of a standard process for software development?
- Has your organization developed a written description of the software process to be used on this project?
- Are staff members "signed up" to the software process as it is documented and willing to use it?
- Is the software process used for other projects?
- Has your organization developed or acquired a series of software engineering training courses for managers and technical staff?
- Are published software engineering standards provided for every software developer and software manager?
- Have document outlines and examples been developed for all deliverables defined as part of the software process?
- Are formal technical reviews of the requirements specification, design, and code conducted regularly?
- Are formal technical reviews of test procedures and test cases conducted regularly?
- Are the results of each formal technical review documented, including errors found and resources used?
- Is there some mechanism for ensuring that work conducted on a project conforms with software engineering standards?
- Is configuration management used to maintain consistency among system/software requirements, design, code, and test cases?
- Is a mechanism used for controlling changes to customer requirements that impact the software?
- Is there a documented statement of work, a software requirements specification, and a software development plan for each subcontract?
- Is a procedure followed for tracking and reviewing the performance of subcontractors?

Technical Issues

- Are facilitated application specification techniques used to aid in communication between the customer and developer?
- Are specific methods used for software analysis?
- Do you use a specific method for data and architectural design?
- Is more that 90 percent of your code written in a high-order language?
- Are specific conventions for code documentation defined and used?
- Do you use specific methods for test case design?
- Are software tools used to support planning and tracking activities?
- Are configuration management software tools used to control and track change activity throughout the software process?
- Are software tools used to support the software analysis and design process?

- Are tools used to create software prototypes?
- Are software tools used to support the testing process?
- Are software tools used to support the production and management of documentation?
- Are quality metrics collected for all software projects?
- Are productivity metrics collected for all software projects?

If a majority of the above questions are answered "no," software process is weak and risk is high.

6.3.5 Technology Risk

Pushing the limits of the technology is challenging and exciting. It's the dream of almost every technical person, because it forces a practitioner to use his or her skills to the fullest. But it's also very risky. Murphy's law seems to hold sway in this part of the development universe, making it extremely difficult to foresee risks, much less plan for them. The following risk item checklist identifies generic risks associated with the technology to be built:

- Is the technology to be built new to your organization?
- Do the customer's requirements demand the creation of new algorithms or input or output technology?
- Does the software interface with new or unproven hardware?
- Does the software to be built interface with vendor supplied software products that are unproven?
- Does the software to be built interface with a database system whose function and performance have not been proven in this application area?
- Is a specialized user interface demanded by product requirements?
- Do requirements for the product demand the creation of program components that are unlike any previously developed by your organization?
- Do requirements demand the use of new analysis, design, or testing methods?
- Do requirements demand the use of unconventional software development methods, such as formal methods, AI-based approaches, and artificial neural networks?
- Do requirements put excessive performance constraints on the product?
- Is the customer uncertain that the functionality requested is "doable"?

If the answer to any of these questions is "yes," further investigation should be undertaken to assess risk potential.

6.3.6 Development Environment Risks

If a carpenter were asked to create a fine piece of furniture with a bent, dull handsaw, the quality of the end product would be suspect. Inappropriate or ineffective tools can blunt the efforts of even a skilled practitioner. The software engineering environment supports the project team, the process, and the product. But if the environment is flawed, it can be the source of significant risk. The following risk item checklist identifies generic risks associated with the development environment[2]:

- Is a software project management tool available?
- Is a software process management tool available?
- Are tools for analysis and design available?
- Do analysis and design tools deliver methods that are appropriate for the product to be built?
- Are compilers or code generators available and appropriate for the product to be built?
- Are testing tools available and appropriate for the product to be built?
- Are software configuration management tools available?
- Does the environment make use of a database or repository?
- Are all software tools integrated with one another?
- Have members of the project team received training in each of the tools?
- Are local experts available to answer questions about the tools?
- Is on-line help and documentation for the tools adequate?

If a majority of the above questions are answered "no," the software development environment is weak and risk is high.

6.3.7 Risks Associated with Staff Size and Experience

Boehm [BOE89] suggests the following questions to assess risks associated with staff size and experience:

- Are the best people available?
- Do the people have the right combination of skills?
- Are enough people available?
- Are staff committed for entire duration of the project?
- Will some project staff be working only part time on this project?
- Do staff have the right expectations about the job at hand?
- Have staff received necessary training?
- Will turnover among staff be low enough to allow continuity?

If the answer to any of these questions is "no," further investigation should be undertaken to assess risk potential.

---

[2]Chapter 29 contains discussions of the tool categories noted in this checklist.

6.3.8 Risk Components and Drivers

The U.S. Air Force [AFC88] has written a pamphlet that contains excellent guidelines for software risk identification and abatement. The Air Force approach requires that the project manager identify the *risk drivers* that affect *software risk components*—performance, cost, support, and schedule. In the context of this discussion, the risk components are defined in the following manner:

- *performance risk*—the degree of uncertainty that the product will meet its requirements and be fit for its intended use
- *cost risk*—the degree of uncertainty that the project budget will be maintained
- *support risk*—the degree of uncertainty that the software will be easy to correct, adapt, and enhance
- *schedule risk*—the degree of uncertainty that the project schedule will be maintained and that the product will be delivered on time

The impact of each risk driver on the risk component is divided into one of four impact categories—negligible, marginal, critical, and catastrophic. Figure 6.1 [BOE89] indicates the potential consequences of errors (rows labeled 1) or a failure to achieve a desired outcome (rows labeled 2). The impact category is chosen based on the characterization that best fits the description in the table.

6.4   RISK PROJECTION

Risk projection, also called *risk estimation,* attempts to rate each risk in two ways—the *likelihood* or probability that the risk is real and the *consequences* of the problems associated with the risk, should it occur. The project planner, along with other managers and technical staff, performs four risk projection activities: (1) establish a scale that reflects the perceived likelihood of a risk; (2) delineate the consequences of the risk; (3) estimate the impact of the risk on the project and the product, and (4) note the overall accuracy of the risk projection so that there will be no misunderstandings.

6.4.1 Developing a Risk Table

A *risk table* provides a project manager with a simple technique for risk projection.[3] The sample risk table is illustrated in Figure 6.2.

A project team begins by listing all risks (no matter how remote) in the first column of the table. This can be accomplished with the help of the risk item

---

[3]The risk table should be implemented as a spreadsheet model. This enables easy manipulation and sorting of the entries.

COMPONENTS ⟍ CATEGORY		PERFORMANCE	SUPPORT	COST	SCHEDULE
CATASTROPHIC	1	Failure to meet the requirement would result in mission failure		Failure results in increased costs and schedule delays with expected values in excess of $500K	
CATASTROPHIC	2	Significant degradation to nonachievement of technical performance	Nonresponsive or unsupportable software	Significant financial shortages, budget overrun likely	Unachievable delivery date
CRITICAL	1	Failure to meet the requirement would degrade system performance to a point where mission suuccess is questionable		Failure results in operational delays and/or increased costs with expected value of $100K to $500K	
CRITICAL	2	Some reduction in technical performance	Minor delays in software modifications	Some shortage of financial resources, possible overruns	Possible slippage in delivery date
MARGINAL	1	Failure to meet the requirement would result in degradation of secondary mission		Costs, impacts, and/or recoverable schedule slips with expected value of $1 to $100k	
MARGINAL	2	Minimal to small reduction in technical performance	Responsive software support	Sufficient financial resources	Realistic, achievable schedule
NEGLIGIBLE	1	Failure to meet the requirement would create inconvenience or nonoperational impact		Error results in minor cost and/or schedule impact with expected value of less than $1K	
NEGLIGIBLE	2	No reduction in technical performance	Easily supportable software	Possible budget underrun	Early achievable delivery date

Note: (1) The potential consequence of undetected software errors or faults.
 (2) The potential consequence if the desired outcome is not achieved.

FIGURE 6.1. Impact assessment [BOE89].

checklists presented in Section 6.3. Each risk is categorized in the second column (e.g., PS implies a project size risk, BU implies a business risk). The probability of occurrence of each risk is entered in the next column of the table. The probability value for each risk can be estimated by team members individually. Individual values are averaged to develop a single consensus probability. Next the impact of each risk is assessed. Each risk component is assessed using the characterization presented in Figure 6.1, and an impact category is determined. The categories for each of the four risk components—performance, support, cost, and schedule—are averaged[4] to determine an overall impact value.

---

[4]A weighted average can be used if one risk component has more significance for the project.

Risks	Category	Probability	Impact	RMMM
Size estimate may be significantly low	PS	60%	2	
Larger number of users than planned	PS	30%	3	
Less reuse than planned	PS	70%	2	
End users resist system	BU	40%	3	
Delivery deadline will be tightened	BU	50%	2	
Funding will be lost	CU	40%	1	
Customer will change requirements	PS	80%	2	
Technology will not meet expectations	TE	30%	1	
Lack of training on tools	DE	80%	3	
Staff inexperienced	ST	30%	2	
Staff turnover will be high	ST	60%	2	

Impact values:
1 – castastrophic
2 – critical
3 – marginal
4 – negligible

FIGURE 6.2. Sample risk table prior to sorting.

Once the first four columns of the risk table have been completed, the table is sorted by probability and by impact. High-probability, high-impact risks percolate to the top of the table, and low-probability risks drop to the bottom. This accomplishes first-order risk prioritization.

The project manager studies the resultant sorted table and defines a cut-off line. The cut-off line (drawn horizontally at some point in the table) implies that only risks which lie above the line will be given further attention. Risks that fall below the line are re-evaluated to accomplish second-order prioritization.

Risk impact and probability have a distinct influence on management concern (Figure 6.3). A risk factor that has a high impact but a very low probability of occurrence should not absorb a significant amount of management time. However, high-impact risks with moderate to high probability and low-impact risks with high probability should be carried forward into the management steps that follow.

All risks that lie above the cut-off line must be managed. The column labeled RMMM contains a pointer into a *Risk Mitigation, Monitoring and Management Plan* developed for all risks that lie above cut-off. The RMMM Plan is discussed in Section 6.5.

Risk probability can be determined by making individual estimates and then developing a single consensus value. Although that approach is workable,

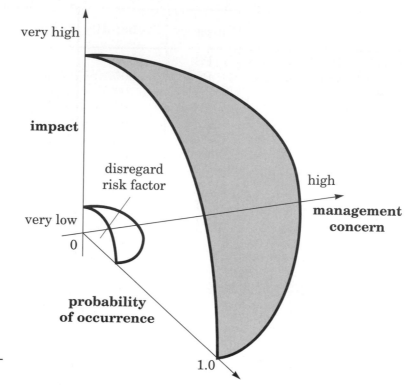

FIGURE 6.3.
Risk and manage-
ment concern.

more sophisticated techniques for determining risk probability have been developed [AFC88]. Risk drivers can be assessed on a qualitative probability scale that has the following values: impossible, improbable, probable, and frequent. Mathematical probability can then be associated with each qualitative value (e.g., a probability of 0.7 to 1.0 implies a highly probable risk).

6.4.2 Assessing Risk Impact

Three factors affect the consequences that are likely if a risk does occur: its nature, its scope, and its timing. The *nature* of the risk indicates the problems that are likely if it occurs. For example, a poorly defined external interface to customer hardware (a technical risk) will preclude early design and testing and will likely lead to system integration problems late in a project. The *scope* of a risk combines the severity (just how serious is it?) with its overall distribution (how much of the project will be affected or how many customers are harmed?). Finally, the *timing* of a risk considers when and for how long the impact will be felt. In most cases, a project manager might want the "bad news" to occur as soon as possible, but in some cases, the longer the delay, the better.

Returning once more to the risk analysis approach proposed by the U.S. Air Force [AFC88], the following steps are recommended to determine the overall consequences of a risk:

1. Determine the average probability of occurrence value for each risk component.

2. Using Figure 6.1, determine the impact for each component based on the criteria shown.

3. Complete the risk table and analyze the results as described in the preceding sections.

The risk projection and analysis techniques described in Sections 6.4.1 and 6.4.2 are applied iteratively as the software project proceeds. The project team should revisit the risk table at regular intervals, re-evaluating each risk to determine when new circumstances cause its probability and impact to change. As a consequence of this activity, it may be necessary to add new risks to the table, remove some risks that are no longer relevant, and change the relative positioning of still others.

6.4.3 Risk Assessment

At this point in the risk management process, we have established a set of triplets of the form [CHA89].

$$[r_i, l_i, x_i]$$

where r_i is risk, l_i is the likelihood (probability) of the risk, and x_i is the impact of the risk. During *risk assessment,* we further examine the accuracy of the estimates that were made during risk projection, attempt to prioritize the risks that have been uncovered, and begin thinking about ways to control and/or avert risks that are likely to occur.

For assessment to be useful, a *risk referent level* [CHA89] must be defined. For most software projects, the risk components discussed earlier—performance, cost, support, and schedule—also represent risk referent levels. That is, there is a level for performance degradation, cost overrun, support difficulty, or schedule slippage (or any combination of the four) that will cause the project to be terminated. If a combination of risks create problems that cause one or more of these referent levels to be exceeded, work will stop. In the context of software risk analysis, a risk referent level has a single point, called the *referent point* or *break point,* at which the decision to proceed with the project or terminate it (problems are just too great) are equally acceptable.

Figure 6.4 represents this situation graphically. If a combination of risks leads to problems that cause cost and schedule overruns, there will be a level, represented by the curve in the figure, that (when exceeded) will cause project termination (the shaded region). At a referent point, the decisions to proceed or to terminate are equally weighted.

In reality, the referent level can rarely be represented as a smooth line on a graph. In most cases it is a region in which there are areas of uncertainty (i.e., attempting to predict a management decision based on the combination of referent values is often impossible).

Therefore, during risk assessment, we perform the following steps:

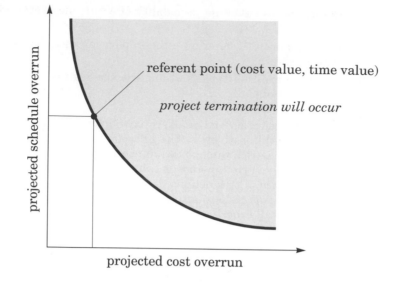

FIGURE 6.4.
Risk referent
level.

1. define the risk referent levels for the project
2. attempt to develop a relationship between each $[r_i, l_i, x_i]$ and each of the referent levels
3. predict the set of referent points that define a region of termination, bounded by a curve or areas of uncertainty
4. try to predict how compound combinations of risks will affect a referent level

A detailed discussion is best left to books that are dedicated to risk analysis (e.g., [CHA89], [ROW88]).

6.5   RISK MITIGATION, MONITORING, AND MANAGEMENT

All of the risk analysis activities presented to this point have a single goal—to assist the project team in developing a strategy for dealing with risk. An effective strategy must consider three issues:

* risk avoidance,
* risk monitoring, and
* risk management and contingency planning.

If a software team adopts a proactive approach to risk, avoidance is always the best strategy. This is achieved by developing a plan for *risk mitigation*. For example, assume that high staff turnover is noted as a project risk, r_1. Based on past history and management intuition, the likelihood, l_1, of high turnover is estimated to be 0.70 (70 percent, rather high) and the impact, x_1, is projected to have a critical impact on project cost and schedule.

To mitigate this risk, project management must develop a strategy for reducing turnover. Among the possible steps to be taken are these:

- meet with current staff to determine causes for turnover (e.g., poor working conditions, low pay, competitive job market)
- act to mitigate those causes that are under management control before the project starts
- once project commences, *assume turnover will occur* and develop techniques to ensure continuity when people leave
- organize project teams so that information about each development activity is widely dispersed
- define documentation standards and establish mechanisms to be sure that documents are developed in a timely manner
- conduct peer reviews of all work so that more than one person is familiar with the work
- define a backup staff member for every critical technologist

As the project proceeds, *risk monitoring* activities commence. The project manager monitors factors that may provide an indication of whether the risk is becoming more or less likely. In the case of high staff turnover, the following factors can be monitored:

- general attitude of team members based on project pressures
- the degree to which the team has jelled
- interpersonal relationships among team members
- potential problems with compensation and benefits
- the availability of jobs within the company and outside it

In addition to monitoring the factors noted above, the project manager should also monitor the effectiveness of risk mitigation steps. For example, a risk mitigation step noted above called for the definition of "documentation standards and mechanisms to be sure that documents are developed in a timely manner." This is one mechanism for ensuring continuity, should a critical individual leave the project. The project manager should monitor documents carefully to ensure that each can stand on its own and that each imparts information that would be necessary if a newcomer were forced to join the project.

Risk management and contingency planning assumes that mitigation efforts have failed and that the risk has become a reality. Continuing the example, suppose that the project is well underway and a number of people announce that they will be leaving. If the mitigation strategy has been followed, backup is available, information is documented, and knowledge has been dispersed across the team. In addition, the project manager may temporarily refocus resources (and readjust the project schedule) to those functions that are fully staffed, enabling newcomers who must be added to the team to "get up to speed." Those individuals who are leaving are asked to stop all work and spend their last weeks in "knowledge transfer mode." This might include video-based knowledge capture, the development of "commentary documents" and/or meeting with other team members who will remain on the project.

It is important to note that RMMM steps incur additional project cost. For example, spending the time to "back up" every critical technologist costs money. Part of risk management, therefore is to evaluate when the benefits accrued by the RMMM steps are outweighed by the costs associated with implementing them. In essence, the project planner performs a classic cost—benefit analysis. If risk aversion steps for high turnover will increase project costs and duration by an estimated 15 percent, but the predominant cost factor is "backup," management may decide not to implement this step. On the other hand if the risk aversion steps are projected to increase costs by 5 percent and duration by only 3 percent, management will likely put all into place.

For a large project, 30 or 40 risks may be identified. If between three and seven risk management steps are identified for each, risk management may become a project in itself! For this reason, we adapt the Pareto 80–20 rule to software risk. Experience indicates that 80 percent of the overall project risk (i.e., 80 percent of the potential for project failure) can be accounted for by only 20 percent of the identified risks. The work performed during earlier risk analysis steps will help the planner to determine which of the risks reside in that 20 percent. For this reason, some of the risks identified, assessed, and projected may not make it into the RMMM plan—they don't comprise the critical 20 percent (the risks with highest project priority).

6.6   SAFETY RISKS AND HAZARDS

Risk is not limited to the software project itself. Risks can occur after the software has been successfully developed and delivered to the customer. These risks are typically associated with the consequences of software failure in the field.

Although the probability of failure of a well-engineered system is small, an undetected fault in a computer-based control or monitoring system could result in enormous economic damage, or worse, significant human injury or loss of life. But the cost and functional benefits of computer-based control and monitoring often outweigh the risk. Today, computer hardware and software are used regularly to control safety-critical systems.

When software is used as part of the control system, complexity can increase by an order of magnitude or more. Subtle design flaws induced by human error—something that can be uncovered and eliminated in hardware-based conventional controls—become much more difficult to uncover when software is used.

Software safety and *hazard analysis* are software quality assurance activities (Chapter 8) that focus on the identification and assessment of potential hazards that may impact software negatively and cause an entire system to fail. If hazards can be identified early in the software engineering process, software design features can be specified that will either eliminate or control potential hazards.

6.7   **THE RMMM PLAN**

A risk management strategy can be included in the software project plan or the risk management steps can be organized into a separate *Risk Mitigation, Monitoring, and Management Plan (RMMM Plan)*. The RMMM Plan documents all work performed as part of risk analysis and is used by the project manager as part of the overall *Project Plan*. An outline for the RMMM Plan follows.

    I. Introduction
       1. Scope and Purpose of Document
       2. Overview of major risks
       3. Responsibilities
          a. Management
          b. Technical staff
   II. Project Risk Table
       1. Description of all risks above cut-off
       2. Factors influencing probability and impact
  III. Risk Mitigation, Monitoring, Management
       n. Risk # n
          a. Mitigation
             i. General strategy
             ii. Specific steps to mitigate the risk
          b. Monitoring
             i. Factors to be monitored
             ii. Monitoring approach
          c. Management
             i. Contingency plan
             ii. Special considerations
  IV. RMMM Plan Iteration Schedule
   V. Summary

Once the RMMM Plan has been developed and the project has begun, risk mitigation and monitoring steps commence. As we have already discussed, risk mitigation is a problem avoidance activity. Risk monitoring is a project tracking activity with three primary objectives: (1) to assess whether a predicted risk does, in fact, occur; (2) to ensure that risk aversion steps defined for the risk are being properly applied; and (3) to collect information that can be used for future risk analysis. In many cases, the problems that occur during a project can be traced to more than one risk. Another job of risk monitoring is to attempt to determine the "origin" (what risk or risks caused which problems) throughout the project.

6.8   **SUMMARY**

Whenever a lot is riding on a software project, common sense dictates risk analysis. And yet, most software project managers do it informally and superficially, if they do it at all. The time spent identifying, analyzing, and managing risk pays itself back in many ways: less upheaval during the project; a greater ability to track and control a project; and the confidence that comes with planning for problems before they occur.

Risk analysis can absorb a significant amount of project planning effort. Identification, projection, assessment, management, and monitoring all take time. But the effort is worth it. To quote Sun Tzu, a Chinese general who lived 2500 years ago, "If you know the enemy and know yourself, you need not fear the result of a hundred battles." For the software project manager, the enemy is risk.

REFERENCES

[AFC88]   *Software Risk Abatement,* AFCS/AFLC Pamphlet 800-45, U.S. Air Force, September 30, 1988.

[BOE89]   Boehm, B.W., *Software Risk Management,* IEEE Computer Society Press, 1989.

[CHA89]   Charette, R.N., *Software Engineering Risk Analysis and Management,* McGraw-Hill/Intertext, 1989.

[CHA92]   Charette, R.N., "Building Bridges over Intelligent Rivers," *American Programmer,* vol. 5, no. 7, September 1992, pp. 2–9.

[DRU75]   Drucker, P., *Management,* W. Heinemann, Ltd., 1975.

[GIL88]   Gilb, T., *Principles of Software Engineering Management,* Addison-Wesley, 1988.

[HIG95]   Higuera, R.P., "Team Risk Management," *CrossTalk,* U.S. Dept. of Defense, January 1995, pp. 2–4.

[LEV95]   Leveson, N.G., *Safeware: System Safety and Computers,* Addison-Wesley, 1995.

[PAR90]   Parnas, D.L., A.J. van Schouwen, and S.P. Kwan, "Evaluation of Safety Critical Software," *CACM,* vol. 33, no. 6, June 1990, pp. 636–648.

[PRE91]   Pressman, R.S., and S.R. Herron, *Software Shock,* Dorset House, 1991.

[PRE95]   *Software Process Assessment Workshop,* R.S. Pressman & Associates, Inc., Orange, CT, 1995.

[ROW88]   Rowe, W.D., *An Anatomy of Risk,* Robert E. Krieger Publishing Co., Malabar, FL, 1988.

[THO92]   Thomsett, R., "The Indiana Jones School of Risk Management," *American Programmer,* vol. 5, no. 7, September 1992, pp. 10–18.

PROBLEMS AND POINTS TO PONDER

6.1. Provide five examples from other fields that illustrate the problems associated with a reactive risk strategy.

6.2. Describe the difference between "known risks" and "predictable risks."

6.3. Add three additional questions or topics to each of the risk item checklists presented in this chapter.

6.4. You've been asked to build software to support a low-cost video-editing system. The system accepts video tape as input, stores the video on disk, and then allows the user to do a wide range of edits to the digitized video. The result can then be output to tape. Do a small amount of research on systems of this type, and then make a list of technology risks that you would face as you begin a project to build the video-editing system.

6.5. You're the project manager for a major software company. You've been asked to lead a team that's developing "next generation" word-processing software (see Section 3.3.2 for a brief description). Create a risk table for the project.

6.6. Describe the difference between risk components and risk drivers.

6.7. Develop a weighting scheme for project risk drivers.

6.8. Develop a risk mitigation strategy and specific risk mitigation activities for three of the risks noted in Figure 6.2.

6.9. Develop a risk monitoring strategy and specific risk monitoring activities for three of the risks noted in Figure 6.2. Be sure to identify the factors that you'll be monitoring to determine whether the risk is becoming more or less likely.

6.10. Develop a risk management strategy and specific risk management activities for three of the risks noted in Figure 6.2.

6.11. Can you think of a situation in which a high-probability, high-impact risk would not be considered as part of your RMMM Plan?

6.12. Referring to the risk referent shown on Figure 6.4, would the curve always have the symmetric arc shown, or would there be situations in which the curve would be more distorted? If so, suggest a scenario in which this might happen.

6.13. Do some research of software safety issues and write a brief paper on the subject. See [LEV95] as a starting point.

6.14. Describe five software application areas in which software safety and hazard analysis would be a major concern.

FURTHER READINGS AND OTHER INFORMATION SOURCES

Capers Jones (*Assessment and Control of Software Risks,* Prentice-Hall, 1994) presents a detailed discussion of software risks that includes data collected from hundreds of software projects. Jones defines 60 risk factors that can affect the outcome of software projects. Boehm [BOE89] suggests excellent questionnaire and checklist formats that can prove invaluable in identifying risk. Charette [CHA89] presents a detailed treatment of the mechanics of risk analysis, calling on probability theory and statistical techniques to analyze risks. In a companion volume, Charette (*Application Strategies for Risk Analysis,* McGraw-Hill, 1990) discusses risk in the context of both system and software engineering and defines pragmatic strategies for risk management.

A useful snapshot of risk assessment has been written by Grey (*Practical Risk Assessment for Project Management,* Wiley, 1995). His abbreviated treatment provides a good introduction to the subject. Karolak (*Software Engineering Risk Management,* IEEE Computer Society Press, 1996) presents a guidebook that introduces an easy-to-use risk analysis model. An entire issue of *American Programmer* magazine (March 1995) was dedicated to risk management.

Air Force Systems Command Pamphlet AFSCP 800-45 [AFC88] describes risk identification and reduction techniques. Gilb [GIL88] presents a set of "principles" (often amusing and frequently profound) that can serve as a worthwhile guide for risk management. Every issue of the *ACM Software Engineering Notes* publishes a section entitled "Risks to the Public" (editor, P.G. Neumann). If you want the latest and best software horror stories, this is the place to go.

A risk factors chart (implemented as a spreadsheet model) is available from Teraquest Metrics (for information via Internet: **statz@acm.org**). The newsgroup **comp.risks** is a source of discussion and commentary.

The *Forum on Risks to the Public* Web site discusses computer and software risks and/or methods for managing them:

http://catless.ncl.ac.uk/Risks.data/info.html

An extensive set of pointers for decision/risk analysis can be obtained at:

http://www.lumina.com/DA/

Riskworld is an on-line publication "providing news and information on the identification, critical analysis, and management of risks" and can be obtained at:

http://www.riskwatch.com/

A good paper on risk and analysis and pointers to a number of excellent risk bibliographies can be obtained at:

http://mijuno.larc.nasa.gov/dfc/rsk.html

The *DOE Risk Management Quarterly* (an on-line publication), although not dedicated to software related risks, contains useful articles and pointers:

http://www.dne.bnl.gov/rmq.html

An up-to-date list of World Wide Web references that are relevant to software risks can be found at: **http://www.rspa.com**

CHAPTER 7

PROJECT SCHEDULING AND TRACKING

In the late 1960s, a bright-eyed young engineer[1] was chosen to "write" a computer program for an automated manufacturing application. The reason for his selection was simple. He was the only person in his technical group who had attended a computer programming seminar. He knew the in's and out's of assembler language and Fortran, but nothing about software engineering and even less about project scheduling and tracking.

His boss gave him the appropriate manuals and a verbal description of what had to be done. He was informed that the project must be completed in two months.

He read the manuals, considered his approach, and began writing code. After two weeks, the boss called him into his office and asked how things were going.

"Really great," said the young engineer with youthful enthusiasm, "This was much simpler than I thought. I'm probably close to 75 percent finished."

The boss smiled. "That's really terrific," he said. He then told the young engineer to keep up the good work and plan to meet again in a week's time.

A week later the boss called the engineer into his office and asked, "Where are we?"

"Everything's going well," said the youngster, "but I've run into a few small snags. I'll get them ironed out and be back on track soon."

"How does the deadline look?" the boss asked.

"No problem," said the engineer. "I'm close to 90 percent complete."

If you've been working in the software world for more than a few years, you can finish the story. It'll come as no surprise that the young engineer stayed 90

---

[1]If you're wondering whether this story is autobiographical, it is!

percent complete for the entire project duration and only finished (with the help of others) one month late.

This story has been repeated tens of thousands of times by software developers during the past three decades. The big question is *"why?"*

7.1   BASIC CONCEPTS

Although there are many reasons why software is delivered late, most can be traced to one or more of the following root causes:

- an unrealistic deadline established by someone outside the software engineering group and forced on managers and practitioners within the group
- changing customer requirements that are not reflected in schedule changes
- an honest underestimate of the amount of effort and/or the number of resources that will be required to do the job
- predictable and/or unpredictable risks that were not considered when the project commenced
- technical difficulties that could not have been foreseen in advance
- human difficulties that could not have been foreseen in advance
- miscommunication among project staff that results in delays
- a failure by project management to recognize that the project is falling behind schedule and a lack of action to correct the problem

Aggressive (read "unrealistic") deadlines are a fact of life in the software business. Sometimes such deadlines are demanded for reasons that are legitimate from the point of view of the person who sets the deadline, but common sense says that legitimacy must also be perceived by the people doing the work.

7.1.1   Comments on "Lateness"

Napoleon once said: "[A]ny commander in chief who undertakes to carry out a plan which he considers defective is at fault; he must put forth his reasons, insist on the plan being changed, and finally tender his resignation rather than be the instrument of his army's downfall." Strong words that many software project managers should ponder.

The estimation and risk analysis activities discussed in Chapters 5 and 6, and the scheduling techniques described in this chapter, are often implemented under the constraint of a defined deadline. If best estimates indicate that the deadline is unrealistic, a competent project manager should "protect his or her team from undue [schedule] pressure [and] reflect the pressure back to its originators" [PAG85].

To illustrate, assume that a software development group has been asked to build a real-time controller for a medical diagnostic instrument that is to be introduced to the market in 9 months. After careful estimation and risk analysis, the software project manager comes to the conclusion that the software, as requested, will require 14 calendar months to create with available staff. How does the project manager proceed?

It is unrealistic to march into the customer's office (in this case the likely customer is marketing/sales) and demand that the delivery date be changed. External market pressures have dictated the date, and the product must be released. It is equally foolhardy to refuse to undertake the work (from a career standpoint). So, what to do?

The following steps are recommended in this situation:

1. Perform a detailed estimate using data from past projects. Determine the estimated effort and duration for the project.

2. Using an incremental process model (Chapter 2), develop a development strategy that will deliver critical functionality by the imposed deadline, but delay other functionality until later. Document the plan.

3. Meet with the customer and (using the detailed estimate), explain why the imposed deadline is unrealistic. Be certain to note that all estimates are based on performance on past projects. Also be certain to indicate the percentage improvement that would be required to achieve the deadline as it currently exists.[2] The following comment is appropriate:

> "I think we may have a problem with the delivery date for the XYZ controller software. I've given each of you an abbreviated breakdown of production rates for past projects and an estimate that we've done a number of different ways. You'll note that I've assumed a 20 percent improvement in past production rates, but we still get a delivery date that's 14 calendar months rather than 9 months away."

4. Offer the incremental development strategy as an alternative.

> "We have a few options, and I'd like you to make a decision based on them. First, we can increase the budget and bring on additional resources so that we'll have a shot at getting this job done in nine months, But understand that this will increase risk of poor quality due to the tight timeline.[3] Second, we can remove a number of the software functions and capabilities that you're requesting. This will make the preliminary version of the product somewhat less functional, but we can announce all functionality and then deliver over the 14 month period. Third, we can dispense with reality and wish the project complete in 9 months. We'll wind up with nothing that can be delivered to a customer. The third option, I hope you'll agree, is unacceptable. Past history and our best estimates say that it is unrealistic and a recipe for disaster."

There will be some grumbling, but if solid estimates based on good historical data are presented, it's likely that negotiated versions of either option 1 or option 2 will be chosen. The unrealistic deadline evaporates.

---

[2] If the percentage improvement is 10 to 25 percent, it may actually be possible to get the job done. But more likely, the percentage improvement in team performance will be greater than 50 percent. This is an unrealistic expectation.

[3] You might also add that adding more people will not reduce calendar time proportionally.

7.1.2 Basic Principles

Fred Brooks, the well-known author of *The Mythical Man-Month* [BRO95], was once asked how software projects fall behind schedule. His response was as simple as it was profound: "One day at a time."

The reality of a technical project (whether it involves building a hydro-electric plant or developing an operating system) is that hundreds of small tasks must occur to accomplish a larger goal. Some of these tasks lie outside the mainstream and may be completed without worry about impact on project completion date. Other tasks lie on the "critical path."[4] If these "critical" tasks fall behind schedule, the completion date of the entire project is put into jeopardy.

The project manager's objective is to define all project tasks, identify the ones that are critical, and then track their progress to ensure that delay is recognized "one day at a time." To accomplish this, the manager must have a schedule that has been defined at a degree of resolution that enables the manager to monitor progress and control the project.

Software project scheduling is an activity that distributes estimated effort across the planned project duration by allocating the effort to specific software engineering tasks. It is important to note, however, that the schedule evolves over time. During early stages of project planning, a *macroscopic schedule* is developed. This type of schedule identifies all major software engineering activities and the product functions to which they are applied. As the project gets under way, each entry on the macroscopic schedule is refined into a *detailed schedule*. Here, specific software tasks (required to accomplish an activity) are identified and scheduled.

Scheduling for software development projects can be viewed from two rather different perspectives. In the first, an end date for release of a computer-based system has already (and irrevocably) been established. The software organization is constrained to distribute effort within the prescribed time frame. The second view of software scheduling assumes that rough chronological bounds have been discussed but that the end date is set by the software engineering organization. Effort is distributed to make best use of resources, and an end date is defined after careful analysis of the software. Unfortunately, the first situation is encountered far more frequently than the second.

Like all other areas of software engineering, a number of basic principles guide software project scheduling:

Compartmentalization. The project must be compartmentalized into a number of manageable activities and tasks. To accomplish compartmentalization, both the product and the process are decomposed (Chapter 3).

Interdependency. The interdependencies of each compartmentalized activity or task must be determined. Some tasks must occur in sequence; others can occur in parallel. Some activities cannot commence until the work product produced by another is available. Other activities can occur independently.

---

[4]The critical path will be discussed in greater detail later in this chapter.

Time allocation.   Each task to be scheduled must be allocated some number of work units (e.g., person-days of effort). In addition, each task must be assigned a start date and a completion date that are functions of the interdependencies and whether work will be conducted on a full-time or part-time basis.

Effort Validation.   Every project has a defined number of staff members. As time allocation occurs, the project manager must ensure that no more than the allocated number of people have been allocated at any given time. For example, consider a project that has three assigned staff members (e.g., three person-days are available per day of assigned effort[5]). On a given day, seven concurrent tasks must be accomplished. Each task requires 0.50 person days of effort. More effort has been allocated than there are people to do the work.

Defined responsibilities.   Every task that is scheduled should be assigned to a specific team member.

Defined outcomes.   Every task that is scheduled should have a defined outcome. For software projects, the outcome is normally a work product (e.g., the design of a module) or a part of a work product. Work products are often combined in *deliverables*.

Defined milestones.   Every task or group of tasks should be associated with a project milestone. A milestone is accomplished when one or more work products have been reviewed for quality (Chapter 8) and have been approved.

Each of the above principles is applied as the project schedule evolves.

7.2   THE RELATIONSHIP BETWEEN PEOPLE AND EFFORT

In a small software development project a single person can analyze requirements, perform design, generate code, and conduct tests. As the size of a project increases, more people must become involved. (We can rarely afford the luxury of approaching a ten person-year effort with one person working for ten years!)

There is a common myth (discussed in Chapter 1) that is still believed by many managers who are responsible for software development effort: "If we fall behind schedule, we can always add more programmers and catch up later in the project." Unfortunately, adding people late in a project often has a disruptive effect, causing schedules to slip even further. People who are added must learn the system, and the people who teach them are the same people who were doing the work. While they are teaching, no work is done and the project falls further behind.

In addition to the time it takes to learn the system, involving more people increases the number of communication paths and the complexity of commu-

---

[5]In reality, less than three person-days are available because of unrelated meetings, sickness, vacation, and a variety of other reasons. For our purposes, however, we assume 100 percent availability.

nication throughout a project. Although communication is absolutely essential to successful software development, every new communication path requires additional effort and therefore additional time.

7.2.1 An Example

Consider four software engineers, each capable of producing 5000 LOC/year when working on an individual project. When these four engineers are placed on a team project, six potential communication paths are possible. Each communication path requires time that could otherwise be spent developing software. We shall assume that team productivity (when measured in LOC) will be reduced by 250 LOC/year for each communication path, due to the overhead associated with communication. Therefore, team productivity is 20,000 − (250 × 6) = 18,500 LOC/year—7.5 percent less than what we might expect.[6]

The one-year project on which the above team is working falls behind schedule and with two months remaining, two additional people are added to the team. The number of communication paths escalates to 14. The productivity input of the new staff is the equivalent of 840 × 2 = 1680 LOC for the two months remaining before delivery. Team productivity now is 20,000 + 1680 − (250 × 14) = 18,180 LOC/year.

Although the above example is a gross oversimplification of real world circumstances, it does serve to illustrate another key point: The relationship between the number of people working on a software project and overall productivity is not linear.

Based on the people—work relationship, are teams counterproductive? The answer is an emphatic "no," if communication serves to improve software quality. In fact, formal technical reviews (see Chapter 8) conducted by software engineering teams can lead to better analysis and design, and more important, can reduce the number of errors that go undetected until testing (thereby reducing testing effort). Hence, productivity and quality, when measured by time to project completion and customer satisfaction, can actually improve.

7.2.2 An Empirical Relationship

Recalling the "software equation" [PUT92] that was introduced in Chapter 5, we can demonstrate the highly nonlinear relationship between chronological time to complete a project and human effort applied to the project. The number of delivered lines of code (source statements), L, are related to effort and development time by the equation:

$$L = P \times (E/B)^{1/3}t^{4/3}$$

---

[6]It is possible to pose a counterargument: Communication, if it is effective, can enhance the quality of the work being performed, thereby reducing the amount of rework and *increasing* the individual productivity of team members. The jury is still out!

where E is development effort in person-months; P is a productivity parameter that reflects a variety of factors that lead to high-quality software engineering work (typical values for P range between 2,000 and 28,000); B is a special skills factor that ranges between 0.16 and 0.39 and is a function of the size of the software to be produced; and t is the project duration in calendar months.

Rearranging the software equation (above), we arrive at an expression for development effort E:

$$E = L^3/(P^3t^4)(7.1)$$

where E is the effort expended (in person-years) over the entire life cycle for software development and maintenance, and t is the development time in years. The equation for development effort can be related to development cost by the inclusion of a burdened labor rate factor ($/person-year).

This leads to some interesting results. Consider a complex, real-time software project estimated at 33,000 LOC, 12 person-years of effort. If eight people are assigned to the project team, the project can be completed in approximately 1.3 years. If, however, we extend the end date to 1.75 years, the highly nonlinear nature of the model described in equation (7.1) yields:

$$E - L^3/(P^3t^4) \sim 3.8 \text{ person-years.}$$

This implies that by extending the end date six months, we can reduce the number of people from eight to four! The validity of such results is open to debate, but the implication is clear: Benefit can be gained by using fewer people over a somewhat longer time span to accomplish the same objective.

7.2.3 Effort Distribution

Each of the software project estimation techniques discussed in Chapter 5 leads to estimates of person-months (or person-years) required to complete software development. A recommended distribution of effort across the definition and development phases is often referred to as the *40–20–40 rule*.[7] Forty percent or more of all effort is allocated to front-end analysis and design tasks. A similar percentage is applied to back-end testing. You can correctly infer that coding (20 percent of effort) is de-emphasized.

This effort distribution should be used as a guideline only. The characteristics of each project dictate the distribution of effort. Effort expended on project planning rarely accounts for more than 2 or 3 percent of effort, unless the plan commits an organization to large expenditures with high risk. Requirements analysis may comprise 10 to 25 percent of project effort. Effort expended on analysis or prototyping should increase in direct proportion with project size and complexity. A range of 20 to 25 percent of effort is normally applied to software design. Time expended for design review and subsequent iteration must also be considered.

---

[7]Today, more than 40 percent of all project effort is often recommended for analysis and design tasks for large software development projects. Hence, the name "40–20–40" no longer applies in a strict sense.

Because of the effort applied to software design, code should follow with relatively little difficulty. A range of 15 to 20 percent of overall effort can be achieved. Testing and subsequent debugging can account for 30 to 40 percent of software development effort. The criticality of the software often dictates the amount of testing that is required. If software is human-rated (i.e., software failure can result in loss of life), even higher percentages may be considered.

7.3   DEFINING A TASK SET FOR THE SOFTWARE PROJECT

A number of different process models were described in Chapter 2. These models offer different paradigms for software development. Regardless of whether a software team chooses a linear sequential paradigm, an iterative paradigm, an evolutionary paradigm, a concurrent paradigm, or some permutation, the process model is populated by a set of tasks that enable the software team to define, develop, and ultimately maintain computer software.

There is no single set of tasks that is appropriate for all projects. The set of tasks that would be appropriate for a large, complex system would likely be perceived as overkill for a small, relatively simple project. Therefore, an effective software process should define a collection of *task sets,* each designed to meet the needs of different types of projects.

A task set is a collection of software engineering work tasks, milestones, and deliverables that must be accomplished to complete a particular project. The task set to be chosen must provide enough discipline to achieve high software quality. But at the same time, it must not burden the project team with unnecessary work.

Task sets are designed to accommodate different types of projects and different degrees of rigor. Although it is difficult to develop a comprehensive taxonomy, most software organizations encounter projects of the following types:

I. **Concept Development Projects** that are initiated to explore some new business concept or application of some new technology,

II. **New Application Development Projects** that are undertaken as a consequence of a specific customer request.

III. **Application Enhancement Projects** that occur when existing software undergoes major modifications to function, performance, or interfaces that are observable by the end user,

IV. **Application Maintenance Projects** that correct, adapt, or extend existing software in ways that may not be immediately obvious to the end user.

V. **Reengineering Projects** that are undertaken with the intent of rebuilding an existing (legacy) system in whole or in part.

Even within a single project type, there are many factors that influence the task set to be chosen. When taken in combination, these factors provide an indication of the *degree of rigor* with which the software process should be applied.

7.3.1   Degree of Rigor

Even for a project of a particular type, the degree of rigor with which the software process is applied may vary significantly. The degree of rigor is a function of many project characteristics. As an example, small, non-business-critical projects can generally be addressed with somewhat less rigor than large, complex, business-critical applications. It should be noted, however, that *all* projects must be conducted in a manner that results in timely, high-quality deliverables. Four different degrees of rigor can be defined:

Casual.   All process framework activities (Chapter 2) are applied, but only a minimum task set is required. In general, umbrella tasks will be minimized and documentation requirements will be reduced. All basic principles of software engineering are still applicable.

Structured.   The process framework will be applied for this project. Framework activities and related tasks appropriate to the project type will be applied and umbrella activities necessary to ensure high quality will be applied. SQA, SCM, documentation, and measurement tasks will be conducted in a streamlined manner.

Strict.   The full process will be applied for this project with a degree of discipline that will ensure high quality. All umbrella activities will be applied, and robust documentation will be produced.

Quick Reaction.   The process framework will be applied for this project, but because of an emergency situation,[8] only those tasks essential to maintaining good quality will be applied. "Back-filling" (i.e., developing a complete set of documentation, conducting additional reviews) will be accomplished after the application/product is delivered to the customer.

The project manager must develop a systematic approach for selecting the degree of rigor that is appropriate for a particular project. To accomplish this, project adaptation criteria are defined and a *task set selector* value is computed.

7.3.2   Defining Adaptation Criteria[9]

Adaptation criteria are used to determine the recommended degree of rigor with which the software process should be applied on a project. Eleven adaptation criteria are defined for software projects:

---

[8]Emergency situations should be rare (they should not occur on more that 10 to 20 percent of all work conducted within the software engineering context). An emergency is *not* the same as a project with tight time constraints.

[9]The adaptation criteria presented in this section and the TSS computation presented in the following sections have been adapted from the *Adaptable Process Model*. They are reproduced with permission of R.S. Pressman & Associates, Inc. E-mail to **info@rspa.com** for further information.

- size of the project
- number of potential users
- mission criticality
- application longevity
- stability of requirements
- ease of customer/developer communication
- maturity of applicable technology
- performance constraints
- embedded/nonembedded characteristics
- project staffing
- reengineering factors

Each of the adaptation criteria is assigned a grade that ranges between 1 and 5, where 1 represents a project in which a small subset of process tasks are required and overall methodological and documentation requirements are minimal, and 5 represents a project in which a complete set of process tasks should be applied and overall methodological and documentation requirements are substantial.

7.3.3 Computing a Task Set Selector Value

To select the appropriate task set for a project, the following steps should be conducted:

1. Review each of the adaptation criteria in Section 7.3.2 and assign the appropriate grades (1 to 5) based on the characteristics of the project. These grades should be entered into Table 7.1.

2. Review the weighting factors assigned to each of the criteria. The value of a weighting factor ranges from 0.8 to 1.2 and provides an indication of the relative importance of a particular adaptation criterion to the types of software developed within the local environment. If modifications are required to better reflect local circumstances, they should be made.

3. Multiply the grade entered in Table 7.1 by the **weighting factor** and by the **entry point multiplier** for the type of project to be undertaken. The entry point multiplier takes on a value of 0 or 1 and indicates the relevance of the adaptation criterion to the project type. The result of the product:

   grade × weighting factor × entry point multiplier

   is placed in the "Product" column of Table 7.1 for each adaptation criterion individually.

4. Compute the average of all entries in the "Product" column and place the result in the space marked *task set selector (TSS)*. This value will be used to help you select the task set that is most appropriate for the project.

TABLE 7.1

COMPUTING THE TASK SET SELECTOR

Adaptation Criteria	Grade	Weight	Entry Point Multiplier					Product
			Conc.	NDev.	Enhan.	Maint.	Reeng.	
Size of project	_____	1.20	0	1	1	1	1	_____
Number of users	_____	1.10	0	1	1	1	1	_____
Business criticality	_____	1.10	0	1	1	1	1	_____
Longevity	_____	0.90	0	1	1	0	0	_____
Stability of requirements	_____	1.20	0	1	1	1	1	_____
Ease of communication	_____	0.90	1	1	1	1	1	_____
Maturity of technology	_____	0.90	1	1	0	0	1	_____
Performance constraints	_____	0.80	0	1	1	0	1	_____
Embedded/nonembedded	_____	1.20	1	1	1	0	1	_____
Project staffing	_____	1.00	1	1	1	1	1	_____
Interoperability	_____	1.10	0	1	1	1	1	_____
Reengineering factors	_____	1.20	0	0	0	0	1	_____

Task set selector (TSS) _____

7.3.4 Interpreting the TSS Value and Selecting the Task Set

Once the task set selector is computed, the following guidelines can be used to select the appropriate task set for a project:

Task Set Selector Value	Degree of Rigor
TSS < 1.2	casual
1.0< TSS< 3.0	structured
TSS > 2.4	strict

The overlap in TSS values from one recommended task set to another is purposeful and is intended to illustrate that sharp boundaries are impossible to define when making task set selections. In the final analysis, the task set selector value, past experience, and common sense must all be factored into the choice of the task set for a project.

Table 7.2 illustrates how TSS might be computed for a hypothetical project. The project manager selects the grades shown in the "Grade" column. The project type is **new application development.** Therefore, entry point multipliers are selected from the "NDev." column. The entry in the "Product" column is computed using

$$\text{Grade} \times \text{Weight} \times \text{NewDev Entry Point Multiplier}$$

The value of TSS (computed as the average of all entries in the product column) is 2.8. Using the criteria discussed above, the manager has the option of using either the **structured** or the **strict** task set. The final decision is made once all project factors have been considered.

TABLE 7.2

COMPUTING THE TASK SET SELECTOR—AN EXAMPLE

Adaptation Criteria	Grade	Weight	Entry Point Multiplier					Product
			Conc.	NDev.	Enhan.	Maint.	Reeng.	
Size of project	2	1.2		1				2.4
Number of users	3	1.1		1				3.3
Business criticality	4	1.1		1				4.4
Longevity	3	0.9		1				2.7
Stability of requirements	2	1.2		1				2.4
Ease of communication	2	0.9		1				1.8
Maturity of technology	2	0.9		1				1.8
Performance constraints	3	0.8		1				2.4
Embedded/nonembedded	3	1.2		1				3.6
Project staffing	2	1.0		1				2.0
Interoperability	4	1.1		1				4.4
Reengineering factors	0	1.2		0				2.8

Task set selector (TSS)   2.8

7.4   SELECTING SOFTWARE ENGINEERING TASKS

In order to develop a project schedule, a task set must be distributed on the project time line. As we noted in Section 7.3, the task set will vary depending upon the project type and the degree of rigor. Each of the project types described in Section 7.3 may be approached using a process model that is linear sequential, iterative (e.g., the prototyping model), or evolutionary (e.g., the spiral model). In some cases, one project type flows smoothly into the next. For example, concept development projects that succeed often evolve into new application development projects. As a new application development project ends, an application enhancement project sometimes begins. This progression is both natural and predictable, and will occur regardless of the process model that is adopted by an organization. As an example, we consider the major software engineering tasks for concept development projects.

Concept development projects are initiated when the potential for some new technology must be explored. There is no certainty that the technology will be applicable, but a customer (e.g., marketing) believes that potential benefit exists. Concept development projects are approached by applying the following major tasks:

Concept scoping   determines the overall scope of the project.

Preliminary concept planning   establishes the organization's ability to undertake the work implied by the project scope.

Technology risk assessment   evaluates the risk associated with the technology to be implemented as part of project scope.

Proof of concept   demonstrates the viability of a new technology in the software context.

Concept implementation   implements the concept representation in a manner that can be reviewed by a customer and is used for "marketing" purposes when a concept must be sold to other customers or management.

Customer reaction to concept   solicits feedback on a new technology concept and targets specific customer applications.

A quick scan of these major tasks should yield few surprises. In fact, the flow of software engineering tasks for concept development projects (and for all other types of projects as well) is little more than common sense.

The software team must understand what must be done (scoping); the team (or manager) must determine whether there's anyone available to do it (planning); consider the risks associated with the work (risk assessment); prove the technology in some way (proof of concept); and implement it in a prototypical manner so that the customer can evaluate it (concept implementation and customer evaluation). Finally, if the concept is viable, a production version (translation) must be produced.

It is important to note that concept development tasks are iterative in nature. That is, an actual concept development project might approach the above tasks in a number of planned increments, each designed to produce a deliverable that can be evaluated by the customer.

If a linear process model flow is chosen, each of these increments is defined in a repeating sequence as illustrated in Figure 7.1. During each sequence, umbrella activities (described in Chapter 2) are applied; quality is monitored, and at the end of each sequence, a deliverable is produced. With each iteration, the deliverable should converge toward the defined end product for the concept development stage. If an evolutionary model is chosen, the layout of tasks I.1 through I.6 would appear as shown in Figure 7.2. Major software engineering tasks for other project types can be defined and applied in a similar manner.

7.5   REFINEMENT OF MAJOR TASKS

The major tasks described in Section 7.4 may be used to define a macroscopic schedule for a project. For example, the tasks described for concept development projects would be used to define a task network (Section 7.6) for the project.

As we noted earlier in this chapter, the macroscopic schedule must be refined to create a detailed project schedule. Refinement begins by taking each major task and decomposing it into a set of subtasks (with related work products and milestones).

As an example of task decomposition, consider the **Concept Scoping** task, discussed in Section 7.4. Task refinement can be accomplished using an outline format, but in this book, a process design language[10] approach is used to illustrate the flow of the concept scoping activity:

---

[10]A process design language is similar in syntax to program design languages discussed in Chapter 14.

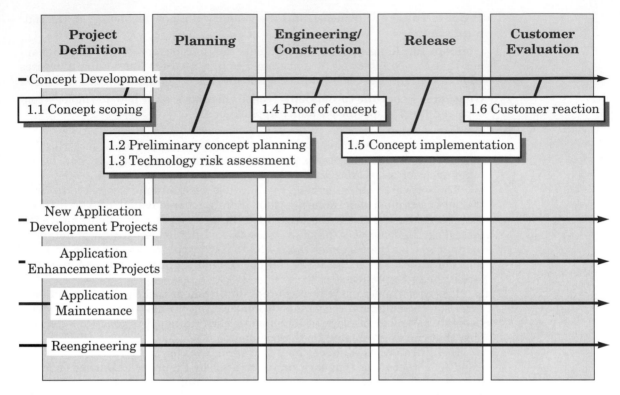

FIGURE 7.1. Concept development tasks in a linear, sequential model.

```
Task I.1 Concept Scoping
    I.1.1  Identify need, benefits and potential customers;
    I.1.2  Define desired output/control and input events
           that drive the application;
  Begin Task 1.1.2
  I.1.2.1  FTR:11 Review written description of need
  I.1.2.2  Derive a list of customer visible outputs/inputs
    case of: mechanics
    mechanics = quality function deployment
      meet with customer to isolate major concept requirements;
      interview end users;
      observe current approach to problem, current process;
      review past requests and complaints;
    mechanics = structured analysis
      make list of major data objects;
      define relationships between objects;
      define object attributes;
    mechanics = object view
      make list of problem classes;
```

---

[11]FTR indicates that a formal technical review (Chapter 8) is to be conducted.

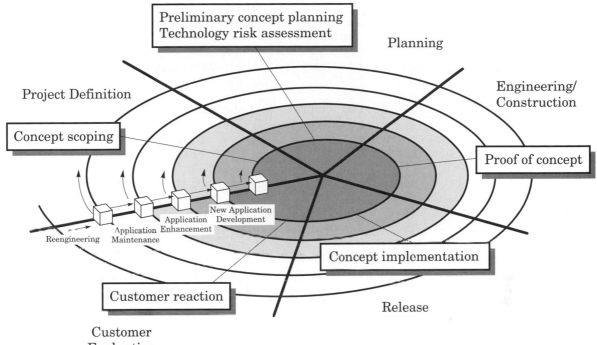

FIGURE 7.2. Concept development tasks using an evolutionary model.

```
          develop class hierarchy and class connections;
          define attributes for classes;
        endcase
  I.1.2.3  FTR: Review outputs/inputs with customer and re-
           vise as required;
  endtask Task I.1.2


  I.1.3  Define the functionality/behavior for each major
         function;
  Begin Task 1.1.3
  I.1.3.1  FTR: Review output and input data objects derived
           in task I.1.2;
  I.1.3.2  Derive a model of functions/behaviors;
    case of: mechanics
    mechanics 5 quality function deployment
      meet with customer to review major concept require-
      ments;
      interview end users;
      observe current approach to problem, current process;
      develop a hierarchical outline of functions/behaviors;
    mechanics 5 structured analysis
      derive a context level data flow diagram;
```

```
            refine the data flow diagram to provide more detail;
            write processing narratives for functions at lowest
            level of refinement;
         mechanics = object view
            define operations/methods that are relevant for each
            class;
         endcase
   I.1.3.3 Review functions/behaviors with customer and re-
            vise as required;
      endtask Task I.1.3
I.1.4 Isolate those elements of the technology to be im-
      plemented in software;
I.1.5 Research availability of existing software;
I.1.6 Define technical feasibility;
I.1.7 Make quick estimate of size;
I.1.8 Create a scope definition;
endTask: Task I.1
```

The tasks and subtasks noted in the process design language refinement form the basis for a detailed schedule for the concept scoping activity.

7.6   DEFINING A TASK NETWORK

Individual tasks and subtasks have interdependencies based on their sequence. In addition, when more than one person is involved in a software engineering project, it is likely that development activities and tasks will be performed in parallel. When this occurs, concurrent tasks must be coordinated so that they will be complete when later tasks require their work product(s).

A *task network* is a graphic representation of the task flow for a project. It is sometimes used as the mechanism through which task sequence and dependencies are input to an automated project scheduling tool. In its simplest form (used when creating a macroscopic schedule), the task network depicts major software engineering tasks. Figure 7.3 shows a schematic *task network* for a concept development project.

The concurrent nature of software engineering activities leads to a number of important scheduling requirements. Because parallel tasks occur asynchronously, the planner must determine intertask dependencies to ensure continuous progress toward completion. In addition, the project manager should be aware of those tasks that lie on the *critical path*. That is, tasks that must be completed on schedule if the project as a whole is to be completed on schedule. These issues are discussed in more detail later in this chapter.

It is important to note that the task network shown in Figure 7.3 is macroscopic. In a detailed task network (a precursor to a detailed schedule) each activity shown in Figure 7.3 would be expanded. For example, Task I.1 would be expanded to show all tasks detailed in the refinement shown in Section 7.5.

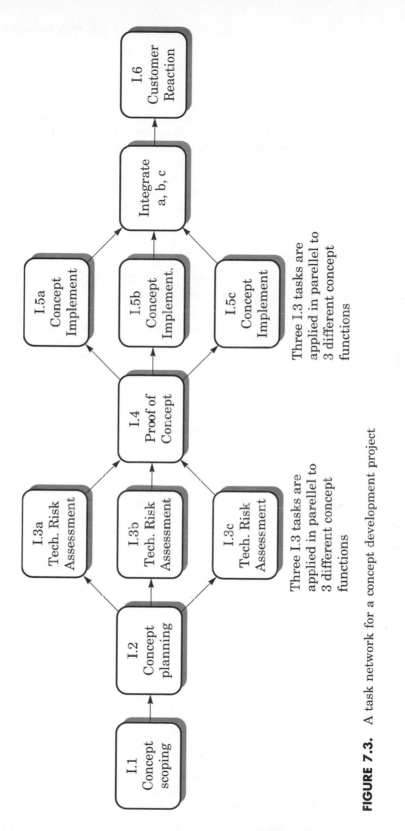

FIGURE 7.3. A task network for a concept development project

Three I.3 tasks are applied in parellel to 3 different concept functions

Three I.3 tasks are applied in parellel to 3 different concept functions

7.7   SCHEDULING

Scheduling of a software project does not differ greatly from scheduling of any multitask engineering effort. Therefore, generalized project scheduling tools and techniques can be applied to software with little modification.

Program evaluation and review technique (PERT) and *critical path method (CPM)* [MOD83] are two project scheduling methods that can be applied to software development. Both techniques are driven by information already developed in earlier project planning activities:

- estimates of effort
- a decomposition of product function
- the selection of the appropriate process model
- the selection of project type and task set

Interdependencies among tasks may be defined using a task network. Tasks, sometimes called the project *work breakdown structure (WBS)*, are defined for the product as a whole or for individual functions.

Both PERT and CPM provide quantitative tools that allow the software planner to (1) determine the *critical path*—the chain of tasks that determines the duration of the project; (2) establish *most likely* time estimates for individual tasks by applying statistical models; and (3) calculate *boundary times* that define a time "window" for a particular task.

Boundary time calculations can be very useful in software project scheduling. Slippage in the design of one function, for example, can retard further development of other functions. Riggs [RIG81] describes important boundary times that may be discerned from a PERT or CPM network: (1) the earliest time that a task can begin when all preceding tasks are completed in the shortest possible time; (2) the latest time for task initiation before the minimum project completion time is delayed; (3) the earliest finish—the sum of the earliest start and the task duration; (4) the latest finish—the latest start time added to task duration; and (5) the *total float*—the amount of surplus time or leeway allowed in scheduling tasks so that the network critical path is maintained on schedule. Boundary time calculations lead to a determination of critical path and provide the manager with a quantitative method for evaluating progress as tasks are completed.

Both PERT and CPM have been implemented in a wide variety of automated tools that are available for virtually every personal computer [THE93]. Such tools are easy to use and make the scheduling methods described above available to every software project manager.

7.7.1   Timeline Charts

When creating a software project schedule, the planner begins with a set of tasks (the work breakdown structure). If automated tools are used, the work breakdown is input as a task network or task outline. Effort, duration, and

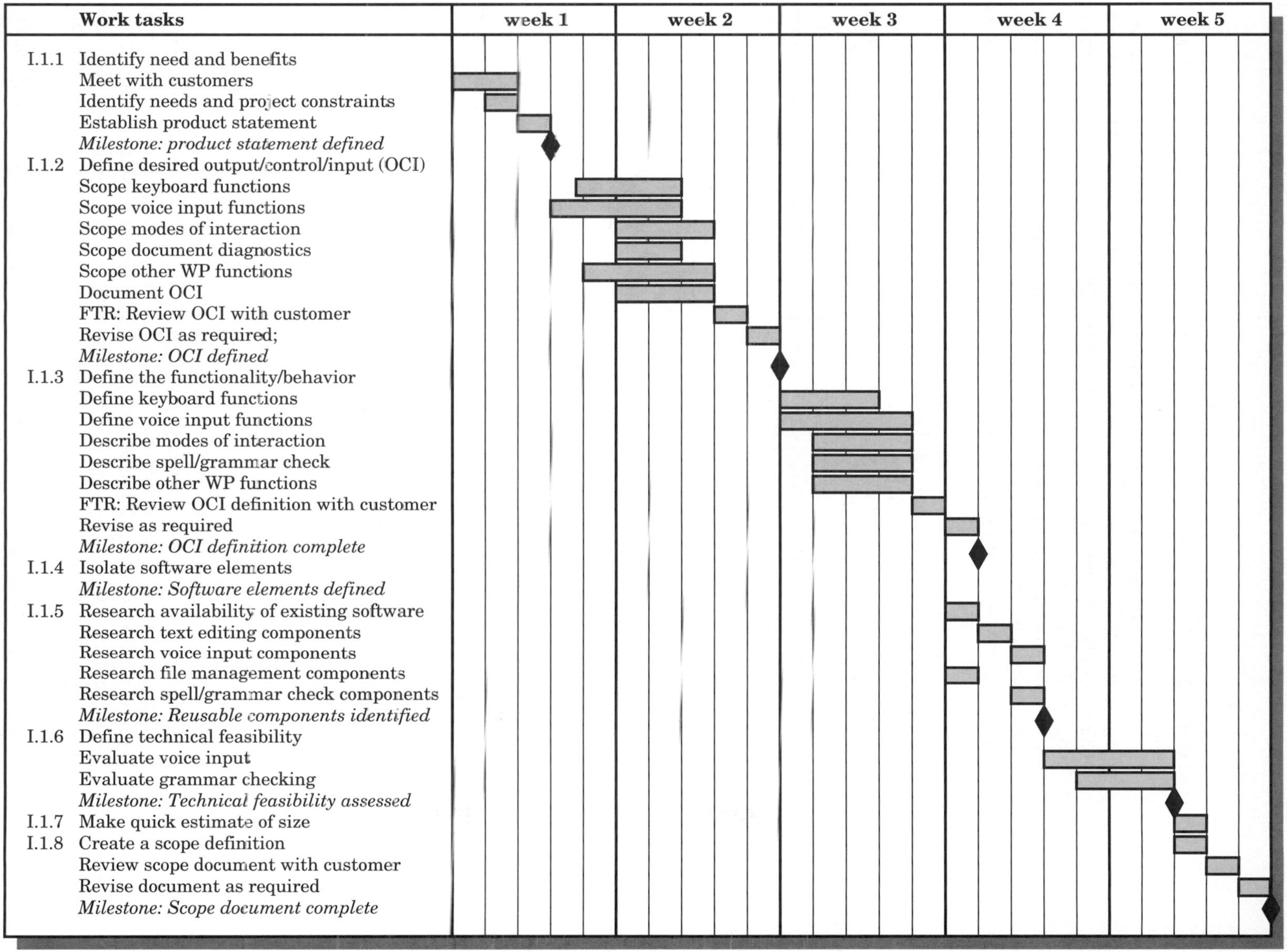

FIGURE 7.4. An example timeline chart.

171

start date are then input for each task. In addition, tasks may be assigned to specific individuals.

As a consequence of this input, a *timeline chart,* also called a *Gantt chart,* is generated. A timeline chart can be developed for the entire project. Alternatively, separate charts can be developed for each project function or for each individual working on the project.

Figure 7.4 illustrates the format of a timeline chart. It depicts a part of a software project schedule that emphasizes the *concept scoping* task (Section 7.5) for a new word-processing software product. All project tasks (for concept scoping) are listed in the left hand column. The horizontal bars indicate the duration of each task. When multiple bars occur at the same time on the calendar, task concurrency is implied. The diamonds indicate milestones.

Once the information necessary for the generation of a timeline chart has been input, the majority of software project scheduling tools produce *project tables*—a tabular listing of all project tasks, their planned and actual start and end dates, and a variety of related information (Figure 7.5). Used in conjunction with the timeline chart, project tables enable the project manager to track progress.

7.7.2 Tracking the Schedule

The project schedule provides a road map for a software project manager. If it has been properly developed, the project schedule defines the tasks and milestones that must be tracked and controlled as the project proceeds. Tracking can be accomplished in a number of different ways:

- conducting periodic project status meetings in which each team member reports progress and problems
- evaluating the results of all reviews conducted throughout the software engineering process
- determining whether formal project milestones (the diamonds shown in Figure 7.4) have been accomplished by the scheduled date
- comparing actual start date to planned start date for each project task listed in the project table (Figure 7.5)
- meeting informally with practitioners to obtain their subjective assessment of progress to date and problems on the horizon

In reality, all of these tracking techniques are used by experienced project managers.

Control is employed by a software project manager to administer project resources, cope with problems, and direct project staff. If things are going well (i.e., the project is on schedule and within budget, reviews indicate that real progress is being made, and milestones are being reached), control is light. But when problems occur, the project manager must exercise control to reconcile them as quickly as possible. After a problem has been diagnosed,[12] additional

---

[12]It is important to note that schedule slippage is a symptom of some underlying problem. The role of the project manager is to diagnose what the underlying problem is and then act to correct it.

Work tasks	Planned start	Actual start	Planned complete	Actual complete	Assigned person	Effort allocated	Notes
I.1.1 Identify needs and benefits							
Meet with customers	wk1, d1	wk1, d1	wk1, d2	wk1, d2	BLS	2 p-d	scoping will require more effort/time
Identify needs and project constraints	wk1, d2	wk1, d2	wk1, d2	wk1, d2	JPP	1 p-d	
Establish product statement	wk1, d3	wk1, d3	wk1, d3	wk1, d3	BLS/JPP	1 p-d	
Milestone: product statement defined	wk1, d3		wk1, d3	wk1, d3			
I.1.2 Define desired output/control/input (OCI)							
Scope keyboard functions	wk1, d4	wk1, d4	wk2, d2		BLS	1.5 p-d	
Scope voice input functions	wk1, d3	wk1, d3	wk2, d2		JPP	2 p-d	
Scope modes of interaction	wk2, d1		wk2, d3		MLL	1 p-d	
Scope document diagnostics	wk2, d1		wk2, d2		BLS	1.5 p-d	
Scope other WP functions	wk1, d4	wk1, d4	wk2, d3		JPP	2 p-d	
Document OCI	wk2, d1		wk2, d3		MLL	3 p-d	
FTR: Review OCI with customer	wk2, d3		wk2, d3		all	3 p-d	
Revise OCI as required;	wk2, d4		wk2, d4		all	3 p-d	
Milestone: OCI defined	wk2, d5		wk2, d5				
I.1.3 Define the functionality/behavior							

FIGURE 7.5. An example project table.

resources may be focused on the problem area: Staff may be redeployed, or the project schedule can be redefined.

When faced with severe deadline pressure, experienced project managers sometimes use a project scheduling and control technique called *time-boxing* [ZAH95]. The time-boxing strategy recognizes that the complete product may not be deliverable by the predefined deadline. Therefore, an incremental software paradigm (Chapter 2) is chosen, and a schedule is derived for each incremental delivery.

The tasks associated with each increment are then time-boxed. This means that the schedule for each task is adjusted by working backward from the delivery date for the increment. A "box" is put around each task. When a task hits the boundary of its time-box (plus or minus 10 percent), work stops and the next task begins.

The initial reaction to the time-boxing approach is often negative: "If the work isn't finished, how can we proceed?" The answer lies in the way work is accomplished. By the time the time-box boundary is encountered, it is likely that 90 percent of the task has been completed.[13] The remaining 10 percent, although important, can (1) be delayed until the next increment, or (2) be completed later if required. Rather than becoming "stuck" on a task, the project proceeds toward the delivery date.

7.8   THE PROJECT PLAN

Each step in the software engineering process should produce a work product that can be reviewed and that can act as a foundation for the steps that follow. The *software project plan* is produced at the culmination of the planning tasks. It provides baseline cost and scheduling information that will be used throughout the software engineering process.

The software project plan is a relatively brief document that is addressed to a diverse audience. It must (1) communicate scope and resources to software management, technical staff, and the customer; (2) define risks and suggest risk management techniques; (3) define cost and schedule for management review; (4) provide an overall approach to software development for all people associated with the project; and (5) outline how quality will be ensured and change will be managed. An outline of the software project plan is presented in Figure 7.6.

A presentation of cost and schedule will vary with the audience to whom it is addressed. If the plan is used only as an internal document, the results of each costing technique can be presented. When the plan is disseminated outside the organization, a reconciled cost breakdown (combining the results of all costing techniques) is provided. Similarly, the degree of detail contained within the schedule section may vary with the audience and formality of the plan.

The software project plan need not be a lengthy, complex document. Its purpose is to help establish the viability of the software development effort. The plan concentrates on a general statement of *what* and a specific statement of

---

[13]A cynic might recall the saying: "The first 90 percent of a system takes 90 percent of the time. The last 10 percent of the system takes 90 percent of the time."

    I. Introduction
        A. Purpose of Plan
        B. Project Scope and Objectives
            1. Statement of Scope
            2. Major Functions
            3. Performance Issues
            4. Management and Technical Constraints
   II. Project Estimates
        A. Historical Data Used for Estimates
        B. Estimation Techniques
        C. Estimates of Effort, Cost, Duration
  III. Risks Management Strategy
        A. Risk Table
        B. Discussion of Risks to be Managed
        C. RMMM Plan for each risk:
            1. Risk Mitigation
            2. Risk Monitoring
            3. Risk Management (contingency plans)
   IV. Schedule
        A. Project Work Breakdown Structure
        B. Task Network
        C. Timeline Chart (Gantt Chart)
        D. Resource Table
    V. Project Resources
        A. People
        B. Hardware and Software
        C. Special Resources
   VI. Staff Organization
        A. Team Structure (if applicable)
        B. Management Reporting
  VII. Tracking and Control Mechanisms
        A. Quality Assurance and Control
        B. Change Management and Control
 VIII. Appendices

FIGURE 7.6.
Software project
plan.

how much and how long. Subsequent steps in the software engineering process will concentrate on definition, development, and maintenance.

7.8   SUMMARY

Scheduling is the culmination of a planning activity that is a primary component of software project management. When combined with estimation methods and risk analysis, scheduling establishes a road map for the project manager.

Scheduling begins with process decomposition. The characteristics of the project are used to adapt an appropriate task set for the work to be done. A task network depicts each engineering task, its dependency on other tasks, and its projected duration. The task network is used to compute the critical project path, a timeline chart, and a variety of project information. Using the schedule as a guide, the project manager can track and control each step in the software engineering process.

REFERENCES

[BRO95]   Brooks, M., *The Mythical Man-Month,* Anniversary Edition, Addison-Wesley, 1995.

[MOD83]   Moder, J.J., C.R. Phillips, and E.W. Davis, *Project Management with CPM, PERT and Precedence Diagramming,* 3rd edition, Van Nostrand Reinhold, 1983.

[PAG85]   Page-Jones, M., *Practical Project Management,* Dorset House, 1985, pp. 90–91.

[PUT92]   Putnam, L., and W. Myers, *Measures for Excellence,* Yourdon Press, 1992.

[RIG81]   Riggs, J., *Production Systems Planning,* Analysis and Control, 3rd edition, Wiley, 1981.

[THE93]   Thé, L., "Project Management Software That's IS Friendly," *Datamation,* October 1, 1993, pp. 55–58.

[ZAH95]   Zahniser, R., "Time-Boxing for Top Team Performance," *Software Development,* March 1995, pp. 34–38.

PROBLEMS AND POINTS TO PONDER

7.1. "Unreasonable" deadlines are a fact of life in the software business. How should you proceed if you're faced with one?

7.2. What is the difference between a macroscopic schedule and a detailed schedule. Is it possible to manage a project if only a macroscopic schedule is developed? Why?

7.3. Is there ever a case where a software project milestone is not tied to a review? If so, provide one or more examples.

7.4. In Section 7.2.1, we present an example of the "communication overhead" that can occur when multiple people work on a software project. Develop a counterexample that illustrates how engineers who are well-versed in good software engineering practices and who make use of formal technical reviews can increase the production rate of a team (when compared to the sum of individual production rates). [Hint: You can assume that reviews reduce rework and that rework can account for 20 to 40 percent of a person's time.]

7.5. Although adding people to a late software project can make it later, there are circumstances in which this is not true. Describe them.

7.6. The relationship between people and time is highly nonlinear. Using Putnam's Software Equation (described in Section 7.2.2), develop a table that relates number of people to project duration for a software project requiring 50,000

LOC and 15 person-years of effort (the productivity parameter is 5000 and $B = 0.37$). Assume that the software must be delivered in 24 months plus or minus 12 months.

7.7. Assume that you have been contracted by a university to develop an on-line course registration system (OLCRS). First, act as the customer (if you're a student, that should be easy!) and specify the characteristics of a good system. Alternatively, your instructor will provide you with a set of preliminary requirements for the system.

Using the COCOMO model described in Chapter 5, develop an effort and duration estimate for OLCRS. Suggest how you would

a. define parallel work activities during the OLCRS project

b. distribute effort throughout the project

c. establish milestones for the project

7.8. Using Section 7.3 as a guide, compute the TSS for OLCRS. Be sure to show all of your work. Select a project type and derive an appropriate task set for the project.

7.9. Define a task network for OLCRS, or alternatively, for another software project that interests you. Be sure to show tasks and milestones and to attach effort and duration estimates to each task. If possible, use an automated scheduling tool to perform this work.

7.10. If an automated scheduling tool is available, determine the critical path for the network defined in problem 7.8.

7.11. Using a scheduling tool (if available) or paper and pencil (if necessary), develop a timeline chart for the OLCRS project.

7.12. Refine a task called **Plan the software project** in much the same way as concept scoping was refined in Section 7.5.

7.13. Suggest practical methods that would enable a manager to monitor compliance with costs and schedules defined in the software project plan.

FURTHER READINGS AND OTHER INFORMATION SOURCES

Project scheduling issues are covered in most books on software project management. Wysoki and his colleagues (*Effective Project Management,* Wiley, 1995) and Whitten (*Managing Software Development Projects,* 2nd edition, Wiley, 1995) consider the topic in detail. Boddie (*Crunch Mode,* Prentice-Hall, 1987) has written a book for all managers who "have 90 days to do a six month project." Gilb (*Principles of Software Engineering Management,* Addison-Wesley, 1988) writes a thought-provoking discussion of software engineering and its management. Kerr and Hunter (*Inside RAD: How to Build Fully Functional Computer Systems in 90 Days or Less,* McGraw-Hill, 1994) discuss project scheduling issues for "accelerated" projects.

Thayer (*Software Engineering Project Management,* IEEE Computer Society Press, 1987) has edited a thorough anthology that contains a number of important papers on project scheduling. Bennatan (*Software Project Management: A Practitioner's Approach,* McGraw-Hill, 1992), Ould (*Strategies for Software Engineering,* Wiley, 1990), Whitten (*Managing Software Development Projects,* Wiley, 1989), and Page-Jones, (*Practical Project Management,*

Dorset House Publishing, New York, 1985), have written good introductions to project management, presenting the basic elements of estimation, planning and scheduling, project tracking, team organization, and other management topics. Youl (*Making Software Development Visible,* Wiley, 1990) has written one of the few books that emphasizes project tracking.

A software management and metrics system, called *Web-Integrated Software Metrics Environment (WISE),* provides a framework for managing software development projects across the Internet. Programmers and managers can log issue reports, track the status of issues, and view project metrics using standard Web browsers at:

http://research.ivv.nasa.gov/projects/WISE/wise.html

An up-to-date list of World Wide Web references for project scheduling and control can be found at: **http://www.rspa.com**

CHAPTER 8

SOFTWARE QUALITY ASSURANCE

The software engineering approach described in this book works toward a single goal: *to produce high-quality software*. Yet many readers will be challenged by the question: "What is software quality?"

Philip Crosby [CRO79], in his landmark book on quality, provides a wry answer to this question:

> The problem of quality management is not what people don't know about it. The problem is what they think they do know. . . .
>
> In this regard, quality has much in common with sex. Everybody is for it. (Under certain conditions, of course.) Everyone feels they understand it. (Even though they wouldn't want to explain it.) Everyone thinks execution is only a matter of following natural inclinations. (After all, we do get along somehow.) And, of course, most people feel that problems in these areas are caused by other people. (If only *they* would take the time to do things right.)

Some software developers continue to believe that software quality is something you begin to worry about after code has been generated. Nothing could be further from the truth! *Software quality assurance (SQA)* is an umbrella activity (Chapter 2) that is applied throughout the software process. SQA encompasses (1) a quality management approach, (2) effective software engineering technology (methods and tools), (3) formal technical reviews that are applied throughout the software process, (4) a multitiered testing strategy, (5) control of software documentation and the changes made to it, (6) a procedure to assure compliance with software development standards (when applicable), and (7) measurement and reporting mechanisms.

In this chapter, we focus on the management issues and the process-specific activities that enable a software organization to ensure that it does "the right things at the right time in the right way." A quantitative discussion of quality is presented in Chapter 18.

8.1   QUALITY CONCEPTS[1]

It has been said that no two snowflakes are alike. Certainly when we watch snow falling it is hard to imagine that snowflakes differ at all, let alone that each flake possesses a unique structure. In order to observe differences between snowflakes, we must examine the specimens closely, perhaps using a magnifying glass. In fact, the closer we look, the more differences we are able to observe.

This phenomenon, *variation between samples,* applies to all products of human as well as natural creation. For example, if two "identical" circuit boards are examined closely enough, we may observe that the copper pathways on the boards differ slightly in geometry, placement, and thickness. In addition, the location and diameter of the holes drilled in the boards varies as well.

All engineered and manufactured parts exhibit variation. The variation between samples may not be obvious without the aid of precise equipment to measure the geometry, electrical characteristics, or other attributes of the parts. However, with sufficiently sensitive instruments, we will likely come to the conclusion that no two samples of any item are exactly alike.

Does this principle apply to software as well as physical items? Imagine a program that, at some point during its execution, needs to sort records in ascending order based on some key field. The nature of the records is not important. They may be employee records, a customer database, map coordinates for a real-time flight control system, or whatever.

The programmer creating the sort routine (or selecting it from a library of reusable components) elects to use *quicksort* to solve the immediate problem. Can an observer of the final product distinguish the software from an otherwise identical product that uses, for example, a bubble sort? Perhaps, but we probably need more information and possibly sensitive instrumentation to distinguish between the two systems.

Variation control is the heart of quality control. A manufacturer wants to minimize the variation among the products that are produced, even when doing something relatively simple like duplicating diskettes. We want to minimize the variation between any pair of allegedly identical diskettes. Surely, this cannot be a problem—duplicating disks is a trivial manufacturing operation, and we can guarantee that exact duplicates of the software are always created.

Or can we? We need to ensure the tracks are placed on the diskettes within a specified tolerance so that the overwhelming majority of floppy drives can read the diskettes. In addition, we need to ensure that the magnetic flux for distinguishing a zero from a one is sufficient for read/write heads to detect. The disk duplication machines can, and do, wear and go out of tolerance. So even a

---

[1]This section, written by Michael Stovsky, has been adapted from "Fundamentals of ISO 9000," a workbook developed for *Essential Software Engineering,* a video curriculum developed by R.S. Pressman & Associates, Inc. Reprinted with permission.

"simple" process such as duplication may encounter problems due to variation between samples.

How might a software development organization need to control variation? From one project to another, we want to minimize the difference between the predicted resources needed to complete a project and the actual resources used, including staffing, equipment, and calendar time. In general, we would like to make sure our testing program covers a known percentage of the software from one release to another. Not only do we want to minimize the number of defects that are released to the field, but we'd like to ensure that the variance in the number of bugs is also minimized from one release to another. (Our customers will likely be upset if the third release of a product has ten times as many defects as the previous release.) We would like to minimize the differences in speed and accuracy of our hotline support responses to customer problems. The list goes on and on.

8.1.1 Quality

The *American Heritage Dictionary* defines quality as "a characteristic or attribute of something." As an attribute of an item, quality refers to measurable characteristics—things we are able to compare to known standards such as length, color, electrical properties, malleability, and so on. However, software, largely an intellectual entity, is more challenging to characterize than physical objects.

Nevertheless, measures of a program's characteristics do exist. These properties include cyclomatic complexity, cohesion, number of function points, lines of code, and many others discussed in Chapters 18 and 23. When we examine an item based on its measurable characteristics, two kinds of quality may be encountered: quality of design and quality of conformance.

Quality of design refers to the characteristics that designers specify for an item. The grade of materials, tolerances, and performance specifications all contribute to the quality of design. As higher-graded materials are used and tighter tolerances and greater levels of performance are specified, the design quality of a product increases, if the product is manufactured according to specifications.

Quality of conformance is the degree to which the design specifications are followed during manufacturing. Again, the greater the degree of conformance, the higher the level of quality of conformance.

In software development, quality of design encompasses requirements, specifications, and the design of the system. Quality of conformance is an issue focused primarily on implementation. If the implementation follows the design and the resulting system meets its requirements and performance goals, conformance quality is high.

8.1.2 Quality Control

Variation control may be equated to quality control. But how do we achieve quality control? *Quality control* is the series of inspections, reviews, and tests used throughout the development cycle to ensure that each work product meets the requirements placed upon it. Quality control includes a feedback loop to the process that created the work product. The combination of measurement and feedback allows us to tune the process when the work products created fail to meet their specifications. This approach views quality control as part of the manufacturing process.

Quality control activities may be fully automated, entirely manual, or a combination of automated tools and human interaction. A key concept of quality control is that all work products have defined and measurable specifications to which we may compare the outputs of each process. The feedback loop is essential to minimize the defects produced.

8.1.3 Quality Assurance

Quality assurance consists of the auditing and reporting functions of management. The goal of quality assurance is to provide management with the data necessary to be informed about product quality, thereby gaining insight and confidence that product quality is meeting its goals. Of course, if the data provided through quality assurance identify problems, it is management's responsibility to address the problems and apply the necessary resources to resolve quality issues.

8.1.4 Cost of Quality

Cost of quality includes all costs incurred in the pursuit of quality or in performing quality related activities. Cost of quality studies are conducted to provide a baseline for the current cost of quality, to identify opportunities for reducing the cost of quality, and to provide a normalized basis of comparison. The basis of normalization is almost always dollars. Once we have normalized quality costs on a dollar basis, we have the necessary data to evaluate where the opportunities lie to improve our processes. Furthermore, we can evaluate the affect of changes in dollar-based terms.

Quality costs may be divided into costs associated with prevention, appraisal, and failure. Prevention costs include:

- quality planning
- formal technical reviews
- test equipment
- training

Appraisal costs include activities to gain insight into product condition the "first time through" each process. Examples of appraisal costs include:

- in-process and interprocess inspection
- equipment calibration and maintenance
- testing

Failure costs are costs that would disappear if no defects appeared before shipping a product to customers. Failure costs may be subdivided into internal failure costs and external failure costs. Internal failure costs are the costs incurred when we detect an error in our product prior to shipment. Internal failure costs include:

- rework
- repair
- failure mode analysis

External failure costs are the costs associated with defects found after the product has been shipped to the customer. Examples of external failure costs are:

- complaint resolution
- product return and replacement
- help line support
- warranty work

As expected, the relative costs to find and repair a defect increase dramatically as we go from prevention to detection and from internal failure to external failure. Figure 8.1, based on data collected by Boehm [BOE81], illustrates this phenomenon.

More recent anecdotal data is reported by Kaplan and his colleagues [KAP95] and is based on work at IBM's Rochester development facility:

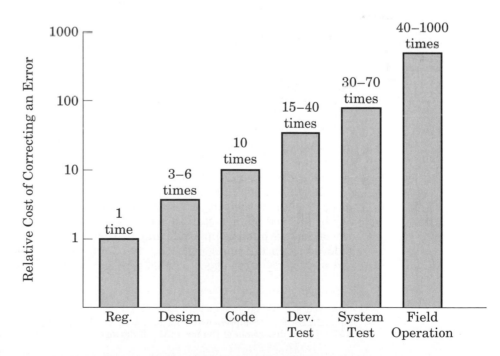

FIGURE 8.1.
Relative cost of
correcting an error.

A total of 7053 hours was spent inspecting 200,000 lines of code with the result that 3112 potential defects were prevented. Assuming a programmer cost of $40.00 per hour, the total cost of preventing 3112 defects was $282,120, or roughly $91.00 per defect.

Compare these numbers to the cost of defect removal once the product has been shipped to the customer. Suppose that there had been no inspections, but that programmers had been extra careful and only one defect per 1000 lines of code [significantly better than industry average] escaped into the shipped product. That would mean that 200 defects would still have to be fixed in the field. At an estimated cost of $25,000 per field fix, the cost would be $5 million, or approximately 18 times more expensive than the total cost of the defect prevention effort.

It is true that IBM produces software that is used by tens of thousands of customers and that their costs for field fixes may be higher than average. This in no way negates the results noted above. Even if the average software organization has field fix costs that are 25 percent of IBM's (most have no idea what their costs are!), the cost savings associated with quality control and assurance activities are compelling.

8.2   THE QUALITY MOVEMENT

Today, senior managers at companies throughout the industrialized world recognize that high product quality translates to cost savings and an improved bottom line. However, this was not always the case. The quality movement began in the 1940s with the seminal work of W. Edwards Deming [DEM86] and had its first true test in Japan. Using Deming's ideas as a cornerstone, the Japanese have developed a systematic approach to the elimination of the root causes of product defects. Throughout the 1970s and 1980s, their work migrated to the Western world and is sometimes called "total quality management (TQM)."[2] Although terminology differs across different companies and authors, a basic four-step progression is normally encountered and forms the foundation of any good TQM program.

The first step is called *kaizen* and refers to a system of continuous process improvement. The goal of *kaizen* is to develop a process (in this case, the software process) that is visible, repeatable, and measurable.

The second step, invoked only after *kaizen* has been achieved, is called *atarimae hinshitsu*. This step examines intangibles that affect the process and works to optimize their impact on the process. For example, the software process may be affected by high staff turnover, which itself is caused by constant reorganizations within a company. It may be that a stable organizational structure could do much to improve the quality of software. *Atarimae hinshitsu* would lead management to suggest changes in the way reorganization occurs.

---

[2]See [ART93] for a comprehensive discussion of TQM and its use in a software context and [KAP95] for a discussion of the use of the Baldridge Award criteria in the software world.

While the first two steps focus on the process, the next step, called *kansei* (translated as "the five senses") concentrates on the user of the product (in this case, software). In essence, by examining the way the user applies the product, *kansei* leads to improvement in the product itself, and potentially, to the process that created it.

Finally, a step called *miryokuteki hinshitsu* broadens management concern beyond the immediate product. This is a business-oriented step that looks for opportunity in related areas that can be identified by observing the use of the product in the marketplace. In the software world, *miryokuteki hinshitsu* might be viewed as an attempt to uncover new and profitable products or applications that are an outgrowth from an existing computer-based system.

For most companies *kaizen* should be of immediate concern. Until a mature software process (Chapter 2) has been achieved, there is little point in moving to the next steps.

8.3 SOFTWARE QUALITY ASSURANCE

Even the most jaded software developers will agree that high-quality software is an important goal. But how do we define quality? A wag once said, "Every program does something right, it just may not be the thing that we want it to do."

There have been many definitions of software quality proposed in the literature. For our purposes, software quality is defined as:

> Conformance to explicitly stated functional and performance requirements, explicitly documented development standards, and implicit characteristics that are expected of all professionally developed software.

There is little question that the above definition could be modified or extended. If fact, a definitive definition of software quality could be debated endlessly. For the purposes of this book, the above definition serves to emphasize three important points:

1. Software requirements are the foundation from which *quality* is measured. Lack of conformance to requirements is lack of quality.
2. Specified standards define a set of development criteria that guide the manner in which software is engineered. If the criteria are not followed, lack of quality will almost surely result.
3. There is a set of *implicit requirements* that often goes unmentioned (e.g., the desire for good maintainability). If software conforms to its explicit requirements but fails to meet implicit requirements, software quality is suspect.

8.3.1 Background Issues

Quality assurance is an essential activity for any business that produces products to be used by others. Prior to the twentieth century, quality assurance was the sole responsibility of the craftsperson who built a product. The first formal quality assurance and control function was introduced at Bell Labs in 1916 and spread rapidly throughout the manufacturing world.

During the early days of computing (the 1950s and 1960s), quality was the sole responsibility of the programmer. Standards for quality assurance for software were introduced in military contract software development during the 1970s and have spread rapidly into software development in the commercial world [IEE94]. Extending the definition presented earlier, software quality assurance is a "planned and systematic pattern of actions" [SCH87] that are required to ensure quality in software. Today, the implication is that many different constituencies in an organization have software quality assurance responsibility—software engineers, project managers, customers, salespeople, and the individuals who serve within an SQA group.

The SQA group serves as the customer's in-house representative. That is, the people who perform SQA must look at the software from the customer's point of view. Does the software adequately meet the quality factors noted in Chapter 18? Has software development been conducted according to pre-established standards? Have technical disciplines properly performed their roles as part of the SQA activity? The SQA group attempts to answer these and other questions to ensure that software quality is maintained.

8.3.2 SQA Activities

Software quality assurance is comprised of a variety of tasks associated with two different constituencies—the software engineers who do technical work and a SQA group that has responsibility for quality assurance planning, oversight, record keeping, analysis, and reporting.

Software engineers address quality (and perform quality assurance) by applying solid technical methods and measures, conducting formal technical reviews, and performing well-planned software testing. Only reviews are discussed in this chapter. Technology topics are discussed in Parts Three through Five of this book.

The charter of the SQA group is to assist the software engineering team in achieving a high quality end product. The Software Engineering Institute [PAU93] recommends a set of SQA activities that address quality assurance planning, oversight, record keeping, analysis, and reporting. It is these activities that are performed (or facilitated) by an independent SQA group:

Prepare a SQA Plan for a project. The plan is developed during project planning and is reviewed by all interested parties. Quality assurance activities performed by the software engineering team and the SQA group are governed by the plan. The plan (Figure 8.5) identifies:

- evaluations to be performed
- audits and reviews to be performed
- standards that are applicable to the project

- procedures for error reporting and tracking
- documents to be produced by the SQA group
- amount of feedback provided to software project team

Participates in the development of the project's software process description. The software engineering team selects a process for the work to be performed. The SQA group reviews the process description for compliance with organizational policy, internal software standards, externally imposed standards (e.g., ISO 9001), and other parts of the software project plan.

Reviews software engineering activities to verify compliance with the defined software process. The SQA group identifies, documents, and tracks deviations from the process and verifies that corrections have been made.

Audits designated software work products to verify compliance with those defined as part of the software process. The SQA group reviews selected work products; identifies, documents, and tracks deviations; verifies that corrections have been made; and periodically reports the results of its work to the project manager.

Ensures that deviations in software work and work products are documented and handled according to a documented procedure. Deviations may be encountered in the project plan, process description, applicable standards, or technical work products.

Records any noncompliance and reports to senior management. Noncompliance items are tracked until they are resolved.

In addition to these activities, the SQA group coordinates the control and management of change (Chapter 9) and helps to collect and analyze software metrics.

8.4   SOFTWARE REVIEWS

Software reviews are a "filter" for the software engineering process. That is, reviews are applied at various points during software development and serve to uncover errors that can then be removed. Software reviews serve to "purify" the software work products that occur as a result of analysis, design, and coding. Freedman and Weinberg [FRE90] discuss the need for reviews this way:

Technical work needs reviewing for the same reason that pencils need erasers: *To err is human.* The second reason we need technical reviews is that although people are good at catching some of their own errors, large classes of errors escape the originator more easily than they escape anyone else. The review process is, therefore, the answer to the prayer of Robert Burns:

O wad some power the giftie give us
to see ourselves as other see us

A review—any review—is a way of using the diversity of a group of people to:

1. point out needed improvements in the product of a single person or team;

2. confirm those parts of a product in which improvement is either not desired or not needed; and

3. achieve technical work of more *uniform,* or at least more *predictable,* quality than can be achieved without reviews, in order to make technical work more *manageable.*

There are many different types of reviews that can be conducted as part of software engineering. Each has its place. An informal meeting around the coffee machine is a form of review, if technical problems are discussed. A formal presentation of software design to an audience of customers, management, and technical staff is a form of review. In this book, however, we focus on the formal technical review—sometimes called a *walkthrough.* A formal technical review is the most effective filter from a quality assurance standpoint. Conducted by software engineers (and others) for software engineers, the FTR is an effective means for improving software quality.

8.4.1 Cost Impact of Software Defects

The *IEEE Standard Dictionary of Electrical and Electronics Terms* (IEEE Standard 100-1992) defines a *defect* as "a product anomaly." The definition for "fault" in the hardware context can be found in IEEE Standard 610.12-1990:

> (a) A defect in a hardware device or component; for example, a short circuit or broken wire. (b) An incorrect step, process, or data definition in a computer program. *Note:* This definition is used primarily by the fault tolerance discipline. In common usage, the terms "error" and "bug" are used to express this meaning. See also: data-sensitive fault; program-sensitive fault; equivalent faults; fault masking; intermittent fault.

Within the context of the software process, the terms "defect" and "fault" are *synonymous.* Both imply a quality problem that is discovered *after* the software has been released to end users. In earlier chapters, we used the term "error" to depict a quality problem that is discovered by software engineers (or others) *before* the software is released to the end user.

The primary objective of formal technical reviews is to find errors during the process so that they do become defects after release of the software. The obvious benefit of formal technical reviews is the early discovery of errors so that they do not propagate to the next step in the software process.

A number of industry studies (TRW, Nippon Electric, and Mitre Corp., among others) indicate that design activities introduce between 50 and 65 percent of all errors (and ultimately, all defects) during the software process. However, formal review techniques have been shown to be up to 75 percent effective [JON86] in uncovering design flaws. By detecting and removing a large percentage of these errors, the review process substantially reduces the cost of subsequent steps in the development and maintenance phases.

To illustrate the cost impact of early error detection, we consider a series of relative costs that are based on actual cost data collected for large software projects [IBM81]. Assume that an error uncovered during design will cost 1.0 monetary unit to correct. Relative to this cost, the same error uncovered just before testing commences will cost 6.5 units; during testing 15 units; and after release, between 60 and 100 units.

8.4.2 Defect Amplification and Removal

A *defect amplification model* [IBM81] can be used to illustrate the generation and detection of errors during preliminary design, detail design, and coding steps of the software engineering process. The model is illustrated schematically in Figure 8.2. A box represents a software development step. During the step, errors may be inadvertently generated. Review may fail to uncover newly generated errors and errors from previous steps, resulting in some number of errors that are passed through. In some cases, errors passed through from previous steps are amplified (amplification factor, x) by current work. The box subdivisions represent each of these characteristics and the percent efficiency for detecting errors, a function of the thoroughness of review.

Figure 8.3 illustrates a hypothetical example of defect amplification for a software development process in which no reviews are conducted. As shown in the figure, each test step is assumed to uncover and correct 50 percent of all incoming errors without introducing any new errors (an optimistic assumption). Ten preliminary design errors are amplified to 94 errors before testing commences. Twelve latent defects are released to the field. Figure 8.4 considers the same conditions except that design and code reviews are conducted as part of each development step. In this case, 10 initial preliminary design errors are amplified to 24 errors before testing commences. Only three latent defects exist. By recalling the relative costs associated with the discovery and correction of errors, overall cost (with and without review for our hypothetical example) can be established. In Table 8.1 it can be seen that total cost for development and maintenance when reviews are conducted is 783 cost units. When no reviews are conducted, total cost is 2177 units—nearly three times more costly.

To conduct reviews, a developer must expend time and effort and the development organization must spend money. However, the results of the preceding example leave little doubt that we have encountered a "pay now or pay much more later" syndrome. Formal technical reviews (for design and other technical activities) provide a demonstrable cost benefit. They should be conducted.

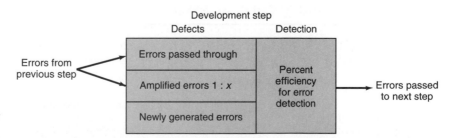

FIGURE 8.2. Defect amplification model

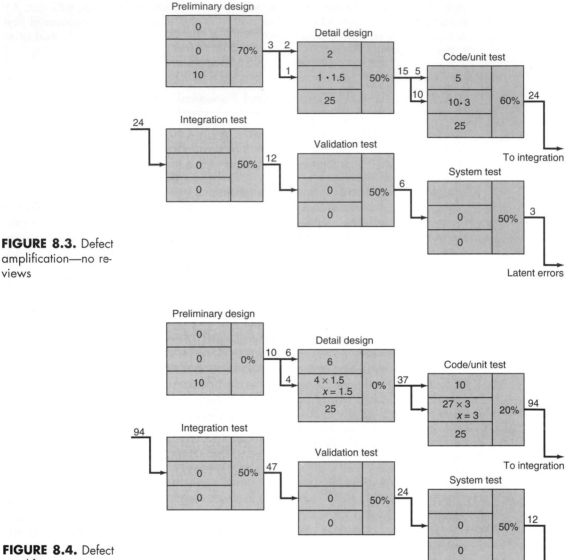

FIGURE 8.3. Defect amplification—no reviews

FIGURE 8.4. Defect amplification—reviews conducted

8.5   FORMAL TECHNICAL REVIEWS

A formal technical review (FTR) is a software quality assurance activity that is performed by software engineers.[3] The objectives of the FTR are (1) to un-

---

[3]In some cases, other constituencies (e.g., customers, marketing, support staff) may also participate in formal technical reviews.

TABLE 8.1

DEVELOPMENT COST COMPARISON

Errors Found	Number	Cost Unit	Total
Reviews Conducted			
During design	22	1.5	33
Before test	36	6.5	234
During test	15	15	315
After release	3	67	201
			783
No Reviews Conducted			
Before test	22	6.5	143
During test	82	15	1230
After release	12	67	804
			2177

cover errors in function, logic, or implementation for any representation of the software; (2) to verify that the software under review meets its requirements; (3) to ensure that the software has been represented according to predefined standards; (4) to achieve software that is developed in a uniform manner; and (5) to make projects more manageable. In addition, the FTR serves as a training ground, enabling junior engineers to observe different approaches to software analysis, design, and implementation. The FTR also serves to promote backup and continuity because a number of people become familiar with parts of the software that they may not have otherwise seen.

The FTR is actually a class of reviews that include *walkthroughs, inspections, round-robin reviews,* and other small group technical assessments of software. Each FTR is conducted as a meeting and will be successful only if it is properly planned, controlled, and attended. In the paragraphs that follow, guidelines similar to those for a *walkthrough* [FRE90, GIL93] are presented as a representative formal technical review.

8.5.1 The Review Meeting

Regardless of the FTR format that is chosen, every review meeting should abide by the following constraints:

- between three and five people (typically) should be involved in the review;
- advance preparation should occur but should require no more than two hours of work for each person; and
- the duration of the review meeting should be less than two hours.

Given the above constraints, it should be obvious that an FTR focuses on a specific (and small) part of the overall software. For example, rather than attempting to review an entire design, walkthroughs are conducted for each module or small group of modules. With a narrower focus, the FTR has a higher likelihood of uncovering errors.

The focus of the FTR is on a work product—a component of the software (e.g., a portion of a requirements specification, a detailed module design, a source code listing for a module). The individual who has developed the work product—the *producer*—informs the project leader that the work product is complete and that a review is required. The project leader contacts a *review leader,* who evaluates the work product for readiness, generates copies, and distributes them to two or three *reviewers* for advance preparation. Each reviewer is expected to spend between one and two hours reviewing the work product, making notes, and otherwise becoming familiar with the work. Concurrently, the review leader also reviews the work product and establishes an agenda for the review meeting, which is typically scheduled for the next day.

The review meeting is attended by the review leader, all reviewers, and the producer. One of the reviewers takes on the role of the *recorder,* that is, the individual who records (in writing) all important issues raised during the review. The FTR begins with an introduction of the agenda and a brief introduction by the producer. The producer then proceeds to "walk through" the work product, explaining the material, while reviewers raise issues based on their advance preparation. When valid problems or errors are discovered, the recorder notes each.

At the end of the review, all attendees of the FTR must decide whether to (1) accept the work product without further modification, (2) reject the work product due to severe errors (once corrected, another review must be performed) or (3) accept the work product provisionally (minor errors have been encountered and must be corrected, but no additional review will be required). The decision made, all FTR attendees complete a *sign-off,* indicating their participation in the review and their concurrence with the review team's findings.

8.5.2 Review Reporting and Record Keeping

During the FTR, a reviewer (the recorder) actively records all issues that have been raised. These are summarized at the end of the review meeting and a *review issues list* is produced. In addition, a simple *review summary report* is completed. A review summary report answers three questions:

1. What was reviewed?
2. Who reviewed it?
3. What were the findings and conclusions?

The review summary report is typically a single page form (with possible attachments). It becomes part of the project historical record and may be distributed to the project leader and other interested parties.

The review issues list serves two purposes: (1) to identify problem areas within the product and (2) to serve as an *action item* checklist that guides the producer as corrections are made. An issues list is normally attached to the summary report.

It is important to establish a follow-up procedure to ensure that items on the issues list have been properly corrected. Unless this is done, it is possible that issues raised can "fall between the cracks." One approach is to assign the responsibility for follow-up to the review leader. A more formal approach assigns responsibility to an independent SQA group.

8.5.3 Review Guidelines

Guidelines for the conduct of formal technical reviews must be established in advance, distributed to all reviewers, agreed upon, and then followed. A review that is uncontrolled can often be worse than no review at all.

The following represents a minimum set of guidelines for formal technical reviews:

1. *Review the product, not the producer.* An FTR involves people and egos. Conducted properly, the FTR should leave all participants with a warm feeling of accomplishment. Conducted improperly, the FTR can take on the aura of an inquisition. Errors should be pointed out gently; the tone of the meeting should be loose and constructive; and the intent should not be to embarrass or belittle. The review leader should conduct the review meeting to ensure that the proper tone and attitude are maintained and should immediately halt a review that has gotten out of control.

2. *Set an agenda and maintain it.* One of the key maladies of meetings of all types is *drift*. An FTR must be kept on track and on schedule. The review leader is chartered with the responsibility for maintaining the meeting schedule and should not be afraid to nudge people when drift sets in.

3. *Limit debate and rebuttal.* When an issue is raised by a reviewer, there may not be universal agreement on its impact. Rather than spending time debating the question, the issue should be recorded for further discussion off-line.

4. *Enunciate problem areas, but don't attempt to solve every problem noted.* A review is not a problem solving session. The solution of a problem can often be accomplished by the producer alone or with the help of only one other individual. Problem solving should be postponed until after the review meeting.

5. *Take written notes.* It is sometimes a good idea for the recorder to make notes on a wall board, so that wording and prioritization can be assessed by other reviewers as information is recorded.

6. *Limit the number of participants and insist upon advance preparation.* Two heads are better than one, but 14 are not necessarily better than 4. Keep the number of people involved to the necessary minimum. However, all review team members must prepare in advance. Written comments should be solicited by the review leader (providing an indication that the reviewer has reviewed the material).

7. *Develop a checklist[4] for each work product that is likely to be reviewed.* A checklist helps the review leader to structure the FTR meeting and helps each reviewer to focus on important issues. Checklists should be developed for analysis, design, coding, and even test documents.

8. *Allocate resources and time schedule for FTRs.* For reviews to be effective, they should be scheduled as a task during the software engineering process. In addition, time should be scheduled for the inevitable modifications that will occur as the result of an FTR.

9. *Conduct meaningful training for all reviewers.* To be effective all review participants should receive some formal training. The training should stress both process related issues and the human psychological side of reviews. Freedman and Weinberg [FRE90] estimate a one month learning curve for every 20 people who are to participate effectively in reviews.

10. *Review your early reviews.* Debriefing can be beneficial in uncovering problems with the review process itself. The very first work product to be reviewed might be the review guidelines themselves.

Because there are many variables (e.g., number of participants, type of work products, timing and length, specific review approach) that have an impact on a successful review, a software organization should experiment to determine what approach works best in a local context. Porter [POR95] and his colleagues provide excellent guidance for this type of experimentation.

8.6   FORMAL APPROACHES TO SQA

In preceding sections, we have argued that software quality is everyone's job and that it can be achieved through competent analysis, design, coding, and testing, as well as through the application of formal technical reviews, a multitiered testing strategy, better control of software documentation and the changes made to it, and the application of accepted software development standards. In addition, quality can be defined in terms of a broad array of quality factors and measured (indirectly) using a variety of indices and metrics.

Over the past two decades, a small, but vocal, segment of the software engineering community has argued that a more formal approach to software quality assurance is required. It can be argued that a computer program is a mathematical object. A rigorous syntax and semantics can be defined for every programming language, and a similarly rigorous approach to the specification of software requirements (Chapter 24) is also available. Once the requirements model (specification) has been represented in a rigorous manner, mathematic proofs of correctness can be applied to demonstrate that a program conforms exactly to its specification.

---

[4]Extensive information on review checklists can be found at the FTR Archive on the World Wide Web. See "Further Readings and Other Information Sources" for additional information.

Attempts to prove programs correct are not new. Dijkstra [DIJ76] and Linger et al. [LIN79], among others, advocated proofs of program correctness and tied these to the use of structured programming concepts (Chapter 14). Today, a number of different approaches to formal proof of correctness have been proposed and are discussed in detail in Chapters 24 and 25.

8.7 STATISTICAL QUALITY ASSURANCE

Statistical quality assurance reflects a growing trend throughout industry to become more quantitative about quality. For software, statistical quality assurance implies the following steps:

1. Information about software defects is collected and categorized.
2. An attempt is made to trace each defect to its underlying cause (e.g., nonconformance to specification, design error, violation of standards, poor communication with customer).
3. Using the Pareto principle (80 percent of the defects can be traced to 20 percent of all possible causes), isolate the 20 percent (the "vital few").
4. Once the vital few causes have been identified, move to correct the problems that have caused the defects.

This relatively simple concept represents an important step toward the creation of an adaptive software engineering process in which changes are made to improve those elements of the process that introduce error.

To illustrate the process, assume that a software development organization collects information on defects for a period of one year. Some errors are uncovered as software is being developed. Other defects are encountered after the software has been released to its end user. Although hundreds of different errors are uncovered, all can be tracked to one (or more) of the following causes:

- incomplete or erroneous specification (IES)
- misinterpretation of customer communication (MCC)
- intentional deviation from specification (IDS)
- violation of programming standards (VPS)
- error in data representation (EDR)
- inconsistent module interface (IMI)
- error in design logic (EDL)
- incomplete or erroneous testing (IET)
- inaccurate or incomplete documentation (IID)
- error in programming language translation of design (PLT)
- ambiguous or inconsistent human–computer interface (HCI)
- miscellaneous (MIS)

To apply statistical SQA, Table 8.2 is built. The table indicates that IES, MCC, and EDR are the vital few causes that account for 53 percent of all errors. It should be noted, however, that IES, EDR, PLT, and EDL would be selected as the vital few causes if only serious errors are considered. Once the vital few causes are determined, the software development organization can begin corrective action. For example, to correct MCC, the software developer might implement facilitated application specification techniques (Chapter 11) to improve the quality of customer communication and specification. To improve EDR, the developer might acquire CASE tools for data modeling and perform more stringent data design reviews. As the vital few causes are corrected, new candidates pop to the top of the stack.

In conjunction with the collection of defect information, software developers can calculate an *error index* (EI) for each major step in the software engineering process [IEE94]. After analysis, design, coding, testing, and release, the following data are gathered:

E_i = the total number of errors uncovered during the ith step in the software engineering process

S_i = the number of serious errors

M_i = the number of moderate errors

T_i = the number of minor errors

PS = size of the product (LOC, design statements, pages of documentation) at the ith step

TABLE 8.2

DATA COLLECTION FOR STATISTICAL SQA

	Total		Serious		Moderate		Minor	
Error	No.	%	No.	%	No.	%	No.	%
IES	205	22%	34	27%	68	18%	103	24%
MCC	156	17%	12	9%	68	18%	76	17%
IDS	48	5%	1	1%	24	6%	23	5%
VPS	25	3%	0	0%	15	4%	10	2%
EDR	130	14%	26	20%	68	18%	36	8%
IMI	58	6%	9	7%	18	5%	31	7%
EDL	45	5%	14	11%	12	3%	19	4%
IET	95	10%	12	9%	35	9%	48	11%
IID	36	4%	2	2%	20	5%	14	3%
PLT	60	6%	15	12%	19	5%	26	6%
HCI	28	3%	3	2%	17	4%	8	2%
MIS	56	6%	0	0%	15	4%	41	9%
Totals	942	100%	128	100%	379	100%	435	100%

w_s, w_m, w_t = weighting factors for serious, moderate and trivial errors, where recommended values are $w_s = 10$, $w_m = 3$, $w_t = 1$. The weighting factors for each phase should become larger as development progresses. This rewards an organization that finds errors early.

At each step in the software engineering process, a phase index, PI_i, is computed:

$$\text{PI}_i = w_s(S_i/E_i) + w_m(M_i/E_i) + w_t(T_i/E_i)$$

The error index (EI) is computed by calculating the cumulative effect or each PI_i, weighting errors encountered later in the software engineering process more heavily than those encountered earlier.

$$\text{EI} = \sum (i \times \text{PI}_i)/\text{PS}$$

$$= (\text{PI}_1 + 2\text{PI}_2 + 3\text{PI}_3 + i\text{PI}_i)/\text{PS}$$

The error index can be used in conjunction with information collected in Table 8.2 to develop an overall indication of improvement in software quality.

The application of statistical SQA and the Pareto principle can be summarized in a single sentence: Spend your time focusing on things that really matter, but first be sure that you understand what really matters! Experienced industry practitioners agree that most really difficult defects can be traced to a relatively limited number of root causes. In fact, most practitioners have an intuitive feeling for the "real" causes of software defects, but few have spent time collecting data to support their feelings. By performing the basic steps of statistical SQA, the vital few causes for defects can be isolated and appropriate corrections can be made.

A comprehensive discussion of statistical SQA is beyond the scope of this book. Interested readers should see [SCH87], [KAP95], or [KAN95].

8.8   SOFTWARE RELIABILITY

There is no doubt that the reliability of a computer program is an important element of its overall quality. If a program repeatedly and frequently fails to perform, it matters little whether other software quality factors are acceptable.

Software reliability, unlike many other quality factors, can be measured, directed, and estimated using historical and developmental data. Software reliability is defined in statistical terms as "the probability of failure free operation of a computer program in a specified environment for a specified time" [MUS87]. To illustrate, program X is estimated to have a reliability of 0.96 over eight elapsed processing hours. In other words, if program X were to be executed 100 times and require eight hours of elapsed processing time (execution time), it is likely to operate correctly (without failure) 96 times out of 100.

Whenever software reliability is discussed, a pivotal question arises: What is meant by the term "failure"? In the context of any discussion of software quality and reliability, failure is nonconformance to software requirements. Yet, even within this definition there are gradations. Failures can be only annoying or catastrophic. One failure can be corrected within seconds while another requires weeks or even months to correct. Complicating the issue even further, the correction of one failure may in fact result in the introduction of other errors that ultimately result in other failures.

8.8.1 Measures of Reliability and Availability

Early work in software reliability attempted to extrapolate the mathematics of hardware reliability theory (e.g., [ALV64]) to the prediction of software reliability. Most hardware related reliability models are predicated on failure due to *wear* rather than failure due to design defects. In hardware, failures due to physical wear (e.g., the effects of temperature, corrosion, shock) are more likely than a design related failure. Unfortunately, the opposite is true for software. In fact, all software failures can be traced to design or implementation problems; wear (see Chapter 1) does not enter into the picture.

There is still debate over the relationship between key concepts in hardware reliability and their applicability to software (e.g., [LIT89], [ROO90]). Although an irrefutable link has yet to be established, it is worthwhile to consider a few simple concepts that apply to both system elements.

If we consider a computer-based system, a simple measure of reliability is *mean time between failure* (MTBF), where

$$MTBF = MTTF + MTTR$$

(The acronyms MTTF and MTTR are *mean time to failure* and *mean time to repair*, respectively.)

Many researchers argue that MTBF is a far more useful measure than defects/KLOC. Stated simply, an end user is concerned with failures, not with the total defect count. Because each defect contained within a program does not have the same failure rate, the total defect count provides little indication of the reliability of a system. For example, consider a program that has been in operation for 14 months. Many defects in this program may remain undetected for decades before they are discovered. The MTBF of such obscure defects might be 50 or even 100 years. Other defects, as yet undiscovered, might have a failure rate of 18 or 24 months. Even if every one of the first category of defects (those with long MTBF) is removed, the impact on software reliability is negligible.

In addition to a reliability measure, we must develop a measure of *availability*. Software availability is the probability that a program is operating according to requirements at a given point in time and is defined as:

$$Availability = MTTF/(MTTF + MTTR) \times 100\%$$

The MTBF reliability measure is equally sensitive to MTTF and MTTR. The availability measure is somewhat more sensitive to MTTR, an indirect measure of the maintainability of software.

8.8.2 Software Safety and Hazard Analysis

Leveson [LEV86] discusses the impact of software in safety critical systems when she writes:

Before software was used in safety critical systems, they were often controlled by conventional (nonprogrammable) mechanical and electronic devices. System safety techniques are designed to cope with random failures in these [nonprogrammable] systems. Human design errors are not considered since it is assumed that all faults caused by human errors can be avoided completely or removed prior to delivery and operation.

When software is used as part of the control system, complexity can increase by an order of magnitude or more. Subtle design faults induced by human error—something that can be uncovered and eliminated in hardware-based conventional control—become much more difficult to uncover when software is used.

Software safety and hazard analysis are software quality assurance activities that focus on the identification and assessment of potential hazards that may impact software negatively and cause an entire system to fail. If hazards can be identified early in the software engineering process, software design features can be specified that will either eliminate or control potential hazards.

A modeling and analysis process is conducted as part of software safety. Initially, hazards are identified and categorized by criticality and risk. For example, some of the hazards associated with a computer-based cruise control for an automobile might be:

- causes uncontrolled acceleration that cannot be stopped
- does not disengage when the brake pedal is depressed
- does not engage when switch is activated
- slowly loses or gains speed

Once these system-level hazards are identified, analysis techniques are used to assign severity and probability of occurrence.[5] To be effective, software must be analyzed in the context of the entire system. For example, a subtle user input error (people *are* system components) may be magnified by a software fault to produce control data that improperly positions a mechanical device. If a set of external environmental conditions are met (and only if they are met), the improper position of the mechanical device will cause a disastrous failure. Analysis techniques such as fault tree analysis [VES81], real-time logic [JAN86], or Petri net models [LEV87] can be used to predict the chain of events that can cause hazards and the probability that each of the events will occur to create the chain.

Fault tree analysis builds a graphical model of the sequential and concurrent combinations of events that can lead to a hazardous event or system state. Using a well-developed fault tree, it is possible to observe the consequences of a sequence of interrelated failures that occur in different system components. *Real-time logic (RTL)* builds a system model by specifying events and corresponding actions. The event–action model can be analyzed using logic operations to test safety assertions about system components and their timing. *Petri net* models can be used to determine the faults that are most hazardous.

---

[5]This approach is analogous to the risk analysis approach described for software project management in Chapter 6. The primary difference is the emphasis on technology issues as opposed to project related topics.

Once hazards are identified and analyzed, safety related requirements can be specified for the software. That is, the specification can contain a list of undesirable events and the desired system responses to these events. The role of software in managing undesirable events is then indicated.

Although software reliability and software safety are closely related to one another, it is important to understand the subtle difference between them. Software reliability uses statistical analysis to determine the likelihood that a software failure will occur. However, the occurrence of a failure does not necessarily result in a hazard or mishap. Software safety examines the ways in which failures result in conditions that can lead to a mishap. That is, failures are not considered in a vacuum, but are evaluated in the context of an entire computer-based system.

A comprehensive discussion of software safety and hazard analysis is beyond the scope of this book. Those readers with further interest should refer to Leveson's [LEV95] book on the subject.

8.9   THE SQA PLAN

The *SQA plan* provides a road map for instituting software quality assurance. Developed by the SQA group and the project team, the plan serves as a template for SQA activities that are instituted for each software project.

Figure 8.5 presents an outline for SQA plans recommended by the IEEE [IEE94]. Initial sections describe the purpose and scope of the document and indicate those software process activities that are covered by quality assurance. All documents noted in the SQA plan are listed and all applicable standards are noted. The *Management* section of the plan describes SQA's place in the organizational structure; SQA tasks and activities and their placement throughout the software process; and the organizational roles and responsibilities relative to product quality.

The *Documentation* section describes (by reference) each of the work products produced as part of the software process. These include:

- project documents (e.g., project plan)
- models (e.g., ERDs, class hierarchies)
- technical documents (e.g., specifications, test plans)
- user documents (e.g., help files)

In addition, this section defines the minimum set of work products that are acceptable to achieve high quality.

Standards, Practices, and Conventions lists all applicable standards/practices that are applied during the software process (e.g., document standards, coding standards, and review guidelines). In addition, all project, process, and (in some instances) product metrics that are to be collected as part of software engineering work are listed.

The *Reviews and Audits* section of the plan identifies the reviews and audits to be conducted by the software engineering team, the SQA group, and the customer. It provides an overview of the approach for each review and audit.

I. Purpose of Plan
II. References
III. Management
    1. Organization
    2. Tasks
    3. Responsibilities
IV. Documentation
    1. Purpose
    2. Required software engineering documents
    3. Other documents
V. Standards, Practices, and Conventions
    1. Purpose
    2. Conventions
VI. Reviews and Audits
    1. Purpose
    2. Review Requirements
        a. software requirements review
        b. design reviews
        c. software verification and validation reviews
        d. functional audit
        e. physical audit
        f. in-process audits
        g. management reviews
VII. Test
VIII. Problem Reporting and Corrective Action
IX. Tools, Techniques, and Methodologies
X. Code Control
XI. Media Control
XII. Supplier Control
XIII. Records Collection, Maintenance, and Retention
XIV. Training
XV. Risk Management

Fig. 8.5.
ANSI/IEEE Std. 730-1984 and 983-1986 software quality assurance plans

The *Test* section references the software test plan and procedure (Chapter 17). It also defines test record-keeping requirements. *Problem Reporting and Corrective Action* defines procedures for reporting, tracking, and resolving errors and defects, and identifies the organizational responsibilities for these activities.

The remainder of the *SQA plan* identifies the tools and methods that support SQA activities and tasks; references software configuration management procedures for controlling change; defines a contract management approach; establishes methods for assembling, safeguarding, and maintaining all records; identifies training required to meet the needs of the plan, and defines methods for identifying, assessing, monitoring, and controlling risks.

8.10   THE ISO 9000 QUALITY STANDARDS[6]

A *quality assurance system* may be defined as the organizational structure, responsibilities, procedures, processes, and resources for implementing quality management [ANS87]. ISO 9000 describes quality assurance elements in generic terms that can be applied to any business regardless of the products or services offered.

To become registered to one of the quality assurance system models contained in ISO 9000, a company's quality system and operations are scrutinized by third party auditors for compliance to the standard and for effective operation. Upon successful registration, a company is issued a certificate from a registration body represented by the auditors. Semiannual surveillance audits ensure continued compliance to the standard.

8.10.1   The ISO Approach to Quality Assurance Systems

The ISO 9000 quality assurance models treat an enterprise as a network of interconnected processes. For a quality system to be ISO-compliant, these processes must address the areas identified in the standard and must be documented and practiced as described. Documenting a process helps an organization understand, control, and improve it. It is the opportunity to understand, control, and improve the process network that offers, perhaps, the greatest benefit to organizations that design and implement ISO-compliant quality systems.

ISO 9000 describes the elements of a quality assurance system in general terms. These elements include the organizational structure, procedures, processes, and resources needed to implement quality planning, quality control, quality assurance, and quality improvement. However, ISO 9000 does not describe how an organization should implement these quality system elements. Consequently, the challenge lies in designing and implementing a quality assurance system that meets the standard and fits the company's products, services, and culture.

8.10.2   The ISO 9001 Standard

ISO 9001 is the quality assurance standard that applies to software engineering. The standard contains 20 requirements that must be present for an effective quality assurance system. Because the ISO 9001 standard is applicable to all engineering disciplines, a special set of ISO guidelines (ISO 9000-3) have been developed to help interpret the standard for use in the software process.

---

[6]This section, written by Michael Stovsky, has been adapted from "Fundamentals of ISO 9000" and "ISO 9001 Standard," workbooks developed for *Essential Software Engineering,* a video curriculum developed by R.S. Pressman & Associates, Inc. Reprinted with permission.

The 20 requirements delineated by ISO 9001 address the following topics:

1. Management responsibility
2. Quality system
3. Contract review
4. Design control
5. Document and data control
6. Purchasing
7. Control of customer supplied product
8. Product identification and traceability
9. Process control
10. Inspection and testing
11. Control of inspection, measuring, and test equipment
12. Inspection and test status
13. Control of nonconforming product
14. Corrective and preventive action
15. Handling, storage, packaging, preservation, and delivery
16. Control of quality records
17. Internal quality audits
18. Training
19. Servicing
20. Statistical techniques

In order for a software organization to become registered to ISO 9001, it must establish policies and procedures to address each of the requirements noted above and then be able to demonstrate that these policies and procedures are being followed. For further information on ISO 9001, the interested reader should see [SCH94] and [ESE95].

8.11 SUMMARY

Software quality assurance is an "umbrella activity" that is applied at each step in the software process. SQA encompasses procedures for the effective application of methods and tools, formal technical reviews, testing strategies and techniques, procedures for change control, procedures for assuring compliance to standards, and measurement and reporting mechanisms.

SQA is complicated by the complex nature of software quality—an attribute of computer programs that is defined as "conformance to explicitly and implicitly defined requirements." But when considered more generally, software quality encompasses many different product and process factors and related metrics.

Software reviews are one of the most important SQA activities. Reviews serve as a filter for the software process, removing errors while they are relatively inexpensive to find and correct. The formal technical review or walk-through is a stylized review meeting that has been shown to be extremely effective in uncovering errors.

To properly conduct software quality assurance, data about the software engineering process should be collected, evaluated, and disseminated. Statistical SQA helps to improve the quality of the product and the software process itself. Software reliability models extend measurements, enabling collected defect data to be extrapolated into projected failure rates and reliability predictions.

In summary, we recall the words of Dunn and Ullman [DUN82]: "Software quality assurance is the mapping of the managerial precepts and design disciplines of quality assurance onto the applicable managerial and technological space of software engineering." The ability to ensure quality is the measure of a mature engineering discipline. When the mapping alluded to above is successfully accomplished, mature software engineering is the result.

REFERENCES

[ALV64] von Alvin, W.H. (ed.), *Reliability Engineering,* Prentice-Hall, 1964.

[ANS87] ANSI/ASQC A3-1987, Quality Systems Terminology, 1987.

[BOE81] Boehm, B., *Software Engineering Economics,* Prentice-Hall, 1981.

[CRO79] Crosby, P., *Quality is Free,* McGraw-Hill, 1979.

[DEM86] Deming, W.W., *Out of the Crisis,* MIT Press, 1986.

[DIJ76] Dijkstra, E., *A Discipline of Programming,* Prentice-Hall, 1976.

[DUN82] Dunn, R., and R. Ullman, *Quality Assurance for Computer Software,* McGraw-Hill, 1982.

[ESE95] "ISO 9000 Software Development," in *Essential Software Engineering,* R.S. Pressman & Associates, Inc., 1995.

[FRE90] Freedman, D.P., and Weinberg, G.M., *Handbook of Walkthroughs, Inspections and Technical Reviews,* 3rd edition, Dorset House, 1990.

[GIL93] Gilb, T., and D. Graham, *Software Inspections,* Addison-Wesley, 1993.

[IBM81] "Implementing Software Inspections," course notes, IBM Systems Sciences Institute, IBM Corporation, 1981.

[IEE94] *Software Engineering Standards,* 1994 edition, IEEE Computer Society, 1994.

[JAN86] Jahanian, F., and A.K. Mok, "Safety Analysis of Timing Properties of Real-Time Systems," *IEEE Trans. Software Engineering,* vol. SE-12, no. 9, September 1986, pp. 890–904.

[JON86] Jones, T.C., *Programming Productivity,* McGraw-Hill, 1986.

[KAN95] Kan, S.H., *Metrics and Models in Software Quality Engineering,* Addison-Wesley, 1995.

[KAP95] Kaplan, C., R. Clark, and V. Tang, *Secrets of Software Quality: 40 Innovations from IBM,* McGraw-Hill, 1995.

[LEV86] Leveson, N.G., "Software Safety: Why, What, and How," *ACM Computing Surveys,* vol. 18, no. 2, June 1986, pp. 125–163.

[LEV87] Leveson, N.G., and J.L. Stolzy, "Safety Analysis using Petri Nets," *IEEE Trans. Software Engineering,* vol. SE-13, no. 3, March 1987, pp. 386–397.

[LEV95] Leveson, N.G., *Safeware: System Safety and Computers,* Addison-Wesley, 1995.

[LIN79]   Linger, R., H. Mills, and B. Witt, *Structured Programming,* Addison-Wesley, 1979.

[LIT89]   Littlewood, B., "Forecasting Software Reliability," in *Software Reliability: Modeling and Identification* (S. Bittanti, ed.), Springer-Verlag, 1989, pp. 141–209.

[MUS87]   Musa, J.D., A. Iannino, and K. Okumoto, *Engineering and Managing Software with Reliability Measures,* McGraw-Hill, 1987.

[PAU93]   Paulk, M. et al. *Capability Maturity Model for Software,* Software Engineering Institute, Carnegie Mellon University, Pittsburgh, PA, 1993.

[POR95]   Porter, A., H. Siy, C.A. Toman, and L.G. Votta, "An Experiment to Assess the Cost-Benefits of Code Inspections in Large Scale Software Development," *Proc. 3rd ACM SIGSOFT Symposium on the Foundations of Software Engineering,* Washington, DC, October 10–13, ACM Press, pp. 92–103.

[ROO90]   Rook, J., *Software Reliability Handbook,* Elsevier, 1990.

[SCH87]   Schulmeyer, G.C., and J.I. McManus (eds.), *Handbook of Software Quality Assurance,* Van Nostrand Reinhold, 1987.

[SCH94]   Schmauch, C.H., *ISO 9000 for Software Developers,* ASQC Quality Press, Milwaukee, WI, 1994.

[VES81]   Veseley, W.E. et al., *Fault Tree Handbook,* U.S. Nuclear Regulatory Commission, NUREG-0492, January 1981.

PROBLEMS AND POINTS TO PONDER

8.1. Early in this chapter we noted that "variation control is the heart of quality control." Since every program that is created is different from every other program, what are the variations that we look for and how do we control them?

8.2. Is it possible to assess the quality of software if the customer keeps changing his mind about what it is supposed to do?

8.3. Quality and reliability are related concepts, but are fundamentally different in a number of ways. Discuss them.

8.4. Can a program be correct and still not be reliable? Explain.

8.5. Can a program be correct and still not exhibit good quality? Explain.

8.6. Why is there often tension between a software engineering group and an independent software quality assurance group? Is this healthy?

8.7. You have been given the responsibility for improving the quality of software across your organization. What is the first thing that you should do? What's next?

8.8. Besides counting errors, are there other countable characteristics of software that imply quality? What are they and can they be measured directly?

8.9. A formal technical review is effective only if everyone has prepared in advance. How do you recognize a review participant who has not prepared? What do you do, if you're the review leader?

8.10. Some people argue that an FTR should assess programming style as well as correctness. Is this a good idea? Why?

8.11. Review Table 8.2 and select the four "vital few" causes of serious and moderate errors. Suggest corrective actions using information presented in other chapters.

8.12. An organization uses a five-step software engineering process in which errors are found according to the following percentage distribution:

Step	Percentage of Error Found
1	20%
2	15%
3	15%
4	40%
5	10%

Using Table 8.2 information and the percentage distribution above, compute the overall defect index for the organization. Assume PS = 100,000.

8.13. Research the literature on software reliability and write a paper that describes one software reliability model. Be sure to provide an example.

8.14. The MTBF concept for software is open to criticism. Can you think of a few reasons why?

8.15. Consider two safety-critical systems that are controlled by computer. List at least three hazards for each that can be directly linked to software failures.

8.16. Acquire a copy of ISO 9001 and ISO 9000-3. Prepare a presentation that discusses three ISO 9001 requirements and how they apply in a software context.

FURTHER READINGS AND OTHER INFORMATION SOURCES

Books by Crosby [CRO79] and Deming [DEM86] are excellent management-level presentations on the benefits of formal quality assurance programs. Although they do not focus on software, both books are must reading for senior managers with software development responsibility. Gluckman and Roome (*Everyday Heros of the Quality Movement,* Dorset House, 1993) humanizes quality issues by telling the story of the players in the quality process. Kan (*Metrics and Models in Software Quality Engineering,* Addison-Wesley, 1995) presents a quantitative view of software quality.

There have been dozens of books written about software quality issues in recent years. The following is a small sampling of useful sources:

Clapp, J.A. et al., *Software Quality Control, Error Analysis and Testing,* Noyes Data Corp., Park Ridge, NJ, 1995.

Dobbins, J.H., *Software Quality Assurance and Evaluation,* ASQC Quality Press, Milwaukee, WI, 1990.

Dunn, R.H., and Ullman, R.S., *TQM for Computer Software,* McGraw-Hill, 1994.

Fenton, N., R. Whitty, and Y. Iizuka, *Software Quality Assurance and Measurement: Worldwide Industrial Applications,* Chapman & Hall, 1994.

Ferdinand, A.E., *Systems, Software, and Quality Engineering,* Van Nostrand Reinhold, 1993.

Ince, D., *ISO 9001 and Software Quality Assurance,* McGraw-Hill, 1994.

Ince, D., *An Introduction to Software Quality Assurance and its Implementation,* McGraw-Hill, 1994.

Sanders, J., *Software Quality: A Framework for Success in Software Development,* Addison-Wesley, 1994.

Schulmeyer, G.G., and J.I. McManus, *Total Quality Management for Software,* Van Nostrand Reinhold, 1992.

Sumner, F.H., *Software Quality Assurance,* Macmillan, 1993.

Wallmuller, E., *Software Quality Assurance: A Practical Approach*, Prentice-Hall, 1995.

Weinberg, G.M., *Quality Software Management*, three volumes, Dorset House, 1992, 1993, 1994.

Wesner, J.W., J.M. Hiatt, and D.C. Trimble, *Winning with Quality: Applying Quality Principles in Product Development,* Addison-Wesley, 1995.

An anthology edited by Wheeler, Brykczynski, and Meeson (*Software Inspection: Industry Best Practice,* IEEE Computer Society Press, 1996) presents useful information on this important SQA activity. Friedman and Voas (*Software Assessment,* Wiley, 1995) discuss both theoretical underpinnings and practical methods for ensuring the reliability and safety of computer programs.

The majority of published work in software reliability and software safety can be found in recent technical papers. Lyu (*Handbook of Software Reliability Engineering,* McGraw-Hill, 1996) has edited a comprehensive handbook on software reliability that is accompanied by a diskette with valuable data on software failure and three reliability tools. Research in reliability modeling is discussed by Pham (*Software Reliability and Testing,* IEEE Computer Society Press, 1995). The *Proceedings of the Symposium on Software Reliability* (*Software Engineering Notes,* special issue, August 1995) is an excellent compendium of recent work.

A reasonably wide variety of Internet sources are available for SQA and related subjects. The newsgroups **comp.software-eng** and **comp.software.testing** often address SQA issues.

General information on SQA can be obtained at the American Society for Quality Control Web site:

http://www.asqc.org/

Quality Assurance Resources Online is a collection of quality related information and groups accessible over the World Wide Web:

http://www.quality.org/qc/homepage.html

Brief discussions and bibliographies on SQA topics can be found at:

http://hissa.ncsl.nist.gov/sw_assurance/

Software Testing Laboratories, Inc. presents a wide array of papers and discussion of software quality assurance:

http://www.stlabs.com

The WWW archive for formal technical reviews is the most extensive on-line repository available for information on formal technical reviews, and includes an extensive bibliography. Review checklists and other information can be found at:

http://www.ics.hawaii.edu/ ~ siro/
http://www.ics.hawaii.edu/ ~ johnson/FTR/

The NASA Formal Inspections Page contains a *Formal Inspection Guidebook* and standard for the inspection process.

http://satc.gsfc.nasa.gov/fi/fipage.html

An extensive repository of information on safety-critical systems, software safety, and hazard analysis can be found at:

http://www.comlab.ox.ac.uk/archive/safety.html

An extensive guide to ISO 9000 can be obtained at:

http://www.outland.ileaf.com/isoguide.html

Additional information on ISO 9000 and related quality issues can be obtained from:

ISO Web Site

http://haas.berkeley.edu/ ~ seidel/iso.html

FAQ on ISO standards

http://www.bedrock.com/patents/readings/standrds.html

An ISO 9000 Bibliography

http://www.exit109.com/ ~ leebee/bibliog.htm

An up-to-date list of World Wide Web references for software quality assurance can be found at: **http://www.rspa.com**

CHAPTER 9

SOFTWARE CONFIGURATION MANAGEMENT

Change is inevitable when computer software is built. And change increases the level of confusion among software engineers who are working on a project. Confusion arises when changes are *not* analyzed before they are made, recorded before they are implemented, reported to those with a need to know, or controlled in a manner that will improve quality and reduce error. Babich [BAB86] discusses this when he states:

> The art of coordinating software development to minimize . . . . confusion is called *configuration management*. Configuration management is the art of identifying, organizing, and controlling modifications to the software being built by a programming team. The goal is to maximize productivity by minimizing mistakes.

Software configuration management (SCM) is an umbrella activity that is applied throughout the software process. Because change can occur at any time, SCM activities are developed to (1) identify change, (2) control change, (3) ensure that change is being properly implemented, and (4) report change to others who may have an interest.

It is important to make a clear distinction between software maintenance and software configuration management. Maintenance is a set of software engineering activities that occur after software has been delivered to the customer and put into operation. Software configuration management is a set of tracking and control activities that begin when a software project begins and terminate only when the software is taken out of operation.

A primary goal of software engineering is to improve the ease with which changes can be accommodated and reduce the amount of effort expended when changes must be made. In this chapter, we discuss the specific activities that enable us to manage change.

9.1   SOFTWARE CONFIGURATION MANAGEMENT

The output of the software process is information that may be divided into three broad categories: (1) computer programs (both source-level and executable forms), (2) documents that describe the computer programs (targeted at both technical practitioners and users), and (3) data (contained within the program or external to it). The items that comprise all information produced as part of the software process are collectively called a *software configuration*.

As the software process progresses, the number of *software configuration items (SCIs)* grows rapidly. A *system specification* spawns a *software project plan* and *software requirements specification* (as well as hardware related documents). These in turn spawn other documents to create a hierarchy of information. If each SCI simply spawned other SCIs, little confusion would result. Unfortunately, another variable enters the process—*change*. Change may occur at any time, for any reason. In fact, the *First Law of System Engineering* [BER80] states: *No matter where you are in the system life cycle, the system will change, and the desire to change it will persist throughout the life cycle.*

What is the origin of these changes? The answer to this question is as varied as the changes themselves. However, there are four fundamental sources of change:

- new business or market conditions that dictate changes in product requirements or business rules
- new customer needs that demand modification of data produced by information systems, functionality delivered by products, or services delivered by a computer-based system
- reorganization and/or business downsizing that causes changes in project priorities or software engineering team structure
- budgetary or scheduling constraints that cause a redefinition of the system or product

Software configuration management is a set of activities that have been developed to manage change throughout the life cycle of computer software. SCM can be viewed as a software quality assurance activity that is applied throughout the software process. In the sections that follow, we examine major SCM tasks and important concepts that help us to manage change.

9.1.1   Baselines

Change is a fact of life in software development. Customers want to modify requirements. Developers want to modify technical approach. Managers want to modify project approach. Why all this modification? The answer is really quite simple. As time passes all constituencies know more (about what they need, which approach would be best, and how to get it done and still make money). This additional knowledge is the driving force behind most changes and leads to a statement of fact that is difficult for many software engineering practitioners to accept: Most changes are justified!

A *baseline* is a software configuration management concept that helps us to control change without seriously impeding justifiable change. The IEEE (IEEE Std. 610.12-1990) defines a baseline as:

> A specification or product that has been formally reviewed and agreed upon, that thereafter serves as the basis for further development, and that can be changed only through formal change control procedures.

One way to describe a baseline is through analogy:

> Consider the doors to the kitchen of a large restaurant. To eliminate collisions, one door is marked OUT and the other is marked IN. The doors have stops that allow them to be opened only in the appropriate direction.
>
> If a waiter picks up an order in the kitchen, places it on a tray, and then realizes he has selected the wrong dish, he may change to the correct dish quickly and informally before he leaves the kitchen.
>
> If, however, he leaves the kitchen, gives the customer the dish and then is informed of his error, he must follow a set procedure: (1) look at the check to determine if an error has occurred; (2) apologize profusely; (3) return to the kitchen through the IN door; (4) explain the problem, and so forth.

A baseline is analogous to a dish as it passes through the kitchen door in the restaurant. Before a software configuration item becomes a baseline, change may be made quickly and informally. However, once a baseline is established, we figuratively pass through a swinging one-way door. Changes can be made, but a specific, formal procedure must be applied to evaluate and verify each change.

In the context of software engineering, a baseline is a milestone in the development of software that is marked by the delivery of one or more software configuration items and the approval of these SCIs that is obtained through a formal technical review (Chapter 8). For example, the elements of a *design specification* have been documented and reviewed. Errors are found and corrected. Once all parts of the specification have been reviewed, corrected and then approved, the design specification becomes a baseline. Further changes to the program architecture (contained in the design specification) can be made only after each has been evaluated and approved. Although baselines can be defined at any level of detail, the most common software baselines are shown in Figure 9.1.

The progression of events that lead to a baseline is illustrated in Figure 9.2. Software engineering tasks produce one or more SCIs. After SCIs are reviewed and approved, they are placed in a *project database* (also called a *project library* or *software repository*). When a member of a software engineering

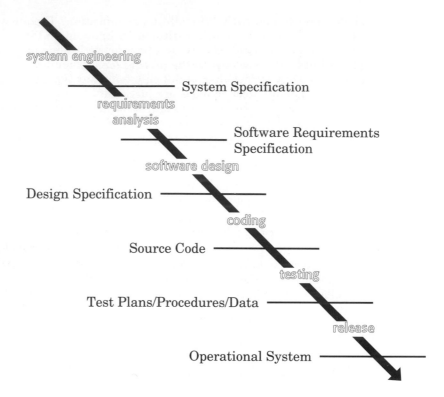

FIGURE 9.1.
Baselines

team wants to make a modification to a baselined SCI, it is copied from the project database into the engineer's private work space. However, this extracted SCI can be modified only if SCM controls (discussed later in this chapter) are followed. The dashed arrows noted in Figure 9.2 illustrate the modification path for a baselined SCI.

9.1.2 Software Configuration Items

We have already defined a software configuration item as information that is created as part of the software engineering process. In the extreme, an SCI could be considered to be a single section of a large specification or one test case in a large suite of tests. More realistically, an SCI is a document, an entire suite of test cases, or a named program component (e.g., a C++ function or an Ada95 package).

The following SCIs become the target for configuration management techniques and form a set of baselines:

1. System Specification
2. Software Project Plan
3. Software Requirements Specification
   a. Graphical analysis models

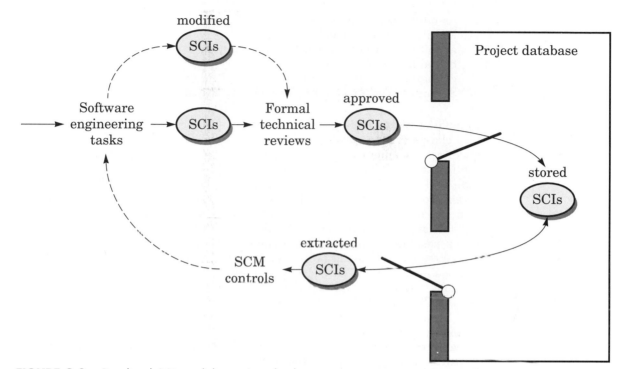

FIGURE 9.2. Baselined SCIs and the project database

        b. Process specifications
        c. Prototype(s)
        d. Mathematical specification
   4. Preliminary User Manual
   5. Design Specification
        a. Data design description
        b. Architectural design description
        c. Module design descriptions
        d. Interface design descriptions
        e. Object descriptions (if object-oriented techniques are used)
   6. Source Code Listing
   7. Test Specification
        a. Test plan and procedure
        b. Test cases and recorded results
   8. Operation and Installation Manuals
   9. Executable Program
        a. Module executable code
        b. Linked modules
  10. Database Description
        a. Schema and file structure
        b. Initial content

11. As-built User Manual
12. Maintenance Documents
    a. Software problem reports
    b. Maintenance requests
    c. Engineering change orders
13. Standards and Procedures for Software Engineering

In addition to the SCIs noted above, many software engineering organizations also place software tools under configuration control. That is, specific versions of editors, compilers, and other CASE tools are "frozen" as part of the software configuration. Because these tools were used to produce documentation, source code, and data, they must be available when changes to the software configuration are to be made. Although problems are rare, it is possible that a new version of a tool (e.g., a compiler) might produce different results than the original version. For this reason, tools, like the software that they help to produce, can be baselined as part of a comprehensive configuration management process.

In reality, SCIs are organized to form *configuration objects* that may be catalogued in the project database with a single name. A configuration object has a name, attributes, and is "connected" to other objects by relationships. In Figure 9.3, the configuration objects **design specification, data model, module N, source code,** and **test specification** are each defined separately. However, each of the objects is related to the others as shown by the arrows. A curved arrow indicates a compositional relation. That is, **data model** and **module N** are part of the object **design specification.** A double headed straight arrow indicates an interrelationship. If a change were made to the **source code** object, interrelationships enable a software engineer to determine what other objects (and SCIs) might be affected.[1]

9.2   THE SCM PROCESS

Software configuration management is an important element of software quality assurance. Its primary responsibility is the control of change. However, SCM is also responsible for the identification of individual SCIs and various versions of the software, the auditing of the software configuration to ensure that it has been properly developed, and the reporting of all changes applied to the configuration.

Any discussion of SCM introduces a set of complex questions:

• How does an organization identify and manage the many existing versions of a program (and its documentation) in a manner that will enable change to be accommodated efficiently?

• How does an organization control changes before and after software is released to a customer?

---

[1]These relationships are discussed in Section 9.2.1, and the structure of the project database will be discussed in greater detail in Chapter 29.

- Who has responsibility for approving and prioritizing changes?
- How can we assure that changes have been made properly?
- What mechanism is used to apprise others of changes that are made?

These questions lead us to the definition of five SCM tasks: *identification, version control, change control, configuration auditing,* and *reporting*.

9.3   IDENTIFICATION OF OBJECTS IN THE SOFTWARE CONFIGURATION

To control and manage software configuration items, each must be separately named and then organized using an object-oriented approach. Two types of objects can be identified [CHO89]: *basic objects* and *aggregate objects*.[2] A basic object is a "unit of text" that has been created by a software engineer during analysis, design, coding, or testing. For example, a basic object might be a section of a requirements specification, a source listing for a module, or a suite of test cases that are used to exercise the code. An aggregate object is a collection of basic objects and other aggregate objects. In Figure 9.3, **design specification** is an aggregate object. Conceptually, it can be viewed as a named (identified) list of pointers that specify basic objects such as **data model** and **module N.**

Each object has a set of distinct features that identify it uniquely: a name, a description, a list of resources, and a "realization." The object name is a character string that identifies the object unambiguously. The object description is a list of data items that identify:

- the SCI type (e.g, document, program, data) that is represented by the object;
- a project identifier; and change and/or version information.

Resources are "entities that are provided, processed, referenced or otherwise required by the object" [CHO89]. For example, data types, specific functions, or even variable names may be considered to be object resources. The realization is a pointer to the "unit of text" for a basic object and *null* for an aggregate object.

Configuration object identification must also consider the relationships that exist between named objects. An object can be identified as **<part-of>** an aggregate object. The relationship **<part-of>** defines a hierarchy of objects. For example, using the simple notation,

```
E-R diagram 1.4 <part-of> data model;
data model <part-of> Design Specification;
we create a hierarchy of SCIs.
```

---

[2]The concept of an aggregate object [GUS89] has been proposed as a mechanism for representing a complete version of a software configuration.

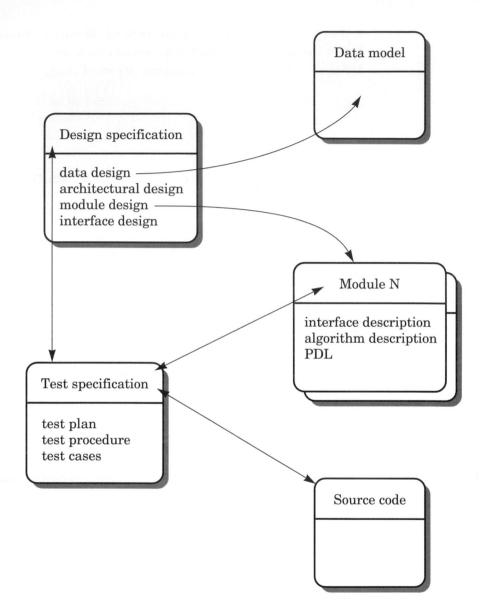

FIGURE 9.3.
Configuration
objects

It is unrealistic to assume that the only relationships among objects in an object hierarchy are along direct paths of the hierarchical tree. In many cases, objects are interrelated across branches of the object hierarchy. For example, **data model** is interrelated to data flow diagrams (assuming the use of structured analysis) and also interrelated to a set of test cases for a specific equivalence class. These cross-structural relationships can be represented in the following manner:

data model <interrelated> data flow model;
data model <interrelated> test case class m;

In the first case, the interrelationship is between a composite object, while the second relationship is between an aggregate object (**data model**) and a basic object (**test case class m**).

The interrelationships between configuration objects can be represented with a *module interconnection language (MIL)* [NAR87]. A MIL describes the interdependencies among configuration objects and enables any version of a system to be constructed automatically.

The identification scheme for software objects must recognize that objects evolve throughout the software process. Before an object is baselined, it may change many times, and even after a baseline has been established, changes may be quite frequent. It is possible to create an *evolution graph* [GUS89] for any object. The evolution graph describes the change history of the object and is illustrated in Figure 9.4. Configuration object 1.0 undergoes revision and becomes object 1.1. Minor corrections and changes result in versions 1.1.1 and 1.1.2, which is followed by a major update that is object 1.2. The evolution of object 1.0 continues through 1.3 and 1.4, but at the same time, a major modification to the object results in a new evolutionary path, version 2.0. Both versions are currently supported.

It is possible that changes may be made to any version, but not necessarily to all versions. How does the developer reference all modules, documents, and test cases for version 1.4? How does the marketing department know what customers currently have version 2.1? How can we be sure that changes to version 2.1 source code are properly reflected in corresponding design documentation? A key element in the answer to all of the above questions is identification.

A variety of automated SCM tools (e.g., CCC, RCS, SCCS, Aide-de-Camp) have been developed to aid in identification (and other SCM) tasks. In some cases, a tool is designed to maintain full copies of only the most recent version. To achieve earlier versions (of documents or programs) changes (catalogued by the tool) are "subtracted" from the most recent version [TIC82]. This scheme makes the current configuration immediately available and other versions easily available.

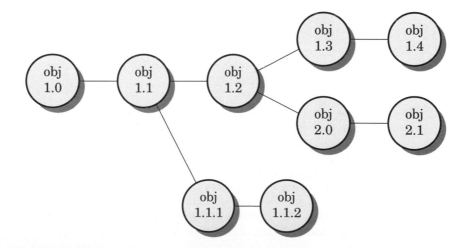

FIGURE 9.4.
Evolution graph

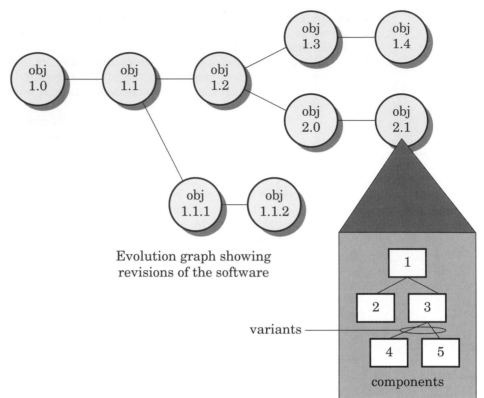

Evolution graph showing
revisions of the software

variants

components

FIGURE 9.5.
Versions and variants

9.4   VERSION CONTROL

Version control combines procedures and tools to manage different versions of
configuration objects that are created during the software engineering process.
Clemm [CLE89] describes version control in the context of SCM:

> Configuration management allows a user to specify alternative configura-
> tions of the software system through the selection of appropriate versions. This
> is supported by associating attributes with each software version, and then al-
> lowing a configuration to be specified [and constructed] by describing the set of
> desired attributes.

The "attributes" mentioned above can be as simple as a specific version number that is attached to each object or as complex as a string of boolean variables (switches) that indicate specific types of functional changes that have
been applied to the system [LIE89].

One representation of the different versions of a system is the evolution
graph presented in Figure 9.4. Each node on the graph is an aggregate object,
that is, a complete version of the software. Each version of the software is a collection of SCIs (source code, documents, data), and each version may be com-

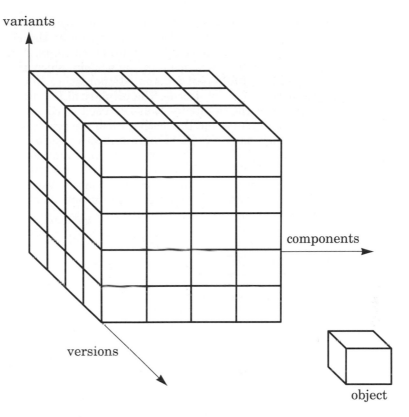

FIGURE 9.6.
Object pool representation of components, variants, and versions [REI89]

posed of different *variants*. To illustrate this concept, consider a version of a simple program that is composed of components 1, 2, 3, 4, and 5 (Figure 9.5).[3] Component 4 is used only when the software is implemented using color displays. Component 5 is implemented when monochrome displays are available. Therefore, two variants of the version can be defined: (1) components 1, 2, 3, and 4; (2) components 1, 2, 3, and 5.

To construct the appropriate variant of a given version of a program, each component can be assigned an "attribute-tuple"—a list of features that will define whether the component should be used when a particular variant of a software version is to be constructed. One or more attributes is assigned for each variant. For example, a *color* attribute could be used to define which component should be included when color displays are to be supported.

Another way to conceptualize the relationship between components, variants and versions (revisions) is to represent them as an *object pool* [REI89]. As Figure 9.6 shows, the relationship between configuration objects and components, variants, and versions can be represented as a three-dimensional space.

---

[3]In this context, the term "component" refers to all composite objects and basic objects that for a baselined SCI. For example, an "input" component might be constructed with six different software modules, each responsible for an input subfunction.

A component is composed of a collection of objects at the same revision level. A variant is a different collection of objects at the same revision level and therefore coexists in parallel with other variants. A new version is defined when major changes are made to one or more objects.

A number of different automated approaches to version control have been proposed over the past decade. The primary difference in approaches is the sophistication of the attributes that are used to construct specific versions and variants of a system and the mechanics of the process for construction. In early systems, such as SCCS [ROC75], attributes took on numeric values. In later systems, such as RCS [TIC82], symbolic revision keys were used. Modern systems, such as NSE or DSEE [ADA89], create version specifications that can be used to construct variants or new versions. These systems also support the baselining concept, thereby precluding uncontrolled modification (or deletion) of a particular version.

9.5   CHANGE CONTROL

For a large software development project, uncontrolled change rapidly leads to chaos. *Change control* combines human procedures and automated tools to provide a mechanism for the control of change. The change control process is illustrated schematically in Figure 9.7. A *change request*[4] is submitted and evaluated to assess technical merit, potential side effects, overall impact on other configuration objects and system functions, and the projected cost of the change. The results of the evaluation are presented as a *change report* that is used by a *change control authority (CCA)*—a person or group who makes a final decision on the status and priority of the change. An *engineering change order (ECO)* is generated for each approved change. The ECO describes the change to be made; the constraints that must be respected, and the criteria for review and audit. The object to be changed is "checked out" of the project database, the change is made, and appropriate SQA activities are applied. The object is then "checked in" to the database and appropriate version control mechanisms (Section 9.4) are used to create the next version of the software.

The "check-in" and "check-out" processes implement two important elements of change control—access control and synchronization control. *Access control* governs which software engineers have the authority to access and modify a particular configuration object. *Synchronization control* helps to ensure that parallel changes, performed by two different people, don't overwrite one another [HAR89].

Access and synchronization control flow is illustrated schematically in Figure 9.8. Based on an approved change request and ECO, a software engineer checks out a configuration object. An access control function ensures that the software engineer has authority to check out the object, and synchroniza-

---

[4]Although many change requests are submitted during the software maintenance phase, we take a broader view in this discussion. A request for change can occur at any time during the software process.

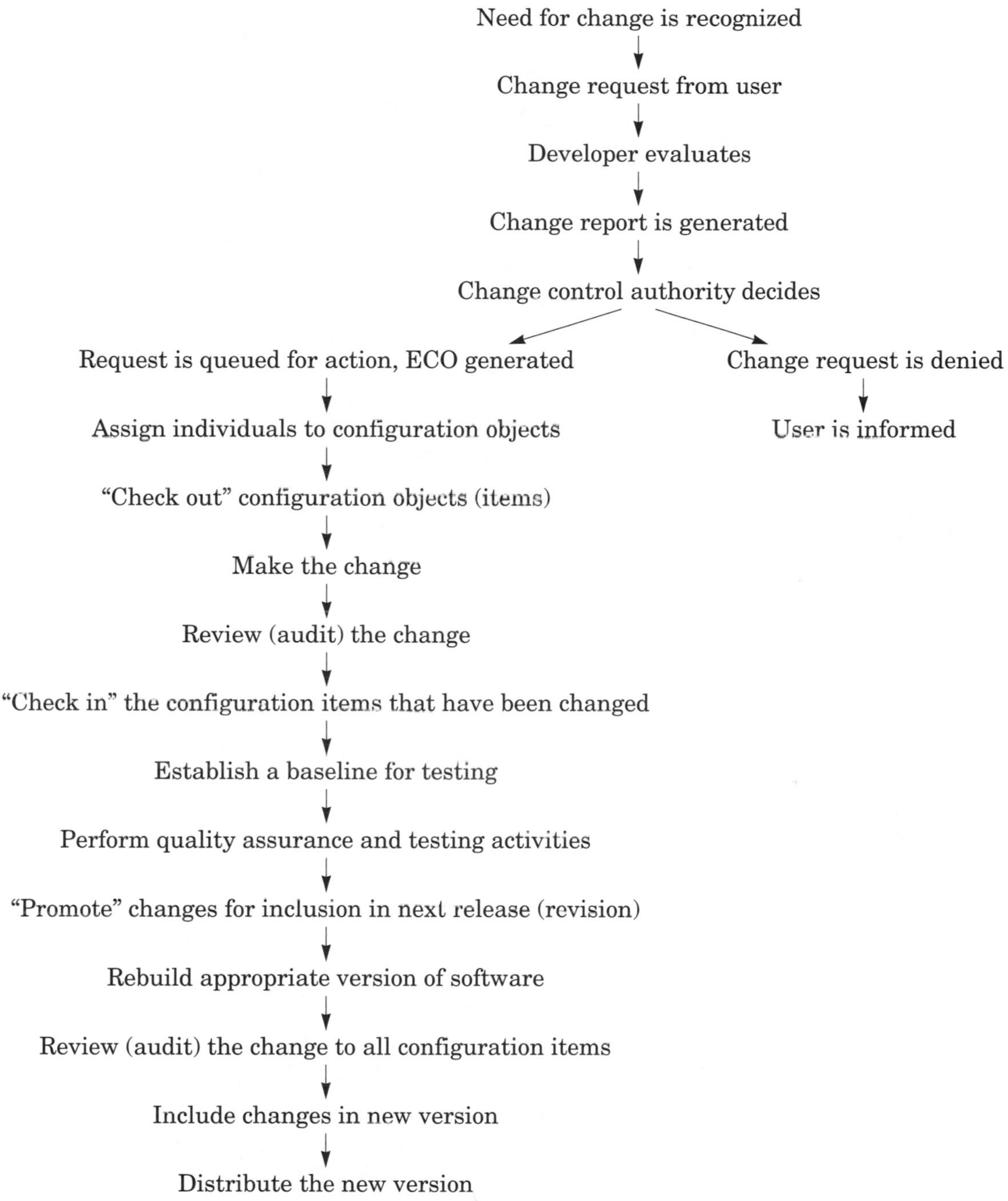

Need for change is recognized

↓

Change request from user

↓

Developer evaluates

↓

Change report is generated

↓

Change control authority decides

Request is queued for action, ECO generated → Change request is denied

↓

Assign individuals to configuration objects → User is informed

↓

"Check out" configuration objects (items)

↓

Make the change

↓

Review (audit) the change

↓

"Check in" the configuration items that have been changed

↓

Establish a baseline for testing

↓

Perform quality assurance and testing activities

↓

"Promote" changes for inclusion in next release (revision)

↓

Rebuild appropriate version of software

↓

Review (audit) the change to all configuration items

↓

Include changes in new version

↓

Distribute the new version

FIGURE 9.7. The change control process

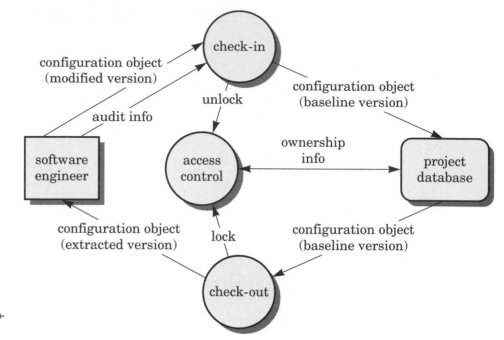

FIGURE 9.8.
Access and synchro-
nization control

tion control locks the object in the project database so that no updates can be
made to it until the version currently checked out has been replaced. Note that
other copies can be checked out, but other updates cannot be made. A copy of
the baselined object, called the "extracted version," is modified by the software
engineer. After appropriate SQA and testing, the modified version of the object
is checked in and the new baseline object is unlocked.

Some readers may begin to feel uncomfortable with the level of bureau-
cracy implied by the change control process description. This feeling is not uncommon. Without proper safeguards, change control can retard progress and
create unnecessary red tape. Most software developers who have change control mechanisms (unfortunately, many have none) have created a number of
layers of control to help avoid the problems alluded to above.

Prior to an SCI becoming a baseline, only *informal change control* need be
applied. The developer of the configuration object (SCI) in question may make
whatever changes are justified by project and technical requirements (as long
as changes do not impact broader system requirements that lie outside the developer's scope of work). Once the object has undergone formal technical review
and has been approved, a baseline is created. Once an SCI becomes a baseline,
project level change control is implemented. Now, to make a change, the developer must gain approval from the project manager (if the change is "local") or
from the CCA if the change impacts other SCIs. In some cases, formal generation of change requests, change reports, and ECOs is dispensed with. However,
assessment of each change is conducted and all changes are tracked and reviewed.

When the software product is released to customers, *formal change control* is instituted. The formal change control procedure has been outlined in Figure 9.7.

The change control authority (CCA) plays an active role in the second and third layer of control. Depending on the size and character of a software project, the CCA may be comprised of one person—the project manager—or a number of people (e.g., representatives from software, hardware, database engineering, support, marketing, etc.). The role of the CCA is to take a global view, that is, to assess the impact of change beyond the SCI in question. How will the change impact hardware? How will the change impact performance? How will the change modify the customer's perception of the product? How will the change affect product quality and reliability? These and many other questions are addressed by the CCA.

9.6 CONFIGURATION AUDIT

Identification, version control, and change control help the software developer to maintain order in what would otherwise be a chaotic and fluid situation. However, even the most successful control mechanisms track a change only until an ECO is generated. How can we ensure that the change has been properly implemented? The answer is twofold: (1) *formal technical reviews* and (2) the *software configuration audit*.

The formal technical review (presented in detail in Chapter 8) focuses on the technical correctness of the configuration object that has been modified. The reviewers assess the SCI to determine consistency with other SCIs, omissions, and potential side effects. A formal technical review should be conducted for all but the most trivial changes.

A software configuration audit complements the formal technical review by assessing a configuration object for characteristics that are generally not considered during review. The audit asks and answers the following questions:

1. Has the change specified in the ECO been made? Have any additional modifications been incorporated?

2. Has a formal technical review been conducted to assess technical correctness?

3. Have software engineering standards been properly followed?

4. Has the change been "highlighted" in the SCI? Have the change date and change author been specified? Do the attributes of the configuration object reflect the change?

5. Have SCM procedures for noting the change, recording it, and reporting it been followed?

6. Have all related SCIs been properly updated?

In some cases, the audit questions are asked as part of a formal technical review. However, when SCM is a formal activity, the SCM audit is conducted separately by the quality assurance group.

9.7   STATUS REPORTING

Configuration status reporting (sometimes called *status accounting*) is an SCM task that answers the following questions: (1) What happened? (2) Who did it? (3) When did it happen? (4) What else will be affected?

The flow of information for configuration status reporting (CSR) is illustrated in Figure 9.7. Each time a SCI is assigned new or updated identification, a CSR entry is made. Each time a change is approved by the CCA (i.e., an ECO is issued), a CSR entry is made. Each time a configuration audit is conducted, the results are reported as part of the CSR task. Output from CSR may be placed in an on-line database [TAY85] so that software developers or maintainers can access change information by keyword category. In addition, a SCR report is generated on a regular basis and is intended to keep management and practitioners appraised of important changes.

Configuration status reporting plays a vital role in the success of a large software development project. When many people are involved, it is likely that "the left hand not knowing what the right hand is doing" syndrome will occur. Two developers may attempt to modify the same SCI with different and conflicting intent. A software engineering team may spend months of effort building software to an obsolete hardware specification. The person who would recognize serious side effects for a proposed change is not aware that the change is being made. CSR helps to eliminate these problems by improving communication among all people involved.

9.8   SCM STANDARDS

Over the past two decades a number of software configuration management standards have been proposed. Many early SCM standards, such as MIL-STD-483, DOD-STD-480A, and MIL-STD-1521A, focused on software developed for military applications. However, more recent ANSI/IEEE standards, such as ANSI/IEEE Std. No. 828-1983, Std. No. 1042-1987, and Std. No. 1028-1988 [IEE94], are applicable for commercial software and are recommended for both large and small software engineering organizations.

9.9   SUMMARY

Software configuration management is an umbrella activity that is applied throughout the software process. SCM identifies, controls, audits, and reports modifications that invariably occur while software is being developed and after it has been released to a customer. All information produced as part of the software process becomes part of a software configuration. The configuration is organized in a manner that enables orderly control of change.

The software configuration is composed of a set of interrelated objects, also called software configuration items, that are produced as a result of some software engineering activity. In addition to documents, programs, and data, the development environment that is used to create software can also be placed under configuration control.

Once a configuration object has been developed and reviewed, it becomes a baseline. Changes to a baselined object result in the creation of a new version of that object. The evolution of a program can be tracked by examining the revision history of all configuration objects. Basic and aggregate objects form an object pool from which variants and versions are created. Version control is the set of procedures and tools for managing the use of these objects.

Change control is a procedural activity that ensures quality and consistency as changes are made to a configuration object. The change control process begins with a change request, leads to a decision to make or reject the request for change, and culminates with a controlled update of the SCI that is to be changed.

The configuration audit is an SQA activity that helps to ensure that quality is maintained as changes are made. Status reporting provides information about each change to those with a need to know.

REFERENCES

[ADA89] Adams, E., M. Honda, and T. Miller, "Object Management in a CASE Environment," *Proc. 11th Intl. Conf. Software Engineering,* IEEE, Pittsburgh, PA, May 1989, pp. 154–163.

[BAB86] Babich, W.A., *Software Configuration Management,* Addison-Wesley, 1986.

[BER80] Bersoff, E.H., V.D. Henderson, and S.G. Siegel, *Software Configuration Management,* Prentice-Hall, 1980.

[CHO89] Choi, S.C., and W. Scacchi, "Assuring the Correctness of a Configured Software Description," *Proc. 2nd Intl. Workshop on Software Configuration Management,* ACM, Princeton, NJ, October 1989, pp. 66–75.

[CLE89] Clemm, G.M., "Replacing Version Control with Job Control," *Proc. 2nd Intl. Workshop on Software Configuration Management,* ACM, Princeton, NJ, October 1989, pp. 162–169.

[GUS89] Gustavsson, A., "Maintaining the Evaluation of Software Objects in an Integrated Environment," *Proc. 2nd Intl. Workshop on Software Configuration Management,* ACM, Princeton, NJ, October 1989, pp. 114–117.

[HAR89] Harter, R., "Configuration Management," *HP Professional,* vol. 3, no. 6, June 1989.

[IEE94] *Software Engineering Standards,* 1994 edition, IEEE Computer Society, 1994.

[LIE89] Lie, A., et al., "Change Oriented Versioning in a Software Engineering Database," *Proc. 2nd Intl. Workshop on Software Configuration Management,* ACM, Princeton, NJ, October 1989, pp. 56–65.

[NAR87] Narayanaswamy, K., and W. Scacchi, "Maintaining Configurations of Evolving Software Systems," *IEEE Trans. Software Engineering,* vol. SE-13, no. 3, March 1987, pp. 324–334.

[REI89] Reichenberger, C., "Orthogonal Version Management," *Proc. 2nd Intl. Workshop on Software Configuration Management,* ACM, Princeton, NJ, October 1989, pp. 137–140.

[ROC75] Rochkind, M., "The Source Code Control System," *IEEE Trans. Software Engineering,* vol. SE-1, no. 4, December 1975, pp. 364–370.

[TAY85]   Taylor, B., "A Database Approach to Configuration Management for Large Projects," *Proc. Conf. Software Maintenance—1985*, IEEE, November 1985, pp. 15–23.

[TIC82]   Tichy, W.F., "Design, Implementation and Evaluation of a Revision Control System," *Proc. 6th Intl. Conf. Software Engineering*, IEEE, Tokyo, September 1982, pp. 58–67.

PROBLEMS AND POINTS TO PONDER

9.1. Why is the First Law of System Engineering true? How does it affect our perception of software engineering paradigms.

9.2. Discuss the reasons for baselines in your own words.

9.3. Assume that you're the manager of a small project. What baselines would you define for the project and how would you control them?

9.4. Design a project database system that would enable a software engineer to store, cross-reference, trace, update, change, etc. all important software configuration items. How would the database handle different versions of the same program? Would source code be handled differently than documentation? How will two developers be precluded from making different changes to the same SCI at the same time?

9.5. Do some research on object-oriented databases and write a paper that describes how they can be used in the context of SCM.

9.6. Use an E-R model (Chapter 12) to describe the interrelationships among the SCIs (objects) listed in section 9.1.2.

9.7. Research an existing SCM tool and describe how it implements control for versions, variants, and configuration objects in general.

9.8. The relations <part-of> and <interrelated> represent simple relationships between configuration objects. Describe five additional relationships that might be useful in the context of a project database.

9.9. Research an existing SCM tool and describe how it implements the mechanics of version control. Alternatively, read two or three of the papers referenced in this chapter and describe the different data structures and referencing mechanisms that are used for version control.

9.10. Using Figure 9.7 as a guide, develop an even more detailed work breakdown for change control. Describe the role of the CCA and suggest formats for the change request, the change report, and the ECO.

9.11. Develop a checklist for use during configuration audits.

9.12. What is the difference between an SCM audit and a formal technical review? Can their function be folded into one review? What are the pros and cons?

FURTHER READINGS AND OTHER INFORMATION SOURCES

The literature on software configuration management has expanded significantly over the past few years. Ayer and Patrinnostro (*Software Configuration*

Management, McGraw-Hill, 1992) present a good overview for those who have not yet been introduced to the subject. Another book by these authors (*Documenting the Software Process,* McGraw-Hill, 1992) is a comprehensive guide to the development and management of the documentation. Berlack (*Software Configuration Management,* Wiley, 1992) presents a survey of SCM concepts, emphasizing the importance of the repository and tools in the management of change. Babich [BAB86] is an abbreviated, yet effective, treatment of pragmatic issues in software configuration management.

Buckley (*Implementing Configuration Management,* IEEE Computer Society Press, 1993) considers configuration management approaches for all system elements—hardware, software, and firmware with detailed discussions of major CM activities. Rawlings (*SCM for Network Development Environments,* McGraw-Hill, 1994) is the first SCM book to address the subject with a specific emphasis on software development in a networked environment. Whitgift (*Methods and Tools for Software Configuration Management,* Wiley, 1991) contains reasonable coverage of all important SCM topics, but is distinguished by discussion of repository and CASE environment issues. Arnold and Bohner (*Software Change Impact Analysis,* IEEE Computer Society Press, 1996) have edited an anthology that discusses how to analyze the impact of change within complex software-based systems.

A number of Internet sources are available for SCM information. The newsgroup **comp.software.config-mgmt** is dedicated to configuration management issues, including discussion of SCM tools. The *Configuration Management Yellow Pages* contains many pointers to SCM information and tools on the internet and can be found at:

> **http://www.cs.colorado.edu/**
> **users/andre/configuration_management.html**

Pointers to the software configuration management FAQ as well as other useful information about SCM can be obtained from:

> **http://www.iac.honeywell.com/Pub/Tech/CM/index.html**
> **http://www.loria.fr/ ~ molli/cm/cm-FAQ/tools_top.html**

Information on software configuration management in the context of the SEI capability maturity model (Chapter 2) can be obtained at:

> **http://www.sei.cmu.edu/**

An up-to-date list of World Wide Web references for software configuration management can be found at: **http://www.rspa.com**

PART THREE

CONVENTIONAL METHODS FOR SOFTWARE ENGINEERING

In this part of *Software Engineering: A Practitioner's Approach* we consider the technical concepts, methods, and measurements that are applicable for the analysis, design, and testing of computer software. In the chapters that follow, we address the following questions:

- How is software defined within the context of a larger system and where do product engineering and information engineering play a role?
- What are the basic concepts and principles that are applicable to the analysis of software requirements?
- What is structured analysis and how do its various models enable a software engineer to understand data, function, and behavior?
- What are the basic concepts and principles that are applied to software design activity?
- How are design models for data, architecture, procedure, and interfaces created?
- What are the unique characteristics of real-time systems and how do these characteristics affect the manner in which such systems are analyzed and designed?
- What are the basic concepts and principles that are applicable to the software testing?
- How are black-box and white-box testing methods used to design effective test cases?
- What is the strategy for software testing?
- What technical metrics are available for assessing the quality of analysis and design models, source code, and test cases?

Once these questions are answered, you'll understand how to build software using a disciplined engineering approach.

CHAPTER 10

SYSTEM ENGINEERING

Four hundred and eighty years ago, Machiavelli said "there is nothing more difficult to take in hand, more perilous to conduct or more uncertain in its success, than to take the lead in the introduction of a new order of things. . . ." During the last quarter of the twentieth century, computer-based systems have introduced a new order. Although technology has made great strides since Machiavelli spoke, his words continue to ring true.

Software engineering occurs as a consequence of a process, called *system engineering*. Instead of concentrating solely on software, system engineering focuses on a variety of elements, analyzing, designing, and organizing those elements into a *system* that can be a product, a service, or a technology for the transformation of information or control.

The system engineering process is called *information engineering* when the context of the engineering work focuses on a business enterprise. When a product is to be built,[1] the process is called *product engineering*.[2]

Both information engineering and product engineering attempt to bring order to the development of computer-based systems. Although each is applied in a different application domain, both strive to put software into context. That is, both information engineering and product engineering work to allocate a role for computer software and to establish the links that tie software to other elements of a computer-based system.

---

[1] In this context, the term "product" includes everything from cellular telephones to a one-of-a kind high-technology system (e.g., an air traffic control system).

[2] In reality, the term "system engineering" is often used in this context. However, in this book, the term "system engineering" is generic and is used to encompass both *information engineering* and *product engineering*.

10.1   COMPUTER-BASED SYSTEMS

The word "system" is possibly the most overused and abused term in the technical lexicon. We speak of political systems and educational systems, of avionics systems and manufacturing systems, of banking systems and subway systems. The word tells us little. We use the adjective describing "system" to understand the context in which the word is used. *Webster's Dictionary* defines "system" as "a set or arrangement of things so related as to form a unity or organic whole ... a set of facts, principles, rules, etc., classified and arranged in an orderly form so as to show a logical plan linking the various parts ... a method or plan of classification or arrangement ... an established way of doing something; method; procedure. ..." Five additional definitions are provided in the dictionary, yet no precise synonym is suggested. "System" is a special word.

Borrowing from Webster's definition, we define a *computer-based system* as:

> A set or arrangement of elements that are organized to accomplish some predefined goal by processing information.

The goal may be to support some business function or to develop a product that can be sold to generate business revenue. To accomplish the goal, a computer-based system makes use of a variety of system elements:

Software.   Computer programs, data structures, and related documentation that serve to effect the logical method, procedure, or control that is required.

Hardware.   Electronic devices that provide computing capability, and electromechanical devices (e.g., sensors, motors, pumps) that provide external world function.

People.   Users and operators of hardware and software.

Database.   A large, organized collection of information that is accessed via software.

Documentation.   Manuals, forms, and other descriptive information that portrays the use and/or operation of the system.

Procedures.   The steps that define the specific use of each system element or the procedural context in which the system resides.

The elements combine in a variety of ways to *transform* information. For example, a marketing department transforms raw sales data into a profile of the typical purchaser of a product, and a robot transforms a command file containing specific instructions into a set of control signals that cause some specific physical action. Creating an information system to assist the marketing department and control software to support the robot both require system engineering.

One complicating characteristic of computer-based systems is that the elements comprising one system may also represent one macro element of a still larger system. The *macro element* is a computer-based system that is one part of a larger computer-based system. As an example, we consider a "factory automation system" that is essentially a hierarchy of systems shown in

Figure 10.1. At the lowest level of the hierarchy we have a numerical control machine, robots, and data entry devices. Each is a computer-based system in its own right. The elements of the numerical control machine include electronic and electromechanical hardware (e.g., processor and memory, motors, sensors); software (for communications, machine control, and interpolation); people (the machine operator); a database (the stored NC program); and documentation and procedures. A similar decomposition could be applied to the robot and data entry device. Each is a computer-based system.

At the next level in the hierarchy (Figure 10.1), a *manufacturing cell* is defined. The manufacturing cell is a computer-based system that may have elements of its own (e.g., computers, mechanical fixtures) and also integrates the macro elements that we have called numerical control machine, robot, and data entry device.

To summarize, the manufacturing cell and its macro elements each are comprised of system elements with the generic labels: software, hardware, people, database, procedures, and documentation. In some cases, macro elements may share a generic element. For example, the robot and the NC machine might both be managed by a single operator (the people element). In other cases, generic elements are exclusive to one system.

The role of the system engineer is to define the elements for a specific computer-based system in the context of the overall hierarchy of systems (macro elements). In the sections that follow, we examine the tasks that constitute computer system engineering.

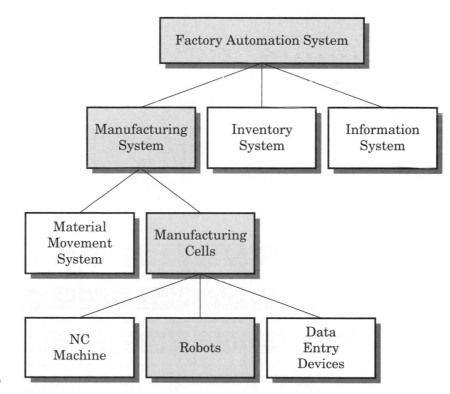

FIGURE 10.1.
A system of systems

10.2   **THE SYSTEM ENGINEERING HIERARCHY**

Regardless of its domain of focus, system engineering encompasses a collection of top-down and bottom-up methods to navigate the hierarchy illustrated in Figure 10.2. The system engineering process usually begins with a "world view." That is, the entire business or product domain is examined to ensure that the

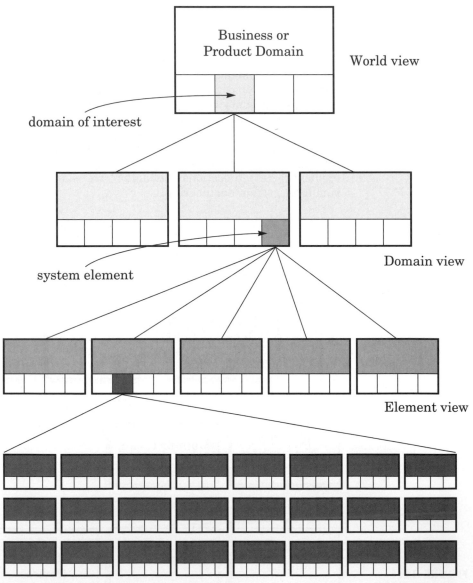

FIGURE 10.2.
The system engineering hierarchy

proper business or technology context can be established. The world view is refined to focus more fully on specific domain of interest. Within a specific domain, the need for targeted system elements (e.g., data, software, hardware, people) is analyzed. Finally, the analysis, design, and construction of a targeted system element is initiated. At the top of the hierarchy a very broad context is established, and at the bottom, detailed technical activities, performed by the relevant engineering discipline (e.g., hardware or software engineering), are conducted.[3]

Stated in a slightly more formal manner, the world view (WV) is composed of a set of domains (D_i), which can each be a system or system of systems in its own right.

$$WV = \{D_1, D_2, D_3, \ldots, D_n\}$$

Each domain is composed of specific elements (E_j), each of which serves some role in accomplishing the objective and goals of the domain:

$$D_i = \{E_1, E_2, E_3, \ldots, E_m\}$$

Finally, each element is implemented by specifying the technical components (C_k) that achieve the necessary function for an element.

$$E_j = \{C_1, C_2, C_3, \ldots, C_k\}$$

In the software context, a component could be a computer program, a reusable program component, a module, an class or object, or even a programming language statement.

It is important to note that the system engineer narrows the focus of work as he or she moves downward in the hierarchy described above. However, the world view portrays a clear definition of overall functionality that will enable the engineer to understand the domain, and ultimately the system or product, in the proper context.

10.2.1 System Modeling

System engineering is a modeling process. Whether the focus is on the world view or the detailed view, the engineer creates models that [MOT92]:

- define the processes that serve the needs of the view under consideration
- represent the behavior of the processes and the assumptions on which the behavior is based
- explicitly define both *exogenous* and *endogenous* input[4] to the model
- represent all linkages (including output) that will enable the engineer to better understand the view

---

[3]In some situations, however, system engineers must first consider individual system elements and/or detailed requirements. Using this approach, subsystems are described bottom-up by first considering constituent detailed components of the subsystem.

[4]Exogenous inputs link one constituent of a given view with other constituents at the same level or other levels; endogenous inputs link individual components of a constituent at a particular view.

To construct a system model, the engineer should consider a number of restraining factors:

1. *Assumptions* that reduce the number of possible permutations and variations, thus enabling a model to reflect the problem in a reasonable manner. As an example, consider a three-dimensional rendering product used by the entertainment industry to create realistic animation. One domain of the product enables the representation of 3D human forms. Input to this domain encompasses the ability to input movement from a live human "actor," from video, or by the creation of graphical models. The system engineer makes certain assumptions about the range of allowable human movement (e.g., legs cannot be wrapped around the torso) so that the range of inputs and processing can be limited.

2. *Simplifications* that enable the model to be created in a timely manner. To illustrate, consider an office products company that sells and services a broad range of copiers, fax machines, and related equipment. The system engineer is modeling the needs of the service organization and is working to understand the flow of information that spawns a service order. Although a service order can be derived from many origins, the engineer categorizes only two sources: internal demand or external request. This enables a simplified partitioning of input that is required to generate the work order.

3. *Limitations* that help to bound the system. For example, an aircraft avionics system is being modeled for a next generation aircraft. Since the aircraft will be a two-engine design, all monitoring domains for propulsion will be modeled to accommodate a maximum of two engines and associated redundant systems.

4. *Constraints* that will guide the manner in which the model is created and the approach taken when the model is implemented. For example, the technology infrastructure for the three-dimensional rendering system described above is a single PowerPC-based processor. The computational complexity of problems must be constrained to fit within the processing bounds imposed by the processor.

5. *Preferences* that indicate the preferred architecture for all data, functions, and technology. The preferred solution sometimes comes into conflict with other restraining factors. Yet, customer satisfaction is often predicated on the degree to which the preferred approach is realized.

The resultant system model (at any view) may call for a completed automated solution, a semi-automated solution, or a manual approach. In fact, it is often possible to characterize models of each type that serve as alternative solutions to the problem at hand. In essence, the system engineer simply modifies the relative influence of different system elements (people, hardware, software) to derive models of each type.

10.2.2 Information Engineering: An Overview

The goal of information engineering (IE) is to define architectures that will enable a business to use information effectively. In addition, information engineering works to create an overall plan for implementing those architectures [SPE93]. Three different architectures must be analyzed and designed within the context of business objectives and goals:

- data architecture
- applications architecture
- technology infrastructure

The *data architecture* provides a framework for the information needs of a business or business function. The individual building blocks of the architecture are the data objects (to be discussed in Chapter 12) that are used by the business. The data objects flow between business functions, are organized within a database, and are transformed to provide information that serves the needs of the business.

The *application architecture* encompasses those elements of a system that transform objects within the data architecture for some business purpose. In the context of this book, we normally consider the application architecture to be the system of programs (software) that performs this transformation. However, in a broader context, the application architecture might incorporate the role of people (who are information transformers and users) and business procedures that have not been automated.

The *technology infrastructure* provides the foundation for the data and application architectures. The infrastructure encompasses the hardware and software that are used to support applications and data. This includes computers and computer networks, telecommunication links, storage technologies, and the architecture (e.g., client/server) that has been designed to implement these technologies.

To model the system architectures described earlier, a hierarchy of information engineering activities is defined. As shown in Figure 10.3, the world view is achieved through *information strategy planning (ISP)*.[5] ISP views the entire business as an entity and isolates the domains of the business (e.g., engineering, manufacturing, marketing, finance, sales) that are important to the overall enterprise. ISP defines the data objects that are visible at the enterprise level, their relationships, and how they flow between the business domains [MAR90].

The domain view is addressed with an IE activity called *business area analysis (BAA)*. Hares [HAR93] describes BAA in the following manner:

---

[5]It should be noted that the terminology used in Figure 10.3 is not used consistently in the literature. However, the area of focus implied by each IE activity is addressed by all who consider the subject.

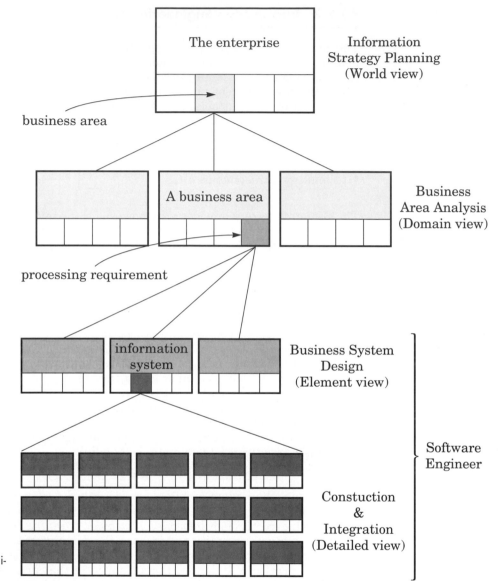

FIGURE 10.3.
The information engineering hierarchy

BAA is concerned with identifying in detail data (in the form of entity [data object] types) and function requirements (in the form of processes) of selected business areas [domains] identified during ISP and ascertaining their interactions (in the form of matrices). It is only concerned with specifying *what* is required in a business area.

As the information engineer begins BAA, the focus narrows to a specific business domain. BAA views the business area as an entity and isolates the business functions and procedures that enable the business area to meet its objectives and goals. BAA, like ISP, defines data objects, their relationships, and how data flow. But at this level, these characteristics are all bounded by the business area being analyzed. The outcome of BAA is to isolate areas of opportunity in which information systems may support the business area.

Once an information system has been isolated for further development, IE makes a transition into software engineering. By invoking a *business system design (BSD)* step, the basic requirements of a specific information system are modeled and these requirements are translated into data architecture, applications architecture, and technology infrastructure.

The final IE step—*construction and integration (C&I)* focuses on implementation detail. The architecture and infrastructure are implemented by constructing an appropriate database and internal data structures, by building applications using program components, and by selecting appropriate elements of a technology infrastructure to support the design created during BSD. Each of these system components must then be integrated to form a complete information system or application. The integration activity also places the new information system into the business area context, performing all user training and logistics support to achieve a smooth transition.

10.2.3   Product Engineering: An Overview

The goal of product engineering is to translate the customer's desire for a set of defined capabilities into a working product.[6] To achieve this goal, *product engineering*—like information engineering—must derive architecture and infrastructure. The architecture encompasses four distinct system components: software, hardware, data (and databases), and people. A *support infrastructure* is established and includes the technology required to tie the components together and the information (e.g., documents, CD-ROM, video) that is used to support the components.

As shown in Figure 10.4, the world view is achieved through *system analysis*. The overall requirements of the product are elicited from the customer. These requirements encompass information and control needs, product function and behavior, overall product performance, design, and interfacing constraints, and other special needs. Once these requirements are known, the job of system analysis is to *allocate* function and behavior to each of the four components noted above.

Once allocation has occurred, component engineering commences. Component engineering is actually a set of concurrent activities that address each of the system components separately: software engineering, hardware engineering, human engineering, and database engineering. Each of these engineering disciplines takes a domain-specific view, but it is important to note that the engineering disciplines must establish and maintain active communication with one another. Part of the role of system analysis is to establish the interfacing mechanisms that will enable this to happen.

---

[6]Product engineering is also applied to the development of one-of-a-kind high-technology systems (e.g., an air traffic control system).

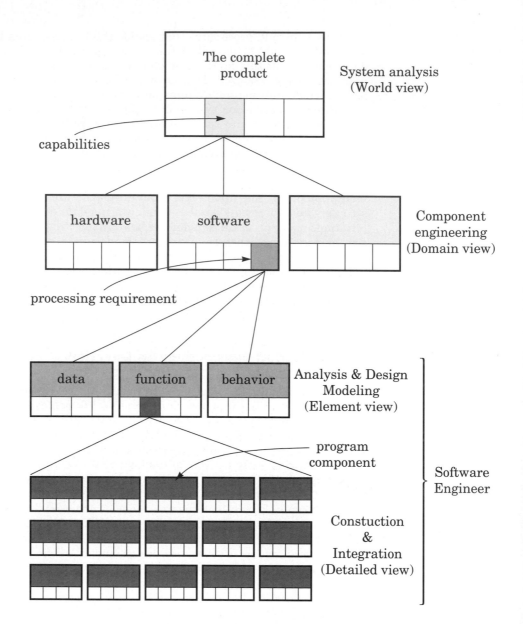

FIGURE 10.4.
The product engineering hierarchy

The element view for product engineering is the engineering discipline it-self applied to the allocated component. For software engineering, this means *analysis and design modeling* activities (covered in detail in later chapters) and *construction and integration* activities that encompass code generation, testing, and support steps. Analysis modeling allocates requirements into representa-tions of data, function, and behavior. Design maps the analysis model into data, architectural, interface, and procedural designs for the software.

10.3   INFORMATION ENGINEERING

When business automation was first introduced in the early 1960s, companies looked for areas of opportunity and simply automated business functions that were previously performed in a manual fashion. As time passed, individual computer programs were combined to encompass business applications. The applications were grouped into major information systems that served specific business areas. Although this approach was workable, it resulted in problems. Systems were difficult to "connect" to one another; redundant data was everywhere; the impact of changes to applications that served one area of the business was difficult to project and even more difficult to implement; and old programs outlived their usefulness, but lack of resources caused them to be used long past their prime.

In their book on "reengineering the corporation," Hammer and Champy [HAM93] state:

> Information technology plays a crucial role in business reengineering, but one that is easily miscast. Modern, state-of-the-art information technology is part of any reengineering effort, an essential enabler [that] permits companies to reengineer business processes. But to paraphrase what is often said about money and governments, merely throwing computers [and software] at an existing business problem does not cause it to be reengineered.

The global objective of information engineering is to apply "information technology" in a way that best serves the overall needs of the business. To accomplish this, IE must begin by analyzing business objectives and goals, understanding the many business areas that must work together to achieve these objectives and goals, and then must define the information needs of each business area and the business as a whole. Only after this is done does IE make a transition into the more technical domain of software engineering—the process where information systems, applications, and programs are analyzed, designed, and built.

10.4   INFORMATION STRATEGY PLANNING

The first information engineering step is *information strategy planning (ISP)*. The overall objectives of ISP are (1) to define strategic business objectives and goals, (2) to isolate the critical success factors that will enable the business to achieve these goals and objectives, (3) to analyze the impact of technology and automation on the goals and objectives, and (4) to analyze existing information to determine its role in achieving goals and objectives. ISP also creates a *business-level data model* that defines key data objects and their relationship to one another and to various business areas.

The terms "objectives" and "goals" take on a specific meaning in ISP. An objective is a general statement of direction. For example, a business objective for a maker of cellular telephones might be to reduce the manufactured cost of the product. Goals define a quantitative course of action. To achieve the objective noted above, the manufacturer might state the following goals:

- decrease reject rate by 20 percent within 9 months
- gain 10 percent price concessions from suppliers
- reengineer keypad to reduce assembly cost by 30 percent
- automate manual assembly of components
- implement a real-time production control system

Objectives tend to be strategic. Goals are tactical.

Critical success factors (CSFs) can be tied to an objective or to individual goals. A CSF must be present if the objective or goal is to be achieved. Therefore management planning must accommodate it. For example, CSFs for the manufacturing objective noted above might be:

- total quality management strategy for the manufacturing organization
- worker training and motivation
- higher-reliability machines
- higher-quality parts
- a "sales plan" to convince suppliers to reduce prices
- availability of engineering staff

Technology impact analysis examines objectives and goals and provides an indication of those technologies that will have a direct or indirect impact on achieving them successfully. The information engineer addresses the following questions: How critical is the technology to the achievement of a business objective? Is the technology available today? How will the technology change the way business is conducted? What are the direct and indirect costs? How should the business adapt or extend objectives and goals to accommodate the technology?

Because every business area makes some use of information technologies, ISP must also identify what currently exists and how it is currently used to achieve objectives and goals. Business process reengineering (BPR) is an activity that examines existing systems with the intent of reengineering them to better meet business needs. BPR is discussed in Chapter 27.

10.4.1 Enterprise Modeling

Enterprise modeling creates a three-dimensional view of a business. The first dimension addresses the organizational structure and the functions that are performed within the business areas defined by the organizational structure. The second dimension decomposes business function to isolate the processes that make function happen. Finally, the third dimension relates objectives, goals, and CSFs to the organization and its functions. In addition, enterprise modeling creates a business-level data model that defines data objects and their relationships to other elements of the enterprise model.

The business organization (Figure 10.5) is defined in a classical business unit hierarchy (e.g., an "org chart"). Each box in the org chart represents a business area of the company. Like all hierarchies, it is generally possible to refine the boxes within the org chart until small working groups or even individuals are noted. However, for ISP purposes, business areas are all that is required.

Business functions are identified and the processes that are required to implement the business functions are defined. Each of the business functions is then related to the business area that has responsibility for it (Figure 10.5). In general a *business function* is some ongoing activity that must be accomplished to support the overall business. It can usually be described as a noun phrase. A *business process* is a transform that accepts specific inputs and produces specific outputs. It can generally be described as a verb phrase.

To illustrate how a business function is refined into a set of supporting processes, consider the market analysis function shown in Figure 10.5. A process refinement follows:

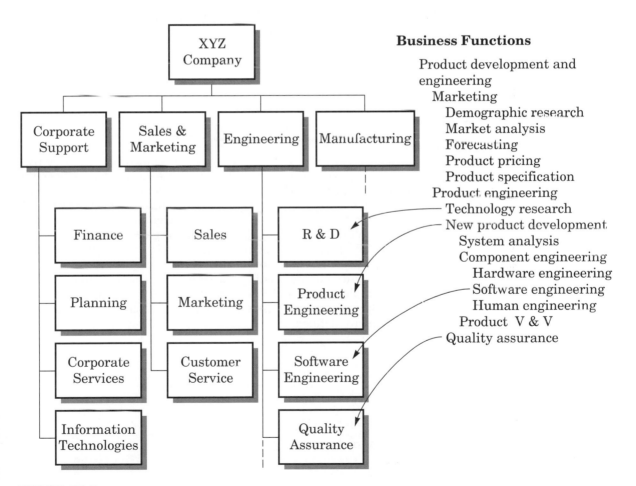

FIGURE 10.5.
Deriving an organizational chart and coupling business areas to function

Market analysis:

- Collect data on all sales inquiries
- Collect data on all sales
- Analyze data on inquires and sales
- Develop buyer profile
- Compare profile to demographic research
- Study industry buying trends
- Establish focus groups to determine best sales message
- Design rough sales materials
- Test sales materials and refine
- Finalize sales approach

Each of the bulleted process steps could be further refined to provide a detailed road map for accomplishing the business function.

During ISP, the information engineer does not become concerned with areas of automation opportunity. The intent is simply to understand and model the business.

10.4.2 Business-Level Data Modeling

Business-level data modeling [SCH92] is an enterprise modeling activity that focuses on the data objects (also called entities) that are required to achieve the business functions noted in Section 10.4.1. At the business level, typical data objects include producers and consumers of information (e.g., a customer), things (e.g., a report), occurrences of events (e.g., a sales conference), organizational roles (e.g., a Vice President of Engineering); organizational units (e.g., Sales and Marketing), places (e.g., manufacturing cell), or information structures (e.g., an employee file). A data object contains a set of attributes that define some aspect, quality, characteristic, or descriptor of the data that is being described. For example, during enterprise modeling an information engineer might define the data object **customer.** To more fully describe **customer,** the following attributes are defined:

Object: **Customer**
Attributes:

    name

    company name

    job classification and purchase authority

    business address and contact information

    product interest(s)

    past purchase(s)

    date of last contact

    status of contact

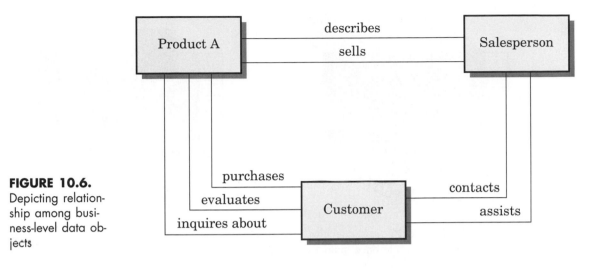

FIGURE 10.6.
Depicting relationship among business-level data objects

Once a set of data objects is defined, their relationships are identified. A *relationship* indicates how objects are connected to one another. As an example, consider the objects **customer, product A,** and **salesperson.** An information engineer creates a diagram[7] (Figure 10.6) to depict these relationships. Referring to the figure, relationships imply a connection between data objects. In general, relationships can be read in either direction; hence, a **customer** *purchases* **product A** and **product A** *is purchased by* a **customer.** In reality additional information is provided as part of the data model, but we postpone discussion of this until Chapter 12.

The culmination of the ISP activity is the creation of a series of cross-reference matrices that establish the overall relationships between the organization (and its business areas), business objectives and goals, business functions, and data objects. Examples of such matrices are shown in Figure 10.7.

10.5　BUSINESS AREA ANALYSIS

In his book on information engineering, Martin [MAR90] describes business area analysis in the following manner:

> Business areas analysis (BAA) establishes a detailed framework for building an information-based enterprise. It takes one business area at a time and analyzes it in detail. It uses diagrams and matrices to model and record the data and activities in the enterprise and to give a clear understanding of the elaborate and subtle ways in which the information aspects of the enterprise interrelate.

---

[7]This diagram, called an *entity-relationship model,* is described in detail in Chapter 12.

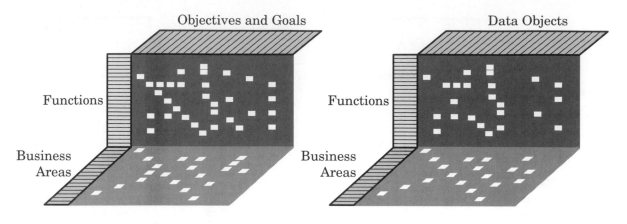

FIGURE 10.7.
Typical cross-reference matrices used during ISP

During BAA, our focus shifts from the world view to the domain view. To model "the elaborate and subtle ways in which the information aspects of the enterprise interrelate," the information engineer must depict how data objects (described during ISP and refined during BAA) are used and transformed within each business area and how the business functions and processes within each business area transform these data objects. In essence, both exogenous and endogenous data are analyzed and modeled for each business area.

To accomplish this work, BAA makes use of a number of different models:

- data models (now refined to the business area level)
- process flow models
- process decomposition diagrams
- a variety of cross-reference matrices

The data objects defined during ISP are refined for use within each business area. For example, the data object **customer** described in the preceding section is used by the sales department. After evaluation of the needs of the sales department (an analysis of the sales domain), the original definition of **customer** is further refined to meet the needs of sales:

Object: **Customer**
Attributes:

  name

  company name → Object: **Company**

  job classification and purchase authority

  business address and contact information

  product interest(s)

  past purchase(s)

date of last contact → record of contacts

status of contact → status of last contact

→ next contact date

→ recommended nature of contact

The attribute *company name* has been modified to point to another object called **Company.** This object contains not only the company name but additional information about the size of the company, its purchasing requirements, the name of other contacts, and so on. This information will be useful in the sales domain. Other attributes have been modified and added as noted above.

10.5.1 Process Modeling

The work performed within a business area encompasses a set of business functions that are further refined into business processes. To illustrate, consider a simplified version of the sales function discussed in Section 10.4.2. The processes that occur to accomplish sales are:

Sales function:

- Establish customer contact
- Provide product literature and related information
- Address questions and concerns
- Provide evaluation product
- Accept sales order
- Check availability of configuration ordered
- Prepare delivery order
- Confirm configuration, pricing, ship date with customer
- Transmit delivery order to fulfillment department
- Follow up with customer

A process flow diagram (Figure 10.8) can be developed for this sequence of processing. It should be noted that each business function relevant to the business area can be refined in a similar manner.

10.5.2 Information Flow Modeling

The process flow model is integrated with the data model to provide an indication of how information flows through a business area. Input and output data objects are shown for each process, providing an indication of how the process transforms information (Figure 10.9) to accomplish a business function.

Once a complete set of process flow models has been created, the information engineer (along with others) examines how the existing process can be

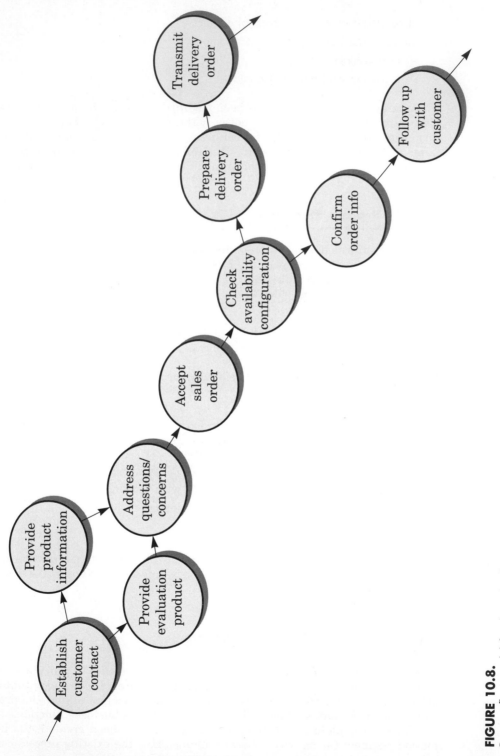

FIGURE 10.8.
Process flow model for the sales function

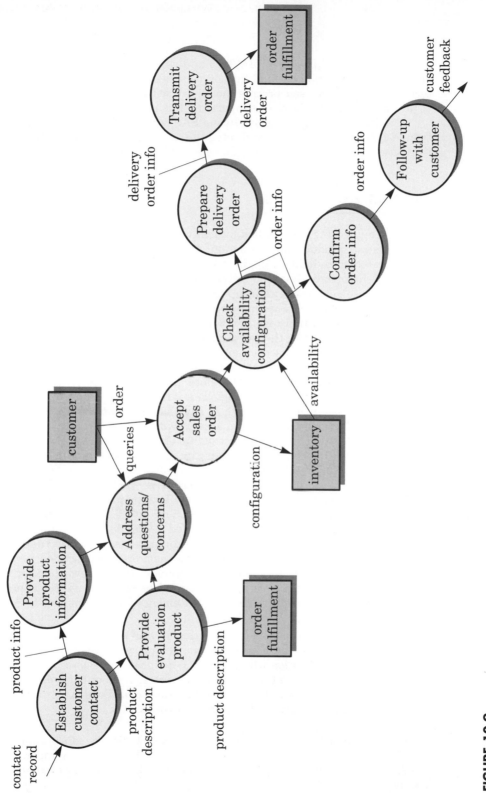

FIGURE 10.9.
Adding information flow to the process flow model for the sales function

reengineered (e.g., [HAM93], [JAY94]) and where existing information systems or applications might be modified or replaced by more efficient information technologies. The revised process model is used as a basis for the specification of new or revised software to support the business function.

The domain view established during BAA serves as the basis for business system design and construction and integration—IE steps that are actually part of the software engineering process. The steps will be considered in later chapters.

10.6   PRODUCT ENGINEERING

Product engineering (also called *system engineering*) is a problem solving activity. Desired product data, function, and behavior are uncovered, analyzed, and allocated to individual engineering components. The system engineer begins with customer-defined objectives and goals for the product and proceeds to model these requirements in a manner that allocates them to a set of engineering components—software, hardware, data (and databases), and people. The components are tied together with a *support infrastructure*—the technology required to integrate the components and the information (e.g., documents, CD-ROM, video) that is used to support the components.

The genesis of most new products and systems begins with a rather nebulous concept of desired function. Therefore, the system engineer must *bound* the product requirements by identifying the scope of function and performance desired. For example, it is not enough to say that the control software for the robot in a manufacturing automation system will "respond rapidly if a parts tray is empty." The system engineer must define (1) what indicates an empty tray to the robot, (2) the precise time bounds (in seconds) within which software response is expected, and (3) what form the response must take. That is, the system engineer must describe the events that drive the behavior of the robot, the nature of the behavior, and the quantitative bounds placed on the behavior.

Once function, performance, constraints, and interfaces are bounded, the system engineer moves on to a task that is called *allocation*. During allocation, function is assigned to one or more engineering components. Often alternative allocations are proposed and evaluated. To illustrate the process of allocation, we consider a macro element of the factory automation system—the conveyor line sorting system (CLSS) that was introduced in Chapter 5. The system engineer is presented with the following (somewhat nebulous) statement of objectives for CLSS:

> CLSS must be developed such that boxes moving along a conveyor line will be identified and sorted into one of six bins at the end of the line. The boxes will pass by a sorting station where they will be identified. Based on an identification number printed on the side of the box (an equivalent bar code is provided), the boxes will be shunted into the appropriate bins. Boxes pass in random order and are evenly spaced. The line is moving slowly.

CLSS is depicted schematically in Figure 5.1. Before continuing, make a list of questions that you would ask if you were the system engineer.

Among the many questions that should be asked and answered are the following:

1. How many different identification numbers must be processed and what is their form?
2. What is the speed of the conveyor line in feet per second and what is the distance between boxes in feet?
3. How far is the sorting station from the bins?
4. How far apart are the bins?
5. What should happen if a box doesn't have an identification number or an incorrect number is present?
6. What happens when a bin fills to capacity?
7. Is information about box destination and bin contents to be passed elsewhere in the factory automation system? Is real-time data acquisition required?
8. What error/failure rate is acceptable?
9. What pieces of the conveyor line system currently exist and are operational?
10. What schedule and budgetary constraints are imposed?

Note that the above questions focus on function, performance, and information flow and content. The system engineer does not ask the customer *how* the task is to be done; rather, the engineer asks *what* is required.

Assuming reasonable answers, the system engineer develops a number of alternative allocations. Note that function and performance are assigned to different generic system elements in each allocation.

Allocation 1.   A sorting operator is training and placed at the sorting station location. He/she reads the box and places it into an appropriate bin.

Allocation 1 represents a purely manual (but nevertheless, effective) solution to the CLSS problem. The primary engineering component is *people* (the sorting operator). The person performs all sorting functions. Some documentation (in the form of a table relating identification number to bin location and procedural description for operator training) may be required. Therefore, this allocation uses only the people and documentation elements.

Allocation 2.   A bar code reader and controller are placed at the sorting station. Bar code output is passed to a programmable controller that controls a mechanical shunting mechanism. The shunt slides the box to the appropriate bin.

For allocation 2, hardware (bar code reader, programmable control, shunt hardware, etc.), software (for the bar code reader and programmable controller) and database (a look-up table that relates box ID with bin location) components are used to provide a fully automated solution. It is likely that each of these components may have corresponding manuals and other documentation, adding another component.

Allocation 3.   A bar code reader and controller are placed at the sorting station. Bar code output is passed to a robot arm that grasps a box and moves it to the appropriate bin location.

Allocation 3 makes use of one macro element—the robot. Like allocation 2, this allocation uses hardware, software, a database, and documentation as engineering components. The robot is a macro element of CLSS and itself contains a set of engineering components.

By examining the three alternative allocations for CLSS, it should be obvious that the same function can be allocated to different components. In order to choose the most effective allocation, a set of trade-off criteria should be applied to each alternative.

The following trade-off criteria govern the selection of a product configuration based on a specific allocation of function and performance to generic system elements:

Project considerations.   Can the configuration be built within pre-established cost and schedule bounds? What is the risk associated with cost and schedule estimates?

Business considerations.   Does the configuration represent the most profitable solution? Can it be marketed successfully? Will ultimate payoff justify development risk?

Technical analysis.   Does the technology exist to develop all elements of the system? Are function and performance assured? Can the configuration be adequately maintained? Do technical resources exist? What is the risk associated with the technology?

Manufacturing evaluation.   Are manufacturing facilities and equipment available? Is there a shortage of necessary components? Can quality assurance be adequately performed?

Human issues.   Are trained personnel available for development and manufacture? Do political problems exist? Does the customer understand what the system is to accomplish?

Environmental interfaces.   Does the proposed configuration properly interface with the system's external environment? Are machine to machine and human to machine communication handled in an intelligent manner?

Legal considerations.   Does this configuration introduce undue liability risk? Can proprietary aspects be adequately protected? Is there potential infringement?

We examine some of these issues in more detail later in this chapter.

It is important to note that the system engineer should also consider off-the-shelf solutions to the customer's problem. Does an equivalent system already exist? Can major parts of a solution be purchased from a third party?

The application of trade-off criteria results in the selection of a specific system configuration and the specification of function and performance allocated to hardware, software (and firmware), people, databases, documentation, and procedures. Essentially, the scope of function and performance is allocated to each engineering component of the product. The role of hardware engineering, software engineering, human engineering, and database engineering is to refine scope and produce an operational product component that can be properly integrated with other components.

10.6.1 System Analysis

System analysis is conducted with the following objectives in mind: (1) identify the customer's need; (2) evaluate the system concept for feasibility; (3) perform economic and technical analysis; (4) allocate functions to hardware, software, people, database, and other system elements; (5) establish cost and schedule constraints; and (6) create a system definition that forms the foundation for all subsequent engineering work. Both hardware and software expertise (as well as human and database engineering) are required to successfully attain the objectives listed above.

10.6.2 Identification of Need

The first step of the system analysis process involves the identification of need. The analyst (system engineer) meets with the customer and the end user (if different from the customer). The customer may be a representative of an outside company, the marketing department of the analyst's company (when a product is being defined), or another technical department (when an internal system is to be developed). Like information engineering, the intent is to understand the product's objective(s) and to define the goals required to meet the objective(s).

Once overall goals are identified, the analyst moves on to an evaluation of supplementary information: Does the technology exist to build the system? What special development and manufacturing resources will be required? What bounds have been placed on costs and schedule? If the new system is actually a product to be developed for sale to many customers, the following questions are also asked: What is the potential market for the product? How does this product compare with competitive products? What position does this product take in the overall product line of the company?

Information gathered during the needs identification step is specified in a *system concept document*. The original concept document is sometimes prepared by the customer before meetings with the analyst. Invariably, customer–analyst communication results in modifications to the document.

10.6.3 Feasibility Study

All projects are feasible—given unlimited resources and infinite time! Unfortunately, the development of a computer-based system or product is more likely plagued by a scarcity of resources and difficult (if not downright unrealistic) delivery dates. It is both necessary and prudent to evaluate the feasibility of a project at the earliest possible time. Months or years of effort, thousands or millions of dollars, and untold professional embarrassment can be averted if an ill-conceived system is recognized early in the definition phase.

Feasibility and risk analysis are related in many ways. If project risk is great (for any of the reasons discussed in Chapter 6), the feasibility of producing quality software is reduced. During product engineering, however, we concentrate our attention on four primary areas of interest:

Economic feasibility.   An evaluation of development cost weighed against the ultimate income or benefit derived from the developed system or product.

Technical feasibility.   A study of function, performance, and constraints that may affect the ability to achieve an acceptable system.

Legal feasibility.   A determination of any infringement, violation, or liability that could result from development of the system.

Alternatives.   An evaluation of alternative approaches to the development of the system or product.

A *feasibility study* is not warranted for systems in which economic justification is obvious, technical risk is low, few legal problems are expected, and no reasonable alternative exists. However, if any of the preceding conditions fail, a study of that area should be conducted.

Economic justification is generally the "bottom-line" consideration for most systems (notable exceptions sometimes include national defense systems, systems mandated by law, and high-technology applications such as the space program).[8] Economic justification includes a broad range of concerns that include cost–benefit analysis, long-term corporate income strategies, impact on other profit centers or products, cost of resources needed for development, and potential market growth.

Technical feasibility is frequently the most difficult area to assess at this stage of the product engineering process. Because objectives, functions, and performance are somewhat hazy, anything seems possible if the "right" assumptions are made. It is essential that the process of analysis and definition be conducted in parallel with an assessment of technical feasibility. In this way concrete specifications may be judged as they are determined.

The considerations that are normally associated with technical feasibility include:

Development risk.   Can the system element be designed so that necessary function and performance are achieved within the constraints uncovered during analysis?

Resource availability.   Are skilled staff available to develop the system element in question? Are other necessary resources (hardware and software) available to build the system?

Technology.   Has the relevant technology progressed to a state that will support the system?

Developers of computer-based systems are optimists by nature. (Who else would be brave enough to attempt what we frequently undertake?) However, during an evaluation of technical feasibility, a cynical, if not pessimistic, attitude should prevail. Misjudgment at this stage can be disastrous.

---

[8]This is beginning to change as attempts to "downsize" government become more widespread. Today, all systems should be economically justified.

Legal feasibility encompasses a broad range of concerns that include contracts, liability, infringement, and myriad other traps frequently unknown to technical staff. A discussion of legal issues and software is beyond the scope of this book. The interested reader should see [SCO89].

The degree to which alternatives are considered is often limited by cost and time constraints; however, a legitimate but "unsponsored" variation should not be buried.

The feasibility study may be documented as a separate report to upper management and included as an appendix to the system specification. Although the format of a feasibility study may vary, the outline provided in Figure 10.10 covers most important topics.

The feasibility study is reviewed first by project management (to assess content reliability) and by upper management (to assess project status). The study should result in a "go/no-go" decision. It should be noted that other go/no-go decisions will be made during the planning, specification, and development steps of both hardware and software engineering.

10.6.4 Economic Analysis

Among the most important information contained in a feasibility study is *cost–benefit analysis*—an assessment of the economic justification for a computer-based system project. Cost–benefit analysis delineates costs for project

FIGURE 10.10.
Feasibility study
outline

    I. Introduction
        A. Statement of the problem
        B. Implementation environment
        C. Constraints
   II. Management Summary and Recommendations
        A. Important findings
        B. Comments
        C. Recommendations
        D. Impact
  III. Alternatives
        A. Alternative system configurations
        B. Criteria used in selecting the final approach
  IV. System Description
        A. Abbreviated statement of scope
        B. Feasibility of allocated elements
    V. Cost–Benefit Analysis
   VI. Evaluation of Technical Risk
  VII. Legal Ramifications
VIII. Other Project-Specific Topics

development and weighs them against tangible (i.e., measurable directly in dollars) and intangible benefits of a system.

Cost–benefit analysis is complicated by criteria that vary with the characteristics of the system to be developed, the relative size of the project, and the expected return on investment desired as part of a company's strategic plan. In addition many benefits derived from computer-based systems are intangible (e.g., better design quality through iterative optimization, increased customer satisfaction through programmable control, and better business decisions through reformatted and preanalyzed sales data). Direct quantitative comparisons may be difficult to achieve.

As we noted above, analysis of benefits will differ depending on system characteristics. To illustrate, consider the benefits for management information systems [KIN78] shown in Table 10.1. Most data-processing systems are developed with "better information quantity, quality, timeliness, or organization" as a primary objective. Therefore, the benefits noted in Table 10.1 concentrate on information access and its impact on the user environment. The benefits that might be associated with an engineering-scientific analysis program or a computer-based product could differ substantially.

Costs associated with the development of a computer-based system [KIN78] are listed in Table 10.2. The analyst can estimate each cost and then use development and ongoing costs to determine a return on investment, a break-even point, and a payback period.

The following excerpt [FRI77] may best characterize cost–benefit analysis:

> Like political rhetoric after the election, the cost-benefit analysis may be forgotten after the project implementation begins. However, it is extremely important because it has been the vehicle by which management approval has been obtained.

Only by spending the time to evaluate feasibility do we reduce the chances for extreme embarrassment (or worse) at later stages of a system project. Effort spent on a feasibility analysis that results in cancellation of a proposed project is not wasted effort.

10.6.5 Technical Analysis

During technical analysis, the analyst evaluates the technical merits of the system concept, at the same time collecting additional information about performance, reliability, maintainability, and producibility. In some cases, this system analysis step also includes a limited amount of research and design.

Technical analysis begins with an assessment of the technical viability of the proposed system. What technologies are required to accomplish system function and performance? What new material, methods, algorithms, or processes are required, and what is their development risk? How will these technology issues affect cost?

The tools available for technical analysis are derived from mathematical modeling and optimization techniques, probability and statistics, queuing the-

TABLE 10.1

POSSIBLE INFORMATION SYSTEM BENEFITS*

Benefits from contributions of calculating and printing tasks
Reduction in per unit costs of calculating and printing (CR)
Improved accuracy in calculating tasks (ER)
Ability to quickly change variables and values in calculation programs (IF)
Greatly increased speed in calculating and printing (IS)

Benefits from contributions to record-keeping tasks
Ability to "automatically" collect and store data from records (CR, IS, ER)
More complete and systematic keeping of records (CR, ER)
Increased capacity for record keeping in terms of space and cost (CR)
Standardization for record keeping (CR, IS)
Increase in amount of data that can be stored per record (CR, IS)
Improved security in records storage (ER, CR, MC)
Improved portability of records (IF, CR, IS)

Benefits from contributions to record-searching tasks
Faster retrieval of records (IS)
Improved ability to access records from large data bases (IF)
Improved ability to change records in data bases (IF, CR)
Ability to link sites that need search capability through telecommunications (IF, IS)
Improved ability to create records of records accessed and by whom (ER, MC)
Ability to audit and analyze record-searching activity (MC, ER)

Benefits from contributions to system restructuring capability
Ability to simultaneously change entire classes of records (IS, IF, CR)
Ability to move large files of data about (IS, IF)
Ability to create new files by merging aspects of other files (IS, IF)

Benefits from contributions of analysis and simulation capability
Ability to perform complex, simultaneous calculations quickly (IS, IF, ER)
Ability to create simulations of complex phenomena to answer "what if?" questions (MC, IF)
Ability to aggregate large amounts of data useful for planning and decision making (MC, IF)

Benefits from contributions to process and resource control
Reduction of need for work force in process and resource control (CR)
Improved ability to "fine tune" process such as assembly lines (CR, MC, IS, ER)
Improved ability to maintain continuous monitoring of resources (MC, ER, IF)

*Abbreviations: CR = cost reduction or avoidance; ER = error reduction; IF = increased flexability; IS = increased speed of activity; MC = improvement in management planning or control.
Source: King and Schrems [KIN78], p. 23. Reprinted with permission.

TABLE 10.2

POSSIBLE INFORMATION SYSTEM COSTS

Procurement costs
    Consulting costs
    Actual equipment purchase or lease costs
    Equipment installation costs
    Costs for modifying the equipment site (air conditioning, security, etc.)
    Cost of capital
    Cost of management and staff dealing with procurement

Start-up costs
    Cost of operating system software
    Cost of communications equipment installation (telephone lines, data lines, etc.)
    Cost of start-up personnel
    Cost of personnel searches and hiring activities
    Cost of disruption to the rest of the organization
    Cost of management required to direct start-up activity

Project related costs
    Cost of applications software purchased
    Cost of software modifications to fit local systems
    Cost of personnel, overhead, etc., from in-house application development
    Cost for training user personnel in application use
    Cost of data collection and installing data collection procedures
    Cost of preparing documentation
    Cost of development management

Ongoing costs
    System maintenance costs (hardware, software, and facilities)
    Rental costs (electricity, telephones, etc.)
    Depreciation costs on hardware
    Cost of staff involved in information systems management, operation, and planning activities

---

Source: King and Schreme [KIN 78], p. 24. Reprinted with permission.

ory, and control theory—to name a few.[9] It is important to note, however, that analytical evaluation is not always possible. Modeling (either mathematical or physical) is an effective mechanism for technical analysis of computer-based systems.

    Blanchard and Fabrycky [BLA81] define a set of criteria for the use of models during technical analysis of systems:

---

[9]A class of CASE tools, called prototyping and simulation tools, can assist greatly in technical analysis. These tools are discussed in Chapter 29.

1. The model should represent the dynamics of the system configuration being evaluated in a way that is simple enough to understand and manipulate, and yet close enough to the operating reality to yield results.

2. The model should highlight those factors that are most relevant to the problem at hand and suppress (with discretion) those that are not as important.

3. The model should be made comprehensive by including *all* relevant factors and should be reliable in terms of repeatability of results.

4. Model design should be simple enough to allow for timely implementation in problem solving. Unless the model can be utilized in a timely and efficient manner by the analyst or the manager, it is of little value. If the model is large and highly complex, it may be appropriate to develop a series of smaller models in which the output of one can be tied to the input of another. Also, it may be desirable to evaluate a specific element of the system independently from other elements.

5. Model design should incorporate provisions for ease of modification and/or expansion to permit the evaluation of additional factors as required. Successful model development often includes a series of trials before the overall objective is met. Initial attempts may suggest information gaps which are not immediately apparent and consequently may suggest beneficial changes.

The results obtained from technical analysis form the basis for another "go/no-go" decision on the system. If technical risk is severe, if models indicate that desired function or performance cannot be achieved, if the pieces just won't fit together smoothly—it's back to the drawing board!

10.7 MODELING THE SYSTEM ARCHITECTURE

Every computer-based system can be modeling as an information transform using an input–processing–output architecture. Hatley and Pirbhai [HAT87] have extended this view to include two additional system features—user interface processing and maintenance and self-test processing. Although these additional features are not present for every computer-based system, they are very common, and their specification makes any system model more robust. Using a representation of input, processing, output, user interface processing, and self-test processing, a system engineer can create a model of system components that sets a foundation for later requirements analysis and design steps in each of the engineering disciplines.

To develop the system model, an *architecture template* [HAT87] is used. The system engineer allocates system elements to each of five processing regions within the template: (1) user interface, (2) input, (3) system function and control, (4) output, and (5) maintenance and self-test. The format of the architecture template is shown in Figure 10.11.

Like nearly all modeling techniques used in system and software engineering, the architecture template enables the analyst to create a hierarchy of detail. An *architecture context diagram (ACD)* resides at the top level of the hierarchy.

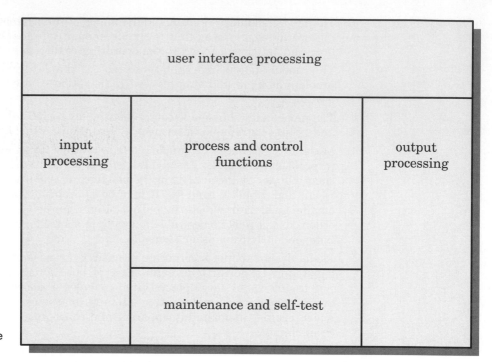

FIGURE 10.11.
Architecture template
[HAT87]

The context diagram "establishes the information boundary between the system being implemented and the environment in which the system is to operate" [HAT87]. That is, the ACD defines all external producers of information used by the system, all external consumers of information created by the system, and all entities that communicate through the interface or perform maintenance and self-test.

To illustrate the use of the ACD, consider an extended version of the conveyor line sorting system (CLSS) discussed earlier in this chapter. The extended version makes use of personal computer at the sorting station site. The PC executes all CLSS software; interfaces with the bar code reader to read part numbers on each box; interfaces with the conveyor line monitoring equipment to acquire conveyor line speed; stores all part numbers sorted; interacts with a sorting station operator to produce a variety of reports and diagnostics; sends control signals to the shunting hardware to sort the boxes; and communicates with a central factory automation mainframe. The ACD for CLSS (extended) is shown in Figure 10.12.

Each box shown in Figure 10.12 represents an *external entity*—that is, a producer or consumer of information from the system. For example, the **bar code reader** produces information that is input to the CLSS system. The symbol for the entire system (or at lower levels, major subsystems) is a rectangle with rounded corners. Hence, CLSS is represented in the processing and control region at the center of the ACD. The labeled arrows shown in the ACD represent information (data and control) as it moves from the external environment into the CLSS system. The external entity **bar code reader** produces

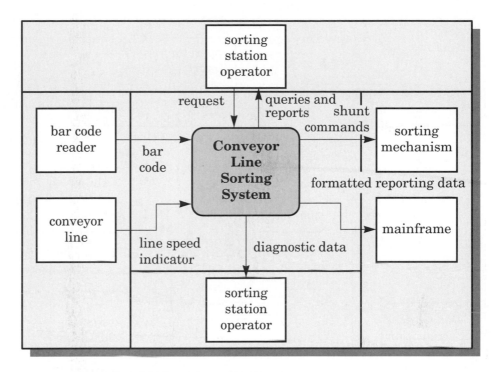

FIGURE 10.12.
Architecture context
diagram for CLSS
(extended)

input information that is labeled **bar code.** In essence, the ACD places any system into the context of its external environment.

The system engineer refines the architecture context diagram by considering the shaded rectangle in Figure 10.12 in more detail. The major subsystems that enable the conveyor line sorting system to function within the context defined by the ACD are identified. In Figure 10.13, the major subsystems[10] are defined in an *architecture flow diagram (AFD)* that is derived from the ACD. Information flow across the regions of the ACD is used to guide the system engineer in developing the AFD—a more detailed "schematic" for CLSS. The architecture flow diagram shows major subsystems and important lines of information (data and control) flow. In addition, the architecture template partitions the subsystem processing into each of the five processing regions discussed earlier. At this stage, each of the subsystems can contain one or more system elements (e.g., hardware, software, people) as allocated by the system engineer.

The initial architecture flow diagram (AFD) becomes the top node of a hierarchy of AFDs. Each rounded rectangle in the original AFD can be expanded into another architecture template dedicated solely to it. This process is illustrated schematically in Figure 10.14. Each of the AFDs for the system can be used as a starting point for subsequent engineering steps for the subsystem that has been described.

---

[10]Hatley and Pirbhai [HAT87] call these *system modules*.

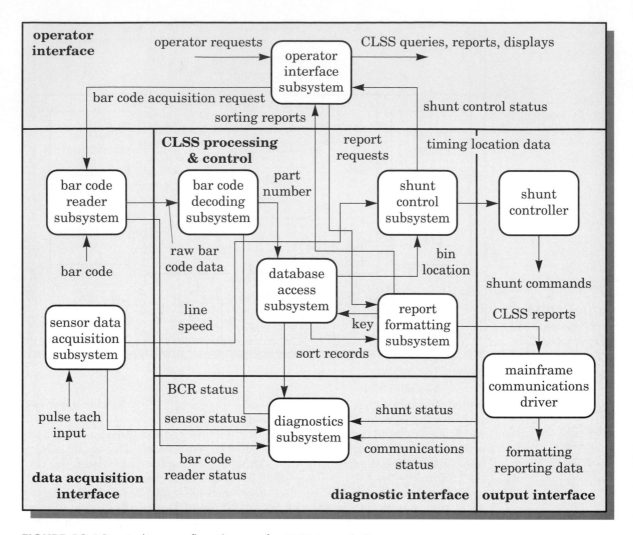

FIGURE 10.13. Architecture flow diagram for CLSS (extended)

Subsystems and the information that flows between them can be specified (bounded) for subsequent engineering work. A narrative description of each subsystem and a definition of all data that flow between subsystems become important elements of the system specification.

10.8   SYSTEM MODELING AND SIMULATION

Almost three decades ago, R.M. Graham [GRA69] made a distressing comment about the way we built computer-based systems: "We build systems like the Wright brothers built airplanes—build the whole thing, push it off a cliff, let it

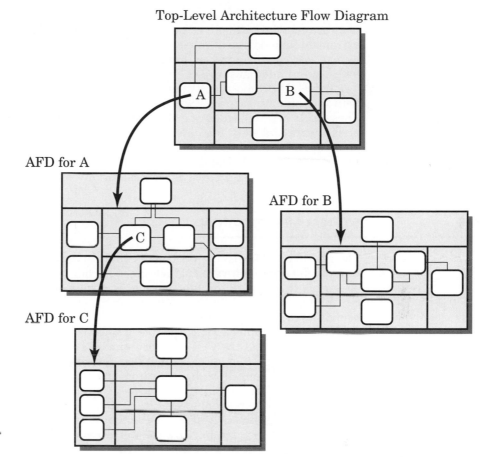

Top-Level Architecture Flow Diagram

AFD for A

AFD for B

AFD for C

FIGURE 10.14.
Building an AFD hierarchy

crash, and start over again." In fact, for at least one class of system—the *reactive system*—we continue to do this today.

Many computer-based systems interact with the real world in a *reactive* fashion. That is, real world events are monitored by the hardware and software that comprise the computer-based system, and based on these events, the system imposes control on the machines, processes, and even people who cause the events to occur. Real-time and embedded systems often fall into the reactive systems category.

Unfortunately, the developers of reactive systems sometimes struggle to make them perform properly. Until recently, it has been difficult to predict the performance, efficiency, and behavior of such systems prior to building them. In a very real sense, the construction of many real-time systems was an adventure in "flying." Surprises (most of them unpleasant) were not discovered until the system was built and "pushed off a cliff." If the system crashed due to incorrect function, inappropriate behavior, or poor performance, we picked up the pieces and started over again.

Many systems in the reactive category control machines and/or processes (e.g., commercial airliners or petroleum refineries) that must operate with an extremely high degree of reliability. If the system fails, significant economic or human loss could occur. For this reason, the approach described by Graham is both painful and dangerous.

Today, CASE tools for system modeling and simulation are being used to help to eliminate surprises when reactive, computer-based systems are built. These tools are applied during the system engineering process, while the roles of hardware and software, databases and people are being specified. Modeling and simulation tools enable a system engineer to "test drive" a specification of the system. The technical details and specialized modeling techniques that are used to enable a test drive are discussed briefly in Chapter 29.

10.9　　SYSTEM SPECIFICATION

The *system specification* is a document that serves as the foundation for hardware engineering, software engineering, data base engineering and human engineering. It describes the function and performance of a computer-based system and the constraints that will govern its development. The specification bounds each allocated system element. For example, it provides the software engineer with an indication of the role of software within the context of the system as a whole and the various subsystems described in the architecture flow diagrams. The system specification also describes the information (data and control) that is input to and output from the system.

A recommended outline for the system specification is presented in Figure 10.15. It should be noted, however, that this is but one of many outlines that can be used to define a system description document. The actual format and content may be dictated by software or system engineering standards or local custom and preference.

10.10　　SUMMARY

A high-technology system encompasses a number of components: software, hardware, people, database, documentation, and procedures. System engineering helps to translate a customer's needs into a model of a system that makes use of one or more of these components.

System engineering begins by taking a "world view." A business domain or product is analyzed to establish all basic requirements. Focus is then narrowed to a "domain view," where each of the system elements is analyzed individually. Each element is allocated to one or more engineering components which are then addressed by the relevant engineering discipline.

Information engineering is a system engineering approach that is used to define architectures that enable a business to use information effectively. The intent of information engineering is to derive comprehensive data architectures, an application architecture, and a technology infrastructure that will meet the needs of the business strategy and the objectives and goals of each

I. Introduction
    A. Scope and Purpose of Document
    B. Overview
        1. Objectives
        2. Constraints
II. Functional and Data Description
    A. System Architecture
        1. Architecture Context Diagram
        2. ACD Description
III. Subsystem Descriptions
    A. Architecture Diagram Specification for Subsystem n
        1. Architecture Flow Diagram
        2. System Module Narrative
        3. Performance Issues
        4. Design Constraints
        5. Allocation of System Components
    B. Architecture Dictionary
    C. Architecture Interconnect Diagrams and Description
IV. System Modeling and Simulation Results
    A. System Model Used for Simulation
    B. Simulation Results
    C. Special Performance Issues
V. Project Issues
    A. Projected Development Costs
    B. Projected Schedule
VI. Appendices

FIGURE 10.15.
System specification outline

business area. Information engineering encompasses information strategy planning (ISP), business area analysis (BAA), and application-specific analysis that is actually part of software engineering.

Product engineering is a system engineering approach that begins with system analysis. The system engineer identifies the customer's needs, determines economic and technical feasibility, and allocates function and performance to software, hardware, people and databases—the key engineering components. An architectural model of the system or product is produced and representations of each major subsystem can be developed. Finally, the system engineer can create a reactive system model that can be used as the basis for a simulation of performance and behavior. The system engineering task culminates with the creation of a system specification—a document that forms the foundation for all engineering work that follows.

System engineering demands intense communication between the customer and the information or system engineer. The customer must understand system objectives and be able to state them clearly. The engineer must know what questions to ask, what advice to give, and what research to do. If communication succeeds and a complete model of the system is created, a solid foundation is established for the construction of the system.

REFERENCES

[BLA81]   Blanchard, B.S., and W.J. Fabrycky, *Systems Engineering and Analysis,* Prentice-Hall, 1981, p. 270.

[FRI77]   Fried, L. "Performing Cost Benefit Analysis," *System Development Management,* Auerbach Publishers, Pennsauken, NJ, 1977.

[GRA69]   Graham, R.M., in *Proceedings 1969 NATO Conference on Software Engineering,* 1969.

[HAM93]   Hammer, M., and J. Champy, *Reengineering the Corporation,* Harper Collins, 1993, p. 83.

[HAR93]   Hares, J.S., *Information Engineering for the Advanced Practitioner,* Wiley, 1993, pp. 12–13.

[HAT87]   Hatley, D.J., and I.A. Pirbhai, *Strategies for Real-Time System Specification,* Dorset House, 1987.

[JAY94]   Jaychandra, Y., *Reengineering the Networked Enterprise,* McGraw-Hill, 1994.

[KIN78]   King, J., and E. Schrems, "Cost Benefit Analysis in Information Systems Development and Operation," *ACM Computing Surveys,* vol. 10, no. 1, March 1978, pp. 19–34.

[MAR90]   Martin, J., *Information Engineering: Book II—Planning and Analysis,* Prentice-Hall, 1990.

[RIS92]   Rishe, N. *Database Design,* McGraw-Hill, 1992.

[MOT92]   Motamarri, S., "Systems Modeling and Description," *Software Engineering Notes,* vol. 17, no. 2., April 1992, pp. 57–63.

[SCH92]   Scheer, A., and A. Hars, "Extending Data Modeling to Cover the Whole Enterprise," *Communication of the ACM,* vol. 35, no. 4, September 1992, pp. 166–172.

[SCO89]   Scott, M.D., *Computer Law,* Wiley, 1989.

[SPE93]   Spewak, S., *Enterprise Architecture Planning,* QED Publishing, 1993.

PROBLEMS AND POINTS TO PONDER

10.1. Find as many single word synonyms for the word "system" as you can. Good luck!

10.2. Build a "system of systems" similar to Figure 10.1 for a large system (other than the one shown). Your hierarchy should extend down to simple system elements (hardware, software, etc.) along at least one branch of the "tree."

10.3. Select any large system or product with which you are familiar. Define the set of domains that describe the world view of the system or product. Describe the set of elements that make up one or two domains. For one element, identify the technical components that must be engineered.

10.4. Select any large system or product with which you are familiar. State the assumptions, simplifications, limitations, constraints, and preferences that would have to be made to build an effective (and realizable) system model.

10.5. Information engineering strives to define data and application architecture as well as technology infrastructure. Describe what each of these terms means and provide an example.

10.6. Information strategy planning begins with the definitions of objectives and goals. Provide examples of each from the business domain.

10.7. You've decided to start a mail-order business for computer software. Because you want to run the business efficiently, you decide to do some information engineering. You'll start with ISP. Build a simple enterprise model that includes an org chart, business function and business process outlines, and a business-level data model.

10.8. Let's assume that one of the business areas that you've identified for the software mail-order business (problem 10.7) is telephone order processing. Do BAA to develop a more detailed data model and process flow diagram for this business area.

10.9. A system engineer can come from one of three sources: the system developer, the customer, or some outside organization. Discuss the pros and cons that apply to each source. Describe an "ideal" system engineer.

10.10. Add at least five additional questions to the list developed for CLSS in Section 10.6. Come up with two additional allocations for CLSS.

10.11. Your instructor will distribute a high-level description of a computer-based system or product.
a. Develop a set of questions that you should ask as a system engineer.
b. Propose at least two different allocations for the system based on answers to your questions provided by your instructor.
c. In class, compare your allocation to those of fellow students.

10.12. Develop a checklist for attributes to be considered when "feasibility" of a system or product is to be evaluated. Discuss the interplay among attributes and attempt to provide a method for grading each so that a quantitative "feasibility number" may be developed.

10.13. Research the accounting techniques that are used for a detailed cost–benefit analysis of a computer-based system that will require some hardware manufacturing and assembly. Attempt to write a "cookbook" set of guidelines that a technical manager could apply.

10.14. Develop an architecture context diagram (ACD) and architecture flow diagrams (AFDs) for the computer-based system of your choice (or one assigned by your instructor).

10.15. Write a system module narrative that would be contained in an architecture diagram specification for one or more of the subsystems defined in the AFDs developed for problem 10.14.

10.16. Research the literature on CASE tools and write a brief paper describing how modeling and simulation tools work. [Alternate: Collect literature from two or more CASE vendors that sell modeling and simulation tools and assess the similarities and differences.]

10.17. Based on documents provided by your instructor, develop an abbreviated system specification for one of the following computer-based systems:
a. a nonlinear, digital video-editing system
b. a digital scanner for a personal computer

    c. an electronic mail system

    d. a university registration system

    e. an Internet access provider

    f. an interactive hotel reservation system

    g. a system of local interest

Be sure to create the architecture models described in Section 10.8.

10.18. Are there characteristics of a system that cannot be established during system engineering activities? Describe the characteristics, if any, and explain why a consideration of them must be delayed until later engineering steps.

10.19. Are there situations in which formal system specification can be abbreviated or eliminated entirely? Explain.

FURTHER READINGS AND OTHER INFORMATION SOURCES

Martin (*Information Engineering,* 3 volumes, Prentice-Hall, 1989, 1990, 1991) presents a comprehensive discussion of information engineering topics. Books by Hares [HAR93], Spewak [SPE93], and Flynn and Fragoso-Diaz (*Information Modeling: An International Perspective,* Prentice-Hall, 1996) also treat the subject in detail.

Because it is an interdisciplinary topic, product engineering is a difficult subject. Books by Armstrong and Sage (*Introduction to Systems Engineering,* Wiley, 1997), Martin (*Systems Engineering Guidebook,* CRC Press, 1996), Wymore (*Model-Based Systems Engineering,* CRC Press, 1993), Lacy (*System Engineering Management,* McGraw-Hill, 1992), Aslaksen and Belcher (*Systems Engineering,* Prentice-Hall, 1992), Athey (*Systematic Systems Approach,* Prentice-Hall, 1982), and Blanchard and Fabrycky [BLA81] present the system engineering process (with a distinct engineering emphasis) and provide worthwhile guidance.

An excellent IEEE tutorial by Thayer and Dorfman (*System and Software Requirements Engineering,* IEEE Computer Society Press, 1990) discusses the interrelationship between system and software level requirements analysis issues. A companion volume by the same authors (*Standards, Guidelines and Examples: System and Software Requirements Engineering,* IEEE Computer Society Press, 1990) presents a comprehensive discussion of standards and guidelines for analysis work.

Books by Robertson and Robertson (*Complete Systems Analysis,* Dorset House, 1994), Silver and Silver (*Systems Analysis and Design,* Addison-Wesley, 1989), Modell (*A Professional's Guide to Systems Analysis,* McGraw-Hill, 1988), and McMenamin and Palmer (*Essential Systems Analysis,* Yourdon Press, 1984) provide useful discussions of the system analysis task as it is applied in the information systems world. Each contains case study supplements that illustrate the problems, approaches, and solutions that may be applied during system analysis.

For those readers actively involved in systems work or interested in a more sophisticated treatment of the topic, Gerald Weinberg's books (*An Introduction to General System Thinking,* Wiley-Interscience, 1976, and *On the Design of Stable Systems,* Wiley-Interscience, 1979) have become classics and provide an excellent discussion of "general systems thinking" that implicitly leads to a general approach to system analysis and design. More recent books by Weinberg (*General Principles of Systems Design,* Dorset House, 1988, and *Rethinking Systems Analysis and Design,* Dorset House, 1988) continue in the tradition of his earlier work.

A comprehensive list of pointers to other servers that have information on "system science" can be obtained at:

http://www.sea.uni-linz.ac.at

The following Web sites discuss research and practical applications of system and information engineering:

Systems Theory and Information Engineering

http://www.cast.uni-linz.ac.at/st/

Information Engineering Initiative

http://www2.echo.lu/programmes/en/fact_sheets/elpub2001.html

Systems Engineering Welcome Page

http://rs712b.gsfc.nasa.gov/704/704home.html

An up-to-date list of World Wide Web references for information engineering and product engineering can be found at: **http://www.rspa.com**

CHAPTER 11

ANALYSIS CONCEPTS AND PRINCIPLES

A complete understanding of software requirements is essential to the success of a software development effort. No matter how well designed or well coded, a poorly analyzed and specified program will disappoint the user and bring grief to the developer.

The requirements analysis task is a process of discovery, refinement, modeling, and specification. The software scope, initially established by the system engineer and refined during software project planning, is refined in detail. Models of the required data, information and control flow, and operational behavior are created. Alternative solutions are analyzed and allocated to various software elements.

Both the developer and customer take an active role in requirements analysis and specification. The customer attempts to reformulate a sometimes nebulous concept of software function and performance into concrete detail. The developer acts as interrogator, consultant, and problem solver.

Requirements analysis and specification may appear to be a relatively simple task, but appearances are deceiving. Communication content is very high. Chances for misinterpretation or misinformation abound. Ambiguity is probable. The dilemma that confronts a software engineer may best be understood by repeating the statement of an anonymous (infamous?) customer: "I know you believe you understood what you think I said, but I am not sure you realize that what you heard is not what I meant."

11.1   REQUIREMENTS ANALYSIS

Requirements analysis is a software engineering task that bridges the gap between system-level software allocation and software design (Figure 11.1).

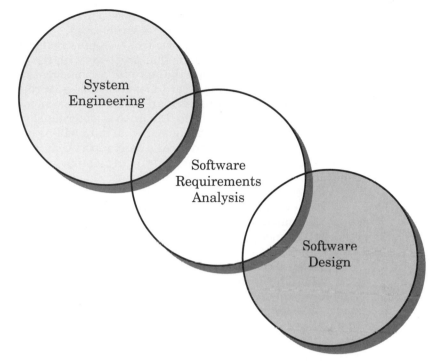

FIGURE 11.1.
Analysis and a
bridge between system engineering and
software design

Requirements analysis enables the system engineer to specify software function and performance, indicate software's interface with other system elements, and establish constraints that software must meet. Requirements analysis allows the software engineer (often called *analyst* in this role) to refine the software allocation and build models of the data, functional, and behavioral domains that will be treated by software. Requirements analysis provides the software designer with models that can be translated in to data, architectural, interface, and procedural design. Finally, the requirements specification provides the developer and the customer with the means to assess quality once software is built.

Software requirements analysis may be divided into five areas of effort: (1) problem recognition; (2) evaluation and synthesis; (3) modeling; (4) specification; and (5) review.

Initially, the analyst studies the *system specification* (if one exists) and the *software project plan*. It is important to understand software in a system context and to review the software scope that was used to generate planning estimates. Next, communication for analysis must be established so that problem recognition is ensured. The goal of the analyst is recognition of the basic problem elements as perceived by the user/customer.

Problem evaluation and solution synthesis is the next major area of effort for analysis. The analyst must define all externally observable data objects, evaluate the flow and content of information; define and elaborate all software functions; understand software behavior in the context of events that affect the system; establish system interface characteristics; and uncover additional design constraints. Each of these tasks serves to describe the problem so that an overall approach or solution may be synthesized.

For example, an inventory control system is required for a major supplier of auto parts. The analyst finds that problems with the current manual system include (1) inability to obtain the status of a component rapidly; (2) two or three day turnaround to update a card file; (3) multiple reorders to the same vendor because there is no way to associate vendors with components, and so on. Once problems have been identified, the analyst determines what information is to be produced by the new system and what data will be provided to the system.[1] For instance, the customer desires a daily report that indicates what parts have been taken from inventory and how many similar parts remain. The customer indicates that inventory clerks will log the identification number of each part as it leaves the inventory area.

Upon evaluating current problems and desired information (input and output), the analyst begins to synthesize one or more solutions. To begin, the data, processing functions, and behavior of the system are defined in detail. Once this information has been established, basic architectures for implementation are considered. A client/server approach would seem to be appropriate, but does it fall within the scope outlined in the software plan? A database management system would seem to be required, but is the user/customer's need for associativity justified? The process of evaluation and synthesis continues until both analyst and customer feel confident that software can be adequately specified for subsequent development steps.

Throughout evaluation and solution synthesis, the analyst's primary focus is on "what," *not* "how." *What* data does the system produce and consume, *what* functions must the system perform, *what* interfaces are defined, and *what* constraints apply?[2]

During the evaluation and solution synthesis activity, the analyst creates models of the system in an effort to better understand data and control flow, functional processing and behavioral operation, and information content. The model serves as a foundation for software design and as the basis for the creation of a specification for the software.

It is important to note that detailed specification may not be possible at this stage. The customer may be unsure of precisely what is required. The developer may be unsure that a specific approach will properly accomplish function and performance. For these and many other reasons, an alternative approach to requirements analysis, called *prototyping,* may be conducted (Chapter 2). We discuss prototyping later in this chapter.

11.2   COMMUNICATION TECHNIQUES

Software requirements analysis always begins with communication between two or more parties. A *customer* has a problem that may be amenable to a com-

---

[1]In reality, much of this information would be acquired as part of an information engineering activity (Chapter 10) if one were conducted.

[2]Davis [DAV93] argues that the terms "what" and "how" are too vague. For an interesting discussion of this issue, the reader should refer to his book.

puter-based solution. A developer responds to the customer's request for help. Communication has begun. But as we have already noted, the road from communication to understanding is often full of potholes.

11.2.1 Initiating the Process

The most commonly used analysis technique to bridge the communication gap between the customer and developer and to get the communication process started is to conduct a preliminary meeting or interview. The first meeting between a software engineer (the analyst) and the customer can be likened to the awkwardness of a first date between two adolescents. Neither person knows what to say or ask; both are worried that what they do say will be misinterpreted; both are thinking about where it might lead (both are likely to have radically different expectations here); both want to get the thing over with; but at the same time, both want it to be a success.

Yet, communication must be initiated. Gause and Weinberg [GAU89] suggest that the analyst start by asking *context free questions.* That is, a set of questions that will lead to a basic understanding of the problem, the people who want a solution, the nature of the solution that is desired, and the effectiveness of the first encounter itself. The first set of context free questions focus on the customer, overall goals, and benefits. For example, the analyst might ask:

- Who is behind the request for this work?
- Who will use the solution?
- What will be the economic benefit of a successful solution?
- Is there another source for the solution that you need?

The next set of questions enables the analyst to gain a better understanding of the problem and the customer to voice his or her perceptions about a solution:

- How would you characterize "good" output that would be generated by a successful solution?
- What problem(s) will this solution address?
- Can you show me (or describe) the environment in which the solution will be used?
- Are there special performance issues or constraints that will affect the way the solution is approached?

The final set of questions focus on the effectiveness of the meeting. Gause and Weinberg [GAU89] call these meta-questions and propose the following (abbreviated) list:

- Are you the right person to answer these questions? Are your answers "official"?

- Are my questions relevant to the problem that you have?
- Am I asking too many questions?
- Is there anyone else who can provide additional information?
- Is there anything else that I should be asking you?

These questions (and others) will help to "break the ice" and initiate the communication that is essential to successful analysis. But a question and answer meeting format is not an approach that has been overwhelmingly successful. In fact, the Q&A session should be used for the first encounter only and then be replaced by a meeting format that combines elements of problem solving, negotiation, and specification. An approach to meetings of this type is presented in the next section.

11.2.2 Facilitated Application Specification Techniques

Customers and software engineers often have an unconscious "us and them" mind set. Rather than working as a team to identify and refine requirements, each constituency defines its own "territory" and communicates through a series of memos, formal position papers, documents, and question and answer sessions. History has shown that this approach doesn't work very well. Misunderstandings abound, important information is omitted, and a successful working relationship is never established.

It is with these problems in mind that a number of independent investigators have developed a team-oriented approach to requirements gathering that is applied during early stages of analysis and specification. Called *facilitated application specification techniques (FAST),* this approach encourages the creation of a joint team of customers and developers who work together to identify the problem, propose elements of the solution, negotiate different approaches, and specify a preliminary set of solution requirements [ZAH90]. Today, FAST is used predominantly by the information systems community, but the technique offers potential for improved communication in applications of all kinds.

Many different approaches to FAST have been proposed.[3] Each makes use of a slightly different scenario, but all apply some variation on the following basic guidelines:

- A meeting is conducted at a neutral site and attended by both developers and customers.
- Rules for preparation and participation are established.
- An agenda is suggested that is formal enough to cover all important points but informal enough to encourage the free flow of ideas.

---

[3]Two of the more popular approaches to FAST are *Joint Application Development (JAD),* developed by IBM, and *The METHOD,* developed by Performance Resources, Inc., Falls Church, VA.

- A "facilitator" (who can be a customer, a developer, or an outsider) controls the meeting.
- A "definition mechanism" (which can be work sheets, flip charts, wall stickers, or a wall board) is used.
- The goal is to identify the problem, propose elements of the solution, negotiate different approaches, and specify a preliminary set of solution requirements in an atmosphere that is conducive to the accomplishment of the goal.

To better understand the flow of events as they occur in a typical FAST meeting, we present a brief scenario that outlines the sequence of events that lead up to the meeting, occur during the meeting, and follow the meeting.

Initial meetings between the developer and customer (Section 11.2.1) occur and basic questions and answers help to establish the scope of the problem and the overall perception of a solution. Out of these initial meetings, the developer and customer write a one- or two-page "product request." A meeting place, time, and date for FAST are selected, and a *facilitator* is chosen. Representatives from both the development and customer organizations are invited to attend. The product request is distributed to all attendees before the meeting date.

While reviewing the request in the days before the meeting, each FAST attendee is asked to make a list of *objects* that are part of the environment that surrounds the system, other objects that are to be produced by the system, and objects that are used by the system to perform its functions. In addition, each attendee is asked to make another list of *services* (processes or functions) that manipulate or interact with the objects. Finally, lists of *constraints* (e.g., cost, size, weight) and *performance criteria* (e.g., speed, accuracy) are also developed. The attendees are informed that the lists are not expected to be exhaustive, but are expected to reflect each person's perception of the system.

As an example,[4] assume that a FAST team working for a consumer products company has been provided with the following product description:

> Our research indicates that the market for home security systems is growing at a rate of 40 percent per year. We would like to enter this market by building a microprocessor-based home security system that would protect against and/or recognize a variety of undesirable "situations" such as illegal entry, fire, flooding and others. The product, tentatively called SafeHome, will use appropriate sensors to detect each situation, can be programmed by the homeowner, and will automatically telephone a monitoring agency when a situation is detected.

In reality, considerably more information would be provided at this stage. But even with additional information, ambiguity would be present, omissions would likely exist, and errors might occur. For now, the above "product description" will suffice.

The FAST team is comprised of representatives from marketing, software and hardware engineering, and manufacturing. An outside facilitator is to be used.

---

[4]This example (with extensions and variations) will be used to illustrate important software engineering methods in many of the chapters that follow. As an exercise, it would be worthwhile to conduct your own FAST meeting and develop a set of lists for it.

Each person on the FAST team (Figure 11.2) develops the lists described above. Objects described for SafeHome might include smoke detectors, window and door sensors, motion detectors, an alarm, an event (a sensor has been activated), a control panel, a display, telephone numbers, a telephone call, and so on. The list of services might include setting the alarm, monitoring the sensors, dialing the phone, programming the control panel, and reading the display (note that services act on objects). In a similar fashion, each FAST attendee will develop lists of constraints (e.g., the system must have a manufactured cost of less than $200, must be user friendly, and must interface directly to a standard phone line) and performance criteria (e.g., a sensor event should be recognized within one second; an event priority scheme should be implemented).

As the meeting begins, the first topic of discussion is the need and justification for the new product—everyone should agree that the product development (or acquisition) is justified. Once agreement has been established, each participant presents his or her lists for discussion. The lists can be pinned to the walls of the room using large sheets of paper, stuck to the walls using adhesive-backed sheets, or written on a wall board. Ideally, each list entry should be capable of being manipulated separately so that lists can be combined, entries can be deleted, and additions can be made. At this stage, critique and debate are strictly prohibited.

After individual lists are presented in one topic area, a combined list is created by the group. The combined list eliminates redundant entries and adds any new ideas that come up during the presentation, but does not delete anything. After combined lists for all topic areas have been created, discussion—coordinated by the facilitator—ensues. The combined list is shortened, lengthened, or reworded to properly reflect the product/system to be developed. The objective is to develop a consensus list in each topic area (objects, services, constraints, and performance). The lists are then set aside for later action.

Once the consensus lists have been completed, the team is divided into smaller subteams; each works to develop a *mini-specification* for one or more entries on each of the lists. The mini-specification is an elaboration of the word or phrase contained on a list. For example, the mini-specification for the SafeHome object **control panel** might be:

FIGURE 11.2.
The FAST meeting

- mounted on wall
- size approximately 9 x 5 inches
- contains standard 12 key pad and special keys
- contains LCD display of the form shown in sketch [not presented here]
- all customer interaction occurs through keys used to enable and disable the system
- software to provide interaction guidance, echoes, etc. connected to all sensors

Each subteam then presents each of its mini-specs to all FAST attendees for discussion. Additions, deletions, and further elaboration are made. In some cases, the development of mini-specs will uncover new objects, services, constraints, or performance requirements that will be added to the original lists. During all discussions, the team may raise an issue that cannot be resolved during the meeting. An issues list is maintained so that these ideas will be acted on later.

After the mini-specs are completed, each FAST attendee makes a list of validation criteria for the product/system and presents his or her list to the team. A consensus list of validation criteria is then created. Finally, one or more participants (or outsiders) is assigned the task of writing the complete draft specification using all inputs from the FAST meeting.

FAST is not a panacea for the problems encountered in early requirements gathering, but the team approach provides the benefits of many points of view, instantaneous discussion and refinement, and a concrete step toward the development of a specification.

11.2.3 Quality Function Deployment

Quality function deployment (QFD) is quality management technique that translates the needs of the customer into technical requirements for software. Originally developed in Japan and first used at the Kobe Shipyard of Mitsubishi Heavy Industries, Ltd. in the early 1970s, QFD "concentrates on maximizing customer satisfaction" [ZUL92]. To accomplish this, QFD emphasizes understanding of what is valuable to the customer and then deploying these values throughout the engineering process.

QFD identifies three types of requirements [ZUL92]:

Normal requirements. Objectives and goals are stated for a product or system during meetings with the customer. If these requirements are present, the customer is satisfied. Examples of normal requirements might be requested types of graphical displays, specific system functions, and defined levels of performance.

Expected requirements. These requirements are implicit to the product or system and may be so fundamental that the customer does not explicitly state them. Their absence will be a cause for significant dissatisfaction. Examples of expected requirements are ease of human–machine interaction, overall operational correctness and reliability, and ease of software installation.

Exciting requirements. These features go beyond the customer's expectations and prove to be very satisfying when present. For example, word-processing software is requested with standard features. The delivered product contains a number of page layout capabilities that are quite pleasing and unexpected.

In actuality, QFD spans the entire engineering process [AKA90]. However, many QFD concepts are applicable to the customer communication problem that faces a software engineer during early stages of requirements analysis. We present an overview of only these concepts (adapted for computer software) in the paragraphs that follow.

In meetings with the customer, *function deployment* is used to determine the value of each function that is required for the system. *Information deployment* identifies both the data objects and events that the system must consume and produce. These are tied to the functions. Finally, *task deployment* examines the behavior of the system or product within the context of its environment. *Value analysis* is conducted to determine the relative priority of requirements determined during each of the three deployments noted above.

QFD uses customer interviews and observation, surveys, and examination of historical data (e.g., problem reports) as raw data for the requirements gathering activity. These data are then translated into a table of requirements—called the *customer voice table*—that is reviewed with the customer. A variety of diagrams, matrices, and evaluation methods are then used to extract expected requirements and to attempt to derive exciting requirements [BOS91].

11.3   ANALYSIS PRINCIPLES

Over the past two decades, investigators have identified analysis problems and their causes, and have developed a variety of modeling notations and corresponding sets of heuristics to overcome them. Each analysis method has a unique point of view. However, all analysis methods are related by a set of operational principles:

1. The information domain of a problem must be represented and understood.
2. The functions that the software is to perform must be defined.
3. The behavior of the software (as a consequence of external events) must be represented.
4. The models that depict information, function, and behavior must be partitioned in a manner that uncovers detail in a layered (or hierarchical) fashion.
5. The analysis process should move from essential information toward implementation detail.

By applying these principles, the analyst approaches a problem systematically. The information domain is examined so that function may be understood more completely. Models are used so that the characteristics of function and behavior can be communicated in a compact fashion. Partitioning is applied to reduce complexity. Essential and implementation views of the software are necessary to accommodate the logical constraints imposed by processing requirements and the physical constraints imposed by other system elements.

In addition to the operational analysis principles noted above, Davis [DAV95a] suggests a set[5] of guiding principles for "requirements engineering":

- *Understand the problem before you begin to create the analysis model*. There is a tendency to rush to a solution, even before the problem is understood. This often leads to elegant software that solves the wrong problem!
- *Develop prototypes that enable a user to understand how human–machine interaction will occur*. Since the perception of the quality of software is often based on the perception of the "friendliness" of the interface, prototyping (and the iteration that results) is highly recommended.
- *Record the origin of and the reason for every requirement*. This is the first step in establishing traceability back to the customer.
- *Use multiple views of requirements*. Building data, functional, and behavioral models provides the software engineer with three different views. This reduces the likelihood that something will be missed and increases the likelihood that inconsistency will be recognized.
- *Prioritize requirements*. Tight deadlines may preclude the implementation of every software requirement. If an incremental process model (Chapter 2) is applied, those requirements to be delivered in the first increment must be identified.
- *Work to eliminate ambiguity*. Because most requirements are described in a natural language, the opportunity for ambiguity abounds. The use of formal technical reviews is one way to uncover and eliminate ambiguity.

A software engineer who takes these principles to heart is more likely to develop a software specification that will provide an excellent foundation for design.

11.3.1 The Information Domain

All software applications can be collectively called *data processing*. It is interesting that this term contains a key to our understanding of software requirements. Software is built to process *data,* to transform data from one form to another, that is, to accept input, manipulate it in some way, and produce output. This fundamental statement of objective is true whether we build batch software for a payroll system or real-time embedded software to control fuel flow to an automobile engine.

It is important to note, however, that software also processes *events*. An event represents some aspect of system control and is really nothing more than boolean data—it is either on or off, true or false, there or not there. For example, a pres-

---

[5]Only a small subset of Davis's requirements engineering principles are noted here. For more information, see [DAV95a].

sure sensor detects that pressure exceeds a safe value and sends an alarm signal to monitoring software. The alarm signal is an event that controls the behavior of the system. Therefore, data (numbers, characters, images, sounds, etc.) and control (events) both reside within the *information domain* of a problem.

The first operational analysis principle requires an examination of the information domain. The information domain contains three different views of the data and control as each is processed by a computer program: (1) information content and relationships, (2) information flow, and (3) information structure. To fully understand the information domain, each of these views should be considered.

Information content represents the individual data and control objects that comprise some larger collection of information that is transformed by the software. For example, the data object **paycheck** is a composite of a number of important pieces of data: the payee's name, the net amount to be paid, the gross pay, deductions, and so forth. Therefore, the *content* of **paycheck** is defined by the *attributes* that are needed to create it. Similarly, the content of a control object called **system status** might be defined by a string of bits. Each bit represents a separate item of information that indicates whether or not a particular device is on- or off-line.

Data and control objects can be related to other data and control objects. For example, the data object **paycheck** has one or more relationships with the objects **timecard, employee, bank,** and others. During the analysis of the information domain, these relationships should be defined.

Information flow represents the manner in which data and control change as each moves through a system. As shown in Figure 11.3, input objects are transformed to intermediate information (data and/or control), which is further transformed to output. Along this transformation path (or paths), additional information may be introduced from an existing *data store* (e.g., a disk file or memory buffer). The transformations that are applied to the data are functions or subfunctions that a program must perform. Data and control that move between two transformations (functions) define the interface for each function.

Information structure represents the internal organization of various data and control items. Are data or control items to be organized as an *n*-dimen-

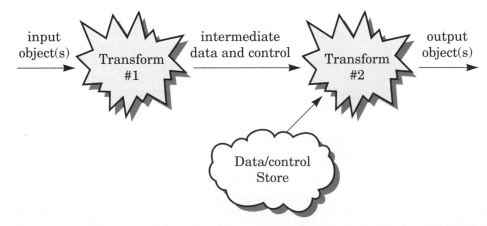

FIGURE 11.3.
Information flow and
transformation

sional table or as a hierarchical tree structure? Within the context of the structure, what information is related to other information? Is all information contained within a single structure or are distinct structures to be used? How does information in one information structure relate to information in another structure? These questions and others are answered by an assessment of information structure. It should be noted that *data structure,* a related concept discussed later in this book, refers to the design and implementation of information structure.

11.3.2 Modeling

We create models to gain a better understanding of the actual entity to be built. When the entity is a physical thing (a building, a plane, a machine), we can build a model that is identical in form and shape, but smaller in scale. However, when the entity is to be built is software, our model must take a different form. It must be capable of modeling the information that software transforms, the functions (and subfunctions) that enable the transformation to occur, and the behavior of the system as the transformation is taking place.

During software requirements analysis, we create models of the system to be built. The models focus on what the system must do, not on how it does it. In many cases, the models that we create make use of a graphical notation that depicts information, processing, system behavior, and other characteristics as distinct and recognizable symbols. Other parts of the model may be purely textual. Descriptive information can be provided using a natural language or a specialized language for describing requirements.

The second and third operational analysis principles require that we build models of function and behavior.

Functional models.   Software transforms information, and in order to accomplish this, it must perform at least three generic functions: input, processing, and output. When functional models of an application are created, the software engineer focuses on problem-specific functions. The functional model begins with a single context level model (i.e., the name of the software to be built). Over a series of iterations, more and more functional detail is provided, until a thorough delineation of all system functionality is represented.

Behavioral models.   Most software responds to events from the outside world. This stimulus–response characteristic forms the basis of the behavioral model. A computer program always exists in some *state*—an externally observable mode of behavior (e.g., waiting, computing, printing, polling) that is changed only when some event occurs. For example software will remain in the *wait state* until (1) an internal clock indicates that some time interval has passed, (2) an external event (e.g., a mouse movement) causes an interrupt, or (3) an external system signals the software to act in some manner. A behavioral model creates a representation of the states of the software and the events that cause software to change state.

Models created during requirements analysis serve a number of important roles:

- The model aids the analyst in understanding the information, function, and behavior of a system, thereby making the requirements analysis task easier and more systematic.
- The model becomes the focal point for review and therefore the key to a determination of completeness, consistency, and accuracy of the specification.
- The model becomes the foundation for design, providing the designer with an essential representation of software that can be translated into an implementation context.

The analysis methods that are discussed in Chapters 12 and 20 are actually modeling methods. Although the modeling method that is used is often a matter of personal (or organizational) preference, the modeling activity is fundamental to good analysis work.

11.3.3 Partitioning

Problems are often too large and complex to be understood as a whole. For this reason, we tend to *partition* (divide) such problems into parts that can be easily understood and establish interfaces between the parts so that overall function can be accomplished. The fourth operational analysis principle suggests that the information, functional, and behavioral domains of software can be partitioned.

In essence, partitioning decomposes a problem into its constituent parts. Conceptually, we establish a hierarchical representation of information or function and then partition the uppermost element by (1) exposing increasing detail by moving vertically in the hierarchy or (2) decomposing the problem by moving horizontally in the hierarchy. To illustrate these partitioning approaches, let us reconsider the SafeHome security system described in Section 11.2.2. The software allocation for SafeHome (derived as a consequence of system engineering and FAST activities) can be stated in the following paragraphs:

> SafeHome software enables the homeowner to configure the security system when it is installed, monitors all sensors connected to the security system, and interacts with the homeowner through a keypad and function keys contained in the SafeHome control panel shown in Figure 11.4.
>
> During installation, the SafeHome control panel is used to "program" and configure the system. Each sensor is assigned a number and type, a master password is programmed for arming and disarming the system, and telephone number(s) are input for dialing when a sensor event occurs.
>
> When a sensor event is recognized, the software invokes an audible alarm attached to the system. After a delay time that is specified by the homeowner during system configuration activities, the software dials a telephone number of a monitoring service and provides information about the location, reporting the nature of the event that has been detected. The number will be redialed every 20 seconds until telephone connection is obtained.

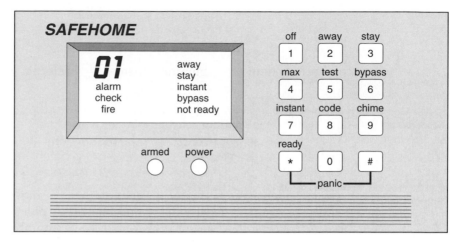

FIGURE 11.4.
SafeHome control panel (a detailed description of the control panel functions will be presented in later chapters)

All interaction with SafeHome is managed by a user-interaction subsystem that reads input provided through the keypad and function keys, displays prompting messages and system status on the LCD display. Keyboard interaction takes the following form. . . .

Requirements for SafeHome software may be analyzed by partitioning the information, functional, and behavioral domains of the product. To illustrate, the functional domain of the problem will be partitioned. Figure 11.5 illustrates a horizontal decomposition of SafeHome software. The problem is partitioned by representing constituent SafeHome software functions, moving horizontally in the functional hierarchy. Three major functions are noted on the first level of the hierarchy.

The subfunctions associated with a major SafeHome function may be examined by exposing detail vertically in the hierarchy, as illustrated in Figure 11.6. Moving downward along a single path below the function **monitor sensors,** partitioning occurs vertically to show increasing levels of functional detail.

The partitioning approach that we have applied to SafeHome functions can also be applied to the information domain and behavioral domain as well. In fact, partitioning of information flow and system behavior (discussed in Chapter 12) will provide additional insight into system requirements. As the problem is partitioned, interfaces between functions are derived. Data and control items that move across an interface should be restricted to inputs required to per-

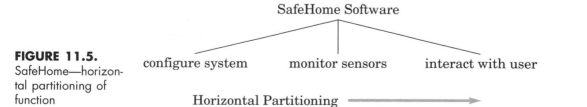

FIGURE 11.5.
SafeHome—horizontal partitioning of function

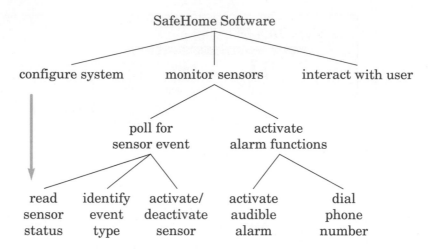

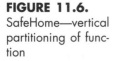

FIGURE 11.6.
SafeHome—vertical
partitioning of function

form the stated function and outputs that are required by other functions or system elements.

11.3.4 Essential and Implementation Views[6]

An *essential view* of software requirements presents the functions to be accomplished and information to be processed without regard to implementation details. For example, the essential view of the SafeHome function **read sensor status** does not concern itself with the physical form of the data or the type of sensor that is used. In fact, it could be argued that **read status** would be a more appropriate name for this function, since it disregards details about the input mechanism altogether. Similarly, an essential *data model* of the data item **phone number** (implied by the function **dial phone number**) can be represented at this stage without regard to the underlying data structure (if any) used to implement the data item. By focusing attention on the essence of the problem at early stages of requirements analysis, we leave our options open to specify implementation details during later stages of requirements specification and software design.

The *implementation* view of software requirements presents the real world manifestation of processing functions and information structures. In some cases, a physical representation is developed as the first step in software design. However, most computer-based systems are specified in a manner that dictates accommodation of certain implementation details. A SafeHome input device is a perimeter sensor (not a watch dog, a human guard, or a booby trap). The sensor detects illegal entry by sensing a break in an electronic circuit. The general characteristics of the sensor should be noted as part of a software requirements specification. The analyst must recognize the constraints imposed

---

[6]Many people use the terms "logical" and "physical" views to connote the same concept.

by predefined system elements (the sensor) and consider the implementation view of function and information when such a view is appropriate.

We have already noted that software requirements analysis should focus on *what* the software is to accomplish, rather than on *how* processing will be implemented. However, the implementation view should not necessarily be interpreted as a representation of *how*. Rather, an implementation model represents the current mode of operation, that is, the existing or proposed allocation for all system elements. The essential model (of function or data) is generic in the sense that realization of function is not explicitly indicated.

11.4   SOFTWARE PROTOTYPING

Analysis should be conducted regardless of the software engineering paradigm that is applied. However, the *form* that analysis takes will vary. In some cases it is possible to apply operational analysis principles and derive a model of software from which a design can be developed. In other situations, requirements gathering (via FAST, QFD, or other "brainstorming" techniques [JOR89]) is conducted, the analysis principles are applied, and a model of the software to be built, called a *prototype,* is constructed for customer and developer assessment. Finally, there are circumstances that require the construction of a prototype at the beginning of analysis, since the model is the only means through which requirements can be effectively derived. The model then evolves into production software.

Boar [BOA84] justifies the prototyping technique in this way:

> Most currently recommended methods for defining business system requirements are designed to establish a final, complete, consistent, and correct set of requirements before the system is designed, constructed, seen or experienced by the user. Common and recurring industry experience indicates that despite the use of rigorous techniques, in many cases users still reject applications as neither correct nor complete upon completion. Consequently, expensive, time-consuming, and divisive rework is required to harmonize the original specification with the definitive test of actual operational needs. In the worst case, rather than retrofit the delivered system, it is abandoned. Developers may build and test against specifications but users accept or reject against current and actual operational realities.

Although the above quote represents an extreme view, its fundamental argument is sound. In many (but not all) cases, the construction of a prototype, possibly coupled with systematic analysis methods, is an effective approach to software engineering.

11.4.1   Selecting the Prototyping Approach

The prototyping paradigm can be either closed-ended or open-ended. The closed-ended approach is often called *throwaway prototyping*. Using this approach, a prototype serves solely as a rough demonstration of requirements. It is then discarded, and the software is engineered using a different paradigm. An open-ended approach, called *evolutionary prototyping,* uses the prototype as the first part of an analysis activity that will be continued into design and construction. The prototype of the software is the first evolution of the finished system.

Before a closed-ended or open-ended approach can be chosen, it is necessary to determine whether the system to be built is amenable to prototyping. A number of prototyping candidacy factors [BOA84] can be defined: application area, application complexity, customer characteristics, and project characteristics.[7]

In general, any application that creates dynamic visual displays, interacts heavily with a human user, or demands algorithms or combinatorial processing that must be developed in an evolutionary fashion is a candidate for prototyping. However, these application areas must be weighed against application complexity. If a candidate application (one that has the characteristics noted above) will require the development of tens of thousands of lines of code before any demonstrable function can be performed, it is likely to be too complex for prototyping.[8] If the complexity can be partitioned, however, it may still be possible to prototype portions of the software.

Because the customer must interact with the prototype in later steps, it is essential that (1) customer resources be committed to the evaluation and refinement of the prototype, and (2) the customer be capable of making requirements decisions in a timely fashion. Finally, the nature of the development project will have a strong bearing on the efficacy of prototyping. Is project management willing and able to work with the prototyping method? Are prototyping tools available? Do developers have experience with prototyping methods?

Andriole [AND92] suggests a set of six questions that will assist in the selection of the prototyping approach:

- Is the application domain for which software is to be built understood by the customer and the developer?
- Does the problem to be solved lend itself to modeling?
- Is the customer fairly certain of basic system requirements?
- Are requirements fairly well established and likely to be reasonably stable?
- Are any requirements ambiguous?
- Are there contradictions in the requirements?

Figure 11.7 indicates typical sets of answers to these questions and the corresponding suggested prototyping approach.

---

[7]A useful discussion of other candidacy factors—"when to prototype"—can be found in [DAV95b].

[8]In some cases, extremely complex prototypes can be constructed rapidly by using fourth generation techniques or reusable software components.

Question	Throwaway Prototype	Evolutionary Prototype	Additional Preliminary Work Required
Is the application domain understood?	Yes	Yes	No
Can the problem be modeling?	Yes	Yes	No
Is the customer certain of basic system requirements?	Yes/No	Yes/No	No
Are requirements established/stable?	No	Yes	Yes
Are any requirements ambiguous?	Yes	No	Yes
Are there contradictions in the requirements?	Yes	No	Yes

FIGURE 11.7. Selecting the appropriate prototyping approach

11.4.2 Prototyping Methods and Tools

For software prototyping to be effective, a prototype must be developed rapidly so that the customer may assess results and recommend changes. To conduct *rapid prototyping,* three generic classes of methods and tools (e.g., [AND92], [TAN89]) are available: fourth generation techniques, reusable software components, formal specification and prototyping environments.

Fourth Generation Techniques Fourth generation techniques (4GT) encompass a broad array of data base query and reporting languages, program and application generators and other very high level nonprocedural languages. Because 4GT enable the software engineer to generate executable code quickly, they are ideal for rapid prototyping.

Reusable Software Components Another approach to rapid prototyping is to assemble, rather than build, the prototype by using a set of existing software components. A software component may be a data structure (or database) or a software architectural component (i.e., a program) or a procedural component (i.e., a module). In each case the software component must be designed in a manner that enables it to be reused without detailed knowledge of its internal workings.

Melding prototyping and program component reuse will work only if a library system is developed so that components that do exist can be catalogued and then retrieved. Although a number of tools have been developed to meet this need (e.g., [ARN87]), much work remains to be done in this area.

It should be noted that an existing software product can be used as a prototype for a "new, improved" competitive product. In a way, this is a form of reusability for software prototyping.

Formal Specification and Prototyping Environments Over the past two decades, a number of formal specification languages and tools have been developed as a replacement for natural language specification techniques. Today, developers of these formal languages are in the process of developing interactive environments that (1) enable an analyst to interactively create a language-based specification of a system or software, (2) invoke automated tools that translate the language-based specification into executable code, and (3) enable the customer to use the prototype executable code to refine formal requirements.

11.5   SPECIFICATION

There is no doubt that the mode of specification has much to do with the quality of solution. Software engineers who have been forced to work with incomplete, inconsistent, or misleading specifications have experienced the frustration and confusion that invariably results. The quality, timeliness, and completeness of the software suffers as a consequence.

11.5.1 Specification Principles

Specification, regardless of the mode through which we accomplish it, may be viewed as a representation process. Requirements are represented in a manner that ultimately leads to successful software implementation. A number of specification principles, adapted from the work of Balzer and Goldman [BAL86], can be proposed:

1. Separate functionality from implementation.
2. Develop a model of the desired behavior of a system that encompasses data and the functional responses of a system to various stimuli from the environment.
3. Establish the context in which software operates by specifying the manner in which other system components interact with software.
4. Define the environment in which the system operates and indicate how "a highly intertwined collection of agents react to stimuli in the environment (changes to objects) produced by those agents" [BAL86].
5. Create a cognitive model rather than a design or implementation model. The cognitive model describes a system as perceived by its user community.
6. Recognize that "the specification must be tolerant of incompleteness and augmentable." A specification is always a model—an abstraction—of some real (or envisioned) situation that is normally quite complex. Hence, it will be incomplete and will exist at many levels of detail.
7. Establish the content and structure of a specification in a way that will enable it to be amenable to change.

The list of basic specification principles noted above provides a basis for representing software requirements. However, principles must be translated into realization. In the next section we examine a set of guidelines for creating a specification of requirements.

11.5.2 Representation

Figure 11.8 is a classic example of a good specification. The drawing, taken from Galileo's work (circa 1638), is used to supplement text that describes his method for the analysis of the strength of a beam. Even without the accompanying text, the diagram helps us to understand what must be done.

We have already seen that software requirements may be specified in a variety of ways. However, if requirements are committed to paper or an electronic presentation medium (and they almost always should be!) a simple set of guidelines is well worth following:

Representation format and content should be relevant to the problem. A general outline for the contents of a software requirements specification can be developed. However, the representation forms contained within the specification are likely to vary with the application area. For example, a specification of a manufacturing automation system would use different symbology, diagrams, and language than the specification for a programming language compiler.

Information contained within the specification should be nested. Representations should reveal layers of information so that a reader can move

FIGURE 11.8.
Representation of specification (Source: Galileo's *Discorsi e Dimonstrazioni Matematiche ubtorno a due nuovo science*, Leyden, 1638; from J. D. Bernal, *Science in History*, London, Watts, 1969)

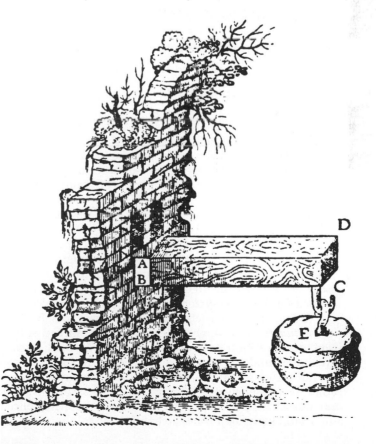

to the level of detail that is required. Paragraph and diagram numbering schemes should indicate the level of detail that is being presented. It is sometimes worthwhile to present the same information at different levels of abstraction to aid in understanding.

Diagrams and other notational forms should be restricted in number and consistent in use.   Confusing or inconsistent notation, whether graphical or symbolic, degrades understanding and fosters errors.

Representations should be revisable.   The content of a specification will change. Ideally, CASE tools should be available to update all representations that are affected by each change.

Investigators have conducted numerous studies (e.g., [HOL95], [CUR85]) on human factors associated with specification. There appears to be little doubt that symbology and arrangement affect understanding. However, software engineers appear to have individual preferences for specific symbolic and diagrammatic forms. Familiarity often lies at the root of a person's preference, but other more tangible factors such as spatial arrangement, easily recognizable patterns, and degree of formality often dictate an individual's choice.

11.5.3   The Software Requirements Specification

The software requirements specification is produced at the culmination of the analysis task. The function and performance allocated to software as part of system engineering are refined by establishing a complete information description, a detailed functional and behavioral description, an indication of performance requirements and design constraints, appropriate validation criteria, and other data pertinent to requirements. The National Bureau of Standards, IEEE (Standard No. 830-1984) and the U.S. Department of Defense have all proposed candidate formats for software requirements specifications (as well as other software engineering documentation). For our purposes, however, the simplified outline presented in Figure 11.9 may be used as a framework for the specification.

The *introduction* states the goals and objectives of the software, describing it in the context of the computer-based system. Actually, the introduction may be nothing more than the software scope of the planning document.

The *information description* provides a detailed description of the problem that the software must solve. Information content and relationships, flow and structure are documented. Hardware, software, and human interfaces are described for external system elements and internal software functions.

A description of each function required to solve the problem is presented in the *functional description*. A processing narrative is provided for each function; design constraints are stated and justified; performance characteristics are stated; and one or more diagrams are included to graphically represent the overall structure of the software and interplay among software functions and other system elements. The *behavioral description* section of the specification examines the operation of the software as a consequence of external events and internally generated control characteristics.

I. Introduction
    A. System reference
    B. Overall description
    C. Software project constraints
II. Information Description
    A. Information content representation
    B. Information flow representation
       1. Data flow
       2. Control flow
III. Functional Description
    A. Functional partitioning
    B. Functional description
       1. Processing narrative
       2. Restrictions/limitations
       3. Performance requirements
       4. Design constraints
       5. Supporting diagrams
    C. Control Description
       1. Control specification
       2. Design constraints
IV. Behavioral Description
    A. System states
    B. Events and actions
V. Validation and Criteria
    A. Performance bounds
    B. Classes of tests
    C. Expected software response
    D. Special considerations
VI. Bibliography
VII. Appendix

FIGURE 11.9.
Software require-
ments specification
outline

Probably the most important, and ironically, the most often neglected section of a software requirements specification is *validation criteria*. How do we recognize a successful implementation? What classes of tests must be conducted to validate function, performance, and constraints? We neglect this section because completing it demands a thorough understanding of software requirements—something that we often do not have at this stage. Yet, specification of validation criteria acts as an implicit review of all other requirements. It is essential that time and attention be given to this section.

Finally, the software requirements specification includes a *bibliography* and *appendix*. The bibliography contains references to all documents that relate to the software. These include other software engineering documentation, technical references, vendor literature, and standards. The appendix contains information that supplements the specification. Tabular data, detailed description of algorithms, charts, graphs, and other material are presented as appendices.

In many cases a software requirements specification may be accompanied by an executable prototype (that in some cases may replace the specification), a paper prototype, or a *preliminary user's manual*. The preliminary user's manual presents the software as a black box. That is, heavy emphasis is placed on user input and resultant output. The manual can serve as a valuable tool for uncovering problems at the human–machine interface.

11.6   SPECIFICATION REVIEW

Review of a software requirements specification (and/or prototype) is conducted by both software developer and customer. Because the specification forms the foundation for design and subsequent software engineering activities, extreme care should be taken in conducting the review.

The review is first conducted at a *macroscopic* level. At this level, the reviewers attempt to ensure that the specification is complete, consistent, and accurate. The following questions are addressed:

- Do stated goals and objectives for software remain consistent with system goals and objectives?
- Have important interfaces to all system elements been described?
- Is information flow and structure adequately defined for the problem domain?
- Are diagrams clear? Can each stand alone without supplementary text?
- Do major functions remain within scope, and has each been adequately described?
- Is the behavior of the software consistent with the information it must process and the functions it must perform?
- Are design constraints realistic?
- Have the technological risks of development been considered?
- Have alternative software requirements been considered?
- Have validation criteria been stated in detail? Are they adequate to describe a successful system?
- Do inconsistencies, omissions, or redundancy exist?
- Is the customer contact complete?
- Has the user reviewed the preliminary user's manual or prototype?
- How are planing estimates affected?

In order to develop answers to many of the above questions, the review may focus at a detailed level. Here, our concern is on the wording of the specification. We attempt to uncover problems that may be hidden within the specification content. The following guidelines for a detailed specification review are suggested:

- Be on the lookout for persuasive connectors (e.g., certainly, therefore, clearly, obviously, it follows that), and ask "why?"

- Watch out for vague terms (e.g., some, sometimes, often, usually, ordinarily, most, mostly); ask for clarification.
- When lists are given, but not completed, be sure all items are understood. Keys to look for: "etc., and so forth, and so on, such as."
- Be sure stated ranges don't contain unstated assumptions (e.g., *Valid codes range from 10 to 100*. Integer? Real? Hex?).
- Beware of vague verbs such as "handled, rejected, processed, skipped, eliminated." They can be interpreted in many ways.
- Beware ambiguous pronouns (e.g., *The I/O module communicates with the data validation module and its control flag is set*. Whose control flag?)
- Look for statements that imply certainty (e.g., always, every, all, none, never), then ask for proof.
- When a term is explicitly defined in one place, try substituting the definition for other occurrences of the term.
- When a structure is described in words, draw a picture to aid in understanding.
- When a calculation is specified, work at least two examples.

Once the review is complete, a software requirements specification is "signed off" by both customer and developer. The specification becomes a "contract" for software development. Changes in requirements requested after the specification is finalized will not be eliminated, but the customer should note that each after-the-fact change is an extension of software scope and therefore can increase cost and/or protract the project schedule.

Even with the best review procedures in place, a number of common specification problems persist. The specification is difficult to "test" in any meaningful way, so inconsistency or omissions may pass unnoticed. During the review, changes to the specification may be recommended. It can be extremely difficult to assess the global impact of a change; that is, how does a change in one function affect requirements for other functions? Modern software engineering environments (Chapter 29) incorporate CASE tools that have been developed to help solve these problems.

11.7   SUMMARY

Requirements analysis is the first technical step in the software engineering process. It is at this point that a general statement of software scope is refined into a concrete specification that becomes the foundation for all software engineering activities that follow.

Analysis must focus on the information, functional, and behavioral domains of a problem. To better understand what is required, models are created, the problem is partitioned, and representations that depict the essence of requirements and later, implementation detail, are developed.

In many cases, it is not possible to completely specify a problem at an early stage. Prototyping offers an alternative approach that results in an executable model of the software from which requirements can be refined. To properly conduct prototyping special tools and techniques are required.

A software requirements specification is developed as a consequence of analysis. Review is essential to ensure that developer and customer have the same perception of the system. Unfortunately, even with the best of methods, the problem is that the problem keeps changing.

REFERENCES

[AKA90]   Akao, Y. (ed.), *Quality Function Deployment: Integrating Customer Requirements in Product Design* (translated by G. Mazur), Productivity Press, Cambridge MA, 1990.

[AND92]   Andriole, S. *Rapid Application Prototyping,* QED, 1992.

[ARN87]   Arnold, S.P., and S.L. Stepoway, "The Reuse System: Cataloging and Retrieval of Reusable Software," *Proc. COMPCON,* 1987, pp. 376–379.

[BAL86]   Balzer, R., and N. Goodman, "Principles of Good Specification and their Implications for Specification Languages," in *Software Specification Techniques* (N. Gehani and A.D. McGettrick, eds.), Addison-Wesley, 1986, pp. 25–39.

[BOA84]   Boar, B., *Application Prototyping,* Wiley-Interscience, 1984.

[BOS91]   Bossert, J.L., *Quality Function Deployment: A Practitioner's Approach,* ASQC Press, 1991.

[CUR85]   Curtis, B., *Human Factors in Software Development,* IEEE Computer Society Press, 1985.

[DAV93]   Davis, A., *Software Requirements: Objects, Functions and States,* Prentice-Hall, 1993.

[DAV95a] Davis, A., *201 Principles of Software Development,* McGraw-Hill, 1995.

[DAV95b] Davis, A., "Software Prototyping," in *Advances in Computers,* vol. 40, Academic Press, 1995.

[GAU89]   Gause, D.C., and G.M. Weinberg, *Exploring Requirements: Quality Before Design,* Dorset House, 1989.

[HOL95]   Holtzblatt, K., and E. Carmel (eds.), *Requirements Gathering: The Human Factor,* a special issue of *Communications of the ACM,* vol. 38, no. 5, May 1995.

[JOR89]   Jordan, P.W. et al., "Software Storming: Combining Rapid Prototyping and Knowledge Engineering," *IEEE Computer,* vol. 22, no. 5, May 1989, pp. 39–50.

[TAN89]   Tanik, M.M., and R.T. Yeh (eds.), "Rapid Prototyping in Software Development," a special issue of *IEEE Computer,* vol. 22, no. 5, May 1989.

[ZAH90]   Zahniser, R.A., "Building Software in Groups," *American Programmer,* vol. 3, no. 7/8, July/August 1990.

[ZUL92]   Zultner, R., "Quality Function Deployment for Software: Satisfying Customers," *American Programmer,* February 1992, pp. 28–41.

PROBLEMS AND POINTS TO PONDER

11.1. Software requirements analysis is unquestionably the most communication intensive step in the software engineering process. Why does the communication path frequently break down?

11.2. There are frequently severe political repercussions when software requirements analysis (and/or system analysis) begins. For example, workers may feel that job security is threatened by a new automated system. What causes such problems? Can the analysis task be conducted so that politics is minimized?

11.3. Discuss your perceptions of the ideal training and background for a systems analyst.

11.4. Throughout this chapter we refer to the "customer." Describe the "customer" for information systems developers, for builders of computer-based products, for systems builders. Be careful here, there may be more to this problem that you first imagine!

11.5. Develop a facilitated application specification techniques (FAST) "kit." The kit should include a set of guidelines for conducting a FAST meeting, materials that can be used to facilitate the creation of lists, and any other items that might help in defining requirements.

11.6. Your instructor will divide the class into groups of four or six students. Half of the group will play the role of the marketing department, and half will take on the role of software engineering. Your job is to define requirements for the SafeHome security system described in this chapter. Conduct a FAST meeting using the guidelines presented in this chapter.

11.7. Is it fair to say that a preliminary user's manual is a form of prototype? Explain your answer.

11.8. Analyze the information domain for SafeHome. Represent (using any notation that seems appropriate) information flow in the system, information content, and any information structure that is relevant.

11.9. Partition the functional domain for SafeHome. First perform horizontal partitioning; then perform vertical partitioning.

11.10. Create essential and implementation representations of the SafeHome system.

11.11. Build a paper prototype (or a real prototype) of SafeHome. Be sure to depict owner interaction and overall system function.

11.12. Try to identify software components of SafeHome that might be "reusable" in other products or systems. Attempt to categorize these components.

11.13. Develop a written specification for SafeHome using the outline provided in Figure 11.9. [Note: Your instructor will suggest which sections to complete at this time.] Be sure to apply the questions that are described for the specification review.

11.14. How did your requirements differ from others who attempted a solution for SafeHome? Who built a "Chevy"? Who built a "Cadillac?"

FURTHER READINGS AND OTHER INFORMATION SOURCES

Requirements analysis is a communication intensive activity. If communication fails, even the best technical approach will fall short. Books by Gause and Weinberg (*Are Your Lights On?,* Dorset House, 1991), Davis [DAV93], and Kilov and Ross (*Information Modeling: An Object-Oriented Approach,* Prentice-Hall, 1994) contain excellent discussion of requirements analysis principles and concepts. A book of short essays by Jackson (*Software Requirements and Specifications,* Addison-Wesley, 1995) presents opinion and guidance from one of the experts in the field.

A comprehensive discussion of one requirements gathering method, Joint Application Design, is presented by Wood and Silver (*Joint Application Design,* 2nd edition, Wiley, 1995). Worthwhile guidelines for conducting FAST meetings are also presented by Cohen (*Quality Function Deployment,* Addison-Wesley, 1995), Gause and Weinberg [GAU89], and Zahniser [ZAH90]. The authors discuss the mechanics of effective meetings, methods for brainstorming, approaches that can be used to clarify results, and a variety of other useful issues. A book by Martin (*User Centered Requirements Analysis,* Prentice-Hall, 1988) also discusses the need for effective customer-developer communication.

Information domain analysis is a fundamental principle of requirements analysis. Books by Mattison (*The Object-Oriented Enterprise,* McGraw-Hill, 1994), Tillman (*A Practical Guide to Logical Data Modelling,* McGraw-Hill, 1993), and Modell (*Data Analysis, Data Modeling and Classification,* McGraw-Hill, 1992) cover various aspects of this important subject. Gehani and McGettrick (*Software Specification Techniques,* Addison-Wesley, 1986) have edited an important anthology of papers on software analysis topics, ranging from basic principles of specification to advanced specification and design environments. The results of more recent research can be obtained from the *Proceedings of the International Symposium on Requirements Engineering* sponsored by the IEEE.

Boar's book on application prototyping [BOA84] and a book by Connell and Shafer (*Structured Rapid Prototyping,* Prentice-Hall, 1989) present this important analysis technique with a definite information systems flavor. However, many topics discussed by the authors are applicable across all application domains. The *Proceedings of the International Conference on Rapid Prototyping* sponsored by the IEEE presents an excellent overview of developments in rapid prototyping.

The Requirements Engineering Newsletter (an on-line publication) can be acquired from:

http://web.cs.city.ac.uk/homes/acwf/rehome.html

An extensive bibliography on requirements engineering can be obtained at:

http://www.ida.liu.se/labs/aslab/people/joaka/re_bib.html

Additional information of requirements engineering, enterprise modeling, and related topics can be found at:

http://mijuno.larc.nasa.gov/dfc/re.html

An up-to-date list of World Wide Web references that are relevant to software analysis activities can be found at: **http://www.rspa.com**

CHAPTER 12

ANALYSIS MODELING

At a technical level, software engineering begins with a series of modeling tasks that lead to a complete specification of requirements and a comprehensive design representation for the software to be built. The analysis model, actually a set of models, is the first technical representation of a system. Over the years many methods have been proposed for analysis modeling. However, two now dominate the analysis modeling landscape. The first, *structured analysis,* is a classical modeling method and is described in this chapter. The other approach, *object-oriented analysis,* is considered in detail in Chapter 20. A brief overview of other commonly used analysis methods is presented in Section 12.8.

Structured analysis is a model building activity. Using a notation that satisfies the operational analysis principles discussed in Chapter 11, we create models that depict information (data and control) content and flow, we partition the system functionally and behaviorally, and we depict the essence of what must be built. Structured analysis is not a single method applied consistently by all who use it. Rather, it is an amalgam that has evolved over almost 20 years.

There is probably no other software engineering method that has generated as much interest, been tried (and often rejected and then tried again) by as many people, provoked as much criticism, and sparked as much controversy, but the method has prospered and has gained a substantial following in the software engineering community.

In his seminal book on the subject, Tom DeMarco [DEM79] describes structured analysis in this way:

> Looking back over the recognized problems and failings of the analysis phase, I suggest that we need to make the following additions to our set of analysis phase goals:

- The products of analysis must be highly maintainable. This applies particularly to the Target Document [software requirements specification].
- Problems of size must be dealt with using an effective method of partitioning. The Victorian novel specification is out.
- Graphics have to be used whenever possible.
- We have to differentiate between logical [essential] and physical [implementation] considerations ...

At the very least, we need ...

- Something to help us partition our requirements and document that partitioning before specification ...
- Some means of keeping track of and evaluating interfaces ...
- New tools to describe logic and policy, something better than narrative text ...

With these words, DeMarco establishes the primary goals of an analysis method that has become the most widely used in the world. In this chapter, we examine this method and its extensions.

12.1   A BRIEF HISTORY

Like many important contributions to software engineering, structured analysis was not introduced with a single landmark paper or book that was a definitive treatment of the subject. Early work in analysis modeling was begun in the late 1960s and early 1970s, but the first appearance of the structured analysis approach was as an adjunct to another important topic—structured design. Researchers (e.g., [STE74], [YOU78]) needed a graphical notation for representing data and the processes that transformed it. These processes would ultimately be mapped into a design architecture.

The term "structured analysis," originally coined by Douglas Ross, was popularized by DeMarco [DEM79]. In his book on the subject, DeMarco introduced and named the key graphical symbols that enabled an analyst to create information flow models, suggested heuristics for the use of these symbols, suggested that a *data dictionary* and *processing narratives* could be used as a supplement to the information flow models, and presented numerous examples that illustrated the use of this new method. In the years that followed, variations of the structured analysis approach were suggested by Page-Jones [PAG80], Gane and Sarson [GAN82], and many others. In every instance, the method focused on information systems applications and did not provide an adequate notation to address the control and behavioral aspects of real-time engineering problems.

By the mid-1980s, the deficiencies of structured analysis (when attempts were made to apply the method to control-oriented applications) became painfully apparent. Real-time "extensions" were introduced by Ward and Mellor [WAR85] and later by Hatley and Pirbhai [HAT87]. These extensions resulted in a more robust analysis method that could be applied effectively to engineering problems. Attempts to develop one consistent notation have been suggested [BRU88], and modernized treatments have been published to accommodate the use of CASE tools [YOU89].

12.2   THE ELEMENTS OF THE ANALYSIS MODEL

The analysis model must achieve three primary objectives: (1) to describe what the customer requires, (2) to establish a basis for the creation of a software design, and (3) to define a set of requirements that can be validated once the software is built. To accomplish these objectives, the analysis model derived during structured analysis takes the form illustrated in Figure 12.1.

At the core of the model lies the *data dictionary*—a repository that contains descriptions of all data objects consumed or produced by the software. Three different diagrams surround the core. The *entity-relationship diagram (ERD)* depicts relationships between data objects. The ERD is the notation that is used to conduct the data modeling activity. The attributes of each data object noted in the ERD can be described using a *data object description*.

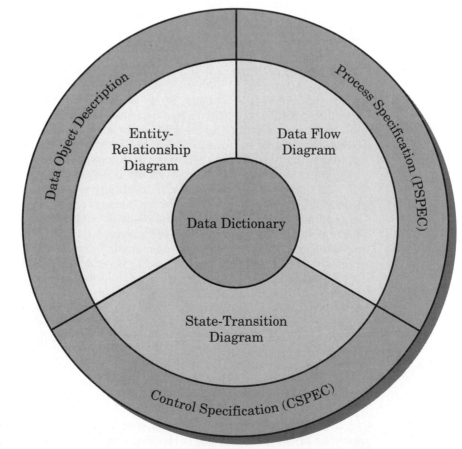

FIGURE 12.1.
The structure of the analysis model

The *data flow diagram (DFD)* serves two purposes: (1) to provide an indication of how data are transformed as they move through the system, and (2) to depict the functions (and subfunctions) that transform the data flow. The DFD provides additional information that is used during the analysis of the information domain and serves as a basis for the modeling of function. A description of each function presented in the DFD is contained in a *process specification (PSPEC)*.

The *state-transition diagram (STD)* indicates how the system behaves as a consequence of external events. To accomplish this, the STD represents the various modes of behavior (called *states*) of the system and the manner in which transitions are made from state to state. The STD serves as the basis for behavioral modeling. Additional information about control aspects of the software is contained in the *control specification (CSPEC)*.

The analysis model encompasses each of the diagrams, specifications, and descriptions, and the dictionary noted in Figure 12.1. A more detailed discussion of these elements of the analysis model is presented in the sections that follow.

12.3   DATA MODELING

Data modeling answers a set of specific questions that are relevant to any data processing application. What are the primary *data objects* to be processed by the system? What is the composition of each data object and what attributes describe the object? Where do the objects currently reside? What are the relationships between each object and other objects? What is the relationship between the objects and the processes that transform them?

To answer these questions, data modeling methods make use of the entity-relationship diagram (ERD). The ERD, described in detail later in this section, enables a software engineer to identify data objects and their relationships using a graphical notation. In the context of structured analysis, the ERD defines all data that are input, stored, transformed, and produced within an application.

The entity-relationship diagram focuses solely on data (and therefore satisfies the first operational analysis principle), representing a "data network" that exists for a given system. The ERD is especially useful for applications in which data and the relationships that govern data are complex. Unlike the data flow diagram (discussed in Section 12.4 and used to represent how data are transformed), data modeling considers data independently of the processing that transforms the data.

12.3.1 Data Objects, Attributes, and Relationships

The data model consists of three interrelated pieces of information: the data object, the attributes that describe the data object, and the relationships that connect data objects to one another.

Data objects   A *data object* is a representation of almost any composite information that must be understood by software. By *composite information,* we mean

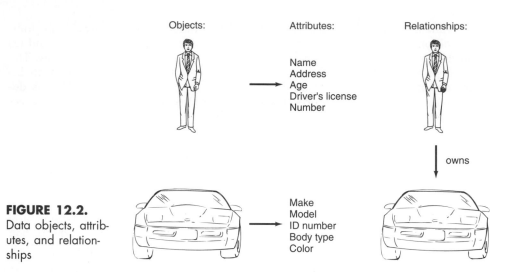

Objects: Attributes: Relationships:

Name
Address
Age
Driver's license
Number

owns

Make
Model
ID number
Body type
Color

FIGURE 12.2.
Data objects, attrib-
utes, and relation-
ships

something that has a number of different properties or attributes. Therefore,
"width" (a single value) would not be a valid data object, but **dimensions** (incorporating height, width, and depth) could be defined as an object.

A data object can be an external entity (e.g., anything that produces or con-
sumes information), a thing (e.g., a report or a display), an occurrence (e.g., a telephone call) or event (e.g., an alarm), a role (e.g., salesperson), an organizational
unit (e.g., accounting department), a place (e.g., a warehouse), or a structure (e.g.,
a file). For example, a **person** or a **car** (Figure 12.2) can be viewed as a data object in the sense that either can be defined in terms of a set of attributes. The
data object description incorporates the data object and all of its attributes.

Data objects are related to one another. For example, **person** can *own* **car,**
where the relationship *own* connotes a specific connection between **person** and
car. The relationships are always defined by the context of the problem that is
being analyzed.

A data object encapsulates data *only*—there is no reference within a data
object to operations that act on the data.[1] Therefore, the data object can be represented as a table as shown in Figure 12.3. The headings in the table reflect
attributes of the object. In this case, a car is defined in terms of make, model,
ID#, body type, color, and owner. The body of the table represents specific instances of the data object. For example, a Chevy Corvette is an instance of the
data object **car.**

Attributes   Attributes define the properties of a data object and take on one of
three different characteristics. They can be used to (1) name an instance of the
data object, (2) describe the instance, or (3) make reference to another instance
in another table. In addition, one or more of the attributes must be defined as
an *identifier*—that is, the identifier attribute becomes a "key" when we want to

---

[1]This distinction separates the data object from the *class* or *object* defined as part of the
object oriented paradigm discussed in Part Four of this book.

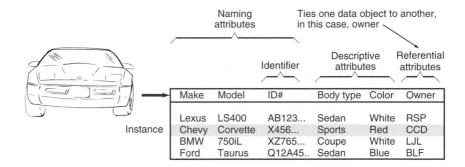

FIGURE 12.3.
Tabular representation of data objects

find an instance of the data object. In some cases, values for the identifier(s) are unique, although this is not a requirement. Referring to the data object **car,** a reasonable identifier might be the ID#.

The set of attributes that is appropriate for a given data object is determined through an understanding of the problem context. The attributes for **car** described above might serve well for an application that would be used by a Department of Motor Vehicles, but these attributes would be useless for an automobile company that needs manufacturing control software. In the latter case, the attributes for **car** might also include ID#, body type, and color, but many additional attributes (e.g., interior code, drive train type, trim package designator, transmission type) would have to be added to make **car** a meaningful object in the manufacturing control context.

Relationships Data objects are connected to one another in a variety of different ways. Consider two data objects, **book** and **bookstore.** These objects can be represented using the simple notation illustrated in Figure 12.4a. A connection is established between **book** and **bookstore** because the two objects are related. But what are the relationships? To determine the answer, we must

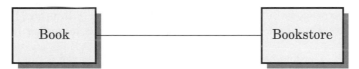

(a) A basic connection between objects

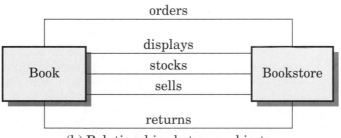

FIGURE 12.4.
Relationships

(b) Relationships between objects

understand the role of books and bookstores within the context of the software to be built. We can define a set of *object–relationship pairs* that define the relevant relationships. For example,

- a bookstore orders books
- a bookstore displays books
- a bookstore stocks books
- a bookstore sells books
- a bookstore returns books

The relationships *orders, displays, stocks, sells,* and *returns* define the relevant connections between **book** and **bookstore.** Figure 12.4b illustrates these object–relationship pairs graphically.

It is important to note that object–relationship pairs are bidirectional; that is, they can be read in either direction. A bookstore *orders* books or books *are ordered by* a bookstore.[2]

12.3.2 Cardinality and Modality

The basic elements of data modeling—data objects, attributes, and relationships—provide the basis for understanding the information domain of a problem. However, additional information related to these basic elements must also be understood.

We have defined a set of objects and represented the object–relationship pairs that bind them. But a simple pair that states: **object X** *relates to* **object Y** does not provide enough information for software engineering purposes. We must understand how many occurrences of **object X** are related to how many occurrences of **object Y.** This leads to a data modeling concept called *cardinality.*

Cardinality The data model must be capable of representing the number of occurrences of objects in a given relationship. Tillmann [TIL93] defines the cardinality of an object–relationship pair in the following manner:

> Cardinality is the specification of the number of occurrences of one [object] that can be related to the number of occurrences of another [object]. Cardinality is usually expressed as simply 'one' or 'many.' For example, a husband can have only *one* wife (in most cultures), while a parent can have *many* children. Taking into consideration all combinations of 'one' and 'many,' two [objects] can be related as
>
> - One-to-one (1:1)—An occurrence of [object] 'A' can relate to one and only one occurrence of [object] 'B,' and an occurrence of 'B' can relate to only one occurrence of 'A.' For example, a husband can have only one wife, and a wife only one husband (at least here in New Jersey).

---

[2]To avoid ambiguity, the manner in which a relationship is labeled must be considered. For example, if context is not considered for a bidirectional relation, Figure 12.4b could be misinterpreted to mean that books *order* bookstores. In such cases, rephrasing is necessary.

- One-to-many (1:N)—One occurrence of [object] 'A' can relate to one or many occurrences of [object] 'B,' but an occurrence of 'B' can relate to only one occurrence of 'A.' For example, a mother can have many children, but a child can have only one mother.

- Many-to-many (M:N)—An occurrence of [object] 'A' can relate to one or more occurrences of 'B,' while an occurrence of 'B' can relate to one or more occurrences of 'A.' For example, an uncle can have many nephews, while a nephew can have many uncles.

Cardinality defines "the maximum number of object relationships that can participate in a relationship" [TIL93]. It does not, however, provide an indication of whether or not a particular data object must participate in the relationship. To specify this information, the data model adds *modality* to the object–relationship pair.

Modality The modality of a relationship is zero if there is no explicit need for the relationship to occur or the relationship is optional. The modality is 1 if an occurrence of the relationship is mandatory. To illustrate, consider software that is used by a local telephone company to process requests for field service. A customer indicates that there is a problem. If the problem is diagnosed as relatively simple, a single repair action occurs. However, if the problem is complex, multiple repair actions may be required. Figure 12.5 illustrates the relationship, cardinality, and modality between the data objects **customer** and **repair action**.

In the figure, a *1 to many* cardinality relationship is established. That is, a single customer can be provided with zero or many repair actions.[3] The symbols[4] on the relationship connection closest to the data object rectangles indicate cardinality. The vertical bar indicates 1, and the three-pronged fork indicates many. Modality is indicated by the symbols that are further away from the data object rectangles. The second vertical bar on the left indicates that there must be a customer for a repair action to occur. The circle on the right indicates that there may be no repair action required for the type of problem reported by the customer.

12.3.3   Entity-Relationship Diagrams

The object–relationship pair (discussed in Section 12.3.1) is the cornerstone of the data model. These pairs can be represented graphically using the *entity-relationship diagram* (ERD).[5] The ERD was originally proposed by Peter Chen [CHE77] for the design of relational database systems and has been extended by others. A set of primary components are identified for the ERD: data objects,

---

[3]There may be a situation in which a repair action is not required.

[4]It is important to note that many different symbols have been proposed for representing relationships, cardinality, and modality. Alternative notations are presented in Section 12.3.4.

[5]Today, the term "data entity" or "entity" has been replaced by "data object." However, the term "entity" remains a part of the name of the graphical notation for object–relationship pairs.

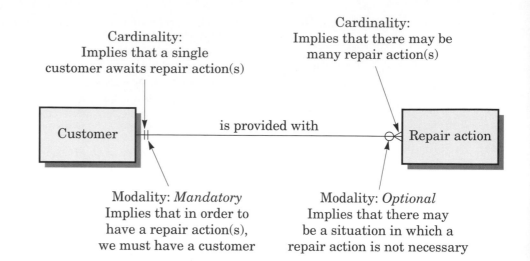

FIGURE 12.5.
Cardinality and
modality

attributes, relationships, and various type indicators. The primary purpose of
the ERD is to represent data objects and their relationships.

Rudimentary ERD notation has already been introduced in Section 12.3.
Data objects are represented by a labeled rectangle. Relationships are indicated
with a labeled line connecting objects. In some variations of the ERD, the connecting line contains a diamond that is labeled with the relationship.
Connections between data objects and relationships are established using a variety of special symbols that indicate cardinality and modality (Section 12.3.2).

The relationship between data objects **car** and **manufacturer** would be
represented as shown in Figure 12.6. One manufacturer builds one or many
cars. Given the context implied by the ERD, the specification of the data object

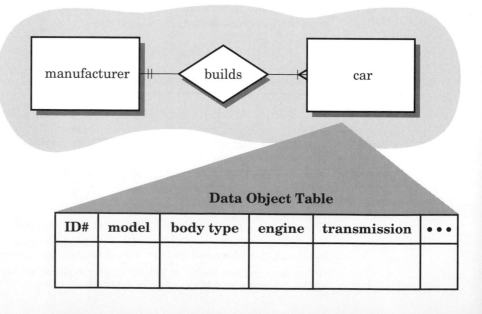

FIGURE 12.6.
A simple ERD and
data object table
(Note: In this ERD
the relationship
builds is indicated
by a diamond on
the connecting line
between data ob-
jects)

Data Object Table

ID#	model	body type	engine	transmission	• • •

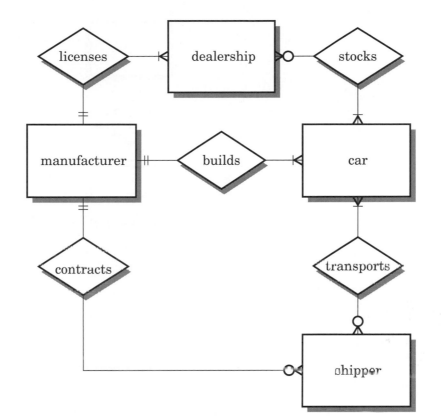

FIGURE 12.7.
An expanded ERD

car (see the data object table in Figure 12.6) would be radically different from
the earlier specification (Figure 12.3). By examining the symbols at the end of
the connection line between objects, it can be seen that the modality of both occurrences is mandatory (the vertical lines).

Expanding the model, we represent a grossly oversimplified ERD (Figure
12.7) of the distribution element of the automobile business. New data objects,
shipper and **dealership,** are introduced. In addition, new relationships —
transports, contracts, licenses and *stocks*—indicate how the data objects shown
in the figure associate with one another. Tables for each of the data objects contained in the ERD would have to be developed according to the rules introduced
earlier in this chapter.

In addition to the basic ERD notation introduced in Figures 12.6 and 12.7,
the analyst can represent *data object type hierarchies*. In many instances, a
data object may actually represent a class or category of information. For example, the data object **car** can be categorized as domestic, European, or Asian.
The ERD notation shown in Figure 12.8 represents this categorization in the
form of a hierarchy.

ERD notation also provides a mechanism that represents the associativity
between objects. An *associative data object* is represented as shown in Figure
12.9. In the figure, the data objects that model individual subsystems are each
associated with the data object **car.**

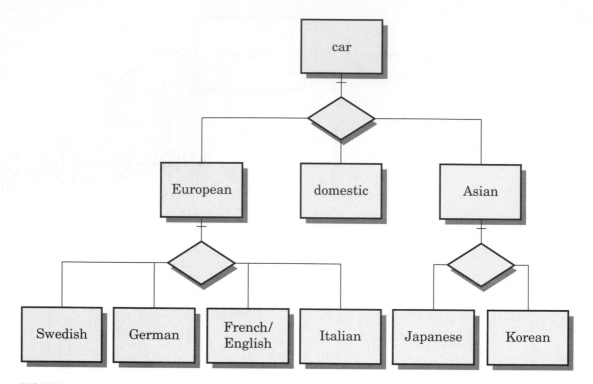

FIGURE 12.8. Data object type hierachies

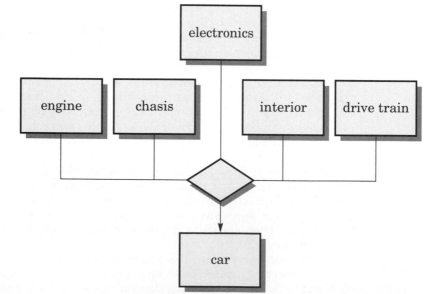

FIGURE 12.9.
Associating data objects

Data modeling and the entity-relationship diagram provide the analyst with a concise notation for examining data within the context of a data processing application. In most cases, the data modeling approach is used to create one piece of the analysis model, but it can also be used for database design and to support any other requirements analysis method.

12.4 FUNCTIONAL MODELING AND INFORMATION FLOW

Information is transformed as it *flows* through a computer-based system. The system accepts input in a variety of forms; applies hardware, software, and human elements to transform input into output; and produces output in a variety of forms. Input may be a control signal transmitted by a transducer, a series of numbers typed by a human operator, a packet of information transmitted on a network link, or a voluminous data file retrieved from a CD-ROM. The transform(s) may comprise a single logical comparison, a complex numerical algorithm or rule-inference approach of an expert system. Output may light a single LED or produce a 200-page report. In effect, we can create a *flow model* for any computer-based system, regardless of size and complexity.

Structured analysis began as an information flow modeling technique. A computer-based system is represented as an information transform as shown in Figure 12.10. Overall function of the system is represented as a single information transform, noted as a *bubble* in the figure. One or more inputs, shown as labeled arrows, originate from external entities, represented as a box. The input drives the transform to produce output information (also represented as labeled arrows) that is passed to the external entities. It should be noted that the model may be applied to the entire system or to the software element only. The key is to represent the information fed into and produced by the transform.

12.4.1 Data Flow Diagrams

As information moves through software, it is modified by a series of transformations. A *data flow diagram (DFD)* is a graphical technique that depicts information flow and the transforms that are applied as data move from input to output. The basic form of a data flow diagram is illustrated in Figure 12.10. The DFD is also known as a *data flow graph* or a *bubble chart*.

The data flow diagram may be used to represent a system or software at any level of abstraction. In fact, DFDs may be partitioned into levels that represent increasing information flow and functional detail. Therefore, the DFD provides a mechanism for functional modeling as well as information flow modeling. In so doing, it satisfies the second operational analysis principle (i.e., creating a functional model) discussed in Chapter 11.

A level 0 DFD, also called a *fundamental system model* or a *context model*, represents the entire software element as a single bubble with input and output data indicated by incoming and outgoing arrows, respectively. Additional processes (bubbles) and information flow paths are represented as the level 0

DFD is partitioned to reveal more detail. For example, a level 1 DFD might contain five or six bubbles with interconnecting arrows. Each of the processes represented at level 1 are subfunctions of the overall system depicted in the context model.

The basic notation[6] used to create a DFD is illustrated in Figure 12.11. A rectangle is used to represent an *external entity,* that is, a system element (e.g., hardware, a person, another program) or another system that produces infor-

---

[6]Extensions to the basic notation are discussed in Section 12.4.2.

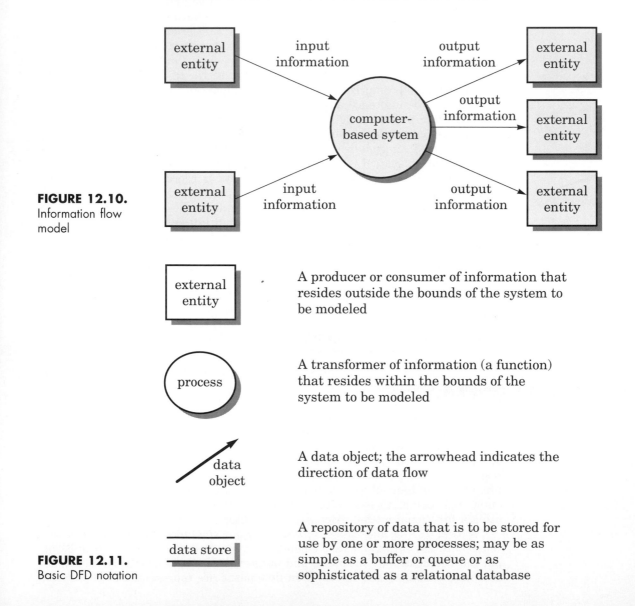

FIGURE 12.10.
Information flow model

FIGURE 12.11.
Basic DFD notation

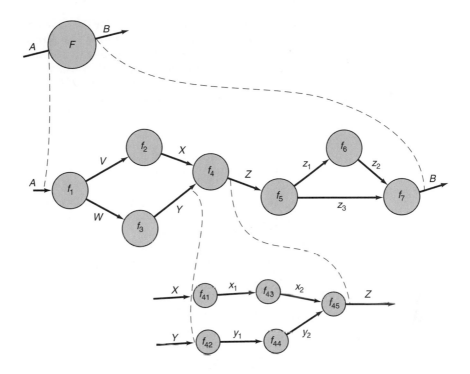

FIGURE 12.12.
Information flow
refinement

mation for transformation by the software or receives information produced by
the software. A circle represents a *process* or *transform* that is applied to data
(or control) and changes it in some way. An arrow represents one or more data
items or data objects. All arrows on a data flow diagram should be labeled. The
double line represents a *data store*—stored information that is used by the software. The simplicity of DFD notation is one reason why structured analysis
techniques are the most widely used.

It is important to note that no explicit indication of the sequence of processing is supplied by the diagram. Procedure or sequence may be implicit in
the diagram, but explicit procedural representation is generally delayed until
software design.

As we noted earlier, each of the bubbles may be refined or layered to depict
more detail. Figure 12.12 illustrates this concept. A fundamental model for system F indicates the primary input is A and ultimate output is B. We refine the
F model into transforms f_1 to f_7. Note that *information flow continuity* must be
maintained, that is, input and output to each refinement must remain the same.
This concept, sometimes called *balancing*, is essential for the development of
consistent models. Further refinement of f_4 depicts detail in the form of transforms f_{41} to f_{45}. Again, the input (X, Y) and output (Z) remain unchanged.

The data flow diagram is a graphical tool that can be very valuable during
software requirements analysis. However, the diagram can be misinterpreted if
its function is confused with the flowchart. A data flow diagram depicts information flow without explicit representation of procedural logic (e.g., conditions
or loops). It is not a flowchart with rounded edges!

The basic notation used to develop a DFD is not in itself sufficient to describe requirements for software. For example, an arrow shown in a DFD represents a data object that is input to or output from a process. A data store represents some organized collection of data. But what is the *content* of the data implied by the arrow or depicted by the store? If the arrow (or the store) represents a collection of objects, what are they? These questions are answered by applying another component of the basic notation for structured analysis—the *data dictionary*.[7] The format and use of the data dictionary are presented later in this chapter.

Finally, the graphical notation represented in Figure 12.11 must be augmented with descriptive text. A *processing specification (PSPEC)* can be used to specify the processing details implied by a bubble within a DFD. The processing specification describes the input to a function, the algorithm that is applied to the input and the output that is produced. In addition, the PSPEC indicates restrictions and limitations imposed on the process (function), performance characteristics that are relevant to the process, and design constraints that may influence the way in which the process will be implemented.

12.4.2 Extensions for Real-Time Systems

Many software applications are time-dependent and process as much or more control-oriented information as data. A real-time system must interact with the real world in a time frame dictated by the real world. Aircraft avionics, manufacturing process control, consumer products, and industrial instrumentation are but a few of hundreds of real-time software applications.

To accommodate the analysis of real-time software, a number of extensions to the basic notation for structured analysis have been proposed. These extensions, developed by Ward and Mellor [WAR85] and Hatley and Pirbhai [HAT87] and shown in Figures 12.13 and 12.14, enable the analyst to represent control flow and control processing as well as data flow and processing.

12.4.3 Ward and Mellor Extensions

Ward and Mellor [WAR85] extend basic structured analysis notation to accommodate the following demands imposed by a real-time system:

- Information flow that is gathered or produced on a time-continuous basis
- Control information passed throughout the system and associated control processing
- Multiple instances of the same transformation, which are sometimes encountered in multitasking situations
- System states and the mechanism that causes transition between states

---

[7]The term "requirements dictionary" is also used.

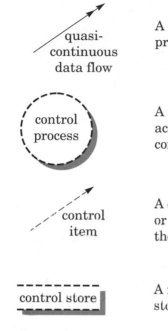

A data object that is input or output from a process on a "continuous" basis

A transformer of control or "events"; accepts control and input and produces control as output

A control item or event; takes on a boolean or discrete value; the arrowhead indicates the direction of data flow

A repository of control items that are to be stored for use by one or more processes

FIGURE 12.13.
Extended structured analysis notation for real-time systems developed by Ward and Mellor [WAR85]

Multiple equivalent instances of the same process; used when multiple processes are created in multitasking system

In a significant percentage of real-time applications, the system must monitor *time-continuous* information generated by some real world process. For example, a real-time test monitoring system for gas turbine engines might be required to monitor turbine speed, combustor temperature, and a variety of pressure probes on a continuous basis. Conventional data flow notation does

A control item or event; takes on a boolean or discrete value; the arrowhead indicates the direction of data flow.

FIGURE 12.14.
Extended structured analysis notation for real-time systems developed by Hatley and Pirbhai [HAT87]

The vertical bar is a reference to a control specification (CSPEC) that describes the behavior of a system and defines how processes are activated as a consequence of events.

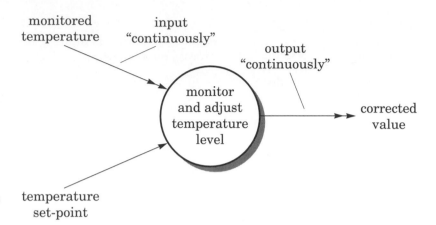

FIGURE 12.15.
Time-continuous data flow

not make a distinction between discrete data and time-continuous data. An extension to basic structured analysis notation, shown in Figure 12.15, provides a mechanism for representing time-continuous data flow. The double headed arrow is used to represent time-continuous flow, and a single headed arrow is used to indicate discrete data flow. In the figure, **monitored temperature** is measured continuously while a single value for **temperature set-point** is also provided. The process shown in the figure produces a time-continuous output, **corrected value**.

The distinction between discrete and time-continuous data flow has important implications for both the system engineer and the software designer. During the creation of the system model, a system engineer will be better able to isolate those processes that may be performance critical (it is likely that the input and output of time-continuous data will be performance sensitive). As the physical or implementation model is created, the designer must establish a mechanism for collection of time-continuous data. Obviously, the digital system collects data in a quasi-continuous fashion using techniques such as high-speed polling. The notation indicates where analog to digital hardware will be required and which transforms are likely to demand high-performance software.

In conventional data flow diagrams, control or *event flows* are not represented explicitly. In fact, the analyst is cautioned to specifically exclude the representation of control flow from the data flow diagram. This exclusion is overly restrictive when real-time applications are considered and for this reason, a specialized notation for representing event flows and control processing has been developed. Continuing the convention established for data flow diagrams, data flow is represented using a solid arrow. *Control flow,* however, is represented using a dashed or shaded arrow. A process that handles only control flows, called a *control process,* is similarly represented using a dashed bubble.

Control flow can be input directly to a conventional process or into a control process. Figure 12.16 illustrates control flow and processing as it would be represented using Ward and Mellor notation. The figure illustrates a top-level view of a data and control flow for a manufacturing cell.[8] As components to be

---

[8]A manufacturing cell is used in factory automation applications. It contains computers and automated machines (e.g., robots, NC machines, specialized fixtures) and performs one discrete manufacturing operation under computer control.

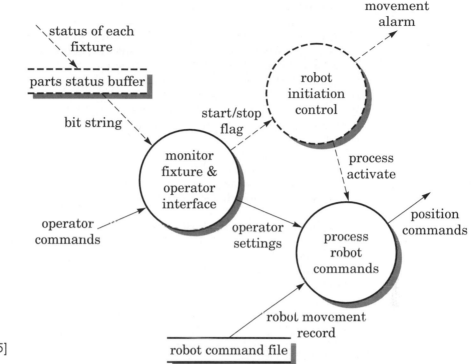

FIGURE 12.16.
Data and control
flows using Ward
and Mellor [WAR85]
notation

assembled by a robot are placed on fixtures, a status bit is set within a **parts status buffer** (a control store) that indicates the presence or absence of each component. Event information contained within the **parts status buffer** is passed as a **bit string** to a process, *monitor fixture and operator interface*. The process will read **operator commands** only when the control information, **bit string,** indicates that all fixtures contain components. An event flag, **start/stop flag,** is sent to *robot initiation control,* a control process that enables further command processing. Other data flows occur as a consequence of the **process activate** event that is sent to *process robot commands*.

In some situations multiple instances of the same control or data transformation process may occur in a real-time system. This can occur in a multitasking environment when tasks are spawned as a result of internal processing or external events. For example, a number of part status buffers may be monitored so that different robots can be signaled at the appropriate time. In addition, each robot may have its own robot control system. The Ward and Mellor notation used to represent *multiple equivalent instances* of the same process is shown in Figure 12.13.

12.4.4   Hatley and Pirbhai Extensions

The Hatley and Pirbhai [HAT87] extensions to basic structured analysis notation focus less on the creation of additional graphical symbols and more on the representation and specification of the control-oriented aspects of the software. In Figure 12.14 the dashed arrow is once again used to represent control or event flow. Unlike Ward and Mellor, Hatley and Pirbhai suggest that dashed and solid notation be represented separately. Therefore, a *control flow diagram (CFD)* is defined. The CFD contains the same processes as the DFD, but shows control flow rather than data flow. Instead of representing control processes directly within the flow model, a notational reference (a solid bar) to a *control specification (CSPEC)* is used. In essence, the solid bar can be viewed as a "window" into an "executive" (the CSPEC) that controls the processes (functions) represented in the DFD based on the event that is passed through the window. The CSPEC, described in detail in Section 12.6.4, is used to indicate (1) how the software behaves when an event or control signal is sensed and (2) which processes are invoked as an consequence of the occurrence of the event. A process specification is used to describe the inner workings of a process represented in a flow diagram.

Using the notation described in Figures 12.11 and 12.14, along with additional information contained in PSPECs and CSPECs, Hatley and Pirbhai create a model of a real-time system. Data flow diagrams are used to represent data and the processes that manipulate it. Control flow diagrams show how events flow among processes and illustrate those external events that cause various processes to be activated. The interrelationship between the process and control models is shown schematically in Figure 12.17. The process model is "connected" to the control model through *data conditions*. The control model is "connected" to the process model through process activation information contained in the CSPEC.

A data condition occurs whenever data input to a process results in a control output. This situation is illustrated in Figure 12.18, part of a flow model for an automated monitoring and control system for pressure vessels in an oil refinery. The process *check & convert pressure* implements the algorithm described in the PSPEC pseudocode shown. When the absolute tank pressure is greater than an allowable maximum, an **above pressure** event is generated. Note that when Hatley and Pirbhai notation is used, the data flow is shown as part of a DFD, while the control flow is noted separately as part of a control flow diagram. To determine what happens when this event occurs, we must check the CSPEC.

The control specification (CSPEC) contains a number of important modeling tools. A *process activation table* (described in Section 12.6.4) is used to indicate which processes are activated by a given event that flows through the vertical bar. For example, a process activation table (PAT) for Figure 12.18 might indicate that the **above pressure** event would cause a process *reduce tank pressure* (not shown) to be invoked. In addition to the PAT, the CSPEC may contain a *state-transition diagram (STD)*. The STD is a behavioral model that relies on the definition of a set of *system states* and is described in the following section.

12.5   BEHAVIORAL MODELING

Behavioral modeling is an operational principle for all requirements analysis methods. Yet, only extended versions of structured analysis ([WAR85], [HAT87])

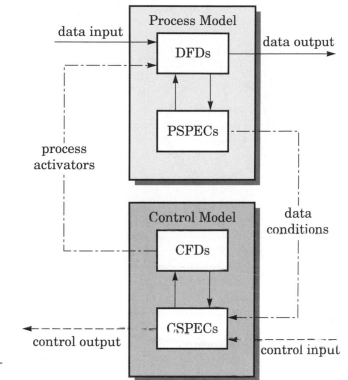

FIGURE 12.17.
The relationship between data and control models [HAT87]

provide a notation for this type of modeling. The state-transition diagram[9] represents the behavior of a system by depicting its states and the events that cause the system to change state. In addition, the STD indicates what actions (e.g., process activation) are taken as a consequence of a particular event.

A *state* is any observable mode of behavior. For example, states for a monitoring and control system for pressure vessel described in Section 12.4.4 might be *monitoring state, alarm state, pressure release state,* and so on. Each of these states represents a mode of behavior of the system. A state transition diagram indicates how the system moves from state to state.

To illustrate the use of the Hatley and Pirbhai control and behavioral extensions, consider software embedded within an office photocopying machine. The photocopier performs a number of functions that are implied by the level 1 DFD shown in Figure 12.19. It should be noted that additional refinement of the data flow and definition of each data item (using a data dictionary) would be required.

The control flow for the photocopier software is shown in Figure 12.20. Control flows are shown entering and exiting individual processes and the CSPEC "window." For example, the **paper feed status** and **start/stop** events flow into the CSPEC bar. This implies that each of these events will cause some

---

[9]Instead of a diagram, a tabular representation for state transition can also be used. For additional information, see [HAT87].

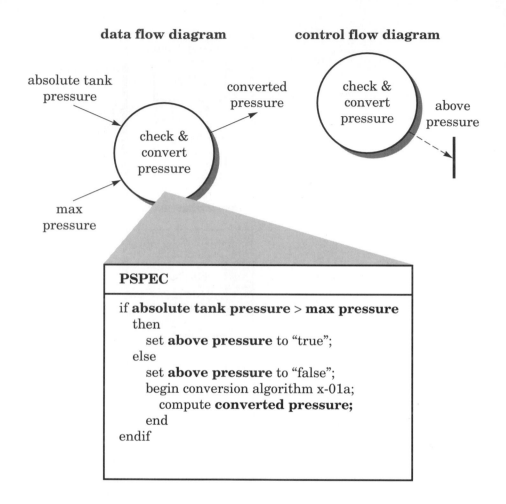

data flow diagram   **control flow diagram**

absolute tank pressure

converted pressure

check & convert pressure

check & convert pressure

above pressure

max pressure

PSPEC

if **absolute tank pressure** > **max pressure**
  then
    set **above pressure** to "true";
  else
    set **above pressure** to "false";
    begin conversion algorithm x-01a;
      compute **converted pressure;**
    end
endif

FIGURE 12.18.
Data conditions

process represented in the CFD to be activated. If we were to examine the CSPEC internals, the **start/stop** event would be shown to activate/deactivate the *manage copying* process. Similarly, the **jammed** event (part of paper feed status) would activate *perform problem diagnosis*. It should be noted that all vertical bars within the CFD refer to the same CSPEC.

An event flow can be input directly into a process as shown with **repro fault**. However, this flow does not activate the process, but rather provides control information for the process algorithm. Data flow arrows have been lightly shaded for illustrative purposes, but in reality they are not shown as part of a control flow diagram.

A simplified state transition diagram for the photocopier software described above is shown in Figure 12.21. The rectangles represent system states and the arrows represent *transitions* between states. Each arrow is labeled with a ruled expression. The top value indicates the event(s) that cause the transition to occur. The bottom value indicates the action that occurs as a consequence of the event. Therefore, when the paper tray is **full** and the **start** button is pressed, the system moves from the *reading commands* state to the *mak-*

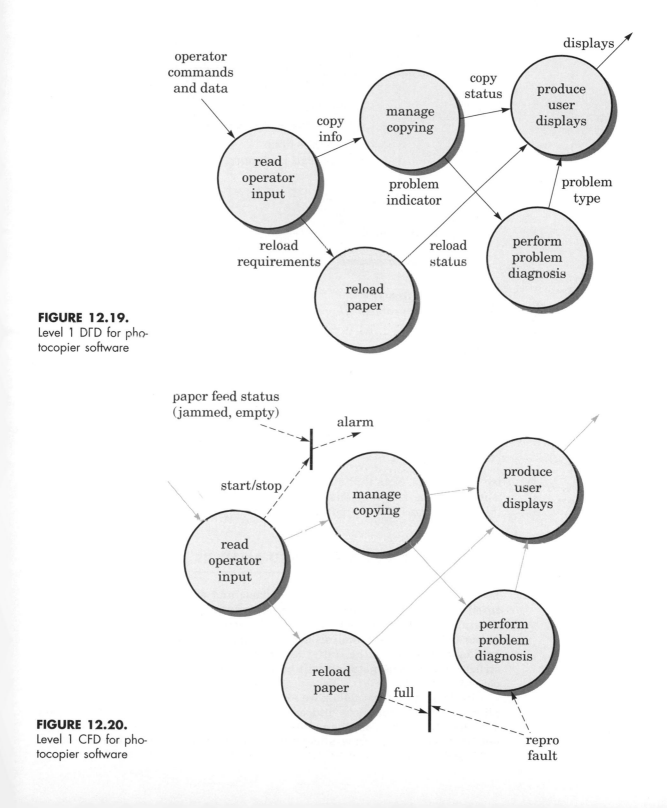

FIGURE 12.19.
Level 1 DFD for photocopier software

FIGURE 12.20.
Level 1 CFD for photocopier software

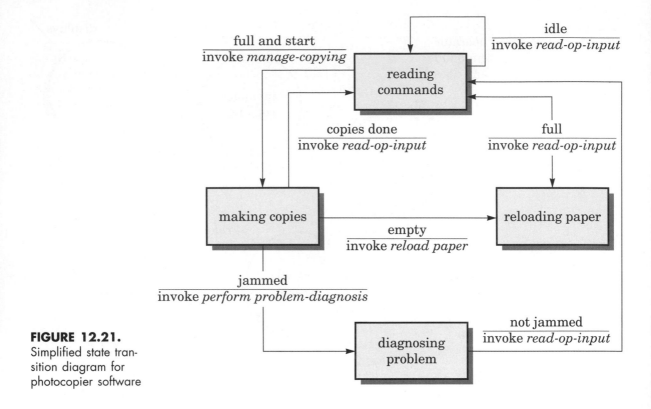

FIGURE 12.21.
Simplified state tran-
sition diagram for
photocopier software

ing copies state. Note that states do not necessarily correspond to processes on a one-to-one basis. For example, the state *making copies* would encompass both the *manage copying* and *produce user displays* processes shown in Figure 12.20.

12.6   THE MECHANICS OF STRUCTURED ANALYSIS

In the previous section, we discussed basic and extended notation for structured analysis. To be used effectively in software requirements analysis, this notation must be combined with a set of heuristics that enable a software engineer to derive a good analysis model. To illustrate the use of these heuristics, an adapted version of the Hatley and Pirbhai [HAT87] extensions to the basic structured analysis notation will be used throughout the remainder of this chapter.

In the sections that follow, we examine each of the steps that should be applied to develop complete and accurate models using structured analysis. Through this discussion, the notation introduced in Section 12.4 will be used, and other notational forms, alluded to earlier, will be presented in some detail.

12.6.1 Creating an Entity-Relationship Diagram

The entity-relationship diagram enables a software engineer to fully specify the data objects that are input and output from a system, the attributes that define the properties of these objects, and the relationships between objects. Like most elements of the analysis model, the ERD is constructed in an iterative manner. The following approach is taken:

1. During requirements gathering, customers are asked to list the "things" that the application or business process addresses. These "things" evolve into a list of input and output data objects as well as external entities that produce or consume information.

2. Taking the objects one at a time, the analyst and customer define whether or not a connection (unnamed at this stage) exists between the data object and other objects.

3. Wherever a connection exists, the analyst and customer create one or more object–relationship pairs.

4. For each object–relationship pair, cardinality and modality are explored.

5. Steps 2 through 4 are continued iteratively until all object–relationship pairs have been defined. It is common to discover omissions as this process continues. New objects and relationships will invariably be added as the number of iterations grows.

6. The attributes of each entity are defined.

7. An entity-relationship diagram is formalized and reviewed.

8. Steps 1 through 7 are repeated until data modeling is complete.

To illustrate the use of these basic guidelines, the SafeHome security system example, discussed in Chapter 11, will be used. A processing narrative for SafeHome is reproduced below:

> SafeHome software enables the homeowner to configure the security system when it is installed, monitors all sensors connected to the security system, and interacts with the homeowner through a keypad and function keys contained in the SafeHome control panel shown in Figure 11.4.
>
> During installation, the SafeHome control panel is used to "program" and configure the system. Each sensor is assigned a number and type, a master password is programmed for arming and disarming the system, and telephone number(s) are input for dialing when a sensor event occurs.
>
> When a sensor event is recognized, the software invokes an audible alarm attached to the system. After a delay time that is specified by the homeowner during system configuration activities, the software dials a telephone number of a monitoring service, provides information about the location, reporting the nature of the event that has been detected. The number will be redialed every 20 seconds until telephone connection is obtained.
>
> All interaction with SafeHome is managed by a user-interaction subsystem that reads input provided through the keypad and function keys, displays

prompting messages and system status on the LCD display. Keyboard interaction takes the following form ...

Discussions between the analyst and the customer indicate the following (partial) list of "things" that are relevant to the problem:

- homeowner
- control panel
- sensors
- security system
- monitoring service

Taking these "things" one at a time, connections are explored. To accomplish this, each object is drawn and lines connecting the objects are noted. For example, Figure 12.22 shows that a direct connection exists between the **homeowner** and **control panel, security system,** and **monitoring service**. A single connection exists between **sensor** and **security system,** and so forth.

Once all connections have been defined, one or more object–relationship pairs are identified for each connection. For example, the connection between **sensor** and **security system** is determined to have the following object–relationship pairs:

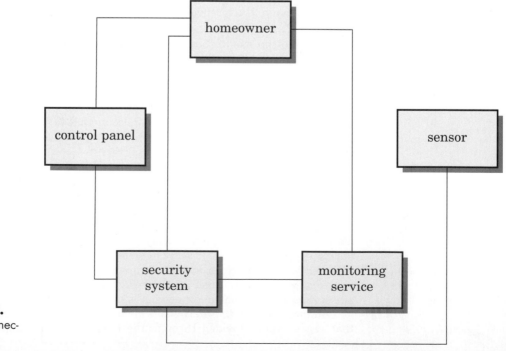

FIGURE 12.22.
Establishing connections

security system *monitors* **sensor**

security system *enables/disables* **sensor**

security system *tests* **sensor**

security system *programs* **sensor**

Each of the above object–relationship pairs is analyzed to determine cardinality and modality. For example, in the object–relationship pair **security system** *monitors* **sensor,** the cardinality between **security system** and **sensor** is one to many. The modality is one occurrence of **security system** (mandatory) and at least one occurrence of **sensor** (mandatory). Using the ERD notation introduced in Section 12.3, the connecting line between **security system** and **sensor** would be modified as shown in Figure 12.23. Similar analysis would be applied to all other data objects.

Each object is studied to determine its attributes. Since we are considering the software that must support SafeHome, the attributes should focus on data that must be stored to enable the system to operate. For example, the **sensor** object might have the following attributes: sensor type, internal identification number, zone location, and alarm level.

12.6.2 Creating a Data Flow Model

The data flow diagram (DFD) enables the software engineer to develop models of the information domain and functional domain at the same time. As the DFD is refined into greater levels of detail, the analyst performs an implicit functional decomposition of the system, thereby accomplishing the fourth operational analysis principle. At the same time, the DFD refinement results in a corresponding refinement of data as it moves through the processes that embody the application.

A few simple guidelines can aid immeasurably during derivation of a data flow diagram: (1) The level 0 data flow diagram should depict the software/system as a single bubble; (2) primary input and output should be carefully noted; (3) refinement should begin by isolating candidate processes, data objects, and stores to be represented at the next level; (4) all arrows and bubbles should be labeled with meaningful names; (5) *information flow continuity* must

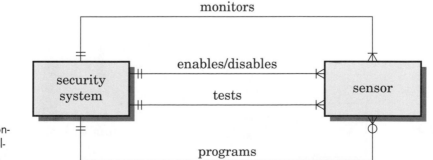

FIGURE 12.23.
Developing relationships and cardinality/modality

be maintained from level to level; and (6) one bubble at a time should be refined. There is a natural tendency to overcomplicate the data flow diagram. This occurs when the analyst attempts to show too much detail too early or represents procedural aspects of the software in lieu of information flow.

Again considering the SafeHome product, a level 0 DFD for the system is shown in Figure 12.24. The primary external entities (boxes) produce information for use by the system and consume information generated by the system. The labeled arrows represent data objects or data object type hierarchies. For example, **user commands and data** encompasses all configuration commands, all activation/deactivation commands, all miscellaneous interactions, and all data that are input to qualify or expand a command.

The level 0 DFD is now expanded into a level 1 model. But how do we proceed? A simple, yet effective approach is to perform a "grammatical parse" on the processing narrative that describes the context level bubble. That is, we isolate all nouns (and noun phrases) and verbs (and verb phrases) in the narrative. To illustrate, we again reproduce the processing narrative underlining the first occurrence of all nouns and italicizing the first occurrence of all verbs. (It should be noted that nouns and verbs that are synonyms or have no direct bearing on the modeling process are omitted.)

SafeHome software *enables* the homeowner to *configure* the security system when it is *installed, monitors* all sensors *connected* to the security system, and *interacts* with the homeowner through a keypad and function keys *contained* in the SafeHome control panel shown in Figure 11.4.

During installation, the SafeHome control panel is *used* to "*program*" and *configure* the system. Each sensor is *assigned* a number and type, a master password in programmed for *arming* and *disarming* the system, and telephone number(s) are *input* for *dialing* when a sensor event occurs.

When a sensor event is *recognized,* the software *invokes* an audible alarm attached to the system. After a delay time that is *specified* by the homeowner during system configuration activities, the software dials a telephone number of a monitoring service, *provides* information about the location, *reporting* and the nature of the event that has been detected. The telephone number will be *redialed* every 20 seconds until telephone connection is *obtained*.

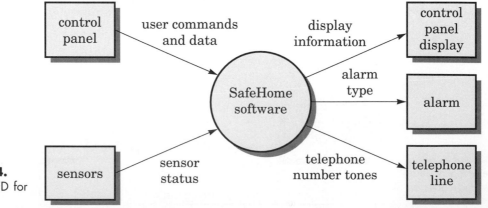

FIGURE 12.24.
Context-level DFD for SafeHome

> All underline{interaction} with SafeHome is *managed* by a underline{user-interaction subsystem} that *reads* underline{input} provided through the keypad and function keys, *displays* underline{prompting messages} and underline{system status} on the underline{LCD display}. Keyboard interaction takes the following form ...

In examining the grammatical parse, we see a pattern begin to emerge. All verbs are SafeHome processes; that is, they may ultimately be represented as bubbles in a subsequent DFD. All nouns are either external entities (boxes), data or control objects (arrows), or data stores (double lines). Note further that nouns and verbs can be attached to one another (e.g., underline{sensor} is *assigned* underline{number} and underline{type}). Therefore, by performing a grammatical parse on the processing narrative for a bubble at any DFD level, we can generate much useful information about how to proceed with the refinement to the next level. Using this information, a level 1 DFD is shown in Figure 12.25. The context-level process shown in Figure 12.24 has been expanded into seven processes derived from an examination of the grammatical parse. Similarly, the information flow between processes at level 1 has been derived from the parse.

It should be noted that information flow continuity is maintained between levels 0 and 1. Elaboration of the content of inputs and output at DFD levels 0 and 1 is postponed until Section 12.7.

The processes represented at DFD level 1 can be further refined into lower levels. For example, the process *monitor sensors* can be refined into a level 2 DFD as shown in Figure 12.26. Note once again that information flow continuity has been maintained between levels.

The refinement of DFDs continues until each bubble performs a simple function, that is, until the process represented by the bubble performs a function that would be easily implemented as a program component. In Chapter 13 we discuss a concept, called *cohesion,* that can be used to assess the simplicity of a given function. For now, we strive to refine DFDs until each bubble is "single minded."

12.6.3 Creating a Control Flow Model

For many types of data processing applications, the data model and the data flow diagram are all that is necessary to obtain meaningful insight into software requirements. As we have already noted, however, there exists a large class of applications that are driven by events rather than data, that produce control information rather than reports or displays, and that process information with heavy concern for time and performance. Such applications require the use of control flow modeling in addition to data flow modeling.

The graphical notation required to create a control flow diagram (CFD) was presented in Section 12.4.4. To review the approach for creating a CFD, a data flow model is "stripped" of all data flow arrows.[10] Events and control items (dashed arrows) are then added to the diagram and a "window" (a vertical bar) into the control specification is shown. But how are events selected?

---

[10]For instructional clarity, the data flow arrows have been shaded lightly and remain in the picture. In practice, they are eliminated altogether.

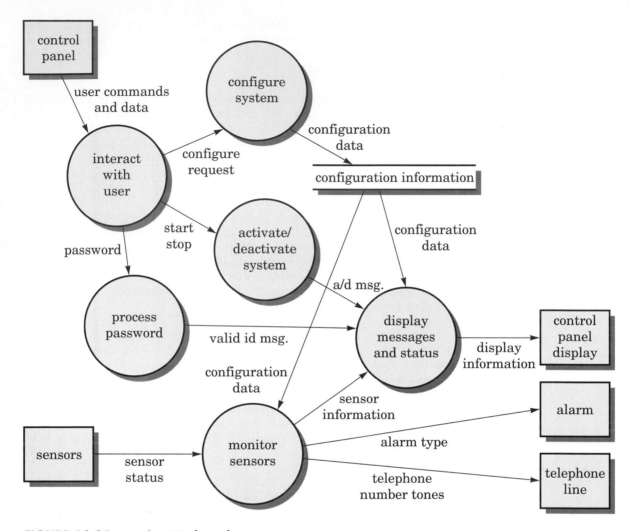

FIGURE 12.25. Level 1 DFD for SafeHome

We have already noted that an event or control item is implemented as a boolean value (e.g., *true* or *false, on* or *off, 1* or *0*) or a discrete list of conditions (*empty, jammed, full*). To select potential candidate events, the following guidelines are suggested:

- List all sensors that are "read" by the software.
- List all interrupt conditions.
- List all "switches" that are actuated by an operator.
- List all data conditions.

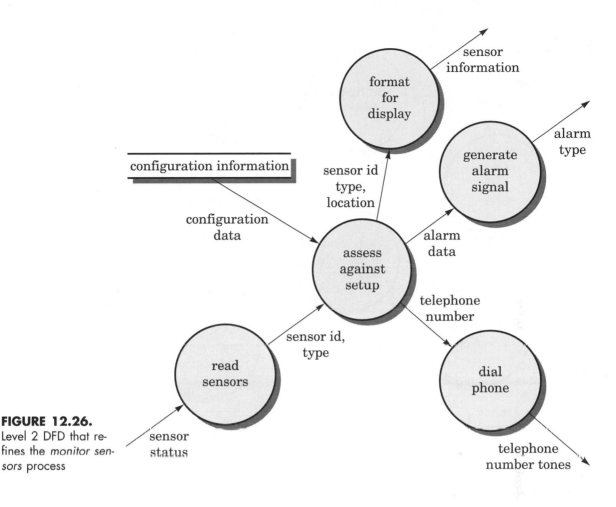

FIGURE 12.26.
Level 2 DFD that refines the *monitor sensors* process

- Recalling the noun–verb parse that was applied to the processing narrative, review all "control items" as possible CSPEC inputs/outputs.
- Describe the behavior of a system by identifying its states; identify how each state is reached and define the transitions between states.
- Focus on possible omissions—a very common error in specifying control (e.g., ask: "Is there any other way I can get to this state or exit from it?")

A level 1 CFD for SafeHome software is illustrated in Figure 12.27. Among the events and control items noted are **sensor event** (i.e., a sensor has been tripped), **blink flag** (a signal to blink the LCD display), and **start/stop switch** (a signal to turn the system on or off). An event flowing into the CSPEC window from the outside world implies that the CSPEC will activate one or more of the processes shown in the CFD. When a control item emanates from a process and flows into the CSPEC window, control and activation of some other process or an outside entity is implied.

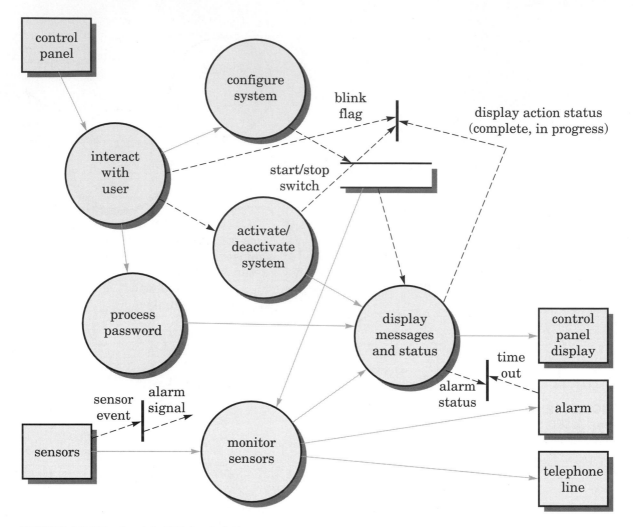

FIGURE 12.27. Level 1 CFD for SafeHome

12.6.4 The Control Specification

The control specification (CSPEC) represents the behavior of the system (at the level from which it has been referenced) in two different ways. The CSPEC contains a state transition diagram (STD) that is a *sequential specification* of behavior. It can also contain a process activation table (PAT)—a *combinatorial specification* of behavior. The underlying attributes of the CSPEC were introduced in Section 12.4.4. It is now time to consider an example of this important modeling notation for structured analysis.

Figure 12.28 depicts a *state-transition diagram* for the level 1 flow model for SafeHome. The labeled transition arrows indicate how the system responds to events as it traverses the four states defined at this level. By studying the STD, a software engineer can determine the behavior of the system and, more important, can ascertain whether there are "holes" in the specified behavior. For example, the STD (Figure 12.28) indicates that the only transition from the *reading user input* state occurs when the **start/stop switch** is encountered and a transition to the *monitoring system status* state occurs. Yet, there appears to be no way, other than the occurrence of **sensor event,** that will allow the system to return to *reading user input*. This is an error in specification and would hopefully be uncovered during review and corrected. Examine the STD to determine whether there are any other anomalies.

A somewhat different mode of behavioral representation is the *process activation table (PAT)*. The PAT represents information contained in the STD in the context of processes, not states. That is, the table indicates which processes (bubbles) in the flow model will be invoked when an event occurs. The PAT can be used as a guide for a designer who must build an executive that controls the processes represented at this level. A PAT for the level 1 flow model of SafeHome software is shown in Figure 12.29.

The CSPEC describes the behavior of the system, but it does not give us any information about the inner working of the processes that are activated as a result of this behavior. The modeling notation that provides this information is discussed in the next section.

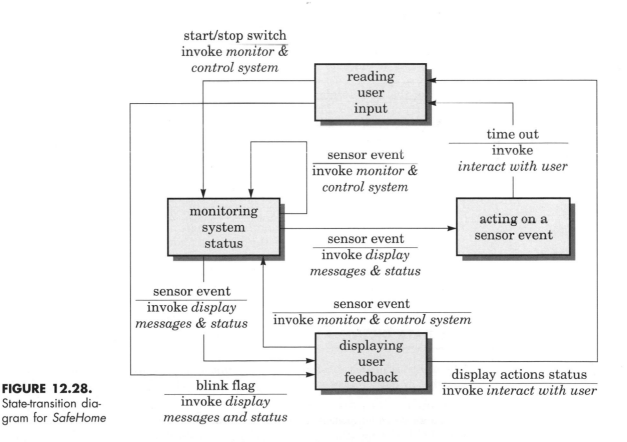

FIGURE 12.28.
State-transition diagram for *SafeHome*

input events						
sensor event	0	0	0	0	1	0
blink flag	0	0	1	1	0	0
start stop switch	0	1	0	0	0	0
display action status						
complete	0	0	0	1	0	0
in-progress	0	0	1	0	0	0
time out	0	0	0	0	0	1
output						
alarm signal	0	0	0	0	1	0
process activation						
monitor and control system	0	1	0	0	1	1
activate/deactivate system	0	1	0	0	0	0
display messages and status	1	0	1	1	1	1
interact with user	1	0	0	1	0	1

FIGURE 12.29.
Process activation
table for SafeHome

12.6.5 The Process Specification

The process specification (PSPEC) is used to describe all flow model processes that appear at the final level of refinement. The content of the process specification can include narrative text, a *program design language (PDL)* description[11] of the process algorithm, mathematical equations, tables, diagrams, or charts. By providing a PSPEC to accompany each bubble in the flow model, the software engineer creates a "mini-spec" that can serve as a first step in the creation of the software requirements specification and as a guide for design of the program component that will implement the process.

To illustrate the use of the PSPEC, consider a software application in which the dimensions of various geometric objects are analyzed to identify the shape of the object. Refinement of a context level data flow diagram continues until level 2 processes are derived. One of these, named *analyze triangle,* is depicted in Figure 12.30. The PSPEC for *analyze triangle* is first written as an English-language narrative as shown in the figure. If additional algorithmic detail is desired at this stage, a program design language representation (Figure 12.31) may also be included as part of the PSPEC. However, many believe that the PDL version should be postponed until design commences.

12.7   THE DATA DICTIONARY

The analysis model encompasses representations of data objects, function, and control. In each representation data objects and/or control items play a role.

---

[11]Program design language is often used as a procedural design notation and is described in detail in Chapter 14.

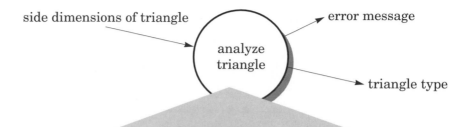

FIGURE 12.30.
Process specification
for a DFD process

PSPEC: Processing Narrative for Analyze Triangle

The analyze-triangle process accepts values A, B, and C that represent the side dimensions of a triangle. The process tests the dimension values to determine whether all values are positive. If a negative value is encountered, an error message is produced. The process evaluates valid input data to determine whether the dimensions define a valid triangle and if so, what type of triangle—equilateral, isosceles or scalene—is implied by the dimensions. The type is output.

Therefore, it is necessary to provide an organized approach for representing the characteristics of each data object and control item. This is accomplished with the data dictionary.

The *data dictionary* has been proposed as a quasi-formal grammar for describing the content of objects defined during structured analysis. This important modeling notation has been defined in the following manner [YOU89]:

> The data dictionary is an organized listing of all data elements that are pertinent to the system, with precise, rigorous definitions so that both user and system analyst will have a common understanding of inputs, outputs, components of stores and [even] intermediate calculations.

Today, the data dictionary is almost always implemented as part of a CASE "structured analysis and design tool." Although the format of dictionaries varies from tool to tool, most contain the following information:

- *name*—the primary name of the data or control item, the data store, or an external entity
- *alias*—other names used for the first entry
- *where-used / how-used*—a listing of the processes that use the data or control item and how it is used (e.g., input to the process, output from the process, as a store, as an external entity)
- *content description*—a notation for representing content
- *supplementary information*—other information about data types, preset values (if known), restrictions or limitations, etc.

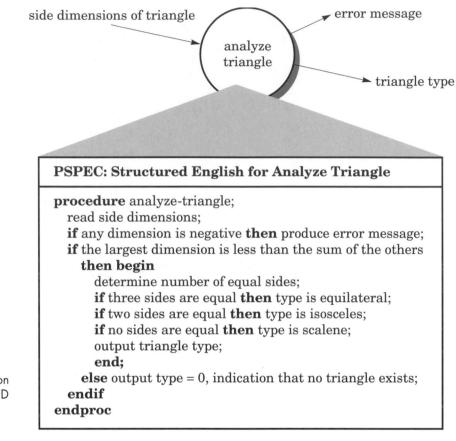

Once a data object or control item name and its aliases are entered into the data dictionary, consistency in naming can be enforced. That is, if an analysis team member decides to name a newly derived data item **xyz,** but **xyz** is already in the dictionary, the CASE tool supporting the dictionary posts a warning to indicate duplicate names. This improves the consistency of the analysis model and helps to reduce errors.

"Where-used/how-used" information is recorded automatically from the flow models. When a dictionary entry is created, the CASE tool scans DFDs and CFDs to determine which processes use the data or control information and how it is used. Although this may appear unimportant, it is actually one of the most important benefits of the dictionary. During analysis there is an almost continuous stream of changes. For large projects, it is often quite difficult to determine the impact of a change. Many a software engineer has asked, "Where is this data object used? What else will have to change if we modify it? What will the overall impact of the change be?" Because the data dictionary can be treated as a database,[12] the analyst can ask "where-used/how-used" questions, and get answers to queries noted above.

---

[12]In reality the data dictionary can be one element of a larger CASE repository. This is discussed in Chapter 29.

The notation used to develop a content description, illustrated in Figure 12.32, enables the analyst to represent *composite data* (i.e., a data object) in one of the three fundamental ways that it can be constructed:

1. as a *sequence* of data items,
2. as a *selection* from among a set of data items, or
3. as a *repeated grouping* of data items.

Each data item entry that is represented as part of a sequence, selection, or repetition may itself be another data object that needs further refinement within the dictionary.

To illustrate the use of the data dictionary and the content description notation shown in Figure 12.32, we return to the level 2 DFD for the *monitor system* process for SafeHome, shown in Figure 12.26. In the figure, the data item **telephone number** is specified as input. But what exactly is a telephone number? It could be a 7 digit local number, a 4 digit extension, or a 25 digit long distance carrier sequence. The data dictionary provides us with a precise definition of **telephone number** for the DFD in question. In addition it indicates where and how this data item is used and any supplementary information that is relevant to it. The data dictionary entry begins as follows:

name:	**telephone number**
aliases:	none
where used / how used:	*assess against setup* (output)
	dial phone (input)

description:
telephone number = [local extension | outside number]

The above content description may be read: **telephone number** is composed of either a **local extension** (for use in a large company) or an **outside number. Local extension** and **outside number** represent composite data and must be refined further in other content description statements. Continuing the content description:

Data construct	Notation	Meaning
	=	is composed of
Sequence	+	and
Selection	[|]	either–or
Repetition	{ }^{n}	*n* repetitions of
	( )	optional data
	* *	delimits comments

FIGURE 12.32.
Content description notation for a data dictionary

> **telephone number** = [**local extension** | **outside number**]
>
> **local extension** = [**2001** | **2002 ...** | **2999**]
>
> **outside number** = **9** + [**local number** | **long distance number**]
>
> **local number** = **prefix** + **access number**
>
> **long distance number** = **(1)** + **area code** + **local number**
>
> **prefix** = [**795** | **799** | **874** | **877**]
>
> **access number** = * **any four number string** *

The content description is expanded until all composite data items (data objects) have been represented as elementary items (items that require no further expansion) or until all data objects are represented in terms that would be well known and unambiguous to all readers (e.g., **area code** is generally understood to mean a 3 digit number that never starts with 0 or 1). It is also important to note that a specification of elementary data often restricts a system. For example, the definition of **prefix** indicates that only four branch exchanges can be accessed locally.

The data dictionary defines information items unambiguously. Although we might assume that the telephone number represented by the DFD in Figure 12.26 could accommodate a 25 digit long distance carrier access number, the data dictionary content description tells us that such numbers are not part of the data that may be used.

For large computer-based systems, the data dictionary grows rapidly in size and complexity. In fact, it is extremely difficult to maintain a dictionary manually. For this reason, CASE tools should be used.

12.8 AN OVERVIEW OF OTHER CLASSICAL ANALYSIS METHODS

Over the years, many other worthwhile software requirements analysis methods have been used throughout the industry. While all follow the operational analysis principles discussed in Chapter 11, each introduces a different notation and heuristics for constructing the analysis model. In this section, we present a very brief overview of three of the more common methods. For further information, the interested reader should refer to the references noted.[13]

12.8.1 Data Structured Systems Development

Data Structured Systems Development (DSSD), also called the Warnier-Orr methodology, evolved from pioneering work on information domain analysis

---

[13]The formal methods approach for the specification of software requirements is considered in detail in Chapter 24.

conducted by J.D. Warnier [WAR74, WAR81]. Warnier developed a notation for representing information hierarchy using the three constructs for sequence, selection, and repetition, and demonstrated that the software structure could be derived directly from the data structure.

Ken Orr [ORR77, ORR81] extended Warnier's work to encompass a somewhat broader view of the information domain that has evolved into Data Structured Systems Development. DSSD considers information flow and functional characteristics as well as data hierarchy.

12.8.2 Jackson System Development

Jackson System Development (JSD) evolved out of work conducted by M.A. Jackson [JAC75, JAC83] on information domain analysis and its relationship to program and system design. Similar in some ways to Warnier's approach and DSSD, JSD focuses on models of the "real world" information domain. In Jackson's words [JAC83], "[t]he developer begins by creating a model of the reality with which the system is concerned, the reality which furnishes its [the system's] subject matter ..."

To conduct JSD, the analyst applies the following steps:

Entity Action Step Using an approach that is quite similar to the object-oriented analysis techniques described in Chapter 20, *entities* (people, objects or organizations that a system needs to produce or use information) and *actions* (the events that occur in the real world that affect entities) are identified.

Entity Structure Step. Actions that affect each entity are ordered by time and represented with *Jackson Diagrams* (a tree-like notation).

Initial Modeling Step. Entities and actions are represented as a process model; connections between the model and the real world are defined.

Function Step. Functions that correspond to defined actions are specified.

System Timing Step. Process scheduling characteristics are assessed and specified.

Implementation Step. Hardware and software are specified as a design.

The last three steps in JSD are closely aligned with system or software design.

12.8.3 SADT

Structured analysis and design technique (SADT)[14] is a technique that has been widely used as a notation for system definition, process representations, software requirements analysis and system/software design [ROS77, ROS85].

---

[14]SADT is a trademark of Softech, Inc.

SADT consists of procedures that allow the analyst to decompose software (or system) functions; a graphical notation, the SADT *actigram* and *datagram,* that communicates the relationships of information (data and control) and function within software, and project control guidelines for applying the methodology.

The SADT methodology encompasses automated tools to support analysis procedures and a well-defined organizational harness through which the tools are applied. Reviews and milestones are specified, allowing validation of developer–customer communication.

12.9   SUMMARY

Structured analysis, the most widely used of requirements modeling methods, relies on data modeling and flow modeling to create the basis for a comprehensive analysis model. Using entity-relationship diagrams, the software engineer creates a representation of all data objects that are important for the system. Data and control flow diagrams are used as a basis for representing the transformation of data and control. At the same time, these models are used to create a functional model of the software and to provide a mechanism for partitioning function. A behavioral model is created using the state transition diagram, and data content is developed with a data dictionary. Process and control specifications provide additional elaboration of detail.

The original notation for structured analysis was developed for conventional data processing applications, but extensions now make the method applicable to real-time systems. Structured analysis is supported by an array of CASE tools that assist in the creation of each element of the model and also help to ensure consistency and correctness.

REFERENCES

[BRU88]   Bruyn, W. et al., "ESML: An Extended Systems Modeling Language Based on the Data Flow Diagram," *ACM Software Engineering Notes,* vol. 13, no. 1, January 1988, pp. 58–67.

[CHE77]   Chen, P., *The Entity-Relationship Approach to Logical Database Design,* QED Information Systems, 1977.

[DEM79]   DeMarco, T., *Structured Analysis and System Specification,* Prentice-Hall, 1979.

[GAN82]   Gane, T., and C. Sarson, *Structured Systems Analysis,* McDonnell Douglas, 1982.

[HAT87]   Hatley, D.J., and I.A. Pirbhai, *Strategies for Real-Time System Specification,* Dorset House, 1987.

[JAC75]   Jackson, M.A., *Principles of Program Design,* Academic Press, 1975.

[JAC83]   Jackson, M.A., *System Development,* Prentice-Hall, 1983.

[ORR77]   Orr, K.T., *Structured Systems Development,* Yourdon Press, New York, 1977.

[ORR81]   Orr, K.T., *Structured Requirements Definition,* Ken Orr & Associates, Inc., Topeka, KS, 1981.

[PAG80]   Page-Jones, M., *The Practical Guide to Structured Systems Design,* Yourdon Press, 1980.

[ROS77]   Ross, D., and K. Schoman, "Structured Analysis for Requirements Definition," *IEEE Trans. Software Engineering,* vol. 3, no. 1, January 1977, pp. 6–15.

[ROS85]   Ross, D. "Applications and Extensions of SADT," *IEEE Computer,* vol. 18, no. 4, April 1984, pp. 25–35.

[STE74]   Stevens, W.P., G.J. Myers, and L.L. Constantine, "Structured Design," *IBM Systems Journal,* vol. 13, no. 2, 1974, pp. 115–139.

[TIL93]   Tillmann, G., *A Practical Guide to Logical Data Modeling,* McGraw-Hill, 1993.

[WAR74]   Warnier, J.D., *Logical Construction of Programs,* Van Nostrand Reinhold, 1974.

[WAR81]   Warnier, J.D., *Logical Construction of Systems,* Van Nostrand Reinhold, 1981.

[WAR85]   Ward, P.T., and S.J. Mellor, *Structured Development for Real-Time Systems,* three volumes, Yourdon Press, 1985.

[YOU78]   Yourdon, E.N., and Constantine, L.L., *Structured Design,* Yourdon Press, 1978.

[YOU89]   Yourdon, E.N., *Modern Structured Analysis,* Prentice-Hall, 1990.

PROBLEMS AND POINTS TO PONDER

12.1.   Acquire at least three of the references discussed in Section 12.1 and write a brief paper that outlines how the perception of structured analysis has changed over time. As a concluding section, suggest ways in which you think the method will change in the future.

12.2.   You have been asked to build one of the following systems:
a. a network-based course registration system for your university
b. an order-processing system for a direct mail advertiser of computer software products
c. a simple invoicing system for a small business
d. a software product that replaces a Rolodex
e. an automated cookbook product
Select the system that is of interest to you and develop an entity-relationship diagram that describes data objects, relationships, and attributes.

12.3.   What is the difference between cardinality and modality?

12.4.   Draw a context-level model (level 0 DFD) for one of the five systems that are listed in problem 12.2. Write a context-level processing narrative for the system.

12.5.   Using the context-level DFD developed in problem 12.4, develop level 1 and level 2 data flow diagrams. Use a "grammatical parse" on the context-level processing narrative to get yourself started. Remember to specify all information flow by labeling all arrows between bubbles. Use meaningful names for each transform.

12.6. Develop CFDs, CSPECs, PSPECs and a data dictionary for the system you selected in problem 12.2. Try to make your model as complete as possible.

12.7. Does the information flow continuity concept mean that if one flow arrow appears as input at level 0, then one flow arrow must appear as input at subsequent levels? Discuss your answer.

12.8. Using the Ward and Mellor extensions, redraw the flow model contained in Figures 12.19 and 12.20. How will you accommodate the CSPEC that is implied in Figure 12.20? Ward and Mellor do not use this notation.

12.9. Using the Hatley and Pirbhai extensions, redraw the flow model contained in Figure 12.16. How will you accommodate the control process (dashed bubble) that is implied in Figure 12.16? (Hatley and Pirbhai do not use this notation.)

12.10. Describe an event flow in your own words.

12.11. Develop a complete flow model for the photocopier software discussed in Section 12.5. You may use either Ward and Mellor or Hatley and Pirbhai notation. Be certain to develop a detailed state-transition diagram for the system.

12.12. Complete the processing narratives for the analysis model for SafeHome software shown in Figure 12.25. Describe the interaction mechanics between the user and the system. Will your additional information change the flow models for SafeHome presented in this chapter? If so, how?

12.13. The department of public works for a large city has decided to develop a "computerized" pothole tracking and repair system (PHTRS). As potholes are reported, they are assigned an identifying number and stored by street address, size (on a scale of 1 to 10), location (middle, curb, etc.), district (determined from street address), and repair priority (determined from the size of the pothole). Work order data are associated with each pothole and include pothole location and size, repair crew identifying number, number of people on crew, equipment assigned, hours applied to repair, hole status (work in progress, repaired, temporary repair, not repaired), amount of filler material used, and cost of repair (computed from hours applied, number of people, material and equipment used). Finally, a damage file is created to hold information about reported damage due to the pothole and includes citizen's name, address, phone number, type of damage, and dollar amount of damage. PHTRS is an on-line system; queries are to be made interactively. Use structured analysis to model the PHTRS.

12.14. Software for a word-processing system is to be developed. Do a few hours of research on the application area and conduct a FAST meeting (see Chapter 11) with your fellow students to develop requirements (your instructor will help you coordinate this). Build a requirements model of the system using structured analysis.

12.15. Software for a real-time test monitoring system for gas turbine engines is to be developed. Proceed as in problem 12.14.

12.16. Software for a manufacturing control system for an automobile assembly plant is to be developed. Proceed as in problem 12.14.

12.17. Software for a video game is to be developed. Proceed as in problem 12.14.

12.18. Contact four or five vendors that sell CASE tools for structured analysis. Review their literature and write a brief paper that summarizes generic features that seem to distinguish one tool from another.

FURTHER READINGS AND OTHER INFORMATION SOURCES

There are literally dozens of books that have been published on structured analysis. Most cover the subject adequately, but only a few do a truly excellent job. DeMarco's book [DEM79] remains a good introduction to the basic notation. Books by Hoffer et al. (*Modern Systems Analysis and Design,* Benjamin-Cummings, 1996), Modell (*Systems Analysis,* 2nd edition, McGraw-Hill, 1996), Robertson and Robertson (*Complete Systems Analysis,* two volumes, Dorset House, 1994), and Page-Jones (*The Practical Guide to Structured Systems Design,* 2nd edition, Prentice-Hall, 1988) are worthwhile references. Yourdon's book on the subject [YOU89] remains the most comprehensive coverage published to date. For an engineering emphasis [WAR85] and [HAT87] are the books of preference. Kirner ("A Tool for Analysis of Real-Time Specification Methods," *Software Engineering Notes,* July 1993) presents an excellent bibliography of real-time analysis methods. The Internet newsgroup **comp.realtime** often contains discussions of real-time analysis and specification methods.

Many variations on structured analysis have evolved over the last decade. Cutts (*Structured Systems Analysis and Design Methodology,* Van Nostrand Reinhold, 1990) and Hares (*SSADM for the Advanced Practitioner,* Wiley, 1990) describe SSADM, a variation on structured analysis that is widely used in the U.K. and Europe.

Reingruber and Gregory (*Data Modeling Handbook,* Wiley, 1995) and Tillman [TIL93] present detailed tutorials for creating industry quality data models. Kim and Salvatore ("Comparing Data Modeling Formalisms," *Communications of the ACM,* June 1995) have written an excellent comparison of data modeling methods. An interesting book by Hay (*Data Modeling Patterns,* Dorset House, 1995) presents typical data model "patterns" that are encountered in many different businesses. A detailed treatment of behavioral modeling can be found in Kowal (*Behavior Models: Specifying User's Expectations,* Prentice-Hall, 1992).

A comprehensive study of CASE tools that are available for analysis modeling has been prepared by Software Technology Support Center (*Requirements Analysis and Design Technology Report,* March 1994), STSC is a government sponsored organization located at Hill Air Force Base in Utah.

A short bibliography on requirements analysis methods and pointers to other bibliographies on function analysis and quality function deployment can be found at:

http://mijuno.larc.nasa.gov/dfc/biblio/reqengBiblio.html

Many major CASE vendors provide Web sites that contain information about tools for structured analysis. A comprehensive set of pointers can be obtained at:

http://www.qucis.queensu.ca/Software-Engineering/toolcat.html

A short tutorial on structured analysis can be examined at:

http://cscmosaic.albany.edu/~gangolly/ssa1.html

An up-to-date list of World Wide Web references for software analysis modeling can be found at: **http://www.rspa.com**

CHAPTER 13

DESIGN CONCEPTS
AND PRINCIPLES

Design is the first step in the development phase for any engineered product or system. It may be defined as *"the process of applying various techniques and principles for the purpose of defining a device, a process or a system in sufficient detail to permit its physical realization"* [TAY59].

The designer's goal is to produce a model or representation of an entity that will later be built. The process by which the model is developed combines intuition and judgment based on experience in building similar entities, a set of principles and/or heuristics that guide the way in which the model evolves, a set of criteria that enable quality to be judged, and a process of iteration that ultimately leads to a final design representation.

Like engineering design approaches in other disciplines, software design changes continually as new methods, better analysis, and broader understanding evolve. Unlike mechanical or electronic design, software design is at a relatively early stage in its evolution. We have given serious thought to software design (as opposed to "programming" or "writing code") for little more than three decades. Therefore, software design methodology lacks the depth, flexibility, and quantitative nature that is normally associated with more classical engineering design disciplines. However, methods for software design do exist; criteria for design quality are available; and design notation can be applied. In this chapter, we explore the fundamental concepts and principles that are applicable to all software design. Chapters 14 and 21 examine a variety of software design methods.

13.1   SOFTWARE DESIGN AND SOFTWARE ENGINEERING

Software design sits at the technical kernel of the software engineering process and is applied regardless of the software process model that is used. Beginning once software requirements have been analyzed and specified, software design is the first of three technical activities—*design, code generation,* and *testing*—that are required to build and verify the software. Each activity transforms information in a manner that ultimately results in validated computer software.

Each of the elements of the analysis model (Chapter 12) provides information that is required to create a design model. The flow of information during software design is illustrated in Figure 13.1. Software requirements, manifested by the data, functional, and behavioral models, feed the design step. Using one of a number of design methods (discussed in later chapters), the design step produces a data design, an architectural design, an interface design, and a procedural design.

The *data design* transforms the information domain model created during analysis into the data structures that will be required to implement the software. The data objects and relationships defined in the entity-relationship diagram and the detailed data content depicted in the data dictionary provide the basis for the data design activity.

The *architectural design* defines the relationship among major structural elements of the program. This design representation—the modular framework of a computer program—can be derived from the analysis model(s) and the interaction of subsystems defined within the analysis model.

The *interface design* describes how the software communicates within itself, to systems that interoperate with it, and with humans who use it. An in-

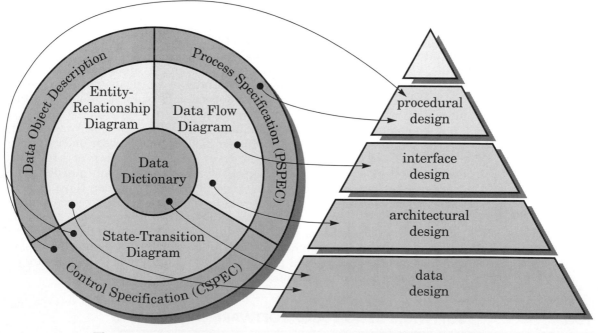

The analysis model   The design model

FIGURE 13.1. Translating the analysis model into a software design

terface implies a flow of information (e.g., data and/or control). Therefore, the data and control flow diagrams provide the information required for interface design.

The *procedural design* transforms structural elements of the program architecture into a procedural description of software components. Information obtained from the PSPEC, CSPEC, and STD serve as the basis for procedural design.

During design we make decisions that will ultimately affect the success of software construction, and as important, the ease with which software can be maintained. But why is design so important?

The importance of software design can be stated with a single word—*quality*. Design is the place where quality is fostered in software development. Design provides us with representations of software that can be assessed for quality. Design is the only way that we can accurately translate a customer's requirements into a finished software product or system. Software design serves as the foundation for all software engineering and software maintenance steps that follow. Without design, we risk building an unstable system—one that will fail when small changes are made; one that may be difficult to test; one whose quality cannot be assessed until late in the software engineering process, when time is short and many dollars have already been spent.

13.2 THE DESIGN PROCESS

Software design is an iterative process through which requirements are translated into a "blueprint" for constructing the software. Initially, the blueprint depicts a holistic view of software. That is, the design is represented at a high level of abstraction—a level that can be directly traced to specific data, functional, and behavioral requirements. As design iterations occur, subsequent refinement leads to design representations at much lower levels of abstraction. These can still be traced to requirements, but the connection is more subtle.

13.2.1 Design and Software Quality

Throughout the design process, the quality of the evolving design is assessed with a series of *formal technical reviews* or *design walkthroughs* discussed in Chapter 8. McGlaughlin [McG91] suggests three characteristics that serve as a guide for the evaluation of a good design:

- The design must implement all of the explicit requirements contained in the analysis model, and it must accommodate all of the implicit requirements desired by the customer.
- The design must be a readable, understandable guide for those who generate code and for those who test and subsequently maintain the software.
- The design should provide a complete picture of the software, addressing the data, functional, and behavioral domains from an implementation perspective.

Each of these characteristics is actually a goal of the design process. But how is each of these goals achieved?

In order to evaluate the quality of a design representation, we must establish technical criteria for good design. Later in this chapter, we discuss design quality criteria in some detail. For the time being, we present the following guidelines:

1. A design should exhibit a hierarchical organization that makes intelligent use of control among elements of software.[1]
2. A design should be modular; that is, the software should be logically partitioned into elements that perform specific functions and subfunctions.
3. A design should contain both data and procedural abstractions.
4. A design should lead to modules (e.g., subroutines or procedures) that exhibit independent functional characteristics.
5. A design should lead to interfaces that reduce the complexity of connections between modules and with the external environment.
6. A design should be derived using a repeatable method that is driven by information obtained during software requirements analysis.

These criteria are not achieved by chance. The software design process encourages good design through the application of fundamental design principles, systematic methodology, and thorough review.

13.2.2 The Evolution of Software Design

The evolution of software design is a continuing process that has spanned the past three decades. Early design work concentrated on criteria for the development of modular programs [DEN73] and methods for refining software architecture in a top-down manner [WIR71]. Procedural aspects of design definition evolved into a philosophy called *structured programming* [DAH71, MIL72]. Later work proposed methods for the translation of data flow [STE74] or data structure [JAC75, WAR74] into a design definition. Newer design approaches (e.g., [JAC92], [GAM95]) propose an *object-oriented* approach to design derivation.

Many design methods, growing out of the work noted above, are being applied throughout the industry. Like the analysis methods presented in Chapter 12, each software design method introduces unique heuristics and notation, as well as a somewhat parochial view of what characterizes lead to design quality. Yet, each of these methods has a number of common characteristics: (1) a mechanism for the translation of an analysis model into a design representation, (2) a notation for representing functional components and their interfaces, (3) heuristics for refinement and partitioning, and (4) guidelines for quality assessment.

---

[1]It should be noted that good object-oriented designs do not necessarily exhibit this characteristic. See Chapters 19 and 21 for more details.

Regardless of the design method that is used, a software engineer should apply a set of fundamental principles and basic concepts to data, architectural, interface, and procedural design. These principles and concepts are considered in the sections that follow.

13.3   DESIGN PRINCIPLES

Software design is both a process and a model. The design process is a set of iterative steps that enable the designer to describe all aspects of the software to be built. It is important to note, however, that the design process is not simply a cookbook. Creative skill, past experience, a sense of what makes "good" software, and an overall commitment to quality are critical success factors for a competent design.

The design model is the equivalent of an architect's plans for a house. It begins by representing the totality of the thing to be built (e.g., a three-dimensional rendering of the house) and slowly refines the thing to provide guidance for constructing each detail (e.g., the plumbing layout). Similarly, the design model that is created for software provides a variety of different views of the computer program.

Basic design principles enable the software engineer to navigate the design process. Davis [DAV95] suggests a set[2] of principles for software design, which have been adapted and extended in the following list:

- *The design process should not suffer from "tunnel vision."* A good designer should consider alternative approaches, judging each based on the requirements of the problem, the resources available to do the job, and the design concepts presented in Section 13.4.

- *The design should be traceable to the analysis model.* Because a single element of the design model often traces to multiple requirements, it is necessary to have a means for tracking how requirements have been satisfied by the design model.

- *The design should not reinvent the wheel.* Systems are constructed using a set of design patterns, many of which have likely been encountered before. These patterns, often called reusable design components, should always be chosen as an alternative to reinvention. Time is short and resources are limited! Design time should be invested in representing truly new ideas and integrating those patterns that already exist.

- *The design should "minimize the intellectual distance" [DAV95] between the software and the problem as it exists in the real world.* That is, the structure of the software design should (whenever possible) mimic the structure of the problem domain.

- *The design should exhibit uniformity and integration.* A design is uniform if it appears that one person developed the entire thing. Rules of style and format

[2]Only a small subset of Davis's design principles are noted here. For more information, see [DAV95].

should be defined for a design team before design work begins. A design is integrated if care is taken in defining interfaces between design components.

- *The design should be structured to accommodate change.* Many of the design concepts discussed in the next section enable a design to achieve this principle.

- *The design should be structured to degrade gently, even when aberrant data, events, or operating conditions are encountered.* A well-designed computer program should never "bomb." It should be designed to accommodate unusual circumstances, and if it must terminate processing, do so in a graceful manner.

- *Design is not coding, coding is not design.* Even when detailed procedural designs are created for program components, the level of abstraction of the design model is higher than source code. The only design decisions made at the coding level address the small implementation details that enable the procedural design to be coded.

- *The design should be assessed for quality as it is being created, not after the fact.* A variety of design concepts (Section 13.4) and design measures (Chapters 18 and 23) are available to assist the designer in assessing quality.

- *The design should be reviewed to minimize conceptual (semantic) errors.* There is sometimes a tendency to focus on minutiae when the design is reviewed, missing the forest for the trees. A designer should ensure that major conceptual elements of the design (omissions, ambiguity, inconsistency) have been addressed before worrying about the syntax of the design model.

When the design principles described above are properly applied, the software engineer creates a design that exhibits both external and internal quality factors [MEY88]. *External quality factors* are those properties of the software that can be readily observed by users (e.g., speed, reliability, correctness, usability).[3] *Internal quality factors* are of importance to software engineers. They lead to a high-quality design from the technical perspective. To achieve internal quality factors, the designer must understand basic design concepts.

13.4   DESIGN CONCEPTS

A set of fundamental software design concepts has evolved over the past three decades. Although the degree of interest in each concept has varied over the years, each has stood the test of time. Each provides the software designer with a foundation from which more sophisticated design methods can be applied. Each helps the software engineer to answer the following questions:

- What criteria can be used to partition software into individual components?
- How is function or data structure detail separated from a conceptual representation of the software?
- Are there uniform criteria that define the technical quality of a software design?

---

[3]A more detailed discussion of quality factors is presented in Chapter 18.

M.A. Jackson once said: "The beginning of wisdom for a [software engineer] is to recognize the difference between getting a program to work, and getting it *right*" [JAC75]. Fundamental software design concepts provide the necessary framework for "getting it right."

13.4.1 Abstraction

When we consider a modular solution to any problem, many *levels of abstraction* can be posed. At the highest level of abstraction, a solution is stated in broad terms using the language of the problem environment. At lower levels of abstraction, a more procedural orientation is taken. Problem-oriented terminology is coupled with implementation-oriented terminology in an effort to state a solution. Finally, at the lowest level of abstraction, the solution is stated in a manner that can be directly implemented. Wasserman [WAS83] provides a useful definition:

> [T]he psychological notion of "abstraction" permits one to concentrate on a problem at some level of generalization without regard to irrelevant low level details; use of abstraction also permits one to work with concepts and terms that are familiar in the problem environment without having to transform them to an unfamiliar structure . . .

Each step in the software engineering process is a refinement in the level of abstraction of the software solution. During system engineering, software is allocated as an element of a computer-based system. During software requirements analysis, the software solution is stated in terms "that are familiar in the problem environment." As we move through the design process, the level of abstraction is reduced. Finally, the lowest level of abstraction is reached when source code is generated.

As we move through different levels of abstraction, we work to create procedural and data *abstractions*. A *procedural abstraction* is a named sequence of instructions that has a specific and limited function. An example of a *procedural abstraction* would be the word "open" on a door. "Open" implies a long sequence of procedural steps (e.g., walk to the door; reach out and grasp knob; turn knob and pull door; step away from moving door, etc.). A *data abstraction* is a named collection of data that describes a data object.

In the context of the procedural abstraction *open* noted above, we can define a data abstraction called **door**. Like any data object, the data abstraction for door would encompass a set of attributes that describe the door (e.g., door type, swing direction, opening mechanism, weight, dimensions). It follows that the procedural abstraction *open* would make use of information contained in the attributes of the data abstraction **door**.

A number of programming languages (e.g., Ada, Modula, CLU) provide mechanisms for creating abstract data types. For example, the Ada *package* is a programming language mechanism that provides support for both data and procedural abstraction. The original abstract data type is used as a template or generic data structure from which other data structures can be *instantiated*.

Control abstraction is the third form of abstraction used in software design. Like procedural and data abstraction, control abstraction implies a program control mechanism without specifying internal details. An example of a control abstraction is the synchronization semaphore [KAI83] used to coordinate activities in an operating system.

13.4.2   Refinement

Stepwise refinement is a top-down design strategy originally proposed by Niklaus Wirth [WIR71]. The architecture of a program is developed by successively refining levels of procedural detail. A hierarchy is developed by decomposing a macroscopic statement of function (a procedural abstraction) in a stepwise fashion until programming language statements are reached. An overview of the concept is provided by Wirth [WIR71]:

> In each step (of the refinement), one or several instructions of the given program are decomposed into more detailed instructions. This successive decomposition or refinement of specifications terminates when all instructions are expressed in terms of any underlying computer or programming language. . . . As tasks are refined, so the data may have to be refined, decomposed, or structured, and it is natural to refine the program and the data specifications in parallel.
>
> Every refinement step implies some design decisions. It is important that . . . the programmer be aware of the underlying criteria (for design decisions) and of the existence of alternative solutions. . . .

The process of program refinement proposed by Wirth is analogous to the process of refinement and partitioning that is used during requirements analysis. The difference is in the level of implementation detail that is considered, not the approach.

Refinement is actually a process of *elaboration*. We begin with a statement of function (or description of information) that is defined at a high level of abstraction. That is, the statement describes function or information conceptually, but provides no information about the internal workings of the function or the internal structure of the information. Refinement causes the designer to elaborate on the original statement, providing more and more detail as each successive refinement (elaboration) occurs.

Abstraction and refinement are complementary concepts. Abstraction enables a designer to specify procedure and data and yet suppress low-level details. Refinement helps the designer to reveal low-level details as design progresses. Both concepts aid the designer in creating a complete design model as the design evolves.

13.4.3   Modularity

The concept of modularity in computer software has been espoused for almost four decades. Software architecture (described in Section 13.4.4) embodies modularity; that is, software is divided into separately named and addressable components, called *modules,* that are integrated to satisfy problem requirements.

It has been stated that "modularity is the single attribute of software that allows a program to be intellectually manageable" [MYE78]. Monolithic software (i.e., a large program comprised of a single module) cannot be easily grasped by a reader. The number of control paths, span of reference, number of variables, and overall complexity would make understanding close to impossible. To illustrate this point, consider the following argument based on observations of human problem solving.

Let $C(x)$ be a function that defines the perceived complexity of a problem x, and $E(x)$ be a function that defines the effort (in time) required to solve a problem x. For two problems, p_1 and p_2, if

$$C(p_1) > C(p_2) \tag{13.1a}$$

it follows that

$$E(p_1) > E(p_2) \tag{13.1b}$$

As a general case, this result is intuitively obvious. It does take more time to solve a difficult problem.

Another interesting characteristic has been uncovered through experimentation in human problem solving. That is,

$$C(p_1 + p_2) > C(p_1) + C(p_2) \tag{13.2}$$

Equation (13.2) implies that the perceived complexity of a problem that combines p_1 and p_2 is greater than the perceived complexity when each problem is considered separately. Considering equation (13.2) and the condition implied by equations (13.1), it follows that

$$E(p_1 + p_2) > E(p_1) + E(p_2) \tag{13.3}$$

This leads to a "divide and conquer" conclusion—it's easier to solve a complex problem when you break it into manageable pieces. The result expressed in inequality (13.3) has important implications with regard to modularity and software. It is, in fact, an argument for modularity.

It is possible to conclude from inequality (13.3) that if we subdivide software indefinitely, the effort required to develop it will become negligibly small! Unfortunately, other forces come into play, causing this conclusion to be (sadly) invalid. As Figure 13.2 shows, the effort (cost) to develop an individual software module does decrease as the total number of modules increases. Given the same set of requirements, more modules means smaller individual size. However, as the number of modules grows, the effort (cost) associated with integrating the modules also grows. These characteristics lead to a total cost or effort curve shown in the figure. There is a number, M, of modules that would result in minimum development cost, but we do not have the necessary sophistication to predict M with assurance.

The curves shown in Figure 13.2 do provide useful guidance when modularity is considered. We should modularize, but care should be taken to stay in the vicinity of M. Undermodularity or overmodularity should be avoided. But how do we know "the vicinity of M"? How modular should we make software? The answers to these questions require an understanding of other design concepts considered later in this chapter.

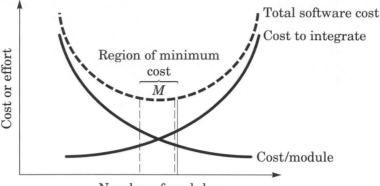

FIGURE 13.2.
Modularity and software cost

Another important question arises when modularity is considered. How do we define an appropriate module of a given size? The answer lies in the method(s) used to define modules within a system.[4] Meyer [MEY88] defines five criteria that enable us to evaluate a design method with respect to its ability to define an effective modular system:

Modular decomposability.   If a design method provides a systematic mechanism for decomposing the problem into subproblems, it will reduce the complexity of the overall problem, thereby achieving an effective modular solution.

Modular composability.   If a design method enables existing (reusable) design components to be assembled into a new system, it will yield a modular solution that does not reinvent the wheel.

Modular understandability.   If a module can be understood as a standalone unit (without reference to other modules) it will be easier to build and easier to change.

Modular continuity.   If small changes to the system requirements result in changes to individual modules, rather than system-wide changes, the impact of change-induced side effects will be minimized.

Modular protection.   If an aberrant condition occurs within a module and its effects are constrained within that module, the impact of error-induced side effects will be minimized.

Finally, it is important to note that a system may be designed modularly, even if its implementation must be "monolithic." There are situations (e.g., real-time software, embedded software) in which relatively minimal speed and memory overhead introduced by subprograms (i.e., subroutines, procedures) is unacceptable. In such situations software can and should be designed with modularity as an overriding philosophy. Code may be developed "in-line."

---

[4]Chapters 14 and 21 discuss methods for design.

Although the program source code may not look modular at first glance, the philosophy has been maintained, and the program will provide the benefits of a modular system.

13.4.4 Software Architecture

Software architecture alludes to "the overall structure of the software and the ways in which that structure provides conceptual integrity for a system" [SHA95a]. In its simplest form, architecture is the hierarchical structure of program components (modules), the manner in which these components interact, and the structure of the data that are used by the components. In a broader sense, however, "components" can be generalized to represent major system elements and their interactions.[5]

One goal of software design is to derive an architectural rendering of a system. This rendering serves as a framework from which more detailed design activities are conducted. A set of architectural patterns enables a software engineer to reuse design-level concepts.

Shaw and Garlan [SHA95a] describe a set of properties that should be specified as part of an architectural design:

Structural properties. This aspect of the architectural design representation defines the components of a system (e.g., modules, objects, filters) and the manner in which those components are packaged and interact with one another. For example, objects are packaged to encapsulate both data and the processing that manipulates the data, and to interact via the invocation of methods (Chapter 19).

Extra-functional properties. The architectural design description should address how the design architecture achieves requirements for performance, capacity, reliability, security, adaptability, and other system characteristics.

Families of related systems. The architectural design should draw upon repeatable patterns that are commonly encountered in the design of families of similar systems. In essence, the design should have the ability to reuse architectural building blocks.

Given the specification of these properties, the architectural design can be represented using one or more of a number of different models [GAR95]. *Structural models* represent architecture as an organized collection of program components. *Framework models* increase the level of design abstraction by attempting to identify repeatable architectural design frameworks (patterns) that are encountered in similar types of applications. *Dynamic models* address the behavioral aspects of the program architecture, indicating how the structure or system configuration may change as a function of external events. *Process mod-*

---

[5]For example, the architectural components of a client/server system are represented at a different level of abstraction. See Chapter 28 for details.

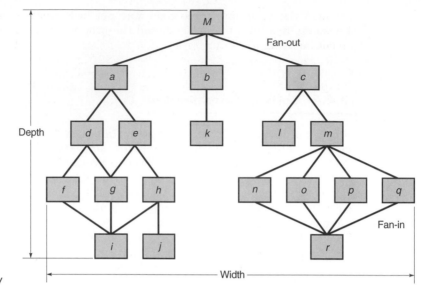

FIGURE 13.3.
Structure terminology

els focus on the design of the business or technical process that the system must accommodate. Finally, *functional models* can be used to represent the functional hierarchy of a system.

A number of different *architectural description languages (ADLs)* have been developed to represent the models noted above [SHA95b]. Although many different ADLs have been proposed, the majority provide mechanisms for describing system components and the manner in which they are connected to one another.

13.4.5 Control Hierarchy

Control hierarchy, also called *program structure,* represents the organization (often hierarchical) of program components (modules) and implies a hierarchy of control. It does not represent procedural aspects of software such as sequence of processes, occurrence/order of decisions, or repetition of operations.

Many different notations are used to represent control hierarchy. The most common is the tree-like diagram (Figure 13.3) that represents the hierarchy. However, other notations, such as Warnier-Orr [ORR77] and Jackson [JAC83] diagrams may also be used with equal effectiveness.[6] In order to facilitate later discussions of structure, we define a few simple measures and terms. In Figure 13.3, *depth* and *width* provide an indication of the number of levels of control and overall span of control, respectively. *Fan-out* is a measure of the number of modules that are directly controlled by another module. *Fan-in* indicates how many modules directly control a given module.

---

[6]For object-oriented designs (Chapter 21) the concept of program structure is less obvious.

The control relationship among modules is expressed in the following way: A module that controls another module is said to be *superordinate* to it; conversely, a module controlled by another is said to be *subordinate* to the controller [YOU79]. For example, as shown in Figure 13.3, module *M* is superordinate to modules *a, b,* and *c.* Module *h* is subordinate to module *e* and is ultimately subordinate to module *M.* Width-oriented relationships (e.g., between modules *d* and *e*), although possible to express in practice, need not be defined with explicit terminology.

The control hierarchy also represents two subtly different characteristics of the software architecture: *visibility* and *connectivity.* Visibility indicates the set of program components that may be invoked or used as data by a given component, even when this is accomplished indirectly. For example, a module in an object-oriented system may have access to a wide array of data attributes that it has inherited, but only make use of a small number of these data attributes. All of the attributes are visible to the module. Connectivity indicates the set of components that are directly invoked or used as data by a given component. For example, a module that directly causes another module to begin execution is connected to it.[7]

13.4.6 Structural Partitioning

The program structure should be partitioned both horizontally and vertically. As shown in Figure 13.4a, *horizontal partitioning* defines separate branches of the modular hierarchy for each major program function. Control modules, represented in a darker shade, are used to coordinate communication between and execution of program functions. The simplest approach to horizontal partitioning defines three partitions—input, data transformation (often called *processing*), and output. Partitioning the architecture horizontally provides a number of distinct benefits:

- results in software that is easier to test
- leads to software that is easier to maintain
- results in propagation of fewer side effects
- results in software that is easier to extend

Because major functions are decoupled from one another, change tends to be less complex and extensions to the system (a common occurrence) tend to be easier to accomplish without side effects. On the negative side, horizontal partitioning often causes more data to be passed across module interfaces and can complicate the overall control of program flow (if processing requires rapid movement from one function to another).

---

[7]In Chapter 19, we explore the concept of inheritance for object-oriented software. A program component can inherit control logic and/or data from another component without explicit reference in the source code. Components of this sort would be visible, but not directly connected. Figure 13.3 indicates connectivity for program modules.

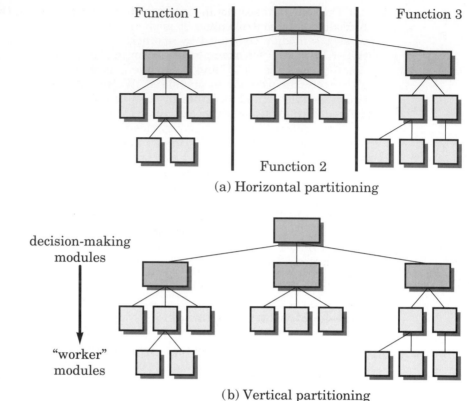

Function 1   Function 3

Function 2

(a) Horizontal partitioning

decision-making modules

"worker" modules

(b) Vertical partitioning

FIGURE 13.4.
Architectural partitioning

Vertical partitioning (Figure 13.4b), often called *factoring,* suggests that control (decision making) and work should be distributed top-down in the program architecture. Top-level modules should perform control functions and do little actual processing work. Modules that reside low in the architecture should be the workers, performing all input, computational, and output tasks.

The nature of change in program architectures justifies the need for vertical partitioning. A change in a control module (high in the architecture) will have a higher probability of propagating side effects to modules that are subordinate to it. A change to a worker module, given its low level in the structure, is less likely to cause the propagation of side effects. In general, changes to computer programs revolve around changes to input, computation or transformation, and output. The overall control structure of the program (i.e., its basic behavior) is far less likely to change. For this reason vertically partitioned architectures are less likely to be susceptible to side effects when changes are made and will therefore be more maintainable—a key quality factor.

13.4.7 Data Structure

Data structure is a representation of the logical relationship among individual elements of data. Because the structure of information will invariably affect the final procedural design, data structure is as important as program structure to the representation of software architecture.

Data structure dictates the organization, methods of access, degree of associativity, and processing alternatives for information. Entire texts (e.g., [AHO83], [KRU84], [GAN89]) have been dedicated to these topics, and a complete discussion is beyond the scope of this book. However, it is important to understand the classic methods available for organizing information and the concepts that underlie information hierarchies.

The organization and complexity of a data structure are limited only by the ingenuity of the designer. There are, however, a limited number of classic data structures that form the building blocks for more sophisticated structures.

A *scalar item* is the simplest of all data structures. As its name implies, a scalar item represents a single element of information that may be addressed by an identifier; that is, access may be achieved by specifying a single address in storage.

When scalar items are organized as a list or contiguous group, a *sequential vector* is formed. Vectors are the most common of all data structures and open the door to variable indexing of information.

When the sequential vector is extended to two, three, and ultimately, an arbitrary number of dimensions, an *n-dimensional* space is created. The most common *n*-dimensional space is the two-dimensional matrix. In most programming languages, an *n*-dimensional space is called an *array*.

Items, vectors, and spaces may be organized in a variety of formats. A *linked list* is a data structure that organizes noncontiguous scalar items, vectors, or spaces in a manner (called *nodes*) that enables them to be processed as a list. Each node contains the appropriate data organization (e.g., a vector) and one or more pointers that indicate the address in storage of the next node in the list. Nodes may be added at any point in the list by redefining pointers to accommodate the new list entry.

Other data structures incorporate or are constructed using the fundamental data structures described above. For example, a *hierarchical data structure* is implemented using multilinked lists that contain scalar items, vectors, and possibly *n*-dimensional spaces. A hierarchical structure is commonly encountered in applications that require information categorization and associativity. Categorization implies a grouping of information by some generic category (e.g., all subcompact automobiles or all 64 bit microprocessors).

Associativity implies the ability to associate information from different categories; for example, find all entries in the microprocessor category that cost less that $100.00 (cost subcategory), run at 100 MHz (cycle time subcategory), and are made by U.S. vendors (vendor subcategory).

It is important to note that data structures, like program structures, can be represented at different levels of abstraction. For example, a **stack** is a conceptual model of a data structure that can be implemented as a vector or a linked list. Depending on the level of design detail, the internal workings of **stack** may or may not be specified.

13.4.8   Software Procedure

Program structure defines control hierarchy without regard to the sequence of processing and decisions. Software procedure focuses on the processing details

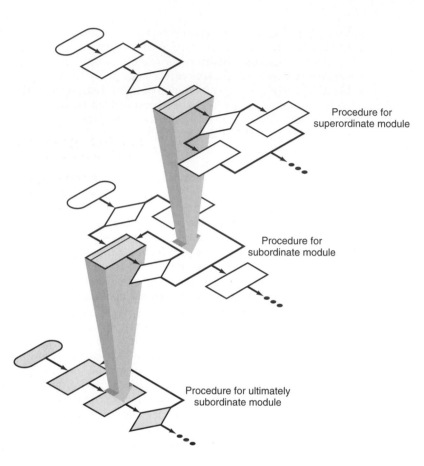

Procedure for
superordinate module

Procedure for
subordinate module

Procedure for ultimately
subordinate module

FIGURE 13.5.
Procedure is layered

of each module individually. Procedure must provide a precise specification of processing, including sequence of events, exact decision points, repetitive operations, and even data organization/structure.

There is, of course, a relationship between structure and procedure. Processing indicated for each module must include a reference to all modules subordinate to the module being described. That is, a procedural representation of software is layered as illustrated in Figure 13.5.

13.4.9 Information Hiding

The concept of modularity leads every software designer to a fundamental question: "How do we decompose a software solution to obtain the best set of modules?" The principle of *information hiding* [PAR72] suggests that modules be "characterized by design decisions that (each) hides from all others." In other words, modules should be specified and designed so that information (procedure and data) contained within a module is inaccessible to other modules that have no need for such information.

Hiding implies that effective modularity can be achieved by defining a set of independent modules that communicate with one another only that information that is necessary to achieve software function. Abstraction helps to define the procedural (or informational) entities that comprise the software. Hiding defines and enforces access constraints to both procedural detail within a module and any local data structure used by the module [ROS75].

The use of information hiding as a design criterion for modular systems provides its greatest benefits when modifications are required during testing and later, during software maintenance. Because most data and procedure are hidden from other parts of the software, inadvertent errors introduced during modification are less likely to propagate to other locations within the software.

13.5   EFFECTIVE MODULAR DESIGN

The fundamental design concepts described in the preceding section all serve to precipitate modular designs. In fact, modularity has become an accepted approach in all engineering disciplines. A modular design reduces complexity (see Section 13.4.3), facilitates change (a critical aspect of software maintainability), and results in easier implementation by encouraging parallel development of different parts of a system.

13.5.1 Functional Independence

The concept of *functional independence* is a direct outgrowth of modularity and the concepts of abstraction and information hiding. In landmark papers on software design Parnas [PAR72] and Wirth [WIR71] allude to refinement techniques that enhance module independence. Later work by Stevens, Myers, and Constantine [STE74] solidified the concept.

Functional independence is achieved by developing modules with "single-minded" function and an "aversion" to excessive interaction with other modules. Stated another way, we want to design software so that each module addresses a specific subfunction of requirements and has a simple interface when viewed from other parts of the program structure. It is fair to ask why independence is important. Software with *effective modularity* (i.e., independent modules), is easier to develop because function may be compartmentalized and interfaces are simplified (consider ramifications when development is conducted by a team). Independent modules are easier to maintain (and test) because secondary effects caused by design/code modification are limited, error propagation is reduced, and reusable modules are possible. To summarize, functional independence is a key to good design, and design is the key to software quality.

Independence is measured using two qualitative criteria: cohesion and coupling. *Cohesion* is a measure of the relative functional strength of a module. *Coupling* is a measure of the relative interdependence among modules.

13.5.2   Cohesion

Cohesion is a natural extension of the information hiding concept described in Section 13.4.9. A cohesive module performs a single task within a software procedure, requiring little interaction with procedures being performed in other parts of a program. Stated simply, an cohesive module should (ideally) do just one thing.

Cohesion may be represented as a "spectrum" shown in Figure 13.6. We always strive for high cohesion, although the mid-range of the spectrum is often acceptable. The scale for cohesion is nonlinear. That is, low-end cohesiveness is much "worse" than the middle range, which is nearly as "good" as high-end cohesion. In practice, a designer need not be concerned with categorizing cohesion in a specific module. Rather, the overall concept should be understood and low levels of cohesion should be avoided when modules are designed.

To illustrate (somewhat facetiously) the low end of the spectrum, we relate the following story:

> In the late 1960s most DP managers began to recognize the worth of modularity. Unfortunately many existing programs were monolithic—e.g., 20,000 lines of undocumented Fortran with one 2500 line subroutine! To bring a large computer program to the state of the art, a manager asked her staff to modularize the program. This was to be done "in your spare time."
>
> Under the gun, one staff member asked (innocently) the proper length for a module. "Seventy-five lines of code," came the reply. He then obtained a red pen and a ruler, measured the linear distance taken by 75 lines of source code, and drew a red line on the source listing, then another and another. Each red line indicated a module boundary. This technique is akin to developing software with coincidental cohesion!

A module that performs a set of tasks that relate to each other loosely, if at all, is termed *coincidentally cohesive*. A module that performs tasks that are related logically (e.g., a module that produces all output regardless of type) is *logically cohesive*. When a module contains tasks that are related by the fact that all must be executed within the same span of time, the module exhibits *temporal cohesion*.

As an example of low cohesion, consider a module that performs error processing for an engineering analysis package. The module is called when computed data exceed prespecified bounds. It performs the following tasks: (1) computes supplementary data based on original computed data; (2) produces an error report (with graphical content) on the user's workstation; (3) performs fol-

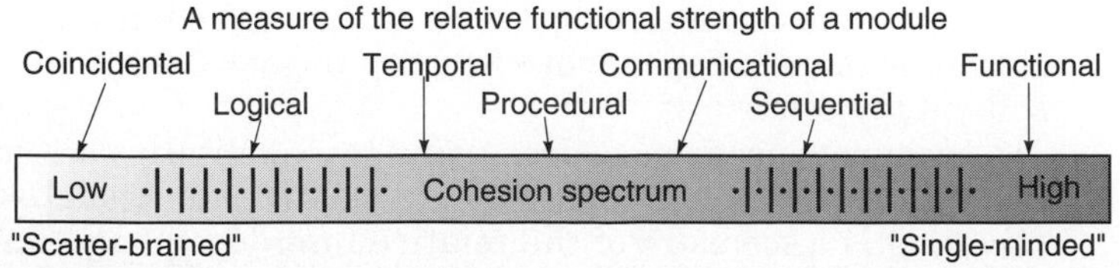

FIGURE 13.6.
Cohesion

low-up calculations requested by the user; (4) updates a data base; and (5) enables menu selection for subsequent processing. Although the preceding tasks are loosely related, each is an independent functional entity that might best be performed as a separate module. Combining the functions into a single module can only serve to increase the likelihood of error propagation when a modification is made to any one of the processing tasks noted above.

Moderate levels of cohesion are relatively close to one another in the degree of module independence. When processing elements of a module are related and must be executed in a specific order, *procedural cohesion* exists. When all processing elements concentrate on one area of a data structure, *communicational cohesion* is present. High cohesion is characterized by a module that performs one distinct procedural task.

As we have already noted, it is unnecessary to determine the precise level of cohesion. Rather it is important to strive for high cohesion and recognize low cohesion so that software design can be modified to achieve greater functional independence.

13.5.4 Coupling

Coupling is a measure of interconnection among modules in a program structure. Like cohesion, coupling may be represented on a spectrum as shown in Figure 13.7. Coupling depends on the interface complexity between modules, the point at which entry or reference is made to a module, and what data pass across the interface.

In software design, we strive for lowest possible coupling. Simple connectivity among modules results in software that is easier to understand and less prone to a "ripple effect" [STE74] caused when errors occur at one location and propagate through a system.

Figure 13.8 provides examples of different types of module coupling. Modules *a* and *d* are subordinate to different modules. Each is unrelated and therefore no direct coupling occurs. Module *c* is subordinate to module *a* and is accessed via a conventional argument list through which data are passed. As long as a simple argument list is present (i.e., simple data are passed; a one-to-one correspondence of items exists), low coupling (*data coupling* on the spectrum) is exhibited in this portion of structure. A variation of data coupling, called *stamp coupling*, is found when a portion of a data structure (rather than simple arguments) is passed via a module interface. This occurs between modules *b* and *a*.

At moderate levels coupling is characterized by passage of control between modules. *Control coupling* is very common in most software designs and is

FIGURE 13.7.
Coupling

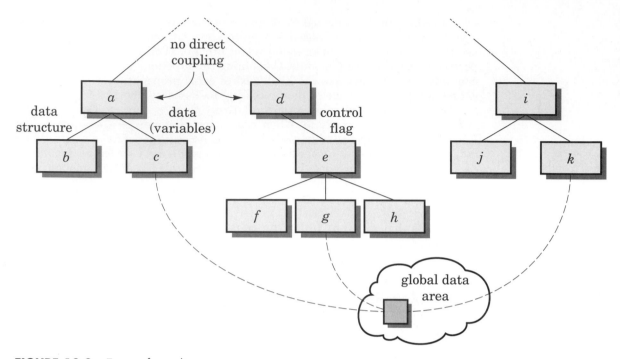

FIGURE 13.8. Types of coupling

shown in Figure 13.8, where a "control flag" (a variable that controls decisions in a subordinate or superordinate module) is passed between modules *d* and *e*.

Relatively high levels of coupling occur when modules are tied to an environment external to software. For example, I/O couples a module to specific devices, formats, and communication protocols. External coupling is essential, but should be limited to a small number of modules with a structure. High coupling also occurs when a number of modules reference a global data area. *Common coupling,* as this mode is called, is shown in Figure 13.8. Modules *c, g,* and *k* each access a data item in a global data area (e.g., a disk file, Fortran COMMON, external data types in the C programming language). Module *c* initializes the item. Later module *g* recomputes and updates the item. Let's assume that an error occurs and *g* updates the item incorrectly. Much later in processing, module *k* reads the item, attempts to process it, and fails, causing the software to abort. The apparent cause of abort is module *k*; the actual cause, module *g*. Diagnosing problems in structures with considerable common coupling is time-consuming and difficult. However, this does not mean that the use of global data is necessarily "bad." It does mean that a software designer must be aware of potential consequences of common coupling and take special care to guard against them.

The highest degree of coupling, *content coupling,* occurs when one module makes use of data or control information maintained within the boundary of another module. Secondarily, content coupling occurs when branches are made into the middle of a module. This mode of coupling can and should be avoided.

The coupling modes discussed above occur because of design decisions made when the program structure was developed. Variants of external coupling, however, may be introduced during coding. For example, compiler coupling ties source code to specific (and often nonstandard) attributes of a compiler; operating system (OS) coupling ties design and resultant code to operating system "hooks" that can create havoc when OS changes occur.

13.6   DESIGN HEURISTICS FOR EFFECTIVE MODULARITY

Once a program structure has been developed, effective modularity can be achieved by applying the design concepts introduced earlier in this chapter. The program architecture is manipulated according to a set of heuristics (guidelines) presented in this section.

I. Evaluate the "first iteration" of the program structure to reduce coupling and improve cohesion.   Once program structure has been developed, modules may be *exploded or imploded* with an eye toward improving module independence. An exploded module becomes two or more modules in the final program structure. An imploded module is the result of combining the processing implied by two or more modules.

An exploded module often results when a common process component exists in two or more modules and can be redefined as a separate cohesive module. When high coupling is expected, modules can sometimes be imploded to reduce passage of control, reference to global data and interface complexity.

II. Attempt to minimize structures with high fan-out; strive for fan-in as depth increases.   The structure shown inside the cloud in Figure 13.9 does not make effective use of factoring. All modules are "pancaked" below a single control module. In general, a more reasonable distribution of control is shown in the upper structure. The structure takes an oval shape, indicating a number of layers of control and highly utilitarian modules at lower levels.

III. Keep scope of effect of a module within the scope of control of that module.   The *scope of effect* of a module *e* is defined as all other modules that are affected by a decision made in module *e*. The *scope of control* of module *e* is all modules that are subordinate and ultimately subordinate to module *e*. As shown in Figure 13.9, if module *e* makes a decision that affects module *r*, we have a violation of heuristic III, because module *r* lies outside the scope of control of module *e*.

IV. Evaluate module interfaces to reduce complexity and redundancy and improve consistency.   Module interface complexity is a prime cause of software errors. Interfaces should be designed to pass information simply and should be consistent with the function of a module. Interface inconsistency (i.e., seemingly unrelated data passed via an argument list or other technique) is an indication of low cohesion. The module in question should be re-evaluated.

V. Define modules whose function is predictable, but avoid modules that are overly restrictive.   A module is predictable when it can

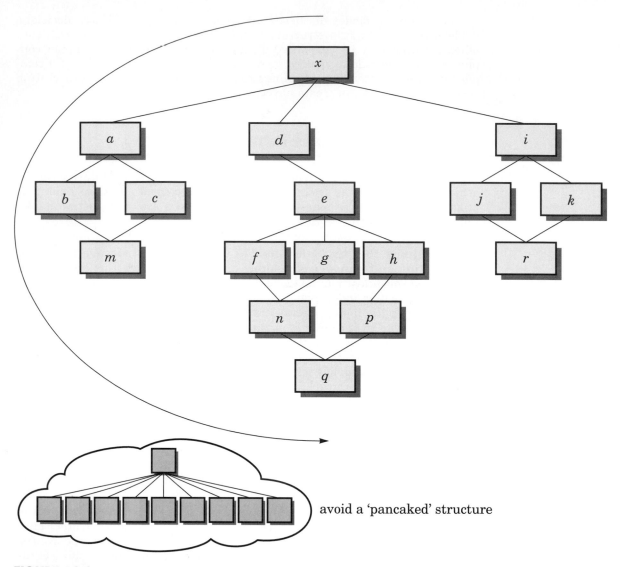

avoid a 'pancaked' structure

FIGURE 13.9. Program structures

be treated as a black box; that is, the same external data will be produced regardless of internal processing details.[8] Modules that have internal "memory" can be unpredictable unless care is taken in their use.

A module that restricts processing to a single subfunction exhibits high cohesion and is viewed with favor by a designer. However, a module that arbitrarily restricts size of a local data structure, options within control

---

[8]A "black-box" module is a *procedural abstraction*.

flow, or modes of external interface will invariably require maintenance to remove such restrictions.

VI. Strive for "controlled entry" modules, avoiding "pathological connections." This design heuristic warns against content coupling. Software is easier to understand and therefore easier to maintain when modules interfaced are constrained and controlled. *Pathological connection* refers to branches or references into the middle of a module.

VII. Package software based on design constraints and portability requirements. *Packaging* alludes to the techniques used to assemble software for a specific processing environment. Design constraints sometimes dictate that a program "overlay" itself in memory. When this must occur, the design structure may have to be reorganized to group modules by degree of repetition, frequency of access and interval between calls. In addition, optional or "one-shot" modules may be separated in the structure so that they may be effectively overlaid.

13.7 THE DESIGN MODEL

The design principles and concepts discussed in this chapter establish a foundation for the creation of the design model that encompasses representations of data, architecture, interfaces, and procedures. Like the analysis model before it, in the design model each of these design representations is tied to the others, and all can be traced back to software requirements.

In Figure 13.1, the design model was represented as a pyramid. The symbolism of this shape is important. A pyramid is an extremely stable object with a wide base and a low center of gravity. Like the pyramid, we want to create a software design that is stable. By establishing a broad foundation using data design, a stable mid-region with architectural and interface design, and a sharp point by applying procedural design, we create a design model that is not easily "tipped over" by the winds of change.

It is interesting to note that some programmers continue to design implicitly, conducting procedural design as they code. This is akin to taking the design pyramid and standing it on its point—an extremely unstable design results. The smallest change may cause the pyramid (and the program) to topple.

The methods that lead to the creation of the design model are presented in Chapters 14 and 21 (for object-oriented systems). Each method enables the designer to create a stable design that conforms to the fundamental concepts that lead to high-quality software.

13.8 DESIGN DOCUMENTATION

The document outlined in Figure 13.10 can be used as a template for a *design specification*. Each numbered paragraph addresses different aspects of the design model. The numbered sections of the design specification are completed as the designer refines his or her representation of the software.

The overall scope of the design effort is described in section I (section numbers refer to design specification outline). Much of the information contained in this section is derived from the *system specification* and the analysis model (*software requirements specification*).

I. Scope
   A. System objectives
   B. Major software requirements
   C. Design constraints, limitations
II. Data Design
   A. Data objects and resultant data structures
   B. File and database structures
      1. external file structure
         a. logical structure
         b. logical record description
         c. access method
      2. global data
      3. file and data cross reference
III. Architectural Design
   A. Review of data and control flow
   B. Derived program structure
IV. Interface Design
   A. Human–machine interface specification
   B. Human–machine interface design rules
   C. External interface design
      1. Interfaces to external data
      2. Interfaces to external systems or devices
   D. Internal interface design rules
V. Procedural Design
   For each module:
   A. Processing narrative
   B. Interface description
   C. Design language (or other) description
   D. Modules used
   E. Internal data structures
   F. Comments/restrictions/limitations
VI. Requirements Cross-Reference
VII. Test Provisions
      1. Test guidelines
      2. Integration strategy
      3. Special considerations
VIII. Special Notes
IX. Appendices

FIGURE 13.10.
Design specification
outline

Section II presents the data design, describing external file structures, internal data structures and a cross reference that connects data objects to specific files. Section III, the architectural design, indicates how the program architecture has been derived from the analysis model. Structure charts (a representation of program structure) are used to represent the module hierarchy.

Sections IV and V evolve as interface and procedural design commence. External and internal program interfaces are represented and a detailed design of the human–machine interface is described. Modules—separately addressable elements of software such as subroutines, functions, or procedures—are initially described with an English-language processing narrative. The processing narrative explains the procedural function of a module. Later, a procedural design tool is used to translate the narrative into a structured description.

Section VI of the design specification contains a *requirements cross-reference*. The purpose of this cross-reference matrix is (1) to establish that all requirements are satisfied by the software design, and (2) to indicate which modules are critical to the implementation of specific requirements.

The first stage in the development of test documentation is contained in section VII of the design document. Once software structure and interfaces have been established, we can develop guidelines for testing of individual modules and integration of the entire package. In some cases, a detailed specification of test procedure occurs in parallel with design. In such cases, this section may be deleted from the design specification.

Design constraints, such as physical memory limitations or the necessity for a specialized external interface, may dictate special requirements for assembling or packaging of software. Special considerations caused by the necessity for program overlay, virtual memory management, high-speed processing, or other factors may cause modification in design derived from information flow or structure. Requirements and considerations for software packaging are presented in section VII. Secondarily, this section describes the approach that will be used to transfer software to a customer site.

Section IX of the design specification contains supplementary data. Algorithm descriptions, alternative procedures, tabular data, excerpts from other documents and other relevant information are presented as a special note or as a separate appendix. It may be advisable to develop a *preliminary operations/installation manual* and include it as an appendix to the design document.

13.9 SUMMARY

Design is the technical kernel of software engineering. During design, progressive refinements of data structure, program architecture, interfaces, and procedural detail are developed, reviewed, and documented. Design results in representations of software that can be assessed for quality.

A number of fundamental software design principles and concepts have been proposed over the past three decades. Design principles guide the software engineer as the design process proceeds. Design concepts provide basic criteria for design quality.

Modularity (in both program and data) and the concept of abstraction enable the designer to simplify and reuse software components. Refinement provides a mechanism for representing successive layers of functional detail. Program and data structure contribute to an overall view of software architecture, while procedure provides the detail necessary for algorithm implementation. Information hiding and functional independence provide heuristics for achieving effective modularity.

We conclude our discussion of design fundamentals with the words of Glenford Myers [MYE78]:

> [W]e try to solve the problem by rushing through the design process so that enough time will be left at the end of the project to uncover errors that were made because we rushed through the design process . . .

The moral is: *don't rush through it!* Design is worth the effort.

We have not concluded our discussion of design. In the chapter that follows, design methods are discussed. These methods, combined with the fundamentals in this chapter and other methods in Chapter 21, form the basis for a complete view of software design.

REFERENCES

[AHO83]   Aho, A.V., J. Hopcroft, and J. Ullmann, *Data Structures and Algorithms,* Addison-Wesley, 1983.

[CAI75]   Caine, S., and K. Gordon, "PDL—A Tool for Software Design," in *Proc. Natl. Computer Conf.*, AFIPS Press, 1975, pp. 271–276.

[CUR85]   Curtis, B., *Human Factors in Software Development,* 2nd edition, IEEE Computer Society Press, 1985.

[DAH72]   Dahl, O. E. Dijkstra, and C. Hoare, *Structured Programming,* Academic Press, 1972.

[DAV95]   Davis, A., *201 Principles of Software Development,* McGraw-Hill, 1995.

[DEN73]   Dennis, J., "Modularity," in *Advanced Course on Software Engineering,* F.L. Bauer (ed.), Springer-Verlag, New York, 1973, pp. 128–182.

[GAM95]   Gamma, E. et al., *Design Patterns,* Addison-Wesley, 1995.

[GAN89]   Gonnet, G., *Handbook of Algorithms and Data Structures,* 2nd edition, Addison-Wesley, 1989.

[GAR95]   Garlan, D., and M. Shaw, "An Introduction to Software Architecture," in *Advances in Software Engineering and Knowledge Engineering,* vol I, V. Ambriola and G. Tortora (eds.), World Scientific Publishing Company, 1995.

[JAC75]   Jackson, M.A., *Principles of Program Design,* Academic Press, 1975.

[JAC83]   Jackson, M.A., *System Development,* Prentice-Hall, 1983.

[JAC92]   Jacobson, I., *Object-Oriented Software Engineering,* Addison-Wesley, 1992.

[KAI83]   Kaiser, S.H., *The Design of Operating Systems for Small Computer Systems,* Wiley-Interscience, 1983, pp. 594ff.

[KRU84]   Kruse, R.L., *Data Structures and Program Design,* Prentice-Hall, 1984.

[McG91]   McGlaughlin, R., "Some Notes on Program Design," *Software Engineering Notes,* vol. 16, no. 4, October 1991, pp. 53–54.

[MEY88]   Meyer, B., *Object-Oriented Software Construction,* Prentice-Hall, 1988.

[MIL72]   Mills, H.D., "Mathematical Foundations for Structured Programming," Technical Report FSC 71-6012, IBM Corp., Federal Systems Division, Gaithersburg, MD, 1972.

[MYE78]   Myers, G., *Composite Structured Design,* Van Nostrand Reinhold, 1978.

[ORR77]   Orr, K.T., *Structured Systems Development,* Yourdon Press, New York, 1977.

[PAR72]   Parnas, D.L., "On Criteria To Be Used in Decomposing Systems into Modules," *CACM,* vol. 14, no. 1, April, 1972, pp. 221–227.

[PET81]   Peters, L.J., Software Design: Methods and Techniques, *Yourdon Press,* New York, 1981.

[ROS75]   Ross, D., J. Goodenough, and C. Irvine, "Software Engineering: Process, Principles and Goals," *IEEE Computer,* vol. 8, no. 5, May 1975.

[SHA95a]   Shaw, M., and D. Garlan, "Formulations and Formalisms in Software Architecture," *Volume 1000—Lecture Notes in Computer Science,* Springer-Verlag, 1995.

[SHA95b]   Shaw, M. et al., "Abstractions for Software Architecture and Tools to Support Them," *IEEE Trans. Software Engineering,* vol. 21, no. 4, April 1995, pp. 314–335.

[STE74]   Stevens, W., G. Myers, and L. Constantine, "Structured Design," *IBM Systems Journal,* vol. 13, no. 2, 1974, pp. 115–139.

[TAY59]   Taylor, E.S., *An Interim Report on Engineering Design,* Massachusetts Institute of Technology, Cambridge, MA, 1959.

[WAR74]   Warnier, J., *Logical Construction of Programs,* Van Nostrand Reinhold, 1974.

[WAS83]   Wasserman, A., "Information System Design Methodology," in *Software Design Techniques,* P. Freeman and A. Wasserman (eds.), 4th edition, IEEE Computer Society Press, 1983, p. 43.

[WIR71]   Wirth, N., "Program Development by Stepwise Refinement," *CACM,* vol. 14, no. 4, 1971, pp. 221–227.

[YOU79]   Yourdon, E., and L. Constantine, *Structured Design,* Prentice-Hall, 1979.

PROBLEMS AND POINTS TO PONDER

13.1. Do you design software when you "write" a program? What makes software design different from coding?

13.2. Develop three additional design principles to add to those noted in Section 13.3.

13.3. Provide examples of three data abstractions and the procedural abstractions that can be used to manipulate them.

13.4. Apply a "stepwise refinement approach" to develop three different levels of procedural abstraction for one or more of the following programs:

a. Develop a check writer that, given a numeric dollar amount, will print the amount in words that is normally required on a check.

b. Iteratively solve for the roots of a transcendental equation.

c. Develop a simple round-robin scheduling algorithm for an operating system.

13.5. Is there a case when inequality (13.2) may not be true? How might such a case affect the argument for modularity.

13.6. When should a modular design be implemented as monolithic software? How can this be accomplished? Is performance the only justification for implementation of monolithic software?

13.7. Develop at least five levels of abstraction for one of the following software problems:

a. a consumer banking application

b. a 3D transformation package for computer graphics applications

c. a BASIC language interpreter

d. a two degree of freedom robot controller

e. any problem mutually agreeable to you and your instructor

As the level of abstraction decreases, your focus may narrow so that at the last level (source code) only a single task need be described.

13.8. Obtain the original Parnas paper [PAR72] and summarize the software example that he uses to illustrate decomposition of a system into modules. How is information hiding used to achieve the decomposition?

13.9. Discuss the relationship between the concept of information hiding as an attribute of effective modularity and the concept of module independence.

13.10. Review some of your recent software development efforts and grade each module (on a scale of 1-low to 7-high). Bring in samples of your best and worst work.

13.11. A number of high-level programming languages support the internal procedure as a modular construct. How does this construct affect coupling? information hiding?

13.12. How are the concepts of coupling and software portability related? Provide examples to support your discussion.

13.13. Discuss how structural partitioning can help to make software more maintainable.

13.14. What is the purpose of developing a program architecture that is factored?

13.15. Describe the concept of information hiding in your own words.

13.16. Why is it a good idea to keep the scope of effect of a module within its scope of control?

FURTHER READINGS AND OTHER INFORMATION SOURCES

An excellent historical survey of important papers on software design is contained in an anthology edited by Freeman and Wasserman (*Software Design*

Techniques, 4th edition, IEEE, 1983). This tutorial reprints many of the classic papers that have formed the basis for current trends in software design. Good discussions of software design fundamentals can be found in books by Myers [MYE78], Peters [PET81], Macro (*Software Engineering: Concepts and Management,* Prentice-Hall, 1990), and Sommerville (*Software Engineering,* Addison-Wesley, 5th edition, 1996). McConnell (*Code Complete,* Microsoft Press, 1993) presents an excellent discussion of the practical aspects of designing high-quality computer software.

A worthwhile survey of different design notations can be found in a book by Martin and McClure (*Diagramming Techniques for Analysts and Programmers,* Prentice-Hall, 1985). Stevens (*Software Design: Concepts and Methods,* Prentice-Hall, 1990) presents a worthwhile treatment of data, architectural and procedural design. Witt and his colleagues (*Software Design,* Van Nostrand Reinhold, 1993) also cover the topic thoroughly. The design issues involved in creating effective software architectures are considered by Shaw and Garlan (*Software Architectures,* Prentice-Hall, 1995) and in an anthology edited by Coplien and Schmidt (*Pattern Languages of Program Design,* Addison-Wesley, 1995).

Mathematically rigorous treatments of computer software and design fundamentals may be found in books by Jones (*Software Development: A Rigorurous Approach,* Prentice-Hall, 1980), Wulf (*Fundamental Structures of Computer Science,* Addison-Wesley, 1981), and Brassard and Bratley (*Fundamentals of Algorithmics,* Prentice-Hall, 1995). Each of these texts helps to supply a necessary theoretical foundation for our understanding of computer software. Kruse (*Data Structures and Program Design,* Prentice-Hall, 1994) and Tucker et al. (*Fundamental of Computing II: Abstraction, Data Structures, and Large Software Systems,* McGraw-Hill, 1995) present worthwhile information on data structures. Measures of design quality, presented from both a technical and management perspective, are considered by Card and Glass (*Measuring Software Design Quality,* Prentice-Hall, 1990).

General discussion of design issues can be found in the Internet newsgroup **comp.software-eng** and many other newsgroups.

An integrated environment for software design is discussed at:

http://www-ksl.stanford.edu/KSL_Abstracts/KSL-91-73.html

A variety of on-line articles on software design as well as other current information can be obtained from the Association for Software Design at:

http://pcd.stanford.edu/asd/index.html

Substantial research has been conducted in the area of software architectures. An excellent technology guide to the subject can be obtained at:

http://www.stars.reston.paramax.com/arch/guide.html

Pointers to current work can be found at:

http://www.cs.cmu.edu/~shaw/Shawparts/ArchPubs.html
http://www.sei.cmu.edu/technology/architecture
http://www2.umassd.edu/SECenter/SAResources.html

An up-to-date list of World Wide Web references for software design can be found at: **http://www.rspa.com**

DESIGN METHODS

Design has been described as a multistep process in which representations of data structure, program structure, interface characteristics, and procedural detail are synthesized from information requirements. This description is extended by Freeman [FRE80]:

> [D]esign is an activity concerned with making major decisions, often of a structural nature. It shares with programming a concern for abstracting information representation and processing sequences, but the level of detail is quite different at the extremes. Design builds coherent, well planned representations of programs that concentrate on the interrelationships of parts at the higher level and the logical operations involved at the lower levels. . . .

As we have noted in the preceding chapter, design is information driven. Software design methods are derived from consideration of each of the three domains of the analysis model. The data, functional, and behavioral domains serve as a guide for the creation of the design.

Methods required to create each of the layers of the design model (Figure 13.1) are presented in this chapter. The objective is to provide a systematic approach for the derivation of the design—the blueprint from which software is constructed.

14.1　　DATA DESIGN

Data design is the first (and some would say the most important) of four design activities that are conducted during software engineering. The impact of data structure on program structure and procedural complexity causes data design to have a profound influence on software quality. The concepts of information hiding and data abstraction provide the foundation for an approach to data design.

The process of data design is summarized by Wasserman [WAS80]:

> The primary activity during data design is to select logical representations of data objects (data structures) identified during the requirements definition and specification phase. The selection process may involve algorithmic analysis of alternative structures in order to determine the most efficient design or may simply involve the use of a set of modules (a "package") that provide the desired operations upon some representation of an object.
>
> An important related activity during design is to identify those program modules that must operate directly upon the logical data structures. In this way the scope of effect of individual data design decisions can be constrained.

Regardless of the design techniques to be used, well-designed data can lead to better program structure and modularity, and reduced procedural complexity.

Wasserman [WAS80] has proposed a set of principles that may be used to specify and design data. In actuality, the design of data begins during the creation of the analysis model (Chapter 12). Recalling that requirements analysis and design often overlap, we consider the following set of principles [WAS80] for data specification:

1. *The systematic analysis principles applied to function and behavior should also be applied to data.* We spend much time and effort deriving, reviewing, and specifying functional requirements and preliminary design. Representations of data objects, relationships, data flow, and content should also be developed and reviewed, alternative data organizations should be considered, and the impact of data modeling on software design should be evaluated. For example, specification of a multiringed linked list may nicely satisfy data requirements but may lead to an unwieldy software design. An alternative data organization may lead to better results.

2. *All data structures and the operations to be performed on each should be identified.* The design of an efficient data structure must take the operations to be performed on the data structure into account (e.g., see [AHO83]). For example, consider a data structure made up of a set of diverse data elements. The data structure is to be manipulated in a number of major software functions. Upon evaluation of the operation performed on the data structure, an abstract data type is defined for use in subsequent software design. Specification of the abstract data type may simplify software design considerably.

3. *A data dictionary should be established and used to define both data and program design.* The concept of a data dictionary was introduced in Chapter 12. A data dictionary explicitly represents the relationships among data objects and the constraints on the elements of a data structure. Algorithms that must take advantage of specific relationships can be more easily defined if a dictionary-like data specification exists.

4. *Low-level data design decisions should be deferred until late in the design process.* A process of stepwise refinement may be used for the design of data. That is, overall data organization may be defined during requirements analysis, refined during preliminary design work, and specified in detail during later design iterations. The top-down approach to data design provides benefits that are analogous to a top-down approach to software design—major structural attributes are designed and evaluated first so that the architecture of the data may be established.

5. *The representation of data structures should be known only to those modules that must make direct use of the data contained within the structure.* The concept of information hiding and the related concept of coupling provide important insight into the quality of a software design. Principle 5 alludes to the importance of these concepts as well as "the importance of separating the logical view of a data object from its physical view" [WAS80].

6. *A library of useful data structures and the operations that may be applied to them should be developed.* Data structures and operations should be viewed as resources for software design. Data structures can be designed for reusability. A library of data structure *templates* (abstract data types) can reduce both specification and design effort for data.

7. *A software design and programming language should support the specification and realization of abstract data types.* The implementation (and corresponding design) of a sophisticated data structure can be made exceedingly difficult if no means for direct specification of the structure exists. For example, implementation (or design) of a linked list structure or a multilevel heterogeneous array would be difficult if the target programming language was Fortran because the language does not support direct specification of these data structures.

The principles described above form a basis for a data design approach that can be integrated into both the definition and development phase of the software engineering process. As we have noted elsewhere in this book, a clear definition of information is essential to successful software development.

14.2   ARCHITECTURAL DESIGN

The primary objective of *architectural design* is to develop a modular program structure and represent the control relationships between modules. In addition, architectural design melds program structure and data structure, defining interfaces that enable data to flow throughout the program.

To understand the importance of architecture design, we present a brief story from everyday life:

You've saved your money, you've purchased a beautiful piece of land, and you've decided to build the house of your dreams. Having no experience in such matters, you visit a builder and explain your desires—number and size of rooms, contemporary styling, spa (of course!), cathedral ceilings, lots of glass, etc. The builder listens carefully, asks a few questions, and then tells you that he'll have a design in a few weeks.

As you wait anxiously for his call, you conjure up many different (and outrageously expensive) images of your new house. What will he come up with? Finally, the phone rings and you rush to his office.

Pulling out a large manila folder, the builder spreads a diagram of the plumbing for the second floor bathroom in front of you and proceeds to explain it in great detail.

"But what about the overall design?" you say.

"Don't worry," says the builder, "we'll get to that later."

Does the builder's approach seem a bit unusual? Do you feel comfortable with the builder's final response? Of course not! You want to see a sketch of the house, a floor plan, and other information that will provide an *architectural view*. Yet many software developers act like the builder in our story. They concentrate on the "plumbing" (procedural details and code) to the exclusion of the software architecture. The design method presented in this section encourages the software engineer to concentrate on architectural design before worrying about the plumbing.

14.2.1 Contributors

Architectural design (and software design generally) has its origins in earlier design concepts that stressed modularity [DEN73], top-down design [WIR71], and structured programming [DAH72, LIN79]. Stevens, Myers, and Constantine [STE74] were early proponents of software design based on the flow of data through a system. Early work was refined and presented in books by Myers [MYE78] and Yourdon and Constantine [YOU79].

More recent work on software architectural design has developed a much more sophisticated focus. A book by Shaw and Garlan [SHA95] and articles by Dean [DEA95] and Moriconi [MOR95] are all representative of work that focuses on developing formalisms for representing architectural design models and patterns.

14.2.2 Areas of Application

Each software design method has strengths and weaknesses. An important selection factor for a design method is the breadth of applications to which it can be applied. Data flow–oriented design is amenable to a broad range of application areas. In fact, because all software can be represented by a data flow diagram, a design method that makes use of the diagram could theoretically be applied in every software development effort. A data flow–oriented approach to design is particularly useful when information is processed sequentially and no formal hierarchical data structure exists. For example, microprocessor control applications; complex, numerical analysis procedures; process control; and many other engineering and scientific software applications fall into this category. Data flow–oriented design techniques are also applicable in data processing applications and can be effectively applied even when hierarchical data structures do exist.

There are cases, however, in which a consideration of data flow is at best a side issue. In such applications (e.g., database systems, expert systems, object-oriented interfaces), other design methods may be more appropriate.

14.3 THE ARCHITECTURAL DESIGN PROCESS

Data flow–oriented design is an architectural design method that allows a convenient transition from the analysis model to a design description of program structure. The transition from information flow (represented as a data flow diagram) to structure is accomplished as part of a five-step process: (1) the type of information flow is established; (2) flow boundaries are indicated; (3) the DFD is mapped into program structure; (4) control hierarchy is defined by *factoring;* and (5) the resultant structure is refined using design measures and heuristics. The information flow type is the driver for the mapping approach required in step 3. In the following sections we examine two flow types.

14.3.1 Transform Flow

In the fundamental system model (level 0 data flow diagram), information must enter and exit software in an "external world" form. For example, data typed on a keyboard, tones on a telephone line, and pictures on a computer graphics display are all forms of external world information. Such externalized data must be converted into an internal form for processing. The time history of data can be illustrated in Figure 14.1. Information enters the system along paths that transform external data into an internal form and will be identified as *incoming flow*. At the kernel of the software, a transition occurs. Incoming data are passed through a *transform center* and begin to move along paths that now lead "out" of the software. Data moving along these paths are called *outgoing flow*. The overall flow of data occurs in a sequential manner and follows one, or only a few, "straight line" paths. When a segment of a data flow diagram exhibits these characteristics, *transform flow* is present.

14.3.2 Transaction Flow

The fundamental system model implies transform flow; therefore, it is possible to characterize all data flow in this category. However, information flow is often characterized by a single data item, called a *transaction,* that triggers other data flow along one of many paths. When a DFD takes the form shown in Figure 14.2, *transaction flow* is present.

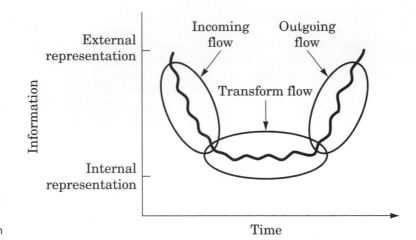

FIGURE 14.1.
Flow of information

Transaction flow is characterized by data moving along an incoming path that converts external world information into a transaction. The transaction is evaluated, and based on its value, flow along one of many *action paths* is initiated. The hub of information flow from which many action paths emanate is called a *transaction center*.

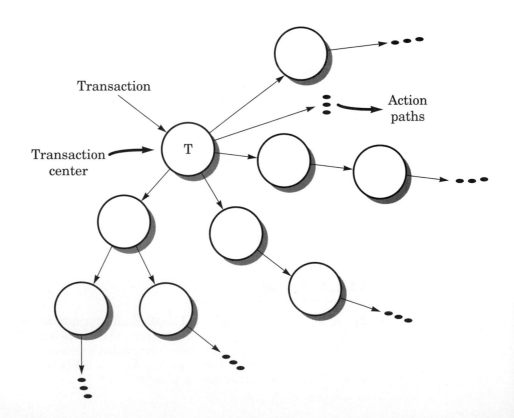

FIGURE 14.2.
Transaction flow

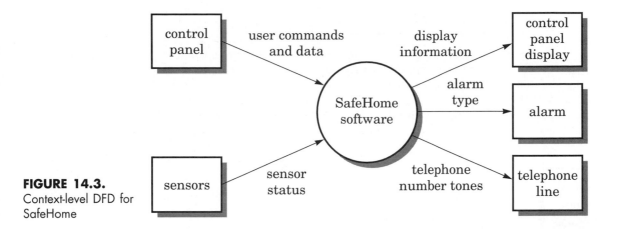

FIGURE 14.3.
Context-level DFD for
SafeHome

It should be noted that within a DFD for a large system, both transform and transaction flow may be present. For example, in a transaction-oriented flow, information flow along an action path may have transform flow characteristics.

14.4 TRANSFORM MAPPING

Transform mapping is set of design steps that allows a DFD with transform flow characteristics to be mapped into a predefined template for program structure. In this section transform mapping is described by applying design steps to an example system—a portion of the SafeHome security software presented in earlier chapters.

14.4.1 An Example

The SafeHome security system, introduced earlier in this book, is representative of many computer-based products and systems in use today. The product monitors the real world and reacts to changes that it encounters. It also interacts with a user through a series of typed inputs and alphanumeric displays. The level 0 data flow diagram for SafeHome, reproduced from Chapter 12, is shown in Figure 14.3.

During requirements analysis, more detailed flow models would be created for SafeHome. In addition, control and process specifications, a data dictionary, and various behavioral models would also be created.[1]

---

[1]Readers who have not read Chapters 11 and 12 are urged to do so before continuing with this chapter.

14.4.2 Design Steps

The above example will be used to illustrate each step in transform mapping. The steps begin with a re-evaluation of work done during requirements analysis and then move to the development of program structure.

Step 1. Review the fundamental system model. The fundamental system model encompasses the level 0 DFD and supporting information. In actuality

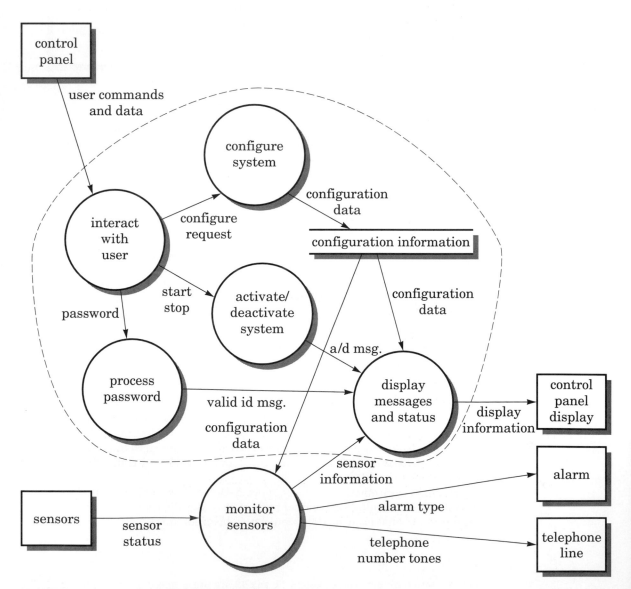

FIGURE 14.4. Level 1 DFD for SafeHome

the design step begins with an evaluation of both the *system specification* and the *software requirements specification*. Both documents describe information flow and structure at the software interface. Figures 14.3 and 14.4 depict level 0 and level 1 data flow for the SafeHome software.

Step 2. Review and refine data flow diagrams for the software. Information obtained from analysis models contained in the software requirements specification is refined to produce greater detail. For example, the level 2 DFDs for *monitor sensors* (Figures 14.4 and 14.5) are examined, and a level 3 data flow diagram is derived as shown in Figure 14.6. At level 3, each transform in the data flow diagram exhibits relatively high *cohesion* (Chapter 13). That is, the process implied by a transform performs a single, distinct function that can be implemented as a module in the SafeHome software. Therefore, the DFD in Figure 14.6 contains sufficient detail for a "first cut" at the design of program structure for the *monitor sensors* subsystem, and we proceed without further refinement.

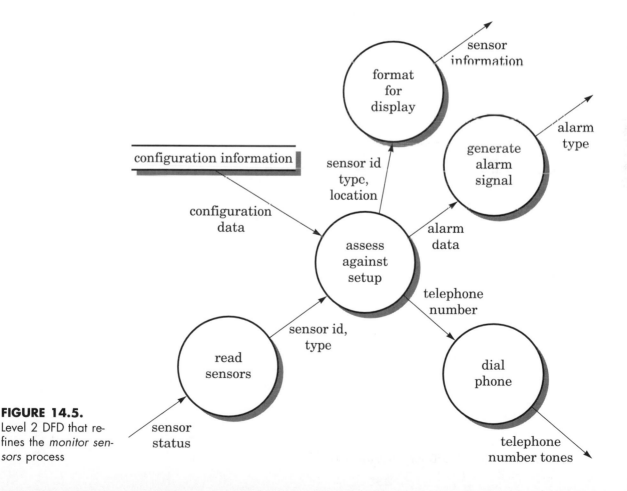

FIGURE 14.5.
Level 2 DFD that refines the *monitor sensors* process

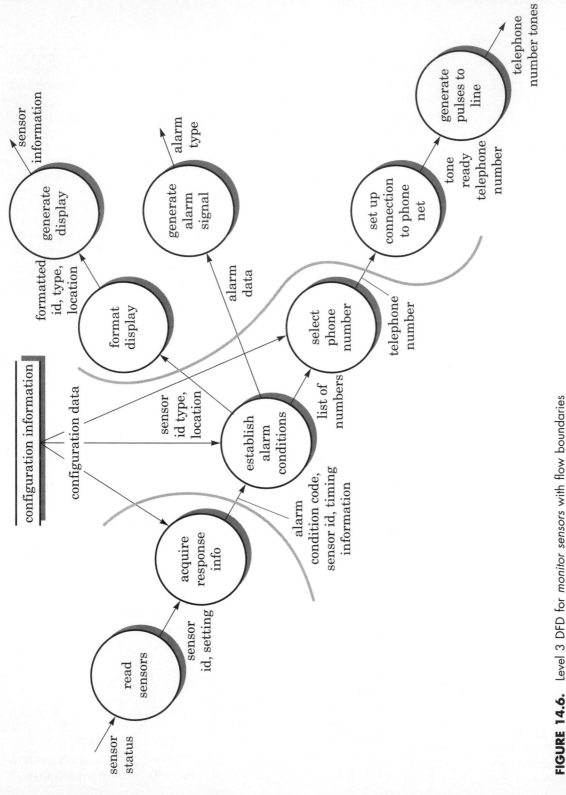

FIGURE 14.6. Level 3 DFD for *monitor sensors* with flow boundaries

Step 3. Determine whether the DFD has transform or transaction flow characteristics. In general, information flow within a system can always be represented as a transform. However, when an obvious transaction characteristic (Figure 14.2) is encountered, a different design mapping is recommended. In this step, the designer selects a global (software-wide) flow characteristic based on the prevailing nature of the DFD. In addition, local regions of transform or transaction flow are isolated. These *subflows* can be used to refine program structure derived from a global characteristic described above. For now, we focus our attention only on the *monitor sensors* subsystem data flow depicted in Figure 14.6.

Evaluating the DFD (Figure 14.6), we see data entering the software along one incoming path and exiting along three outgoing paths. No distinct transaction center is implied (although the transform *acquire alarm conditions* could be perceived as such). Therefore, an overall transform characteristic will be assumed for information flow.

Step 4. Isolate the transform center by specifying incoming and outgoing flow boundaries. In the preceding section incoming flow was described as a path in which information is converted from external to internal form; outgoing flow converts from internal to external form. Incoming and outgoing flow boundaries are open to interpretation. That is, different designers may select slightly different points in the flow as boundary locations. In fact, alternative design solutions can be derived by varying the placement of flow boundaries. Although care should be taken when boundaries are selected, a variance of one bubble along a flow path will generally have little impact on the final program structure.

Flow boundaries for the example are illustrated as shaded curves running vertically through the flow in Figure 14.6. The transforms (bubbles) that comprise the transform center lie within the two shaded boundaries that run from top to bottom in the figure. An argument can be made to readjust a boundary (e.g., an incoming flow boundary separating *read sensors* and *acquire response info* could be proposed). The emphasis in this design step should be on selecting reasonable boundaries, rather than lengthy iteration on placement of divisions.

Step 5. Perform "first-level factoring." Program structure represents a top-down distribution of control. *Factoring* results in a program structure in which top-level modules perform decision making and low-level modules perform most input, computational, and output work. Middle-level modules perform some control and do moderate amounts of work.

When transform flow is encountered, a DFD is mapped to a specific structure that provides control for incoming, transform, and outgoing information processing. This *first-level factoring* for the *monitor sensors* subsystem is illustrated in Figure 14.7. A main controller (called **monitor sensors executive**) resides at the top of the program structure and serves to coordinate the following subordinate control functions:

an incoming information processing controller, called **sensor input controller,** coordinates receipt of all incoming data;

a transform flow controller, called **alarm conditions controller,** supervises all operations on data in internalized form (e.g., a module that invokes various data transformation procedures;

an outgoing information processing controller, called **alarm output controller,** coordinates production of output information.

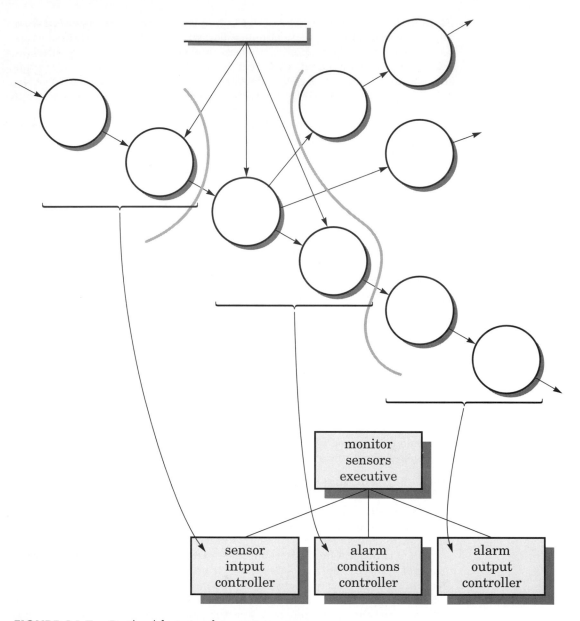

FIGURE 14.7.   First-level factoring for *monitor sensors*

Although a three-pronged structure is implied by Figure 14.7, complex flows in large systems may dictate two or more control modules for each of the generic control functions described above. The number of modules at the first level should be limited to the minimum that can accomplish control functions and still maintain good coupling and cohesion characteristics.

Step 6. Perform "second-level factoring." *Second-level factoring* is accomplished by mapping individual transforms (bubbles) of a DFD into appropriate modules within the program structure. Beginning at the transform center boundary and moving outward along incoming and then outgoing paths, transforms are mapped into subordinate levels of the software structure. The general approach to second-level factoring for the SafeHome data flow is illustrated in Figure 14.8.

Although Figure 14.8 illustrates a one-to-one mapping between DFD transforms and software modules, different mappings frequently occur. Two or even three bubbles can be combined and represented as one module (recalling potential problems with cohesion), or a single bubble may be expanded to two or more modules. Practical considerations and measures of design quality dictate the outcome of second-level factoring. Review and refinement may lead to changes in this structure, but it can serve as a first design iteration.

Second-level factoring for incoming flow follows in the same manner. Factoring is again accomplished by moving outward from the transform center boundary on the incoming flow side. The transform center of *monitor sensors* subsystem software is mapped somewhat differently. Each of the data conversion or calculation transforms of the transform portion of the DFD is mapped into a module subordinate to the transform controller. A completed first iteration program structure is shown in Figure 14.9.

The modules mapped in the manner described above and shown in Figure 14.9 represent an initial design of program structure. Although modules are named in a manner that implies function, a brief processing narrative (adapted from the PSPEC created during analysis modeling) should be written for each. The narrative describes:

- information that passes into and out of the module (an interface description);

- information that is retained by a module, e.g., data stored in a local data structure;

- a procedural narrative that indicates major decisions points and tasks; and

- a brief discussion of restrictions and special features (e.g., file I/O, hardware dependent characteristics, special timing requirements).

The narrative serves as a first generation design specification. However, further refinement and additions occur regularly during this period of design.

Step 7. Refine the first iteration program structure using design heuristics for improved software quality. A first program structure can always be refined by applying concepts of module independence (Chapter 13). Modules are *exploded* or *imploded* to produce sensible factoring, good cohesion, minimal coupling, and most important, a structure that can be implemented without difficulty, tested without confusion, and maintained without grief.

Refinements are dictated by practical considerations and common sense. There are times, for example, when the controller for incoming data flow is totally unnecessary, when some input processing is required in a module that is subordinate to the transform controller, when high coupling due to global data cannot be avoided, or when optimal structural characteristics (see Section 13.6)

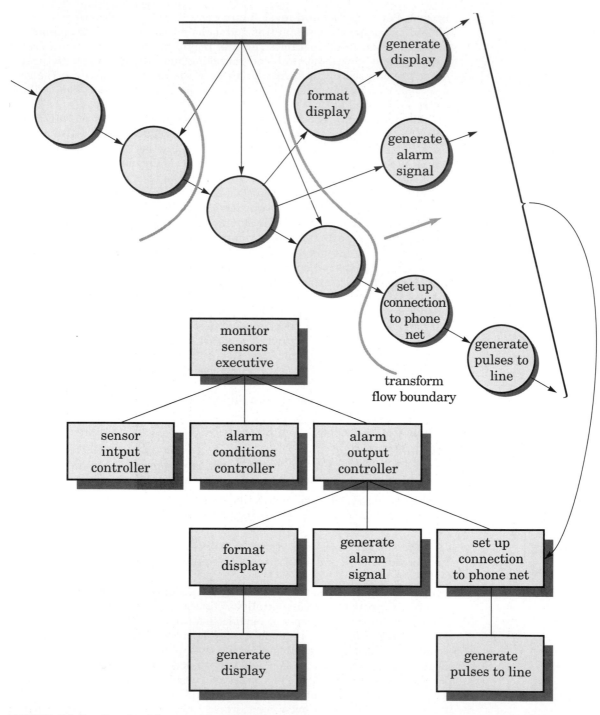

FIGURE 14.8. First level factoring for *monitor sensors*

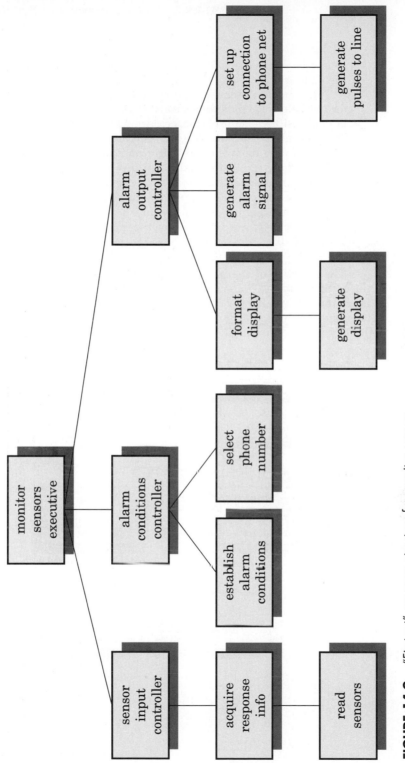

FIGURE 14.9. "First-cut" program structure for *monitor sensors*

cannot be achieved. Software requirements coupled with human judgment is the final arbiter.

Many modifications can be made to the first iteration structure developed for the SafeHome *monitor sensors* subsystem: (1) The incoming controller can be removed because it is unnecessary when a single incoming flow path is to be managed. (2) The substructure generated from the transform flow can be imploded into the module **establish alarm conditions** (which will now include the processing implied by **select phone number**). The transform controller will not be needed and the small decrease in cohesion is tolerable. (3) The modules **format display** and **generate display** can be imploded (we assume that display formatting is quite simple) into a new module called **produce display**. The refined software structure for the *monitor sensors* subsystem is shown in Figure 14.10.

The objective of the preceding seven steps is to develop a global representation of software. That is, once structure is defined, we can evaluate and refine software architecture by viewing it as a whole. Modifications made at this time require little additional work, yet can have a profound impact on software quality and maintainability.

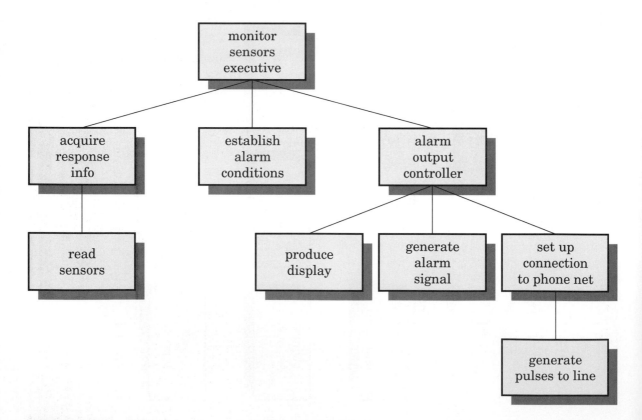

FIGURE 14.10. Refined program structure for *monitor sensors*

The reader should pause for a moment and consider the difference between the design approach described above and the process of "writing programs." If code is the only representation of software, the developer will have great difficulty evaluating or refining at a global or holistic level and will, in fact, have difficulty "seeing the forest for the trees."

14.5   TRANSACTION MAPPING

In many software applications, a single data item triggers one or a number of information flows that effect a function implied by the triggering data item. The data item, called a *transaction,* and its corresponding flow characteristics were discussed in Section 14.3.2. In this section we consider design steps used to treat transaction flow.

14.5.1   An Example

Transaction mapping will be illustrated by considering the *user interaction* subsystem of the SafeHome software. Level 1 data flow for this subsystem is shown as part of Figure 14.4. Refining the flow, a level 2 data flow diagram (a corresponding data dictionary, CSPEC, and PSPECs would also be created) is developed and shown in Figure 14.11.

As shown in the figure, **user commands** flows into the system and results in additional information flow along one of three action paths. A single data item, **command type,** causes the data flow to fan outward from a hub. Therefore, the overall data flow characteristic is transaction-oriented.

It should be noted that information flow along two of the three action paths accommodate additional incoming flow (e.g., **system parameters and data** are input on the "configure" action path. Each action path flows into a single transform, *display messages and status.*

14.5.2   Design Steps

Design steps for transaction mapping are similar and in some cases identical to steps for transform mapping (Section 14.4). A major difference lies in the mapping of the DFD to software structure.

Step 1. Review the fundamental system model.

Step 2. Review and refine data flow diagrams for the software.

Step 3. Determine whether the DFD has transform or transaction flow characteristics. Steps 1, 2, and 3 are identical to corresponding steps in transform mapping. The DFD shown in Figure 14.11 has a classic transaction flow characteristic. However, flow along two of the action paths emanating from the *invoke command processing* bubble appears to have transform flow characteristics. Therefore, flow boundaries must be established for both flow types.

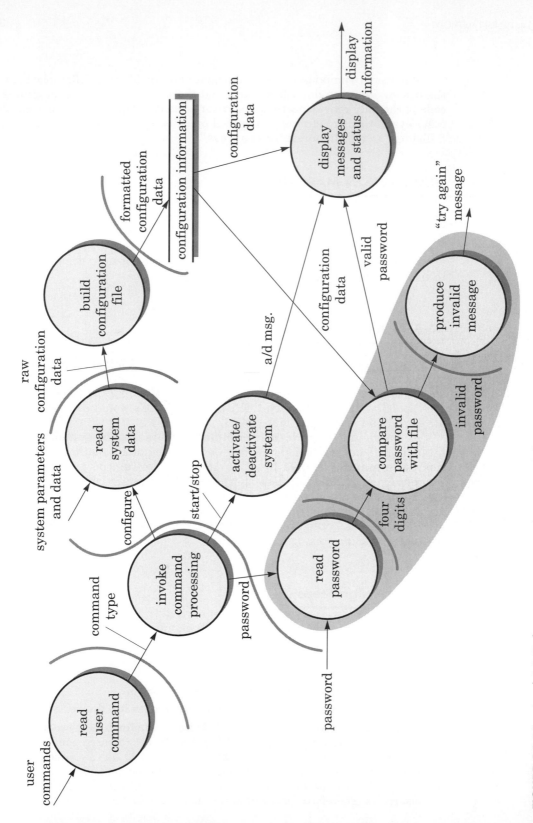

FIGURE 14.11. Level 2 DFD for *user interaction* subsystem with flow boundaries

Step 4. Identify the transaction center and the flow characteristics along each of the action paths. The location of the transaction center can be immediately discerned from the DFD. The transaction center lies at the origin of a number of actions paths that flow radially from it. For the flow shown in Figure 14.11, the *invoke command processing* bubble is the transaction center.

The incoming path (i.e., the flow path along which a transaction is received) and all action paths must also be isolated. Boundaries that define a reception path and action paths are also shown in the figure. Each action path must be evaluated for its individual flow characteristic. For example, the "password" path (shown enclosed by a shaded area in Figure 14.11) has transform characteristics. Incoming, transform, and outgoing flow are indicated with boundaries.

Step 5. Map the DFD in a program structure amenable to transaction processing. Transaction flow is mapped into a program structure that contains an incoming branch and a dispatch branch. Structure for the incoming branch is developed in much the same way as transform mapping. Starting at the transaction center, bubbles along the incoming path are mapped into modules. The structure of the dispatch branch contains a dispatcher module that controls all subordinate action modules. Each action flow path of the DFD is mapped to a structure that corresponds to its specific flow characteristics. This process is illustrated in Figure 14.12.

Considering the *user interaction* subsystem data flow, first-level factoring for step 5 is shown in Figure 14.13. The bubbles *read user command* and *activate/deactivate system* map directly into the program structure without the need for intermediate control modules. The transaction center, *invoke command processing,* maps directly into a dispatcher module of the same name. Controllers for system configuration and password processing are mapped as indicated in Figure 14.12.

Step 6. Factor and refine the transaction structure and the structure of each action path. Each action path of the data flow diagram has its own information flow characteristics. We have already noted that transform or transaction flow may be encountered. The action path–related "substructure" is developed using the design steps discussed in this and the preceding section.

As an example, consider the password processing information flow shown (inside shaded area) in Figure 14.11. The flow exhibits classic transform characteristics. A password is input (incoming flow) and transmitted to a transform center where it is compared against stored passwords. An alarm and warning message (outgoing flow) are produced (if a match is not obtained). The "configure" path is drawn similarly using the transform mapping. The resultant program structure is shown in Figure 14.14.

Step 7. Refine the first iteration program structure using design heuristics for improved software quality. This step for transaction mapping is identical to the corresponding step for transform mapping. In both design approaches, criteria such as module independence, practicality (efficacy of implementation and test), and maintainability must be carefully considered as structural modifications are proposed.

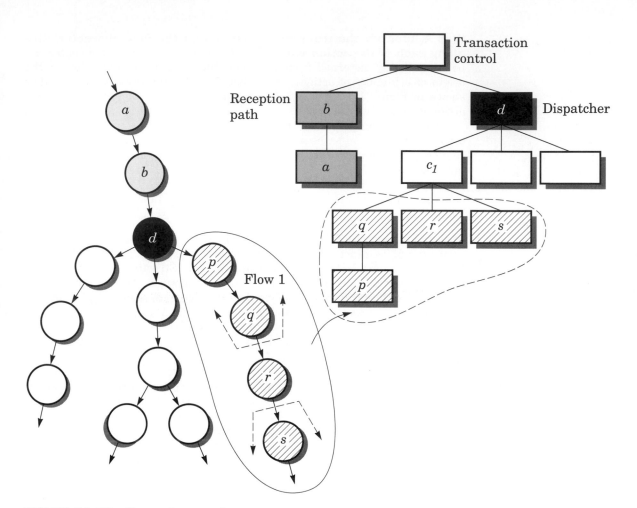

FIGURE 14.12. Transaction mapping

14.6   **DESIGN POSTPROCESSING**

Successful application of transform or transaction mapping is supplemented by additional documentation that is required as part of architectural design. After structure has been developed and refined, the following tasks must be completed:

- A processing narrative must be developed for each module.
- An interface description is provided for each module.
- Local and global data structures are defined.
- All design restrictions/limitations are noted.
- A design review is conducted.
- "Optimization" is considered (if required and justified).

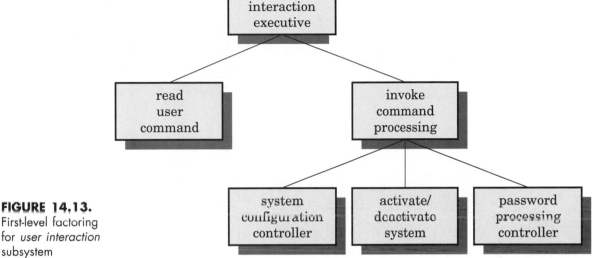

FIGURE 14.13.
First-level factoring
for *user interaction*
subsystem

A processing narrative is (ideally) an unambiguous, bounded description of processing that occurs within a module. The narrative describes processing tasks, decisions, and I/O.

The interface description requires the design of internal module interfaces, external system interfaces and the human–computer interface. These topics are discussed in Section 14.8.

The design of data structures can have a profound impact on program structure and the procedural details for each module. Techniques described in Chapter 12 establish the basic data model and identify all important data objects. These then serve as the basis for the design of both local and global data structures.

Restrictions and/or limitations for each module are also documented. Typical topics for discussion include restriction of data type or format, memory or timing limitations, bounding values or quantities of data structures, special cases not considered, and specific characteristics of an individual module. The purpose of a restrictions/limitations section is to reduce the number of errors introduced because of assumed functional characteristics.

Once design documentation has been developed for all modules, a design review is conducted (see Chapter 8 for review guidelines). The review emphasizes traceability to software requirements, quality of program structure, interface descriptions, data structure descriptions, implementation and test practicality, and maintainability.

14.7   ARCHITECTURAL DESIGN OPTIMIZATION

Any discussion of design optimization should be prefaced with the following comment: "Remember that an 'optimal design' that doesn't work has question-

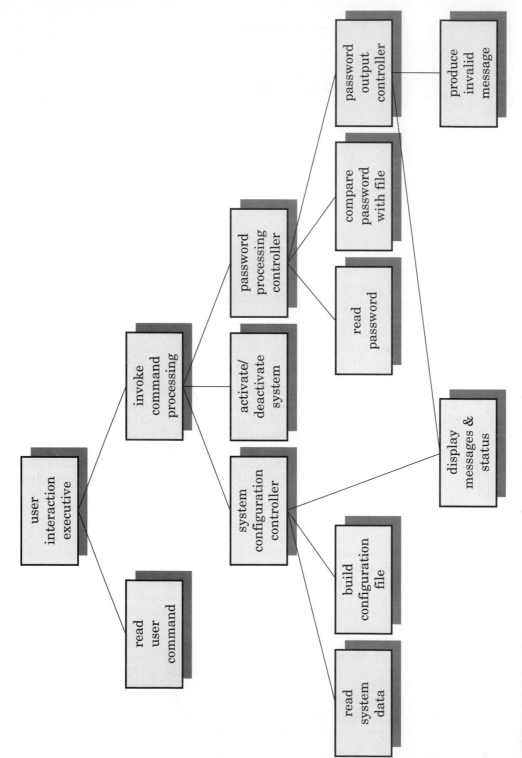

FIGURE 14.14. First-cut program structure for *user interaction subsystem*

able merit." The software designer should be concerned with developing a representation of software that will meet all functional and performance requirements and merit acceptance based on design quality measures.

Refinement of program structure during the early stages of design is to be encouraged. Alternative representations may be derived, refined, and evaluated for the "best" approach. This approach to optimization is one of the true benefits derived from developing a representation of software architecture.

It is important to note that structural simplicity often reflects both elegance and efficiency. Design optimization should strive for the smallest number of modules that is consistent with effective modularity and the least complex data structure that adequately serves information requirements.

For performance-critical applications, it may be necessary to "optimize" during later design iterations, and possibly during coding. The software engineer should note, however, that a relatively small percentage (typically, 10–20 percent) of a program often accounts for a large percentage (50–80 percent) of all processing time. It is not unreasonable to propose the following approach for performance-critical software:

1. Develop and refine program structure without concern for performance-critical optimization.
2. Use CASE tools that simulate run-time performance to isolate areas of inefficiency.
3. During later design iterations, select modules that are suspect "time hogs" and carefully develop procedures (algorithms) for time efficiency.
4. Code in an appropriate programming language.
5. Instrument the software to isolate modules that account for heavy processor utilization.
6. If necessary, redesign or recode in machine-dependent language to improve efficiency.

This approach follows a dictum that will be further discussed in a later chapter: "Get it to work, then make it fast."

14.8   INTERFACE DESIGN

The architectural design provides a software engineer with a picture of the program structure. Like the blueprint for a house, the overall design is not complete without a representation of doors, windows, and utility connections for water, electricity, and telephone (not to mention cable TV). The "doors, windows, and utility connections" for computer software comprise the interface design of a system.

Interface design focuses on three areas of concern: (1) the design of interfaces between software modules; (2) the design of interfaces between the software and other nonhuman producers and consumers of information (i.e., other external entities); and (3) the design of the interface between a human (i.e., the user) and the computer.

14.8.1   Internal and External Interface Design

The design of internal program interfaces, sometimes called *intermodular interface design,* is driven by the data that must flow between modules and the characteristics of the programming language in which the software is to be implemented.[2] In general, the analysis model contains much of the information required for intermodular interface design. The data flow diagram (Chapter 12) describes how data objects are transformed as they move through a system. The transforms (i.e., bubbles) of the DFD are mapped into modules within the program structure (Sections 14.4 and 14.5). Therefore, the arrows (data objects) flowing into and out of each DFD transform must be mapped into a design for the interface of the module that corresponds to that DFD transform.

External interface design begins with an evaluation of each external entity represented in the DFDs of the analysis model. The data and control requirements of the external entity are determined and appropriate external interfaces are designed. For example, the SafeHome software discussed earlier in this chapter requires interfacing with a variety of external security sensors. The design of the external interface for each sensor is predicated on the specific data and control items required for the sensor.

Both internal and external interface designs must be coupled with data validation and error handling algorithms within a module. Because side effects propagate across program interfaces, it is essential to check all data flowing from module to module (or to the outside world) to ensure that the data conform to bounds established during requirements analysis.

14.8.2   User Interface Design

In the preface to his book on user interface design, Ben Shneiderman [SHN87] states:

> Frustration and anxiety are part of daily life for many users of computerized information systems. They struggle to learn command language or menu selection systems that are supposed to help them do their job. Some people encounter such serious cases of computer shock, terminal terror, or network neurosis that they avoid using computerized systems.

The problems to which Shneiderman alludes are real. We have all encountered "interfaces" that are difficult to learn, difficult to use, confusing, unforgiving, and in many cases, totally frustrating. Yet, someone spent time and energy building each of these interfaces, and it is likely that the builder did not create these problems purposely.

---

[2]Conventional programming languages typically make use of an argument list to transfer data across interfaces. Object-oriented languages make use of messages to accomplish data transfer. Design issues in these two contexts are different.

User interface design has as much to do with the study of people as it does with technology issues. Who is the user? How does the user learn to interact with a new computer-based system? How does the user interpret information produced by the system? What will the user expect of the system? These are only a few of the many questions that must be asked and answered as part of user interface design.

14.9   HUMAN–COMPUTER INTERFACE DESIGN

The overall process for designing a user interface begins with the creation of different models of system function (as perceived from the outside). The human- and computer-oriented tasks that are required to achieve system function are then delineated; design issues that apply to all interface designs are considered; tools are used to prototype and ultimately implement the design model; and the result is evaluated for quality.

14.9.1   Interface Design Models

Four different models come into play when a human–computer interface (HCI) is to be designed. The software engineer creates a *design model,* a human engineer (or the software engineer) establishes a *user model,* the end user develops a mental image that is often called the *user's model* or the *system perception,* and the implementers of the system create a *system image* [RUB88]. Unfortunately, these models may differ significantly. The role of interface designer is to reconcile these differences and derive a consistent representation of the interface.

A *design model* of the entire system incorporates data, architectural, interface, and procedural representations of the software. The requirements specification may establish certain constraints that help to define the user of the system, but the interface design is often only incidental to the design model.[3]

The *user model* depicts the profile of end users of the system. To build an effective user interface, "all design should begin with an understanding of the intended users, including profiles of their age, sex, physical abilities, education, cultural or ethnic background, motivation, goals and personality" [SHN87]. In addition, users can be categorized as:

- *novices*—no syntactic knowledge[4] of the system and little semantic knowledge[5] of the application or computer usage in general;

---

[3]Of course, this is not as it should be. For interactive systems, the interface design is as important as the data, architectural, or procedural design.

[4]In this context *syntactic knowledge* refers to the mechanics of interaction that is required to use the interface effectively.

[5]*Semantic knowledge* refers to an underlying sense of the application—an understanding of the functions that are performed, the meaning of input and output, and the goals and objectives of the system.

- *knowledgeable, intermittent users*—reasonable semantic knowledge of the application, but relatively low recall of syntactic information necessary to use the interface; and

- *knowledgeable, frequent users*—good semantic and syntactic knowledge that often leads to the "power-user syndrome," that is, individuals who look for shortcuts and abbreviated modes of interaction.

The *system perception* (user's model) is the image of the system that an end user carries in his or her head. For example, if the user of a particular word processor were asked to describe its operation, the system perception would guide the response. The accuracy of the description will depend upon the user's profile (e.g., novices would provide a sketchy response at best) and overall familiarity with software in the application domain. A user who understands word processors fully, but has only worked with the specific word processor once, might actually be able to provide a more complete description of its function than the novice who has spent weeks trying to learn the system.

The *system image* couples the outward manifestation of the computer-based system (the look and feel of the interface), with all supporting information (books, manuals, video tapes) that describe system syntax and semantics. When the system image and the system perception are coincident, users generally feel comfortable with the software and use it effectively. To accomplish this "melding" of the models, the design model must have been developed to accommodate the information contained in the user model and the system image must accurately reflect syntactic and semantic information about the interface. The interrelationship among the models is shown in Figure 14.15.

The models described in this section are "abstractions of what the user is doing or thinks he is doing or what somebody else thinks he ought to be doing when he uses an interactive system" [MON84]. In essence, these models enable the interface designer to satisfy a key element of the most important principle of user interface design: "Know the user, know the tasks."

14.9.2   Task Analysis and Modeling

Task analysis and modeling can be applied to understand the tasks that people currently perform (when using a manual or semiautomated approach) and then map these into a similar (but not necessarily identical) set of tasks that are implemented in the context of the HCI. This can be accomplished by observation or by studying an existing specification for a computer-based solution and deriving a set of user tasks that will accommodate the user model, the design model, and the system perception.

Regardless of the overall approach to task analysis, the human engineer must first define and classify tasks. One approach is stepwise elaboration (Chapter 13). For example, assume that a small software company wants to build a computer-aided design system explicitly for interior designers. By observing a designer at work, the engineer notices that the interior design is comprised of a number of major activities: furniture layout, fabric and material selection, wall and window covering selection, presentation (to the customer),

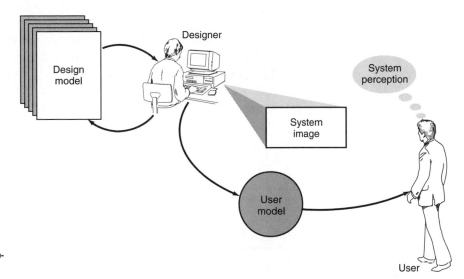

FIGURE 14.15.
Relating interface design models

costing, and shopping. Each of these major tasks can be elaborated into subtasks. For example, furniture layout can be refined into the following tasks: (1) Draw floor plan based on room dimensions; (2) place windows and doors at appropriate locations; (3) use furniture templates to draw scaled furniture outlines on floor plan; (4) move furniture outlines to get best placement; (5) label all furniture outlines; (6) draw dimensions to show location; and (7) draw perspective view for customer. A similar approach could be used for each of the other major tasks.

Subtasks 1 to 7 can each be refined further. Subtasks 1 to 6 will be performed by manipulating information and performing actions with the user interface. On the other hand, subtask 7 can be performed automatically in software and will result in little direct user interaction. The design model of the interface should accommodate each of these tasks in a way that is consistent with the user model (the profile of a "typical" interior designer) and system perception (what the interior designer expects from a automated system).

An alternative approach to task analysis takes an object-oriented point of view.[6] The human engineer observes the physical objects that are used by the interior designer and the actions that are applied to each object. For example, the furniture template would be an object in this approach to task analysis. The interior designer would *select* the appropriate template, *move* it to a position on the floor plan, *trace* the furniture outline and so forth. The design model for the interface would not describe implementation details for each of these actions, but it would define user tasks that accomplish the end result (drawing furniture outlines on the floor plan).

Once each task or action has been defined, interface design begins. The first steps in the interface design process [NOR86] can be accomplished using the following approach:

---

[6]See Part Four of this book for further discussion of the object-oriented viewpoint.

1. Establish the goals and intentions for the task.
2. Map each goal/intention to a sequence of specific actions.
3. Specify the action sequence as it will be executed at the interface level.
4. Indicate the state of the system; i.e., what does the interface look like at the time that an action in the sequence is performed?
5. Define control mechanisms, i.e., the devices and actions available to the user to alter the system state.
6. Show how control mechanisms affect the state of the system.
7. Indicate how the user interprets the state of the system from information provided through the interface.

14.9.3 Design Issues

As the design of a user interface evolves, four common design issues almost always surface: system response time, user help facilities, error information handling, and command labeling. Unfortunately, many designers do not address these issues until relatively late in the design process (sometimes the first inkling of a problem doesn't occur until an operational prototype is available). Unnecessary iteration, project delays, and customer frustration almost always result. It is far better to establish each as a design issue to be considered at the beginning of software design, when changes are easy and costs are low.

System response time is *the* primary complaint for many interactive systems. In general, system response time is measured from the point at which the user performs some control action (e.g., hits the return key or clicks a mouse) until the software responds with desired output or action.

System response time has two important characteristics: *length* and *variability*. If the length of time for system response is too long, user frustration and stress is the inevitable result. However, a very brief response time can also be detrimental if the user is being paced by the interface. A rapid response may force the user to rush and therefore make mistakes.

Variability refers to the deviation from average response time, and in many ways, it is the more important of the response time characteristics. Low variability enables the user to establish a rhythm, even if response time is relatively long. For example, one second response to a command is preferable to a response that varies from 0.1 to 2.5 seconds. The user is always off balance, always wondering whether something "different" has occurred behind the scenes.

Almost every user of an interactive, computer-based system requires help now and then, In some cases, a simple question addressed to a knowledgeable colleague can do the trick. In others, detailed research in a multivolume set of user manuals may be the only option. In many cases, however, modern software provides on-line help facilities that enable a user to get a question answered or resolve a problem without leaving the interface.

Two different types of help facilities are encountered: *integrated* and *add-on* [RUB88]. An *integrated help facility* is designed into the software from the beginning. It is often context sensitive, enabling the user to select from those topics that are relevant to the actions currently being performed. Obviously, this reduces the time required for the user to obtain help and increases the "friendliness" of the interface. An *add-on help facility* is added to the software after the system has been built. In many ways, it is really an on-line user's manual with limited query capability. The user may have to search through a list of hundreds of topics to find appropriate guidance, often making many false starts and receiving much irrelevant information. There is little doubt that the integrated help facility is preferable to the add-on approach.

A number of design issues [RUB88] must be addressed when a help facility is considered:

- Will help be available for all system functions and at all times during system interaction? Options include help only for a subset of all functions and actions, and help for all functions.

- How will the user request help? Options include a help menu, a special function key, and a HELP command.

- How will help be represented? Options include a separate window, a reference to a printed document (less than ideal), and a one or two line suggestion produced in a fixed screen location.

- How will the user return to normal interaction? Options include a return button displayed on the screen and a function key or control sequence.

- How will help information be structured? Options include a "flat" structure in which all information is accessed through a keyword, a layered hierarchy of information that provides increasing detail as the user proceeds into the structure, and the use of hypertext.

Error messages and warnings are "bad news" delivered to users of interactive systems when something has gone awry. At their worst, error messages and warnings impart useless or misleading information and serve only to increase user frustration. Few computer users have not encountered an error of the form:

SEVERE SYSTEM FAILURE—14A

Somewhere, an explanation for error 14A must exist; otherwise, why would the designers have added the identification? Yet the error message provides no real indication of what is wrong or where to look to get additional information. An error message presented in the manner shown above does nothing to assuage user anxiety or to help correct the problem.

In general, every error message or warning produced by an interactive system should have the following characteristics:

- The message should describe the problem in jargon that the user can understand.

- The message should provide constructive advice for recovering from the error.

- The message should indicate any negative consequences of the error (e.g., potentially corrupted data files) so that the user can check to ensure that they have not occurred (or correct them if they have).

- The message should be accompanied by an audible or visual cue. That is, a beep might be generated to accompany the display of the message, or the message might flash momentarily or be displayed in a color that is easily recognizable as the "error color."
- The message should be "nonjudgmental." That is, the wording should never place blame on the user.

Because no one really likes bad news, few users will like an error message no matter how well it is designed. But an effective error message philosophy can do much to improve the quality of an interactive system and will significantly reduce user frustration when problems do occur.

The typed command was once the most common mode of interaction between user and system software and was commonly used for applications of every type. Today, the use of window-oriented, point and pick interfaces has reduced reliance on typed commands, but many power-users continue to prefer a command-oriented mode of interaction. In many situations, the user can be provided with an option—software functions can be selected from a static or pull-down menu or invoked through some keyboard command sequence.

A number of design issues arise when commands are provided as a mode of interaction:

- Will every menu option have a corresponding command?
- What form will commands take? Options include a control sequence (e.g., **^P**), function keys, and a typed word.
- How difficult will it be to learn and remember the commands? What can be done if a command is forgotten? (See the discussion of help earlier in this section.)
- Can commands be customized or abbreviated by the user?

In a growing number of applications, interface designers provide a *command macro facility* that allows the user to store a sequence of commonly used commands under a user-defined name. Instead of each command being typed individually (and repetitively), the command macro is typed and all commands implied by it are executed in sequence.

In an ideal setting, conventions for command usage should be established across all applications. It is confusing and often error-prone for a user to type **^D** when a graphics object is to be duplicated in one application and **^D** when a graphics object is to be deleted in another. The potential for error is obvious.

14.9.4   Implementation Tools

The process of user interface design is iterative. That is, a design model is created, implemented as a prototype,[7] examined by users (who fit the user model described earlier), and modified based on their comments. To accommodate this

---

[7]It should be noted that in some cases (e.g., aircraft cockpit displays) the first step might be to simulate the interface on a display device rather than prototyping it using cockpit hardware.

iterative design approach a broad class of interface design and prototyping tools has evolved. Called *user interface toolkits or user interface development systems (UIDS),* these tools provide routines or objects that facilitate creation of windows, menus, device interaction, error messages, commands, and many other elements of an interactive environment.

Using prepackaged software that can be used directly by the designer and implementer or a user interface, a UIDS provides built-in mechanisms [MYE89] for:

- managing input devices (such as the mouse or keyboard);
- validating user input;
- handling errors and displaying error messages;
- providing feedback (e.g., automatic input echo);
- providing help and prompts;
- handling windows and fields, scrolling within windows;
- establishing connections between application software and the interface;
- insulating the application from interface management functions; and
- allowing the user to customize the interface.

The functions described above can be implemented using either a language-based or a graphical approach.

14.9.5 Design Evaluation

Once an operational user interface prototype has been created, it must be evaluated to determine whether it meets the needs of the user. Evaluation can span a formality spectrum that ranges from an informal "test drive" in which a user provides impromptu feedback to a formally designed study that uses statistical methods for the evaluation of questionnaires completed by a population of end users.

The user interface evaluation cycle takes the form shown in Figure 14.16. After the preliminary design has been completed, a first-level prototype is created. The prototype is evaluated by the user, who provides the designer with direct comments about the efficacy of the interface. In addition, if formal evaluation techniques are used (e.g., questionnaires, rating sheets), the designer may extract information from this information (e.g., 80 percent of all users did not like the mechanism for saving data files). Design modifications are made based on user input and the next-level prototype is created. The evaluation cycle continues until no further modifications to the interface design are necessary. But is it possible to evaluate the quality of a user interface before a prototype is built? If potential problems can be uncovered and corrected early, the number of loops through the evaluation cycle will be reduced and development time will shorten.

When a design model of the interface has been created, a number of evaluation criteria [MOR81] can be applied during early design reviews:

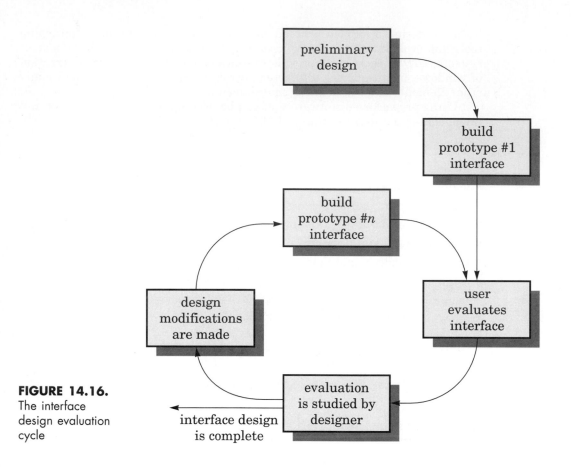

FIGURE 14.16.
The interface design evaluation cycle

1. The length and complexity of the written specification of the system and its interface provide an indication of the amount of learning required by users of the system.

2. The number of commands or actions specified and the average number of arguments per command or individual operations per action provide an indication of interaction time and the overall efficiency of the system.

3. The number of actions, commands, and system states indicated by the design model indicate the *memory load* on users of the system.

4. Interface style, help facilities, and error handling protocols provide a general indication of the complexity of the interface and the degree to which it will be accepted by the user.

Once the first prototype is built, the designer can collect a variety of qualitative and quantitative data that will assist in evaluating the interface. To collect qualitative data, questionnaires can be distributed to users of the prototype. Question responses can be (1) simple yes/no, (2) numeric, (3) scaled (subjective), or (4) percentage (subjective). Examples are:

1. Were the commands easy to remember? (yes/no)
2. How many different commands did you use?
3. How easy was it to learn basic system operations? (scale of 1 to 5)
4. Compared to other interfaces you've used, how would this rate? (top 1%, top 10%, top 25%, top 50%, bottom 50%)

If quantitative data are desired, a form of time study analysis can be conducted. Users are observed during interaction, and data such as number of tasks correctly completed over a standard time period, frequency of command use, sequence of commands, time spent "looking" at the display, number of errors, types of error and error recovery time, time spent using help, and number of help references per standard time period are collected and used as a guide for interface modification.

A complete discussion of user interface evaluation methods is beyond the scope of this book. For further information, see [LEA88].

14.10   INTERFACE DESIGN GUIDELINES

The design of user interfaces draws heavily on the experience of the designer and on anecdotal experience presented in hundreds of technical papers and dozens of books. Many sources in the literature (e.g., [DUM88]) present a set of HCI design guidelines that will result in a "friendly," efficient interface. In this section, some of the more important HCI design guidelines are presented.

Three categories of HCI design guidelines are suggested: general interaction, information display, and data entry.

14.10.1   General Interaction

Guidelines for general interaction often cross the boundary into information display, data entry, and overall system control. They are therefore all-encompassing and are ignored at great risk. The following guidelines focus on general interaction:

Be consistent.   Use a consistent format for menu selection, command input, data display, and the myriad other functions that occur in a HCI.

Offer meaningful feedback.   Provide the user with visual and auditory feedback to ensure that two-way communication (between user and interface) is established.

Ask for verification of any nontrivial destructive action.   If a user requests the deletion of a file, indicates that substantial information is to be overwritten, or asks for the termination of a program, an "Are you sure....?" message should appear.

Permit easy reversal of most actions.   UNDO or REVERSE functions have saved tens of thousands of end users from millions of hours of frustration. Reversal should be available in every interactive application.

Reduce the amount of information that must be memorized between actions. The user should not be expected to remember a list of numbers or names so that he or she can reuse them in a subsequent function. Memory load should be minimized.

Seek efficiency in dialog, motion, and thought. Keystrokes should be minimized, the distance a mouse must travel between picks should be considered in designing screen layout, the user should rarely encounter a situation where he or she asks, "Now what does this mean?"

Forgive mistakes. The system should protect itself from errors that might cause it to fail.

Categorize activities by function and organize screen geography accordingly. One of the key benefits of the pull-down menu is the ability to organize commands by type. In essence, the designer should strive for "cohesive" placement of commands and actions.

Provide help facilities that are context sensitive. See Section 14.9.3.

Use simple action verbs or short verb phrases to name commands. A lengthy command name is more difficult to recognize and recall. It may also take up unnecessary space in menu lists.

14.10.2 Information Display

If information presented by the HCI is incomplete, ambiguous, or unintelligible, the application will fail to satisfy the needs of a user. Information is "displayed" in many different ways: with text, pictures, and sound; by placement, motion, and size; and using color, resolution, and even omission. The following guidelines focus on information display:

Display only that information that is relevant to the current context. The user should not have to wade through extraneous data, menus, and graphics to obtain information relevant to a specific system function.

Don't bury the user with data, use a presentation format that enables rapid assimilation of information. Graphs or charts should replace voluminous tables.

Use consistent labels, standard abbreviations, and predictable colors. The meaning of a display should be obvious without reference to some outside source of information.

Allow the user to maintain visual context. If graphical representations are scaled up and down, the original image should be displayed constantly (in reduced form at the corner of the display) so that the user understands the relative location of the portion of the image that is currently being viewed.

Produce meaningful error messages. See Section 14.9.3.

Use upper and lower case, indentation, and text grouping to aid in understanding. Much of the information imparted by a HCI is textual, and the layout and form of the text has a significant impact on the ease with which information is assimilated by the user.

Use windows to compartmentalize different types of information. Windows enable the user to "keep" many different types of information within easy reach.

Use 'analog' displays to represent information that is more easily assimilated with this form of representation. For example, a display of holding tank pressure in an oil refinery would have little impact if a numeric representation were used. However, if a thermometer-like display were used, vertical motion and color changes could be used to indicate dangerous pressure conditions. This would provide the user with both absolute and relative information.

Consider the available geography of the display screen and use it efficiently. When multiple windows are to be used, space should be available to show at least some portion of each. In addition, screen size (a system engineering issue) should be selected to accommodate the type of application that is to be implemented.

14.10.3 Data Input

Much of the user's time is spent picking commands, typing data, and otherwise providing system input. In many applications, the keyboard remains the primary input medium, but the mouse, digitizer, and even voice recognition systems are rapidly becoming effective alternatives. The following guidelines focus on data input:

Minimize the number of input actions required of the user. Above all, reduce the amount of typing that is required. This can be accomplished by using the mouse to select from predefined sets of input, using a "sliding scale" to specify input data across a range of values, and using macros that enable a single keystroke to be transformed into a more complex collection of input data.

Maintain consistency between information display and data input. The visual characteristics of the display (e.g., text size, color, and placement) should be carried over to the input domain.

Allow the user to customize input. An expert user might decide to create custom commands or dispense with some types of warning messages and action verification. The HCI should allow this.

Interaction should be flexible but also tuned to the user's preferred mode of input. The user model will assist in determining which mode of input is preferred. A clerical worker might be very happy with keyboard input, while a manager might be more comfortable using a point and pick device such as a mouse.

Deactivate commands that are inappropriate in the context of current actions. This protects the user from attempting some action that could result in an error.

Let the user control the interactive flow. The user should be able to jump unnecessary actions, change the order of required actions (when possible in the context of an application), and recover from error conditions without exiting from the program.

Provide help to assist with all input actions.   See Section 14.9.3.

Eliminate "mickey mouse" input.   Do not require the user to specify units for engineering input (unless there may be ambiguity). Do not require the user to type .00 for whole number dollar amounts, provide default values whenever possible, and never require the user to enter information that can be acquired automatically or computed within the program.

14.11   PROCEDURAL DESIGN

Procedural design occurs after data, architectural, and interface designs have been established. In an ideal world, the procedural specification required to define algorithmic details would be stated in a natural language such as English. After all, members of a software development organization all speak a natural language (in theory, at least), people outside the software domain could more readily understand the specification, and no new learning would be required.

Unfortunately, there is one small problem. Procedural design must specify procedural detail unambiguously, and a lack of ambiguity in a natural language is not natural. Using a natural language, we can write a set of procedural steps in too many different ways. We frequently rely on context to get a point across. We often write as if a dialog with the reader were possible (it isn't). For these and many other reasons, a more constrained mode for representing procedural detail must be used.

14.11.1   Structured Programming

The foundations of procedural design were formed in the early 1960s and were solidified with the work of Edsgar Dijkstra and his colleagues [BOH66, DIJ65, DIJ76]. In the late 1960s Dijkstra and others proposed the use of a set of existing logical constructs from which any program could be formed. The constructs emphasized "maintenance of functional domain." That is, each construct had a predictable logical structure, was entered at the top, and exited at the bottom, enabling a reader to follow procedural flow more easily.[8]

The constructs are *sequence, condition,* and *repetition*. Sequence implements processing steps that are essential in the specification of any algorithm, condition provides the facility for selected processing based on some logical occurrence, and repetition provides for looping. These three constructs are fundamental to *structured programming*—an important procedural design technique.

----

[8]A little used but extremely important feature of structured programming is "proof of correctness." Procedural designs can be *proved* correct as they are created. An introduction to correctness verification of design is presented in Chapter 25.

The structured constructs were proposed to limit the procedural design of software to a small number of predictable operations. Complexity metrics (Chapter 18) indicate that the use of the structured constructs reduces program complexity and thereby enhances readability, testability, and maintainability. The use of a limited number of logical constructs also contributes to a human understanding process that psychologists call *chunking*. To understand this process, consider how you are reading this page. You do not read individual letters; rather, you recognize patterns or chunks of letters that form words or phrases. The structured constructs are logical chunks that allow a reader to recognize procedural elements of a module rather than read the design or code line by line. Understanding is enhanced when readily recognizable logical forms are encountered.

Any program, regardless of application area or technical complexity, can be designed and implemented using only the three structured constructs. It should be noted, however, that dogmatic use of only these constructs can sometimes cause practical difficulties. Section 14.11.2 considers this issue in further detail.

14.11.2 Graphical Design Notation

"A picture is worth a thousand words," but it's rather important to know which picture and which 1000 words. There is no question that graphical tools, such as the flowchart or box diagram, provide excellent pictorial patterns that readily depict procedural detail. However, if graphical tools are misused, the wrong picture may lead to the wrong software.

The *flowchart* was once the most widely used graphical representation for procedural design. Unfortunately, it was the most widely abused method as well.

The flowchart is quite simple pictorially. A box is used to indicate a processing step. A diamond represents a logical condition, and arrows show the flow of control. Figure 14.17 illustrates the three structured constructs discussed in Section 14.11.1. Sequence is represented as two processing boxes connected by a line (arrow) of control. Condition, also called *if-then-else* is depicted as a decision diamond which if true causes *then-part* processing to occur, and if false, invokes *else-part* processing. Repetition is represented using two slightly different forms. The *do-while* tests a condition and executes a *loop task* repetitively as long as the condition holds true. A *repeat-until* executes the loop task first, then tests a condition and repeats the task until the condition fails. The selection (or *select-case*) construct shown in the figure is actually an extension of the *if-then-else*. A parameter is tested by successive decisions until a true condition occurs and a *case part* processing path is executed.

The structured constructs may be nested within one another as shown in Figure 14.18. In the figure, a *repeat-until* forms the *then-part* of an *if-then-else* (shown enclosed by the outer dashed boundary). Another *if-then-else* forms the *else-part* of the larger condition. Finally, the condition itself becomes a second block in a sequence. By nesting constructs in this manner, a complex logical schema may be developed. It should be noted that any one of the blocks in Figure 14.18 could reference another module, thereby accomplishing *procedural layering* implied by program structure.

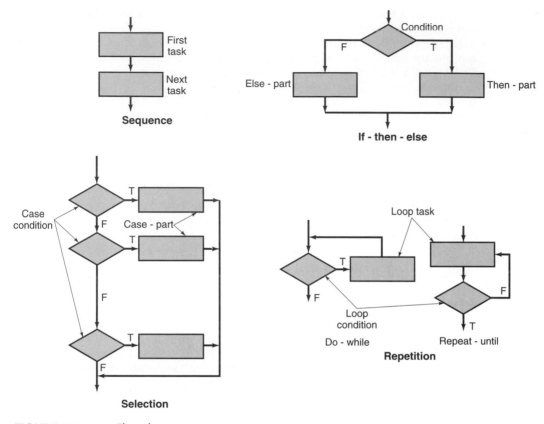

FIGURE 14.17. Flowchart constructs

In general, the dogmatic use of only the structured constructs can introduce inefficiency when an escape from a set of nested loops or nested conditions is required. More important, additional complication of all logical tests along the path of escape can cloud software control flow, increase the possibility of error, and have a negative impact on readability and maintainability. What can we do?

The designer is left with two options: (1) The procedural representation is redesigned so that the "escape branch" is not required at a nested location in the flow of control; or (2) the structured constructs are violated in a controlled manner; that is, a constrained branch out of the nested flow is designed. Option 1 is obviously the ideal approach, but option 2 can be accommodated without violating of the spirit of structured programming.

Another graphical design tool, the *box diagram,* evolved from a desire to develop a procedural design representation that would not allow violation of the structured constructs. Developed by Nassi and Shneiderman [NAS73] and extended by Chapin [CHA74], the diagrams (also called *Nassi-Shneiderman charts, N-S charts,* or *Chapin charts*) have the following characteristics: (1) *functional domain* (that is, the scope of repetition or an *if-then-else*) is well defined and clearly visible as a pictorial representation; (2) arbitrary transfer of

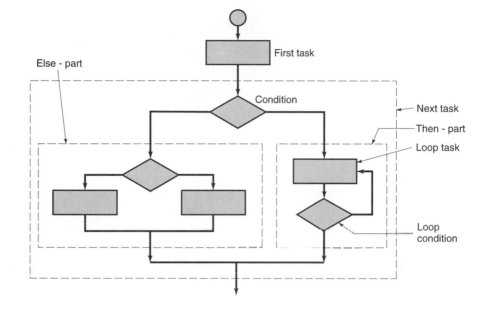

FIGURE 14.18.
Nesting
constructs

control is impossible; (3) the scope of local and/or global data can be easily determined; and (4) recursion is easy to represent.

The graphical representation of structured constructs using the box diagram is illustrated in Figure 14.19. The fundamental element of the diagram is a box. To represent sequence, two boxes are connected bottom to top. To represent an *if-then-else,* a condition box is followed by a *then-part* box and *else-part* box. Repetition is depicted with a bounding pattern that encloses the process (*do-while-part* or *repeat-until-part*) to be repeated. Finally, selection is represented using the graphical form shown at the bottom right of the figure.

Like flowcharts, a box diagram is layered on multiple pages as processing elements of a module are refined. A "call" to a subordinate module can be represented by a box with the module name enclosed by an oval.

14.11.3   Tabular Design Notation

In many software applications, a module may be required to evaluate a complex combination of conditions and select appropriate actions based on these conditions. *Decision tables* provide a notation that translates actions and conditions (described in a processing narrative) into a tabular form. The table is difficult to misinterpret and may even be used as a machine readable input to a table driven algorithm. In a comprehensive treatment of this design tool, Ned Chapin states [HUR83]:

> Some old software tools and techniques mesh well with new tools and techniques of software engineering. Decision tables are an excellent example.

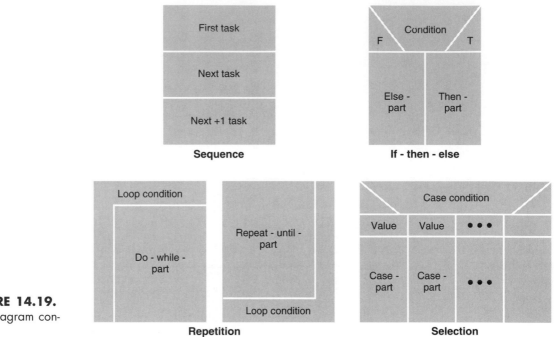

FIGURE 14.19.
Box diagram constructs

Decision tables preceded software engineering by nearly a decade, but fit so well with software engineering that they might have been designed for that purpose.

Decision table organization is illustrated in Figure 14.20. The table is divided into four sections. The upper left hand quadrant contains a list of all conditions. The lower left hand quadrant contains a list of all actions that are possible based on combinations of conditions. The right hand quadrants form a matrix that indicates condition combinations and the corresponding actions that will occur for a specific combination. Therefore, each column of the matrix may be interpreted as a processing *rule*.

The following steps are applied to develop a decision table:

1. List all actions that can be associated with a specific procedure (or module).
2. List all conditions (or decisions made) during execution of the procedure.
3. Associate specific sets of conditions with specific actions, eliminating impossible combinations of conditions; alternatively, develop every possible permutation of conditions.
4. Define *rules* by indicating what action or actions occur for a set of conditions.

To illustrate the use of a decision table consider the following excerpt from a processing narrative for a public utility billing system:

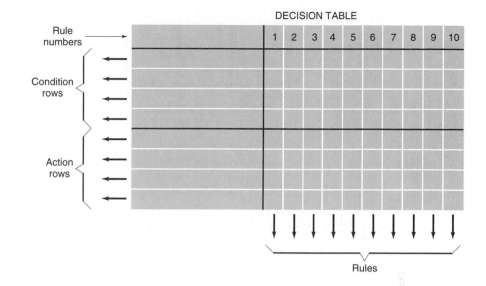

FIGURE 14.20.
Decision table
nomenclature

[I]f the customer account is billed using a fixed rate method, a minimum monthly charge is assessed for consumption of less than 100 kWh (kilowatt-hours). Otherwise, computer billing applies a Schedule A rate structure. However, if the account is billed using a variable rate method, a Schedule A rate structure will apply to consumption below 100 kWh, with additional consumption billed according to Schedule B.

Figure 14.21 illustrates a decision table representation of the preceding narrative. Each of the five rules indicates one of five viable conditions (e.g., a "T" (true) in both fixed rate and variable rate account makes no sense in the context of this procedure). As a general rule, the decision table can be effectively used to supplement other procedural design notation.

14.11.4 Program Design Language

Program Design Language (PDL), also called *structured English* or *pseudocode,* is "a pidgin language in that it uses the vocabulary of one language (i.e., English) and the overall syntax of another (i.e., a structured programming language)" [CAI75]. In this chapter PDL is used as a generic reference for a design language.

At first glance PDL looks something like any modern programming language. The difference between PDL and a modern programming language lies in the use of narrative text (e.g., English) embedded directly within PDL statements. Because narrative text is embedded directly into a syntactical structure, PDL cannot be compiled (at least not yet). However, PDL "processors" currently exist to translate PDL into a graphical representation (e.g., a flowchart) of design and produce nesting maps, a design operation index, cross-reference tables, and a variety of other information.

A program design language may be a simple transposition of a language such as Ada or C. Alternatively, it may be a product purchased specifically for

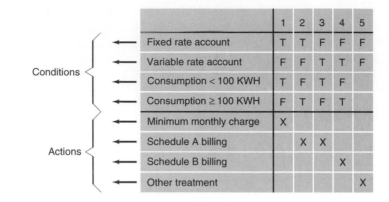

	1	2	3	4	5
Fixed rate account	T	T	F	F	F
Variable rate account	F	F	T	T	F
Consumption < 100 KWH	T	F	T	F	
Consumption ≥ 100 KWH	F	T	F	T	
Minimum monthly charge	X				
Schedule A billing		X	X		
Schedule B billing				X	
Other treatment					X

Conditions {first four rows}
Actions {last four rows}

FIGURE 14.21.
Resultant decision table

procedural design. Regardless of origin, a design language should have the following characteristics:

- a fixed syntax of *keywords* that provide for all structured constructs, data declarations, and modularity characteristics;
- a free syntax of natural language that describes processing features;
- data declaration facilities that should include both simple (scalar, array) and complex (linked list or tree) data structures; and
- subprogram definition and calling techniques that support various modes of interface description. Today, a high-order programming language is often used as the basis for a PDL. For example, Ada-PDL is widely used in the Ada community as a design definition tool. Ada language constructs and format are "mixed" with English narrative to form the design language.

A basic PDL syntax should include constructs for subprogram definition, interface description, and data declaration; and techniques for *block structuring,* condition constructs, repetition constructs, and I/O constructs. The format and semantics for some of these PDL constructs are presented in the section that follows.

It should be noted that PDL can be extended to include keywords for multitasking and/or concurrent processing, interrupt handling, interprocess synchronization, and many other features. The application design for which PDL is to be used should dictate the final form for the design language.

14.11.5   A PDL Example

To illustrate the use of PDL, we present an example of a procedural design for the SafeHome security system software introduced in earlier chapters. The SafeHome system in question monitors alarms for fire, smoke, burglars, water (flooding), and temperature (e.g., furnace breaks while home owner is away during winter); produces an alarm signal; and calls a monitoring service, generating a voice synthesized message. In the PDL that follows, we illustrate some of the important constructs noted in Section 14.11.4.

Recall that PDL is not a programming language. The designer can adapt as required without worry of syntax errors. However, the design for the monitoring software would have to be reviewed (do you see any problems?) and further refined before code could be written. The following PDL defines an elaboration of the procedural design for the **security monitor** procedure.

```
PROCEDURE security.monitor;
INTERFACE RETURNS system.status;
TYPE signal IS STRUCTURE DEFINED
    name IS STRING LENGTH VAR;
    address IS HEX device location;
    bound.value IS upper bound SCALAR;
    message IS STRING LENGTH VAR;
END signal TYPE;
TYPE system.status IS BIT (4);
TYPE alarm.type DEFINED
    smoke.alarm IS INSTANCE OF signal;
    fire.alarm IS INSTANCE OF signal;
    water.alarm IS INSTANCE OF signal;
    temp.alarm IS INSTANCE OF signal;
    burglar.alarm IS INSTANCE OF signal;
TYPE phone.number IS area code + 7-digit number;
    o
    o
    o

initialize all system ports and reset all hardware;
CASE OF control.panel.switches (cps):
    WHEN cps = "test" SELECT
        CALL alarm PROCEDURE WITH
            "on" for test.time in seconds;
    WHEN cps = "alarm-off" SELECT
        CALL alarm PROCEDURE WITH
            "off";
    WHEN cps = "new.bound.temp" SELECT
    CALL keypad.input PROCEDURE;
    WHEN cps = "burglar.alarm.off" SELECT
        deactivate signal [burglar.alarm];
    o
    o
    o

    DEFAULT none;
ENDCASE
REPEAT UNTIL activate.switch is turned off
    reset all signal.values and switches;
    DO FOR alarm.type = smoke, fire, water, temp, burglar;
        READ address [alarm.type] signal.value;
        IF signal.value > bound [alarm.type]
            THEN phone.message = message [alarm.type];
            set alarm.bell to "on" for alarm.timeseconds;
        PARBEGIN
```

```
                    CALL alarm PROCEDURE WITH "on", alarm.time in seconds;
                    CALL phone PROCEDURE WITH message [alarm.type],
                    phone.number;
              ENDPAR
        ELSE skip
        ENDIF
        ENDFOR
ENDREP
END security.monitor
```

Note that the designer for the security.monitor procedure has used a new construct PARBEGIN. . . . ENDPAR that specifies a *parallel block*. All tasks specified within the PARBEGIN block are executed in parallel. In this case, implementation details are not considered.

Program design language is often used in conjunction with CASE design tools that in some cases overlay a graphical component on the procedural design representation. For example, the *control structure diagram (CSD)* [CRO96] can be used in conjunction with either programming language source code or PDL. The design text is augmented with graphical symbols that depict all important structured programming constructs and special language forms (e.g., the Ada task or rendezvous). CSD notation is illustrated in Figure 14.22.

A natural question arises in any discussion of design notation: "What notation is really the best?" Any answer to this question is admittedly subjective

FIGURE 14.22.

Control structure diagram notation

and open to debate. However, it appears that program design language offers the best combination of characteristics. PDL may be embedded directly into source listings, improving documentation and making design maintenance less difficult. Editing can be accomplished with any text editor or word-processing system; automatic processors already exist, and the potential for "automatic code generation" is good.

However, it does not follow that other design notation is necessarily inferior to PDL. The pictorial nature of flowcharts and box diagrams provides a perspective on control flow that many designers prefer; the precise tabular content of decision tables is an excellent tool for table driven applications; and many other design representations (e.g., see [PET81], [SOM89]), not presented in this book, offer their own unique benefits. In the final analysis, the choice of a design tool may be more closely related to human factors than to technical attributes.

14.12   SUMMARY

Software design encompasses four distinct but interrelated activities: data design, architectural design, interface design, and procedural design. When each of these design activities has been completed, a comprehensive design model exists for the software.

Data design translates the data objects defined in the analysis model into data structures that reside within the software. The attributes that describe data objects, the relationships between data objects, and their use within the program all influence the choice of data structures.

The architectural design method presented in this chapter use information flow characteristics described in the analysis model to derive program structure. A data flow diagram is mapped into program structure using one of two mapping approaches—transform mapping and/or transaction mapping. Transform mapping is applied to an information flow that exhibits distinct boundaries between incoming and outgoing data. The DFD is mapped into a structure that allocates control to input, processing, and output along three separately factored module hierarchies. Transaction mapping is applied when a single information item causes flow to branch along one of many paths. The DFD is mapped into a structure that allocates control to a substructure that acquires and evaluates a transaction. Another substructure controls all potential processing actions based on a transaction.

Interface design encompasses internal and external program interfaces and the design of the user interface. Internal and external interface design are guided by information obtained from the analysis model. The user interface design process begins with task analysis and modeling, a design activity that defines user tasks and actions using either a elaborative or object-oriented approach. Design issues such as response time, command structure, error handling, and help facilities are considered, and a design model for the system is refined. A variety of implementation tools are used to build a prototype for evaluation by the user. A set of generic design guidelines govern general interaction, information display, and data entry.

Design notation, coupled with structured programming concepts, enables the designer to represent procedural detail in a manner that facilitates translation to code. Graphical, tabular, and textual notations are available.

The design methods presented in this chapter lead to a design model of the software. Data structure is developed, program architecture is established, modules are defined, and interfaces are established. This blueprint for implementation forms the basis for all subsequent software engineering work.

REFERENCES

[AHO83]   Aho, A.V., J. Hopcroft, and J. Ullmann, *Data Structures and Algorithms,* Addison-Wesley, 1983.

[BOH66]   Bohm, C., and G. Jacopini, "Flow Diagrams, Turing Machines and Languages with Only Two Formation Rules," *CACM,* vol. 9, no. 5, May 1966, pp. 366–371.

[CAI75]   Caine, S., and K. Gordon, "PDL—A Tool for Software Design," in *Proc. Natl. Computer Conference,* AFIPS Press, 1975, pp. 271–276.

[CHA74]   Chapin, N., "A New Format for Flowcharts," *Software—Practice and Experience,* vol. 4, no. 4, 1974, pp. 341–357.

[CRO96]   Cross, J.H., K.H. Chang, and T.D. Hendrix, "Grasp/Ada 95—Visualization with Control Structure Diagrams," *CrossTalk Journal of Defense Software Engineering,* January 1996, vol.9, no. 1, pp. 20–24.

[DAH72]   Dahl, O., E. Dijkstra, and C. Hoare, *Structured Programming,* Academic Press, 1972.

[DEA95]   Dean, T.R., and J.R. Cordy, "A Syntactic Theory of Software Architecture," *IEEE Trans. Software Engineering,* vol. 21, no. 4, April 1995, pp. 302–313.

[DEN73]   Dennis, J.B., "Modularity," in *Advanced Course on Software Engineering,* F.L. Bauer (ed.), Springer-Verlag, New York, 1973, pp. 128–182.

[DIJ65]   Dijkstra, E., "Programming Considered as a Human Activity," in *Proc. 1965 IFIP Congress,* North Holland Publishing Co., 1965.

[DIJ76]   Dijkstra, E., "Structured Programming," in *Software Engineering, Concepts and Techniques,* J. Buxton et al. (eds.), Van Nostrand Reinhold, 1976.

[DUM88]   Dumas, J.S., *Designing User Interfaces for Software,* Prentice-Hall, 1988.

[FRE80]   Freeman, P., "The Context of Design," in *Software Design Techniques,* 3rd ed., P. Freeman and A. Wasserman (eds.), IEEE Computer Society Press, pp. 2–4.

[GOM84]   Gomaa, H., "A Software Design Method for Real Time Systems," *CACM,* vol. 27, no. 9, September 1984, pp. 938–949.

[HUR83]   Hurley, R.B., *Decision Tables in Software Engineering,* Van Nostrand Reinhold, 1983.

[LEA88]   Lea, M., "Evaluating User Interface Designs," *User Interface Design for Computer Systems,* Halstead Press (Wiley), 1988.

[LIN79]   Linger, R.C, H.D. Mills, and B.I. Witt, *Structured Programming,* Addison-Wesley, 1979.

[MON84]   Monk, A. (ed.), *Fundamentals of Human–Computer Interaction,* Academic Press, 1984.

[MOR81]   Moran, T.P., "The Command Language Grammar: A Representation for the User Interface of Interactive Computer Systems," *Intl. Journal of Man-Machine Studies,* vol. 15, pp. 3–50.

[MOR95]   Moriconi, M., X. Qian, and R.A. Riemenschneider, "Correct Architecture Refinement," *IEEE Trans. Software Engineering,* vol. 21, no. 4, April 1995, pp. 356–372.

[MYE78]   Myers, G., *Composite Structured Design,* Van Nostrand Reinhold, 1978.

[MYE89]   Myers, B.A., "User Interface Tools: Introduction and Survey," *IEEE Software,* January 1989, p. 15–23.

[NAS73]   Nassi, I., and B. Shneiderman, "Flowchart Techniques for Structured Programming," *SIGPLAN Notices,* ACM, August 1973.

[NOR86]   Norman, D.A., "Cognitive Engineering," in *User Centered Systems Design,* Lawrence Erlbaum Associates, New Jersey, 1986.

[PET81]   Peters, L.J., Software Design: Methods and Techniques, *Yourdon Press,* New York, 1981.

[RUB88]   Rubin, T., *User Interface Design for Computer Systems,* Halstead Press (Wiley), 1988.

[SHA95]   Shaw, M., and D. Garlan, "Formulations and Formalisms in Software Architecture," *Volume 1000—Lecture Notes in Computer Science,* Springer-Verlag, 1995.

[SHN87]   Shneiderman, B., *Designing the User Interface,* Addison-Wesley, 1987.

[SOM89]   Sommerville, I., *Software Engineering,* 3rd edition, Addison-Wesley, 1989.

[STE74]   Stevens, W., G. Myers, and L. Constantine, "Structured Design," *IBM System Journal,* vol. 13, no. 2, 1974, pp. 115–139.

[WAS80]   Wasserman, A., "Principles of Systematic Data Design and Implementation," in *Software Design Techniques,* (P. Freeman and A. Wasserman, eds.), 3rd ed., IEEE Computer Society Press, 1980, pp. 287–293.

[WIR71]   Wirth, N., "Program Development by Stepwise Refinement," *CACM,* vol. 14, no. 4, 1971, pp. 221–227.

[YOU79]   Yourdon, E., and L. Constantine, *Structured Design,* Prentice-Hall, 1979.

PROBLEMS AND POINTS TO PONDER

14.1.   Write a three- to five-page paper that presents guidelines for selecting data structures based on the nature of problem. Begin by delineating the classical data structures encountered in software work and then describe criteria for selecting from these for particular types of problems.

14.2.   Some designers contend that all data flow may be treated as transform oriented. Discuss how this contention will affect the software structure that is derived when a transaction-oriented flow is treated as a transform. Use an example flow to illustrate important points.

14.3.   If you haven't done so, complete problem 12.13 in Chapter 12. Use the design methods described in this chapter to develop a program structure for the PHTRS.

14.4.   Propose an approach to the design of real-time software applications that makes use of data flow–oriented techniques. To begin your discussion, list problems with real-time systems (e.g., interrupt driven) that make direct application of data flow–oriented design somewhat unwieldy.

14.5.   Using a data flow diagram and a processing narrative, describe a computer-based system that has distinct transform flow characteristics. Define flow boundaries and map the DFD into a software structure using the technique described in Section 14.4.

14.6. Using a data flow diagram and a processing narrative, describe a computer-based system that has distinct transaction flow characteristics. Define flow boundaries and map the DFD into a software structure using the technique described in Section 14.5.

14.7. Using requirements that are derived from a classroom discussion, complete the DFDs and architectural design for the SafeHome example presented in Sections 14.4 and 14.5. Assess the functional independence of all modules. Document your design.

14.8. For readers with a background in compiler design: Develop a DFD for a simple compiler, assess its overall flow characteristic, and derive a program structure using the techniques described in this chapter. Provide processing narratives for each module.

14.9. How does the concept of *recursive modules* (i.e., modules that invoke themselves) fit into the design philosophy and techniques presented in this chapter?

14.10. Using the DFD shown in Figure 14.23, apply transaction analysis to the DFD and derive a program structure. The overall flow characteristic should be assumed to be transaction flow (with transaction center at transform c). Flow in region I is transform; flow in region II is transaction, with transform subflows as shown; flow in region III is transform. Your program structure should have modules that correspond on a one-to-one basis with the transforms in the figure. It will be necessary to derive a number of control modules.

14.11. Discuss the relative merits and difficulties of applying data flow–oriented design in the following areas:
a. embedded microprocessor applications
b. engineering/scientific analysis
c. computer graphics
d. operating system design
e. business applications
f. database management system design
g. communications software design
h. compiler design
i. process control applications
j. artificial intelligence applications

14.12. Given a set of requirements provided by your instructor (or a set of requirements for a problem on which you are currently working) develop a complete design including all design documentation. Conduct a design review (Chapter 8) to assess the quality of your design. This problem may assigned to a team, rather than an individual.

14.13. Describe the worst interface that you have ever worked with and critique it relative to the concepts introduced in this chapter. Describe the best interface that you have ever worked with and critique it relative to the concepts introduced in this chapter.

14.14. Consider one of the following interactive applications:
a. a desk-top publishing system
b. a computer-aided design system
c. an interior design system (as described in Section 14.9.2)

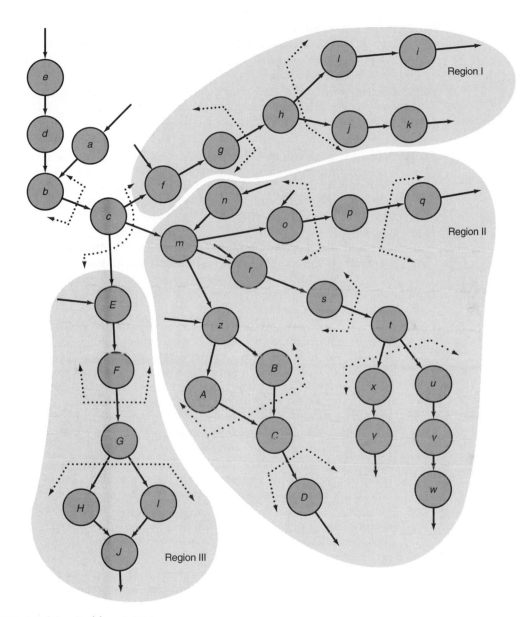

FIGURE 14.23. Problem 14.10

d. an automated course registration system for a university
e. a library management system
f. a next generation polling booth for elections
g. a home banking system
h. an interactive application assigned by your instructor
Develop a design model, a user model, a system image, and a system perception for any one of the above systems.

14.15. Perform a detailed task analysis for any one of the systems listed in problem 14.14. Use either an elaborative or object-oriented approach.

14.16. Continuing problem 14.15, apply the seven-step interface design process described in this chapter.

14.17. Describe your approach to user help facilities for the design model and task analysis you have performed as part of problems 14.15 and 14.16.

14.18. Provide a few examples that illustrate why response time variability can be a issue.

14.19. Develop an approach that would automatically integrate error messages and a user help facility. That is, the system would automatically recognize the error type and provide a help window with suggestions for correcting it. Perform a reasonably complete software design that considers appropriate data structures and algorithms.

14.20. Develop an interface evaluation questionnaire that contains 20 generic questions that would apply to most interfaces. Have ten classmates complete the questionnaire for an interactive system that you all use. Summarize the results and report them to your class.

14.21. Attempt to add at least five additional design guidelines to each category discussed in Section 14.10.

14.22. An enormous literature has evolved on the topic of structured programming. Write a brief paper that highlights the published arguments—pro and con—about the exclusive use of structured constructs.

Problems 23 to 31 may be represented using any one (or more) of the procedural design notations that have been presented in this chapter. Your instructor may assign specific notation to specific problems.

14.23. Develop a procedural design for modules that implement the following sorts: Shell-Metzner sort; heapsort; BSST (tree) sort. Refer to a book on data structures if you are unfamiliar with these sorts.

14.24. Develop a procedural design for an interactive user interface that queries for basic income tax information. Derive your own requirements and assume that all tax computations are performed by other modules.

14.25. Develop a procedural design for garbage collection function for a variable partitioned memory management scheme. Define all appropriate data structures in the design representation. Refer to a book on operating systems for more information.

14.26. Develop a procedural design for a program that accepts an arbitrarily long text as input and produces a list of words and their frequency of occurrence as output.

14.27. Develop a procedural design of a program that will numerically integrate a function f in the bounds a to b.

14.28. Develop a procedural design for a generalized Turing machine that will accept a set of quadruples as program input and produce output as specified.

14.29. Develop a procedural design for a program that will solve the Towers of Hanoi problem. Many books on artificial intelligence discuss this problem in some detail.

14.30. Develop a procedural design for all or major portions of an LR parser for a compiler. Refer to one or more books on compiler design.

14.31. Develop a procedural design for an encryption/decryption algorithm of your choosing.

FURTHER READINGS AND OTHER INFORMATION SOURCES

Treatments of software design are contained in most books dedicated to software engineering. More rigorous treatments of the subject can be found in Feijs (*Formalization of Design Methods,* Prentice-Hall, 1993), Witt et al., (*Software Architecture and Design Principles,* Thomson Publishing, 1994), and Budgen (*Software Design,* Addison-Wesley, 1994).

Complete presentations of data flow–oriented design may be found in Myers [MYE78], Yourdon and Constantine [YOU79], Buhr (*System Design with Ada,* Prentice-Hall, 1984), and Page-Jones (*The Practical Guide to Structured Systems Design,* 2nd edition, Prentice-Hall, 1988). These books are dedicated to design alone and provide comprehensive tutorials in the data flow approach.

The literature on human–computer interfaces and human factors has expanding dramatically over the past decade. Books by Thimbley (*The User Interface Design Book,* Addison-Wesley, 1989), Barfield (*The User Interface: Concepts and Design,* Addison-Wesley, 1993), Nielsen (*Usability Engineering,* Academic Press, 1993), Preece (*A Guide to Usability,* Addison-Wesley, 1993), and Lee (*Object-Oriented GUI Application Development,* Prentice-Hall, 1994) provide worthwhile treatments of the subject. Books by Rubinstein and Hersh (*The Human Factor,* Digital Press, 1984), Dumas [DUM88], Helander (*Handbook of Human–Computer Interaction,* Elsevier Science Publishers, 1988), and Laurel (*The Art of Human–Computer Interface Design,* Addison-Wesley, 1990) each contain worthwhile lists of interface design guidelines. Norman (*The Psychology of Everyday Things,* Basic Books, 1988) uses examples from everyday life to highlight good and bad design. He contends that good interface designs take account of our strong perceptual abilities, while bad interfaces fight against them.

The work of Linger, Mills, and Witt (*Structured Programming—Theory and Practice,* Addison-Wesley, 1979) remains a definitive treatment of the subject. The text contains a good PDL as well as detailed discussions of the ramifications of structured programming. Other books that focus on procedural design issues include books by Bentley (*Programming Pearls,* Addison-Wesley, 1986, and *More Programming Pearls,* Addison-Wesley, 1988) and Dahl, Dijkstra, and Hoare (*Structured Programming,* Academic Press, 1972).

A collection of articles and commentary of software design methods can be found at the Web site for the Association for Software Design:

http://www-pcd.stanford.edu/asd/info/articles/

A bibliography, pointers and advanced discussion of software architecture technology and a "Software Architecture Technology Guide" are available at:

http://www.stars.reston.unisysgsg.com/arch/guide.html

http://www.sci.cmu.edu/technology/architecture/bibliography.html

An on-line edition of Geo Wiederhold's classic book (*Database Design*, 3rd edition, McGraw-Hill, 1988) can be found at:

http://db.stanford.edu/pub/gio/dbd/intro.html

A brief tutorial, "Comments on Human Computer Interface Design," can be found at:

http://infolabwww.kub.nl:2080/w3thesis/Hci/user_centered.html

Lewis and Rieman have provided an on-line textbook (as shareware) entitled *Task Centered User Interface Design* at:

ftp://ftp.cs.colorado.edu/pub/cs/distribs/clewis/HCI-Design-Book/

An up-to-date list of World Wide Web references for software design methods can be found at: **http://www.rspa.com**

DESIGN FOR REAL-TIME SYSTEMS

The design of real-time computing systems is the most challenging and complex task that can be undertaken by a software engineer. By its very nature, software for real-time systems makes demands on analysis, design, and testing techniques that are unknown in other application areas.

Real-time software is highly coupled to the external world. That is, real-time software must respond to the problem domain (the real world) in a time frame dictated by the problem domain. Because real-time software must operate under rigorous performance constraints, software design is often driven by hardware as well as software architecture, operating system characteristics as well as application requirements, programming language vagaries as well as design issues.

In his book on real-time software, Robert Glass [GLA83] provides a useful introduction to the subject of real-time systems:

> The digital computer is becoming ever more present in the daily lives of all of us. Computers allow our watches to play games as well as tell time, optimize the gas mileage of our latest generation cars, and sequence our appliances. . . . [In industry, computers control machines, coordinate processes, and increasingly, replace manual skills and human recognition with automated systems and "artificial intelligence."]
>
> All these computing interactions—whether helpful or intrusive—are examples of real-time computing. The computer is controlling something that interacts with reality on a timely basis. In fact, timing is the essence of the interaction. . . . An unresponsive real-time system may be worse than no system at all.

No more than a decade ago, real-time software development was considered a black art, applied by anointed wizards who guarded their closed world with jealousy. Today, there aren't enough wizards to go around! Yet, there is no question that the engineering of real-time software requires special skills. In this chapter we examine real-time software and discuss at least some of the skills that are required to build it.

15.1   SYSTEM CONSIDERATIONS

Like any computer-based system, a real-time system must integrate hardware, software, human, and database elements to properly achieve a set of functional and performance requirements. In Chapter 10, we examined the allocation task for computer-based systems, indicating that the system engineer must allocate function and performance among the system elements. The problem for real-time systems is proper allocation. Real-time performance is often as important as function, yet allocation decisions that relate to performance are often difficult to make with assurance. Can a processing algorithm meet severe timing constraints, or should we build special hardware to do the job? Can an off-the-shelf operating system meet our need for efficient interrupt handling, multi-tasking, and communication, or should we build a custom executive? Can specified hardware coupled with proposed software meet performance criteria? These and many other questions must be answered by the real-time system engineer.

A comprehensive discussion of all elements of real-time systems is beyond the scope of this book. Among a number of good sources of information are [SAV85], [ELL94], and [SEL94]. However, it is important that we understand each of the elements of a real-time system before discussing software analysis and design issues.

Everett [EVE95] defines three characteristics that differentiate real-time software development from other software engineering efforts:

- *The design of a real-time system is resource constrained.* The primary resource for a real-time system is time. It is essential to complete a defined task within a given number of CPU cycles. In addition, other system resources, such as memory size, may be traded against time to achieve system objectives.

- *Real-time systems are compact, yet complex.* Although a sophisticated real-time system may contain well over a million lines of code, the time-critical portion of the software typically represents a very small percentage of the total. It is this small percentage of code that is the most complex (from an algorithmic point of view).

- *Real-time systems often work without the presence of a human user.* Therefore, real-time software must detect problems that lead to failure and automatically recover from these problems before damage to data and the controlled environment occurs.

In the section that follows, we examine some of the key attributes that differentiate real-time systems from other types of computer software.

15.2   REAL-TIME SYSTEMS[1]

Real-time systems generate some action in response to external events. To accomplish this function, they perform high-speed data acquisition and control under severe time and reliability constraints. Because these constraints are so stringent, real-time systems are frequently dedicated to a single application.

Real-time systems are used widely for diverse applications that include military command and control systems, consumer electronics, process control, industrial automation, medical and scientific research, computer graphics, local and wide area communications, aerospace systems, computer-aided testing, and a vast array of industrial instrumentation.

15.2.1   Integration and Performance Issues

Putting together a real-time system presents the system engineer with difficult hardware and software decisions. (The allocation issues associated with hardware for real-time systems are beyond the scope of this book; see [SAV85] for additional information.) Once the software element has been allocated, detailed software requirements are established and a fundamental software design must be developed. Among many real-time design concerns are coordination between the real-time tasks, processing of system interrupts, I/O handling to ensure that no data are lost, specifying the system's internal and external timing constraints, and ensuring the accuracy of its database.

Each real-time design concern for software must be applied in the context of system *performance*. In most cases, the performance of a real-time system is measured as one or more time related characteristics, but other measures such as fault-tolerance may also be used.

Some real-time systems are designed for applications in which only the response time or the data transfer rate is critical. Other real-time applications require optimization of both parameters under peak loading conditions. What's more, real-time systems must handle their peak loads while performing a number of simultaneous tasks.

Since the performance of a real-time system is determined primarily by the system response time and its data transfer rate, it is important to understand these two parameters. System *response time* is the time within which a system must detect an internal or external event and respond with an action. Often, event detection and response generation are simple. It is the processing of the information about the event to determine the appropriate response that may involve complex, time-consuming algorithms.

Among the key parameters that affect the response time are *context switching* and *interrupt latency*. Context switching involves the time and overhead to switch among tasks, and interrupt latency is the time lag before the switch is

---

[1]Based on an article, "Real-Time Systems" by H.J. Hinden and W.B. Rausch Hinden [HIN83]. Reproduced with permission of *Electronic Design* and Heyden Publishing.

actually possible. Other parameters that affect response time are the speed of computation and the speed of access to mass storage.

The *data transfer rate* indicates how fast serial or parallel data, as well as analog or digital data, must be moved into or out of the system. Hardware vendors often quote timing and capacity values for performance characteristics. However, hardware specifications for performance are usually measured in isolation and are often of little value in determining overall real-time system performance. Therefore, I/O device performance, bus latency, buffer size, disk performance, and a host of other factors, although important, are only part of the story of real-time system design.

Real-time systems are often required to process a continuous stream of incoming data. Design must ensure that data are not missed. In addition, a real-time system must respond to events that are asynchronous. Therefore, the arrival sequence and data volume cannot be easily predicted in advance.

Although all software applications must be reliable, real-time systems make special demands on reliability, restart, and fault recovery. Because the real world is being monitored and controlled, loss of monitoring or control (or both) is intolerable in many circumstances (e.g., an air traffic control system). Consequently, real-time systems contain restart and fault-recovery mechanisms, and frequently have built-in redundancy to ensure backup.

The need for reliability, however, has spurred an ongoing debate about whether *on-line* systems, such as airline reservation systems and automatic bank tellers, also qualify as real-time. On one hand, such on-line systems must respond to external interrupts within prescribed response times on the order of one second. On the other hand, nothing catastrophic occurs if an on-line system fails to meet response requirements; instead, only system degradation results.

15.2.2 Interrupt Handling

One characteristic that serves to distinguish real-time systems from any other type is *interrupt handling*. A real-time system must respond to external stimuli—*interrupts*—in a time frame dictated by the external world. Because multiple stimuli (interrupts) are often present, priorities and priority interrupts must be established. In other words, the most important task must always be serviced within predefined time constraints regardless of other events.

Interrupt handling entails not only storing information so that the computer can correctly restart the interrupted task, but also avoiding deadlocks and endless loops. The overall approach to interrupt handling is illustrated in Figure 15.1. Normal processing flow is "interrupted" by an event that is detected by processor hardware. An *event* is any occurrence that requires immediate service and may be generated by either hardware or software. The state of the interrupted program is saved (i.e., all register contents, control blocks, etc. are saved) and control is passed to an interrupt service routine that branches to appropriate software for handling the interrupt. Upon completion of interrupt servicing, the state of the machine is restored and normal processing flow continues.

In many situations, interrupt servicing for one event may itself be interrupted by another, higher-priority event. Interrupt priority levels (Figure 15.2)

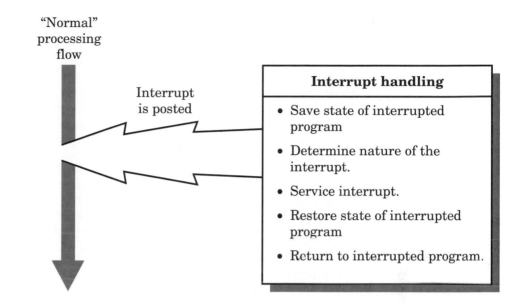

FIGURE 15.1.
Interrupts

may be established. If a lower-priority process is accidentally allowed to interrupt a higher-priority one, it may be difficult to restart the processes in the right order and an endless loop may result.

To handle interrupts and still meet the system time constraints, many real-time operating systems make dynamic calculations to determine whether the system goals can be met. These dynamic calculations are based on the average frequency of occurrence of events, the amount of time it takes to service them (if they can be serviced), and the routines that can interrupt them and temporarily prevent their servicing.

If the dynamic calculations show that it is impossible to handle the events that can occur in the system and still meet the time constraints, the system

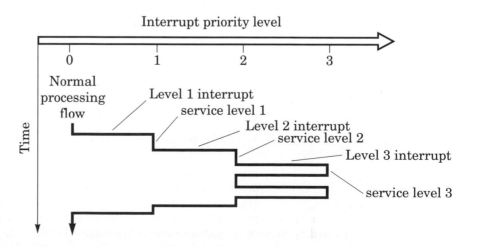

FIGURE 15.2.
An example of interrupt priority levels

must decide on a plan of action. One possible approach involves buffering the data so that it can be processed quickly when the system is ready.

15.2.3   Real-Time Data Bases

Like many data processing systems, real-time systems often are coupled with a database management function. However, *distributed databases* would seem to be a preferred approach in real-time systems because multitasking is commonplace and data are often processed in parallel. If the database is distributed, individual tasks can access their data faster and more reliably, and with fewer bottlenecks than with a centralized database. The use of a distributed database for real-time applications divides input/output "traffic" and shortens queues of tasks waiting for access to a database. Moreover, a failure of one database will rarely cause the failure of the entire system, if redundancy is built in.

The performance efficiencies achieved through the use of a distributed database must be weighed against potential problems associated with data partitioning and replication. Although data redundancy improves response time by providing multiple information sources, replication requirements for distributed files also produce logistical and overhead problems, since all the file copies must be updated. In addition, the use of distributed databases introduces the problem of *concurrency control*. Concurrency control involves synchronizing the databases so that all copies have the correct, identical information free for access.

The conventional approach to concurrency control is based on what are known as *locking* and *time stamps*. At regular intervals, the following tasks are initiated: (1) The database is "locked" so that concurrency control is assured; no I/O is permitted; (2) updating occurs as required; (3) the database is unlocked; (4) files are validated to ensure that all updates have been correctly made; (5) the completed update is acknowledged. All locking tasks are monitored by a master clock (i.e., time stamps). The delays involved in these procedures, as well as the problems of avoiding inconsistent updates and deadlock, militate against the widespread use of distributed databases.

Some techniques, however, have been developed to speed updating and to solve the concurrency problem. One of these, called the *exclusive-writer protocol* maintains the consistency of replicated files by allowing only a single, exclusive writing task to update a file. It therefore eliminates the high overhead of locking or time stamp procedures.

15.2.4   Real-Time Operating Systems

Some real-time operating systems (RTOS) are applicable to a broad range of system configurations, while others are geared to a particular board or even microprocessor, regardless of the surrounding electronic environment. RTOS achieve their capabilities through a combination of software features and (increasingly) a variety of micro-coded capabilities implemented in hardware.

Today, two broad classes of operating systems are used for real-time work: (1) dedicated RTOS designed exclusively for real-time applications and (2) general-purpose operating systems that have been enhanced to provide real-time capability. The use of a *real-time executive* makes real-time performance feasible for a general-purpose operating system. Behaving like application software, the executive performs a number of operating system functions—particularly those that affect real-time performance—faster and more efficiently than the general-purpose operating system.

All operating systems must have a priority scheduling mechanism, but RTOS must provide a *priority mechanism* that allows high-priority interrupts to take precedence over less important ones. Moreover, because interrupts occur in response to asynchronous, nonrecurring events, they must be serviced without first taking time to swap in a program from disk storage. Consequently, to guarantee the required response time, a real-time operating system must have a mechanism for *memory locking*—that is, locking at least some programs in main memory so that swapping overhead is avoided.

To determine which kind of real-time operating system best matches an application, measures of RTOS quality can be defined and evaluated. Context switching time and interrupt latency (discussed earlier) determine interrupt-handling capability, the most important aspect of a real-time system. Context switching time is the time the operating system takes to store the state of the computer and the contents of the registers so that it can return to a processing task after servicing the interrupt.

Interrupt latency, the maximum time lag before the system gets around to switching a task, occurs because in an operating system there are often non-reentrant or critical processing paths that must be completed before an interrupt can be processed.

The length of these paths (the number of instructions) before the system can service an interrupt indicates the worst-case time lag. The worst case occurs if a high-priority interrupt is generated immediately after the system enters a critical path between an interrupt and interrupt service. If the time is too long, the system may miss data that are unrecoverable. It is important that the designer know the time lag so that the system can compensate for it.

Many operating systems perform multitasking [WOO90], or concurrent processing, another major requirement for real-time systems. But to be viable for real-time operation, the system overhead must be low in terms of switching time and memory space used.

15.2.5 Real-Time Languages

Because of the special requirements for performance and reliability demanded of real-time systems, the choice of a programming language is important. Many general-purpose programming languages (e.g., C, Fortran, Modula-2) can be used effectively for real-time applications. However, a class of so-called "real-time languages" (e.g., Ada, Jovial, HAL/S, Chill, and others) is often used in specialized military and communications applications.

A combination of characteristics makes a real-time language different from a general-purpose language. These include the multitasking capability, constructs to directly implement real-time functions, and modern programming features that help ensure program correctness.

A programming language that directly supports multitasking is important because a real-time system must respond to asynchronous events. Although many RTOS provide multitasking capabilities, embedded real-time software often exists without an operating system. Instead, embedded applications are written in a language that provides sufficient run-time support for real-time program execution. Run-time support requires less memory than an operating system, and it can be tailored to an application, thus increasing performance.

15.2.6 Task Synchronization and Communication

A multitasking system must furnish a mechanism for the tasks to pass information to each other as well as to ensure their synchronization. For these functions, operating systems and languages with run-time support commonly use queuing semaphores, mailboxes, or message systems. A semaphore enables concurrent tasks to be synchronized. It supplies synchronization and signaling but contains no information. Messages are similar to semaphores except that they carry the associated information. Mailboxes, on the other hand, do not signal information but instead contain it.

Queuing semaphores are software primitives that help manage traffic. They provide a method of directing several queues—for example, queues of tasks waiting for resources, database access, and devices, as well as queues of the resources and devices. The semaphores coordinate (synchronize) the waiting tasks with whatever they are waiting for without letting tasks or resources interfere with each other.

In a real-time system, semaphores are commonly used to implement and manage *mailboxes*. Mailboxes are temporary storage places (also called a *message pools* or *buffers*) for messages sent from one process to another. One process produces a piece of information, puts it in the mailbox, and then signals a consuming process that there is a piece of information in the mailbox for it to use.

Some approaches to real-time operating systems or run-time support systems view mailboxes as the most efficient way to implement communications between processes. Some real-time operating systems furnish a place to send and receive pointers to mailbox data. This eliminates the need to transfer all of the data—thus saving time and overhead.

A third approach to communication and synchronization among processes is a message system. With a message system, one process sends a message to another. The latter is then automatically activated by the run-time support system or operating system to process the message. Such a system incurs overhead because it transfers the actual information, but it provides greater flexibility and ease of use.

15.3   ANALYSIS AND SIMULATION OF REAL-TIME SYSTEMS

In the preceding section, we discussed a set of dynamic attributes that cannot be divorced from the functional requirements of a real-time system:

- interrupt handling and context switching
- response time
- data transfer rate and throughput
- resource allocation and priority handling
- task synchronization and intertask communication

Each of these performance attributes can be specified, but it is extremely difficult to verify whether system elements will achieve desired response, system resources will be sufficient to satisfy computational requirements, or processing algorithms will execute with sufficient speed.

The analysis of real-time systems requires modeling and simulation that enables the system engineer to assess "timing and sizing" issues. Although a number of analysis techniques have been proposed in the literature (e.g., [LIU90], [WIL90], and [ZUC89]), it is fair to state that analytical approaches for the analysis and design of real-time systems are still in their early stages of development.

15.3.1 Mathematical Tools for Real-Time System Analysis

A set of mathematical tools that enable the system engineer to model real-time system elements and assess timing and sizing issues has been proposed by Thomas McCabe [MCC85]. Based loosely on data flow analysis techniques (Chapter 12), McCabe's approach enables the analyst to model both hardware and software elements of a real-time system; represent control in a probabilistic manner; and apply network analysis, queuing and graph theory, and a Markovian mathematical model [GRO85] to derive system timing and resource sizing. Unfortunately, the mathematics involved is beyond the scope of this book, making a detailed explication of McCabe's work difficult. However, an overview of the technique will provide a worthwhile view of an analytical approach to the engineering of real-time systems.

McCabe's real time analysis technique is predicated on a data flow model of the real-time system. However, rather than using a DFD in the conventional manner, McCabe [MCC85] contends that the transforms (bubbles) of a DFD can be represented as process states of a Markov chain (a probabilistic queuing model) and the data flows themselves represent transitions between the process states. The analyst can assign transitional probabilities to each data flow path. As shown in Figure 15.3, a value,

$$0 < p_{ij} \leq 1.0$$

may be specified for each flow path, where p_{ij} represents the probability that flow will occur between process i and process j. The processes correspond to information transforms (bubbles) in the DFD.

Each process in the DFD-like model can be given a "unit cost" that represents the estimated (or actual) execution time required to perform its function and an "entrance value" that depicts the number of system interrupts corresponding to the process. The model is then analyzed using a set of mathematical tools that compute (1) the expected number of visits to a process, (2) the

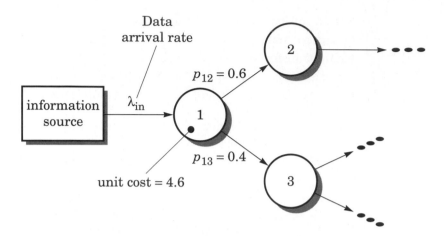

time spent in the system when processing begins at a specific process, and (3) the total time spent in the system.

To illustrate the McCabe technique on a realistic example, we consider a DFD for an electronic countermeasures system shown in Figure 15.4. The data flow diagram takes the standard form, but data flow identification has been replaced by p_{ij}. A queue network model is derived from the DFD is shown in Figure 15.5. The values lambda (λ_i) correspond to the arrival rate (arrivals per second) at each process. Depending on the type of queue encountered, the analyst must determine statistical information such as the mean service rate (mean run-time per process), variance of service rate, variance of arrival rate, and so forth.

The arrival rates for each process are determined using the flow path probabilities, p_{ij} and the arrival rate into the system, λ_{in}. A set of flow balance equations are derived and solved simultaneously to compute the flow through each process. For the example shown in Figure 15.5, the following flow balance equations result [MCC85]:

$$\lambda_1 = \lambda_{in} + \lambda_4$$

$$\lambda_2 = p_{12}\lambda_1$$

$$\lambda_3 = p_{13}\lambda_1 + p_{23}\lambda_2$$

$$\lambda_4 = p_{64}\lambda_6$$

$$\lambda_5 = p_{25}\lambda_2 = \lambda_3$$

$$\lambda_6 = \lambda_5$$

$$\lambda_7 = p_{67}\lambda_6$$

For the p_{ij} shown and an arrival rate, $\lambda_{in} = 5$ arrivals per second, the above equations can be solved [MCC85] to yield:

$$\lambda_1 = 8.3$$

$$\lambda_2 = 5.8$$

$$\lambda_3 = 5.4$$

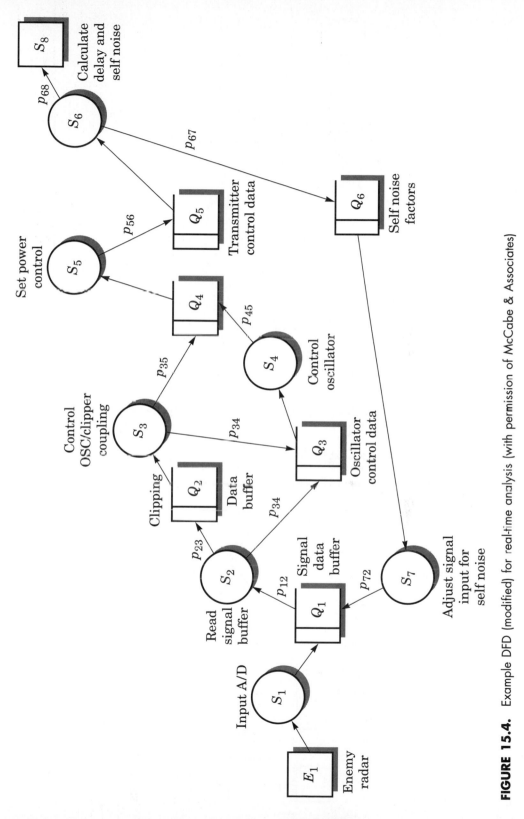

FIGURE 15.4. Example DFD (modified) for real-time analysis (with permission of McCabe & Associates)

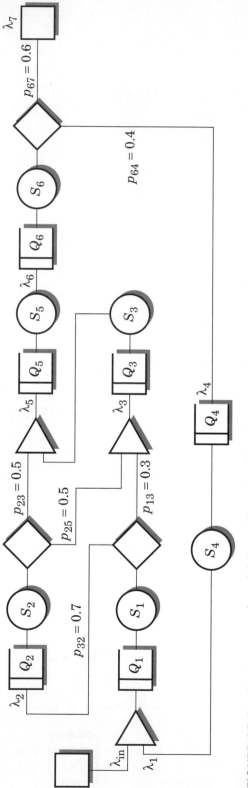

FIGURE 15.5. Queuing network model derived from data flow diagram (with permission of McCabe & Associates)

$$\lambda_4 = 3.3$$

$$\lambda_5 = 8.3$$

$$\lambda_6 = 8.3$$

$$\lambda_7 = 5.0$$

Once the arrival rates have been computed, standard queuing theory can be used to compute system timing. Each subsystem (a queue, Q, and a server, S) may be evaluated using formulas that correspond to the queue type. For $(m/m/1)$ queues [KLI75]:

utilization: $\rho = \lambda/\mu$

expected queue length: $N_q = \rho^2/(1 - \rho)$

expected number in subsystem: $N_s = \rho_1/(1 - \rho)$

expected time in queue: $T_q = \lambda/(\mu(\mu - \lambda))$

expected time in subsystem: $T_s = 1/(\mu - \lambda)$

where μ is completion rate (completions/sec). Applying standard queuing network reduction rules, illustrated in Figure 15.6, the original queuing network (Figure 15.5) derived from the data flow diagram (Figure 15.4) can be simplified by applying the steps shown in Figure 15.7. The total time spent in the system is 2.37 seconds.

Obviously, the accuracy of McCabe's analysis approach is only as good as estimates for flow probability, arrival rate, and completion rate. However, significant benefit can be achieved by taking a more analytical view of real-time systems during analysis. To quote McCabe [MCC85]:

> By changing such variables as arrival rates, interrupt rates, splitting probabilities, priority structure, queue discipline, configurations, requirements, physical implementation and variances we can easily show the program manager what affect it will have on the system at hand. These iterative methodologies are necessary to fill a void in real-time specification modeling.

15.3.2 Simulation and Modeling Techniques

Mathematical analysis of a real-time system represents one approach that can be used to understand projected performance. However, a growing number of real-time software developers use simulation and modeling tools that not only analyze a system's performance, but also enable the software engineer to build a prototype, execute it, and thereby gain an understanding of a system's behavior.

The overall rationale behind simulation and modeling for real-time systems is discussed [ILO89] by i-Logix (a company that develops tools for systems engineers):

(a) *Series rule*—The arrivals are served by the subsystem in series.

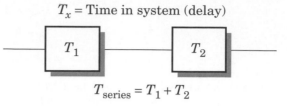

$$T_x = \text{Time in system (delay)}$$

$$T_{\text{series}} = T_1 + T_2$$

(b) *Parallel rule*—The arrivals are served by the subsystem in parallel.

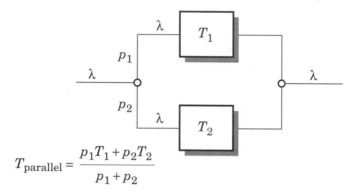

$$T_{\text{parallel}} = \frac{p_1 T_1 + p_2 T_2}{p_1 + p_2}$$

p_1 = probability of entering the server 1 system.

p_2 = probability of entering the server 2 system.

(c) *Looping rule*—A server with delay $T(\lambda\mu)$ and a "feedback" loop with looping probability P.

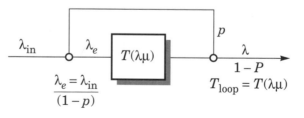

FIGURE 15.6.
Queuing network
reduction rules
[MCC85]

$$\lambda_e = \frac{\lambda_{\text{in}}}{(1-p)}$$

$$T_{\text{loop}} = T(\lambda\mu)$$

The understanding of a system's behavior in its environment over time is most often addressed in the design, implementation and testing phases of a project, through iterative trial and error. The Statemate [a system engineering tool for simulation and modeling] approach provides an alternative to this costly process. It allows you to build a comprehensive system model that is accurate enough to be relied on and clear enough to be useful. The model addresses the usual functional and flow issues, but also covers the dynamic, behavioral aspects of a system. This model can then be tested with the Statemate analysis and retrieval tools, which provide extensive mechanisms for inspecting and debugging the specification and retrieving information from it. By test-

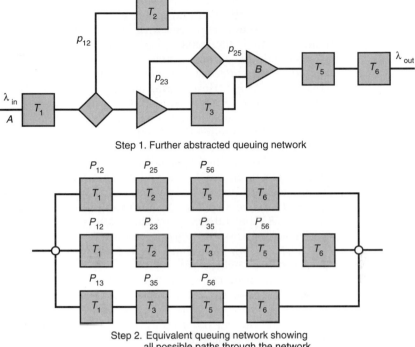

Step 1. Further abstracted queuing network

Step 2. Equivalent queuing network showing
all possible paths through the network

Step 3. Final reduction

FIGURE 15.7.
Simplifying the
queuing network

ing the implementation model, the system engineer can see how the system as specified would behave if implemented.

The i-Logix approach [HAR90] makes use of a notation that combines three different views of a system: the *activity-chart,* the *module-chart,* and the *state-chart.* In the paragraphs that follow, the i-Logix approach to real-time system simulation and modeling is described.[2]

The Conceptual View

Functional issues are treated using *activities* that represent the processing capabilities of the system. Dealing with a customer's confirmation request in an airline reservation system is an example of an activity, as is updating the aircraft's position in an avionics system. Activities can be nested, forming a hierarchy that constitutes a functional decomposition of the system. Items of in-

---

[2]The text that follows has been adapted from [ILO89], which describes Statemate® and is used with the permission of i-Logix Inc.

formation, such as the distance to a target or a customer's name, will typically flow between activities and might also be kept in data stores. This functional view of a system is captured with *activity-charts,* which are similar to conventional data flow diagrams.

Dynamic behavioral issues, commonly referred to as control aspects, are treated using *statecharts,* a notation developed by Harel and his colleagues [HAR88], [HAR92]. Here, states (or modes) can be nested and linked in a number of ways to represent sequential or concurrent behavior. An avionics mission computer, for example, could be in one of three states: air-to-air, air-to-ground, or navigation. At the same time it must be in the state of either automatic or manual flight control. Transitions between states are typically triggered by events, which may be qualified by conditions. Flipping a certain switch on the throttle, for example, is an event that will cause a transition from the navigate state to the air-to-ground state, but only on condition that the aircraft has air-to-ground ammunition available. As a simple example, consider the digital watch shown in Figure 15.8. The statechart for the watch is shown in Figure 15.9.

These two views of a system are integrated in the following way. Associated with each level of an activity-chart, there will usually be a statechart, called a control activity, whose role is to control the activities and data flows of that level [this is similar in some ways to the relationship between flow models and CSPEC described in Chapter 12]. A statechart is able to exercise control over the activities. For example, it can instruct activities to start and stop and to suspend and resume their work. It is able to change the values of variables and thus to influence the processing carried out by the activities. It is also able to send signals to other activities and thus cause them to change their own behavior. In addition to being able to generate actions, a controlling statechart is able to sense such actions being carried out by other statecharts. For example, if one statechart starts an activity or increments the value of a variable, another can sense that event and use it, say, to trigger a transition.

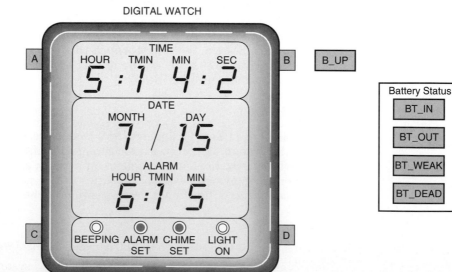

FIGURE 15.8.
Digital watch prototype (courtesy i-Logix)

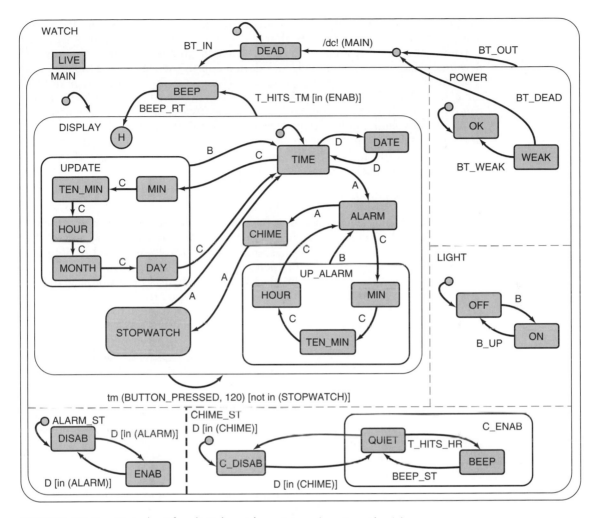

FIGURE 15.9. Statechart for digital watch prototype (courtesy i-Logix)

It is important to realize that activity-charts and statecharts are strongly linked, but they are not different representations of the same thing. Activity-charts on their own are incomplete as a model of the system, since they do not address behavior. Statecharts are also incomplete, since without activities they have nothing to control. Together, a detailed activity-chart and its controlling statecharts provide the conceptual model. The activity-chart is the backbone of the model; its decomposition of the capabilities of the system is the dominant hierarchy of the specification, and its controlling statecharts are the driving force behind the system's behavior.

The Physical View

A specification that uses activity-charts and statecharts in the form of a conceptual model is an excellent foundation, but it is not a real system. What is missing is a means for describing the system from a physical (implementation) perspective and a means to be sure that the system is implemented in a way that is true to that specification. An important part of this is describing the physical decomposition of the system and its relationship to the conceptual model.

The physical aspects are treated in Statemate using the language of *module-charts*. The terms "physical" and "module" are used generically to denote components of a system, whether hardware, software, or hybrid. Like activities in an activity-chart, modules are arranged in a hierarchy to show the decomposition of a system into its components and subcomponents. Modules are connected by flow lines, which one can think of as being the carriers of information between modules.

Analysis and Simulation

Once we have constructed a conceptual model, consisting of an activity-chart and its controlling statecharts, it can be thoroughly analyzed and tested. The model might describe the entire system, down to the lowest level of detail, or it might be only a partial specification.

We must first be sure that the model is syntactically correct. This gives rise to many relatively straightforward tests: for example, that the various charts are not blatantly incomplete (e.g., missing labels or names, dangling arrows); that the definitions of nongraphical elements, such as events and conditions, employ legal operations only, and so on. Syntax checking also involves more subtle tests, such as the correctness of inputs and outputs. A example of this is a test for elements that are used in the statechart but are neither input nor affected internally, such as a power-on event that is meant to cause a transition in the statechart but is not defined in the activity-chart as an input. All of these are usually referred to as consistency and completeness tests, and most of them are analogous to the checking carried out by a compiler prior to the actual compilation of a programming language.

Running Scenarios

A syntactically correct model accurately describes some system. However, it might not be the system we had in mind. In fact, the system described might be seriously flawed—syntactic correctness does not guarantee correctness of function or behavior. The real objective of analyzing the model is to find out whether it truly describes the system that we want. The analysis should enable us to learn more about the model that has been constructed, to examine how a system based on it would behave, and to verify that it indeed meets expectations. This requires a modeling language with more than a formal syntax. It requires that the system used to create the model recognize formal semantics as well.

If the model is based on a formal semantics, the system engineer can execute the model. The engineer can create and run a *scenario* that allows him to "press buttons" and observe the behavior of the model before the system is actually built. For example, to exercise a model of an automated teller machine (ATM) the following steps occur: (1) a conceptual model is created; (2) the engineer plays the role of the customer and the bank computer, generating events such as insertion of a bank card, buttons being pressed, and new balance information arriving; (3) the reaction of the system to these events is monitored and (4) inconsistencies in behavior are noted; (5) the conceptual model is modified to reflect proper behavior; and (6) iteration occurs until the system that is desired evolves.

The system engineer runs scenarios and views the system's response graphically. "Active" elements of the model (e.g., states that the system is in at the moment and activities that are active) are highlighted graphically, and the dynamic execution results in an animated representation of the model. The execution of a scenario simulates the system running in real time and keeps track of time-dependent information. At any point during the execution, the engineer can ask to see the status of any other, nongraphical, element, such as the value of a variable or a condition.

Programming Simulations

A scenario enables the system engineer to exercise the model interactively. At times, however, more extensive simulation may be desirable. Performance under random conditions in both typical and atypical situations may need to be assessed. For situations in which a more extensive simulation of a real-time model is desired, Simulation Control Language (SCL) enables the engineer to retain general control over how the executions proceed, but at the same time exploits the power of the tool to take over many of the details.

One of the simplest things that can be done with SCL is to read lists of events from a batch file. This means that lengthy scenarios or parts of them can be prepared in advance and executed automatically. These can be observed by the system engineer. Alternatively, the system engineer can program with SCL to set break points and to monitor certain variables, states, or conditions. For example, running a simulation of an avionics system, the engineer might ask the SCL program to stop whenever the radar locks on target and switch to interactive mode. Once "lock on" is recognized, the engineer takes over interactively, so that this state can be examined in more detail.

The use of scenarios and simulations also enables the engineer to gather meaningful statistics about the operation of the system that is to be built. For example, we might want to know how many times, in a typical flight of the aircraft, the radar loses a locked-on target. Since it might be difficult for the engineer to put together a single, all-encompassing flight scenario, a programmed simulation can be developed using accumulated results from other scenarios to obtain average-case statistics. A simulation control program generates random events according to predefined probabilities. Thus, events that occur very rarely (say, seat ejection in a fighter aircraft) can be assigned very low probabilities while others are assigned higher probabilities, and the random selection of events thus becomes realistic. In order to be able to gather the desired statistics, we insert appropriate break points in the SCL program.

Automatic Translation Into Code

Once the system model has been built, it can be translated in its entirety into executable code using a prototyping function. Activity-charts and their controlling statecharts can be translated into a high-level programming language, such as Ada or C. Today, the primary use of the resulting code is to observe a system perform under circumstances that are as close to the real world as possible. For example, the prototype code can be executed in a full-fledged simulator of the target environment or in the final environment itself. The code produced by such CASE tools should be considered to be "prototypical." It is not production or final code. Consequently, it might not always reflect accurate real-time performance of the intended system. Nevertheless, it is useful for testing the system's performance in close to real circumstances.

15.4   REAL-TIME DESIGN

The design of real-time software must incorporate all of the fundamental concepts and principles (Chapter 13) associated with high-quality software. In addition, real-time software poses a set of unique problems for the designer:

- representation of interrupts and context switching
- concurrency as manifested by multitasking and multiprocessing
- intertask communication and synchronization
- wide variations in data and communication rates
- representation of timing constraints
- asynchronous processing
- necessary and unavoidable coupling with operating systems, hardware, and other external system elements

It is worthwhile to address a set of specialized design principles that are particularly relevant during the design of real-time systems. Kurki-Suono [KUR93] discusses the design model for real-time ("reactive") software:

> All reasoning, whether formal or intuitive, is performed with some abstraction. Therefore, it is important to understand which kinds of properties are expressible in the abstraction in question. In connection with reactive systems, this is emphasized by the more stringent need for formal methods, and by the fact that no general consensus has been reached about the models that should be used. Rigorous formalisms for reactive systems range from process algebras and temporal logics to concrete state-based models and Petri nets, and different schools keep arguing about their relative merits.

He then defines a number of "modeling principles" that should be considered in the design of real-time software [KUR93]:

> **Explicit atomicity.** It is necessary to define "atomic actions" explicitly as part of the real-time design model. An atomic action or event is a well-constrained and limited function that can be executed by a single task or executed concurrently by several tasks. An atomic action is invoked only by those tasks ("participants") that require it, and the results of its execution affect only those participants; no other parts of the system are affected.
>
> **Interleaving.** Although processing can be concurrent, the history of some computation should be characterized in a way that can be obtained by a linear sequence of actions. Starting with an initial state, a first action is

enabled and executed. As a result of this action, the state is modified and a second action occurs. Because several actions can occur in any given state, different results (histories) can be spawned from the same initial state. "This nondeterminism is essential in interleaved modeling of concurrency" [KUR93].

Nonterminating histories and fairness. The processing history of a reactive system is assumed to be infinite, By this we mean that processing continues indefinitely or "stutters" until some event causes it to continue processing. *Fairness* requirements prevent a system from stopping at some arbitrary point.

Closed system principle. A design model of a real-time system should encompass the software and the environment in which the software resides. "Actions can therefore be partitioned into those for which the system itself is responsible, and to those that are assumed to be executed by the environment" [KUR93].

Structuring of state. A real-time system can be modeled as a set of objects,[3] each of which has a state of its own.

The software engineer should consider each of the concepts noted above as the design of a real-time system evolves.

Over the past two decades, a number of real-time software design methods have been proposed to grapple with some or all of the problems noted above. Some approaches to real-time design extend the design methods discussed in Chapters 14 and 21 (e.g., data flow [WAR85], [HAT87]; data structure [JAC83]; or object-oriented [LEV90] methods). Others introduce an entirely separate approach, using finite state machine models or message passing systems, Petri nets, or a specialized language as a basis for design. A comprehensive discussion of software design for real-time systems is beyond the scope of this book. For further details, the reader should refer to [LEV90], [SHU92], [SEL94], and [GOM95].

15.5   SUMMARY

The design of real-time software encompasses all aspects of conventional software design while introducing a new set of design criteria and concerns. Because real-time software must respond to real-world events in a time frame dictated by those events, all classes of design become more complex.

It is difficult, and often impractical, to divorce software design from larger system-oriented issues. Because real-time software is either clock or event driven, the designer must consider function and performance of hardware and software. Interrupt processing and data transfer rate, distributed databases and operating systems, specialized programming languages and synchronization methods are just some of the concerns of the real-time system designer.

---

[3]See Part Four of this book.

The analysis of real-time systems encompasses both mathematical modeling and simulation. Queuing and network models enable the system engineer to assess overall response time, processing rate and other timing and sizing issues. Formal analysis tools provide a mechanism for real-time system simulation.

Software design for real-time systems can be predicated on a conventional design methodology that extends data flow-oriented or object-oriented design by providing a notation and approach that addresses real-time system characteristics. Alternatively, design methods that make use of unique notation or specialized languages can also be applied.

Software design for real-time systems remains a challenge. Progress has been made; methods do exist, but a realistic assessment of the state-of-the-art suggests much remains to be done.

REFERENCES

[ELL94]   Ellison, K.S., *Developing Real-Time Embedded Software in a Market Driven Company,* Wiley, 1994.

[EVE95]   Everett, W.W., "Reliability and Safety of Real-Time Systems, *Computer,* May 1995, pp. 13–16.

[GLA83]   Glass, R.L., *Real-Time Software,* Prentice-Hall, 1983.

[GOM95]   Gomaa, H., *Software Design Methods for Concurrent and Real-Time Systems,* Addison-Wesley, 1995.

[GRO85]   Gross, D., and C.M. Harris, *Fundamentals of Queuing Theory,* 2nd edition, Wiley, 1985.

[HAR88]   Harel, D., "On Visual Formalisms," *Communications of the ACM,* vol. 31, no. 5, May 1988, pp. 514–530.

[HAR90]   Harel, D. et al., "STATEMATE: A Working Environment for the Development of Complex Reactive Systems," *IEEE Trans. Software Engineering,* vol. 16, no. 3, April 1990, pp. 403–414.

[HAR92]   Harel, D., "Biting the Bullet: Toward a Brighter Future for System Development," *Computer,* January 1992, pp. 8–24.

[HAT87]   Hatley, D.J., and I.A. Pirbhai, *Strategies for Real-Time System Specification,* Dorset House, 1987.

[HIN83]   Hinden, H.J., and W.B. Rauch-Hinden, "Real-Time Systems," *Electronic Design,* January 6, 1983, pp. 288–311.

[ILO89]   "The Statemate Approach to Complex Systems," I-Logix Inc., Burlington, MA, 1989.

[JAC83]   Jackson, M., *System Development,* Van Nostrand Reinhold, 1983.

[KLI75]   Kleinrock, L., *Queueing Systems, Volume 1: Theory,* Wiley, 1975.

[KUR93]   Kurki-Suonio, R., "Stepwise Design of Real-Time Systems," *IEEE Trans. Software Engineering,* vol. 19, no. 1, January 1993, pp. 56–69.

[LEV90]   Levi, S.T., and A.K. Agrawala, *Real-Time System Design,* McGraw-Hill, 1990.

[LIU90]   Liu, L.Y., and R.K. Shyamasundar, "Static Analysis of Real-Time Distributed Systems," *IEEE Trans. Software Engineering,* vol. 16, no. 3, April 1990, pp. 373–388.

[MCC85]   McCabe, T.J. et al., "Structured Real-Time Analysis and Design," *COMPSAC-85,* IEEE, October 1985, pp. 40–51.

[SAV85]   Savitsky, S., *Real-Time Microprocessor Systems,* Van Nostrand Reinhold, 1985.

[SEL94]   Selic, B., G. Gullekson, and P. Ward, *Real-Time Object-Oriented Modeling Wiley, 1994.,*

[SHU92]   Shumate, K., and M. Keller, *Software Specification and Design—A Disciplined Approach For Real-Time Systems,* Wiley 1992.

[WAR85]   Ward, P.T., and S.J. Mellor, *Structured Development for Real-Time Systems,* three volumes, Yourdon Press, 1985, 1986.

[WIL90]   Wilson, R.G., and B.H. Krogh, Petri Net Tools for the Specification and Analysis of Discrete Controllers," *IEEE Trans. Software Engineering,* vol. 16, no. 1, January 1990, pp. 39–50.

[WOO90]   Wood, M., and T. Barrett, "A Real-Time Primer," *Embedded Systems Programming,* vol. 3, no. 2, February 1990, pp. 20–28.

[ZUC89]   Zucconi, L., "Techniques and Experiences in Capturing Requirements for Real-Time Systems, *ACM Software Engineering Notes,* vol. 14, no. 6, October 1989, pp. 51–55.

PROBLEMS AND POINTS TO PONDER

15.1. List five examples of computer-based real time systems. Indicate what "stimuli" feed the system and what devices or situations the system controls or monitors.

15.2. Obtain information on a commercial real-time operating system (RTOS) and write a short paper that presents a discussion of RTOS internals. What special features are present? How are interrupts handled? How does the RTOS effect task synchronization?

15.3. Write a brief comparison of the real-time constructs in the programming languages Ada and Modula-2. Do these constructs provide distinct benefits over other languages such as C or Pascal?

15.4. Provide three examples in which semaphores would be an appropriate task synchronization mechanism.

15.5. The analysis technique for real-time systems presented in Section 15.3 assumes a knowledge of queuing models. Do some research using the references indicated and:
a. describe how Figure 15.5 was derived from Figure 15.4.
b. show how the flow balance equations are derived from Figure 15.5.

15.6. Get information on one or more formal analysis tools for real-time systems (Section 15.3.2). Write a paper that outlines each tool's use in specification and design of a real-time system.

FURTHER READINGS AND OTHER INFORMATION SOURCES

Hatley and Pirbhai [HAT87] and Ward and Mellor (*Structured Development for Real-Time Systems,* Yourdon Press, 1986) are widely used books for analysis and design of real-time systems. Mattai (*Real Time Systems,* Prentice-Hall, 1996) addresses program structures, timing analysis using scheduling theory, and specification and verification of real-time systems. Cooling (*Software Design for Real-Time Systems,* Thomsen Publishing, 1996), considers the application of formal specification methods for time-dependent applications. Ellison (*Developing Real-Time Software in a Market Driven Company,* Wiley, 1994) considers both management and technical aspects of real-time development.

Heath (*Real-Time Software Techniques,* Van Nostrand Reinhold, 1991) focuses on implementation issues for the design and development of real-time machine control software. Books by Shumate and Keller (*Software Specification and Design—A Disciplined Approach For Real-Time Systems,* Wiley, 1992) and Braek and Oystein (*Engineering Real Time Systems,* Prentice-Hall, 1993) provide a wealth of information on both analysis and design modeling for real-time software. Klein (*A Practitioner's Handbook for Real-Time Analysis: Guide to Rate Monotonic Analysis for Real-Time Systems,* Kluwer Academic Publishers, 1994) addresses the detailed mathematical analysis required to predict the timing behavior of many real-time systems. Mahar et al. (*Object-Oriented Technology for Real-Time Systems,* Prentice-Hall, 1996) and Levi and Agrawala [LEV90] consider real-time systems from the object technologies perspective.

Van Tilborg and Koob (*Foundations of Real-Time Systems,* Kluwer Academic Publishers, 1992) and Krishua and Lee (*Readings in Real-Time Systems,* IEEE Computer Society Press, 1993) have each edited excellent tutorials on real time systems. Schiebe (*Real-Time Systems Engineering and Applications,* Kluwer Academic Publishers, 1994) has edited an anthology that addresses the engineering methods required for real-time hardware and software.

Sources for real-time system design and real-time software are distributed across many Web sites dedicated to software and software engineering. The Internet newsgroup **comp.realtime** is a source for timely discussion. The IEEE technical committee on real-time systems presents an array of Web pointers for real-time topics at:

http://cs-www.bu.edu/pub/ieee-rts/Home.html

Other information on real-time embedded systems, prototyping as a design approach, and a variety of real-time resources and selected papers can be obtained at the following sites:

http://borneo.gmd.de
http://wwwsel.iit.nrc.ca/ harmony.html
http://www.cera2.com/ebox.htm
http://www.ee.umd.edu/serts/
http://www.cs.unc.edu/dirt/real-time.html

Information about *Real-Time Engineering* magazine can be obtained at:

http://www.primenet.com/~magpub/RTE_home_page.html

and the FAQ for the newsgroup **comp.realtime** can be obtained from:

ftp://rtfm.mit.edu/usenet/comp.realtime

An up-to-date list of World Wide Web references for software design for real-time systems can be found at: **http://www.rspa.com**

CHAPTER 16

SOFTWARE TESTING TECHNIQUES

he importance of software testing and its implications with respect to software quality cannot be overemphasized. To quote Deutsch [DEU79]:

> The development of software systems involves a series of production activities where opportunities for injection of human fallibilities are enormous. Errors may begin to occur at the very inception of the process where the objectives. . . may be erroneously or imperfectly specified, as well as [in] later design and development stages. . . . Because of human inability to perform and communicate with perfection, software development is accompanied by a quality assurance activity.

Software testing is a critical element of software quality assurance and represents the ultimate review of specification, design, and coding.

The increasing visibility of software as a system element and the attendant "costs" associated with a software failure are motivating forces for well-planned, thorough testing. It is not unusual for a software development organization to expend between 30 and 40 percent of total project effort on testing. In the extreme, testing of human-rated software (e.g., flight control, nuclear reactor monitoring) can cost three to five times as much as all other software engineering activities combined!

In this chapter, we discuss software testing fundamentals and techniques for software test case design. Software testing fundamentals define the overriding objectives for software testing. Test case design focuses on a set of techniques for the creation of test cases that meet overall testing objectives. In Chapter 17, testing strategies and software debugging are presented.

16.1   **SOFTWARE TESTING FUNDAMENTALS**

Testing presents an interesting anomaly for the software engineer. Earlier in the software process, the engineer attempts to build software from an abstract concept to a tangible implementation. Now comes testing. The engineer creates a series of test cases that are intended to "demolish" the software that has been built. In fact, testing is the one step in the software engineering process that could be viewed (psychologically, at least) as destructive rather than constructive.

Software developers are by their nature constructive people. Testing requires that the developer discard preconceived notions of the "correctness" of software just developed and overcome a conflict of interest that occurs when errors are uncovered. Beizer [BEI90] describes this situation effectively when he states:

> There's a myth that if we were really good at programming, there would be no bugs to catch. If only we could really concentrate, if only everyone used structured programming, top-down design, decision tables, if programs were written in SQUISH, if we had the right silver bullets, then there would be no bugs. So goes the myth. There are bugs, the myth says, because we are bad at what we do; and if we are bad at it, we should feel guilty about it. Therefore, testing and test case design is an admission of failure, which instills a goodly dose of guilt. And the tedium of testing is just punishment for our errors. Punishment for what? For being human? Guilt for what? For failing to achieve inhuman perfection? For not distinguishing between what another programmer thinks and what he says? For failing to be telepathic? For not solving human communications problems that have been kicked around. . . for forty centuries?

Should testing instill guilt? Is testing really destructive? The answer to these questions is "no!" However, the objectives of testing are somewhat different than we might expect.

16.1.1 Testing Objectives

In his classic book on software testing, Glen Myers [MYE79] states a number of rules that can serve well as testing objectives:

1. Testing is a process of executing a program with the intent of finding an error.
2. A good test case is one that has a high probability of finding an as-yet undiscovered error.
3. A successful test is one that uncovers an as-yet undiscovered error.

The above objectives imply a dramatic change in viewpoint. They move counter to the commonly held view that a successful test is one in which no errors are found. Our objective is to design tests that systematically uncover different classes of errors and do so with a minimum amount of time and effort.

If testing is conducted successfully (according to the objective stated above), it will uncover errors in the software. As a secondary benefit, testing demonstrates that software functions appear to be working according to specification and that performance requirements appear to have been met. In addition, data collected as testing is conducted provides a good indication of software reliability and some indication of software quality as a whole. But there is one thing that testing cannot do:

> Testing cannot show the absence of defects, it can only show that software errors are present.

It is important to keep this (rather gloomy) statement in mind as testing is being conducted.

16.1.2 Testing Principles

Before applying methods to design effective test cases, a software engineer must understand the basic principles that guide software testing. Davis [DAV95] suggests a set[1] of testing principles which have been adapted for use in this book:

- *All tests should be traceable to customer requirements*. As we have seen, the objective of software testing is to uncover errors. It follows that the most severe defects (from the customer's point of view) are those that cause the program to fail to meet its requirements.

- *Tests should be planned long before testing begins*. Test planning (Chapter 17) can begin as soon as the requirements model is complete. Detailed definition of test cases can begin as soon as the design model has been solidified. Therefore, all tests can be planned and designed *before* any code has been generated.

- *The Pareto principle applies to software testing*. Stated simply, the Pareto principle implies that 80 percent of all errors uncovered during testing will likely be traceable to 20 percent of all program modules. The problem, of course, is to isolate these suspect modules and to thoroughly test them.

- *Testing should begin "in the small" and progress toward testing "in the large."* The first tests planned and executed generally focus on individual program modules. As testing progresses, testing shifts focus in an attempt to find errors in integrated clusters of modules and ultimately in the entire system (Chapter 17).

- *Exhaustive testing is not possible*. The number of path permutations for even a moderately sized program is exceptionally large (see Section 16.2 for further discussion). For this reason, it is impossible to execute every combination of

---

[1]Only a small subset of Davis's requirements engineering principles are noted here. For more information, see [DAV95].

paths during testing. It is possible, however, to adequately cover program logic and to ensure that all conditions in the procedural design have been exercised.

• *To be most effective, testing should be conducted by an independent third party*. By "most effective," we mean testing that has the highest probability of finding errors (the primary objective of testing). For reasons that have been introduced earlier in this chapter and are considered in more detail in Chapter 17, the software engineer who created the system is not the best person to conduct all tests for the software.

16.1.3 Testability

In ideal circumstances, a software engineer designs a computer program, a system, or a product with "testability" in mind. This enables the individuals charged with testing to design effective test cases more easily. But what is "testability?" James Bach[2] describes testability in the following manner:

Software testability is simply how easily a computer program can be tested. Since testing is so profoundly difficult, it pays to know what can be done to streamline it. Sometimes programmers are willing to do things that will help the testing process, and a checklist of possible design points, features, and so on can be useful in negotiating with them.

There are certainly metrics that could be used to measure testability in most of its aspects. Sometimes, testability is used to mean how adequately a particular set of tests will cover the product. It's also used by the military to mean how easily a tool can be checked and repaired in the field. Those two meanings are not the same as "software testability." The checklist that follows provides a set of characteristics that lead to testable software.

Operability. "The better it works, the more efficiently it can be tested."

- The system has few bugs (bugs add analysis and reporting overhead to the test process).
- No bugs block the execution of tests.
- The product evolves in functional stages (allows simultaneous development and testing).

Observability. "What you see is what you test."

- Distinct output is generated for each input.
- System states and variables are visible or queriable during execution.
- Past system states and variables are visible or queriable (e.g., transaction logs).
- All factors affecting the output are visible.

---

[2]The paragraphs that follow are copyright 1994 by James Bach and have been adapted from an Internet posting that first appeared in the newsgroup **comp.software-eng**. This material is used with permission.

- Incorrect output is easily identified.
- Internal errors are automatically detected through self-testing mechanisms.
- Internal errors are automatically reported.
- Source code is accessible.

Controllability. "The better we can control the software, the more the testing can be automated and optimized."

- All possible outputs can be generated through some combination of input.
- All code is executable through some combination of input.
- Software and hardware states and variables can be controlled directly by the test engineer.
- Input and output formats are consistent and structured.
- Tests can be conveniently specified, automated, and reproduced.

Decomposability. "By controlling the scope of testing, we can more quickly isolate problems and perform smarter retesting."

- The software system is built from independent modules.
- Software modules can be tested independently.

Simplicity. "The less there is to test, the more quickly we can test it."

- Functional simplicity (e.g., the feature set is the minimum necessary to meet requirements).
- Structural simplicity (e.g., architecture is modularized to limit the propagation of faults).
- Code simplicity (e.g., a coding standard is adopted for ease of inspection and maintenance).

Stability. "The fewer the changes, the fewer the disruptions to testing."

- Changes to the software are infrequent.
- Changes to the software are controlled.
- Changes to the software do not invalidate existing tests.
- The software recovers well from failures.

Understandability. "The more information we have, the smarter we will test."

- The design is well understood.
- Dependencies between internal, external, and shared components are well understood.
- Changes to the design are communicated.

- Technical documentation is instantly accessible.
- Technical documentation is well organized.
- Technical documentation is specific and detailed.
- Technical documentation is accurate.

The attributes suggested by James Bach can be used by a software engineer to develop a software configuration (i.e., programs, data, and documents) that is amenable to testing.

And what about the tests themselves? Kaner, Falk, and Nguyen [KAN93] suggest the following attributes of a "good" test:

1. *A good test has a high probability of finding an error*. To achieve this goal, the tester must understand the software and attempt to develop a mental picture of how the software might fail. Ideally, the classes of failure are probed. For example, one class of potential failure in a GUI (graphical user interface) is a failure to recognize proper mouse position. A set of tests would be designed to exercise the mouse in an attempt to demonstrate an error in mouse position recognition.

2. *A good test is not redundant*. Testing time and resources are limited. There is no point in conducting a test that has the same purpose as another test. Every test should have a different purpose (even if it is subtly different). For example, a module of the SafeHome software[3] is designed to recognize a user password to activate and deactivate the system. In an effort to uncover an error in password input, the tester designs a series of tests that input a sequence of passwords. Valid and invalid passwords (four numeral sequences) are input as separate tests. However, each valid/invalid password should probe a different mode of failure. For example, the invalid password 1234 should not be accepted by a system programmed to recognize 8080 as the valid password. If 1234 is accepted, an error is present. Another test input, say 1235, would have the same purpose as 1234 and is therefore redundant. However, the invalid input 8081 or 8180 has a subtle difference, attempting to demonstrate that an error exists for passwords "close to" but not identical with the valid password.

3. *A good test should be "best of breed"* [KAN93]. In a group of tests that have a similar intent, time and resource limitations may militate for the execution of only a subset of these tests. In such cases, the test that has the highest likelihood of uncovering a whole class of errors should be used.

4. *A good test should be neither too simple nor too complex*. Although it is sometimes possible to combine a series of tests into one test case, the possible side effects associated with this approach may mask errors. In general, each test should be executed separately.

16.2   TEST CASE DESIGN

The design of tests for software and other engineered products can be as challenging as the initial design of the product itself. Yet for reasons that we have al-

---

[3]SafeHome is a home security system that has been used as an example application in earlier chapters.

ready discussed, software engineers often treat testing as an afterthought, developing test cases that may "feel right" but have little assurance of being complete. Recalling the objectives of testing, we must design tests that have the highest likelihood of finding the most errors with a minimum amount of time and effort.

Over the past two decades a rich variety of test case design methods have evolved for software. These methods provide the developer with a systematic approach to testing. More important, methods provide a mechanism that can help to ensure the completeness of tests and provide the highest likelihood for uncovering errors in software.

Any engineered product (and most other things) can be tested in one of two ways: (1) knowing the specified function that a product has been designed to perform, tests can be conducted that demonstrate each function is fully operational, at the same time searching for errors in each function; (2) knowing the internal workings of a product, tests can be conducted to ensure that "all gears mesh," that is, that internal operation performs according to specification and all internal components have been adequately exercised. The first test approach is called *black-box testing* and the second, *white-box testing*.

When computer software is considered, black-box testing alludes to tests that are conducted at the software interface. Although they are designed to uncover errors, black-box tests are used to demonstrate that software functions are operational; that input is properly accepted and output is correctly produced; and that the integrity of external information (e.g., data files) is maintained. A black-box test examines some fundamental aspect of a system with little regard for the internal logical structure of the software.

White-box testing of software is predicated on close examination of procedural detail. Logical paths through the software are tested by providing test cases that exercise specific sets of conditions and/or loops. The "status of the program" may be examined at various points to determine if the expected or asserted status corresponds to the actual status.

At first glance it would seem that very thorough white-box testing would lead to "100 percent correct programs." All we need do is define all logical paths, develop test cases to exercise them, and evaluate results, that is, generate test cases to exercise program logic exhaustively. Unfortunately, exhaustive testing presents certain logistical problems. For even small programs, the number of possible logical paths can be very large. For example, consider the 100 line program in the language C. After some basic data declaration, the program contains two nested loops that execute from 1 to 20 times each, depending on conditions specified at input. Inside the interior loop, four *if-then-else* constructs are required. There are approximately 10^{14} possible paths that may be executed in this program!

To put this number in perspective, we assume that a magic test processor ("magic" because no such processor exists) has been developed for exhaustive testing. The processor can develop a test case, execute it, and evaluate the results in one millisecond. Working 24 hours a days, 365 days a year, the processor would work for 3170 years to test the program. This would undeniably cause havoc in most development schedules. Exhaustive testing is impossible for large software systems.

White-box testing should not, however, be dismissed as impractical. A limited number of important logical paths can be selected and exercised. Important data structures can be probed for validity. The attributes of both black- and white-box testing can be combined to provide an approach that validates the software interface and selectively assures that the internal workings of the software are correct.

16.3   WHITE-BOX TESTING

White-box testing, sometimes called *glass-box testing,* is a test case design method that uses the control structure of the procedural design to derive test cases. Using white-box testing methods, the software engineer can derive test cases that (1) guarantee that all *independent paths* within a module have been exercised at least once; (2) exercise all logical decisions on their *true* and *false* sides; (3) execute all loops at their boundaries and within their operational bounds; and (4) exercise internal data structures to assure their validity.

A reasonable question might be posed at this juncture: "Why spend time and energy worrying about (and testing) logical minutiae when we might better expend effort ensuring that program requirements have been met?" Stated another way, why don't we spend all of our energies on black-box tests? The answer lies in the nature of software defects (e.g., [JON81]):

- *Logic errors and incorrect assumptions are inversely proportional to the probability that a program path will be executed.* Errors tend to creep into our work when we design and implement function, conditions, or control that are out of the mainstream. Everyday processing tends to be well understood (and well scrutinized), while "special case" processing tends to fall into the cracks.

- *We often believe that a logical path is not likely to be executed when, in fact, it may be executed on a regular basis.* The logical flow of a program is sometimes counterintuitive, meaning that our unconscious assumptions about flow of control and data may lead us to make design errors that are uncovered only once path testing commences.

- *Typographical errors are random.* When a program is translated into programming language source code, it is likely that some typing errors will occur. Many will be uncovered by syntax checking mechanisms, but others will go undetected until testing begins. It is as likely that a typo will exist on an obscure logical path as on a mainstream path.

Each of these reasons provides an argument for conducting white-box tests. Black-box testing, no matter how thorough, may miss the kinds of errors noted above. As Beizer has stated [BEI90]: "Bugs lurk in corners and congregate at boundaries." White-box testing is far more likely to uncover them.

16.4   BASIS PATH TESTING

Basis path testing is a white-box testing technique first proposed by Tom McCabe [MCC76]. The basis path method enables the test case designer to derive a logical complexity measure of a procedural design and use this measure

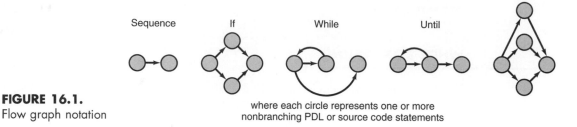

The structured constructs in flow graph form:

Sequence If While Until Case

where each circle represents one or more
nonbranching PDL or source code statements

FIGURE 16.1.
Flow graph notation

as a guide for defining a *basis set* of execution paths. Test cases derived to exercise the basis set are guaranteed to execute every statement in the program at least one time during testing.

16.4.1 Flow Graph Notation

Before the basis path method can be introduced, a simple notation for the representation of control flow, called a *flow graph* (or *program graph*) must be introduced.[4] The flow graph depicts logical control flow using the notation illustrated in Figure 16.1. Each structured construct (Chapter 14) has a corresponding flow graph symbol.

To illustrate the use of a flow graph, we consider the procedural design representation in Figure 16.2a. Here, a flowchart is used to depict program control structure. Figure 16.2b maps the flowchart into a corresponding flow graph (assuming that no compound conditions are contained in the decision diamonds of the flowchart). In Figure 16.2b, each circle, called a flow graph *node,* represents one or more procedural statements. A sequence of process boxes and a decision diamond can map into a single node. The arrows on the flow graph, called *edges* or *links,* represent flow of control and are analogous to flowchart arrows. An edge must terminate at a node, even if the node does not represent any procedural statements (e.g, see the symbol for the if-then-else construct). Areas bounded by edges and nodes are called *regions*. When counting regions we include the area outside the graph and count it as a region.[5]

Any procedural design representation can be translated into a flow graph. In Figure 16.3, a program design language (PDL) segment and its corresponding flow graph are shown. Note that the PDL statements have been numbered and corresponding numbering is used for the flow graph.

When compound conditions are encountered in a procedural design, the generation of a flow graph becomes slightly more complicated. A compound condition occurs when one or more Boolean operators (logical OR, AND, NAND,

---

[4]In actuality, the basis path method can be conducted without the use of flow graphs. However, they serve as a useful tool for understanding control flow and illustrating the approach.

[5]A more detailed discussion of graphs and their use in testing is contained in Section 16.6.1.

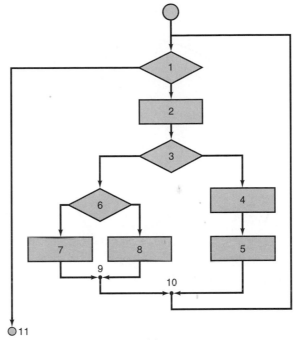

(a)

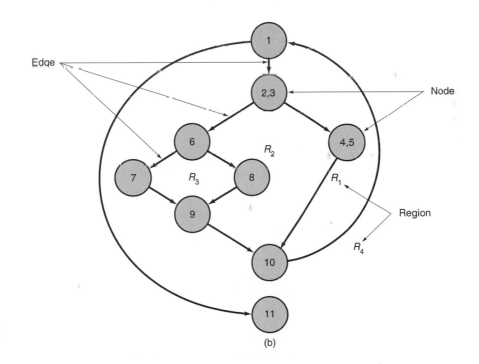

FIGURE 16.2.
(a) Flow chart; (b)
flow graph

(b)

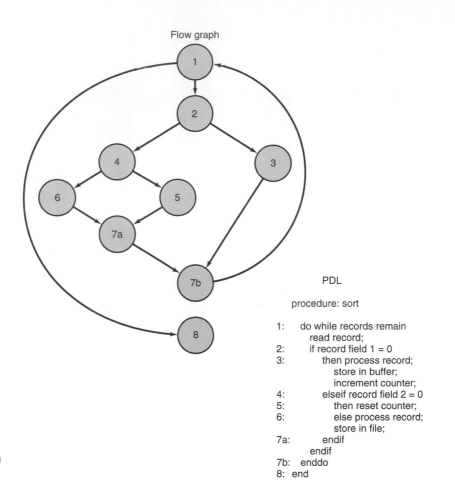

FIGURE 16.3.
Translating PDL to a
flow graph

Flow graph

PDL

procedure: sort

1:	do while records remain
	read record;
2:	if record field 1 = 0
3:	then process record;
	store in buffer;
	increment counter;
4:	elseif record field 2 = 0
5:	then reset counter;
6:	else process record;
	store in file;
7a:	endif
	endif
7b:	enddo
8:	end

NOR) are present in a conditional statement. In Figure 16.4, a PDL segment translates into the flow graph shown. Note that a separate node is created for each of the conditions *a* and *b* in the statement IF *a* OR *b*. Each node that contains a condition is called a *predicate node* and is characterized by two or more edges emanating from it.

16.4.2 Cyclomatic Complexity

Cyclomatic complexity is a software metric that provides a quantitative measure of the logical complexity of a program. When this metric is used in the context of the basis path testing method, the value computed for cyclomatic complexity defines the number of *independent paths* in the *basis set* of a program and provides us with an upper bound for the number of tests that must be conducted to ensure that all statements have been executed at least once.

An independent path is any path through the program that introduces at least one new set of processing statements or a new condition. When stated in

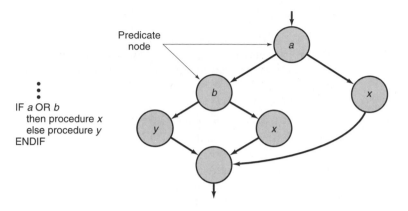

IF *a* OR *b*
   then procedure *x*
   else procedure *y*
ENDIF

FIGURE 16.4.
Compound logic

terms of a flow graph, an independent path must move along at least one edge that has not been traversed before the path is defined. For example, a set of independent paths for the flow graph illustrated in Figure 16.2b is:

> path 1: 1-11
> path 2: 1-2-3-4-5-10-1-11
> path 3: 1-2-3-6-8-9-10-1-11
> path 4: 1-2-3-6-7-9-10-1-11

Note that each new path introduces a new edge. The path

$$1\text{-}2\text{-}3\text{-}4\text{-}5\text{-}10\text{-}1\text{-}2\text{-}3\text{-}6\text{-}8\text{-}9\text{-}10\text{-}1\text{-}11$$

is not considered to be an independent path because it is simply a combination of already specified paths and does not traverse any new edges.

Paths 1, 2, 3, and 4 defined above comprise a *basis set* for the flow graph in Figure 16.2b. That is, if tests can be designed to force execution of these paths (a basis set), every statement in the program will be executed at least one time and every condition will have been executed on its true and false side. It should be noted that the basis set is not unique. In fact, any number of different basis sets can be derived for a given procedural design.

How do we know how many paths to look for? The computation of cyclomatic complexity provides the answer. Cyclomatic complexity has a foundation in graph theory and provides us with an extremely useful software metric. Complexity is computed in one of three ways:

1. The number of regions of the flow graph correspond to the cyclomatic complexity.

2. Cyclomatic complexity, $V(G)$, for a flow graph G is defined as

$$V(G) = E - N + 2$$

where E is the number of flow graph edges and N is the number of flow graph nodes.

3. Cyclomatic complexity, $V(G)$, for a flow graph G is also defined as

$$V(G) = P + 1$$

where P is the number of predicate nodes contained in the flow graph G.

Refer once more to the flow graph in Figure 16.2b. The cyclomatic complexity can be computed using each of the algorithms noted above:

1. The flow graph has 4 regions
2. $V(G) = 11$ edges $- 9$ nodes $+ 2 = 4$
3. $V(G) = 3$ predicate nodes $+ 1 = 4$

Therefore, the cyclomatic complexity of the flow graph in Figure 16.2b is 4.

More important, the value for $V(G)$ provides us with an upper bound for the number of independent paths that comprise the basis set, and by implication, *an upper bound on the number of tests that must be designed and executed* to guarantee coverage of all program statements.

16.4.3 Deriving Test Cases

The basis path testing method can be applied to a procedural design or to source code. In this section, we present basis path testing as a series of steps. The procedure **average,** depicted in PDL in Figure 16.5, will be used as an ex-

```
PROCEDURE average;

    *   This procedure computes the average of 100 or fewer
        numbers that lie between bounding values; it also computes the
        sum and the total number valid.

    INTERFACE RETURNS average, total.input, total.valid;
    INTERFACE ACCEPTS value, minimum, maximum;

    TYPE value[1:100] IS SCALAR ARRAY;
    TYPE average, total.input, total.valid;
        minimum, maximum, sum IS SCALAR;
    TYPE i IS INTEGER;
    i = 1;
    total.input = total.valid = 0;
    sum = 0;
      DO WHILE value[ i ] < > –999 and total.input < 100
        increment total.input by 1;
          IF value[ i ] > = minimum AND value[ i ] < = maximum
            THEN increment total.valid by 1;
                 sum = sum + value[ i ]
            ELSE skip
          ENDIF
          increment i by 1;
      ENDDO
    IF total.valid > 0
      THEN average = sum / total.valid;
      ELSE average = –999;
    ENDIF
END average
```

FIGURE 16.5.
PDL for test case design with nodes identified

ample to illustrate each step in the test case design method. Note that **average,** although an extremely simple algorithm, contains compound conditions and loops.

1. **Using the design or code as a foundation, draw a corresponding flow graph.** A flow graph is created using the symbols and construction rules presented in Section 16.4.1. Refer to the PDL for **average** in Figure 16.5. A flow graph is created by numbering those PDL statements that will be mapped into corresponding flow graph nodes. The corresponding flow graph is shown in Figure 16.6.

2. **Determine the cyclomatic complexity of the resultant flow graph.** The cyclomatic complexity, $V(G)$, is determined by applying one of the algorithms described above. It should be noted that $V(G)$ can be determined without developing a flow graph by counting all conditional statements in the PDL (for the procedure **average,** compound conditions count as 2) and adding 1.

   In Figure 16.6,

$$V(G) = 6 \text{ regions}$$

$$V(G) = 18 \text{ edges} - 14 \text{ nodes} + 2 = 6$$

$$V(G) = 5 \text{ predicates nodes} + 1 = 6$$

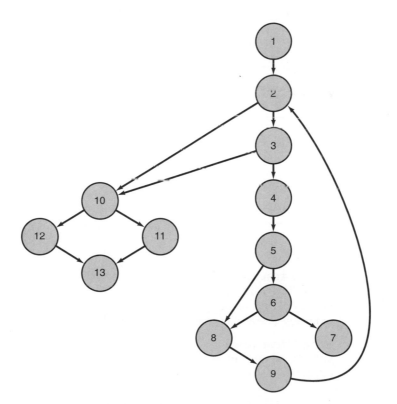

FIGURE 16.6.
Flow graph of the procedure *average*

3. **Determine a basis set of linearly independent paths.**   The value of $V(G)$ provides the number of linearly independent paths through the program control structure. In the case of procedure **average,** we expect to specify six paths:

   path 1: 1-2-10-11-13
   path 2: 1-2-10-12-13
   path 3: 1-2-3-10-11-13
   path 4: 1-2-3-4-5-8-9-2- · · ·
   path 5: 1-2-3-4-5-6-8-9-2- · · ·
   path 6: 1-2-3-4-5-6-7-8-9-2- · · ·

   The ellipsis (· · ·) following paths 4, 5, and 6 indicates that any path through the remainder of the control structure is acceptable. It is often worthwhile to identify predicate nodes as an aid in the derivation of test cases. In this case, nodes 2, 3, 5, 6, and 10 are predicate nodes.

4. **Prepare test cases that will force execution of each path in the basis set.** Data should be chosen so that conditions at the predicate nodes are appropriately set as each path is tested. Test cases that satisfy the basis set described above are:

   Path 1 test case:
   value(k) = valid input, where $k < i$ defined below
   value(i) = − 999, where $2 \leq i \leq 100$
   expected results: correct average based on k values and proper totals
   Note: Path 1 cannot be tested standalone but must be tested as part of path 4, 5, and 6 tests.

   Path 2 test case:
   value(1) = − 999
   expected results: average = − 999; other totals at initial values

   Path 3 test case:
   attempt to process 101 or more values
   first 100 values should be valid
   expected results: same as test case 1

   Path 4 test case:
   value(i) = valid input, where $i < 100$
   value(k) < minimum, where $k < i$
   expected results: correct average based on k values and proper totals

   Path 5 test case:
   value(i) = valid input, where $i < 100$
   value(k) > maximum, where $k \leq i$
   expected results: correct average based on n values and proper totals

   Path 6 test case:
   value(i) = valid input, where $i < 100$
   expected results: correct average based on n values and proper totals

Each test case is executed and compared to expected results. Once all test cases have been completed, the tester can be sure that all statements in the program have been executed at least once.

It is important to note that some independent paths (e.g., Path 1 in our example) cannot be tested in standalone fashion. That is, the combination of data required to traverse the path cannot be achieved in the normal flow of the program. In such cases, these paths are tested as part of another path test.

16.4.4 Graph Matrices

The procedure for deriving the flow graph and even determining a set of basis paths is amenable to mechanization. To develop a software tool that assists in basis path testing, a data structure, called a *graph matrix,* can be quite useful.

A graph matrix is a square matrix whose size (i.e., number of rows and columns) is equal to the number of nodes on the flow graph. Each row and column corresponds to an identified node, and matrix entries correspond to *connections* (edges) between nodes. A simple example of a flow graph and it corresponding graph matrix [BEI90] is shown in Figure 16.7.

In the figure, each node on the flow graph is identified by numbers, while each edge is identified by letters. A letter entry is made in the matrix to correspond to a connection between two nodes. For example, node 3 is connected to node 4 by edge *b*.

To this point, the graph matrix is nothing more that a tabular representation of a flow graph. However, by adding a *link weight* to each matrix entry, the graph matrix can become a powerful tool for evaluating program control structure during testing. The link weight provides additional information about control flow. In its simplest form, the link weight is 1 (a connection exists) or 0 (a

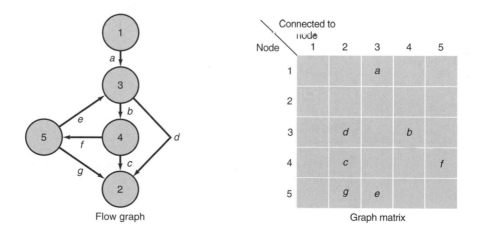

FIGURE 16.7.
Connection matrix

Flow graph

Graph matrix

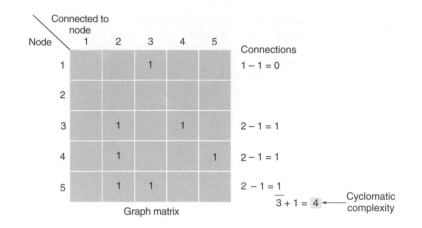

FIGURE 16.8.
Connection matrix

connection does not exist). But link weights can be assigned other, more interesting properties:

- the probability that a link (edge) will be executed;
- the processing time expended during traversal of a link;
- the memory required during traversal of a link; and
- the resources required during traversal of a link.

To illustrate, we use the simplest weighting to indicate connections (0 or 1). The graph matrix in Figure 16.7 is redrawn as shown in Figure 16.8. Each letter has been replaced with a 1, indicating that a connection exists (zeros have been excluded for clarity). Represented in this form, the graph matrix is called a *connection matrix*. In Figure 16.8, each row with two or more entries represents a predicate node. Therefore, performing the arithmetic shown to the right of the connection matrix provides us with still another method for determining cyclomatic complexity (Section 16.4.2).

Beizer [BEI90] provides a thorough treatment of additional mathematical algorithms that can be applied to graph matrices. Using these techniques, the analysis required to design test cases can be partially or fully automated.

16.5   CONTROL STRUCTURE TESTING

The basis path testing technique described in Section 16.4 is one of a number of techniques for *control structure testing*. Although basis path testing is simple and highly effective, it is not sufficient in itself. In this section, other variations on control structure testing are discussed. These broaden testing coverage and improve quality of white-box testing.

16.5.1 Condition Testing[6]

Condition testing is a test case design method that exercises the logical conditions contained in a program module. A *simple condition* is a Boolean variable or a relational expression, possibly preceded with one NOT ("¬") operator. A *relational expression* takes the form

$$E_1(\text{relational-operator})E_2$$

where E_1 and E_2 are arithmetic expressions and (relational-operator) is one of the following: "<" , "≤", "=", "≠" ("¬ =") (non-equality), ">", or "≥". A *compound condition* is composed of two or more simple conditions, Boolean operators, and parentheses. We assume that Boolean operators allowed in a compound condition include OR ("|"), AND ("&") and NOT ("¬"). A condition without relational expressions is referred to as a *Boolean expression*.

Therefore, the possible types of components in a condition include a Boolean operator, a Boolean variable, a pair of Boolean parentheses (surrounding a simple or compound condition), a relational operator, or an arithmetic expression.

If a condition is incorrect, then at least one component of the condition is incorrect. Thus, types of errors in a condition include the following:

- Boolean operator error (existence of incorrect/missing/extra Boolean operators)
- Boolean variable error
- Boolean parenthesis error
- relational operator error
- arithmetic expression error

The *condition testing* method focuses on testing each condition in the program. Condition testing strategies (discussed later in this section) generally have two advantages. First, measurement of test coverage of a condition is simple. Second, the test coverage of conditions in a program provides guidance for the generation of additional tests for the program.

The purpose of condition testing is to detect not only errors in the conditions of a program but also other errors in the program. If a test set for a program P is effective for detecting errors in the conditions contained in P, it is likely that this test set is also effective for detecting other errors in P. In addition, if a testing strategy is effective for detecting errors in a condition, then it is likely that this strategy will also be effective for detecting errors in a program.

A number of condition testing strategies have been proposed. *Branch testing* is probably the simplest condition testing strategy. For a compound condition C, the true and false branches of C and every simple condition in C need to be executed at least once [MYE79].

---

[6]Sections 16.5.1 and 16.5.2 were adapted from [TAI89] with permission of Professor K.C. Tai.

Domain testing [WHI80] requires three or four tests to be derived for a rational expression. For a rational expression of the form

$$E_1 \text{(relational-operator)} E_2$$

three tests are required to make the value of E_1 greater than, equal to, or less than that of E_2 respectively [HOW82]. If (relational-operator) is incorrect and E_1 and E_2 are correct, then these three tests guarantee the detection of the relational operator error. To detect errors in E_1 and E_2, a test that makes the value of E_1 greater or less than that of E_2 should make the difference between these two values as small as possible.

For a Boolean expression with n variables, all of 2^n possible tests are required ($n > 0$). This strategy can detect Boolean operator, variable, and parenthesis errors, but it is practical only if n is small.

Error-sensitive tests for Boolean expressions can also be derived [FOS84, TAI87]. For a singular Boolean expression (a Boolean expression in which each Boolean variable occurs only once) with n Boolean variables ($n > 0$), we can easily generate a test set with less than 2^n tests such that this test set guarantees the detection of multiple Boolean operator errors and is also effective for detecting other errors.

Tai [TAI89] suggests a condition testing strategy that builds on the techniques outlined above. Called *BRO (branch and relational operator) testing,* the technique guarantees the detection of branch and relational operator errors in a condition provided that all Boolean variables and relational operators in the condition occur only once and have no common variables.

The BRO strategy uses *condition constraints* for a condition C. A condition constraint for C with n simple conditions is defined as $(D_1, D_2, \ldots, D_n)$, where D_i ($0 < i \leq n$) is a symbol specifying a constraint on the outcome of the ith simple condition in condition C. A condition constraint D for condition C is said to be covered by an execution of C if during this execution of C the outcome of each simple condition in C satisfies the corresponding constraint in D.

For a Boolean variable, B, we specify a constraint on the outcome of B that states that B must be either true (t) or false (f). Similarly, for a relational expression, the symbols $>$, $=$, and $<$ are used to specify constraints on the outcome of the expression.

As an example, consider the condition

$$C_1: B_1 \,\&\, B_2$$

where B_1 and B_2 are Boolean variables. The condition constraint for C_1 is of the form (D_1, D_2), where each of D_1 and D_2 is "t" or "f". The value (t, f) is a condition constraint for C_1 and is covered by the test that makes the value of B_1 to be true and the value of B_2 to be false. The BRO testing strategy requires that the constraint set {(t, t),(f, t),(t, f)} be covered by the executions of C_1. If C_1 is incorrect due to one or more Boolean operator errors, at least one member of the constraint set will force C_1 to fail.

As a second example, consider a condition of the form

$$C_2: B_1 \,\&\, (E_3 = E_4)$$

where B_1 is a Boolean expression and E_3 and E_4 are arithmetic expressions. A condition constraint for C_2 is of the form (D_1, D_2), where each of D_1 is "t" or "f" and D_2 is $>$, $=$, or $<$. Since C_2 is the same as C_1 except that the second simple condition in C_2 is a relational expression, we can construct a constraint set for C_2 by modifying the constraint set {(t, t), (f, t), (t, f)} defined for C_1. Note that "t" for $(E_3 = E_4)$ implies " $=$ " and that "f" for $(E_3 = E_4)$ implies either " $<$ " or " $>$." By replacing (t, t) and (f, t) with (t, $=$) and (f, $=$) respectively and by replacing (t, f) with (t, $<\setminus<$) and (t, $>$), the resulting constraint set for C_2 is {(t, $=$), (f, $=$), (t, $<$), (t, $>$) }. Coverage of the above constraint set will guarantee detection of Boolean and relational operator errors in C_2.

As a third example, we consider a condition of the form:

$$C_3\colon (E_1 > E_2) \ \& \ (E_3 = E_4)$$

where E_1, E_2, E_3, and E_4 are arithmetic expressions. A condition constraint for C_3 is of the form (D_1, D_2), where each of D_1 and D_2 is $>$, $=$, or $<$. Since C_3 is the same as C_2 except that the first simple condition in C_3 is a relational expression, we can construct a constraint set for C_3 by modifying the constraint set for C_2, obtaining:

$$\{(>, =), (=, =), (<, =), (>, >), (>, <)\}$$

Coverage of the above constraint set will guarantee detection of relational operator errors in C_3.

16.5.2 Data Flow Testing

The *data flow testing* method selects test paths of a program according to the locations of definitions and uses of variables in the program. A number of data flow testing strategies have been studied and compared (e.g., [FRA88], [NTA88], [FRA93]).

To illustrate the data flow testing approach, assume that each statement in a program is assigned a unique statement number and that each function does not modify its parameters or global variables. For a statement with S as its statement number,

$$\text{DEF}(S) = \{X \,|\, \text{statement } S \text{ contains a definition of } X\}$$

$$\text{USE}(S) = \{X \,|\, \text{statement } S \text{ contains a use of } X\}$$

If statement S is an *if* or loop statement, its DEF set is empty and its USE set is based on the condition of statement S. The definition of variable X at statement S is said to be *live* at statement S' if there exists a path from statement S to statement S' that does not contain any other definition of X.

A *definition-use chain* (or *DU chain*) of variable X is of the form [X, S, S'], where S and S' are statement numbers, X is in DEF(S) and USE(S'), and the definition of X in statement S is live at statement S'.

One simple data flow testing strategy is to require that every DU chain be covered at least once. We refer to this strategy as the *DU testing strategy*. It has been shown that DU testing does not guarantee the coverage of all branches of a program. However, a branch is not guaranteed to be covered by DU testing only in rare situations such as *if-then-else* constructs in which the *then* part has no definition of any variable and the *else* part does not exist. In this situation, the *else* branch of the above *if* statement is not necessarily covered by DU testing.

Data flow testing strategies are useful for selecting test paths of a program containing nested *if* and *loop* statements. To illustrate this, consider the application of DU testing to select test paths for the PDL that follows:

```
proc x
    B1;
    do while C1
      if C2
        then
          if C4
            then B4;
            else B5;
          endif;
        else
          if C3
            then B2;
            else B3;
          endif;
      endif;
    enddo;
    B6;
end proc;
```

To apply the DU testing strategy to select test paths of the control flow diagram, we need to know the definitions and uses of variables in each condition or blocks in the PDL. Assume that variable X is defined in the last statement of blocks B1, B2, B3, B4, and B5, and is used in the first statement of blocks B2, B3, B4, B5, and B6. The DU testing strategy requires an execution of the shortest path from each of B_i, $0 < i \leq 5$, to each of B_j, $1 < j \leq 6$. (Such testing also covers any use of variable X in conditions C1, C2, C3, and C4.) Although there are twenty-five DU chains of variable X, we only need five paths to cover these DU chains. The reason is that five paths are needed to cover the DU chain of X from B_i, $0 < i \leq 5$, to B6, and other DU chains can be covered by making these five paths containing iterations of the loop.

Note that if we apply the branch testing strategy to select test paths of the PDL noted above, we do not need any additional information. To select paths of the diagram for BRO testing, we need to know the structure of each condition or block. (After the selection of a path of a program, we need to determine whether the path is feasible for the program, i.e., whether there exists at least one input that exercises the path.)

Since the statements in a program are related to each other according to the definitions and uses of variables, the data flow testing approach is effective for error protection. However, the problems of measuring test coverage and selecting test paths for data flow testing are more difficult than the corresponding problems for condition testing.

16.5.3 Loop Testing

Loops are the cornerstone for the vast majority of all algorithms implemented in software. And yet, we often pay them little heed while conducting software testing.

Loop testing is a white-box testing technique that focuses exclusively on the validity of loop constructs. Four different classes of loops [BEI90] can be defined: *simple loops, concatenated loops, nested loops,* and *unstructured loops* (Figure 16.9).

Simple loops. The following set of tests should be applied to simple loops, where n is the maximum number of allowable passes through the loop.

1. Skip the loop entirely.
2. Only one pass through the loop.

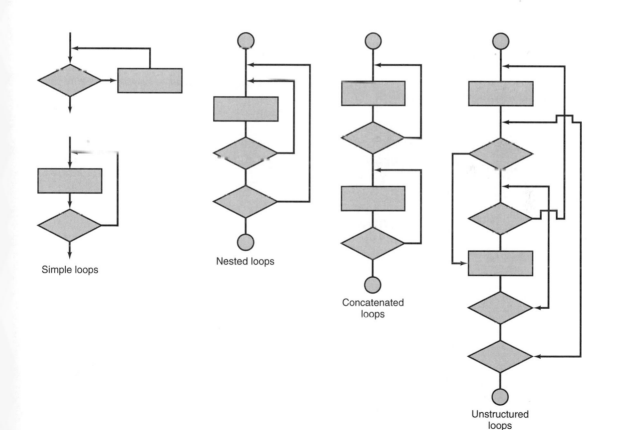

Simple loops

Nested loops

Concatenated loops

Unstructured loops

FIGURE 16.9. Loops

3. Two passes through the loop.

4. m passes through the loop where $m < n$

5. $n - 1, n, n + 1$ passes through the loop

Nested loops.   If we were to extend the test approach for simple loops to nested loops, the number of possible tests would grow geometrically as the level of nesting increases. This would result in an impractical number of tests. Beizer [BEI90] suggests an approach that will help to reduce the number of tests:

1. Start at the innermost loop. Set all other loops to minimum values.

2. Conduct simple loop tests for the innermost loop while holding the outer loops at their minimum iteration parameter (e.g., loop counter) values. Add other tests for out-of-range or excluded values.

3. Work outward, conducting tests for the next loop, but keeping all other outer loops at minimum values and other nested loops to "typical" values.

4. Continue until all loops have been tested.

Concatenated loops.   Concatenated loops can be tested using the approach defined above for simple loops if each of the loops is independent of the other. However, if two loops are concatenated and the loop counter for loop 1 is used as the initial value for loop 2, then the loops are *not* independent. When the loops are not independent, the approach applied to nested loops is recommended.

Unstructured loops.   Whenever possible, this class of loops should be *redesigned* to reflect the use of the structured programming constructs (Chapter 14).

16.6   BLACK-BOX TESTING

Black-box testing, focuses on the functional requirements of the software. That is, black-box testing enables the software engineer to derive sets of input conditions that will fully exercise all functional requirements for a program. Black-box testing is *not* an alternative to white-box techniques. Rather, it is a complementary approach that is likely to uncover a different class of errors than white-box methods.

Black-box testing attempts to find errors in the following categories: (1) incorrect or missing functions, (2) interface errors, (3) errors in data structures or external data base access, (4) performance errors, and (5) initialization and termination errors.

Unlike white-box testing, which is performed early in the testing process, black-box testing tends to be applied during later stages of testing (see Chapter 17). Because black-box testing purposely disregards control structure, attention is focused on the information domain. Tests are designed to answer the following questions:

- How is functional validity tested?
- What *classes* of input will make good test cases?
- Is the system particularly sensitive to certain input values?
- How are the boundaries of a data class isolated?
- What data rates and data volume can the system tolerate?
- What effect will specific combinations of data have on system operation?

By applying black-box techniques, we derive a set of test cases that satisfy the following criteria [MYE79]: (1) test cases that reduce, by a count that is greater than one, the number of additional test cases that must be designed to achieve reasonable testing, and (2) test cases that tell us something about the presence or absence of classes of errors, rather than errors associated only with the specific test at hand.

16.6.1 Graph-Based Testing Methods

The first step in black-box testing[7] is to understand the objects[8] that are modeled in software and the relationships that connect these objects. Once this has been accomplished, the next step is to define a series of tests that verify "all objects have the expected relationship to one another" [BEI95]. Stated in another way, software testing begins by creating a graph of important objects and their relationships and then devising a series of tests that will cover the graph so that each object and relationship is exercised and errors are uncovered.

To accomplish these steps, the software engineer begins by creating a graph—a collection of *nodes* that represent objects; *links* that represent the relationships between objects; *node weights* that describe the properties of a node (e.g., a specific data value or state behavior), and *link weights* that describe some characteristic of a link.[9]

The symbolic representation of a graph is shown in Figure 16.10a. Nodes are represented as circles connected by links that take a number of different forms. A directed link (represented by an arrow) indicates that a relationship moves in only one direction. A *bidirectional link,* also called a *symmetric link,* implies that the relationship applies in both directions. Parallel links are used when a number of different relationships are established between graph nodes.

As a simple example, consider a portion of a graph for a word-processing application (Figure 16.10b) where:

---

[7]Black-box testing is sometimes called *behavioral testing* or *partition testing*.

[8]In this context, the term "object" encompasses the data objects that we discussed in Chapters 11 and 12 as well as program objects such as modules or collections of programming language statements.

[9]If the above concepts seem vaguely familiar, recall that graphs were also used in Section 16.4.1 to create a program graph for the basis path testing method. The nodes of the program graph contained instructions (program objects) characterized as either procedural design representations or source code, and the directed links indicated the control flow between these program objects. Here, the use of graphs is extended to encompass black-box testing as well.

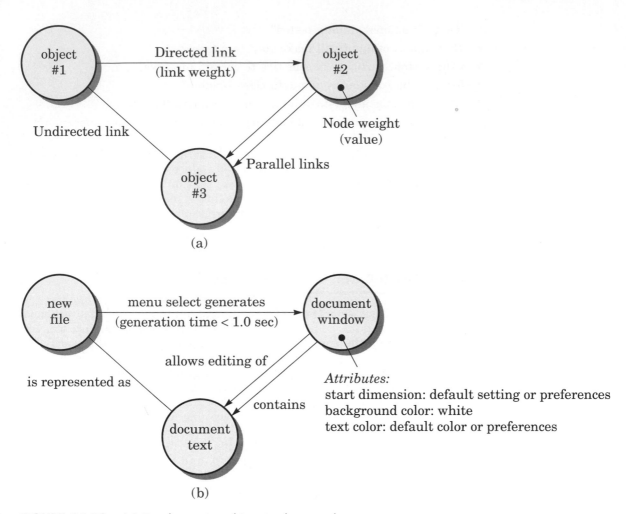

FIGURE 16.10.   (a) Graph notation; (b) a simple example

object #1 = **new file menu select**

object #2 = **document window**

object #3 = **document text**

As shown in the figure, a menu select on **new file** generates a **document window**. The node weight of **document window** provides a list of the window attributes that are to be expected when the window is generated. The link weight indicates that the window must be generated in less than 1.0 second. An undirected link establishes a symmetric relationship between the **new file menu select** and **document text,** and parallel links indicate relationships between **document window** and **document text**. In reality, a far more detailed graph would have to be generated as a precursor to test case design. The software engineer then derives test cases by traversing the graph and covering each of the relationships shown. These test cases are designed in an attempt to find errors in any of the relationships.

Beizer [BEI95] describes a number of behavioral testing methods that can make use of graphs:

Transaction flow modeling. The nodes represent steps in some transaction (e.g., the steps required to make an airline reservation using an online service), and the links represent the logical connection between steps (e.g., **flight.information.input** *is followed* by **validation/availability. processing**). The data flow diagram (Chapter 12) can be used to assist in creating graphs of this type.

Finite state modeling. The nodes represent different user observable states of the software (e.g., each of the "screens" that appear as an order entry clerk takes a phone order), and the links represent the transitions that occur to move from state to state (e.g., **order-information** *is verified during* **inventory-availability-look-up** *is followed by* **customer-billing-information input**). The state-transition diagram (Chapter 12) can be used to assist in creating graphs of this type.

Data flow modeling. The nodes are data objects, and the links are the transformations that occur to translate one data object into another. For example, the node **FICA.tax.withheld** (FTW) *is computed from* **gross.wages** (GW) using the relationship, FTW = 0.062 × GW.

Timing modeling. The nodes are program objects and the links are the sequential connections between those objects. Link weights are used to specify the required execution times as the program executes.

A detailed discussion of each of these graph-based testing methods is beyond the scope of this book. The interested reader should see [BEI95] for a comprehensive discussion. It is worthwhile, however, to provide a generic outline of the graph-based testing approach.

Graph-based testing begins with the definition of all nodes and node weights. That is, objects and attributes are identified. The data model (Chapter 12) can be used as a starting point, but it is important to note that many nodes may be program objects (not explicitly represented in the data model). To provide an indication of the start and stop points for the graph, it is useful to define *entry* and *exit nodes*.

Once nodes have been identified, links and link weights should be established. In general, links should be named, although links that represent control flow between program objects need not be named.

In many cases, the graph model may have loops (i.e., a path through the graph in which one or more nodes is encountered more than one time). Loop testing (Section 16.5.3) can also be applied at the behavioral (black-box) level. The graph will assist in identifying those loops that need to be tested.

Each relationship is studied separately so that test cases can be derived. The *transitivity* of sequential relationships is studied to determine how the impact of relationships propagates across objects defined in a graph. Transitivity can be illustrated by considering three objects, **X**, **Y**, and **Z**. Consider the following relationships:

X *is required to compute* **Y**

Y *is required to compute* **Z**

Therefore, a transitive relationship has been established between **X** and **Z**:

X *is required to compute* **Z**

Based on this transitive relationship, tests to find errors in the calculation of **Z** must consider a variety of values for both **X** and **Y**.

The *symmetry* of a relationship (graph link) is also an important guide to the design of test cases. If a link is indeed bidirectional (symmetric), it is important to test this feature. The UNDO feature [BEI95] in many personal computer applications implements limited symmetry. That is, UNDO allows an action to be negated after it has been completed. This should be thoroughly tested and all exceptions (i.e., places where UNDO cannot be used) should be noted. Finally, every node in the graph should have a relationship that leads back to itself; in essence, a "no action" or "null action" loop. These *reflexive* relationships should also be tested.

As test case design begins, the first objective is to achieve *node coverage*. By this we mean that tests should be designed to demonstrate that no nodes have been inadvertently omitted and that node weights (object attributes) are correct.

Next, *link coverage* is addressed. Each relationship is tested based on its properties. For example, a symmetric relationship is tested to demonstrate that it is, in fact, bidirectional. A transitive relationship is tested to demonstrate that transitivity is present. A reflexive relationship is tested to ensure that a null loop is present. When link weights have been specified, tests are devised to demonstrate that these weights are valid. Finally, loop testing is invoked (Section 16.5.3).

16.6.2 Equivalence Partitioning

Equivalence partitioning is a black-box testing method that divides the input domain of a program into classes of data from which test cases can be derived. An ideal test case single-handedly uncovers a class of errors (e.g., incorrect processing of all character data) that might otherwise require many cases to be executed before the general error is observed. Equivalence partitioning strives to define a test case that uncovers classes of errors, thereby reducing the total number of test cases that must be developed.

Test case design for equivalence partitioning is based on an evaluation of equivalence classes for an *input condition*. Using concepts introduced in the preceding section, if a set of objects can be linked by relationships that are symmetric, transitive, and reflexive, an equivalence class is present [BEI95]. An *equivalence class* represents a set of valid or invalid states for input conditions. Typically, an input condition is either a specific numeric value, a range of values, a set of related values, or a Boolean condition. Equivalence classes may be defined according to the following guidelines:

1. If an input condition specifies a *range,* one valid and two invalid equivalence classes are defined.

2. If an input condition requires a specific *value,* one valid and two invalid equivalence classes are defined.

3. If an input condition specifies a member of a *set,* one valid and one invalid equivalence class are defined.

4. If an input condition is *Boolean,* one valid and one invalid class are defined.

As an example, consider data maintained as part of an automated banking application. The user can "dial" the bank using his or her personal computer, provide a six digit password, and follow with a series of keyword commands that trigger various banking functions. The software supplied for the banking application accepts data in the form:

area code—blank or three digit number

prefix—three digit number not beginning with 0 or 1

suffix—four digit number

password—six digit alphanumeric value

commands—"check," "deposit," "bill pay," etc.

The input conditions associated with each data element for the banking application can be specified as:

area code: input condition, *Boolean*—the area code may or may not be present
input condition, *range*—values defined between 200 and 999, with specific exceptions

prefix: input condition, *range*—specified value > 200 with no 0 digits

suffix: input condition, *value*—four digit length

password: input condition, *Boolean*—a password may or may not be present
input condition, *value* six character string

command: input condition, *set*—containing commands noted above

Applying the guidelines for the derivation of equivalence classes, test cases for each input domain data item could be developed and executed. Test cases are selected so that the largest number of attributes of an equivalence class are exercised at once.

16.6.3 Boundary Value Analysis

For reasons that are not completely clear, a greater number of errors tend to occur at the boundaries of the input domain than in the "center." It is for this reason that *boundary value analysis (BVA)* has been developed as a testing technique. Boundary value analysis leads to a selection of test cases that exercise bounding values.

Boundary value analysis is a test case design technique that complements equivalence partitioning. Rather than selecting any element of an equivalence class, BVA leads to the selection of test cases at the "edges" of the class. Rather than focusing solely on input conditions, BVA derives test cases from the output domain as well [MYE79].

Guidelines for BVA are similar in many respects to those provided for equivalence partitioning:

1. If an input condition specifies a *range* bounded by values a and b, test cases should be designed with values a and b, just above and just below a and b, respectively.

2. If an input condition specifies a number of values, test cases should be developed that exercise the minimum and maximum numbers. Values just above and below minimum and maximum are also tested.

3. Guidelines 1 and 2 are applied to output conditions. For example, assume that a temperature vs. pressure table is required as output from an engineering analysis program. Test cases should be designed to create an output report that produces the maximum (and minimum) allowable number of table entries.

4. If internal program data structures have prescribed boundaries (e.g., an array has a defined limit of 100 entries), be certain to design a test case to exercise the data structure at its boundary.

Most software engineers intuitively perform BVA to some degree. By applying the guidelines noted above, boundary testing will be more complete, thereby having a higher likelihood for error detection.

16.6.4 Comparison Testing

There are some situations (e.g., aircraft avionics, nuclear power plant control) in which the reliability of software is absolutely critical. In such applications redundant hardware *and* software are often used to minimize the possibility of error. When redundant software is developed, separate software engineering teams develop independent versions of an application using the same specification. In such situations, each version can be tested with the same test data to ensure that all provide identical output. Then all versions are executed in parallel with real-time comparison of results to ensure consistency.

Using lessons learned from redundant systems, researchers (e.g., [BRI87]) have suggested that independent versions of software be developed for critical applications, even when only a single version will be used in the delivered computer-based system. These independent versions form the basis of a black-box testing technique called *comparison testing* or *back-to-back testing* [KNI89].

When multiple implementations of the same specification have been produced, test cases designed using other black-box techniques (e.g., equivalence partitioning) are provided as input to each version of the software. If the output from each version is the same, it is assumed that all implementations are correct. If the output is different, each of the applications is investigated to determine if a defect in one or more versions is responsible for the difference. In most cases, the comparison of outputs can be performed by a automated tool.

Comparison testing is not foolproof. If the specification from which all versions have been developed is in error, all versions will likely reflect the error. In addition, if each of the independent versions produces identical, but incorrect, results, condition testing will fail to detect the error.

16.7   TESTING FOR SPECIALIZED ENVIRONMENTS AND APPLICATIONS

As computer software has become more complex, the need for specialized testing approaches has also grown. The white-box and black-box testing methods discussed in Sections 16.5 and 16.6 are applicable across all environments, architectures, and applications, but unique guidelines and approaches to testing are sometime warranted. In this section we consider testing guidelines for specialized environments, architectures, and applications that are commonly encountered by software engineers.

16.7.1   Testing GUIs

Graphical user interfaces (GUIs) present interesting challenges for software engineers. Because of reusable components provided as part of GUI development environments, the creation of the user interface has become less time-consuming and more precise. At the same time, the complexity of GUIs has grown, leading to more difficulty in the design and execution of test cases.

Because modern GUIs have the same look and feel, a series of standard tests can be derived. The following questions can serve as a guideline for creating a series of generic tests for GUIs:

For windows:

- Will the window open properly based on related typed or menu-based commands?
- Can the window be resized, moved, and scrolled?
- Is all data content contained within the window properly addressable with a mouse, function keys, directional arrows, and keyboard?
- Does the window properly regenerate when it is overwritten and then recalled?
- Are all functions that relate to the window available when needed?
- Are all functions that relate to the window operational?
- Are all relevant pull-down menus, tool bars, scroll bars, dialog boxes, and buttons, icons, and other controls available and properly displayed for the window?
- When multiple windows are displayed, is the name of the window properly represented?

- Is the active window properly highlighted?
- If multitasking is used, are all windows updated at appropriate times?
- Do multiple or incorrect mouse picks within the window cause unexpected side effects?
- Are audio and/or color prompts within the window or as a consequence of window operations presented according to specification?
- Does the window properly close?

For pull-down menus and mouse operations:

- Is the appropriate menu bar displayed in the appropriate context?
- Does the application menu bar display system related features (e.g., a clock display)?
- Do pull-down operations work properly?
- Do breakaway menus, palettes, and tool bars work properly?
- Are all menu functions and pull-down subfunctions properly listed?
- Are all menu functions properly addressable by the mouse?
- Is text typeface, size, and format correct?
- Is it possible to invoke each menu function using its alternative text-based command?
- Are menu functions highlighted (or grayed-out) based on the context of current operations within a window?
- Does each menu function perform as advertised?
- Are the names of menu functions self-explanatory?
- Is help available for each menu item, and is it context sensitive?
- Are mouse operations properly recognized throughout the interactive context?
- If multiple clicks are required, are they properly recognized in context?
- If the mouse has multiple buttons, are they properly recognized in context?
- Do the cursor, processing indicator (e.g., an hour glass or clock), and pointer properly change as different operations are invoked?

Data entry:

- Is alphanumeric data entry properly echoed and input to the system?
- Do graphical modes of data entry (e.g., a slide bar) work properly?
- Is invalid data properly recognized?
- Are data input messages intelligible?

In addition to the above guidelines, finite state modeling graphs (Section 16.6.1) may be used to derive a series of tests that address specific data and program objects that are relevant to the GUI.

Because of the large number of permutations associated with GUI operations, testing should be approached using automated tools. A wide array of GUI testing tools has appeared on the market over the past few years. For further discussion, see Chapter 29.

16.7.2 Testing of Client/Server Architectures

Client/server (C/S) architectures (e.g., [BER92], [VAS93]) represent a significant challenge for software testers. The distributed nature of client/server environments, the performance issues associated with transaction processing, the potential presence of a number of different hardware platforms, the complexities of network communication, the need to service multiple clients from a centralized (or in some cases, distributed) database, and the coordination requirements imposed on the server all combine to make testing of C/S architectures and the software that reside within them considerably more difficult than testing standalone applications. In fact, recent industry studies indicate a significant increase in testing time and cost when C/S environments are developed. For further information on client/server testing, see Chapter 28.

16.7.3 Testing Documentation and Help Facilities

The term "software testing" conjures images of large numbers of test cases prepared to exercise computer programs and the data that they manipulate. Recalling the definition of software presented in the first chapter of this book, it is important to note that testing must also extend to the third element of the software configuration—documentation.[10]

Errors in documentation can be as devastating to the acceptance of the program as errors in data or source code. Nothing is more frustrating than following the user guide exactly and getting results or behaviors that do not coincide with those predicted by the document. For this reason, documentation testing should be a meaningful part of every software test plan.

Documentation testing can be approached in two phases. The first phase, formal technical review (Chapter 8), examines the document for editorial clarity. The second phase, live test, uses the documentation in conjunction with the use of the actual program.

It is surprising, but live test for documentation can be approached using techniques that are analogous to many of the black-box testing methods discussed in Section 16.6. Graph-based testing can be used to describe the use of the program; equivalence partitioning and boundary value analysis can be used to define various classes of input and associated interactions. Program usage is then tracked through the documentation:

- Does the documentation accurately describe how to accomplish each mode of use?
- Is the description of each interaction sequence accurate?
- Are examples accurate?
- Are terminology, menu descriptions, and system responses consistent with the actual program?
- Is it relatively easy to locate guidance within the documentation?

---

[10]In this context, *documentation* refers to printed manuals and online help facilities.

- Can troubleshooting be accomplished easily with the documentation?
- Are the document table of contents and index accurate and complete?
- Is the design of the document (layout, typefaces, indentation, graphics) conducive to understanding and quick assimilation of information?
- Are all error messages displayed for the user described in more detail in the document?
- If hypertext links are used, are they accurate and complete?

The only viable way to answer these questions is to have an independent third party (e.g., selected users) test the documentation in the context of program usage. All discrepancies are noted, and areas of document ambiguity or weakness are defined for potential rewrite.

16.7.4   Testing for Real-Time Systems

The time-dependent, asynchronous nature of many real-time applications (Chapter 15) adds a new and potentially difficult element to the testing mix— *time*. Not only does the test case designer have to consider white- and blackbox test cases, but also event handling (i.e., interrupt processing), the timing of the data, and the parallelism of the tasks (processes) that handle the data. In many situations, test data provided when a real-time system is in one state will result in proper processing, while the same data provided when the system is in a different state may lead to error.

For example, the real-time software that controls a new photocopier accepts operator interrupts (i.e., the machine operator hits control keys such as "reset" or "darken") with no error when the machine is making copies (in the "copying" state). These same operator interrupts, if input when the machine is in the "jammed" state, cause a diagnostic code indicating the location of the jam to be lost (an error).

In addition, the intimate relationship that exists between real-time software and its hardware environment can also cause testing problems. Software tests must consider the impact of hardware faults on software processing. Such faults can be extremely difficult to simulate realistically.

Comprehensive test case design methods for real-time systems have yet to evolve. However, an overall four-step strategy can be proposed:

Task testing.   The first step in the testing of real-time software is to test each task independently.[11] That is, white-box and black-box tests are designed and executed for each task. Each task is executed independently during these tests. Task testing uncovers errors in logic and function, but will not uncover timing or behavioral errors.

---

[11]In this context, we view a task as a separate program that accepts input and produces output. A task may be composed of many modules and can be tested using methods discussed earlier in this chapter.

Behavioral testing. Using system models created with CASE tools (Section 15.3), it is possible to simulate the behavior of a real-time system and examine its behavior as a consequence of external events. These analysis activities can serve as the basis for the design of test cases that are conducted when the real-time software has been built. Using a technique that is similar to equivalence partitioning (Section 16.6.2), events (e.g., interrupts, control signals, data) are categorized for testing. For example, events for the photocopier might be user interrupts (e.g., reset counter), mechanical interrupts (e.g., paper jammed), system interrupts (e.g., toner low) and failure modes (e.g., roller overheated). Each of these events is tested individually and the behavior of the executable system is examined to detect errors that occur as a consequence of processing associated with these events. The behavior of the system model (developed during the analysis activity) and the executable software can be compared for conformance. Once each class of events has been tested, events are presented to the system in random order and with random frequency. The behavior of the software is examined to detect behavior errors.

Intertask testing. Once errors in individual tasks and in system behavior have been isolated, testing shifts to time related errors. Asynchronous tasks that are known to communicate with one another are tested with different data rates and processing load to determine if intertask synchronization errors will occur. In addition, tasks that communicate via a message queue or data store are tested to uncover errors in the sizing of these data storage areas.

System testing. Software and hardware are integrated, and a full range of system tests (Chapter 17) are conducted in an attempt to uncover errors at the software/hardware interface.

Most real-time systems process interrupts. Therefore, testing the handling of these Boolean events is essential. Using the state-transition diagram and the control specification (Chapter 12), the tester develops a list of all possible interrupts and the processing that occurs as a consequence of the interrupt. Tests are then designed to assess the following system characteristics:

- Are interrupt priorities properly assigned and properly handled?
- Is processing for each interrupt handled correctly?
- Does the performance (e.g., processing time) of each interrupt handling procedure conform to requirements?
- Does a high volume of interrupts arriving at critical times create problems in function or performance?

In addition, global data areas that are used to transfer information as part of interrupt processing should be tested to assess the potential for the generation of side effects.

16.8   SUMMARY

The primary objective for test case design is to derive a set of tests that have the highest likelihood for uncovering errors in the software. To accomplish this objective, two different categories of test case design techniques are used: white-box testing and black-box testing.

White-box tests focus on the program control structure. Test cases are derived to ensure that all statements in the program have been executed at least once during testing and that all logical conditions have been exercised. Basis path testing, a white-box technique, makes use of program graphs (or graph matrices) to derive the set of linearly independent tests that will ensure coverage. Condition and data flow testing further exercise program logic, and loop testing complements other white-box techniques by providing a procedure for exercising loops of varying degrees of complexity.

Hetzel [HET84] describes white-box testing as "testing in the small." His implication is that the white-box tests that we have considered in this chapter are typically applied to small program components (e.g., modules or small groups of modules). Black-box testing, on the other hand, broadens our focus and might be called "testing in the large."

Black-box tests are designed to uncover errors in functional requirements without regard to the internal workings of a program. Black-box testing techniques focus on the information domain of the software, deriving test cases by partitioning the input and output domain of a program in a manner that provides thorough test coverage. Graph-based testing methods explore the relationships between and behavior of program objects. Equivalence partitioning divides the input domain into classes of data that are likely to exercise specific software function. Boundary value analysis probes the program's ability to handle data at the limits of acceptability.

Specialized testing methods encompass a broad array of software capabilities and application areas. Graphical user interfaces, client/server architectures, documentation and help facilities, and real-time systems each require specialized guidelines and techniques for software testing.

Experienced software developers often say, "Testing never ends, it just gets transferred from you (the software engineer) to your customer. Every time your customer uses the program, a test is being conducted." By applying test case design, the software engineer can achieve more complete testing and thereby uncover and correct the highest number of errors before the "customer's tests" begin.

REFERENCES

[BEI90] Beizer, B., *Software Testing Techniques,* 2nd edition, Van Nostrand Reinhold, 1990.

[BEI95] Beizer, B., *Black-Box Testing,* Wiley, 1995.

[BER92] Berson, A., *Client/Server Architectures,* McGraw-Hill, 1992.

[BRI87] Brilliant, S.S., J.C. Knight, and N.G. Levenson, "The Consistent Comparison Problem in N-Version Software," *ACM Software Engineering Notes,* vol. 12, no. 1, January 1987, pp. 29–34.

[DAV95] Davis, A., *201 Principles of Software Development,* McGraw-Hill, 1995.

[DEU79] Deutsch, M., "Verification and Validation," in *Software Engineering,* R. Jensen and C. Tonies (eds.), Prentice-Hall, 1979, pp. 329–408.

[DUN84] Dunn, R., *Software Defect Removal,* McGraw-Hill, 1984.

[FOS84]   Foster, K.A., "Sensitive Test Data for Boolean Expressions," *ACM Software Engineering Notes,* vol. 9, no. 2, April 1984, pp. 120–125.

[FRA88]   Frankl, P.G., and E.J. Weyuker, "An Applicable Family of Data Flow Testing Criteria," *IEEE Trans. Software Engineering,* vol. 14, no. 10, October 1988, pp. 1483–1498.

[FRA93]   Frankl, P.G., and S. Weiss, "An Experimental Comparison of the Effectiveness of Branch Testing and Data Flow," *IEEE Trans. Software Engineering,* vol. 19, no. 8, August 1993, pp. 770–787.

[HET84]   Hetzel, W., *The Complete Guide to Software Testing,* QED Information Sciences, Inc., Wellesley, MA, 1984.

[HOW82]   Howden, W.E., "Weak Mutation Testing and the Completeness of Test Cases," *IEEE Trans. Software Engineering,* vol. SE-8, no. 4, July 1982, pp. 371–379.

[JON81]   Jones, T.C., *Programming Productivity: Issues for the 80s,* IEEE Computer Society Press, 1981.

[KAN93]   Kaner, C., J. Falk, and H.Q. Nguyen, *Testing Computer Software,* 2nd edition, Van Nostrand Reinhold, 1993.

[KNI89]   Knight, J., and P. Ammann, "Testing Software Using Multiple Versions," Software Productivity Consortium, Report No. 89029N, Reston, VA, June 1989.

[MCC76]   McCabe, T., "A Software Complexity Measure," *IEEE Trans. Software Engineering,* vol. 2, December 1976, pp. 308–320.

[MYE79]   Myers, G., *The Art of Software Testing,* Wiley, 1979.

[NTA88]   Ntafos, S.C., A Comparison of Some Structural Testing Strategies," *IEEE Trans. Software Engineering,* vol. 14, no. 6, June 1988, pp. 868–874.

[TAI87]   Tai, K.C., and H.K. Su, "Test Generation for Boolean Expressions," *Proc. COMPSAC '87,* October 1987, pp. 278–283.

[TAI89]   Tai, K.C., "What to Do Beyond Branch Testing," *ACM Software Engineering Notes,* vol. 14, no. 2, April 1989, pp. 58–61.

[VAS93]   Vaskevitch, D., *Client/Server Strategies,* IDG Books, 1993.

[WHI80]   White, L.J., and E.I. Cohen, "A Domain Strategy for Program Testing," *IEEE Trans. Software Engineering,* vol. SE-6, no. 5, May 1980, pp. 247–257.

PROBLEMS AND POINTS TO PONDER

16.1.   Myers [MYE79] uses the following program as a self-assessment for your ability to specify adequate testing: A program reads three integer values. The three values are interpreted as representing the lengths of the sides of a triangle. The program prints a message that states whether the triangle is scalene, isosceles, or equilateral. Develop a set of test cases that you feel will adequately test this program.

16.2.   Design and implement the program (with error handling where appropriate) specified in problem 16.1. Derive a flow graph for the program and apply basis path testing to develop test cases that will guarantee that all statements in the program have been tested. Execute the cases and show your results.

16.3. Can you think of any additional testing objectives that are not discussed in Section 16.1.1?

16.4. Apply the basis path testing technique to any one of the programs that you have implemented in problems 14.23 through 14.31.

16.5. Specify, design, and implement a software tool that will compute the cyclomatic complexity for the programming language of your choice. Use the graph matrix as the operative data structure in your design.

16.6. Read Beizer [BEI95] and determine how the program you have developed in problem 16.5 can be extended to accommodate various *link weights*. Extend your tool to process execution probabilities or link processing times.

16.7. Use the condition testing approach described in Section 16.5.1 to design a set of test cases for the program you created in problem 16.2.

16.8. Using the data flow testing approach described in Section 16.5.2, make a list of definition-use chains for the program you created in problem 16.2.

16.9. Design an automated tool that will recognize loops and categorize them as indicated in Section 16.5.3.

16.10. Extend the tool described in problem 16.9 to generate test cases for each loop category, once encountered. It will be necessary to perform this function interactively with the tester.

16.11. Give at least three examples in which black-box testing might give the impression that "everything's O.K.," while white-box tests might uncover an error. Give at least three examples in which white-box testing might give the impression that "everything's O.K.," while black-box tests might uncover an error.

16.12. Will exhaustive testing (even if it is possible for very small programs) guarantee that the program is 100 percent correct?

16.13. Using the equivalence partitioning method, derive a set of test cases for the SafeHome system described earlier in this book.

16.14. Using boundary value analysis, derive a set of test cases for the PHTRS system described in problem 12.13.

16.15. Select a specific GUI for a program with which you are familiar and design a series of tests to exercise the GUI.

16.16. Test a user manual (or help facility) for an application that you use frequently. Find at least one error in the documentation.

FURTHER READINGS AND OTHER INFORMATION SOURCES

A number of excellent books are now available for those readers who desire additional information on software testing. Myers [MYE79] remains a classic text, covering black-box techniques in considerable detail. Beizer [BEI90] provides comprehensive coverage of white-box techniques, introducing a level of mathematical rigor that has often been missing in other treatments of testing. His later book [BEI95] presents a concise treatment of important methods. Perry (*Effective Methods for Software Testing*, Wiley-QED, 1995), Marnick (*The Craft of Software Testing,* Prentice-Hall, 1995) and Friedman and Voas (*Software Assessment: Reliability, Safety, Testability,* Wiley, 1995) present good introductions to testing strategies and tactics. Mosley (*The Handbook of MIS Application Software Testing,* Prentice-Hall, 1993) discusses testing issues for large information systems, and Marks (*Testing Very Big Systems,* McGraw-Hill, 1992) discusses the special issues that must be considered when testing major programming systems. Jorgensen (*Software Testing: A Craftman's Approach,* CRC Press, 1995) presents a detailed discussion of a wide variety of black- and white-box testing methods. Rubin (*Handbook of Usability Testing,* Wiley, 1994) has written a useful guide for those who must exercise human interfaces.

Howden (*Functional Program Testing and Analysis,* McGraw-Hill, 1987) presents a mathematically rigorous discussion that attempts to unify different test case design strategies. Perry (*How to Test Software Packages,* Wiley, 1986) provides practical guidelines and useful checklists for testing purchased software (as well as software developed internally). Miller and Howden (*Software Testing and Validation Techniques,* 2nd edition, IEEE Computer Society Press, 1981) have edited an excellent anthology of early papers on testing.

An excellent source of information on automated tools for software testing is the *Testing Tools Reference Guide* (Software Quality Engineering, Inc., Jacksonville, FL, updated yearly). This directory contains descriptions of hundreds of testing tools, categorized by testing activity, hardware platform, and software support.

The Internet newsgroup **comp.software.testing** contains debate, discussion, and guidelines on all aspects of software testing. The *Testing Techniques Newsletter (TTN),* On-Line Edition, is available via the Internet and is e-mailed monthly. It provides information of general use to the software testing community. For further information, contact: **ttn@soft.com**

Software Testing Laboratories and the Software Testing Institute provide useful information on testing. Information on training and publications can be obtained at:

http://www.stlabs.com/default.htm
http://www.metronet.com/ ~ sarcher/sti/

An archive containing all articles posted to the newsgroup **comp.software.testing** can be found at:

http://tsunami.jpl.nasa.gov/TEL-bin/browse

A database of software testing resources has been developed by Reliable Software Technologies and can be found at:

http://www.rstcorp.com

A variety of publications on software verification and testing can be acquired from:

http://www.rai.com/soft_eng/indexes/svt.html

Bugnet, an online journal of "of computer bugs, glitches, incompatibilities. . . . and their fixes" can be found at:

http://www.pacificrim.net/ ~ bugnet/

An up-to-date list of World Wide Web references for software testing can be found at: **http://www.rspa.com**

SOFTWARE TESTING STRATEGIES

A strategy for software testing integrates software test case design methods into a well-planned series of steps that result in the successful construction of software. As important, a software testing strategy provides a road map for the software developer, the quality assurance organization, and the customer—a road map that describes the steps to be conducted as part of testing, when these steps are planned and then undertaken, and how much effort, time, and resources will be required. Therefore, any testing strategy must incorporate test planning, test case design, test execution, and resultant data collection and evaluation.

A software testing strategy should be flexible enough to promote the creativity and customization that are necessary to adequately test all large software-based systems. At the same time, the strategy must be rigid enough to promote reasonable planning and management tracking as the project progresses. Shooman [SHO83] discusses these issues:

> In many ways, testing is an individualistic process, and the number of different types of tests varies as much as the different development approaches. For many years, our only defense against programming errors was careful design and the native intelligence of the programmer. We are now in an era in which modern design techniques [and formal technical reviews] are helping us to reduce the number of initial errors that are inherent in the code. Similarly, different test methods are beginning to cluster themselves into several distinct approaches and philosophies.

These approaches and philosophies are what we shall call *strategy*. In Chapter 16, the technology of software testing was presented.[1] In this chapter, we focus our attention on the strategy for software testing.

---

[1]Testing for object-oriented systems is discussed in Chapter 22.

17.1   A STRATEGIC APPROACH TO SOFTWARE TESTING

Testing is a set of activities that can be planned in advance and conducted systematically. For this reason a *template* for software testing—a set of steps into which we can place specific test case design methods—should be defined for the software engineering process.

A number of software testing strategies have been proposed in the literature. All provide the software developer with a template for testing, and all have the following generic characteristics:

- Testing begins at the module level[2] and works "outward" toward the integration of the entire computer-based system.
- Different testing techniques are appropriate at different points in time.
- Testing is conducted by the developer of the software and (for large projects) an independent test group.
- Testing and debugging are different activities, but debugging must be accommodated in any testing strategy.

A strategy for software testing must accommodate low-level tests that are necessary to verify that a small source code segment has been correctly implemented as well as high-level tests that validate major system functions against customer requirements. A strategy must provide guidance for the practitioner and a set of milestones for the manager. Because the steps of the test strategy occur at a time when deadline pressure begins to rise, progress must be measurable and problems must surface as early as possible.

17.1.1   Verification and Validation

Software testing is one element of a broader topic that is often referred to as *verification and validation (V&V)*. Verification refers to the set of activities that ensure that software correctly implements a specific function. Validation refers to a different set of activities that ensure that the software that has been built is traceable to customer requirements. Boehm [BOE81] states this another way:

> *Verification:*   "Are we building the product right?"
>
> *Validation:*   "Are we building the right product?"

The definition of V&V encompasses many of the activities that we have referred to as software quality assurance (SQA).

Recall the discussion of software quality in Chapter 8. The activities required to achieve it may be viewed as a set of components depicted in Figure 17.1. Software engineering methods provide the foundation from which quality is built. Analysis, design, and construction (coding) methods act to enhance

---

[2]For object-oriented systems, testing begins at the class or object level. See Chapter 22 for details.

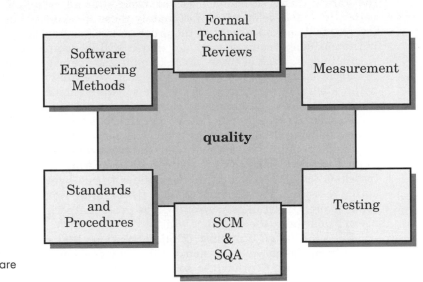

FIGURE 17.1.
Achieving software
quality

quality by providing uniform techniques and predictable results. Formal technical reviews (walkthroughs) help to ensure the quality of work products produced as a consequence of each software engineering step. Throughout the process, measurement and control are applied to every element of a software configuration. Standards and procedures help to ensure uniformity, and a formal SQA process enforces a "total quality philosophy."

Testing provides the last bastion from which quality can be assessed and, more pragmatically, errors can be uncovered. But testing should *not* be viewed as a safety net. As they say, "You can't test in quality. If it's not there before you begin testing, it won't be there when you're finished testing." Quality is incorporated into software throughout the software process. Proper application of methods and tools, effective formal technical reviews, and solid management and measurement all lead to quality that is confirmed during testing.

Miller [MIL77] relates software testing to quality assurance by stating that "the underlying motivation of program testing is to affirm software quality with methods that can be economically and effectively applied to both large-scale and small-scale systems."

It is important to note that verification and validation encompass a wide array of SQA activities that include formal technical reviews, quality and configuration audits, performance monitoring, simulation, feasibility study, documentation review, database review, algorithm analysis, development testing, qualification testing, and installation testing [WAL89]. Although testing plays an extremely important role in V&V, many other activities are also necessary.

17.1.2 Organizing for Software Testing

For every software project, there is an inherent conflict of interest that occurs as testing begins. The people who have built the software are now asked to test the software. This seems harmless in itself: After all, who knows the program better than its developers? Unfortunately, these same developers have a vested interest in demonstrating that the program is error-free, that it works according to customer requirements, and that it will be completed on schedule and within budget. Each of these interests militates against thorough testing.

From a psychological point of view, software analysis and design (along with coding) are *constructive* tasks. The software engineer creates a computer program, its documentation, and related data structures. Like any builder, the software engineer is proud of the edifice that has been built and looks askance at anyone who attempts to tear it down. When testing commences, there is a subtle, yet definite, attempt to "break" the thing that the software engineer has built. From the point of view of the builder, testing can be considered to be (psychologically) *destructive.* So the builder treads lightly, designing and executing tests that will demonstrate that the program works, rather than uncovering errors. Unfortunately, errors will be present. And if the software engineer doesn't find them, the customer will!

There are often a number of misconceptions that can be erroneously inferred from the above discussion: (1) that the developer of software should do no testing at all; (2) that the software should be "tossed over the wall" to strangers who will test it mercilessly; and (3) that testers get involved with the project only when the testing steps are about to begin. Each of these statements is incorrect.

The software developer is always responsible for testing the individual units (modules) of the program, ensuring that each performs the function for which it was designed. In many cases, the developer also conducts *integration testing*—a testing step that leads to the construction (and testing) of the complete program structure. Only after the software architecture is complete does an independent test group become involved.

The role of an *independent test group (ITG)* is to remove the inherent problems associated with letting the builder test the thing that has been built. Independent testing removes the conflict of interest that may otherwise be present. After all, personnel in the independent group team are paid to find errors.

However, the software developer doesn't turn the program over to ITG and walk away. The developer and the ITG work closely throughout a software project to ensure that thorough tests will be conducted. While testing is conducted, the developer must be available to correct errors that are uncovered.

The ITG is part of the software development project team in the sense that it becomes involved during the specification process and stays involved (planning and specifying test procedures) throughout a large project. However, in many cases the ITG reports to the software quality assurance organization, thereby achieving a degree of independence that might not be possible if it were a part of the software development organization.

17.1.3 A Software Testing Strategy

The software engineering process may be viewed as a spiral, illustrated in Figure 17.2. Initially, system engineering defines the role of software and leads to software requirements analysis, where the information domain, function, be-

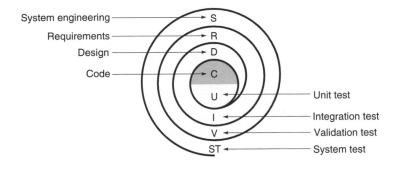

System engineering
Requirements
Design
Code

Unit test
Integration test
Validation test
System test

FIGURE 17.2.

Testing strategy

havior, performance, constraints, and validation criteria for software are established. Moving inward along the spiral, we come to design and finally to coding. To develop computer software, we spiral in along streamlines that decrease the level of abstraction on each turn.

A strategy for software testing may also be viewed in the context of the spiral (Figure 17.2). *Unit testing* begins at the vortex of the spiral and concentrates on each unit of the software as implemented in source code. Testing progresses by moving outward along the spiral to *integration testing,* where the focus is on design and the construction of the software architecture. Taking another turn outward on the spiral, we encounter *validation testing,* where requirements established as part of software requirements analysis are validated against the software that has been constructed. Finally, we arrive at *system testing,* where the software and other system elements are tested as a whole. To test computer software, we spiral out along streamlines that broaden the scope of testing with each turn.

Considering the process from a procedural point of view, testing within the context of software engineering is actually a series of four steps that are implemented sequentially. The steps are shown in Figure 17.3. Initially, tests focus on each module individually, assuring that it functions properly as a unit. Hence, the name *unit testing.* Unit testing makes heavy use of white-box testing techniques, exercising specific paths in a module's control structure to ensure complete coverage and maximum error detection. Next, modules must be assembled or integrated to form the complete software package. *Integration testing* addresses the issues associated with the dual problems of verification and program construction. Black-box test case design techniques are the most prevalent during integration, although a limited amount of white-box testing may be used to ensure coverage of major control paths. After the software has been integrated (constructed), a set of *high-order tests* are conducted. Validation criteria (established during requirements analysis) must be tested. *Validation testing* provides final assurance that software meets all functional, behavioral, and performance requirements. Black-box testing techniques are used exclusively during validation.

The last high-order testing step falls outside the boundary of software engineering and into the broader context of computer system engineering. Software, once validated, must be combined with other system elements (e.g., hardware, people, databases). *System testing* verifies that all elements mesh properly and that overall system function/performance is achieved.

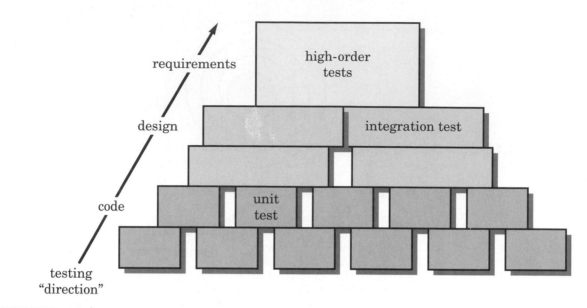

requirements

design

code

testing
"direction"

high-order
tests

integration test

unit
test

FIGURE 17.3. Software testing steps

17.1.4 Criteria for Completion of Testing

A classic question arises every time software testing is discussed: "When are we done testing—how do we know that we've tested enough?" Sadly, there is no definitive answer to this question, but there are a few pragmatic responses and early attempts at empirical guidance.

One response to the above question is this: "You're never done testing, the burden simply shifts from you (the developer) to your customer." Every time the customer/user executes a computer program, the program is being tested on a new set of data. This sobering fact underlines the importance of other software quality assurance activities. Another response (somewhat cynical, but nonetheless accurate) is "You're done testing when you run out of time or you run out of money."

Although few practitioners would argue with these responses, a software engineer needs more rigorous criteria for determining when sufficient testing has been conducted. Musa and Ackerman [MUS89] suggest a response that is based on statistical criteria: "No, we cannot be absolutely certain that the software will never fail, but relative to a theoretically sound and experimentally validated statistical model, we have done sufficient testing to say with 95 percent confidence that the probability of 1000 CPU hours of failure-free operation in a probabilistically defined environment is at least 0.995."

Using statistical modeling and software reliability theory, models of software failures (uncovered during testing) as a function of execution time can be developed [MUS89]. A version of the failure model, called a *logarithmic Poisson execution-time model,* takes the form:

$$f(t) = (1/p)\ln(l_0 pt + 1) \tag{17.1}$$

where $f(t)$ = cumulative number of failures that are expected to occur once the software has been tested for a certain amount of execution time, t,

l_0 = the initial software *failure intensity* (failures per unit time) at the beginning of testing,

p = the exponential reduction in failure intensity as errors are uncovered and repairs are made.

The instantaneous failure intensity, $l(t)$ can be derived by taking the derivative of $f(t)$,

$$l(t) = l_0/(l_0pt + 1) \qquad (17.2)$$

Using the relationship noted in equation (17.2), testers can predict the drop-off of errors as testing progresses. The actual error intensity can be plotted against the predicted curve (Figure 17.4). If the actual data gathered during testing and the logarithmic Poisson execution-time model are reasonably close to one another over a number of data points, the model can be used to predict total testing time required to achieve an acceptably low failure intensity.

By collecting metrics during software testing and making use of existing software reliability models, it is possible to develop meaningful guidelines for answering the question: "When are we done testing?" There is little debate that further work remains to be done before quantitative rules for testing can be established, but the empirical approaches that currently exist are considerably better than raw intuition.

17.2   STRATEGIC ISSUES

Later in this chapter, we explore a systematic strategy for software testing. But even the best strategy will fail if a series on overriding issues are not ad-

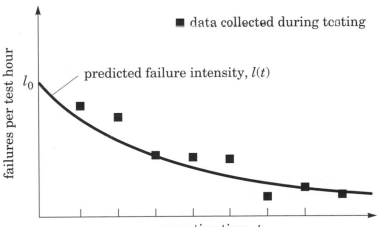

FIGURE 17.4.

Failure intensity as a function of execution time

dressed. Tom Gilb [GIL95] argues that the following issues must be addressed if a successful software testing strategy is to be implemented:

Specify product requirements in a quantifiable manner long before testing commences. Although the overriding objective of testing is to find errors, a good testing strategy also assesses other quality characteristics such as portability, maintainability, and usability (Chapter 18). These should be specified in a way that is measurable so that testing results are unambiguous.

State testing objectives explicitly. The specific objectives of testing should be stated in measurable terms. For example, test effectiveness, test coverage, mean time to failure, the cost to find and fix defects, remaining defect density or frequency of occurrence, and test work-hours per regression test should all be stated within the test plan [GIL95].

Understand the users of the software and develop a profile for each user category. Use cases (Chapter 20), which describe the interaction scenario for each class of user can reduce overall testing effort by focusing testing on actual use of the product.

Develop a testing plan that emphasizes "rapid cycle testing." Gilb [GIL95] recommends that a software engineering team "learn to test in rapid cycles (2 percent of project effort) of customer-useful, at least field 'trialable,' increments of functionality and/or quality improvement." The feedback generated from these rapid cycle tests can be used to control quality levels and the corresponding test strategies.

Build "robust" software that is designed to test itself. Software should be designed in a manner that uses antibugging (Section 17.3.1) techniques. That is, software should be capable of diagnosing certain classes of errors. In addition, the design should accommodate automated testing and regression testing.

Use effective formal technical reviews as a filter prior to testing. Formal technical reviews (Chapter 8) can be as effective as testing in uncovering errors. For this reason, reviews can reduce the amount of testing effort that is required to produce high-quality software.

Conduct formal technical reviews to assess the test strategy and test cases themselves. Formal technical reviews can uncover inconsistencies, omissions, and outright errors in the testing approach. This saves time and also improves product quality.

Develop a continuous improvement approach for the testing process. The test strategy should be measured. The metrics collected during testing should be used as part of a statistical process control approach for software testing.

17.3   UNIT TESTING

Unit testing focuses verification effort on the smallest unit of software design—the module. Using the procedural design description as a guide, important control paths are tested to uncover errors within the boundary of the module. The relative complexity of tests and uncovered errors is limited by the constrained scope established for unit testing. The unit test is normally white-box oriented, and the step can be conducted in parallel for multiple modules.

17.3.1   Unit Test Considerations

The tests that occur as part of unit testing are illustrated schematically in Figure 17.5. The module *interface* is tested to ensure that information properly flows into and out of the program unit under test. The local data structure is examined to ensure that data stored temporarily maintains its integrity during all steps in an algorithm's execution. *Boundary conditions* are tested to ensure that the module operates properly at boundaries established to limit or restrict processing. All independent paths (basis paths) through the control structure are exercised to ensure that all statements in a module have been executed at least once. And finally, all error handling paths are tested.

Tests of data flow across a module interface are required before any other test is initiated. If data do not enter and exit properly, all other tests are moot. In his text on software testing, Myers [MYE79] proposes a checklist for interface tests:

1. Number of input parameters equal to number of arguments?
2. Parameter and argument attributes match?
3. Parameter and argument units systems match?

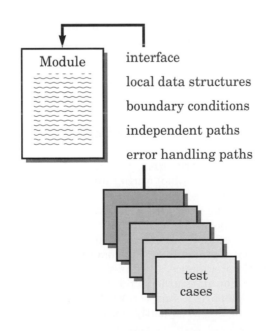

FIGURE 17.5.
Unit test

4. Number of arguments transmitted to called modules equal to number of parameters?

5. Attributes of arguments transmitted to called modules equal to attributes of parameters?

6. Unit system of arguments transmitted to called modules equal to unit system of parameters?

7. Number attributes and order of arguments to built-in functions correct?

8. Any references to parameters not associated with current point of entry?

9. Input-only arguments altered?

10. Global variable definitions consistent across modules?

11. Constraints passed as arguments?

When a module performs external I/O, additional interface tests must be conducted. Again, from Myers [MYE79]:

1. File attributes correct?

2. OPEN/CLOSE statements correct?

3. Format specification matches I/O statement?

4. Buffer size matches record size?

5. Files opened before use?

6. End-of-file conditions handled?

7. I/O errors handled?

8. Any textual errors in output information?

The local data structure for a module is a common source of errors. Test cases should be designed to uncover errors in the following categories:

1. improper or inconsistent typing

2. erroneous initialization or default values

3. incorrect (misspelled or truncated) variable names

4. inconsistent data types

5. underflow, overflow, and addressing exceptions

In addition to local data structures, the impact of global data on a module should be ascertained (if possible) during unit testing.

Selective testing of execution paths is an essential task during the unit test. Test cases should be designed to uncover errors due to erroneous computations, incorrect comparisons, or improper control flow. Basis path and loop testing are effective techniques for uncovering a broad array of path errors.

Among the more common errors in computation are (1) misunderstood or incorrect arithmetic precedence; (2) mixed mode operations; (3) incorrect initialization; (4) precision inaccuracy; and (5) incorrect symbolic representation of an expression. Comparison and control flow are closely coupled to one another (i.e., change of flow frequently occurs after a comparison). Test cases should uncover errors such as (1) comparison of different data types; (2) incorrect logical operators or precedence; (3) expectation of equality when precision error makes equality unlikely; (4) incorrect comparison or variables; (5) improper or nonexistent loop termination; (6) failure to exit when divergent iteration is encountered; and (7) improperly modified loop variables.

Good design dictates that error conditions be anticipated and error handling paths set up to reroute or cleanly terminate processing when an error does occur. Yourdon [YOU75] calls this approach *antibugging*. Unfortunately, there is a tendency to incorporate error handling into software and then never test it. A real-life anecdote may serve to illustrate:

> A major interactive design system was developed under contract. In one transaction processing module, a practical joker placed the following error handling message after a series of conditional tests that invoked various control flow branches: ERROR! THERE IS NO WAY YOU CAN GET HERE. This "error message" was uncovered by a customer during user training!

Among the potential errors that should be tested when error handling is evaluated are:

1. Error description is unintelligible.
2. Error noted does not correspond to error encountered.
3. Error condition causes system intervention prior to error handling.
4. Exception-condition processing is incorrect.
5. Error description does not provide enough information to assist in the location of the cause of the error.

Boundary testing is the last (and probably most important) task of the unit test step. Software often fails at its boundaries. That is, errors often occur when the nth element of an n-dimensional array is processed; when the ith repetition of a loop with i passes is invoked; or when the maximum or minimum allowable value is encountered. Test cases that exercise data structure, control flow, and data values just below, at, and just above maxima and minima are very likely to uncover errors.

17.3.2 Unit Test Procedures

Unit testing is normally considered as an adjunct to the coding step. After source-level code has been developed, reviewed, and verified for correct syntax, unit test case design begins. A review of design information provides guidance for establishing test cases that are likely to uncover errors in each of the categories discussed above. Each test case should be coupled with a set of expected results.

Because a module is not a standalone program, *driver* and/or *stub* software must be developed for each unit test. The unit test environment is illustrated in Figure 17.6. In most applications a driver is nothing more than a "main pro-

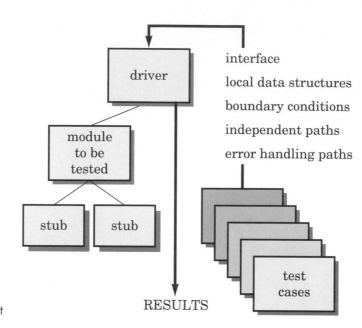

interface

local data structures

boundary conditions

independent paths

error handling paths

RESULTS

FIGURE 17.6.
Unit test environment

gram" that accepts test case data, passes such data to the module (to be tested), and prints relevant results. Stubs serve to replace modules that are subordinate to (called by) the module to be tested. A stub or "dummy subprogram" uses the subordinate module's interface, may do minimal data manipulation, prints verification of entry, and returns.

Drivers and stubs represent overhead. That is, both are software that must be developed but that is not delivered with the final software product. If drivers and stubs are kept simple, actual overhead is relatively low. Unfortunately, many modules cannot be adequately unit tested with "simple" overhead software. In such cases, complete testing can be postponed until the integration test step (where drivers or stubs are also used).

Unit testing is simplified when a module with high cohesion is designed. When only one function is addressed by a module, the number of test cases is reduced and errors can be more easily predicted and uncovered.

17.4   INTEGRATION TESTING[3]

A neophyte in the software world might ask a seemingly legitimate question once all modules have been unit tested: "If they all work individually, why do you doubt that they'll work when we put them together?" The problem, of course, is "putting them together"—interfacing. Data can be lost across an interface; one module can have an inadvertent, adverse affect on another; subfunctions, when combined, may not produce the desired major function; indi-

---

[3]Integration strategies for object-oriented systems are discussed in Chapter 22.

vidually acceptable imprecision may be magnified to unacceptable levels; global data structures can present problems—sadly, the list goes on and on.

Integration testing is a systematic technique for constructing the program structure while conducting tests to uncover errors associated with interfacing. The objective is to take unit tested modules and build a program structure that has been dictated by design.

There is often a tendency to attempt *non-incremental integration;* that is, to construct the program using a "big bang" approach. All modules are combined in advance. The entire program is tested as a whole. And chaos usually results! A set of errors are encountered. Correction is difficult because isolation of causes is complicated by the vast expanse of the entire program. Once these errors are corrected, new ones appear and the process continues in a seemingly endless loop.

Incremental integration is the antithesis of the big bang approach. The program is constructed and tested in small segments, where errors are easier to isolate and correct; interfaces are more likely to be tested completely; and a systematic test approach may be applied. In the sections that follow, a number of different incremental integration strategies are discussed.

17.4.1 Top-Down Integration

Top-down integration is an incremental approach to construction of program structure. Modules are integrated by moving downward through the control hierarchy, beginning with the main control module (main program). Modules subordinate (and ultimately subordinate) to the main control module are incorporated into the structure in either a *depth-first* or *breadth-first* manner.

As shown in Figure 17.7, depth-first integration would integrate all modules on a major control path of the structure. Selection of a major path is somewhat arbitrary and depends on application-specific characteristics. For example, selecting the left hand path, modules M_1, M_2, and M_5 would be integrated

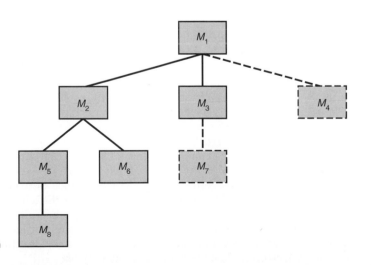

FIGURE 17.7.
Top-down integration

first. Next, M_8 or (if necessary for proper functioning of M_2) M_6 would be integrated. Then, the central and right hand control paths are built. Breadth-first integration incorporates all modules directly subordinate at each level, moving across the structure horizontally. From the figure, modules M_2, M_3, and M_4 would be integrated first. The next control level, M_5, M_6, and so on, follows.

The integration process is performed in a series of five steps:

1. The main control module is used as a test driver, and stubs are substituted for all modules directly subordinate to the main control module.

2. Depending on the integration approach selected (i.e., depth- or breadth-first), subordinate stubs are replaced one at a time with actual modules.

3. Tests are conducted as each module is integrated.

4. On completion of each set of tests, another stub is replaced with the real module.

5. Regression testing (Section 17.4.3) may be conducted to ensure that new errors have not been introduced.

The process continues from step 2 until the entire program structure is built.

The top-down integration strategy verifies major control or decision points early in the test process. In a well-factored program structure, decision making occurs at upper levels in the hierarchy and is therefore encountered first. If major control problems do exist, early recognition is essential. If depth-first integration is selected, a complete function of the software may be implemented and demonstrated. For example, consider a classic transaction structure (Chapter 14) in which a complex series of interactive inputs are requested, acquired, and validated via an incoming path. The incoming path may be integrated in a top-down manner. All input processing (for subsequent transaction dispatching) may be demonstrated before other elements of the structure have been integrated. Early demonstration of functional capability is a confidence builder for both the developer and the customer.

Top-down strategy sounds relatively uncomplicated, but in practice, logistical problems can arise. The most common of these problems occurs when processing at low levels in the hierarchy is required to adequately test upper levels. *Stubs* replace low-level modules at the beginning of top-down testing; therefore, no significant data can flow upward in the program structure. The tester is left with three choices: (1) delay many tests until stubs are replaced with actual modules, (2) develop stubs that perform limited functions that simulate the actual module, or (3) integrate the software from the bottom of the hierarchy upward. Figure 17.8 illustrates typical classes of stubs, ranging from the simplest (stub A) to the most complex (stub D).

The first approach (delay tests until stubs are replaced by actual modules) causes us to lose some control over correspondence between specific tests and incorporation of specific modules. This can lead to difficulty in determining the cause of errors and tends to violate the highly constrained nature of the top-down approach. The second approach is workable, but can lead to significant overhead, as stubs become more and more complex. The third approach, called *bottom-up testing* is discussed in the next section.

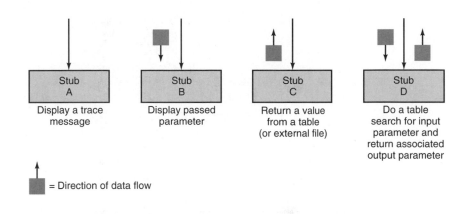

FIGURE 17.8.
Stubs

17.4.2 Bottom-Up Integration

Bottom-up integration testing, as its name implies, begins construction and testing with *atomic modules* (i.e., modules at the lowest levels in the program structure). Because modules are integrated from the bottom up, processing required for modules subordinate to a given level is always available and the need for stubs is eliminated.

A bottom-up integration strategy may be implemented with the following steps:

1. Low-level modules are combined into *clusters* (sometimes called *builds*) that perform a specific software subfunction.
2. A driver (a control program for testing) is written to coordinate test case input and output.
3. The cluster is tested.
4. Drivers are removed and clusters are combined moving upward in the program structure.

Integration follows the pattern illustrated in Figure 17.9. Modules are combined to form clusters 1, 2, and 3. Each of the clusters is tested using a driver (shown as a dashed block). Modules in clusters 1 and 2 are subordinate to M_a. Drivers D_1 and D_2 are removed, and the clusters are interfaced directly to M_a. Similarly, driver D_3 for cluster 3 is removed prior to integration with module M_b. Both M_a and M_b will ultimately be integrated with module M_c, and so forth. Different categories of drivers are illustrated in Figure 17.10.

As integration moves upward, the need for separate test drivers lessens. In fact, if the top two levels of program structure are integrated top-down, the number of drivers can be reduced substantially and integration of clusters is greatly simplified.

17.4.3 Regression Testing

Each time a new module is added as part of integration testing, the software changes. New data flow paths are established, new I/O may occur, and new con-

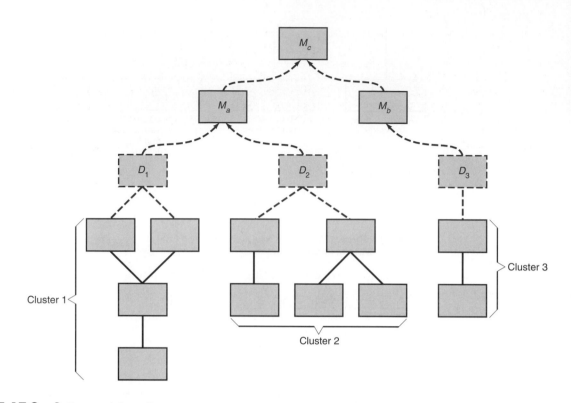

FIGURE 17.9. Bottom-up integration

trol logic is invoked. These changes may cause problems with functions that previously worked flawlessly. In the context of an integration test strategy, *regression testing* is the re-execution of some subset of tests that have already been conducted to ensure that changes have not propagated unintended side effects.

In a broader context, successful tests (of any kind) result in the discovery of errors, and errors must be corrected. Whenever software is corrected, some aspect of the software configuration (the program, its documentation, or the data that support it) is changed. *Regression testing* is the activity that helps to

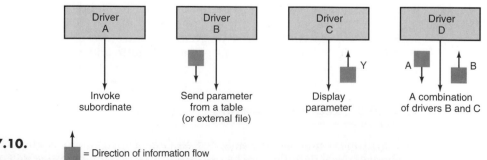

FIGURE 17.10.
Drivers

 = Direction of information flow

ensure that changes (due to testing or for other reasons) do not introduce unintended behavior or additional errors.

Regression testing may be conducted manually, by re-executing a subset of all test cases or using automated capture playback tools. *Capture-playback tools* enable the software engineer to capture test cases and results for subsequent playback and comparison. The regression test suite (the subset of tests to be executed) contains three different classes of test cases:

- A representative sample of tests that will exercise all software functions.
- Additional tests that focus on software functions that are likely to be affected by the change.
- Tests that focus on the software components that have been changed.

As integration testing proceeds, the number of regression tests can grow quite large. Therefore, the regression test suite should be designed to include only those tests that address one or more classes of errors in each of the major program functions. It is impractical and inefficient to re-execute every test for every program function once a change has occurred.

17.4.4 Comments on Integration Testing

There has been much discussion (e.g., [BEI84]) of the relative advantages and disadvantages of top-down versus bottom-up integration testing. In general, the advantages of one strategy tend to result in disadvantages for the other strategy. The major disadvantage of the top-down approach is the need for stubs and the attendant testing difficulties that can be associated with them. Problems associated with stubs may be offset by the advantage of testing major control functions early. The major disadvantage of bottom up integration is that "the program as an entity does not exist until the last module is added" [MYE79]. This drawback is tempered by easier test case design and a lack of stubs.

Selection of an integration strategy depends upon software characteristics and sometimes, project schedule. In general, a combined approach (sometimes called *sandwich testing*) that uses a top-down strategy for upper levels of the program structure, coupled with a bottom-up strategy for subordinate levels may be the best compromise.

As integration testing is conducted, the tester should identify *critical modules*. A critical module has one or more of the following characteristics: (1) addresses several software requirements; (2) has a high level of control (resides relatively high in the program structure); (3) is complex or error-prone (cyclomatic complexity may be used as an indicator); or (4) has definite performance requirements. Critical modules should be tested as early as is possible. In addition, regression tests should focus on critical module function.

17.4.5 Integration Test Documentation

An overall plan for integration of the software and a description of specific tests are documented in a *test specification*. The specification is a deliverable in the

I. Scope of Testing
II. Test Plan
    A. Test phases and builds
    B. Schedule
    C. Overhead software
    D. Environment and resources
III. Test Procedure n (description of test for build n)
    A. Order of integration
        1. purpose
        2. modules to be tested
    B. Unit tests for modules in build
        1. description of test for module n
        2. overhead software description
        3. expected results
    C. Test environment
        1. special tools or techniques
        2. overhead software description
    D. Test case data
    E. Expected results for build n
IV. Actual Test Results
V. References
VI. Appendices

FIGURE 17.11.
Test specification outline

software engineering process and becomes part of the software configuration. Figure 17.11 presents a test specification outline that may be used as a framework for this document.

"Scope of Testing" summarizes specific functional, performance and internal design characteristics that are to be tested. Testing effort is bounded; criteria for completion of each test phase are described; and schedule constraints are documented.

The "Test Plan" section describes the overall strategy for integration. Testing is divided into *phases* and *builds* that address specific functional and behavioral characteristics of the software. For example, integration testing for a computer graphics–oriented CAD system might be divided into the following test phases:

- user interaction (command selection; drawing creation; display representation; error processing and representation)

- data manipulation and analysis (symbol creation; dimensioning; rotation; computation of physical properties)

- display processing and generation (two-dimensional displays; three-dimensional displays; graphs and charts)

- database management (access; update; integrity; performance)

Each of these phases and subphases (denoted in parentheses) delineates a broad functional category within the software and can generally be related to a specific domain of the program structure. Therefore, program builds (groups of modules) are created to correspond to each phase.

The following criteria and corresponding tests are applied for all test phases:

Interface integrity. Internal and external interfaces are tested as each module (or cluster) is incorporated into the structure.

Functional validity. Tests designed to uncover functional errors are conducted.

Information content. Tests designed to uncover errors associated with local or global data structures are conducted.

Performance. Tests designed to verify performance bounds established during software design are conducted.

These criteria and tests associated with them are discussed in this section of the test specification.

A schedule for integration, overhead software, and related topics are also discussed as part of the "Test Plan" section. Start and end dates for each phase are established and availability windows for unit tested modules are defined. A brief description of overhead software (stubs and drivers) concentrates on characteristics that might require special effort. Finally, test environments and resources are described. Unusual hardware configurations, exotic simulators, special test tools or techniques are a few of many topics that may be discussed in this section.

A detailed testing procedure that is required to accomplish the test plan is described in the "Test Procedure" section. In outline item III of the test specification, the order of integration and corresponding tests at each integration step are described. A listing of all test cases (annotated for subsequent reference) and expected results is also included.

A history of actual test results, problems or peculiarities is recorded in the fourth section of the test specification. Information contained in this section can be vital during software maintenance. Appropriate references and appendices are presented in the final two sections.

Like all other elements of a software configuration, test specification format may be tailored to the local needs of a software development organization. It is important to note, however, that an integration strategy, contained in a test plan, and testing details, described in a test procedure, are essential ingredients and must appear.

17.5   VALIDATION TESTING

At the culmination of integration testing, software is completely assembled as a package; interfacing errors have been uncovered and corrected, and a final series of software tests—*validation testing*—may begin. Validation can be defined in many ways, but a simple (albeit harsh) definition is that validation succeeds when software functions in a manner that can be reasonably expected by the customer. At this point a battle-hardened software developer might protest: "Who or what is the arbiter of *reasonable expectations*?"

Reasonable expectations are defined in the software requirements specification—a document (Chapter 12) that describes all user-visible attributes of the software. The specification contains a section titled "Validation Criteria." Information contained in that section forms the basis for a validation testing approach.

17.5.1   Validation Test Criteria

Software validation is achieved through a series of black-box tests that demonstrate conformity with requirements. A test plan outlines the classes of tests to be conducted, and a test procedure defines specific test cases that will be used in an attempt to uncover errors in conformity with requirements. Both the plan and procedure are designed to ensure that all functional requirements are satisfied; all performance requirements are achieved; documentation is correct and human-engineered; and other requirements are met (e.g., transportability, compatibility, error recovery, maintainability).

After each validation test case has been conducted, one of two possible conditions exist: (1) The function or performance characteristics conform to specification and are accepted, or (2) a deviation from specification is uncovered and a deficiency list is created. Deviation or error discovered at this stage in a project can rarely be corrected prior to scheduled completion. It is often necessary to negotiate with the customer to establish a method for resolving deficiencies.

17.5.2   Configuration Review

An important element of the validation process is a *configuration review*. The intent of the review is to ensure that all elements of the software configuration have been properly developed, are catalogued, and have the necessary detail to support the maintenance phase of the software life cycle. The configuration review, sometimes called an *audit*, has been discussed in more detail in Chapter 9.

17.5.3   Alpha and Beta Testing

It is virtually impossible for a software developer to foresee how the customer will *really* use a program. Instructions for use may be misinterpreted; strange combinations of data may be regularly used; and output that seemed clear to the tester may be unintelligible to a user in the field.

When custom software is built for one customer, a series of *acceptance tests* are conducted to enable the customer to validate all requirements. Conducted by the end user rather than the system developer, an acceptance test can range from an informal "test drive" to a planned and systematically executed series of tests. In fact, acceptance testing can be conducted over a period of weeks or months, thereby uncovering cumulative errors that might degrade the system over time.

If software is developed as a product to be used by many customers, it is impractical to perform formal acceptance tests with each one. Most software product builders use a process called *alpha* and *beta testing* to uncover errors that only the end user seems able to find.

The alpha test is conducted at the developer's site by a customer. The software is used in a natural setting with the developer "looking over the shoulder" of the user and recording errors and usage problems. Alpha tests are conducted in a controlled environment.

The beta test is conducted at one or more customer sites by the end user(s) of the software. Unlike alpha testing, the developer is generally not present. Therefore, the beta test is a "live" application of the software in an environment that cannot be controlled by the developer. The customer records all problems (real or imagined) that are encountered during beta testing and reports these to the developer at regular intervals. As a result of problems reported during beta test, the software developer makes modifications and then prepares for release of the software product to the entire customer base.

17.6   SYSTEM TESTING

At the beginning of this book, we stressed the fact that software is only one element of a larger computer-based system. Ultimately, software is incorporated with other system elements (e.g., new hardware, information), and a series of system integration and validation tests are conducted. These tests fall outside the scope of the software engineering process and are not conducted solely by the software developer. However, steps taken during software design and testing can greatly improve the probability of successful software integration in the larger system.

A classic system testing problem is "finger pointing." This occurs when an error is uncovered, and each system element developer blames the other for the problem. Rather than indulging in such nonsense, the software engineer should anticipate potential interfacing problems and (1) design error-handling paths that test all information coming from other elements of the system; (2) conduct a series of tests that simulate bad data or other potential errors at the software interface; (3) record the results of tests to use as "evidence" if finger pointing does occur; and (4) participate in planning and design of system tests to ensure that software is adequately tested.

System testing is actually a series of different tests whose primary purpose is to fully exercise the computer-based system. Although each test has a different purpose, all work to verify that all system elements have been properly integrated and perform allocated functions. In the sections that follow, we discuss the types of system tests [BEI84] that are worthwhile for software-based systems.

17.6.1   Recovery Testing

Many computer-based systems must recover from faults and resume processing within a prespecified time. In some cases, a system must be fault tolerant;

that is, processing faults must not cause overall system function to cease. In other cases, a system failure must be corrected within a specified period of time or severe economic damage will occur.

Recovery testing is a system test that forces the software to fail in a variety of ways and verifies that recovery is properly performed. If recovery is automatic (performed by the system itself), re-initialization, checkpointing mechanisms, data recovery, and restart are each evaluated for correctness. If recovery requires human intervention, the mean time to repair is evaluated to determine whether it is within acceptable limits.

17.6.2   Security Testing

Any computer-based system that manages sensitive information or causes actions that can improperly harm (or benefit) individuals is a target for improper or illegal penetration. Penetration spans a broad range of activities: *hackers* who attempt to penetrate systems for sport; disgruntled employees who attempt to penetrate for revenge; and dishonest individuals who attempt to penetrate for illicit personal gain.

Security testing attempts to verify that protection mechanisms built into a system will in fact protect it from improper penetration. To quote Beizer [BEI84]: "The system's security must, of course, be tested for invulnerability from frontal attack—but must also be tested for invulnerability from flank or rear attack."

During security testing, the tester plays the role(s) of the individual who desires to penetrate the system. Anything goes! The tester may attempt to acquire passwords through external clerical means, may attack the system with custom software designed to break down any defenses that have been constructed; may overwhelm the system, thereby denying service to others; may purposely cause system errors, hoping to penetrate during recovery; may browse through insecure data, hoping to find the key to system entry; and so on.

Given enough time and resources, good security testing will ultimately penetrate a system. The role of the system designer is to make penetration cost greater than the value of the information that will be obtained.

17.6.3   Stress Testing

During earlier software testing steps, white-box and black-box techniques resulted in thorough evaluation of normal program functions and performance. *Stress tests* are designed to confront programs with abnormal situations. In essence, the tester who performs stress testing asks: "How high can we crank this up before it fails?"

Stress testing executes a system in a manner that demands resources in abnormal quantity, frequency, or volume. For example, (1) special tests may be designed that generate 10 interrupts per second, when one or two is the average rate; (2) input data rates may be increased by an order of magnitude to determine how input functions will respond; (3) test cases that require maximum memory or other resources may be executed; (4) test cases that may cause thrashing in a virtual operating system may be designed; or (5) test cases that may cause excessive hunting for disk resident data may be created. Essentially, the tester attempts to break the program.

A variation of stress testing is a technique called *sensitivity testing*. In some situations (the most common occur in mathematical algorithms) a very small range of data contained within the bounds of valid data for a program may cause extreme and even erroneous processing or profound performance degradation. This situation is analogous to a singularity in a mathematical function. Sensitivity testing attempts to uncover data combinations within valid input classes that may cause instability or improper processing.

17.6.4 Performance Testing

For real-time and embedded systems, software that provides required function but does not conform to performance requirements is unacceptable. *Performance testing* is designed to test run-time performance of software within the context of an integrated system. Performance testing occurs throughout all steps in the testing process. Even at the unit level, the performance of an individual module may be assessed as white-box tests are conducted. However, it is not until all system elements are fully integrated that the true performance of a system can be ascertained.

Performance tests are often coupled with stress testing and often require both hardware and software *instrumentation*. That is, it is often necessary to measure resource utilization (e.g., processor cycles) in an exacting fashion. External instrumentation can monitor execution intervals, log events (e.g., interrupts) as they occur, and sample machine states on a regular basis. By instrumenting a system, the tester can uncover situations that lead to degradation and possible system failure.

17.7   THE ART OF DEBUGGING

Software testing is a process that can be systematically planned and specified. Test case design can be conducted, a strategy can be defined, and results can be evaluated against prescribed expectations.

Debugging occurs as a consequence of successful testing. That is, when a test case uncovers an error, debugging is the process that results in the removal of the error. Although debugging can and should be an orderly process, it is still very much an art. A software engineer, evaluating the results of a test, is often confronted with a "symptomatic" indication of a software problem. That is, the external manifestation of the error and the internal cause of the error may have no obvious relationship to one another. The poorly understood mental process that connects a symptom to a cause is debugging.

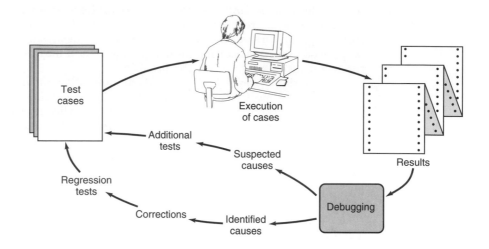

FIGURE 17.12.
Debugging

17.7.1   The Debugging Process

Debugging is *not* testing, but it always occurs as a consequence of testing.[4] As shown in Figure 17.12, the debugging process begins with the execution of a test case. Results are assessed and a lack of correspondence between expected and actual is encountered. In many cases, the non-corresponding data is a symptom of an underlying cause as yet hidden. The debugging process attempts to match symptom with cause, thereby leading to error correction.

The debugging process will always have one of two outcomes: (1) The cause will be found, corrected, and removed, or (2) the cause will not be found. In the latter case, the person performing debugging may suspect a cause, design a test case to help validate his or her suspicion, and work toward error correction in an iterative fashion.

Why is debugging so difficult? In all likelihood, human psychology (see the next section) has more to do with an answer than does software technology. However, a few characteristics of bugs provide some clues:

1. The symptom and the cause may be geographically remote. That is, the symptom may appear in one part of a program, while the cause may actually be located at a site that is far removed. Highly coupled program structures (Chapter 14) exacerbate this situation.

2. The symptom may disappear (temporarily) when another error is corrected.

3. The symptom may actually be caused by nonerrors (e.g., round-off inaccuracies).

4. The symptom may be caused by human error that is not easily traced.

---

[4]In making this statement, we take the broadest possible view of *testing*. Not only does the developer test software prior to release, but the customer/user tests software every time it is used!

5. The symptom may be a result of timing problems, rather than processing problems.

6. It may be difficult to accurately reproduce input conditions (e.g., a real-time application in which input ordering is indeterminate).

7. The symptom may be intermittent. This is particularly common in embedded systems that couple hardware and software inextricably.

8. The symptom may be due to causes that are distributed across a number of tasks running on different processors [CHE90].

During debugging, we encounter errors that range from mildly annoying (e.g., an incorrect output format) to catastrophic (e.g. the system fails, causing serious economic or physical damage). As the consequences of an error increase, the amount of pressure to find the cause also increases. Often, pressure forces a software developer to fix one error and at the same time introduce two more.

17.7.2 Psychological Considerations

Unfortunately, there appears to be some evidence that debugging prowess is an innate human trait. Some people are good at it, and others aren't. Although experimental evidence on debugging is open to many interpretations, large variances in debugging ability have been reported for programmers with the same educational and experiential background.

Commenting on the human aspects of debugging, Shneiderman [SHN80] states:

> Debugging is one of the more frustrating parts of programming. It has elements of problem solving or brain teasers, coupled with the annoying recognition that you have made a mistake. Heightened anxiety, and the unwillingness to accept the possibility of errors, increases the task difficulty. Fortunately, there is a great sigh of relief and a lessening of tension when the bug is ultimately . . . corrected.

Although it may be difficult to "learn" debugging, a number of approaches to the problem can be proposed. We examine these in the next section.

17.7.3 Debugging Approaches

Regardless of the approach that is taken, debugging has one overriding objective: to find and correct the cause of a software error. The objective is realized by a combination of systematic evaluation, intuition, and luck. Bradley [BRA85] describes the debugging approach in this way:

> Debugging is a straightforward application of the scientific method that has been developed over 2,500 years. The basis of debugging is to locate the prob-

lem's source [the cause] by binary partitioning, through working hypotheses that predict new values to be examined.

Take a simple non-software example: A lamp in my house does not work. If nothing in the house works, the cause must be in the main circuit breaker or outside; I look around to see whether the neighborhood is blacked out. I plug the suspect lamp into a working socket and a working appliance into the suspect circuit. So goes the alternation of hypothesis and test.

In general, three categories for debugging approaches may be proposed [MYE79]:

- brute force
- backtracking
- cause elimination

The *brute force* category of debugging is probably the most common and least efficient method for isolating the cause of a software error. We apply brute force debugging methods when all else fails. Using a "let the computer find the error" philosophy, memory dumps are taken, run-time traces are invoked, and the program is loaded with WRITE statements. We hope that somewhere in the morass of information that is produced we will find a clue that can lead us to the cause of an error. Although the mass of information produced may ultimately lead to success, it more frequently leads to wasted effort and time. Thought must be expended first!

Backtracking is a fairly common debugging approach that can be used successfully in small programs. Beginning at the site where a symptom has been uncovered, the source code is traced backward (manually) until the site of the cause is found. Unfortunately, as the number of source lines increases, the number of potential backward paths may become unmanageably large.

The third approach to debugging—*cause elimination*—is manifested by induction or deduction and introduces the concept of *binary partitioning*. Data related to the error occurrence are organized to isolate potential causes. A "cause hypothesis" is devised and the data are used to prove or disprove the hypothesis. Alternatively, a list of all possible causes is developed and tests are conducted to eliminate each. If initial tests indicate that a particular cause hypothesis shows promise, the data are refined in an attempt to isolate the bug.

Each of the above debugging approaches can be supplemented with debugging tools. We can apply a wide variety of debugging compilers, dynamic debugging aids ("tracers"), automatic test case generators, memory dumps, and cross-reference maps. However, tools are not a substitute for careful evaluation based on a complete software design document and clear source code.

Any discussion of debugging approaches and tools is incomplete without mention of a powerful ally: other people! Each of us can recall puzzling for hours or days over a persistent bug. A colleague wanders by and in desperation we explain the problem and throw open the listing. Instantaneously (it seems), the cause of the error is uncovered. Smiling smugly, our colleague wanders off. A fresh viewpoint, unclouded by hours of frustration, can do wonders. A final maxim for debugging might be: "When all else fails, get help!"

Once a bug has been found, it must be corrected. But as we have already noted, the correction of a bug can introduce other errors and therefore do more harm than good. Van Vleck [VAN89] suggests three simple questions that every software engineer should ask before making the "correction" that removes the cause of a bug:

1. *Is the cause of the bug reproduced in another part of the program?* In many situations, a program error is caused by an erroneous pattern of logic that may be reproduced elsewhere. Explicit consideration of the logical pattern may result in the discovery of other errors.

2. *What "next bug" might be introduced by the fix I'm about to make?* Before the correction is made, the source code (or better, the design) should be evaluated to assess coupling of logic and data structures. If the correction is to be made in a highly coupled section of the program, special care must be taken when any change is made.

3. *What could we have done to prevent this bug in the first place?* This question is the first step toward establishing a statistical software quality assurance approach (Chapter 8). If we correct the process as well as the product, the bug will be removed from the current program *and* may be eliminated from all future programs.

17.8   SUMMARY

Software testing accounts for the largest percentage of technical effort in the software process. Yet we are only beginning to understand the subtleties of systematic test planning, execution and control.

The objective of software testing is to uncover errors. To fulfill this objective, a series of test steps—unit, integration, validation, and system tests—are planned and executed. Unit and integration tests concentrate on functional verification of a module and incorporation of modules into a program structure. Validation testing demonstrates traceability to software requirements, and system testing validates software once it has been incorporated into a larger system.

Each test step is accomplished through a series of systematic test techniques that assist in the design of test cases. With each testing step, the level of abstraction with which software is considered is broadened.

Unlike testing (a systematic, planned activity), debugging must be viewed as an art. Beginning with a symptomatic indication of a problem, the debugging activity tracks down the cause of an error. Of the many resources available during debugging, the most valuable is the counsel of other software engineers.

The requirement for higher-quality software demands a more systematic approach to testing. To quote Dunn and Ullman [DUN82]:

What is required is an overall strategy, spanning the strategic test space, quite as deliberate in its methodology as was the systematic development on which analysis, design and code were based.

In this chapter, we have examined the "strategic test space," considering the steps that have the highest likelihood of meeting the overriding test objective: to find and remove errors in an orderly and effective manner.

REFERENCES

[BEI84]   Beizer, B., *Software System Testing and Quality Assurance,* Van Nostrand Reinhold, 1984.

[BOE81]   Boehm, B., *Software Engineering Economics,* Prentice-Hall, 1981, p. 37.

[BRA85]   Bradley, J.H., "The Science and Art of Debugging," *Computerworld,* August 19, 1985, pp. 35–38.

[BRO73]   Brown, A., and W. Sampson, *Programming Debugging,* American Elsevier, New York, 1973.

[CHE90]   Cheung, W.H., J.P. Black, and E. Manning, "A Framework for Distributed Debugging," *IEEE Software,* January 1990, pp. 106–115.

[DUN82]   Dunn, R., and R. Ullman, *Quality Assurance for Computer Software,* McGraw-Hill, 1982, p. 158.

[GIL95]   Gilb, T., "What We Fail To Do In Our Current Testing Culture," *Testing Techniques Newsletter,* (on-line edition, **ttn@soft.com**), Software Research, Inc., San Francisco, January 1995.

[MIL77]   Miller, E., "The Philosophy of Testing," in *Program Testing Techniques,* IEEE Computer Society Press, 1977, pp. 1–3.

[MUS89]   Musa, J.D., and Ackerman, A.F., "Quantifying Software Validation: When to Stop Testing?" *IEEE Software,* May 1989, pp. 19–27.

[MYE79]   Myers, G., *The Art of Software Testing,* Wiley, 1979.

[SHO83]   Shooman, M.L., *Software Engineering,* McGraw-Hill, 1983.

[SHN80]   Shneiderman, B., *Software Psychology,* Winthrop Publishers, 1980, p. 28.

[VAN89]   Van Vleck, T., "Three Questions About Each Bug You Find," *ACM Software Engineering Notes,* vol. 14, no. 5, July 1989, pp. 62–63.

[WAL89]   Wallace, D.R., and R.U. Fujii, "Software Verification and Validation: An Overview," *IEEE Software,* May 1989, pp. 10–17.

[YOU75]   Yourdon, E., *Techniques of Program Structure and Design,* Prentice-Hall, 1975.

PROBLEMS AND POINTS TO PONDER

17.1. Using your own words, describe the difference between verification and validation. Do both make use of test case design methods and testing strategies?

17.2. List some problems that might be associated with the creation of an independent test group. Are an ITG and an SQA group made up of the same people?

17.3. Is it always possible to develop a strategy for testing software that uses the sequence of testing steps described in section 17.1.3? What are possible complications that might arise for embedded systems?

17.4. If you could only select three test case design methods to apply during unit testing, what would they be and why?

17.5. Add at least three additional questions to each segment of the unit test checklist presented in Section 17.3.1.

17.6. The concept of "antibugging" (Section 17.3.1) is an extremely effective way to provide built-in debugging assistance when an error is uncovered.
a. Develop a set of guidelines for antibugging.
b. Discuss advantages of using the technique.
c. Discuss disadvantages.

17.7. Develop an integration testing strategy for the any one of the systems implemented in problems 14.23 through 14.31. Define test phases, note the order of integration, specify additional test software, and justify your order of integration. Assume that all modules have been unit tested and are available. [Note: it may be necessary to do a bit of design work first.]

17.8. How can project scheduling affect integration testing?

17.9. Is unit testing possible or even desirable in all circumstances? Provide examples to justify your answer.

17.10. Who should perform the validation test—the software developer or the software user? Justify your answer.

17.11. Develop a complete test strategy for the SafeHome system discussed earlier in this book. Document it in a test specification.

17.12. As a class project, develop a debugging guide for your installation. The guide should provide language and system oriented hints that have been learned through the school of hard knocks! Begin with an outline of topics that will be reviewed by the class and your instructor. Publish the guide for others in your local environment.

FURTHER READINGS AND OTHER INFORMATION RESOURCES

A detailed discussion on testing strategies can be found in books by Kit (*Software Testing in the Real World,* Addison-Wesley, 1995), Evans (*Productive Software Test Management,* Wiley-Interscience, 1984), Hetzel (*The Complete Guide to Software Testing,* QED Information Sciences, 1984), Beizer [BEI84], Ould and Unwin (*Testing in Software Development,* Cambridge University Press, 1986), Marks (*Testing Very Big Systems,* McGraw-Hill, 1992), and Kaner et al. (*Testing Computer Software,* 2nd edition, Van Nostrand Reinhold, 1993). Each delineates the steps of an effective strategy, provides a set of techniques and guidelines and suggests procedures for controlling and tracking the testing process. Hutcheson (*Software Testing Methods and Metrics,* McGraw-Hill, 1996) presents testing methods and strategies but also provides a detailed discussion of how measurement can be used to achieve efficient testing.

For individuals that build product software, Gunther's book (*Management Methodology for Software Product Engineering,* Wiley-Interscience, 1978) remains a useful guide for the establishment and conduct of effective test strategies. In addition, Perry (*How to Test Software Packages,* Wiley, 1986) provides useful information for both the product builder and the purchaser. Mosley (*Real World Issues in Client-Server Software Testing,* Prentice-Hall, 1996) addresses strategies and techniques for testing client/server based applications.

Guidelines for debugging are contained in a book by Dunn (*Software Defect Removal,* McGraw-Hill, 1984). Beizer [BEI84] presents an interesting "taxonomy of bugs" that can lead to effective methods for test planning. McConnell (*Code Complete,* Microsoft Press, 1993) presents pragmatic advice on unit and integration testing as well as debugging.

Internet sources for software testing are presented in the "Further Readings and Other Information Resources" sections of Chapters 16 and 22.

CHAPTER 18

TECHNICAL METRICS FOR SOFTWARE

A key element of any engineering process is measurement. We use measures to better understand the attributes of the models that we create. But most important, we use measurement to assess the quality of the engineered products or systems that we build.

Unlike other engineering disciplines, software engineering is not grounded in the basic quantitative laws of physics. Absolute measures, such as voltage, mass, velocity, or temperature, are uncommon in the software world. Instead, we attempt to derive a set of indirect measures that lead to metrics that provide an indication of the quality of some representation of software. Because software measures and metrics are not absolute, they are open to debate. Fenton [FEN91] addresses this issue when he states:

> Measurement is the process by which numbers or symbols are assigned to the attributes of entities in the real world in such a way as to define them according to clearly defined rules. . . .
>
> In the physical sciences, medicine, economics, and more recently the social sciences, we are now able to measure attributes that we previously thought to be unmeasurable. . . . Of course, such measurements are not as refined as many measurements in the physical sciences. . . , but they exist [and important decisions are made based on them]. We feel that the obligation to attempt to "measure the unmeasurable" in order to improve our understanding of particular entities is as powerful in software engineering as in any discipline.

But some members of the software community continue to argue that software is unmeasurable or that attempts at measurement should be postponed until we better understand software and the attributes that should be used to describe it. This is a mistake.

Although technical metrics for computer software are not absolute, they provide us with a systematic way to assess quality based on a set of "clearly defined rules." They also provide the software engineer with on-the-spot rather than after-the-fact insight. This enables the engineer to discover and correct potential problems before they become catastrophic defects.

In Chapter 4 we discussed software metrics as they are applied at the process and project level. In this chapter, our focus shifts to measures that can be used to assess the quality of the product as it is being engineered. These measures of internal product attributes provide the software engineer with a real-time indication of the efficacy of the analysis, design, and code models; the effectiveness of test cases; and the overall quality of the software to be built.

18.1   SOFTWARE QUALITY

Even the most jaded software developers will agree that high-quality software is an important goal. But how do we define quality? A wag once said, "Every program does something right, it just may not be the thing that we want it to do."

In Chapter 8 we proposed a number of different ways to look at software quality and introduced a definition that stressed conformance to explicitly stated functional and performance requirements, explicitly documented development standards, and implicit characteristics that are expected of all professionally developed software.

There is little question that the above definition could be modified or extended and debated endlessly. For the purposes of this book, the definition serves to emphasize three important points:

1. Software requirements are the foundation from which quality is measured. Lack of conformance to requirements is lack of quality.[1]

2. Specified standards define a set of development criteria that guide the manner in which software is engineered. If the criteria are not followed, lack of quality will almost surely result.

3. There is a set of *implicit requirements* that often goes unmentioned (e.g., the desire for good maintainability). If software conforms to its explicit requirements, but fails to meet implicit requirements, software quality is suspect.

Software quality is a complex mix of factors that will vary across different applications and the customers who request them. In the sections that follow, software quality factors are identified and the human activities required to achieve them are described.

---

[1] It is important to note that quality extends to the technical attributes of the analysis, design, and code models. Models that exhibit high quality (in the technical sense) will lead to software that exhibits high quality from the customer's point of view.

18.1.1 McCall's Quality Factors

The factors that affect software quality can be categorized in two broad groups: (1) factors that can be directly measured (e.g., defects per function point) and (2) factors that can be measured only indirectly (e.g., usability or maintainability). In each case *measurement* must occur. We must compare the software (documents, programs, data) to some datum and arrive at an indication of quality.

McCall and his colleagues [MCC77] proposed a useful categorization of factors that affect software quality. These *software quality factors,* shown in Figure 18.1, focus on three important aspects of a software product: its operational characteristics, its ability to undergo change, and its adaptability to new environments.

Referring to the factors noted in Figure 18.1, McCall provides the following descriptions:

Correctness. The extent to which a program satisfies its specification and fulfills the customer's mission objectives.

Reliability. The extent to which a program can be expected to perform its intended function with required precision. It should be noted that other, more complete, definitions of reliability have been proposed (see Chapter 8).

Efficiency. The amount of computing resources and code required by a program to perform its function.

Integrity. The extent to which access to software or data by unauthorized persons can be controlled.

Usability. The effort required to learn, operate, prepare input, and interpret output of a program.

Maintainability. The effort required to locate and fix an error in a program. (This is a very limited definition.)

Flexibility. The effort required to modify an operational program.

Testability. The effort required to test a program to ensure that it performs its intended function.

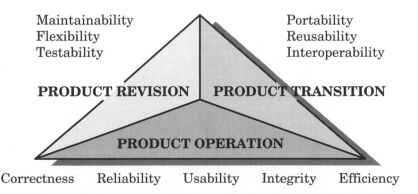

FIGURE 18.1.
McCall's software
quality factors

Portability. The effort required to transfer the program from one hardware and/or software system environment to another.

Reusability. The extent to which a program [or parts of a program] can be reused in other applications—related to the packaging and scope of the functions that the program performs.

Interoperability. The effort required to couple one system to another.

It is difficult, and in some cases impossible, to develop direct measures of the above quality factors. Therefore, a set of metrics are defined and used to develop expressions for each of the factors according to the following relationship:

$$F_q = c_1 \times m_1 + c_2 \times m_2 + \cdots + c_n \times m_n$$

where F_q is a software quality factor, c_n are regression coefficients, and m_n are the metrics that affect the quality factor. Unfortunately, many of the metrics defined by McCall can only be measured subjectively. The metrics may be in the form of a checklist that is used to "grade" specific attributes of the software [CAV78]. The grading scheme proposed by McCall is a 0 (low) to 10 (high) scale. The following metrics are used in the grading scheme:

Audibility. The ease with which conformance to standards can be checked.

Accuracy. The precision of computations and control.

Communication commonality. The degree to which standard interfaces, protocols, and bandwidth are used.

Completeness. The degree to which full implementation of required function has been achieved.

Conciseness. The compactness of the program in terms of lines of code.

Consistency. The use of uniform design and documentation techniques throughout the software development project.

Data commonality. The use of standard data structures and types throughout the program.

Error tolerance. The damage that occurs when the program encounters an error.

Execution efficiency. The run-time performance of a program.

Expandability. The degree to which architectural, data, or procedural design can be extended.

Generality. The breadth of potential application of program components.

Hardware independence. The degree to which the software is decoupled from the hardware on which it operates.

Instrumentation. The degree to which the program monitors its own operation and identifies errors that do occur.

Modularity. The functional independence (Chapter 13) of program components.

Operability. The ease of operation of a program.

Security. The availability of mechanisms that control or protect programs and data.

Self-documentation. The degree to which the source code provides meaningful documentation.

Simplicity. The degree to which a program can be understood without difficulty.

Software system independence. The degree to which the program is independent of nonstandard programming language features, operating system characteristics, and other environmental constraints.

Traceability. The ability to trace a design representation or actual program component back to requirements.

Training. The degree to which the software assists in enabling new users to apply the system.

The relationship between software quality factors and the metrics listed above is shown in Figure 18.2. It should be noted that the weight given to each metric depends on local products and concerns.

18.1.2 FURPS

The quality factors described by McCall and his colleagues [MCC77] represent one of a number of suggested "checklists" for software quality. Hewlett-Packard [GRA87] has developed a set of software quality factors that has been given the acronym FURPS—functionality, usability, reliability, performance, and supportability. The FURPS quality factors draw liberally from earlier work, defining the following attributes for each of the five major factors:

- *Functionality* is assessed by evaluating the feature set and capabilities of the program, the generality of the functions that are delivered, and the security of the overall system.

- *Usability* is assessed by considering human factors (Chapter 14), overall aesthetics, consistency, and documentation.

- *Reliability* is evaluated by measuring the frequency and severity of failure, the accuracy of output results, the mean time between failures (MTBF), the ability to recover from failure, and the predictability of the program.

- *Performance* is measured by processing speed, response time, resource consumption, throughput, and efficiency.

- *Supportability* combines the ability to extend the program (extensibility), adaptability, and serviceability (these three attributes represent a more common term—*maintainability*), as well as testability, compatibility, configurability [the ability to organize and control elements of the software configuration (Chapter 9)], the ease with which a system can be installed, and the ease with which problems can be localized.

The FURPS quality factors and attributes described above can be used to establish quality metrics for each activity in the software process.

Quality factor \ Software quality metric	Correctness	Reliability	Efficiency	Integrity	Maintainability	Flexibility	Testability	Portability	Reusability	Interoperability	Usability
Auditability				x			x				
Accuracy		x									
Communication commonality										x	
Completeness	x										
Complexity		x				x	x				
Concision			x		x	x					
Consistency	x	x			x	x					
Data commonality										x	
Error tolerance		x									
Execution efficiency			x								
Expandability						x					
Generality						x		x	x	x	
Hardware Indep.								x	x		
Instumentation				x	x		x				
Modularity		x			x	x	x	x	x	x	
Operability			x								x
Security				x							
Self documentation					x	x	x	x	x		
Simplicity		x			x	x	x				
System Indep.								x	x		
Traceability	x										
Training											x

FIGURE 18.2.
Quality factors and metrics

(Adapted from Arthur, L. A., *Measuring Programmer Productivity and Software Quality*, Wiley-Interscience, 1985.)

18.1.3   The Transition to a Quantitative View

In the preceding sections, a set of qualitative factors for the "measurement" of software quality were discussed. We strive to develop precise measures for software quality and are sometimes frustrated by the subjective nature of the activity. Cavano and McCall [CAV78] discuss this situation:

> The determination of quality is a key factor in everyday events—wine tasting contests, sporting events [e.g., gymnastics], talent contests, etc. In these situations, quality is judged in the most fundamental and direct manner: side by side comparison of objects under identical conditions and with predetermined concepts. The wine may be judged according to clarity, color, bouquet, taste, etc. However, this type of judgement is very subjective; to have any value at all, it must be made by an expert.

Subjectivity and specialization also apply to determining software quality. To help solve this problem, a more precise definition of software quality is needed as well as a way to derive quantitative measurements of software quality for objective analysis. . . . Since there is no such thing as absolute knowledge, one should not expect to measure software quality exactly, for every measurement is partially imperfect. Jacob Bronkowski described this paradox of knowledge in this way: "Year by year we devise more precise instruments with which to observe nature with more fineness. And when we look at the observations we are discomfited to see that they are still fuzzy, and we feel that they are as uncertain as ever."

In the sections that follow, we examine a set of software metrics that can be applied to the quantitative assessment of software quality. In all cases, the metrics represent indirect measures; that is, we never really measure *quality* but rather some manifestation of quality. The complicating factor is the precise relationship between the variable that is measured and the quality of software.

18.2   A FRAMEWORK FOR TECHNICAL SOFTWARE METRICS

As we noted in the introduction to this chapter, measurement assigns numbers or symbols to attributes of entities in the real world. To accomplish this, a measurement model encompassing a consistent set of rules is required. Although the theory of measurement (e.g., [KYB84]) and its application to computer software (e.g., [DEM81], [BRI96]) are topics that are beyond the scope of this book, it is worthwhile to establish a fundamental framework and a set of basic principles for the measurement of technical metrics for software.

18.2.1   The Challenge of Technical Metrics

Over the past two decades, many researchers have attempted to develop a single metric that provides a comprehensive measure of software complexity. Fenton [FEN94] characterizes this research as a search for "the impossible holy grail." Although dozens of complexity measures have been proposed [ZUS90], each takes a somewhat different view of what complexity is and what attributes of a system lead to complexity. By analogy, consider a metric for evaluating an attractive car. Some observers might emphasize body design, others might consider mechanical characteristics, still others might tout cost, or performance, or fuel economy, or the ability to recycle when the car is junked. Since any one of these characteristics may be at odds with others, it is difficult to derive a single value for "attractiveness." The same problem occurs for computer software.

Yet there is a need to measure and control software complexity. And if a single value of this "quality metric" is difficult to derive, it should be possible to develop measures of different internal program attributes (e.g., effective modularity, functional independence, and other attributes discussed in Chapter 13). These measures and the metrics derived from them can be used as independent indicators of the quality of analysis and design models. But here again, problems arise. Fenton [FEN94] notes this when he states:

> The danger of attempting to find measures which characterize so many different attributes is that inevitably the measures have to satisfy conflicting aims. This is counter to the representational theory of measurement.

Although Fenton's statement is correct, many people argue that technical measurement conducted during the early stages of the software process provides software engineers with a consistent and objective mechanism for assessing quality.

It is fair to ask, however, just how valid technical metrics are. That is, how closely aligned are technical metrics to the long-term reliability and quality of a computer-based system? Fenton [FEN91] addresses this question in the following way:

> In spite of the intuitive connections between the internal structure of software products [technical metrics] and its external product and process attributes, there have actually been very few scientific attempts to establish specific relationships. There are a number of reasons why this is so; the most commonly cited is the impracticality of conducting relevant experiments.

Each of the challenges noted above is a cause for caution, but it is not reason to dismiss technical metrics.[2] Measurement is essential if quality is to be achieved.

18.2.2 Measurement Principles

Before we introduce a series of technical metrics that (1) assist in the evaluation of the analysis and design models, (2) provide an indication of the complexity of procedural designs and source code, and (3) facilitate the design of more effective testing, it is important to understand basic measurement principles. Roche [ROC94] suggests a measurement process that can be characterized by five activities:

- *formulation*—the derivation of software measures and metrics that are appropriate for the representation of software that is being considered
- *collection*—the mechanism used to accumulate data required to derive the formulated metrics

---

[2]A vast literature on software metrics (e.g., see [FEN94], [ROC94] for extensive bibliographies) has been spawned, and criticism of specific metrics (including some of those presented in this chapter) is common. However, many of the critiques focus on esoteric issues and miss the primary objective of measurement in the real world: to help the engineer establish a systematic and objective way to gain insight into his or her work and to improve product quality as a result.

- *analysis*—the computation of metrics and the application of mathematical tools
- *interpretation*—the evaluation of metrics results in an effort to gain insight into the quality of the representation
- *feedback*—recommendations derived from the interpretation of technical metrics transmitted to the software team

The principles that can be associated with the formulation of technical metrics are these [ROC94]:

- The objectives of measurement should be established before data collection begins.
- Each technical metric should be defined in an unambiguous manner.
- Metrics should be derived based on a theory that is valid for the domain of application (e.g., metrics for design should draw upon basic design concepts and principles, and should attempt to provide an indication of the presence of an attribute that is deemed desirable).
- Metrics should be tailored to best accommodate specific products and processes [BAS84].

Although formulation is a critical starting point, collection and analysis are the activities that drive the measurement process. Roche [ROC94] suggests the following principles for these activities:

- Whenever possible, data collection and analysis should be automated.
- Valid statistical techniques should be applied to establish relationships between internal product attributes and external quality characteristics (e.g., is the level of architectural complexity correlated with the number of defects reported in production use?).
- Interpretative guidelines and recommendations should be established for each metric.

In addition to the principles noted above, the success of a metrics activity is also tied to management support. Funding, training, and promotion must all be considered if a technical measurement program is to be established and sustained.

18.2.3 The Attributes of Effective Software Metrics

Hundreds of metrics have been proposed for computer software, but not all provide practical support to the software engineer. Some demand measurement that is too complex, others are so esoteric that few real-world professionals have any hope of understanding them, and others violate the basic intuitive notions of what high-quality software really is.

Ejiogu [EJI91] defines a set of attributes that should be encompassed by effective software metrics. The derived metric and the measures that lead to it should be:

- *simple and computable*. It should be relatively easy to learn how to derive the metric, and its computation should not demand inordinate effort or time.
- *empirically and intuitively persuasive*. The metric should satisfy the engineer's intuitive notions about the product attribute under consideration (e.g., a metric that measures module cohesion should increase in value as the level of cohesion increases).
- *consistent and objective*. The metric should always yield results that are unambiguous. An independent third party should be able to derive the same metric value using the same information about the software.
- *consistent in its use of units and dimensions*. The mathematical computation of the metric should use measures that do not lead to bizarre combinations of units. For example, multiplying people on the project teams by programming language variables in the program results in a suspicious mix of units that are not intuitively persuasive.
- *programming language independent*. Metrics should be based on the analysis model, the design model, or the structure of the program itself. They should not depend on the vagaries of programming language syntax or semantics.
- *an effective mechanism for quality feedback*. The metric should provide a software engineer with information that can lead to a higher quality end product.

Although most software metrics satisfy the above attributes, some commonly used metrics may fail to satisfy one or two. An example is the function point (discussed in Chapter 4 and again in this chapter). It can be argued[3] that the *consistent and objective* attribute fails because an independent third party may not be able to derive the same function point value as a colleague using the same information about the software. Should we therefore reject the FP measure? The answer is "of course not!" FP provides useful insight and therefore provides distinct value, even if it fails to satisfy one attribute perfectly.

18.3   METRICS FOR THE ANALYSIS MODEL

Technical work in software engineering begins with the creation of the analysis model.[4] It is at this stage that requirements are derived and that a foundation for design is established. Therefore, technical metrics that provide insight into the quality of the analysis model are desirable.

Although relatively few analysis and specification metrics have appeared in the literature, it is possible to adapt metrics derived for project application (Chapter 4) for use in this context. These metrics examine the analysis model

---

[3]Please note that an equally vigorous counterargument can also be made. Such is the nature of software metrics.

[4]The analysis model encompasses representations of data, function, and behavior. For additional information, see Chapters 11 and 12.

with the intent of predicting the "size" of the resultant system. It is likely that size and design complexity will be directly correlated.

18.3.1 Function-Based Metrics

The function point (FP) metric (Chapter 4) can be used as a means for predicting the size of a system that will be derived from the analysis model. To illustrate the use of the FP metric in this context, we consider a simple analysis model representation illustrated in Figure 18.3. In the figure, a data flow diagram (Chapter 12) for a function within the SafeHome software[5] is represented. The function manages user interaction, accepting a user password to activate/deactivate the system and allowing inquiries on the status of security zones and various security sensors. The function displays a series of prompting messages and sends appropriate control signals to various components of the security system.

The data flow diagram is evaluated to determine the key measures required for computation of the function point metric (Chapter 4):

- number of user inputs
- number of user outputs
- number of user inquiries
- number of files
- number of external interfaces

---

[5]SafeHome is a home security system that has been used as an example application in earlier chapters.

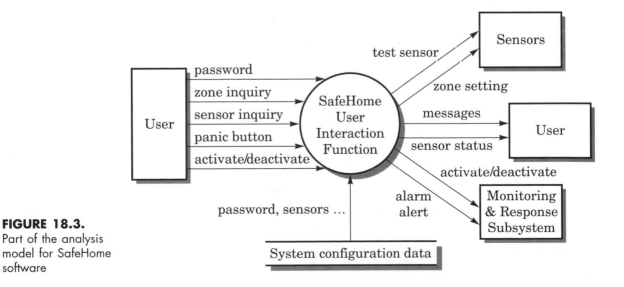

FIGURE 18.3.
Part of the analysis model for SafeHome software

Three user inputs: **password, panic button,** and **activate/deactivate** are shown in the figure along with two inquires: **zone inquiry** and **sensor inquiry.** One file (**system configuration file**) is shown. Two user outputs (**messages** and **sensor status**) and four external interfaces (**test sensor, zone setting, activate/deactivate,** and **alarm alert**) are also present. These data, along with the appropriate complexity, are shown in Figure 18.3.

The *count-total* shown in Figure 18.4 must be adjusted using equation (4.1):

$$FP = \text{count-total} \times (0.65 + 0.01 \times \Sigma\, F_i)$$

where count-total is the sum of all FP entries obtained from Figure 18.3 and F_i (i = 1 to 14) are "complexity adjustment values." For the purposes of this example, we assume that $\Sigma\, F_i$ is 46 (a moderately complex product). Therefore,

$$FP = 50 \times [0.65 + (0.01 \times 46)] = 56$$

Based on the projected FP value derived from the analysis model, the project team can estimate the overall implemented size of the SafeHome user interaction function. Assume that past data indicate that one FP translates into 60 lines of code (an object-oriented language is to be used) and that 12 FP are produced for each person-month of effort. These historical data provide the project manager with important planning information that is based on the analysis model rather than preliminary estimates.

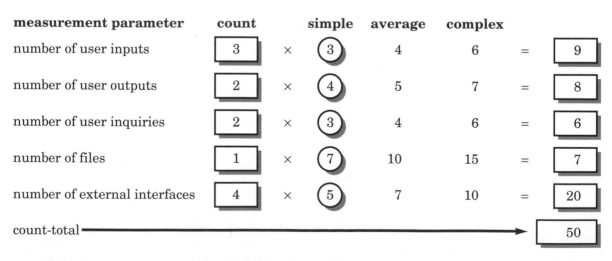

Weighting Factor

measurement parameter	count		simple	average	complex		
number of user inputs	3	×	3	4	6	=	9
number of user outputs	2	×	4	5	7	=	8
number of user inquiries	2	×	3	4	6	=	6
number of files	1	×	7	10	15	=	7
number of external interfaces	4	×	5	7	10	=	20
count-total							50

FIGURE 18.4. Computing function-points: SafeHome *user interaction* function

18.3.2 The Bang Metric

Like the function point metric, the *bang metric* can be used to develop an indication of the size of the software to be implemented as a consequence of the analysis model. Developed by Tom DeMarco [DEM82], the bang metric is "an implementation independent indication of system size." To compute the bang metric, the software engineer must first evaluate a set of *primitives*—elements of the analysis model that are not further subdivided at the analysis level. Primitives [DEM82] are determined by evaluating the analysis model and developing counts for the following items[6]:

Functional primitives (FuP). Transformations (bubbles) that appear at the lowest level of a data flow diagram (Chapter 12).

Data elements (DE). The attributes of a data object, data elements are *not* composite data and appear within the data dictionary.

Objects (OB). Data objects as described in Chapter 11.

Relationships (RE). The connections between data objects as described in Chapter 12.

States (ST). The number of user observable states in the state-transition diagram (Chapter 12).

Transitions (TR). The number of state transitions in the state-transition diagram (Chapter 12).

In addition to the six primitives noted above, the additional counts are determined for:

Modified manual function primitives (FuPM). Functions that lie outside the system boundary and that must be modified to accommodate the new system.

Input data elements (DEI). Those data elements that are input to the system.

Output data elements (DEO). Those data elements that are output from the system.

Retained data elements (DER). Those data elements that are retained (stored) by the system.

Data Tokens (TC_i). The data tokens (data items that are not subdivided within a functional primitive) that exist at the boundary of the ith functional primitive (evaluated for each primitive).

Relationship connections (RE_i). The relationships that connect the ith object in the data model to other objects.

---

[6]The acronym noted in parentheses following the primitive is used to denote the *count* of the particular primitive; e.g., FuP indicates the number of functional primitives present in an analysis model.

DeMarco [DEM82] suggests that most software can be allocated to one of two domains, *function-strong* or *data-strong,* depending upon the ratio RE/FuP. Function-strong applications (commonly encountered in engineering and scientific applications) emphasize the transformation of data and do not generally have complex data structures. Data-strong applications (commonly encountered in information systems applications) tend to have complex data models.

RE/FuP < 0.7 implies a function-strong application

0.8 < RE/FuP < 1.4 implies a hybrid application

RE/FuP > 1.5 implies a data-strong application

Because different analysis models will partition the model to greater or lessor degrees of refinement, DeMarco suggests that an average token count per primitive

$$TC_{avg} = \Sigma\ TC_i/FuP$$

be used to control uniformity of partitioning across many different models within an application domain.

To compute the bang metric for function-strong applications, the following algorithm is used:

```
set initial value of bang = 0;
do while functional primitives remain to be evaluated
  compute token-count around the boundary of primitive i;
  compute corrected FuP increment (CFuPI);
  Allocate primitive to class;
  Assess class and note assessed weight;
  Multiply CFuPI by the assessed weight;
  bang = bang + weighted CFuPI;
enddo
```

The token-count is computed by determining how many separate tokens are "visible" [DEM82] within the primitive. It is possible that the number of tokens and the number of data elements will differ, if data elements can be moved from input to output without any internal transformation. The corrected CFuPI is determined from a table published by DeMarco. A much abbreviated version is shown below:

TC$_i$	CFuPI
2	1.0
5	5.8
10	16.6
15	29.3
20	43.2

The assessed weight noted in the above algorithm is determined from 16 different classes of functional primitives defined by DeMarco. A weight ranging from 0.6 (simple data routing) to 2.5 (data management functions) is assigned depending on the class of the primitive.

For data-strong applications, the bang metric is computed using the following algorithm:

```
set initial value of bang = 0;
do while objects remain to be evaluated in the data model;
  compute count of relationships for object i;
  compute corrected OB increment (COBI);
  bang = bang + COBI;
enddo
```

The corrected COBI is also determined from a table published by DeMarco. An abbreviated version is shown below:

RE_i	COBI
1	1.0
3	4.0
6	9.8

Once the bang metric has been computed, past history can be used to associate it with size and effort. DeMarco suggests that an organization build its own versions of the CFuPI and COBI tables to use for calibrating information from completed software projects.

18.3.3 Metrics for Specification Quality

Davis and his colleagues [DAV93] propose a list of characteristics that can be used to assess the quality of the analysis model and the corresponding requirements specification: specificity (lack of ambiguity), completeness, correctness, understandability, verifiability, internal and external consistency, achievability, concision, traceability, modifiability, precision, and reusability. In addition, the authors note that high-quality specifications are electronically stored, executable or at least interpretable, annotated by relative importance and stability, versioned, organized, cross-referenced, and specified at the right level of detail.

Although many of the above characteristics appear to be qualitative in nature, Davis et al. [DAV93] suggest that each can be represented using one or more metrics.[7] For example, we assume that there are n_r requirements in a specification, such that

$$n_r = n_f + n_{nf}$$

---

[7] A complete discussion of specification quality metrics is beyond the scope of this chapter. See [DAV93] for more details.

where n_f is the number of functional requirements and n_{nf} is the number of nonfunctional (e.g., performance) requirements.

To determine the *specificity* (lack of ambiguity) of requirements, Davis et al. suggest a metric that is based on the consistency of the reviewers' interpretation of each requirement:

$$Q_1 = n_{ui}/n_r$$

where n_{ui} is the number of requirements for which all reviewers had identical interpretations. The closer the value of Q is to 1, the lower the ambiguity of the specification.

The *completeness* of functional requirements can be determined by computing the ratio

$$Q_2 = n_u/(n_i \times n_s)$$

where n_u is the number of unique function requirements, n_i is the number of inputs (stimuli) defined or implied by the specification, and n_s is the number of states specified. The Q_2 ratio measures the percentage of necessary functions that have been specified for a system. However, it does not address nonfunctional requirements. To incorporate these into an overall metric for completeness, we must consider the degree to which requirements have been validated.

$$Q_3 = n_c/(n_c + n_{nv})$$

where n_c is the number of requirements that have been validated as correct and n_{nv} is the number of requirements that have not yet been validated.

18.4 METRICS FOR THE DESIGN MODEL

It is inconceivable that the design of a new aircraft, a new computer chip, or a new office building would be conducted without defining design measures, determining metrics for various aspects of design quality, and using them to guide the manner in which the design evolves. And yet, the design of complex software-based systems often proceeds with virtually no measurement. The irony of this is that design metrics for software are available, but the vast majority of software engineers continue to be unaware of their existence.

Design metrics for computer software, like all other software metrics, are not perfect. Debate continues over their efficacy and how they should be applied. Many experts argue that further experimentation is required before design measures can be used. And yet, design without measurement is an unacceptable alternative.

In the sections that follow we examine some of the more common design metrics for computer software. Although none of them are perfect, all can provide the designer with improved insight and all can help the design to evolve to a higher level of quality.

18.4.1 High-Level Design Metrics

High-level design metrics focus on characteristics of the program architecture (Chapter 14) with an emphasis on the architectural structure and the effectiveness of modules. These metrics are black-box in the sense that they do not require any knowledge of the inner working of a particular module with the system.

Card and Glass [CAR90] define three software design complexity measures: *structural complexity, data complexity,* and *system complexity.* Structural complexity, $S(i)$, of a module i is defined in the following manner:

$$S(i) = f_{out}^2(i) \tag{18.1}$$

where $f_{out}(i)$ is the fan-out[8] of module i.

Data complexity, $D(i)$, provides an indication of the complexity in the internal interface for a module i and is defined as:

$$D(i) = v(i)/[f_{out}(i) + 1] \tag{18.2}$$

where $v(i)$ is the number of input and output variables that are passed to and from module i.

Finally, system complexity, $C(i)$, is defined as the sum of structural and data complexity and is defined as:

$$C(i) = S(i) + D(i) \tag{18.3}$$

As each of these complexity values increases, the overall architectural complexity of the system also increases. This leads to a greater likelihood that integration and testing effort will also increase.

An earlier high-level architectural design metric proposed by Henry and Kafura [HEN81] also makes use of the fan-in and fan-out. The authors define a complexity metric of the form:

$$HKM = length(i) \times [f_{in}(i) + f_{out}(i)]^2 \tag{18.4}$$

where length(i) is the number of programming language statements in module i and $f_{in}(i)$ is the fan-in of module i. Henry and Kafura extend the definition of fan-in and fan-out presented in this book to include not only the number of module control connections (module calls) but also the number of data structures from which module i retrieves (fan-in) or updates (fan-out) data. To compute HKM during design, the procedural design may be used to estimate the number of programming language statements for module i. Like the Card and Glass metrics noted above, an increase in the Henry-Kafura metric leads to a greater likelihood that integration and testing effort will also increase for a module.

---

[8]As was noted in the discussion presented in Chapter 13, *fan-out* indicates the number of modules immediately subordinate to module i, that is, the number of modules that are directly invoked by module i.

Fenton [FEN91] suggests a number of simple *morphology* (i.e., shape) *metrics* that enable different program architectures to be compared using a set of straightforward dimensions. In Figure 18.5, the following metrics can be defined:

$$size = n + a$$

where n is the number of nodes (modules) and a is the number of arcs (lines of control). For the architecture shown in Figure 18.5,

$$size = 17 + 18 = 35$$

depth = the longest path from the root (top) node to a leaf node. For the architecture shown in Figure 18.5, depth = 4.

width = maximum number of nodes at any one level of the architecture. For the architecture shown in Figure 18.5, width = 6.

$$\text{arc-to-node ratio, } r = a/n,$$

which measures the connectivity density of the architecture and may provide a simple indication of the coupling of the architecture. For the architecture shown in Figure 18.5, $r = 18/17 = 1.06$.

The U.S. Air Force Systems Command [USA87] has developed a number of software quality indicators that are based on measurable design characteristics of a computer program. Using concepts similar to those proposed in IEEE Std. 982.1-1988 [IEE94], the Air Force uses information obtained from data and architectural design to derive a *design structure quality index (DSQI)* that

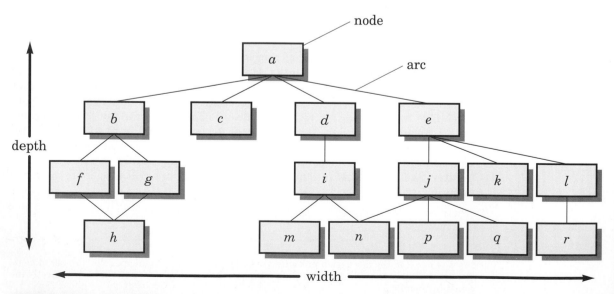

FIGURE 18.5. Morphology metrics

ranges from 0 to 1. The following values must be ascertained to compute the DSQI [CHA89]:

S_1 = the total number of modules defined in the program architecture

S_2 = the number of modules whose correct function depends on the source of data input or produces data to be used elsewhere [in general, control modules (among others) would not be counted as part of S_2]

S_3 = the number of modules whose correct function depends on prior processing

S_4 = the number of database items (includes data objects and all attributes that define objects)

S_5 = the total number of unique database items

S_6 = the number of database segments (different records or individual objects)

S_7 = the number of modules with a single entry and exit (exception processing is not considered to be a multiple exit)

Once values S_1 through S_7 are determined for a computer program, the following intermediate values can be computed:

Program structure: D_1, where D_1 is defined as follows: If the architectural design was developed using a distinct method (e.g., data flow-oriented design or object-oriented design, then $D_1 = 1$, otherwise $D_1 = 0$.

Module independence: $D_2 = 1 - (S_2/S_1)$

Modules not dependent on prior processing: $D_3 = 1 - (S_3/S_1)$

Database size: $D_4 = 1 - (S_5/S_4)$

Database compartmentalization: $D_5 = 1 - (S_6/S_4)$

Module entrance/exit characteristic: $D_6 = 1 - (S_7/S_1)$

With these intermediate values determined, the DSQI is computed in the following manner:

$$\text{DSQI} = \Sigma\, w_i D_i \qquad (18.5)$$

where $i = 1$ to 6, w_i is the relative weighting of the importance of each of the intermediate values and $\Sigma\, w_i = 1$ (if all D_i are weighted equally, then $w_i = 0.167$).

The value of DSQI for past designs can be determined and compared to a design that is currently under development. If the DSQI is significantly lower than average, further design work and review are indicated. Similarly, if major changes are to be made to an existing design, the effect of those changes on DSQI can be calculated.

18.4.2   Component-Level Design Metrics

Component-level design metrics focus on internal characteristics of software components and include measures of module cohesion, coupling, and complexity. These "3-C's" can help a software engineer to judge the quality of a component level design.

The metrics presented in this section are glass-box in the sense that they require knowledge of the inner working of the module under consideration. Component-level design metrics may be applied once a procedural design has been developed. Alternatively, they may be delayed until source code is available.

Cohesion metrics   Bieman and Ott [BIE94] define a collection of metrics that provide an indication of the cohesiveness (Chapter 13) of a module. The metrics are defined in terms of five concepts and measures:

> *Data slice.* Stated simply, a data slice is a backward walk through a module that looks for data values that affect the module location at which the walk began. It should be noted that both *program slices* (which focus on statements and conditions) and data slices can be defined.
>
> *Data tokens.* The variables defined for a module can be defined as data tokens for the module.
>
> *Glue tokens.* The set of data tokens that lie on one or more data slice.
>
> *Superglue tokens.* The data tokens that are common to every data slice in a module.
>
> *Stickiness.* The relative stickiness of a glue token is directly proportional to the number of data slices that it binds.

Bieman and Ott develop metrics for strong functional cohesion (SFC), weak functional cohesion (WFC), and adhesiveness (the relative degree to which glue tokens bind data slices together). These metrics can be interpreted in the following manner [BIE94]:

> All of these cohesion metrics range in value between 0 and 1. They have a value of 0 when a procedure has more than one output and exhibits none of the cohesion attributes indicated by a particular metric. A procedure with no superglue tokens, no tokens that are common to all data slices, has zero strong functional cohesion—there are no data tokens that contribute to all outputs. A procedure with no glue tokens, that is, no tokens common to more than one data slice (in procedures with more than one data slice), exhibits zero weak functional cohesion and zero adhesiveness—there are no data tokens that contribute to more than one output.

Strong functional cohesion and adhesiveness are encountered when the Bieman and Ott metrics take on a maximum value of 1.

A detailed discussion of the Bieman and Ott metrics is best left to the authors [BIE94]. However, to illustrate the character of these metrics, consider the metric for strong functional cohesion:

$$\text{SFC}(i) = \text{SG}(\text{SA}(i))/\text{tokens}(i) \tag{18.6}$$

where $\text{SG}(\text{SA}(i))$ denotes superglue tokens—the set of data tokens that lie on all data slices for a module i. As the ratio of superglue tokens to the total number of tokens in a module i increases toward a maximum value of 1, the functional cohesiveness of the module also increases.

Coupling metrics   Module coupling provides an indication of the "connectedness" of a module to other modules, global data, and the outside environment. In Chapter 13, coupling was discussed in qualitative terms.

Dhama [DHA95] has proposed a metric for module coupling that encompasses data and control flow coupling, global coupling, and environmental coupling. The measures required to compute module coupling are defined in terms of each of the three coupling types noted above.

For data and control flow coupling:

  d_i = number of input data parameters
  c_i = number of input control parameters
  d_o = number of output data parameters
  c_o = number of output control parameters

For global coupling:

  g_d = number of global variables used as data
  g_c = number of global variables used as control

For environmental coupling:

  w = number of modules called (fan-out)
  r = number of modules calling the module under consideration (fan-in)

Using these measures, a module coupling indicator, m_c, is defined in the following way:

$$m_c = k/M$$

where $k = 1$, a proportionality constant.[9]

$$M = d_i + a \cdot c_i + d_o + b \cdot c_o + g_d + c \cdot g_c + w + r$$

where

$$a = b = c = 2.$$

---

[9]The author [DHA95] notes that the values of k and a, b, and c (discussed in the next equation) may be adjusted as more experimental verification occurs.

The higher the value of m_c, the lower the overall module coupling. For example. If a module has a single input and output data parameter, accesses no global data, and is called by a single module:

$$m_c = 1/(1 + 0 + 1 + 0 + 0 + 0 + 1 + 0) = 1/3 = 0.33$$

We would expect that such a module would exhibit low coupling. Hence, a value of $m_c = 0.33$ implies low coupling. Alternatively, if a module has 5 input and 5 output data parameters, an equal number of control parameters, accesses 10 items of global data, and has a fan-in of 3 and a fan-out of 4,

$$m_c = 1/(5 + 2 \cdot 5 + 5 + 2 \cdot 5 + 10 + 0 + 3 + 4) = 0.02$$

and the implied coupling is high.

In order to have the coupling metric move upward as the degree of coupling increases, a revised coupling metric may be defined as:

$$C = 1 - m_c$$

where the degree of coupling increases nonlinearly between a minimum value in the range 0.66 to a maximum value that approaches 1.0.

Complexity metrics   A variety of software metrics can be computed to determine the complexity of program control flow. Many of these are based on a representation called a *flow graph*. As we discussed in Chapter 16, a graph is a representation composed of nodes and links (also called edges). When the links (edges) are directed, the flow graph is a *directed graph*.

McCabe [MCC94] identifies a number of important uses for complexity metrics:

> Complexity metrics can be used to predict critical information about reliability and maintainability of software systems from automatic analysis of source code [or procedural design information]. Complexity metrics also provide feedback during the software project to help control the [design activity]. During testing and maintenance, they provide detailed information about software modules to help pinpoint areas of potential instability.

The most widely used (and debated) complexity metric for computer software is *cyclomatic complexity*, originally developed by Thomas McCabe [MCC76, MCC89] and discussed in detail in Section 16.4.2.

The McCabe metric provides a quantitative measure of testing difficulty and an indication of ultimate reliability. Experimental studies indicate a strong correlation between the McCabe metric and the number of errors existing in source code, as well as the time required to find and correct such errors.

McCabe also contends that cyclomatic complexity may be used to provide a quantitative indication of maximum module size. Collecting data from a number of actual programming projects, he has found that a cyclomatic complexity of 10 appears to be a practical upper limit for module size. When the cyclomatic complexity of modules exceeded this number, it became extremely difficult to adequately test a module. See Chapter 16 for a discussion of cyclomatic complexity as a guide for the design of white-box test cases.

Zuse [ZUS90] presents an encyclopedic discussion of no fewer than 18 different categories of software complexity metrics. The author presents the basic definitions for metrics in each category (e.g., there are a number of variations on the cyclomatic complexity metric) and then analyzes and critiques each. Zuse's work is the most comprehensive published to date.

18.4.3 Interface Design Metrics

Although there is a significant literature on the design of human-computer interfaces (see Chapter 14), relatively little information has been published on metrics that would provide insight into the quality and usability of the interface.

Sears [SEA93] suggests *layout appropriateness (LA)* as a worthwhile design metric for human-computer interfaces. A typical GUI uses *layout entities*—graphic icons, text, menus, windows, and the like—to assist the user in completing tasks. To accomplish a given task using a GUI, the user must move from one layout entity to the next. The absolute and relative position of each layout entity, the frequency with which it is used, and the "cost" of the transition from one layout entity to the next will all contribute to the appropriateness of the interface.

For a specific layout (i.e., a specific GUI design), cost can be assigned to each sequence of actions according to the following relationship:

$$\text{cost} = \Sigma \; [\text{frequency of transition}(k) \times \text{cost of transition}(k)] \qquad (18.7)$$

where k is a specific transition from one layout entity to the next as a specific task is accomplished. The summation occurs across all transitions for a particular task or set of tasks required to accomplish some application function. Cost may be characterized in terms of time, processing delay, or any other reasonable value, such as the distance that a mouse must travel between layout entities.

Layout appropriateness is defined as:

$$\text{LA} = 100 \times [(\text{cost of LA-optimal layout})/(\text{cost of proposed layout})] \qquad (18.8)$$

where LA = 100 for an optimal layout.

To compute the optimal layout for a GUI, interface real estate (the area of the screen) is divided into a grid. Each square of the grid represents a possible position for a layout entity. For a grid with N possible positions and K different layout entities to place, the number of possible layouts is represented in the following manner [SEA93]:

$$\text{number of possible layouts} = [N!/(K! \times (N - K)!] \times K! \qquad (18.9)$$

As the number of layout positions increases, the number of possible layouts grows very large. To find the optimal (lowest-cost) layout, Sears [SEA93] proposes a tree searching algorithm.

LA is used to assess different proposed GUI layouts and the sensitivity of a particular layout to changes in task descriptions (i.e., changes in the sequence and/or frequency of transitions). The interface designer can use the change in layout appropriateness, ΔLA, as a guide in choosing the best GUI layout for a particular application.

It is important to note that the selection of a GUI design can be guided with metrics such as LA, but the final arbiter should be user feedback based on GUI prototypes. Nielsen and Levy [NIE94] report that "one has a reasonably large chance of success if one chooses between interface [designs] based solely on user's opinions. Users' average task performance and their subjective satisfaction with a GUI are highly correlated."

18.5　METRICS FOR SOURCE CODE

Halstead's theory of *software science* [HAL77] is "probably the best known and most thoroughly studied . . . composite measures of (software) complexity" [CUR80]. Software science proposed the first analytical "laws" for computer software.[10]

Software science assigns quantitative laws to the development of computer software. Halstead's theory is derived from one fundamental assumption [HAL77]: "the human brain follows a more rigid set of rules (in developing algorithms) than it has been aware of. . . ." Software science uses a set of primitive measures that may be derived after code is generated or estimated once design is complete. These are listed below.

n_1—the number of distinct operators that appear in a program

n_2—the number of distinct operands that appear in a program

N_1—the total number of operator occurrences

N_2—the total number of operand occurrences

To illustrate how these primitive measures are obtained, refer to the simple SORT program [FIT78] shown in Figure 18.6.

Halstead uses the primitive measures to develop expressions for the overall program *length;* potential minimum *volume* for an algorithm; the actual volume (number of bits required to specify a program); the *program level* (a measure of software complexity); *language level* (a constant for a given language); and other features such as development effort, development time, and even the projected number of faults in the software.

Halstead shows that length N can be estimated by:

$$N = n_1 \log_2 n_1 + n_2 \log_2 n_2 \qquad (18.10)$$

and program volume may be defined by:

$$V = N \log_2(n_1 + n_2) \qquad (18.11)$$

---

[10]It should be noted that Halstead's "laws" have generated substantial controversy and that not everyone agrees that the underlying theory is correct. However, experimental verification of Halstead's findings have been made for a number of programming languages (e.g., [FEL89]).

Interchange sort program
SUBROUTINE SORT (X,N)
DIMENSION X(N)
IF (N.LT.2) RETURN
DO 20 I = 2,N
DO 10 J = 1,I
IF (X(I).GE.X(J)) GO TO 10
SAVE = X(I)
X(I) = X(J)
X(J) = SAVE
10 CONTINUE
20 CONTINUE
RETURN
END

Operators of the interchange sort program	
Operator	Count
1 End of statement	7
2 Array subscript	6
3 =	5
4 IF ( )	2
5 DO	2
6 ,	2
7 End of program	1
8 .LT.	1
9 .GE.	1
n_1 = 10 GO TO 10	1
	$28 = N_1$

Operands of the interchange sort program	
Operand	Count
1 X	6
2 I	5
3 J	4
4 N	2
5 2	2
6 SAVE	2
n_2 = 7 1	1
	$22 = N_2$

FIGURE 18.6. Operators and operand for a simple program
(*Source*: A. Fitzsimmons and T. Love, "A Review and Evaluation of Software Science," ACM Computing Surveys, vol. 10, no. 1, March 1978. Copyright 1978, Association of Computing Machinery, Inc. Reprinted with permission.)

It should be noted that V will vary with programming language and represents the volume of information (in bits) required to specify a program. For the SORT module shown in Figure 18.6, it can be shown [FIT78] that the volume for the Fortran version is 204. Volume for an equivalent assembler language version would be 328. As we would suspect, it takes more effort to specify a program in assembler language.

Theoretically, a minimum volume must exist for a particular algorithm. Halstead defines a volume ratio L as the ratio of volume of the most compact form of a program to the volume of the actual program. In actuality, L must always be less than one. In terms of primitive measures, the volume ratio may be expressed as

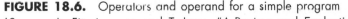

$$L = 2/n_1 \times n_2/N_2 \tag{18.12}$$

Halstead proposed that each language may be categorized by language level, l, which will vary among languages. Halstead theorized that language level is constant for a given language, but other work [ZEL81] indicates that language level is a function of both language and programmer. The following language level values have been empirically derived:

Language	Mean/l
English prose	2.16
PL/1	1.53
ALGOL/68	2.12
FORTRAN	1.14
Assembler	0.88

It appears that language level implies a level of abstraction in the specification of procedure. High-level languages allow specification of code at a higher level of abstraction than does assembler (machine-oriented) language.

Halstead's work is amenable to experimental verification, and a large body of research has been conducted to investigate software science. A discussion of this work is beyond the scope of this text, but it can be said that good agreement has been found between analytically predicted and experimental results. For further information, see [ZUS90] and [FEN91].

18.6   METRICS FOR TESTING

Although much has been written on software metrics for testing (e.g., [HET93]), the majority of metrics proposed focus on the process of testing, not the technical characteristics of the tests themselves. In general, testers must rely on analysis, design, and code metrics to guide them in the design and execution of test cases.

Function-based metrics (Section 18.3.1) can be used as a predictor for overall testing effort. Various project-level characteristics (e.g., testing effort and time, errors uncovered, number of test cases produced) for past projects can be collected and correlated with the number of FP produced by a project team. The team can then project "expected" values for these characteristics for the current project.

The bang metric can provide an indication of the number of test cases required by examining the primitive measures discussed in Section 18.3.2. The number of functional primitives (FuP), data elements (DE), objects (OB), relationships (RE), states (ST), and transitions (TR) can be used to project the number and types of black-box and white-box tests for the software. For example, the number of tests associated with the human–computer interface can be estimated by examining (1) the number of transitions (TR) contained in the state-transition representation of the HCI and evaluating the tests required to exercise each transition, (2) the number of data objects (OB) that move across the interface, and (3) the number of data elements that are input or output.

High-level design metrics provide information on the ease or difficulty associated with integration testing (Chapter 17) and the need for specialized testing software (e.g., stubs and drivers). Cyclomatic complexity (a component design metric) lies at the core of basis path testing, a test case design method presented in Chapter 16. In addition, cyclomatic complexity can be used to target modules as candidates for extensive unit testing (Chapter 17). Modules with high cyclomatic complexity are likely more error-prone than modules whose cyclomatic complexity is lower. For this reason, the tester should expend above average effort to uncover errors in the module before it is integrated in a system. Testing effort can also be estimated using metrics derived from Halstead measures (Section 18.5). Using the definitions for program volume, V, and program level, PL, software science effort, e, can be computed as:

$$PL = 1/[(n_1/2) \cdot (N_2/n_2)] \qquad (18.13a)$$

$$e = V/PL \qquad (18.13b)$$

The percentage of overall testing effort to be allocated to a module k can be estimated using the following relationship:

$$\text{percentage of testing effort } (k) = e(k)/\Sigma\, e(i) \qquad (18.14)$$

where $e(k)$ is computed for module k using equations (18.13) and the summation in the denominator of equation (18.14) is the sum of software science effort across all modules of the system.

As tests are conducted, three different measures provide an indication of testing completeness. A measure of the *breadth of testing* provides an indication how many requirements (of the total number of requirements) have been tested. This provides an indication of the completeness of the test plan. *Depth of testing* is a measure of the percentage of independent basis paths covered by testing versus the total number of basis paths in the program. A reasonably accurate estimate of the number of basis paths can be computed by adding the cyclomatic complexity of all program modules. Finally, as tests are conducted and error data are collected, *fault profiles* may be used to prioritize and categorize errors uncovered. Priority indicates the severity of the problem. Fault categories provide a description of an error so that statistical error analysis can be conducted.

18.7 METRICS FOR MAINTENANCE

All of the software metrics introduced in this chapter can be used for the development of new software and the maintenance of existing software. However, metrics designed explicitly for maintenance activities have been proposed.

IEEE Std. 982.1-1988 [IEE94] suggests a *software maturity index (SMI)* that provides an indication of the stability of a software product (based on changes that occur for each release of the product). The following information is determined:

M_T = the number of modules in the current release

F_c = the number of modules in the current release that have been changed

F_a = the number of modules in the current release that have been added

F_d = the number of modules from the preceding release that were deleted in the current release

The software maturity index is computed in the following manner:

$$SMI = [M_T - (F_a + F_c + F_d)]/M_T \qquad (18.15)$$

As SMI approaches 1.0, the product begins to stabilize. SMI may also be used as a metric for planning software maintenance activities. The mean time to produce a release of a software product can be correlated with SMI, and empirical models for maintenance effort can be developed.

18.8 SUMMARY

Software metrics provide a quantitative way to assess the quality of internal product attributes, thereby enabling the software engineer to assess quality before the product is built. Metrics provide the insight necessary to create effective analysis and design models, solid code, and thorough tests.

To be useful in a real world context, a software metric must be simple and computable, persuasive, and consistent and objective. It should be programming language-independent and provide effective feedback to the software engineer.

Metrics for the analysis model focus on function, data, and behavior—the three components of the analysis model. The function point and the bang metric each provide a quantitative means for evaluating the analysis model. Metrics for design consider high-level, component-level, and interface design issues. High-level design metrics consider the architectural and structural aspects of the design model. Component-level design metrics provide an indication of module quality by establishing indirect measures for cohesion, coupling, and complexity. Interface design metrics provide an indication of layout appropriateness for a GUI.

Software science provides an intriguing set of metrics at the source code level. Using the number of operators and operands present in the code, software science provides a variety of metrics that can be used to assess program quality.

Few technical metrics have been proposed for direct use in software testing and maintenance. However, many other technical metrics can be used to guide the testing process and as a mechanism for assessing the maintainability of a computer program.

REFERENCES

[BAS84]   Basili, V.R., and D.M. Weiss, "A Methodology for Collecting Valid Software Engineering Data," *IEEE Trans. Software Engineering,* vol. SE-10, 1984, pp. 728–738.

[BIE94]   Bieman, J.M., and L.M. Ott, "Measuring Functional Cohesion," *IEEE Trans. Software Engineering,* vol. 20, no. 8, August 1994, pp. 308–320.

[BRI96]   Briand, L.C., S. Morasca, and V.R. Basili, "Property-Based Software Engineering Measurement," *IEEE Trans. Software Engineering,* vol. 22, no. 1, January 1996, pp. 68–85.

[CAR90]   Card, D.N., and R.L. Glass, *Measuring Software Design Quality,* Prentice-Hall, 1990.

[CAV78]   Cavano, J.P., and J.A. McCall, "A Framework for the Measurement of Software Quality," *Proc. ACM Software Quality Assurance Workshop,* November 1978, pp. 133–139.

[CHA89]   Charette, R.N., *Software Engineering Risk Analysis and Management,* McGraw-Hill/Intertext, 1989.

[CUR80]   Curtis, W. "Management and Experimentation in Software Engineering," *Proc. IEEE,* vol. 68, no. 9, September 1980.

[DAV93]   Davis, A. et al., "Identifying and Measuring Quality in a Software Requirements Specification, *Proc. 1st Intl. Software Metric Symposium,* IEEE, Baltimore, MD, May 1993, pp. 141–152.

[DEM81]   DeMillo, R.A., and R.J. Lipton, "Software Project Forecasting," in *Software Metrics,* A.J. Perlis, F.G. Sayward, and M. Shaw (eds.), MIT Press, 1981, pp. 77–89.

[DEM82]   DeMarco, T., *Controlling Software Projects,* Yourdon Press, 1982.

[DHA95]   Dhama, H., "Quantitative Models of Cohesion and Coupling in Software," *Journal of Systems and Software,* vol. 29, no. 4, April 1995.

[EJI91]   Ejiogu, L., *Software Engineering with Formal Metrics,* QED Publishing, 1991.

[FEL89]   Felican, L., and G. Zalateu, "Validating Halstead's Theory for Pascal Programs," *IEEE Trans. Software Engineering,* vol. 15, no. 2, December 1989, pp. 1630–1632.

[FEN91]   Fenton, N., *Software Metrics,* Chapman & Hall, 1991.

[FEN94]   Fenton, N., "Software Measurement: A Necessary Scientific Basis," *IEEE Trans. Software Engineering,* vol. 20, no. 3, March 1994, pp. 199–206.

[FIT78]   Fitzsimmons, A., and T. Love, "A Review and Evaluation of Software Science," *ACM Computing Surveys,* vol. 10, no. 1, March 1978, pp. 3–18.

[GRA87]   Grady, R.B., and D.L. Caswell, *Software Metrics: Establishing a Company-Wide Program,* Prentice-Hall, 1987.

[HAL77]   Halstead, M., *Elements of Software Science,* North Holland, 1977.

[HEN81]   Henry, S., and D. Kafura, "Software Structure Metrics Based on Information Flow," *IEEE Trans. Software Engineering,* vol. SE-7, no. 5, September 1981, pp. 510–518.

[HET93]   Hetzel, B., *Making Software Measurement Work,* QED Publishing, 1993.

[IEE94]   *IEEE Software Engineering Standards,* 1994 edition, IEEE, 1994.

[KYB84]   Kyburg, H.E., *Theory and Measurement,* Cambridge University Press, 1984.

[MCC76]   McCabe, T.J., "A Software Complexity Measure," *IEEE Trans. Software Engineering,* vol. 2, December 1976, pp. 308–320.

[MCC77]   McCall, J., P. Richards, and G. Walters, "Factors in Software Quality," three volumes, NTIS AD-A049-014, 015, 055, November 1977.

[MCC89]   McCabe, T.J., and C.W. Butler, "Design Complexity Measurement and Testing," *CACM,* vol. 32, no. 12, December 1989, pp. 1415–1425.

[MCC94]   McCabe, T.J., and A.H. Watson, "Software Complexity," *Crosstalk,* vol. 7, no. 12, December 1994, pp. 5–9.

[NIE94]   Nielsen, J., and J. Levy, "Measuring Usability: Preference vs. Performance," *CACM,* vol. 37, no. 4, April 1994, pp. 65–75.

[ROC94]   Roche, J.M., "Software Metrics and Measurement Principles," *Software Engineering Notes,* ACM, vol. 19, no. 1, January 1994, pp. 76–85.

[SEA93]   Sears, A., "Layout Appropriateness: A Metric for Evaluating User Interface Widget Layout," *IEEE Trans. Software Engineering,* vol. 19, no. 7, July 1993, pp. 707–719.

[USA87]   *Management Quality Insight,* AFCSP 8u.   ' (U.S. Air Force), January 20, 1987.

[ZEL81]   Zelkowitz, M., private communication, 1981.

[ZUS90]   Zuse, H., *Software Complexity: Measures and Methods,* DeGruyter, New York, 1990.

PROBLEMS AND POINTS TO PONDER

18.1. Measurement theory is an advanced topic that has a strong bearing on software metrics. Using [FEN91], [ZUS90], [KYB84], or some other source, write a brief paper that outlines the main tenets of measurement theory. Individual project: Develop a presentation on the subject and present it to your class.

18.2. McCall's quality factors were developed during the 1970s. Almost every aspect of computing has changed dramatically since the time that they were developed, and yet, McCall's factors continue to apply to modern software. Can you draw any conclusions based on this fact?

18.3. Why is it that a single, all-encompassing metric cannot be developed for program complexity or program quality?

18.4. Review the analysis model you developed as part of problem 12.13. Using the guidelines presented in Section 18.3.1, develop an estimate for the number of function points associated with PHTRS.

18.5. Review the analysis model you developed as part of problem 12.13. Using the guidelines presented in Section 18.3.2, develop primitive counts for the bang metric. Is the PHTRS system function-strong or data-strong?

18.6. Compute the value of the bang metric using the measures you developed in problem 18.5.

18.7. Create a complete design model for a system that is proposed by your instructor. Compute structural and data complexity using the metrics described in Section 18.4.1. Also compute the Henry-Kafura and morphology metrics for the design model.

18.8. A major information system has 1140 modules. There are 96 modules that perform control and coordination functions and 490 modules whose function depends on prior processing. The system processes approximately 220 data objects that each have an average of 3 attributes. There are 140 unique data base items and 90 different database segments. 600 modules have single entry and exit points. Compute the DSQI for this system.

18.9. Research Bieman and Ott's [BIE94] paper and develop a complete example that illustrates the computation of their cohesion metric. Be sure to indicate how data slices, data tokens, and glue and superglue tokens are determined.

18.10. Select five modules in an existing computer program. Using Dhama's metric described in Section 18.4.2, compute the coupling value for each module.

18.11. Develop a software tool that will compute cyclomatic complexity for a programming language module. You may choose the language.

18.12. Develop a software tool that will compute layout appropriateness for a GUI. The tool should enable you to assign the transition cost between layout entities. [Note: Recognize that the size of the potential population of layout alternatives grows very large as the number of possible grid positions grows.]

18.13. Develop a small software tool that will perform a Halstead analysis on programming language source code of your choosing.

18.14. Research the literature and write a paper on the relationship of Halstead's metric and McCabe's metric on software quality (as measured by error count). Are the data compelling? Recommend guidelines for the application of these metrics.

18.15. Research the literature for any recent papers of metrics specifically designed to assist in test case design. Present your findings to the class.

18.16. A legacy system has 940 modules. The latest release required that 90 of these modules be changed. In addition, 40 new modules were added and 12 old modules were removed. Compute the software maturity index for the system.

FURTHER READINGS AND OTHER INFORMATION SOURCES

There are a surprisingly large number of books that are dedicated to software metrics, although the majority focus on process and project metrics to the exclusion of technical metrics. Books by Card and Glass [CAR90], Zuse [ZUS90], Fenton [FEN91], Ejiogu [EJI91], Moeller and Paulish (*Software Metrics,* Chapman & Hall, 1993), and Hetzel [HET93] all address technical metrics in some detail. In addition, the following books are worth examining:

Conte, S.D., H.E. Dunsmore, and V.Y. Shen, *Software Engineering Metrics and Models,* Benjamin Cummings, 1984

Grady, R.B., *Practical Software Metrics for Project Management and Process Improvement,* Prentice-Hall, 1992.

Grady, R.B., and D.L. Caswell, *Practical Software Metrics for Project Management and Process Improvement,* Prentice-Hall, 1992.

Perlis, A., F. Sayward, and M. Shaw, *Software Metrics: An Analysis and Evaluation,* MIT Press, 1981.

Sheppard, M., *Software Engineering Metrics,* McGraw-Hill, 1992.

The theory of software measurement is presented by Denvir, Herman, and Whitty in a edited collection of papers (*Proceedings of the International BCS-FACS Workshop: Formal Aspects of Measurement,* Springer-Verlag, 1992). Shepperd (*Foundations of Software Measurement,* Prentice-Hall, 1996) also addresses measurement theory in some detail.

A comprehensive summary of dozens of useful software metrics is presented in [IEE94]. In general, a discussion of each metric has been distilled to the essential "primitives" (measures) required to compute the metric and the appropriate relationships to effect the computation. An appendix provides discussion and many references.

An extensive software metrics bibliography covering process, project, and product metrics has been assembled by the Software Measurement Laboratory at the University of Magdeburg and can be found at:

http://irb.cs.uni-magdeburg.de/se/metrics_eng.html

A number of consulting companies specialize in software metrics. Their Web sites contain useful information:

Software Productivity Research, Inc.	**http://www.spr.com/**
Quantitative Software Management, Inc.	**http://www.qsm.com/**

The United States Department of Defense and other government agencies have active metrics programs that are described at the following sites:

http://www.army.mil/optec-pg/homepage.htm

http://vislab-www.nps.navy.mil/~sm/metrics.shtml

The Software Productivity Center of Canada also has an active metrics program that provides tools and handbooks as well as other useful information at:

http://www.spc.ca/spc/metrovrv.htm

A set of educational materials tailored to the specific needs of industry and academia, called METKIT, is available at:

http://www.sbu.ac.uk/ ~ csse/metkit.html

An extensive database of technical metrics with over 500 entries has been compiled by Professor Horst Zuse, who has also written an on-line history of software metrics with extensive bibliographic references:

http://www.cs.tu-berlin.de/ ~ zuse/3-hist.html

An up-to-date list of World Wide Web references for technical metrics can be found at: **http://www.rspa.com**

PART FOUR

OBJECT-ORIENTED SOFTWARE ENGINEERING

In this part of *Software Engineering: A Practitioner's Approach* we consider the technical concepts, methods, and measurements that are applicable for the analysis, design, and testing of object-oriented software. In the chapters that follow, we address the following questions:

- What are the basic concepts and principles that are applicable to object-oriented thinking?
- How should object-oriented software projects be planned and managed?
- What is object-oriented analysis and how do its various models enable a software engineer to understand classes, their relationships and behaviors?
- What is a 'use case' and how can it be applied to analyze the requirements of a system?
- How do conventional and object-oriented approaches differ?
- What are the components of an object-oriented design model?
- How are 'patterns' used in the creation of an object-oriented design?
- What are the basic concepts and principles that are applicable for testing of object-oriented software?
- How do testing strategies and test case design methods change when object-oriented software is considered?
- What technical metrics are available for assessing the quality of object-oriented software?

Once these questions are answered, you'll understand how to analyze, design, implement, and test software using the object-oriented paradigm.

OBJECT-ORIENTED CONCEPTS AND PRINCIPLES

We live in a world of objects. These objects exist in nature, in man-made entities, in business, and in the products that we use. They can be categorized, described, organized, combined, manipulated, and created. Therefore, it is no surprise that an object-oriented view would be proposed for the creation of computer software—an abstraction that models the world in ways that help us to better understand and navigate it.

An object-oriented approach to the development of software was first proposed in the late 1960s. However, it took almost 20 years for object technologies[1] to become widely used. During the first half of the 1990s, object-oriented software engineering became the paradigm of choice for many software product builders and a growing number of information systems and engineering professionals. As time passes, object technologies are replacing classical software development approaches. An important question is "Why?"

The answer (like many answers to questions about software engineering) is not a simple one. Some people would argue that software professionals simply yearned for a "new" approach, but that view is overly simplistic. Object technologies do lead to a number of inherent benefits that provide advantages at both the management and technical level.

Object technologies lead to reuse, and reuse (of program components) leads to faster software development and higher-quality programs.[2] Object-oriented software is easier to maintain because its structure is inherently decoupled.

---

[1]The term "object technologies" is often used to encompass all aspects of an object-oriented view and includes analysis, design, and testing methods; programming languages; tools; databases; and the applications that are created using an object-oriented approach.

[2]A detailed discussion of software reuse is presented in Chapter 26.

This leads to fewer side effects when changes have to be made and less frustration for the software engineer and the customer. In addition, object-oriented systems are easier to adapt and easier to scale (i.e., large systems can be created by assembling reusable subsystems).

In this chapter we introduce the basic principles and concepts that form a foundation for the understanding of object technologies. Throughout the remainder of Part Four of this book, we consider methods that form the basis for an engineering approach to the creation of object-oriented products and systems.

19.1   THE OBJECT-ORIENTED PARADIGM

For many years, the term "object-oriented" (OO) was used to denote a software development approach that used one of a number of object-oriented programming languages (e.g., Ada 95, C++, Eiffel, Smalltalk). Today, the OO paradigm encompasses a complete view of software engineering. Edward Berard notes this when he states [BER93]:

> The benefits of object-oriented technology are enhanced if it is addressed early-on and throughout the software engineering process. Those considering object-oriented technology must assess its impact on the entire software engineering process. Merely employing object-oriented programming (OOP) will *not* yield the best results. Software engineers and their managers must consider such items as object-oriented requirements analysis (OORA), object-oriented design (OOD), object-oriented domain analysis (OODA), object-oriented database systems (OODBMS) and object-oriented computer aided software engineering (OOCASE).

A reader who is familiar with the conventional approach to software engineering (presented in Part Three of this book) might react to the above statement with a shrug: "What's the big deal? We use analysis, design, programming, testing, and related technologies when we engineer software using the classical methods. Why should OO be any different?" Indeed, why should OO be any different? In short, it shouldn't!

In Chapter 2, we discussed a number of different process models for software engineering. Although any one of these models could be adapted for use with OO, the best choice would recognize that OO systems tend to evolve over time. Therefore, an evolutionary process model coupled with an approach that encourages component assembly (reuse) is the best paradigm for OO software engineering. In Figure 19.1 the component assembly process model (Chapter 2) has been tailored for OO software engineering.

The OO process moves through an evolutionary spiral that starts with customer communication. It is here that the problem domain is defined and that basic problem classes (discussed later in this chapter) are identified. Planning and risk analysis establish a foundation for the OO project plan. The technical work associated with OO software engineering follows the iterative path shown in the shaded box. OO software engineering emphasizes reuse. Therefore,

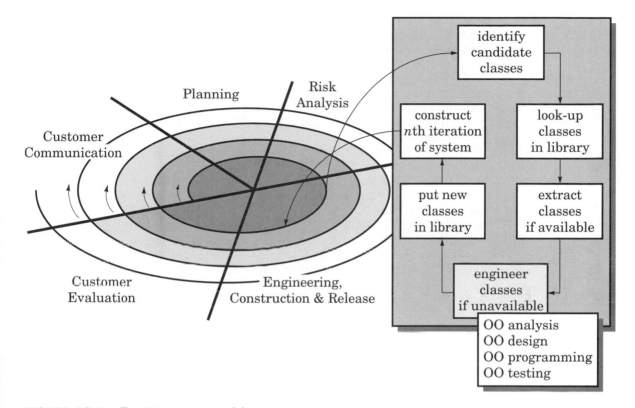

FIGURE 19.1. The OO process model

classes are "looked up" in a library (of existing OO classes) before they are built. When a class cannot be found in the library, the software engineer applies object-oriented analysis (OOA), object-oriented design (OOD), object-oriented programming (OOP), and object-oriented testing (OOT) to create the class and the objects derived from the class. The new class is then put into the library so that it may be reused in the future.

The object-oriented view demands an evolutionary approach to software engineering. As we will see throughout this and the following chapters, it would be exceedingly difficult to define all necessary classes for a major system or product in a single iteration. As the OO analysis and design models evolve, the need for additional classes becomes apparent. It is for this reason that the paradigm described above works best for OO. Further discussion of the OO process model is presented in Section 19.4.1.

19.2 OBJECT-ORIENTED CONCEPTS

Any discussion of object-oriented software engineering must begin by addressing the term "object-oriented." What is an object-oriented viewpoint? Why is a method considered to be object-oriented? What is an object? Over the years, there have been many different opinions (e.g., [BER93], [TAY90], [STR88], [BOO86]) about the correct answers to these questions. In the discussion that follows, we attempt to synthesize the most common of these.

To understand the object-oriented point of view, consider an example of a real world object—the thing you are sitting in right now—a chair. **Chair** is a member (the term "instance" is also used) of a much larger *class* of objects that we call **furniture**. A set of generic *attributes* can be associated with every object in the class **furniture**. For example, all furniture has a *cost, dimensions, weight, location,* and *color,* among many possible attributes. These apply whether we are talking about a table or a chair, a sofa or an armoire. Because **chair** is a *member* of the class **furniture,** chair *inherits* all attributes defined for the class. This concept is illustrated schematically in Figure 19.2.

Once the class has been defined, the attributes can be reused when new instances of the class are created. For example, assume that we were to define a new object called **chable** (a cross between a chair and a table) that is a member of the class **furniture. Chable** inherits all of the attributes of **furniture**.

We have attempted an anecdotal definition of a class by describing its attributes, but something is missing. Every object in the class **furniture** can be manipulated in a variety of ways. It can be bought and sold, physically modified (e.g., you can saw off a leg or paint the object purple) or moved from one place to another. Each of these *operations* (other terms are "services" or "meth-

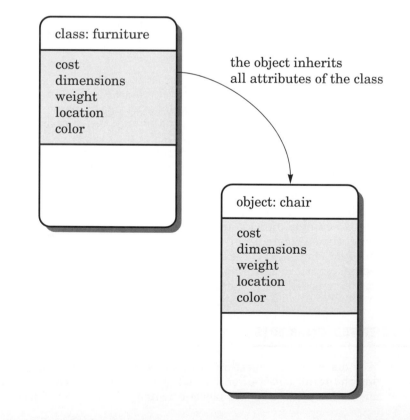

FIGURE 19.2.
Inheritance from
class to object

ods") will modify one or more attributes of the object. For example, if the attribute *location* is actually a composite data item defined (using data dictionary notation from Chapter 12) as:

location = building + floor + room

then an operation named *move* would modify one or more of the data items (*building, floor* or *room*) that comprise the attribute *location*. To do this, *move* must have "knowledge" of these data items. The operation *move* could be used for a chair or a table, as long as both are instances of the class **furniture**. All valid operations (e.g., *buy, sell, weigh*) for the class **furniture** are "connected" to the object definition as shown in Figure 19.3 and are inherited by all instances of the class.

The object **chair** (and all objects in general) *encapsulates* data (the attribute values that define the chair), operations (the actions that are applied to change the attributes of **chair**), other objects (*composite objects* can be defined [EVB89]), constants (set values), and other related information. *Encapsulation*

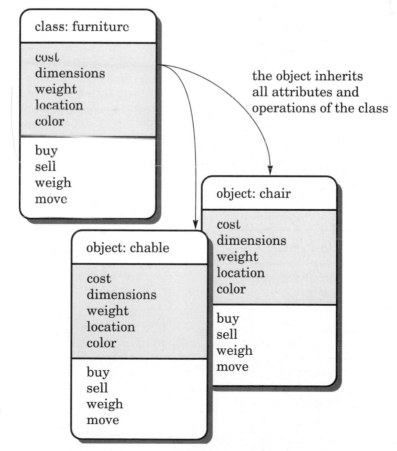

FIGURE 19.3.
Inheritance of operations from class to object

means that all of this information is packaged under one name and can be reused as one specification or program component.

Now that we have introduced a few basic concepts, a more formal definition of *object-oriented* will prove more meaningful. Coad and Yourdon [COA91] define the term this way:

object-oriented = objects + classification + inheritance + communication.

Three of these concepts have already been introduced. We will postpone a discussion of communication until later.

19.2.1 Classes and Objects

The fundamental concepts that lead to high-quality design (Chapter 13) apply equally to systems developed using conventional and object-oriented methods. For this reason, an OO model of computer software must exhibit data and procedural abstractions that lead to effective modularity. A *class* is an OO concept that encapsulates the data and procedural abstractions that are required to describe the content and behavior of some real world entity. Taylor [TAY90] uses the notation shown on the right side of Figure 19.4 to describe a class (and objects derived from a class).

The data abstractions (attributes) that describe the class are enclosed by a "wall" of procedural abstractions (called operations, methods, or services) that are capable of manipulating the data in some way. The only way to reach the attributes (and operate on them) is to go through one of the methods that comprise the wall. Therefore, the class encapsulates data (inside the wall) and the processing that manipulates the data (the methods that make up the wall). This achieves information hiding and reduces the impact of side effects associated with change. Since the methods tend to manipulate a limited number of attributes, they are cohesive, and because communication occurs only through the methods that comprise the "wall," the class tends to be decoupled from

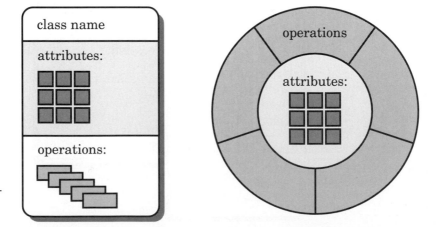

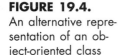

FIGURE 19.4.
An alternative representation of an object-oriented class

other elements of a system. All of these design characteristics (Chapter 13) lead to high-quality software.

Stated another way, a class is a generalized description (e.g., a template, pattern, or blueprint) that describes a collection of similar objects. By definition, all objects that exist within a class inherit its attributes and the operations that are available to manipulate the attributes. A *superclass* is a collection of classes, and a *subclass* is an instance of a class.

These definitions imply the existence of a *class hierarchy* in which the attributes and operations of the superclass are inherited by subclasses that may each add additional "private" attributes and methods. A class hierarchy for the class **furniture** is illustrated in Figure 19.5.

19.2.2 Attributes

We have already seen that attributes are attached to classes and objects, and that they describe the class or object in some way. A discussion of attributes is presented by de Champeaux and his colleagues [CHA93]:

Real life entities are often described with words that indicate stable features. Most physical objects have features such as shape, weight, color, and type of material. People have features including data of birth, parents, names, and eye color. A feature may be seen as a binary relation between a class and a certain domain.

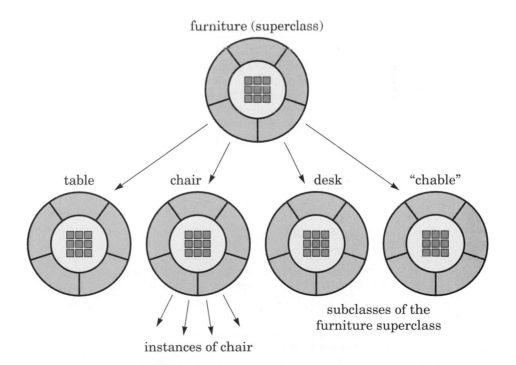

FIGURE 19.5.
A class hierarchy

The binary relation noted above implies that an attribute can take on a value defined by an enumerated domain. In most cases, a domain is simply a set of specific values. For example, assume that a class **automobile** has an attribute *color*. The domain of values for *color* is {white, black, silver, gray, blue, red, yellow, green}. In more complex situations, the domain can be a set of classes. Continuing the example, the class **automobile** also has an attribute *power train* that encompasses the following domain of values: {16 value economy option, 16 valve sport option, 24 valve sport option, 32 valve luxury option}. Each of the "options" noted has a set of specific attributes of its own.

The features (values of the domain) can be augmented by assigning a default value (feature) to an attribute. For example, the *power train* attribute noted above defaults to 16 valve sport option. It may also be useful to associate a probability with a particular feature by assigned (value, probability) pairs. Consider the *color* attribute for **automobile**. In some applications (e.g., manufacturing planning) it might be necessary to assign a probability to each of the colors (white and black are highly probable as automobile colors).

19.2.3 Operations, Methods, and Services

An object encapsulates data (represented as a collection of attributes) and the algorithms that process the data. These algorithms are called *operations, methods,* or *services*[3] and can be viewed as modules in a conventional sense.

Each of the operations that is encapsulated by an object provides a representation of one of the behaviors of the object. For example, the operation *GetColor* for the object **automobile** will extract the color stored in the *color* attribute. The implication of the existence of this operation is that the class **automobile** has been designed to receive a stimulus [JAC92] (we call the stimulus a "message") that requests the color of the particular instance of a class. Whenever an object receives a stimulus, it initiates some behavior. This can be as simple as retrieving the color of automobile or as complex as the initiation of a chain of stimuli that are passed among a variety of different objects. In the latter case, consider an example in which the initial stimulus received by object #1 results in the generation of two other stimuli that are sent to object #2 and object #3. Operations encapsulated by the second and third objects act on the stimuli, returning necessary information to the first object. Object #1 then uses the returned information to satisfy the behavior demanded by the initial stimulus.

19.2.4 Messages

Messages are the means by which objects interact. Using the terminology introduced in the preceding section, a message stimulates some behavior to oc-

---

[3]In the context of this discussion we use the term "operations," but "methods" and "services" are equally popular.

cur in the receiving object. The behavior is accomplished when an operation is executed.

The interaction between objects is illustrated schematically in Figure 19.6. An operation within a *sender object* generates a message of the form:

message: [destination, operation, parameters]

where *destination* defines the *receiver* object that is stimulated by the message, *operation* refers to the method that is to receive the message, and *parameters* provides information that is required for the operation to be successful.

As an example of message passing within an OO system, consider the objects shown in Figure 19.7. Four objects, **A, B, C,** and **D,** communicate with one another by passing messages. For example, if object **B** required processing associated with operation *op10* of object **D,** it would send **D** a message that would contain:

message: [**D,** *op10,* (data)]

As part of the execution of *op10,* object **D** may send a message to object **C** of the form:

message: [**C,** *op08,* (data)]

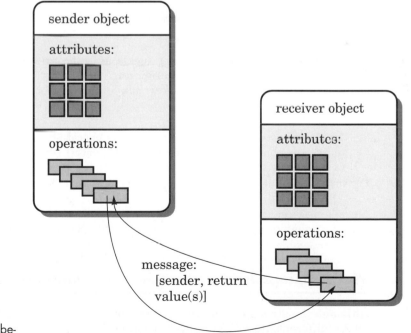

FIGURE 19.6.
Message passing between objects

message: [receiver, operation, parameters]

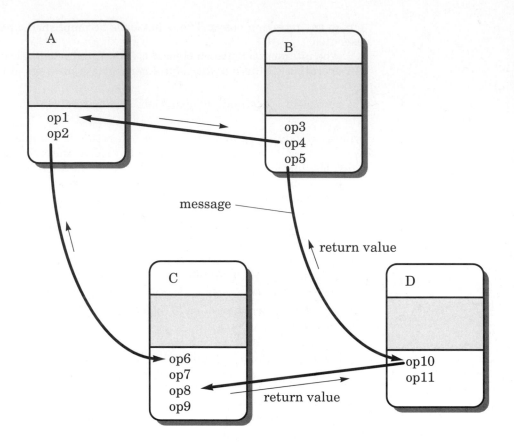

FIGURE 19.7.
Messaging

C finds *op08*, performs it, and then sends an appropriate return value to **D**. Operation *op10* completes its execution and sends a return value to **B**.

Cox [COX86] describes the interchange between objects in the following manner:

> An object is requested to perform one of its operations by sending it a message telling the object what to do. The receiver [object] responds to the message by first choosing the operation that implements the message name, executing this operation, and then returning control to the caller.

Messaging ties an object-oriented system together. Messages provide insight into the behavior of individual objects and the OO system as a whole.

19.2.5 Encapsulation, Inheritance, and Polymorphism

Although the structure and terminology introduced in Sections 19.2.1 through 19.2.4 differentiate OO systems from their conventional counterparts, three characteristics of object-oriented systems make them unique. As we have already noted, the OO class and the objects spawned from the class encapsulate data and the operations that work on the data in a single package. This provides a number of important benefits:

- The internal implementation details of data and procedures are hidden from the outside world (information hiding). This reduces the propagation of side effects when changes occur.
- Data structures and the operations that manipulate them are merged in a single named entity—the class. This facilitates component reuse.
- Interfaces among encapsulated objects are simplified. An object that sends a message need not be concerned with the details of internal data structures in the receiving object. Hence, interfacing is simplified and the system coupling tends to be reduced.

Inheritance is one of the key differentiators between conventional and OO systems. A subclass **Y** inherits all of the attributes and operations associated with its superclass **X**. This means that all data structures and algorithms originally designed and implemented for **X** are immediately available for **Y**—no further work need be done. Reuse has been accomplished directly.

Any change to the data or operations contained within a superclass is immediately inherited by all subclasses that have inherited from the superclass.[4] Therefore, the class hierarchy becomes a mechanism through which changes (at high levels) can be immediately propagated through a system.

It is important to note that at each level of the class hierarchy, new attributes and operations may be added to those that have been inherited from higher levels in the hierarchy. In fact, whenever a new class is to be created, the software engineer has a number of options:

- The class can be designed and built from scratch. That is, inheritance is not used.
- The class hierarchy can be searched to determine if an ancestor class contains most of the required attributes and operations.
- The new class inherits from the ancestor class, and additions may then be added as required.
- The class hierarchy can be restructured so that the required attributes and operations can be inherited by the new class.
- Characteristics of an existing class can be overridden and private versions of attributes or operations implemented for the new class.

To illustrate how restructuring of the class hierarchy might lead to a desired class, consider the example shown in Figure 19.8. The class hierarchy illus-

---

[4]The terms "descendants" and "ancestors" [JAC92] are sometimes used to replace "subclass" and "superclass," respectively.

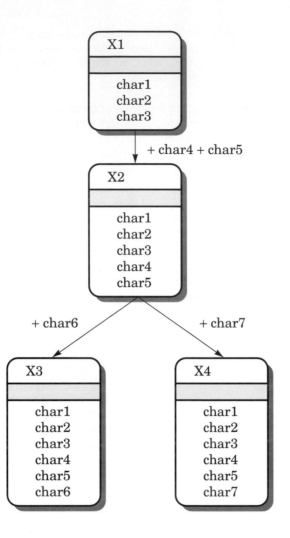

FIGURE 19.8a.
Original class hierarchy

trated in Figure 19.8a enables us to derive classes **X3** and **X4** with characteristics 1, 2, 3, 4, 5 and 6, and 1, 2, 3, 4, 5, and 7, respectively.[5] Now, suppose that a new class with *only* characteristics 1, 2, 3, 4, and 8 is desired. To derive this class, called **X2b** in the example, the hierarchy may be restructured as shown in Figure 19.8b. It is important to note that restructuring the hierarchy can be difficult, and for this reason, *overriding* is sometimes used.

In essence, overriding occurs when attributes and operations are inherited in the normal manner, but are then modified to the specific needs of the new class. As Jacobson notes, when overriding is used, "inheritance is not transitive." [JAC92]

---

[5]For the purposes of this example, "characteristics" may be either attributes or operations.

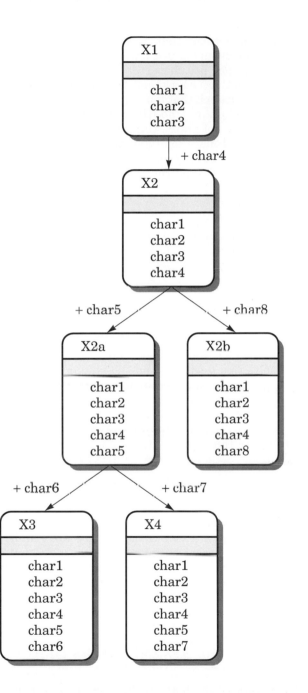

FIGURE 19.8b.
Restructured class hierarchy

In some cases, it is tempting to inherit some attributes and operations from one class and others from another class. This is called *multiple inheritance,* and it is controversial. In general, multiple inheritance complicates the class hierarchy and creates potential problems in configuration control (Chapter 9). Because multiple inheritance sequences are more difficult to trace, changes to the definition of a class that resides high in the hierarchy may have unintended impact(s) on classes defined lower in the architecture.

Polymorphism is a characteristic that greatly reduces the effort required to extend an existing OO system. To understand polymorphism, consider a conventional application that must draw four different types of graphs: line graphs, pie charts, histograms, and Kiviat diagrams. Ideally, once data are collected for a particular type of graph, the graph should draw itself. To accomplish this in a conventional application (and maintain module cohesion), it would be necessary to develop drawing modules for each type of graph. Then, within the design for each graph type, control logic similar to the following would have to be embedded:

```
case of graphtype:
    if graphtype = linegraph then DrawLineGraph (data);
    if graphtype = piechart  then DrawPieChart (data);
    if graphtype = histogram then DrawHisto (data);
    if graphtype = kiviat    then DrawKiviat (data);
end case;
```

Although this design is reasonably straightforward, adding new graph types could be tricky. A new drawing module would have to be created for each graph type and then the control logic would have to be updated for each graph.

To solve this problem in an OO system, each of the graphs noted above become a subclass of a general class called **graph**. Using a concept called *overloading* [TAY90], each subclass defines an operation called *draw*. An object can send a *draw* message to any one of the objects instantiated from any one of the subclasses. The object receiving the message will invoke its own *draw* operation to create the appropriate graph. Therefore, the design noted above is reduced to:

```
graphtype draw
```

When a new graphtype is to be added to the system, a subclass is created with its own *draw* operation. But no changes are required within any object that wants a graph drawn because the message `graphtype draw` remains unchanged. To summarize, polymorphism enables a number of different operations to have the same name. This in turn decouples objects from one another, making each more independent.

19.3   IDENTIFYING THE ELEMENTS OF AN OBJECT MODEL

The elements of an object model—classes and objects, attributes, operations, and messages—were each defined and discussed in the preceding section. But how do we go about identifying these elements for an actual problem? The sections that follow present a series of informal guidelines that will assist in the identification of the elements of the object model.

19.3.1 Identifying Classes and Objects

If you look around a room, there is a set of physical objects that can be easily identified, classified, and defined (in terms of attributes and operations). But when you "look around" the problem space of a software application, the objects may be more difficult to comprehend.

We can begin to identify objects[6] by examining the problem statement or (using the terminology Chapter 12) by performing a "grammatical parse" on the processing narrative for the system to be built. Objects are determined by underlining each noun or noun clause and entering it in a simple table. Synonyms should be noted. If the object is required to implement a solution, then it is part of the *solution space;* otherwise, if an object is necessary only to describe a solution, it is part of the *problem space*. But what should we look for once all of the nouns have been isolated?

Objects manifest themselves in one of the ways represented in Figure 19.9. Objects can be:

- *external entities* (e.g., other systems, devices, people) that produce or consume information to be used by a computer-based system;
- *things* (e.g., reports, displays, letters, signals) that are part of the information domain for the problem;

---

[6]In reality, OOA actually attempts to define *classes* from which objects are *instantiated*. Therefore, when we isolate potential objects, we also identify members of potential classes.

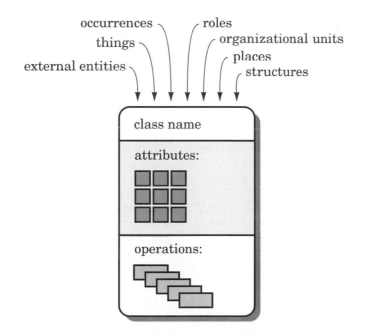

FIGURE 19.9.
How objects manifest themselves

- *occurrences* or *events*[7] (e.g., a property transfer or the completion of a series of robot movements) that occur within the context of system operation;
- *roles* (e.g., manager, engineer, salesperson) played by people who interact with the system;
- *organizational units* (e.g., division, group, team) that are relevant to an application;
- *places* (e.g., manufacturing floor or loading dock) that establish the context of the problem and the overall function of the system; or
- *structures* (e.g., sensors, four-wheeled vehicles or computers) that define a class of objects or, in the extreme, related classes of objects.

The categorization noted above is but one of many that have been proposed in the literature. For example, Budd [BUD96] suggests a taxonomy of classes that includes producers (sources) and consumers (sinks) of data, data managers, view or observer classes, and helper classes.

It is also important to note what objects are not. In general, an object should never have an "imperative procedural name." [CAS89] For example, if the developers of software for a medical imaging system defined an object with the name **image inversion,** they would be making a subtle mistake. The **image** obtained from the software could, of course, be an object (it is a thing that is part of the information domain). *Inversion* of the image is an operation that is applied to the object. It is likely that *inversion* would be defined as an operation for the object **image,** but it would not be defined as a separate object to connote "image inversion." As Cashman [CAS89] states, "the intent of object-orientation is to encapsulate, but still keep separate, data and operations on the data."

To illustrate how objects might be defined during the early stages of analysis, we return to the SafeHome security system example introduced earlier in this book. In Chapter 12, we performed a "grammatical parse" on a processing narrative for the SafeHome system. The processing narrative is reproduced below:

> SafeHome software enables the homeowner to configure the security system when it is installed, monitors all sensors connected to the security system, and interacts with the homeowner through a key pad and function keys contained in the SafeHome control panel shown in Figure 11.4.
>
> During installation, the SafeHome control panel is used to "program" and configure the system. Each sensor is assigned a number and type, a master password is programmed for arming and disarming the system, and telephone number(s) are input for dialing when a sensor event occurs.
>
> When a sensor event is recognized, the software invokes an audible alarm attached to the system. After a delay time that is specified by the homeowner during system configuration activities, the software dials a telephone number of a monitoring service, provides information about the location, reporting na-

---

[7]In this context, the term "event" connotes any occurrence. It does not necessarily imply control as it did in Chapter 12.

ture of the event that has been detected. The number will be redialed every 20 seconds until telephone connection is obtained.

All interaction with SafeHome is managed by a user-interaction subsystem that reads input provided through the keypad and function keys, and displays prompting messages and system status on the LCD display. Keyboard interaction takes the following form. . . .

Extracting the nouns, we can propose a number of potential objects:

Potential Object/Class	General Classification
homeowner	role or external entity
sensor	external entity
control panel	external entity
installation	occurrence
system (alias security system)	thing
number, type	*not objects, attributes of sensor*
master password	thing
telephone number	thing
sensor event	occurrence
audible alarm	external entity
monitoring service	organizational unit or external entity

The above list would be continued until all nouns in the processing narrative have been considered. Note that we call each entry in the list a *potential* object. We must consider each further before a final decision is made.

Coad and Yourdon [COA91] suggest six selection characteristics that should be used as an analyst considers each potential object for inclusion in the analysis model:

1. *retained information*—the potential object will be useful during analysis only if information about it must be remembered so that the system can function;
2. *needed services*—the potential object must have a set of identifiable operations that can change the value of its attributes in some way;
3. *multiple attributes*—during requirement analysis, the focus should be on "major" information (an object with a single attribute may, in fact, be useful during design, but is probably better represented as an attribute of another object during the analysis activity);
4. *common attributes*—a set of attributes can be defined for the potential object, and these attributes apply to all occurrences of the object;
5. *common operations*—a set of operations can be defined for the potential object, and these operations apply to all occurrences of the object; and
6. *essential requirements*—external entities that appear in the problem space and produce or consume information that is essential to the operation of

any solution for the system will almost always be defined as objects in the requirements model.

To be considered a legitimate object for inclusion in the requirements model, a potential object should satisfy all (or almost all) of the above characteristics. The decision for inclusion of potential objects in the analysis model is somewhat subjective, and later evaluation may cause an object to be discarded or reinstated. However, the first step of OOA must be a definition of objects, and decisions (even subjective ones) must be made. With this in mind, we apply the selection characteristics to the list of potential SafeHome objects:

Potential Object/Class	Characteristic Number that Applies
homeowner	rejected: 1, 2 fail even though 6 applies
sensor	accepted: all apply
control panel	accepted: all apply
installation	rejected
system (alias security system)	accepted: all apply
number, type	rejected: 3 fails, attributes of sensor
master password	rejected: 3 fails
telephone number	rejected: 3 fails
sensor event	accepted: all apply
audible alarm	accepted: 2, 3, 4, 5, 6 apply
monitoring service	rejected: 1, 2 fail even though 6 applies

It should be noted that (1) the above list is not all-inclusive, additional objects would have to be added to complete the model; (2) some of the rejected potential objects will become attributes for those objects that were accepted (e.g., *number* and *type* are attributes of **sensor,** and *master password* and *telephone number* may become attributes of **system**); and (3) different statements of the problem might cause different "accept or reject" decisions to be made (e.g., if each homeowner had his or her own password or was identified by voice print, the **homeowner** object would satisfy characteristics 1 and 2 and would have been accepted).

19.3.2 Specifying Attributes

Attributes describe an object that has been selected for inclusion in the analysis model. In essence, it is the attributes that define the object—that clarify what is meant by the object in the context of the problem space. For example, if we were to build a system that tracks statistics for professional baseball players, the attributes of the object **player** would be quite different from the attributes of the same object when it is used in the context of the professional baseball pension system. In the former, attributes such as name, position, batting average, fielding percentage, years played, and games played might be relevant. For the latter, some of these attributes would be meaningful, but others would be replaced (or augmented) by attributes like average salary, credit toward full vesting, pension plan options chosen, mailing address, and so on.

To develop a meaningful set of attributes for an object, the analyst can again study the processing narrative (or statement of scope) for the problem and select those things that reasonably "belong" to the object. In addition, the following question should be answered for each object: "What data items (composite and/or elementary) fully define this object in the context of the problem at hand?"

To illustrate, we consider the **system** object defined for SafeHome. We noted earlier in the book that the homeowner can configure the security system to reflect sensor information, alarm response information, activation/deactivation information, identification information, and so forth. Using the content description notation defined for the data dictionary and presented in Chapter 12, we can represent these composite data items in the following manner:

sensor information = sensor type + sensor number + alarm threshold

alarm response information = delay time + telephone number + alarm type

activation/deactivation information = master password + number of allowable tries + temporary password

identification information = system ID + verification phone number + system status

Each of the data items on the right of the equal sign could be further defined to an elementary level. But for our purposes, they comprise a reasonable list of attributes for the **system** object (shaded portion of Figure 19.10).

19.3.3 Defining Operations

Operations define the behavior of an object and change the object's attributes in some way. More specifically, an operation changes one or more attribute values that are contained within the object. Therefore, an operation must have "knowledge" of the nature of the object's attributes and must be implemented in a manner that enables it to manipulate the data structures that have been derived from the attributes.

Although many different types of operations exist, they can generally be divided into three broad categories: (1) operations that *manipulate* data in some way (e.g., adding, deleting, reformatting, selecting); (2) operations that perform a *computation;* and (3) operations that *monitor* an object for the occurrence of a controlling event.

As a first iteration at deriving a set of operations for the objects of the analysis model, the analyst can again study the processing narrative (or statement of scope) for the problem and select those operations that reasonably belong to the object. To accomplish this, the grammatical parse is again studied and verbs are isolated. Some of these verbs will be legitimate operations and can be easily connected to a specific object. For example, from the SafeHome

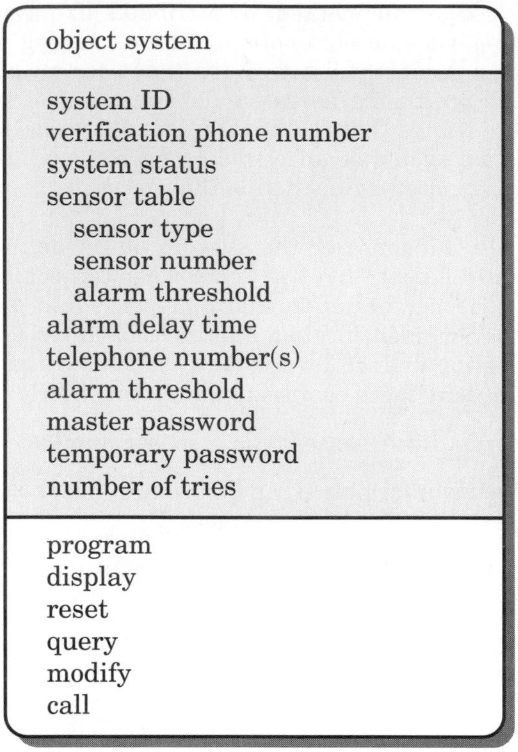

```
object system

  system ID
  verification phone number
  system status
  sensor table
     sensor type
     sensor number
     alarm threshold
  alarm delay time
  telephone number(s)
  alarm threshold
  master password
  temporary password
  number of tries

  program
  display
  reset
  query
  modify
  call
```

FIGURE 19.10.
The **system** object with operations attached

processing narrative presented earlier in this chapter, we see that "sensor is assigned a number and type" or that "a master password is programmed for arming and disarming the system." These two phrases indicate a number of things:

- that an *assign* operation is relevant for the **sensor** object;
- that a *program* operation will be applied to the **system** object;
- that *arm* and *disarm* are operations that apply to **system** (also that *system status* may ultimately be defined using data dictionary notation) as

system status = [armed | disarmed]

Upon further investigation, it is likely that the operation *program* will be divided into a number of more specific suboperations required to configure the system. For example, *program* implies specifying phone numbers, configuring system characteristics (e.g., creating the sensor table, inputting alarm characteristics), and inputting password(s), but for now, we specify *program* as a single operation.

In addition to the grammatical parse, we can gain additional insight into other operations by considering the *communication* that occurs between objects. As we have seen, objects communicate by passing messages to one another. The messages that pass among objects imply a set of operations that must be present.

19.3.4 Finalizing the Object Definition

The definition of operations is the last step in completing the specification of an object. In Section 19.3.3, operations were culled from a grammatical parse of the processing narrative for the system. Additional operations may be determined by considering the "life history" [COA91] of an object and the messages that are passed among objects defined for the system.

The generic life history of an object can be defined by recognizing that the object must be created, modified, manipulated or read in other ways, and possibly deleted. For the **system** object, this can be expanded to reflect known activities that occur during its life (in this case, during the time that SafeHome is operational). Some of the operations can be ascertained from likely communication between objects. For example, **sensor event** will send a message to **system** to *display* the event location and number; **control panel** will send a *reset* message to update *system status* (an attribute); the **audible alarm** will send a *query* message; the **control panel** will send a *modify* message to change one or more attributes without reconfiguring the entire **system** object; **sensor event** will also send a message to call the phone number(s) contain in the object. Other messages can be considered and operations derived. The resulting object definition is shown in Figure 19.10.

A similar approach would be used for each of the objects defined for SafeHome. After attributes and operations are defined for each of the objects defined to this point, the beginnings of an OOA model would be created. A more detailed discussion of the analysis model that is created as part of OOA is presented in Chapter 20.

19.4 Management of Object-Oriented Software Projects

As we discussed in Part Two of this book, modern software project management can be subdivided into the following activities:

1. Establishing a common process framework for the project
2. Using the framework and historical metrics to develop effort and time estimates
3. Specifying work products and milestones that will enable progress to be measured
4. Defining checkpoints for quality assurance and control
5. Managing the changes that invariably occur as the project progresses
6. Tracking, monitoring, and controlling progress

The technical manager who is faced with an object-oriented project applies these six activities. But because of the unique nature of object-oriented software, each of these management activities has a subtly different feel and must be approached using a somewhat different mind-set.

In the sections that follow, we explore software project management for object-oriented projects. The fundamental principles of management stay the same, but the technique must be adapted so that an OO project is properly managed.

19.4.1   The Common Process Framework for OO

A *common process framework (CPF)* defines an organization's approach to software development and maintenance. It identifies the software engineering paradigm that is applied to build and maintain software, and the tasks, milestones, and deliverables that will be required. It establishes the degree of rigor with which different kinds of projects will be approached.

The CPF is always adaptable so that it can meet the individual needs of a project team. This is its single most important characteristic.

An effective CPF for OO projects is *not* a linear sequential model. Linear sequential models, best known as life cycle or waterfall models, assume that requirements are defined at the front end of the project and that engineering activities progress in a linear sequential fashion. By its nature, object-oriented software engineering must apply a paradigm that encourages iterative development. That is, OO software evolves through a number of cycles. The common process framework that is used to manage an OO project must be evolutionary in nature. A process model for OO was presented in Section 19.1.

Ed Berard [BER93] and Grady Booch [BOO91] among others suggest the use of a "recursive/parallel model" for object-oriented software development. In essence the recursive/parallel model works in the following way:

- Do enough analysis to isolate major problem classes and connections.
- Do a little design to determine whether the classes and connections can be implemented in a practical way.
- Extract reusable objects from a library to build a rough prototype.
- Conduct some tests to uncover errors in the prototype.
- Get customer feedback on the prototype.
- Modify the analysis model based on what you've learned from the prototype, from doing design, and from customer feedback.
- Refine the design to accommodate your changes.
- Engineer special objects (that are not available from the library).
- Assemble a new prototype using objects from the library and the new objects you've created.
- Conduct some tests to uncover errors in the prototype.
- Get customer feedback on the prototype.

This approach continues until the prototype evolves into a production application.

The recursive/parallel model is quite similar to the OO process model presented earlier in this chapter. Progress occurs iteratively. What makes the recursive/parallel model different is the recognition that (1) analysis and design modeling for OO systems cannot be accomplished at an even level of abstraction, and (2) analysis and design can be applied to independent system components concurrently.

Berard [BER93] describes the model in the following manner:

- Systematically decompose the problem into highly independent components.
- Reapply the decomposition process to each of the independent components to decompose each further (the recursive part).

- Conduct this reapplication of decomposition concurrently on all components (the parallel) part.
- Continue this process until completion criteria are attained.

It's important to note that the decomposition process noted above is discontinued if the analyst/designer recognizes that the component or subcomponent required is available in a reuse library.

To control the recursive/parallel process framework, the project manager must recognize that progress is planned and measured incrementally. That is, project tasks and the project schedule are tied to each of the "highly independent components," and progress is measured for each of these components individually.

Each iteration of the recursive/parallel process requires planning, engineering (analysis, design, class extraction, prototyping, and testing) and evaluation activities (Figure 19.11). During planning, activities associated with each of the independent program components are planned and scheduled. [Note: With each iteration the schedule is adjusted to accommodate changes associated with the preceding iteration.] During early stages of engineering, analysis and design occur iteratively. The intent is to isolate all important elements of the OO analysis and design models. As engineering work proceeds, incremental versions of the software are produced. During evaluation, reviews, customer evaluation, and testing are performed for each increment, with feedback affecting the next planning activity and subsequent increment.

19.4.2 Object-Oriented Project Metrics and Estimation

Conventional software project estimation techniques require estimates of lines of code (LOC) or function points (FP) as the primary driver for estimation. Because an overriding goal for OO projects should be reuse, LOC estimates make little sense. FP estimates can be used effectively because the information domain counts that are required are readily obtainable from the problem statement. FP analysis may provide value for estimating OO projects, but the FP measure does not provide enough granularity for the schedule and effort adjustments that are required as we iterate through the recursive/parallel paradigm.

Lorenz and Kidd [LOR94] suggest the following set of project metrics:[8]

Number of scenario scripts. A *scenario script*[9] is a detailed sequence of steps that describe the interaction between the user and the application. Each script is organized into triplets of the form

{initiator, action, participant}

---

[8]Technical metrics for OO systems are discussed in detail in Chapter 23.

[9]The *scenario script* defined by Lorenz and Kidd is analogous to the *use case* discussed in Chapter 20.

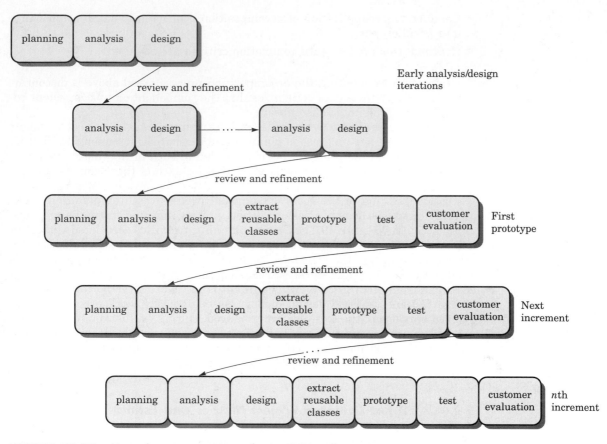

FIGURE 19.11. Typical process sequence for an OO project

where *initiator* is the object that requests some service (that initiates a message); *action* is the result of the request; and *participant* is the server object that satisfies the request.

The number of scenario scripts is directly correlated to the size of the application and to the number of test cases that must be developed to exercise the system once it is constructed.

Number of key classes. Key classes are the "highly independent components" [LOR94] that are defined early in OOA. Because key classes are central to the problem domain, the number of such classes is an indication of the amount of effort required to develop the software and also an indication of the potential amount of reuse to be applied during system development.

Number of support classes. Support classes are required to implement the system, but are not immediately related to the problem domain. Examples might be GUI classes, database access and manipulation, and communication classes. In addition, support classes can be developed for each of the key classes. Support classes are defined iteratively throughout the recursive/parallel process.

The number of support classes is an indication of the amount of effort required to develop the software and also an indication of the potential amount of reuse to be applied during system development.

Average number of support classes per key class. In general, key classes are known early in the project. Support classes are defined throughout. If the average number of support classes per key class were known for a given problem domain, estimating (based on total number of classes) would be much simplified.

Lorenz and Kidd suggest that applications with a GUI have between two and three times the number of support classes as key classes. Non-GUI applications have up to twice the number of support classes as key classes.

Number of subsystems. A subsystem is an aggregation of classes that support a function that is visible to the end user of a system. Once subsystems are identified, it is easier to lay out a reasonable schedule in which work on subsystems is partitioned among project staff.

19.4.3 An OO Estimating and Scheduling Approach

Software project estimation is an art, not a science. However, this in no way precludes the use of a systematic approach. To develop reasonable estimates it is essential to develop multiple data points. That is, estimates should be derived using a number of different techniques. Effort and duration estimates used for conventional software development (Chapter 5) are applicable to the OO world, but the historical database for OO projects is relatively small for many organizations. Therefore, it is worthwhile to supplement conventional software cost estimation with an approach that has been designed explicitly for OO software. Lorenz and Kidd [LOR94] suggest the following approach:

1. Develop estimates using effort decomposition, FP analysis, and any other method that is applicable for conventional applications.
2. Using OOA (Chapter 20), develop scenario scripts and determine a count. Recognize that the number of scenario scripts may change as the project progresses.
3. Using OOA, determine the number of key classes.
4. Categorize the type of interface for the application and develop a multiplier for support classes:

Interface Type	Multiplier
No GUI	2.0
Text-based user interface	2.25
GUI	2.5
Complex GUI	3.0

Multiply the number of key classes (step 3) by the above multiplier to obtain an estimate for the number of support classes.

5. Multiply the total number of classes (key + support) by the average number of work-units per class. Lorenz and Kidd suggest 15 to 20 person-days per class.

6. Cross check the class based estimate by multiplying the average number of work units per scenario script

Scheduling for object-oriented projects is complicated by the iterative nature of the process framework. Lorenz and Kidd suggest a set of metrics that may assist during project scheduling:

> **Number of major iterations.** Thinking back to the OO process model, a major iteration would correspond to one 360 degree traversal of the spiral. The recursive/parallel process model would spawn a number of mini-spirals (localized iterations) that occur as the major iteration progresses. Lorenz and Kidd suggest that iterations of between 2.5 and 4 months in length are easiest to track and manage.

> **Number of completed contracts.** A contract is "a group of related public responsibilities that are provided by subsystems and classes to their clients" [LOR94]. A contract is an excellent milestone, and at least one contract should be associated with each project iteration. A project manager can use completed contracts as a good indicator of progress on an OO project.

19.4.4 Tracking Progress for an Object-Oriented Project

Although the recursive/parallel process model is the best framework for an OO project, task parallelism makes project tracking difficult. The project manager can have difficulty establishing meaningful milestones for an OO project because a number of different things are happening at once. In general, the following major milestones can be considered "completed" when the criteria noted have been met:

Technical milestone: OO analysis completed

• All classes and the class hierarchy have been defined and reviewed.

• Class attributes and operations associated with a class have been defined and reviewed.

• Class relationships (Chapter 20) have been established and reviewed.

• A behavioral model (Chapter 20) has been created and reviewed.

• Reusable classes have been noted.

Technical milestone: OO design completed

• The set of subsystems (Chapter 21) have been defined and reviewed.

• Classes are allocated to subsystems and reviewed.

• Task allocation has been established and reviewed.

• Responsibilities and collaborations (Chapter 21) have been identified.

- Attributes and operations have been designed and reviewed.
- The messaging model has been created and reviewed.

Technical milestone: OO programming completed

- Each new class has been implemented in code from the design model.
- Extracted classes (from a reuse library) have been integrated.
- A prototype or increment has been built.

Technical milestone: OO testing

- The correctness and completeness of OO analysis and design models have been reviewed.
- A class–responsibility–collaboration network (Chapter 22) has been developed and reviewed.
- Test cases are designed and class-level tests (Chapter 22) have been conducted for each class.
- Test cases are designed and cluster testing (Chapter 22) is completed, and the classes are integrated.
- System-level tests are completed.

Recalling the recursive/parallel process model discussed earlier in this chapter, it is important to note that each of these milestones may be revisited as different increments are delivered to the customer.

19.5   SUMMARY

Object technologies reflect a natural view of the world. Objects are categorized into classes and class hierarchies. Each class contains a set of attributes that describe it and a set of operations that define its behavior. Objects model almost any identifiable aspect of the problem domain: External entities, things, occurrences, roles, organizational units, places, and structures can all be represented as objects. As important, objects (and the classes from which they are derived) encapsulate both data and process. Processing operations are part of the object and are initiated by passing the object a message. A class definition, once defined, forms the basis for reusability at the modeling, design, and implementation levels. New objects can be instantiated from a class.

Three important concepts differentiate the OO approach from conventional software engineering. Encapsulation packages data and the operations that manipulate the data into a single named object. Inheritance enables the attributes and operations of a class to be inherited by all subclasses and the objects that are instantiated from them. Polymorphism enables a number of different operations to have the same name, reducing the number of lines of code required to implement a system and facilitating changes when they are made.

Object-oriented products and systems are engineered using an evolutionary model, sometimes called a recursive/parallel model. OO software evolves iteratively and must be managed with the recognition that the final product will be developed over a series of increments.

REFERENCES

[BER93] Berard, E.V., *Essays on Object-Oriented Software Engineering,* Addison-Wesley, 1993.

[BOO86] Booch, G., "Object-Oriented Development," *IEEE Trans. Software Engineering,* vol. SE-12, no. 2, February 1986, pp. 211ff.

[BOO91] Booch, G., *Object-Oriented Design,* Benjamin Cummings, 1991.

[BUD96] Budd, T., *An Introduction to Object-Oriented Programming,* 2nd edition, Addison-Wesley, 1996.

[CAS89] Cashman, M., "Object Oriented Domain Analysis," *ACM Software Engineering Notes,* vol. 14, no. 6, October 1989, p. 67.

[CHA93] de Champeaux, D., D. Lea, and P. Faure, *Object-Oriented System Development,* Addison-Wesley, 1993.

[COA91] Coad, P., and E. Yourdon, *Object-Oriented Analysis,* 2nd edition, Prentice-Hall, 1991.

[COX86] Cox, B.J., *Object-Oriented Programming,* Addison-Wesley, 1986.

[EVB89] *Object-Oriented Requirements Analysis* (course notebook), EVB Software Engineering, Inc., Frederick, MD, 1989.

[JAC92] Jacobson, I., *Object-Oriented Software Engineering,* Addison-Wesley, 1992.

[LOR94] Lorenz, M., and J. Kidd, *Object-Oriented Software Metrics,* Prentice-Hall, 1994.

[STR88] Stroustrup, B., "What is Object-Oriented Programming?" *IEEE Software,* vol. 5, no. 3, May 1988, pp. 10–20.

[TAY90] Taylor, D.A., *Object-Oriented Technology: A Manager's Guide,* Addison-Wesley, 1990.

PROBLEMS AND POINTS TO PONDER

19.1. The object-oriented paradigm is "hot." Articles at every level of technical sophistication have been written about it. Using the *Reader's Guide* in your library, find three current nontechnical (not published in engineering journals or magazines; PC magazines are O.K.) articles and write a brief paper summarizing what they have to say.

19.2. In this chapter we did not consider the case in which a new object requires an attribute or operation that is not contained in the class from which it inherited all other attributes and operations. How do you think this is handled?

19.3. Do some research and find the real answer to problem 19.2.

19.4. Using your own words and a few examples, define the terms "class," "encapsulation," "inheritance," and "polymorphism."

19.5. Review the objects defined for the SafeHome system. Are there other objects that you feel should be defined as modeling begins?

19.6. Consider a typical graphical user interface (GUI). Define a set of classes (and subclasses) for the interface entities that typically appear in the GUI. Be sure to define appropriate attributes and operations.

19.7. Provide an example of a composite object.

19.8. You have been assigned the job of engineering new word-processing software. A class named **document** is identified. Define the attributes and operations that are relevant for **document**.

19.9. Research two different OO programming languages and show how messages are implemented in the language syntax. Provide a few examples for each language.

19.10. Provide a concrete example of class hierarchy restructuring as described in the discussion of Figure 19.8.

19.11. Provide a concrete example of multiple inheritance. Research one or more papers on this subject and provide the pro and con arguments for multiple inheritance.

19.12. Develop a statement of scope for a system requested by your instructor. Use the grammatical parse to isolate candidate classes, attributes, and operations for the system. Apply the selection criteria discussed in Section 19.3.1 to determine whether the class should be used in the analysis model.

19.13. In your own words, describe why the recursive/parallel process model is appropriate for OO systems.

19.14. Provide three or four specific examples of the key class and support class described in Section 19.4.2.

FURTHER READINGS AND OTHER INFORMATION SOURCES

The explosion of interest in object technologies has resulted in the publication of literally hundreds of books during the past decade. Taylor's abbreviated treatment [TAY90] remains the best basic introduction to the subject. Books by Baudoin and Hollowell (*Realizing the Object-Oriented Life Cycle,* Prentice-Hall, 1996), Khoshafian and Abnous (*Object-Orientation,* Wiley, 1995), Meyer (*Object Success: A Manager's Guide to Object-Orientation,* Prentice-Hall, 1995), Berard [BER93], Wilkie (*Object-Oriented Software Engineering,* Addison-Wesley, 1993), and Winblad et al. (*Object-Oriented Software,* Addison-Wesley, 1990) provide additional insight into basic concepts, languages, databases, and user interfaces.

An excellent anthology of early papers on object-oriented issues has been compiled by Peterson (*Object-Oriented Computing: Concepts,* IEEE Computer Society Press, 1987). Sigfried (*Understanding Object-Oriented Software Engineering,* IEEE Computer Society Press, 1996) discusses techniques for class and object definition.

The OOPSLA Proceedings, a publication that summarizes the ACM's yearly conference on object-oriented programming systems, is dedicated to object-oriented topics and contains many useful papers. *Object Magazine, Journal of Object-Oriented Programming, C++ Report,* and *The Smalltalk Report* are all published by SIGS Publications, Inc. in Langhorne, Pennsylvania. In October 1995, entire issues of *Communications of the ACM, IEEE Computer,* and *Software Development* were all dedicated to object technologies.

The Internet newsgroup **comp.object** is a useful source for information, discussion, and debate on object technologies. The FAQ for this newsgroup is one of the most comprehensive collections of OO information on the Internet.

The FAQ contains a discussion of most important OO concepts, as well as detailed discussion of OO languages, databases, tools, and associated vendors, and can be found at:

> **http://www.cs.cmu.edu/Web/Groups/AI/html/faqs/lang/oop/faq.html**

Further discussion of OO issues may be found in **comp.software-eng, comp.databases.object, comp.specification,** and **comp.testing**. Pointers to dozens of Web sites, archive information, and related topics on object technologies can be obtained at:

> **http://www.eg3.com/object.htm**
> **http://cuiwww.unige.ch/OSG/OOinfo/index.html**

An excellent OO tutorial that is very useful for those who are first learning about the subject can be found at:

> **http://www.soft-design.com/softinfo/objects.html**

Detailed summaries of dozens of books on OO methods can be obtained at:

> **http://www.amazon.com**

A comprehensive bibliography with references to concepts, methods and languages and tools can be obtained at:

> **http://zgdv.igd.fhg.de/papers/se/oop/**

A collection of useful white papers, general information, references, and pointers can be acquired by visiting:

> **http://www.toa.com**

An up-to-date list of World Wide Web references for object technologies can be found at: **http://www.rspa.com**

CHAPTER 20

OBJECT-ORIENTED ANALYSIS

When a new product or system is to be built, how do we characterize it in a way that is amenable to OO software engineering? What are the relevant objects? How do they relate to one another? How do objects behave in the context of the system? How do we specify or model a problem so that we can create an effective design?

Each of these questions is answered within the context of *object-oriented analysis (OOA)*—the first technical activity that is performed as part of OO software engineering. OOA is grounded in a set of basic principles that were introduced in Chapter 11. In order to build an analysis model, five basic principles are applied: (1) The information domain is modeled; (2) module function is described; (3) model behavior is represented; (4) the models are partitioned to expose greater detail; and (5) early models represent the essence of the problem while later models provide implementation details. These principles form the foundation for the approach to OOA presented in this chapter.

The intent of OOA is to define all classes (and the relationships and behavior associated with them) that are relevant to the problem to be solved. To accomplish this, a number of tasks must occur:

1. Basic user requirements must be communicated between the customer and the software engineer.
2. Classes must be identified (i.e., attributes and methods are defined).
3. A class hierarchy must be specified.
4. Object-to-object relationships (object connections) should be represented.
5. Object behavior must be modeled.
6. Tasks 1 through 5 are reapplied iteratively until the model is complete.

Instead of examining a problem using the classic input–processing–output (information flow) model or a model derived exclusively from hierarchical information structures, OOA introduces a number of new concepts. These new concepts may seem a bit unusual, but they are really quite natural. Coad and Yourdon [COA91] consider this issue when they write:

> OOA—object-oriented analysis—is based upon concepts that we first learned in kindergarten: objects and attributes, classes and members, wholes and parts. Why it has taken us so long to apply these concepts to the analysis and specification of information systems is anyone's guess—perhaps we've been too busy "following the flow" during the heyday of structured analysis to consider the alternatives.

It is important to note that there is no universal agreement on the "concepts" that serve as a foundation for OOA, but a limited number of key ideas appear repeatedly, and it is these that we will consider in this chapter.

20.1   OBJECT-ORIENTED ANALYSIS

The objective of object-oriented analysis is to develop a series of models that describe computer software as it works to satisfy a set of customer-defined requirements. OOA, like the conventional analysis methods described in Chapter 12, builds a multipart analysis model to satisfy this objective. The analysis model depicts information, function, and behavior within the context of the elements of the object model described in Chapter 19.

20.1.1 Conventional vs. OO approaches

Is object-oriented analysis really different from the structured analysis approach that was presented in Chapter 12? Although debate continues, Fichman and Kemerer [FIC92] address the question head-on:

> We conclude that the object-oriented analysis approach . . . represents a radical change over process-oriented methodologies such as structured analysis, but only an incremental change over data oriented methodologies such as information engineering. Process-oriented methodologies focus attention away from the inherent properties of objects during the modeling process and lead to a model of the problem domain that is orthogonal to the three essential principles of object-orientation: encapsulation, classification of objects, and inheritance.

Stated simply, structured analysis takes a distinct input–process–output view of requirements. Data are considered separately from the processes that transform the data. System behavior, although important, tends to play a secondary role in structured analysis. The structured analysis approach makes heavy use of functional decomposition (partitioning of the data flow diagram, Chapter 12).

Fichman and Kemerer [FIC92] suggest 11 "modeling dimensions" that may be used to compare various conventional and object-oriented analysis methods:

1. identification/classification of entities[1]
2. general to specific and whole to part entity relationships
3. other entity relationships
4. description of attributes of entities
5. large scale model partitioning
6. states and transitions between states
7. detailed specification for functions
8. top-down decomposition
9. end-to-end processing sequences
10. identification of exclusive services
11. entity communication (via messages or events)

Because many variations exist for structured analysis and dozens of OOA methods (see Section 20.1.3) are available, it is difficult to develop a generalized comparison between the two methods. It can be stated, however, that modeling dimensions 8 and 9 are always present with SA and rarely present when OOA is used.

20.1.2 The OOA Landscape

The popularity of object technologies has spawned dozens of OOA methods.[2] Each of these introduces a process for the analysis of a product or system, a set of models that evolves out of the process, and a notation that enables the software engineer to create each model in a consistent manner. In the paragraphs that follow, some of the more popular OOA methods[3] are presented in outline form. The intent is to provide a snapshot of the OOA process that has been proposed by the author(s) of the method.[4]

The Booch Method   The Booch method [BOO94] encompasses both a "micro development process" and a "macro development process." The micro level defines

---

[1]In this context, "entity" refers to either a data object (in the structured analysis sense) or an object (in the OOA sense).

[2]A detailed discussion of these methods and their differences is beyond the scope of this book. The interested reader should refer to Berard [BER92] and Graham [GRA94] for detailed comparisons.

[3]In general, OOA methods are identified using the name(s) of the developer of the method, even if the method has been given a unique name or acronym.

[4]The meaning of many of the steps outlined in the process descriptions that follow will be discussed in Sections 20.3 and 20.4. It should also be noted that each of these methods also has a design component that will be discussed briefly in Chapter 21.

a set of analysis tasks that are re-applied for each step in the macro process. Hence, an evolutionary approach is maintained. The Booch method is supported by a variety of automated tools. A brief outline of Booch's OOA micro development process follows:

- Identify classes and objects.
  - Propose candidate objects.
  - Conduct behavior analysis.
  - Identify relevant scenarios.
  - Define attributes and operations for each class.
- Identify the semantics of classes and objects.
  - Select scenarios and analyze.
  - Assign responsibility to achieve desired behavior.
  - Partition responsibilities to balance behavior.
  - Select an object and enumerate its roles and responsibilities.
  - Define operations to satisfy the responsibilities.
  - Look for collaborations among objects.
- Identify relationships among classes and objects.
  - Define dependencies that exist between objects.
  - Describe the role of each participating object.
  - Validate by walking through scenarios.
- Conduct a series of refinements.
  - Produce appropriate diagrams for the work conducted above.
  - Define class hierarchies as appropriate.
  - Perform clustering based on class commonality.
- Implement classes and objects (in the context of OOA, this implies completion of the analysis model).

The Coad and Yourdon Method   The Coad and Yourdon method [COA91] is often viewed as one of the easiest OOA methods to learn. Modeling notation is relatively simple and guidelines for developing the analysis model are straightforward. A brief outline of Coad and Yourdon's OOA process follows:

- Identify objects using "what to look for" criteria.
- Define a generalization–specification structure.
- Define a whole–part structure.
- Identify subjects (representations of subsystem components).
- Define attributes.
- Define services.

The Jacobson Method   Also called OOSE (object-oriented software engineering), the Jacobson method [JAC92] is a simplified version of the proprietary Objectory method, also developed by Jacobson. This method is differentiated from others by heavy emphasis on the *use case*—a description or scenario that depicts how the user interacts with the product or system. A brief outline of Jacobson's OOA process follows:

- Identify the users of the system and their overall responsibilities.
- Build a requirements model.
    Define the actors and their responsibilities.
    Identify use cases for each actor.
    Prepare initial view of system objects and relationships.
    Review model using use cases as scenarios to determine validity.
- Build analysis model.
    Identify interface objects using actor-interaction information.
    Create structural views of interface objects.
    Represent object behavior.
    Isolate subsystems and models for each.
    Review the model using use cases as scenarios to determine validity.

The Rambaugh Method   Rambaugh [RAM91] and his colleagues developed the Object Modeling Technique (OMT) for analysis, system design, and object-level design. The analysis activity creates three models: the object model (a representation of objects, classes, hierarchies, and relationships), the dynamic model (a representation of object and system behavior), and the functional model (a high-level DFD-like representation of information flow through the system). A brief outline of Rambaugh's OOA process follows:

- Develop a statement of scope for the problem.
- Build an object model.
    Identify classes that are relevant for the problem.
    Define attributes and associations.
    Define object links.
    Organize object classes using inheritance.
- Develop a dynamic model.
    Prepare scenarios.
    Define events and develop an event trace for each scenario.
    Construct an event flow diagram.
    Develop a state diagram.
    Review behavior for consistency and completeness.
- Construct a functional model for the system.
    Identify inputs and outputs.
    Use data flow diagrams to represent flow transformations.
    Develop PSPECs (Chapter 12) for each function.
    Specify constraints and optimization criteria.

It should be noted that work is underway to merge the Booch and Rambaugh methods. The resultant set of notation and heuristics, called the *Unified Method* ([BOO96], [LOC96]) combines the strong data emphasis of Rambaugh with the behavioral and operational emphasis of Booch.

The Wirfs-Brock Method Wirfs-Brock method [WIR90] does not make a clear distinction between analysis and design tasks. Instead, a continuous process that begins with the assessment of a customer specification and ends with design is proposed. A brief outline of Wirfs-Brock's analysis-related tasks follows:

- Evaluate the customer specification.
- Use a grammatical parse to extract candidate classes from the specification.
- Group classes in an attempt to identify superclasses.
- Define responsibilities for each class.
- Assign responsibilities to each class.
- Identify relationships between classes.
- Define collaboration between classes based on responsibilities.
- Build hierarchical representations of classes to show inheritance relationships.
- Construct a collaboration graph for the system.

Although the terminology and process steps for each of these OOA methods differ, the overall OOA processes are really quite similar. To perform object-oriented analysis, a software engineer should perform the following generic steps:

- Obtain customer requirements for the OO System.
    - Identify scenarios or use cases.
    - Build a requirements model.
- Select classes and objects using basic requirements as a guide.
- Identify attributes and operations for each system object.
- Define structures and hierarchies that organize classes.
- Build an object-relationship model.
- Build an object-behavior model.
- Review the OO analysis model against use cases/scenarios.

These generic steps are considered in greater detail in Sections 20.3 and 20.4.

20.2   DOMAIN ANALYSIS

Analysis for object-oriented systems can occur at many different levels of abstraction. At the business or enterprise level, the techniques associated with OOA can be coupled with an information engineering approach (Chapter 10) in an effort to define classes, objects, relationships, and behaviors that model the entire business. This level of OOA is analogous to information strategy planning. At the business area level, an object model that describes the workings of a particular business area (or a category of products or systems) can be defined. At an application level, the object model focuses on specific customer requirements as those requirements affect an application to be built.

OOA at the highest level of abstraction (the enterprise level) is beyond the scope of this book. Interested readers should see [DUE92], [MAT94], [SUL94], and [TAY95] for a detailed discussion. OOA at the lowest level of abstraction falls within the general purview of object-oriented software engineering and is the focus of all other sections of this chapter. In this section, we focus on OOA that is conducted at the middle level of abstraction. This activity, called *domain analysis,* is conducted when an organization wants to create a library of reusable classes (components) that will be broadly applicable to an entire category of applications.

20.2.1 Reuse and Domain Analysis

Object technologies are leveraged through reuse. Consider a simple example. The analysis of requirements for a new application indicates that 100 classes are needed. Two teams are assigned to build the application. Each will design and construct a final product. Each is populated by people with the same skill levels and experience.

Team A does not have access to a class library, so it must develop all 100 classes from scratch. Team B uses a robust class library and finds that 55 classes already exist. It is highly likely that:

1. Team B will finish the project much sooner than team A.
2. The cost of team B's product will be significantly lower than the cost of team A's product.
3. The product produced by team B will have fewer delivered defects than team A's product.

Although the margin by which team B's work would exceed team A's accomplishments is open to debate, few would argue that reuse provides team B will a substantial advantage.

But where did the "robust class library" come from? And how were the entries in the library determined to be appropriate for use in new applications? To answer these questions, the organization that created and maintained the library had to apply domain analysis.

20.2.2 The Domain Analysis Process

Firesmith [FIR93] describes software domain analysis in the following way:

> Software domain analysis is the identification, analysis, and specification of common requirements from a specific application domain, typically for reuse on multiple projects within that application domain. . . . [Object-oriented domain

analysis is] the identification, analysis, and specification of common, reusable capabilities within a specific application domain, in terms of common objects, classes, subassemblies, and frameworks. . . .

The "specific application domain" can range from avionics to banking, from multimedia video games to applications within a CAT scanner. The goal of domain analysis is straightforward: to find or create those classes that are broadly applicable, so that they may be reused.[5]

Using jargon that was introduced earlier in this book, domain analysis may be viewed as an umbrella activity for the software process. By this we mean that domain analysis is an ongoing software engineering activity that is not connected to any one software project. In a way, the role of a domain analyst is similar to the role of a master toolsmith in a heavy manufacturing environment. The job of the toolsmith is to design and build tools that may be used by many people doing similar, but not necessarily the same jobs. The role of the domain analyst is to design and build reusable components that may be used by many people working on similar, but not necessarily the same applications.

Figure 20.1 [ARA89] illustrates key inputs and outputs for the domain analysis process. Sources of domain knowledge are surveyed in an attempt to identify objects that can be reused across the domain. In essence domain analysis is quite similar to knowledge engineering. The knowledge engineer investigates a specific area of interest in an attempt to extract key facts that may be of use in creating an expert system or artificial neural network. During domain analysis, object (and class) extraction occurs.

The domain analysis process can be characterized by a series of activities that begin with the identification of the domain to be investigated and end with a specification of the objects and classes that characterize the domain. Berard [BER93] suggests the following activities:

Define the domain to be investigated. To accomplish this, the analyst must first isolate the business area, system type, or product category of

---

[5]The technology associated with software reuse is discussed in detail in Chapter 26.

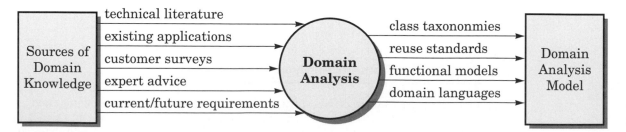

FIGURE 20.1. Input and outputs for domain analysis

interest. Next, both OO and non-OO "items" must be extracted. OO items include specifications, designs, and code for existing OO application classes; support classes (e.g., GUI classes or database access classes); commercial off-the shelf (COTS) component libraries that are relevant to the domain; and test cases. Non-OO items encompass policies, procedures, plans, standards, and guidelines; parts of existing non-OO applications (including specification, design and test information); metrics; and COTS non-OO software.

Categorize the items extracted from the domain. The items are organized into categories, and the general defining characteristics of the category are defined. A classification scheme for the categories is proposed, and naming conventions for each item are defined. When appropriate, classification hierarchies are established.

Collect a representative sample of applications in the domain. To accomplish this activity, the analyst must ensure that the application in question has items that fit into the categories that have already been defined. Berard [BER93] notes that during the early stages of use of object technologies, a software organization will have few if any OO applications. Therefore, the domain analyst must "identify the *conceptual* (as opposed to *physical*) objects in each [non-OO] application."

Analyze each application in the sample. The following steps [BER93] occur during domain analysis:

- identify candidate reusable objects;
- indicate the reasons that the object has been identified for reuse;
- define adaptations to the object that may also be reusable;
- estimate the percentage of applications in the domain that might make reuse of the object; and
- identify the objects by name, and use configuration management techniques (Chapter 9) to control them.

In addition, once the objects have been defined, the analysis should estimate what percentage of a typical application could be constructed using the reusable objects.

Develop an analysis model for the objects. The analysis model will service as the basis for design and construction of the domain objects.

In addition to these steps, the domain analyst should also create a set of reuse guidelines and develop an example that illustrates how the domain objects could be used to create a new application.

Domain analysis is the first technical activity in a broader discipline that some call *domain engineering* (Chapter 26). When a business, system, or product domain is defined to be business strategic in the long term, a continuing effort to create a robust reuse library can be undertaken. The goal is to be able to create software within the domain with a very high percentage of reusable components. Lower cost, higher quality, and improved time to market are the arguments in favor of a dedicated domain engineering effort.

20.3   GENERIC COMPONENTS OF THE OO ANALYSIS MODEL

The object-oriented analysis process conforms to the basic analysis concepts and principles discussed in Chapter 11. Although the terminology, notation, and activities differ from conventional methods, OOA (at its kernel) addresses the same underlying objectives. Rambaugh et al. [RAM91] discuss this when they state:

> Analysis . . . is concerned with devising a precise, concise, understandable, and correct model of the real world. . . . The purpose of object-oriented analysis is to model the real world so that it can be understood. To do this, you must examine requirements, analyze their implications, and restate them rigorously. You must abstract real-world features first, and defer small details until later.

To develop a "precise, concise, understandable, and correct model of the real world," a software engineer must select from one of a number of OOA notations and processes. As we noted in Section 20.1.2, each OOA method (and there are dozens of them) has a unique process and a distinct notation. And yet, all conform to a set of generic process steps (Section 20.1.2) and all provide a notation that implements a set of generic components of an OO analysis model.

Monarchi and Puhr [MON92] define a set of generic representational components that appear in all OO analysis models.[6] *Static components* are structural in nature and indicate characteristics that hold throughout the operational life of an application. These characteristics distinguish one object from other objects. *Dynamic components* focus on control and are sensitive to timing and event processing. They define how one object interacts with other objects over time. The following components are identified [MON92]:

Static view of semantic classes. A taxonomy of typical classes was identified in Chapter 19. Requirements are assessed and classes are extracted (and represented) as part of the analysis model. These classes persist throughout the life of the application and are derived based on the semantics of the customer requirements.

Static view of attributes. Every class must be explicitly described. The attributes associated with the class provide a description of the class as well as a first indication of the operations that are relevant to the class.

Static view of relationships. Objects are "connected" to one another in a variety of ways. The analysis model must represent these relationships so that operations (that affect these connections) can be identified and so that the design of an messaging approach can be accomplished.

Static view of behaviors. The relationships noted above define a set of behaviors that accommodate the usage scenario (use cases) of the system.

---

[6]The authors [MON92] also provide an analysis of 23 OOA methods and indicate how they address these components.

These behaviors are implemented by defining a sequence of operations that achieve them.

Dynamic view of communication. Objects must communicate with one another and do so based on a series of events that cause transitions from one state of a system to another.

Dynamic view of control and time. The nature and timing of events that cause transitions among states must be described.

As shown in Figure 20.2, de Champeaux and his colleagues [CHA93] define a slightly different view of OOA representations. Static and dynamic components are identified for object internals and for inter-object representations. A dynamic view of object internals can be characterized as an *object life history,* that is, the states of the object over time as various operations are performed on its attributes.

20.4   THE OOA PROCESS

The OOA process does not begin with a concern for objects. Rather, it begins with an understanding of the manner in which the system will be used—by people, if the system is human-interactive; by machines, if the system is involved in process control; or by other programs, if the system coordinates and controls applications. Once the scenario of usage has been defined, the modeling of the software begins.

The sections that follow define a series of techniques that may be used to gather basic customer requirements and then define an analysis model for an object-oriented system.

	object internals	interobject representations
static components	class attributes operations	object relationships states transitions
dynamic components	object life history	communication timing

FIGURE 20.2.
OOA representations [CHA93]

20.4.1 Use Cases

Requirements gathering is always the first step in any software analysis activity. As we discussed in Chapter 11, requirements gathering can take the form of a FAST meeting in which customer and developer meet to define basic system and software requirements. Based on these requirements, the software engineer (analyst) can create a set of scenarios that each identify a thread of usage for the system to be constructed. The scenarios, often called *use cases* [JAC92], provide a description of how the system will be used.

To create a use case, the analyst must first identify the different types of people (or devices) that use the system or product. These *actors* actually represent roles that people (or devices) play as the system operates. Defined somewhat more formally, an actor is anything that communicates with the system or product and that is external to the system itself.

It is important to note that an actor and a user are *not* the same thing. A typical user may play a number of different roles when using a system, whereas an actor represents a class of external entities (often, but not always people) that play just one role. As an example, consider a machine operator (a user) who interacts with the control computer for a manufacturing cell that contains a number of robots and numerically controlled machines. After careful review of requirements, the software for the control computer requires four different modes (roles) for interaction: programming mode, test mode, monitoring mode, and troubleshooting mode. Therefore, four actors can be defined: programmer, tester, monitor, and troubleshooter. In some cases, the machine operator can play all of these roles. In others, different people may play the role of each actor.

Like other aspects of the OO analysis model, not all actors are identified during the first iteration. It is possible to identify *primary actors* [JAC92] during the first iteration and *secondary actors* as more is learned about the system. Primary actors interact to achieve required system function and derive the intended benefit from the system. They work directly and frequently with the software. Secondary actors exist to support the system so that primary actors can do their work.

Once actors have been identified, use cases can be developed. The use case describes the manner in which an actor interacts with the system. Jacobson [JAC92] suggests a number of questions that should be answered by the use case:

- What are the main tasks or functions that are performed by the actor?
- What system information will the actor acquire, produce, or change?
- Will the actor have to inform the system about changes in the external environment?
- What information does the actor desire from the system?
- Does the actor wish to be informed about unexpected changes?

In general, a use case is simply a written narrative that describes the role of an actor as interaction with the system occurs.

The SafeHome security system, discussed in earlier chapters, can be used to illustrate how use cases can be developed. Recalling basic SafeHome requirements, we can define three actors: the homeowner (the user), sensors (devices attached to the system), and the monitoring and response subsystem (the central station that monitors SafeHome). For the purposes of this example, we consider only the homeowner actor. The homeowner interacts with the product in a number of different ways:

- inputs a password to allow all other interactions
- inquires about the status of a security zone
- inquires about the status of a sensor
- presses the panic button in an emergency
- activates/deactivates the security system

A use case for system activation follows:

1. The homeowner observes the SafeHome control panel (Figure 11.4) to determine if the system is ready for input. If the system is *not ready,* the homeowner must physically close windows/doors so that the ready indicator is present. (A *not ready* indicator implies that a sensor is open, i.e., that a door or window is open.)

2. The homeowner uses the key pad to key in a four digit password. The password is compared with the valid password stored in the system. If the password is incorrect, the control panel will beep once and reset itself for additional input. If the password is correct, the control panel awaits further action.

3. The homeowner selects and keys in *stay* or *away* (see Figure 11.4) to activate the system. *Stay* activates only perimeter sensors (inside motion detecting sensors are deactivated). *Away* activates all sensors.

4. When activation occurs, a red alarm light can be observed by the homeowner.

Use cases for other homeowner interactions would be developed in a similar manner. It is important to note that each use case must be reviewed with care. If some element of the interaction is ambiguous, it is likely that a review of the use case will indicate a problem.

Each use case provides an unambiguous scenario of interaction between an actor and the software. It can also be used to specify timing requirements or other constraints for the scenario. For example, in the use case noted above, requirements indicate that activation occurs 30 seconds after the *stay* or *away* key is hit. This information can be appended to the use case.

Use cases describe scenarios that will be perceived differently by different actors. Wyder [WYD96] suggests that quality function deployment (QFD)[7] can be used to develop a weighted priority value for each use case. To accomplish this, use cases are evaluated from the point of view of all actors defined for the system. A priority value is assigned to each use case (e.g., a value from 1 to 10) by each of the actors.[8] An average priority is then computed, indicating the perceived importance of each of the use cases. When an iterative or incremental

---

[7]QFD is discussed briefly in Chapter 11.

[8]Ideally, this evaluation should be performed by individuals from the organization or business function represented by an actor.

process model is used for object-oriented software engineering, the priorities can influence which system functionality is delivered first.

20.4.2 Class–Responsibility–Collaborator Modeling

Once basic usage scenarios have been developed for the system, it is time to identify candidate classes, and indicate their responsibilities and collaborations. *Class–responsibility–collaborator (CRC) modeling* [WIR90] provides a simple means for identifying and organizing the classes that are relevant to system or product requirements. Ambler [AMB95] describes CRC modeling in the following way:

> A CRC model is really a collection of standard index cards that represent classes. The cards are divided into three sections. Along the top of the card you write the name of the class. In the body of the card you list the class responsibilities on the left and the collaborators on the right.

In reality, the CRC model may make use of actual or virtual index cards. The intent is to develop an organized representation of classes. *Responsibilities* are the attributes and operations that are relevant for the class. Stated simply, a responsibility is "anything the class knows or does" [AMB95]. *Collaborators* are those classes that are required to provide a class with the information needed to complete a responsibility. In general, a collaboration implies either a request for information or a request for some action.

Classes

Basic guidelines for identifying classes and objects were presented in Chapter 19. To summarize, objects manifest themselves in a variety of forms (Section 19.3.1): external entities, things, occurrences or events, roles, organizational units, places, or structures. One technique for identifying these in the context of a software problem is to perform a grammatical parse on the processing narrative for the system. All nouns become potential objects. However, not every potential object makes the cut. Six selection characteristics were defined in Chapter 19: retained information, needed services, multiple attributes, common attributes, common operations, and essential requirements. A potential object should satisfy all six of these selection characteristics if it is to be considered for inclusion in the CRC model.

Firesmith [FIR93] extends the taxonomy of class types noted above by suggesting the following additions:

Device classes. Model external entities such as sensors, motors, and keyboards.

Property classes. Represent some important property of the problem environment (e.g., credit rating within the context of a mortgage loan application).

Interaction classes. Model interactions that occur among other objects (e.g., a purchase or a license).

In addition, objects and classes may be categorized by a set of characteristics:

Tangibility. Does the class represent a tangible thing (e.g., a keyboard or sensor), or does it represent more abstract information (e.g., a predicted outcome)?

Inclusiveness. Is the class *atomic* (i.e., it does not include any other classes) or is it *aggregate* (it includes at least one nested object)?

Sequentiality. Is the class *concurrent* (i.e., it has its own thread of control) or *sequential* (it is controlled by outside resources)?

Persistence. Is the class *transient* (i.e., it is created and removed during program operation); *temporary* (it is created during program operation and removed once the program terminates); or *permanent* (it is stored in a database)?

Integrity. Is the class corruptible (i.e., it does not protect its resources from outside influence) or is it guarded (the class enforces controls on access to its resources)?

Using the class categories noted above, the "index card" created as part of the CRC model might be extended to include the type of class and its characteristics (Figure 20.3).

Responsibilities

Basic guidelines for identifying responsibilities (attributes and operations) were also presented in Chapter 19. To summarize, attributes represent stable features of a class, that is, information about the class that must be retained

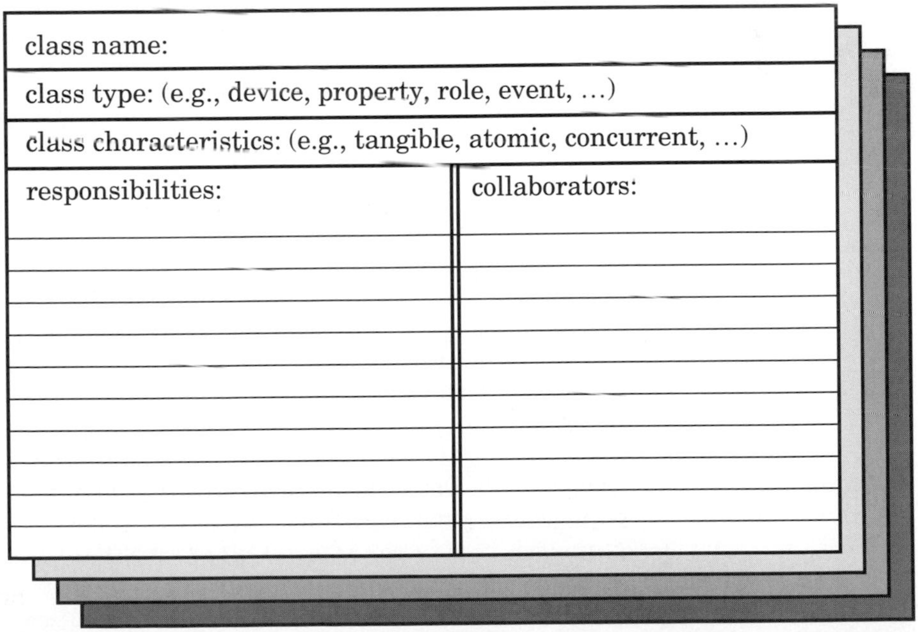

FIGURE 20.3.
A CRC model index card

to accomplish the objectives of the software specified by the customer. Attributes can often be extracted from the statement of scope or discerned from an understanding of the nature of the class. Operations can be extracted by performing a grammatical parse on the processing narrative for the system. Verbs become candidate operations. Each operation that is chosen for a class exhibits a behavior of the class.

Wirfs-Brock and her colleagues [WIR90] suggest five guidelines for allocating responsibilities to classes:

1. *System intelligence should be evenly distributed.* Every application encompasses a certain degree of intelligence, i.e., what the system knows and what it can do. This intelligence can be distributed across classes in a number of different ways. "Dumb" classes (those that have few responsibilities) can be modeled to act as servants to a few "smart" classes (those having many responsibilities). Although this approach makes the flow of control in a system straightforward, it has a few disadvantages:

   - It concentrates all intelligence within a few classes, making changes more difficult.

   - It tends to require more classes and therefore more development effort.

   Therefore, system intelligence should be evenly distributed across the classes in an application. Because each object knows about and does only a few things (that are generally well-focused), the cohesiveness of the system is improved. In addition, side effects due to change tend to be dampened because system intelligence has been decoupled across many objects.

   To determine whether system intelligence is evenly distributed, the responsibilities noted on each CRC model index card should be evaluated to determine if any class has an extraordinarily long list of responsibilities. This indicates a concentration of intelligence. In addition, the responsibilities for each class should exhibit the same level of abstraction. For example, among the operations listed for an aggregate class called **checking account** are two responsibilities: *balance-the-account* and *check-off-cleared-checks*. The first operation (responsibility) implies a complex mathematical and logical procedure. The second is a simple clerical activity. Since these two operations are not at the same level of abstraction, *check-off-cleared-checks* should be placed within the responsibilities of **check-entry,** a class that is encompassed by the aggregate class **checking account**.

2. *Each responsibility should be stated as generally as possible.* This guideline implies that general responsibilities (both attributes and operations) should reside high in the class hierarchy (because they are generic, they will apply to all subclasses). In addition, polymorphism (Chapter 19) should be used in an effort to define operations that generally apply to the superclass but are implemented differently in each of the subclasses.

3. *Information and the behavior that is related to it should reside within the same class.* This achieves the OO principle that we call encapsulation (Chapter 19). Data and the processes that manipulate the data should be packaged as a cohesive unit.

4. *Information about one thing should be localized within a single class, not distributed across multiple classes.* A single class should take on the re-

sponsibility for storing and manipulating a specific type of information. This responsibility should not, in general, be shared across a number of classes. If information is distributed, software becomes more difficult to maintain and more challenging to test.

5. *Share responsibilities among related classes, when appropriate.* There are many cases in which a variety of related objects must all exhibit the same behavior at the same time. As an example, consider a video game that must display the following objects: **player, player-body, player-arms, player-head.** Each of these objects has its own attributes (e.g., *position, orientation, color, speed*), and all must be updated and displayed as the user manipulates a joy stick. The responsibilities *update* and *display* must therefore be shared by each of the objects noted. **Player** knows when something has changed and *update* is required. It collaborates with the other objects to achieve a new position or orientation, but each object controls its own display.

Collaborators

Classes fulfill their responsibilities in one of two ways: (1) A class can use its own operations to manipulate its own attributes, thereby fulfilling a particular responsibility, or (2) a class can collaborate with other classes.

Wirfs-Brock [WIR90] and her colleagues define collaborations in the following way:

> Collaborations represent requests from a client to a server in fulfillment of a client responsibility. A collaboration is the embodiment of the contract between the client and the server. . . . We say that an object collaborates with another object if, to fulfill a responsibility, it needs to send the other object any messages. A single collaboration flows in one direction—representing a request from the client to the server. From the client's point of view, each of its collaborations is associated with a particular responsibility implemented by the server.

Collaborations identify relationships between classes. When a set of classes all collaborate to achieve some requirement, they can be organized into a subsystem (a design issue).

Collaborations are identified by determining whether a class can fulfill each responsibility itself. If it cannot, then it needs to interact with another class. Hence, a collaboration.

As an example, consider the SafeHome application.[9] As part of the activation procedure (see the use case for activation in Section 20.4.1), the **control panel** object must determine whether any sensors are open. A responsibility named *determine-sensor-status* is defined. If sensors are open, **control panel** must set a *status* attribute to "not ready." Sensor information can be acquired from the **sensor** object. Therefore, the responsibility *determine-sensor-status* can be fulfilled only if **control panel** works in collaboration with **sensor**.

---

[9]See Section 19.3 for a delineation of classes for SafeHome.

To help in the identification of collaborators, the analyst can examine three different generic relationships between classes [WIR90]: (1) the *is-part-of* relationship, (2) the *has-knowledge-of* relationship, and (3) the *depends-upon* relationship. By creating a class-relationship diagram (Section 20.4.4), the analyst develops the connections necessary to identify these relationships. Each of the three generic relations is considered briefly in the paragraphs that follow.

All classes that are part of an aggregate class are connected to the aggregate class via an *is-part-of* relationship. Consider the classes defined for the video game noted earlier, the class **player-body** *is-part-of* **player,** as are **player-arms, player-legs,** and **player-head**.

When one class must acquire information from another class, the *has-knowledge-of* relationship is established. The *determine-sensor-status* responsibility noted earlier is an example of a *has-knowledge-of* relationship.

The *depends-upon* relationship implies that two classes have a dependency that is not achieved by *has-knowledge-of* or *is-part-of.* For example, **player-head** must always be connected to **player-body** (unless the video game is particularly violent), yet each object could exist without direct knowledge of the other. An attribute of the **player-head** object called *center-position* is determined from the *center-position* of **player-body.** This information is obtained via a third object, **player,** which acquires it from **player-body.** Hence, **player-head** *depends-upon* **player-body**.

In all cases, the collaborator class name is recorded on the CRC model index card next to the responsibility that has spawned the collaboration. Therefore, the index card contains a list of responsibilities and the corresponding collaborations that enable responsibilities to be fulfilled.

When a complete CRC model has been developed, the representatives from the customer and software engineering organizations can walk through the model using the following approach [AMB95]:

1. All participants in the review (of the CRC model) are given a subset of the CRC model index cards. Cards that collaborate should be separated (i.e., no reviewer should have two cards that collaborate).

2. All use case scenarios should be organized into categories.

3. The review leader reads the use case deliberately. As the review leader comes to a named object, she passes the token to the person holding the corresponding class index card. For example, the use case noted in Section 20.4.1 contains the following narrative:

   1. The homeowner observes the SafeHome **control panel** (Figure 11.4) to determine if the system is ready for input. If the system is *not ready,* the homeowner must physically close windows/doors so that the ready indicator is present. [A *not ready* indicator implies that a **sensor** is open, i.e., that a door or window is open.]

When the review leader comes to "control panel," in the use case narrative, the token is passed to the person holding the **control panel** card. The phrase "implies that a sensor is open" requires that the index card contains a responsibility that will validate this implication (the responsibility *determine-sensor-status* accomplishes this). Next to the responsibility on the index card is the collaborator **sensor.** The token is then passed to the **sensor** object.

4. When the token is passed, the holder of the class card is asked to describe the responsibilities noted on the card. The group determines whether one (or more) of the responsibilities satisfies the use case requirement.

5. If the responsibilities and collaborations noted on the index cards cannot accommodate the use case, modifications are made to the cards. This may include the definition of new classes (and corresponding CRC index cards) or the specification of new or revised responsibilities or collaborations on existing cards. This modus operandi continues until the use case is finished.

The CRC model is a first representation of the analysis model for an OO system. It can be "tested" by conducting a review that is driven by use cases derived for the system.

20.4.3   Defining Structures and Hierarchies

Once classes and objects have been identified using the CRC model, the analyst begins to focus on the *structure* of the class model and the resultant hierarchies that arise as classes and subclasses emerge. Coad and Yourdon [COA91] suggest that a *generalization–specialization (gen–spec) structure* should be derived for the identified classes.

To illustrate, consider the **sensor** object defined for SafeHome and shown in Figure 20.4. Here, the generalization, **sensor,** is refined into a set of specializations—**entry sensor, smoke sensor,** and **motion sensor.** We have created a simple class hierarchy.

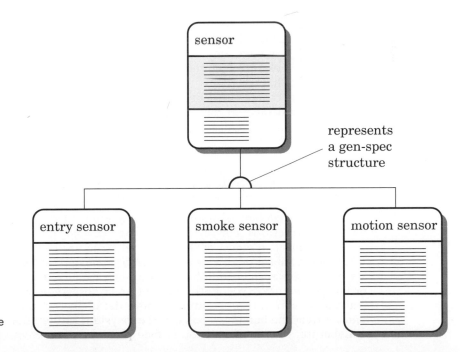

represents
a gen-spec
structure

FIGURE 20.4.
Gen–spec structure
notation

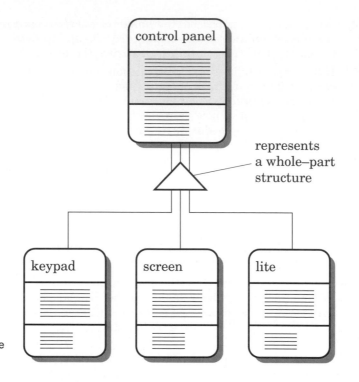

represents
a whole–part
structure

FIGURE 20.5.
Whole–part structure
notation

In other cases, an object represented in the initial model might actually be composed of a number of component parts that could themselves be defined as objects. These aggregate objects can be represented as a *whole–part structure* [COA91] and are defined using the notation represented in Figure 20.5. The triangle implies as assembly relationship. It should be noted that the connecting lines may be augmented with additional symbols (not shown) to represent cardinality. These are adapted from the entity-relationship modeling notation discussed in Chapter 12.

Structure representations provide the analyst with a means for partitioning the CRC model and representing that partitioning graphically. The expansion of each class provides needed detail for review and for subsequent design.

20.4.4 Defining Subjects and Subsystems

An analysis model for a complex application may have hundreds of classes and dozens of structures. For this reason, it is necessary to define a concise representation that is a digest of the CRC and structure models described above.

When a subset of all classes collaborate among themselves to accomplish a set of cohesive responsibilities, they are often referred to as *subjects* [COA91] or *subsystems* [WIR90]. Both subjects and subsystems are abstractions that provide a reference or pointer to more detail in the analysis model. When viewed from the outside, a subject or subsystem can be treated as a black box that contains a set of responsibilities and that has its own (outside) collaborators. A subsystem implements one or more *contracts* with its outside collaborators. A contract is a specific list of requests that collaborators can make of the subsystem.[10]

Subsystems can be represented within the context of CRC modeling by creating a subsystem index card. The subsystem index card indicates the name of the subsystem, the contracts that the subsystem must accommodate, and the classes or (other) subsystems that support the contract.

Subjects are identical to subsystems in intent and content, but are represented graphically. For example, assume that the control panel for SafeHome is considerably more complex than the one implied by Figure 20.5, containing multiple display areas, a sophisticated key arrangement, and other features. It might be modeled as an whole–part structure shown in Figure 20.6. If the overall requirements model contains dozens of these structures (SafeHome would not), it would be difficult to absorb the entire representation at one time. By defining a subject reference as shown in the figure, the entire structure can be referenced by a single icon (the rectangle). Subject references are generally created for any structure that has more than five or six objects.

At the most abstract level, the OOA model would contain only subject references such as those illustrated at the top of Figure 20.7. Each of the references would be expanded into a structure. Structures for the **control panel** and **sensor** objects (Figures 20.6 and 20.4) are illustrated; structures for **system, sensor event,** and **audible alarm** would also be created if these objects required more than five or six classification or assembly objects.

The doubled-headed arrows shown in at the top of Figure 20.7 represent communication (message) paths between objects contained within the subject references. These are derived as a consequence of the modeling activities described in the next section.

20.5   THE OBJECT-RELATIONSHIP MODEL

The CRC modeling approach that has been used in earlier sections has established the first elements of class and object relationships. The first step in establishing relationships is to understand the responsibilities for each class. The CRC model index card contains a list of responsibilities. The next step is to define those collaborator classes that help in achieving each responsibility. This establishes the "connection" between classes.

A *relationship* exists between any two classes that are connected.[11] Therefore, collaborators are always related in some way. The most common type of relationship is binary—a connection exists between two classes. When considered within the context of an OO system, a binary relationship has a spe-

---

[10]Recall that classes interact using a client/server philosophy. In this case the subsystem is the server and outside collaborators are clients.

[11]Other terms for relationship are "association" [RAM91] and "connection" [COA91].

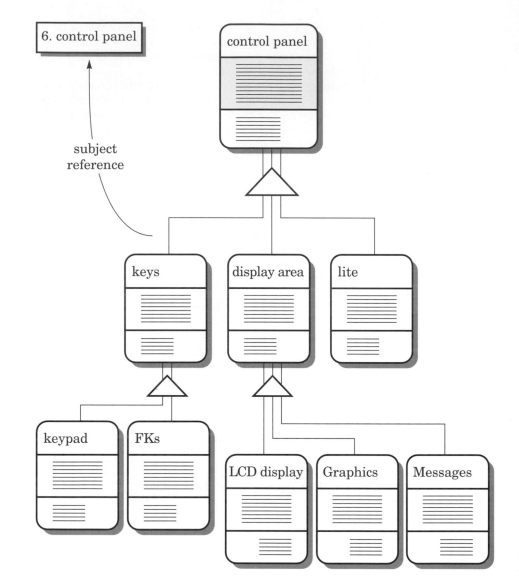

FIGURE 20.6.
Subject reference

cific direction[12] that is defined by which class plays the role of the client and
which acts as a server.

Rambaugh and his colleagues [RAM91] suggest that relationships can be
derived by examining the verbs or verb phrases in the statement of scope or
use cases for the system. Using a grammatical parse, the analyst isolates verbs
that indicate physical location or placement (*next to, part of, contained in*), communications (*transmits to, acquires from*), ownership (*incorporated by, is com-*

---

[12]It is important to note that this is a departure from the bidirectional nature of relationships
used in data modeling (Chapter 12).

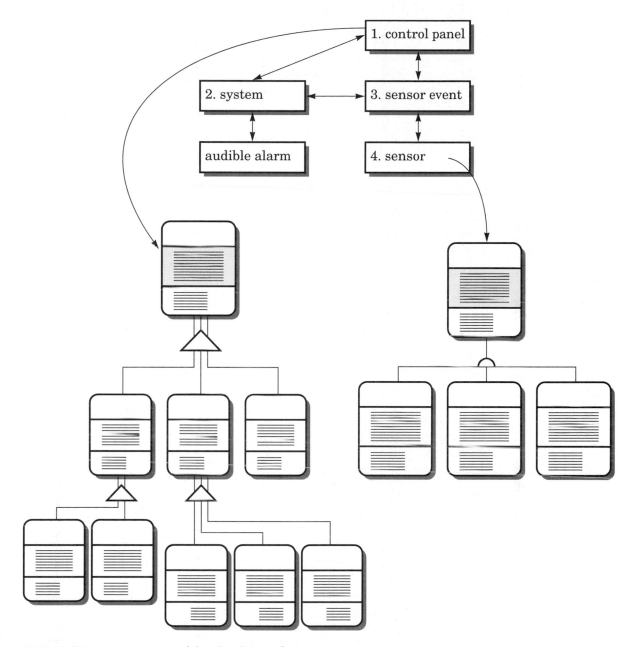

FIGURE 20.7. An OOA model with subject references

posed of), and satisfaction of a condition (*manages, coordinates, controls*). These provide an indication of a relationship.

A variety of different graphical notations has been proposed for the object-relationship model (e.g., [COA91], [RAM91], [EMB92], [BOO94]). Although each makes use of its own symbology, all are adapted from the entity-relationship

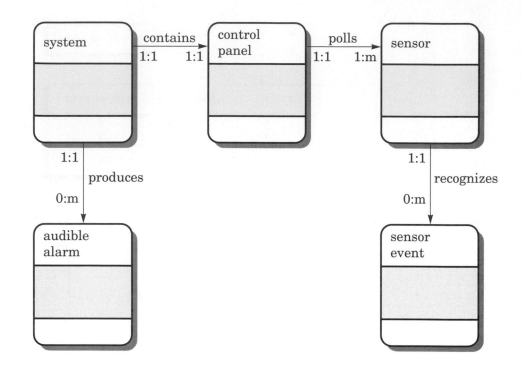

FIGURE 20.8.
Cardinality is
defined

modeling techniques discussed in Chapter 12. In essence, objects are connected
to other objects using named relationships. The cardinality of the connection (see
Chapter 12) is specified, and an overall network of relationships is established.

The object-relationship model (like the entity-relationship model) can be
derived in three steps:

1. Using the CRC index cards, a network of collaborator objects can be drawn.
   Figure 20.8 represents the class connections for SafeHome objects. First the
   objects are drawn connected by unlabeled lines (not shown in the figure)
   that indicate some relationship exists between the connected objects.

2. Reviewing the CRC model index card, responsibilities and collaborators are
   evaluated and each unlabeled connected line is named. To avoid ambiguity,
   an arrowhead indicates the "direction" of the relationship (Figure 20.8).

3. Once the named relationships have been established, each end is evaluated
   to determine cardinality (Figure 20.8). Four options exist: 0 to 1, 1 to 1, 0
   to many, or 1 to many. For example, the SafeHome system contains a single control panel (the 1:1 cardinality notation indicates this). At least one
   sensor must be present for polling by the control panel. However, there may
   be many sensors present (the 1:m notation indicates this). One sensor can
   recognize from 0 to many sensor events (e.g., smoke is detected or a break-
   in has occurred).

The steps noted above continue until a complete object-relationship model has
been produced.

By developing an object-relationship model, the analyst adds still another dimension to the overall analysis model. Not only are the relationships between objects identified, but all important *message paths* are defined (Chapter 19). In our discussion of Figure 20.7, we made reference to the arrows that connect subject symbols. These are also message paths. Each arrow implies the interchange of messages among subsystems in the model.

20.6   THE OBJECT-BEHAVIOR MODEL

The CRC model and the object-relationship model represent static elements of the OO analysis model. It is now time to make a transition to the dynamic behavior of the OO system or product. To accomplish this, we must represent the behavior of the system as a function of specific events and time.

The *object-behavior model* indicates how an OO system will respond to external events or stimuli. To create the model, the analyst must perform the following steps:

1. Evaluate all use cases (Section 20.4.1) to fully understand the sequence of interaction within the system.
2. Identify events that drive the interaction sequence and understand how these events relate to specific objects.
3. Create an event trace [RAM91] for each use case.
4. Build a state-transition diagram for the system.
5. Review the object-behavior model to verify accuracy and consistency.

Each of the above steps is discussed in the sections that follow.

20.6.1   Event Identification with Use Cases

As we noted in Section 20.4.1, the use case represents a sequence of activities that involve actors and the system. In general, an *event* occurs whenever an OO system and an actor (recall that an actor can be a person, a device, or even an external system) exchange information. Recalling the discussion presented in Chapter 12, it is important to note that an event is Boolean. That is, an event is *not* the information that has been exchanged; it is the fact that information has been exchanged.

A use case is examined for points of information exchange. To illustrate, reconsider the use case described in Section 20.4.1:

1. The homeowner observes the SafeHome control panel (Figure 11.4) to determine if the system is ready for input. If the system is *not ready,* the homeowner must physically close windows/doors so that the ready indicator is present. [A *not ready* indicator implies that a sensor is open, i.e., that a door or window is open.]
2. The homeowner uses the key pad to key in a four digit password. The password is compared with the valid password stored in the system. If the pass-

word is incorrect, the <u>control panel will beep once</u> and reset itself for additional input. If the password is correct, the control panel awaits further action.

3. The homeowner <u>selects and keys in *stay* or *away*</u> (see Figure 11.4) to activate the system. <u>*Stay* activates only perimeter sensors</u> (inside motion detecting sensors are deactivated). <u>*Away* activates all sensors.</u>

4. When activation occurs, <u>a red alarm light can be observed by the homeowner.</u>

The underlined portions of the use case scenario noted above indicate events. An actor should be identified for each event; the information that is exchanged should be noted, and any conditions or constraints should be indicated.

As an example of a typical event, consider the underlined use case phrase <u>homeowner uses the key pad to key in a four digit password</u>. In the context of the OO analysis model, the actor **homeowner** transmits an event to the object **control panel.** The event might be called *password entered*. The information transferred is the four digits that comprise the password, but this is not an essential part of the behavioral model. It is important to note that some events have an explicit impact on the flow of control of the use case, while others have no direct impact on the flow of control. For example, the event *password entered* does not explicitly change the flow of control of the use case, but the results of the event *compare password* (derived from the interaction <u>password is compared with the valid password stored in the system</u>) will have an explicit impact on the information and control flow of the SafeHome software.

Once all events have been identified, they are allocated to the objects involved. Actors (external entities) and objects can be responsible for generating events (e.g., **homeowner** generates the *password entered* event) or recognizing events that have occurred elsewhere (e.g., **control panel** recognizes the binary result of the *compare password* event).

20.6.2 State Representations

In the context of OO systems, two different characterizations of states must be considered:

- the state of each object as the system performs its function
- the state of the system as observed from the outside as the system performs its function

The state of an object takes on both passive and active characteristics [CHA93]. A *passive state* is simply the current status of all of an object's attributes. For example, the passive state of the aggregate object **player** (in the video game application discussed earlier) would include the *current position* and *orientation* of **player** (object attributes) as well as an other features of **player** that are relevant to the game (e.g., an attribute that indicates *magic wishes remaining*). The *active state* of an object indicates the current status of the object as it undergoes a continuing transformation or process. The object **player** might have the following active states: *moving, at rest, injured, being cured, trapped, lost,* and so on. An event (sometimes called a *trigger*) must oc-

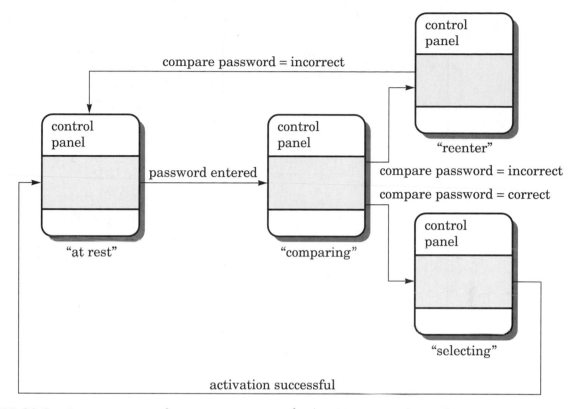

FIGURE 20.9. A representation of active state transitions for the object **control panel**

cur to force an object to make a transition from one active state to another. One component of an object-behavior model is a simple representation of the active states for each object and the events (triggers) that cause changes between these active states. Figure 20.9 illustrates a simple representation of active states for the **control panel** object in the SafeHome system.

Each arrow shown in Figure 20.9 represents a transition from one active state of an object to another. The labels shown for each arrow represent the event that triggers the transition. Although the active state model provides useful insight into the "life history" of an object, it is possible to specify additional information to provide more depth in understanding the behavior of an object. In addition to specifying the event that causes the transition to occur, the analysis can also specify a *guard* and an *action* [CHA93]. A guard is a Boolean condition that must be satisfied in order for the transition to occur. For example, the guard for the transition from the "at rest" state to the "comparing state" in Figure 20.9 can be determined by examining the use case:

if (password input = 4 digits) then make transition to comparing state;

In general, the guard for a transition usually depends upon the value of one or more attributes of an object. In other words, the guard depends on the passive state of the object.

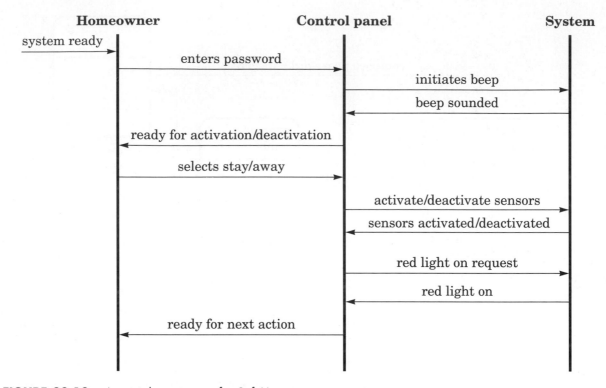

FIGURE 20.10. A partial event trace for SafeHome

An action occurs concurrently with the transition or as a consequence of it and generally involves one or more operations (responsibilities) of the object. For example, the action connected to the *password entered* event (Figure 20.9) is an operation that accesses a **password** object and performs a digit by digit comparison to validate the entered password.

The second type of behavioral representation for OOA considers a state representation for the overall product or system. This representation encompasses a simple event trace model [RAM91] that indicates how events cause transitions from object to object and a state-transition diagram that depicts the processing behavior of each object.

Once events have been identified for a use case, the analyst creates a representation of how events cause flow from one object to another. Called an *event trace,* this representation is a shorthand version of the use case. It represents key objects and the events that cause behavior to flow from object to object.

Figure 20.10 illustrates a partial event trace for the SafeHome system. Each of the arrows represents an event (derived from a use case) and indicates how the event channels behavior between SafeHome objects. The first event, *system ready,* is derived from the external environment and channels behavior to the **homeowner**. The homeowner enters a password. The events *initiates beep* and *beep sounded* indicate how behavior is channeled if the password is invalid. A valid password results in flow back to **homeowner.** The remaining events and traces follow the behavior as the system is activated or deactivated.

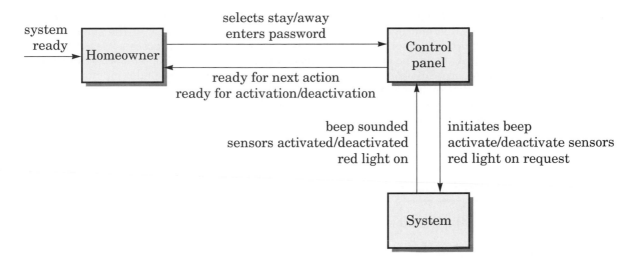

FIGURE 20.11. A partial event flow diagram for SafeHome

Once a complete event trace has been developed, all of the events that cause transitions between system objects can be collated into a set of input events and output events (from an object) This can be represented using an *event flow diagram* [RAM91] All events that flow into and out of an object are noted as shown in Figure 20.11. A state-transition diagram (Chapter 12) can then be developed to represent the behavior associated with responsibilities for each class.[13]

Like the structured analysis diagrams presented in Chapter 12, graphical representation forms the basis for the OO analysis model and provides an excellent foundation for the creation of a *software requirements specification.*

20.8   SUMMARY

Object-oriented analysis methods enable a software engineer to model a problem by representing objects, attributes, and operations as the primary modeling components. A wide variety of object-oriented analysis methods have been proposed in the literature, but all have a set of common characteristics: (1) representation of classes and class hierarchies, (2) creation of object-relationship models, and (3) derivation of object-behavior models.

Analysis for object-oriented systems occurs at many different levels of abstraction. At the business or enterprise level, the techniques associated with OOA can be coupled with an information engineering approach. This technique is often called domain analysis. At an application level, the object model focuses on specific customer requirements as those requirements affect an application to be built.

The OOA process begins with the definition of use cases—scenarios that describe how the OO system is to be used. The class–responsibility–collabora-

---

[13]An excellent tutorial on "object behavior analysis" can be found in [RUB92].

tor (CRC) modeling technique is then applied to document classes and their attributes and operations. It also provides an initial view of the collaborations that occur among objects. The next step in the OOA process is classification of objects and the creation of a class hierarchy. Subsystems (subjects) can be used to encapsulate related objects. The object-relationship model provides an indication of how classes are connected to one another, and the object-behavior model indicates the behavior of individual objects and the overall behavior of the OO system.

REFERENCES

[AMB95]   Ambler, S., "Using Use Cases," *Software Development,* July 1995, pp. 53–61.

[ARA89]   Arango, G., and R. Prieto-Diaz, "Domain Analysis: Concepts and Research Directions," in *Domain Analysis: Acquisition of Reusable Information for Software Construction,* G. Arango and R. Prieto-Diaz (eds.), IEEE Computer Society Press, 1989.

[BER92]   Berard, E.V., *A Comparison of Object-Oriented Development Methodologies,* Berard Software Engineering, Inc., Gaithersburg, MD, 1992.

[BER93]   Berard, E.V., *Essays on Object-Oriented Software Engineering,* Addison-Wesley, 1993.

[BOO94]   Booch, G., *Object-Oriented Analysis and Design,* 2nd edition, Benjamin Cummings, 1994.

[BOO96]   Booch, G., and J. Rambaugh, *Unified Method for Object-Oriented Development,* Rational Software Corp., 1996.

[CHA93]   de Champeaux, D., D. Lea, and P. Faure, *Object-Oriented System Development,* Addison-Wesley, 1993.

[COA91]   Coad, P., and E. Yourdon, *Object-Oriented Analysis,* 2nd edition, Prentice-Hall, 1991.

[DUE92]   Due, R., "Enterprise Modeling: Still in Pursuit," *Database Programming and Design,* November 1992, pp. 62–65.

[EMB92]   Embley, D.W., B.D. Kurtz, and S.N. Woodfield, *Object-Oriented Systems Analysis,* Yourdon Press, 1992.

[FIC92]   Fichman, R.G., and C.F. Kemerer, "Object-Oriented and Conventional Analysis and Design Methodologies," *Computer,* vol. 25, no. 10, October 1992, pp. 22–39.

[FIR93]   Firesmith, D.G., *Object-Oriented Requirements Analysis and Logical Design,* Wiley, 1993.

[GRA94]   Graham, I., *Object-Oriented Methods,* Addison-Wesley, 1994.

[JAC92]   Jacobson, I., *Object-Oriented Software Engineering,* Addison-Wesley, 1992.

[LOC96]   *Succeeding with the Booch and OMT Methods,* Lockheed-Martin and Rational Software Corporation, Addison-Wesley, 1996.

[MAT94]   Mattison, R., *The Object-Oriented Enterprise,* McGraw-Hill, 1994.

[MON92]   Monarchi, D.E., and G.I. Puhr, "A Research Typology for Object-Oriented Analysis and Design," *Communications of the ACM,* vol. 35, no. 9, September 1992, pp. 35–47.

[RAM91]   Rambaugh, J. et al., *Object-Oriented Modeling and Design,* Prentice-Hall, 1991.

[RUB92]   Rubin, K.S., and A. Goldberg, "Object Behavior Analysis," *Communications of the ACM,* vol. 35, no. 9, September 1992, pp. 48–62.

[SUL94]   Sullo, G.C., *Object Engineering,* Wiley, 1994.

[TAY95]   Taylor, D.A., *Business Engineering with Object Technology,* Wiley, 1995.

[WIR90]   Wirfs-Brock, R., B. Wilkerson, and L. Weiner, *Designing Object-Oriented Software,* Prentice-Hall, 1990.

[WYD96]   Wyder, T., "Capturing Requirements with Use Cases," *Software Development,* February 1996, pp. 37–40.

PROBLEMS AND POINTS TO PONDER

20.1.   Select five object-oriented analysis methods and structured analysis (Chapter 12) and compare them using the modeling dimensions proposed by Fichman and Kemerer [FIC92] in Section 20.1.1.

20.2.   Develop a classroom presentation on one of the OOA methods discussed in Section 20.1.2. Present the method in the context of a simple example. Note areas where a unique notation or approach is used.

20.3.   Conduct an abbreviated domain analysis for one of the following areas:
a. a university student record-keeping system
b. an on-line service
c. customer service for a bank
d. a video game developer
e. an application area suggested by your instructor
Be sure to isolate classes that can be applied across a number of applications in the domain.

20.4.   In your own words describe the difference between static and dynamic views of an OO system.

20.5.   Write use cases for the SafeHome system discussed in this book. The use cases should address the scenario required to define a security zone. A security zone encompasses a set of sensors that can be addressed, activated, and deactivated as a set, rather than individually. As many as 10 security zones can be defined. Be creative here, but stay within the bounds of the control panel as it is defined earlier in the book.

20.6.   Develop a set of use cases for the PHTRS system introduced in problem 12.13. You'll have to make a number of assumptions about the manner in which a user interacts with this system.

20.7.   Develop a set of use cases listed in Table 20.1. or for a system or product suggested by your instructor. Do a few hours of research on the application area and conduct a FAST meeting (Chapter 11) with your fellow students to develop basic requirements (your instructor will help you coordinate this).

20.8.   Develop a complete set of CRC model index cards for the product or system you chose as part of problem 20.7.

20.9.   Conduct a review of the CRC index cards developed in problem 20.8 with your colleagues. How many additional classes, responsibilities, and collaborators were added as a consequence of the review?

TABLE 20.1

SUGGESTED APPLICATION FOR PROBLEMS 20.7 THROUGH 20.12

The PHTRS application introduced in problem 12.13

Software for a personal computer–based word-processing system

Real-time test monitoring system for gas turbine engines

Software for a manufacturing control system

Software for a video game of your choosing

A spreadsheet application

A PC-based 3D graphics package

A system suggested by your instructor

20.10. Develop a class hierarchy for the product or system you chose as part of problem 20.7.

20.11. Develop a set of subsystems for the product or system you chose as part of problem 20.7.

20.12. Develop an object-relationship model for the product or system you chose as part of problem 20.7.

20.13. Develop an object-behavior model for the product or system you chose as part of problem 20.7. Be sure to list all events, provide an event trace, develop an event flow diagram, and define a state diagram for each class.

20.14. In your own words, describe how collaborators for a class are determined.

20.15. What strategy would you propose for defining subsystems for a collection of classes?

20.16. What role does cardinality play in the development of an object-relationship model?

20.17. What is the difference between an active and a passive state for an object?

FURTHER READINGS AND OTHER INFORMATION SOURCES

Dozens of books address object-oriented analysis. Before selecting one, the reader should select an OOA method that appears to serve local needs and then select a book that describes the appropriate method. An excellent survey of available methods is presented in [MON92] and [FIC92].

Detailed discussions of OOA may be found in [BER93], [BOO94], [CHA93], [COA91], [FIR93], [JAC92], [RAM91], and [WIR90]. In addition, books by Shlaer and Mellor (*Object-Oriented Systems Analysis: Modeling the World in States,* Prentice-Hall, 1992), Martin and Odell (*Object-Oriented Analysis and Design,* Prentice-Hall, 1992), Goldstein and Alger (*Developing Object-Oriented Software for the Macintosh,* Addison-Wesley, 1992), and Lorenz (*Object-Oriented Software Development,* Prentice-Hall, 1993) contain useful discussion. Yourdon and Argila (*Case Studies in Object-Oriented Analysis and Design,* Prentice-Hall, 1995) present two realistic case studies that illustrate the OOA process in detail.

Worthwhile discussions of OO techniques for prototyping are presented by Connell and Shafer (*Object-Oriented Rapid Prototyping,* Prentice-Hall, 1994) and Krief (*Using Object Oriented Languages for Rapid Prototyping,* Prentice-Hall, 1996).

The same Internet sources noted for Chapter 19 are equally applicable for OOA. The Internet newsgroup **comp.object** is a useful source for information, discussion, and debate on OOA methods and tools. The FAQ for this newsgroup contains a brief summary of OOA methods and points to additional references. It can be found at:

http://www.cs.cmu.edu/Web/Groups/AI/html/faqs/lang/oop/faq.html.

Discussion of OOA issues can sometimes be found in **comp.software-eng** and **comp.specification.** *A Comparison of Object-Oriented Development Methodologies* by Edward Berard is available. Select "on-line documents" at:

http://www.toa.com

Additional information on OOA and object technologies in general can be obtained at:

http://www.rational.com

Many references to OOA papers and books can be obtained at:

http://www.cera2.com/object.htm

An up-to-date list of World Wide Web references for object-oriented analysis can be found at: **http://www.rspa.com**

CHAPTER 21

OBJECT-ORIENTED DESIGN

bject-oriented design (OOD) transforms the analysis model created using object-oriented analysis (Chapter 20) into a design model that serves as a blueprint for software construction. Unlike conventional software design methods, OOD results in a design that achieves a number of different levels of modularity. Major system components are organized into system-level "modules" called subsystems. Data and the operations that manipulate the data are encapsulated into objects—a modular form that is the building block of an OO system. In addition, OOD must describe the specific data organization of attributes and the procedural detail of individual operations. These represent data and algorithmic pieces of an OO system and are a contributor to overall modularity.

The unique nature of object-oriented design lies in its ability to build upon four important software design concepts: abstraction, information hiding, functional independence, and modularity (Chapter 13). All design methods strive for software that exhibits these fundamental characteristics, but only OOD provides a mechanism that enables the designer to achieve all four with less complexity and compromise.

The job of the software designer can be daunting. Gamma [GAM95] and his colleagues provide a reasonably accurate picture of OOD when they state:

Designing object-oriented software is hard, and designing *reusable* object-oriented software is even harder. You must find pertinent objects, factor them into classes at the right granularity, define class interfaces and inheritance hierarchies, and establish key relationships among them. Your design should be specific to the problem at hand but also general enough to address future problems and requirements. You also want to avoid redesign, or at least minimize it. Experienced object-oriented designers will tell you that a reusable and flexible design is difficult if not impossible to get "right" the first time. Before a design is finished, they usually try to reuse it several times, modifying it each time.

Object-oriented design, object-oriented programming, and object-oriented testing are the construction activities for OO systems. In this chapter, we consider the first step in construction.

21.1   DESIGN FOR OBJECT-ORIENTED SYSTEMS

In Chapter 13 we introduced the concept of the design pyramid for conventional software. Four design layers—data, architectural, interface, and procedural—were each defined and discussed. For object-oriented systems, we can also define a design pyramid, but the layers are a bit different. As shown in Figure 21.1, the four layers of the OO design pyramid are:

The subsystem layer. Contains a representation of each of the subsystems that enable the software to achieve its customer defined requirements and to implement the technical infrastructure that supports customer requirements.

The class and object layer. Contains the class hierarchies that enable the system to be created using generalizations and increasingly more targeted specializations. This layer also contains design representations of each object.

The message layer. Contains the details that enable each object to communicate with its collaborators. This layer establishes the external and internal interfaces for the system.

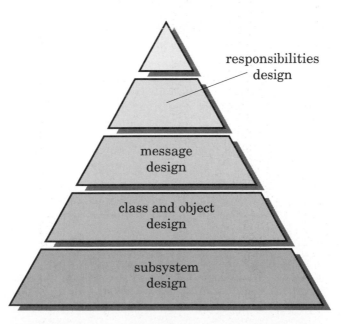

FIGURE 21.1.
The OO design pyramid

The responsibilities layer. Contains the data structure and algorithmic design for all attributes and operations for each object.

The design pyramid focuses exclusively on the design of a specific product or system. It should be noted, however, that another "layer" of design exists, and this layer forms the foundation on which the pyramid rests. The foundation layer focuses on the design of *domain objects* (called design patterns later in this chapter). Domain objects play a key role in building the infrastructure for the OO system by providing support for human–computer interface activities, task management, and data management. Domain objects can also be used to flesh out the design of the application itself.

21.1.1   Conventional vs. OO Approaches

Conventional approaches to software design apply a distinct notation and set of heuristics to map the analysis model into a design model. Recall Figure 13.1. Each element of the conventional analysis model maps into one or more layers of the design model. Like conventional software design, OOD applies data design (when attributes are represented), interface design (when a messaging model is developed), and procedural design (in the design of operations). However, architectural design is different. Unlike the architectural designs derived using conventional software engineering methods, an OO design does not exhibit a hierarchical control structure.[1] In fact, the "architecture" of an OO design has more to do with the collaborations among objects that with the flow of control.

Although similarity between the conventional and OO design models does exist, we have chosen to rename the layers of the design pyramid to reflect more accurately the nature of an OO design. Figure 21.2 illustrates the relationship between the OO analysis model (Chapter 20) and the design model that will be derived from it.[2]

The subsystem design is derived by considering overall customer requirements (represented with use cases) and the events and states that are externally observable (the object-behavior model). Class and object design is mapped from the description of attributes, operations, and collaborations contained in the CRC model. Message design is driven by the object-relationship model, and responsibilities design is derived using the attributes, operations, and collaborations described in the CRC model.

Fichman and Kemerer [FIC92] suggest 10 design modeling components that may be used to compare various conventional and object-oriented design methods:

1. representation of hierarchy of modules
2. specification of data definitions

---

[1]Recall the discussion of factored control hierarchies presented in Chapter 13.

[2]It is important to note that the derivation is not always straightforward. For further discussion, see [DAV95].

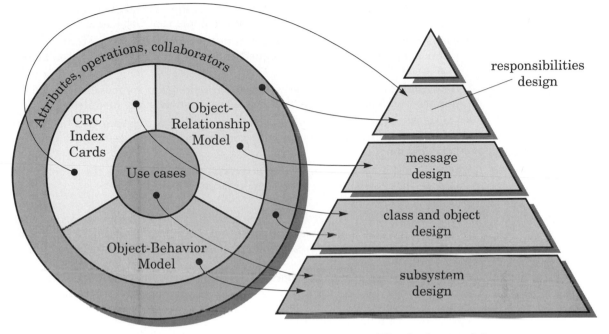

FIGURE 21.2. Translating the OO analysis model into an OO design model

3. specification of procedural logic
4. indication of end-to-end processing sequences
5. representation of object states and transitions
6. definition of classes and hierarchies
7. assignment of operations to classes
8. detailed definition of operations
9. specification of message connections
10. identification of exclusive services

Because many conventional and object-oriented design approaches are available, it is difficult to develop a generalized comparison between the two methods. It can be stated, however, that modeling dimensions 5 through 10 are not supported using structured design (Chapter 14) or its derivatives.

21.1.2 Design Issues

Bertrand Meyer [MEY90] suggests five criteria for judging a design method's ability to achieve modularity and relates these to object-oriented design:

- *decomposability*—the facility with which a design method helps the designer to decompose a large problem into subproblems that are easier to solve;
- *composability*—the degree to which a design method ensures that program components (modules), once designed and built, can be reused to create other systems;
- *understandability*—the ease with which a program component can be understood without reference to other information or other modules;
- *continuity*—the ability to make small changes in a program and have these changes manifest themselves with corresponding changes in just one or a very few modules; and
- *protection*—an architectural characteristic that will reduce the propagation of side affects if an error does occur in a given module.

From these criteria, Meyer [MEY90] suggests five basic design principles that can be derived for modular architectures: (1) linguistic modular units; (2) few interfaces; (3) small interfaces (weak coupling); (4) explicit interfaces; and (5) information hiding.

Modules are defined as *linguistic modular units* when they "correspond to syntactic units in the language used" [MEY90]. That is, the programming language to be used should be capable of supporting the modularity defined directly. For example, if the designer creates a *subroutine,* even the classical programming languages (e.g., Fortran, C, Pascal) could implement it as a syntactic unit. But if a *package* that contains data structures and procedures and identifies them as a single unit were defined, a language such as Ada (or other object-oriented languages) would be necessary to directly represent this type of module in the language syntax.

To achieve low coupling (a design concept introduced in Chapter 13), the number of interfaces between modules should be minimized (few interfaces) and the amount of information that moves across an interface should be minimized (small interfaces). Whenever modules do communicate, they should do so in an obvious and direct way (explicit interfaces). For example, if module X and module Y communicate through a global data area (what we have called common coupling in Chapter 13), they violate the principle of explicit interfaces because the communication between the modules is not obvious to an outside observer. Finally, we achieve the principle of information hiding when all information about a module is hidden from outside access, unless that information is specifically defined as "public information."

The design criteria and principles presented in this section can be applied to any design method (e.g., we can apply them to structured design). As we will see, however, the object-oriented design method achieves each of the criteria more efficiently than other approaches and results in modular architectures that allow us to meet each of the modularity criteria most effectively.

21.1.3 The OOD Landscape

A snapshot of a number of popular OOA methods was presented in Chapter 20. Each of the methods presented has a corresponding process for OOD that spawns a set of design representations and a notation that enables the software engineer to create the design model in a consistent manner. In the paragraphs that follow, corresponding OOD methods[3] are presented in outline form. The intent is to provide a snapshot of the OOD process that has been proposed by the author(s) of the method.[4]

The Booch Method   As we noted in Chapter 20, the Booch method [BOO94] encompasses both a "micro-development process" and a "macro-development process." The micro level defines a set of design tasks that are re-applied for each step in the macro process. Hence, an evolutionary approach is maintained. A brief outline of Booch's OOD micro-development process follows:

Architectural planning:
- Cluster similar objects in separate architectural partitions.
- Layer objects by level of abstraction.
- Identify relevant scenarios.
- Create a design prototype.
- Validate the design prototype by applying it to usage scenarios.

Tactical design:
- Define domain-independent policies (i.e., the "rules" that govern the use of operations and attributes).
- Define domain-specific policies for memory management, error handling, and other infrastructure functions.
- Develop a scenario that describes the semantics of the policy.
- Create a prototype for each policy.
- Instrument and refine the prototype.
- Review each policy to ensure that it "broadcasts its architectural vision" [BOO94].

Release planning:
- Organize scenarios developed during OOA by priority.
- Allocate corresponding architectural releases to the scenarios.
- Design and construct each architectural release incrementally.
- Adjust goals and schedule of incremental release as required.

The Coad and Yourdon Method   The Coad and Yourdon method for OOD [COA91] was developed by studying how "effective object-oriented designers" do their design work. The design approach addresses not only the application but also the

---

[3]In general, OOD methods are identified using the name(s) of the developer of the method, even if the method has been given a unique name or acronym.

[4]The meaning of many of the steps outlined in the process descriptions that follow will be discussed in Sections 21.3 and 21.4.

infrastructure for the application. A brief outline of Coad and Yourdon's OOD process follows:

Problem domain component:

- Group all domain specific classes.
- Design an appropriate class hierarchy for the application classes.
- Work to simplify inheritance, when appropriate.
- Refine design to improve performance.
- Develop an interface with the data management component.
- Refine and add low-level objects as required.
- Review design and challenge any additions to the analysis model.

Human interaction component:

- Define the human actors.
- Develop task scenarios.
- Design a hierarchy of user commands.
- Refine the user interaction sequence.
- Design relevant classes and class hierarchy.
- Integrate GUI classes as appropriate.

Task management component:

- Identify types of tasks (e.g., event driven, clock driven).
- Establish priorities.
- Identify a task to serve as coordinator for other tasks.
- Design appropriate objects for each task.

Data management component

- Design the data structures and layout.
- Design services required to manage the data structures.
- Identify tools that can assist in implementing data management.
- Design appropriate classes and class hierarchy.

The Jacobson Method   The design activity for OOSE (object-oriented software engineering) [JAC92] is a simplified version of the proprietary Objectory method, also developed by Jacobson. The design model emphasizes traceability to the OOSE analysis model. A brief outline of Jacobson's OOD process follows:

- Consider adaptations to make the idealized analysis model fit the real world environment.
- Create *blocks* as the primary design object.[5]

---

[5]A block is the design abstraction that allows for the representation of an aggregate object.

Define a block to implement related analysis objects.

Identify interface blocks, entity blocks, and control blocks.

Describe how blocks communicate during execution.

Identify stimuli that are passed between blocks and their order of communication.

- Create an interaction diagram that shows how stimuli are passed between blocks.
- Organize blocks into subsystems.
- Review the design work.

The Rambaugh Method The Object Modeling Technique (OMT) [RAM91] encompasses a design activity that encourages design to be conducted at two different levels of abstraction. System design focuses on the layout for the components that are needed to construct a complete product or system. Object design emphasizes the detailed layout of an individual object. A brief outline of Rambaugh's OOD process follows:

- Perform system design

Partition the analysis model into subsystems.

Identify concurrency that is dictated by the problem.

Allocate subsystems to processors and tasks.

Choose a basic strategy for implementing data management.

Identify global resources and the control mechanisms required to access them.

Design an appropriate control mechanism for the system.

Consider how boundary conditions should be handled.

Review and consider trade-offs.

- Conduct object design

Select operations from the analysis model.

Define algorithms for each operation.

Select data structures that are appropriate for algorithms.

Define any internal classes.

Revise class organization to optimize access to data and improve computational efficiency.

Design class attributes.

- Implement control mechanisms defined in system design.
- Adjust class structure to strengthen inheritance.
- Design messaging to implement the object relationships (associations).
- Package classes and associations into modules.

As we noted in Chapter 20, work is underway to merge the Booch and Rambaugh methods ([BOO96], [LOC96]).

The Wirfs-Brock Method   Wirfs-Brock [WIR90] defines a continuum of technical tasks in which analysis leads seamlessly into design. A brief outline of Wirfs-Brock's design-related tasks follows:

- Construct *protocols* for each class.[6]
  > Refine contracts between objects into refined protocols.
  > Design each operation (responsibility).
  > Design each protocol (interface design).

- Create a design specification for each class.
  > Describe each contract in detail.
  > Define private responsibilities.
  > Specify algorithms for each operation.
  > Note special considerations and constraints.

- Create a design specification for each subsystem.
  > Identify all encapsulated classes.
  > Describe contracts in detail for which the subsystem is a server.
  > Note special considerations and constraints.

Although the terminology and process steps for each of these OOD methods differ, the overall OOD processes are reasonably consistent. To perform object-oriented design, a software engineer should perform the following generic steps:

- Describe each of the subsystems in a manner that is implementable.
  > Allocate subsystems to processors and tasks.
  > Choose a design strategy for implementing data management, interface support, and task management.
  > Design an appropriate control mechanism for the system.
  > Review and consider trade-offs.

- Object design:
  > Design each operation at a procedural level.
  > Define any internal classes.
  > Design internal data structures for class attributes.

- Message design:
  > Using collaborations between objects and object-relationships, design the messaging model.

---

[6]A protocol is a formal description of the messages to which a class will respond.

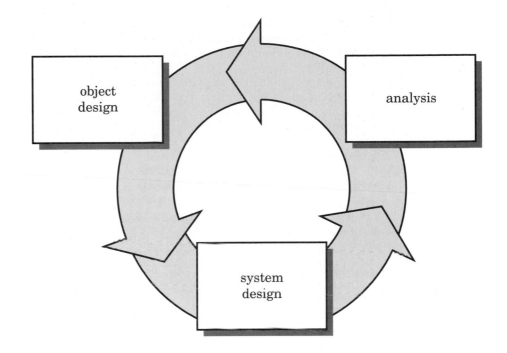

FIGURE 21.3.
Process flow for
OOD

• Review the design model and iterate as required.

It is important to note that the design steps discussed in this section are iterative. That is, they may be executed incrementally, along with addition OOA activities, until a completed design is produced.

21.2   THE GENERIC COMPONENTS OF THE OO DESIGN MODEL

It is sometimes difficult to make a clear distinction between object-oriented analysis (Chapter 20) and object oriented design.[7] In essence, object-oriented analysis (OOA) is a classification activity. That is, a problem is analyzed in an effort to determine the classes of objects that will be applicable as a solution is developed. Analysis also determines object relationships and behavior. Object-oriented design (OOD) enables a software engineer to indicate the objects that are derived from each class and how these objects interrelate with one another. In addition, OOD depicts how the relationships among objects are achieved, how behavior is to be implemented, and how communication is to be implemented between objects.

The generic process flow from analysis to design is illustrated in Figure 21.3. Once a reasonably complete analysis model has been developed,[8] the soft-

---

[7]Readers who have not yet read Chapter 20 in its entirety are urged to do so.

[8]Recall that OOA is an iterative activity. It is entirely possible that the analysis model will be revised as a consequence of design work.

ware engineer concentrates on the design of the system. This is accomplished by describing characteristics of the subsystems required to implement both customer requirements and the support environment that is necessary for their realization.

As subsystems are defined, they must be coordinated within the overall context of customer requirements. Which subsystems are responsible for which customer requirements? Within which subsystems do objects reside that were defined during OOA? Which subsystems must operate concurrently and what system components coordinate and control them? How are global resources managed by the subsystems?

During subsystem design, it is necessary for the software engineer to define four important design components [COA91]:

- *problem domain*—the subsystems that are responsible for implementing customer requirements directly;
- *human interaction*—the subsystems that implement the user interface (this included reusable GUI subsystems);
- *task management*—the subsystems that are responsible for controlling and coordinating concurrent tasks that may be packaged within a subsystem or among different subsystems; and
- *data management*—the subsystem that is responsible for the storage and retrieval of objects.

Each of these generic components may be modeled (during OOA) with a series of classes as well as requisite relationships and behaviors. In addition, the design components are implemented by defining the *protocol* [WIR90] that formally describes the messaging model for each of the components.

Once a subsystem has been defined and the design of each of the components noted above begins, the emphasis shifts to object design. At this level, the elements of the CRC model (Chapter 20) are translated into a design realization. In essence the translation illustrated in Figure 21.4 is accomplished.

21.3   THE SYSTEM DESIGN PROCESS

Although a number of authors suggest process models for OO system design, the sequence of activities proposed by Rambaugh and his colleagues [RAM91] is one of the more definitive treatments of the subject. In the outline presented in Section 21.1.3, the following design steps were defined:

- Partition the analysis model into subsystems.
- Identify concurrency that is dictated by the problem.
- Allocate subsystems to processors and tasks.
- Choose a basic strategy for implementing data management.
- Identify global resources and the control mechanisms required to access them.

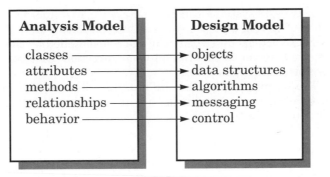

FIGURE 21.4.
Translating the analysis model into a design model during object design

- Design an appropriate control mechanism for the system.
- Consider how boundary conditions should be handled.
- Review and consider trade-offs.

In the sections that follow, design activities that are related to each of these steps are considered in more detail.

21.3.1 Partitioning the Analysis Model

One of the fundamental analysis principles (Chapter 11) is partitioning. In OO system design we partition the analysis model to define cohesive collections of classes, relationships, and behavior. These design elements are packaged as a *subsystem*.

In general, all of the elements of a subsystem share some property in common. They may all be involved in accomplishing the same function; they may reside within the same product hardware; or they may manage the same class of resources. Subsystems are characterized by their responsibilities; that is, a subsystem can be identified by the services that it provides [RAM91]. When used in the OO system design context, a *service* is a collection of operations that perform a specific function (e.g., managing word-processor files, producing a three-dimensional rendering, translating an analog video signal into a compressed digital image).

As subsystems are defined (and designed), they should conform to the following design criteria:

- The subsystem should have a well-defined interface through which all communication with the rest of the system occurs.
- With the exception of a small number of "communication classes," the classes within a subsystem should collaborate only with other classes within the subsystem.
- The number of subsystems should be kept small.
- Subsystems can be partitioned internally to help reduce complexity.

When two subsystems communicate with one another, they can establish a client/server link or a peer-to-peer link [RAM91]. In a *client/server link*, each of the subsystems takes on one of the roles implied by client and server. Service flows from server to client in only one direction. In a *peer-to-peer link*, services may flow in either direction.

The communication and information flow implied by the links described above can be represented using a data flow diagram (Chapter 12). In this case, each "bubble" in the DFD is a subsystem.

21.3.2 Concurrency and Subsystem Allocation

The dynamic aspects of the object-behavior model provide an indication of concurrency among objects (or subsystems). If objects (or subsystems) are not active at the same time, there is no need for concurrent processing. This means that the objects (or subsystems) can be implemented on the same processor hardware. On the other hand, if objects (or subsystems) must act on events asynchronously and at the same time, they are viewed as concurrent. When subsystems are concurrent, two allocation options exist:

- Allocate each subsystem to an independent processor.
- Allocate the subsystems to the same processor and provide concurrency support through operating system features.

Concurrent tasks are defined [RAM91] by examining the state diagram for each object. If the flow of events and transitions indicates that only a single object is active at any one time, a *thread of control* has been established. The thread of control continues even when one object sends a message to another object, as long as the first object waits for a response. If, however, the first object continues processing after sending a message, the thread of control splits.

Tasks in an OO system are designed by isolating threads of control. For example, while the SafeHome security system is monitoring its sensors, it can also be dialing the central monitoring station for verification of connection. Since the objects involved in both of these behaviors are active at the same time, each represents a separate thread of control and each can be defined as a separate task. If the monitoring and dialing activities occur sequentially, a single task could be implemented.

To determine which of the processor allocation options noted above is appropriate, the designer must consider performance requirements, costs, and the overhead imposed by interprocessor communication.

21.3.3 The Task Management Component

Coad and Yourdon [COA91] suggest the following strategy for the design of the objects that manage concurrent tasks:

- The characteristics of the task are determined.
- A coordinator task and associated objects are defined.
- The coordinator and other tasks are integrated.

The characteristics of a task are determined by understanding how the task is initiated. Event driven and clock driven tasks are the most commonly encountered. Both are activated by an interrupt, but the former receives an interrupt from some outside source (e.g., another processor, a sensor) whereas the latter is governed by a system clock.

In addition to the manner in which a task is initiated, the priority and criticality of the task must also be determined. High-priority tasks must have immediate access to system resources. High-criticality tasks must continue to operate even if resource availability is reduced or the system is operating in a degraded state.

Once the characteristics of the task have been determined, object attributes and operations required to achieve coordination and communication with other tasks are defined. The basic task template (for a task object) takes the form [COA91]:

Task name—the name of the object

Description—a narrative describing the purpose of the object

Priority—task priority (e.g., low, medium, high)

Services—a list of operations that are object responsibilities

Coordinates by—the manner in which object behavior is invoked

Communicates via—input and output data values relevant to the task

This template description can then be translated into the standard design model (incorporating a representation of attributes and operations) for the task object(s).

21.3.4 The Data Management Component

Data management encompasses two distinct areas of concern: (1) the management of data that are critical to the application itself, and (2) the creation of an infrastructure for storage and retrieval of objects. In general, data management is designed in a layered fashion. The idea is to isolate the low-level requirements for manipulating data structures from the higher-level requirements for handling system attributes.

Within the system context, a database management system is often used as a common data store for all subsystems. The objects required to manipulate that database are members of reusable classes that are identified using domain analysis (Chapter 20) or are supplied directly by the database vendor. A detailed discussion of database design for OO systems is beyond the scope of this book.[9]

---

[9]Interested readers should refer to [BRO91], [TAY92], or [RAO94].

The design of the data management component includes the design of the attributes and operations required to manage objects. The relevant attributes are appended to every object in the problem domain and provide information that answers the question: How do I store myself? Coad and Yourdon [COA91] suggest the creation of an **object-server** class "with services to (a) tell each object to save itself and (b) retrieve stored objects for use by other design components."

As an example of data management for the **sensor** object discussed as part of the SafeHome security system, the design could specify a flat file called *sensor.* Each field would correspond to a named instance of **sensor** and would contain the values of each **sensor** attribute for that named instance. Operations within the **object-server** class would enable a specific object to be stored and retrieved when it is needed by the system. For more complex objects, it might be necessary to specify a relational database or an object-oriented database to accomplish the same function.

21.3.5 The Resource Management Component

A variety of different resources are available to an OO system or product, and in many instances, subsystems compete for these resources at the same time. Global system resources can be external entities (e.g., a disk drive, processor, or communication line) or abstractions (e.g., a database, an object). Regardless of the nature of the resource, the software engineer should design a control mechanism for it. Rambaugh and his colleagues [RAM91] suggest that each resource should be owned by a "guardian object." The guardian object is the gatekeeper for the resource, controlling access to it and moderating conflicting requests for it.

21.3.6 The Human–Computer Interface Component

Although the human–computer interface (HCI) component is implemented within the context of the problem domain, the interface itself represents a critically important subsystem for most modern applications. The OO analysis model (Chapter 20) contains usage scenarios (called use cases) and a description of the roles that users (called actors) play as they interact with the system. These serve as input to the HCI design process.

Once the actor and his usage scenario are defined, a command hierarchy is identified. The command hierarchy defines the major system menu categories (the menu bar or tool palette) and all subfunctions that are available within the context of a major system menu category (the menu windows). The command hierarchy is refined iteratively until every use case can be implemented by navigating the hierarchy of functions.

Because a wide variety of HCI development environments already exist (e.g, MacApp or Windows), the design of GUI elements is not necessary. Reusable classes (with appropriate attributes and operations) already exist for windows, icons, mouse operations, and a wide variety of other interaction functions. The implementer need only instantiate objects that have appropriate characteristics for the problem domain.

21.3.7 Intersubsystem Communication

Once each subsystem has been specified, it is necessary to define the collaborations that exist between the subsystems. The model that we use for object-to-object collaboration can be extended to subsystems as a whole. Figure 21.5 provides a schematic representation of collaboration. As we noted earlier in this chapter, communication can occur by establishing a client/server link or a peer-to-peer link. As the figure shows, we must specify the contract that exists between subsystems. Recall that a contract provides an indication of the ways in which one subsystem can interact with another.

The following design steps can be applied to specify a contract for a subsystem [WIR90]:

1. List each request that can be made by collaborators of the subsystem. Organize the requests by subsystem and define them within one or more appropriate contracts. Be sure to note contracts that are inherited from superclasses.

2. For each contract, note the operations (both inherited and private) that are required to implement the responsibilities implied by the contract. Be sure to associate the operations with specific classes that reside within a subsystem.

3. Considering one contract at a time, create a table of the form shown in Figure 21.6. For each contract, the following entries are made in the table:

   Type—the type of contract (i.e., client/server or peer-to-peer)

   Collaborators—the names of the subsystems that are parties to the contract

   Class—the names of the classes (contained within a subsystem) that support services implied by the contract

   Operation—the names of the operations (within the class) that implement the services

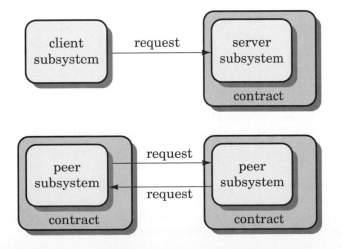

FIGURE 21.5.
A model of collaboration between subsystems

Contract	Type	Collaborators	Class(es)	Operation(s)	Message Format

FIGURE 21.6.   Subsystem collaboration table

Message format—the message format required to implement the interaction between collaborators.

An appropriate message description is drafted for each interaction between the subsystems.

4. If the modes of interaction between subsystems are complex, a subsystem-collaboration graph, illustrated in Figure 21.7, is created. The collaboration graph is similar in form to the event flow diagram discussed in Chapter 20. Each subsystem is represented along with its interactions with other subsystems. The contracts that are invoked during an interaction are noted as shown. The details of the interaction are determined by looking up the contract in the subsystem collaboration table (Figure 21.6).

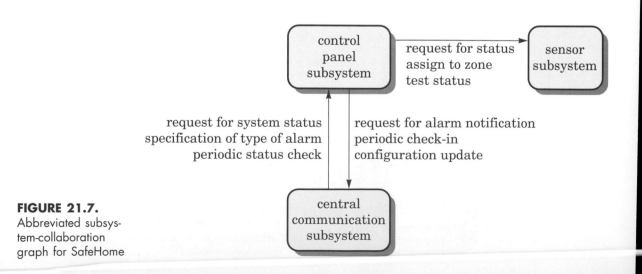

FIGURE 21.7.
Abbreviated subsystem-collaboration graph for SafeHome

21.4   THE OBJECT DESIGN PROCESS

To borrow from a metaphor that was introduced earlier in this book, the OO system design might be viewed as the floor plan of a house. The floor plan specifies the purpose of each room and the mechanisms that connect the rooms to one another and to the outside environment. It is now time to provide the details that are required to build each room.

In the context of OOD, *object design* focuses on the "rooms." We must develop a detailed design of the attributes and operations that comprise each class, and a thorough specification of the messages that connect the class with their collaborators.

21.4.1   Object Descriptions

A design description of an object (an instance of a class or subclass) can take one of two forms [GOL83]:

1. a *protocol description* that establishes the interface of an object by defining each message that the object can receive and the related operation that the object performs when it receives the message, and

2. an *implementation description* that shows implementation details for each operation implied by a message that is passed to an object. Implementation details include information about the object's private part, that is, internal details about the data structures that describe the object's attributes and procedural details that describe operations.

The protocol description is nothing more than a set of messages and a corresponding comment for each message. For example, a portion of the protocol description for the object **motion sensor** (described earlier) might be:

MESSAGE (motion sensor) → read: RETURNS sensor ID, sensor status;

which describes the message required to read the sensor. Similarly,

MESSAGE (motion sensor) → set: SENDS sensor ID, sensor status;

sets or resets the status of the sensor.

For a large system with many messages, it is often possible to create message categories. For example, message categories for the SafeHome **system** object might include system configuration messages, monitoring messages, event messages, and so forth.

An implementation description of an object provides the internal ("hidden") details that are required for implementation but are not necessary for invocation. That is, the designer of the object must provide an implementation description and must therefore create the internal details of the object. However, another designer or implementer who uses the object or an other instance of the object requires only the protocol description but not the implementation description.

An implementation description is composed of the following information: (1) a specification of the object's name and reference to class; (2) a specification of private data structures with indication of data items and types; (3) a procedural description of each operation or alternatively, pointers to such procedural descriptions. The implementation description must contain sufficient information to provide for proper handling of all messages described in the protocol description.

Cox [COX85] characterizes the difference between the information contained in the protocol description and that contained in the implementation description in terms of "users" and "suppliers" of services. A user of the "service" provided by an object must be familiar with the protocol for invoking the service, that is, for specifying *what* is desired. The supplier of the service (the object itself) must be concerned with *how* the service is to be supplied to the user, that is, with implementation details. This is the objective of encapsulation, a concept introduced in Chapter 19.

21.4.2 Designing Algorithms and Data Structures

A variety of representations contained in the analysis model and the system design provide a specification for all operations and attributes. Algorithms and data structures are designed using an approach that differs little from the data design and procedural design approaches discussed for conventional software engineering.[10]

An algorithm is created to implement the specification for each operation. In many cases, the algorithm is a simple computational or procedural sequence that can be implemented as a self-contained software module. However, if the specification of the operation is complex, it may be necessary to modularize the operation. Conventional procedural design techniques can be used to accomplish this.

Data structures are designed concurrently with algorithms. Since operations invariably manipulate the attributes of a class, the design of the data structures that best reflect the attributes will have a strong bearing on the algorithmic design of the corresponding operations.

Although many different types of operations exist, they can generally be divided into three broad categories: (1) operations that *manipulate* data in some way (e.g., adding, deleting, reformatting, selecting); (2) operations that perform a *computation;* and (3) operations that *monitor* an object for the occurrence of a controlling event.

For example, the SafeHome processing narrative contains the sentence fragments: "sensor *is assigned* a number and type" and "a master password is *programmed* for *arming* and *disarming* the system." These two phrases indicate a number of things:

---

[10]See Chapter 14 for details.

- that an *assign* operation is relevant for the **sensor** object;
- that a *program* operation will be applied to the **system** object; and
- that *arm* and *disarm* are operations that apply to **system** (also that system status may ultimately be defined (using data dictionary notation) as

    system status = [armed | disarmed]

The operation *program* is allocated during OOA, but during object design it will be refined into a number of more specific operations that are required to configure the system. For example, after discussions with product engineering, the analyst, and possibly the marketing department, the designer might elaborate the original processing narrative and write the following for **program**:[11]

> Program enables the SafeHome user to configure the system once it has been installed. The user can (1) install phone numbers; (2) define delay times for alarms; (3) build a sensor table that contains each sensor ID, its type, and its location; and (4) load a master password.

Therefore, the designer has refined the single operation *program* and replaced it with the operations *install, define, build,* and *load.* Each of these new operations becomes part of the **system** object, has knowledge of the internal data structures that implement the object's attributes, and is invoked by sending the object messages of the form:

    MESSAGE (system) → install: SENDS telephone number;

which implies that to provide the system with an emergency phone number, an *install* message will be sent to **system**.

Verbs connote actions or occurrences. In the context of object design formalization, we consider not only verbs but also *descriptive verb phrases* and *predicates* (e.g., "is equal to") as potential operations. The grammatical parse is applied recursively until each operation has been refined to its most detailed level.

Once the basic object model is created, optimization should occur. Rambaugh and his colleagues [RAM91] suggest three major thrusts for OOD optimization:

- Review the object-relationship model to ensure that the implemented design leads to efficient utilization of resources and ease of implementation. Add redundancy where necessary.
- Revise attribute data structures and corresponding operation algorithms to enhance efficient processing.
- Create new attributes to save derived information, thereby avoiding recomputation.

---

[11]Underlining has been added to isolate important verbs.

A detailed discussion of OO design optimization is beyond the scope of this book. The interested reader should refer to [RAM91] and [DEC93].

21.4.3 Program Components and Interfaces

An important aspect of software design quality is *modularity*—that is, the specification of *program components* (modules) that are combined to form a complete program. The object-oriented approach defines the object as a program component that is itself linked to other components (e.g., private data, operations). But defining objects and operations is not enough. During design, we must also identify the *interfaces* that exist between objects and the overall structure (considered in an architectural sense) of the objects.

Although a program component is a design abstraction, it should be represented in the context of the programming language with which the design is to be implemented. To accommodate OOD, the programming language to be used for implementation should be capable of creating the following program component (modeled after Ada):

```
PACKAGE program-component-name IS
   TYPE specification of data objects
   .
   .
   .
   PROC specification of related operations . . .
PRIVATE
   data structure details for objects
PACKAGE BODY program-component-name IS
   PROC operation.1 (interface description) IS
   .
   .
   .
   END
   PROC operation.n (interface description) IS
   .
   .
   .
   END
END program-component-name
```

In the Ada-like PDL (program design language) shown above, a program component is specified by indicating both data objects and operations. The *specification-part* of the component indicates all data objects (declared with the TYPE statement) and the operations (PROC for *procedure*) that act on them. The private part (PRIVATE) of the component provides otherwise hidden details of data structure and processing. In the context of our earlier discussion, the PACKAGE is conceptually similar to objects discussed throughout this chapter.

The first program components to be identified should be the highest-level module from which all processing originates and all data structures evolve

Referring once again to the SafeHome example, we can define the highest-level program component as:

```
PROCEDURE SafeHome software
```

The *SafeHome* software component can be coupled with a preliminary design for the following packages (objects):

```
PACKAGE system IS
   TYPE system data
   PROC install, define, build, load
   PROC display, reset, query, modify, call
   PRIVATE
      PACKAGE BODY system IS
      PRIVATE
         system.id IS STRING LENGTH (8);
         verification phone number, telephone number,  . . .
         IS STRING LENGTH (8);
         sensor table DEFINED
            sensor type IS STRING LENGTH (2),
            sensor number, alarm threshold IS NUMERIC;
      PROC install RECEIVES (telephone number)
         {design detail for operation install}
   .
   .
   .
END system
PACKAGE sensor IS
   TYPE sensor data
   PROC read, set, test
   PRIVATE
      PACKAGE BODY sensor IS
      PRIVATE
         sensor.id IS STRING LENGTH (8);
         sensor status IS STRING LENGTH (8);
         alarm characteristics DEFINED
            threshold, signal type, signal level IS NUMERIC,
         hardware interface DEFINED
            type, a/d.characteristics, timing.data IS NUMERIC,
END sensor
   .
   .
   .
END SafeHome software
```

Data objects and corresponding operations are specified for each of the program components for SafeHome software. The final step in the object design process completes all information required to fully implement the data structures and types contained in the PRIVATE portion of the package and all procedural detail contained in the PACKAGE BODY.

To illustrate the detail design of a program component, we reconsider the **sensor** package described above. The data structures for sensor attributes have already been defined. Therefore, the first step is to define the interfaces for each of the operations attached to **sensor**:

```
PROC read (sensor.id, sensor status: OUT);
PROC set (alarm characteristics, hardware interface: IN)
PROC test (sensor.id, sensor status, alarm characteristics:
OUT);
```

The next step requires stepwise refinement of each operation associated with the **sensor** package. To illustrate the refinement, we develop a processing narrative (an informal strategy) for *read:*

> When the sensor object receives a *read* message, the *read* process is invoked. The process determines the interface and signal type, polls the sensor interface, converts A/D characteristics into an internal signal level, and compares the internal signal level to a threshold value. If the threshold is exceeded, the sensor status is set to "event." Otherwise, the sensor status is set to "no event." If an error is sensed while polling the sensor, the sensor status is set to "error."

Given the processing narrative, a PDL description of the *read* process can be developed:

```
PROC read (sensor.id, sensor.status: OUT);
    raw.signal IS BIT STRING
    IF (hardware.interface.type = "s" &
    alarm.characteristics.signal.type = "B"
    THEN
        GET (sensor, exception: sensor status : = error) raw.
        signal;
        CONVERT raw.signal TO internal.signal.level;
        IF internal.signal.level > threshold
            THEN sensor status : = "event";
            ELSE sensor status : = "no event";
        ENDIF
    ELSE {processing for other types of s interfaces would be
    specified}
    ENDIF
    RETURN sensor.id, sensor status;
END read
```

The PDL representation of the *read* operation can be translated into the appropriate implementation language. The functions GET and CONVERT are assumed to be available as part of a run-time library.

21.5   DESIGN PATTERNS

The best designers in any field have an uncanny ability to see patterns that characterize a problem and corresponding patterns that can be combined to create a solution. Gamma and his colleagues [GAM95] discuss this when they state:

> [Y]ou'll find recurring patterns of classes and communicating objects in many object-oriented systems. These patterns solve specific design problems and make object-oriented design more flexible, elegant, and ultimately reusable. They help designers reuse successful designs by basing new designs on prior experience. A designer who is familiar with such patterns can apply them immediately to design problems without having to rediscover them.

Throughout the OOD process, a software engineer should look for every opportunity to reuse existing design patterns and to create new ones if reuse cannot be achieved.

21.5.1 Describing a Design Pattern

Mature engineering disciplines make use of thousands of design patterns. For example, a mechanical engineer uses a two-step, keyed shaft as a design pattern. Inherent in the pattern are attributes (the diameters of the shaft, the dimensions of the keyway, etc.) and operations (e.g., shaft rotation, shaft connection). An electrical engineer uses an integrated circuit (an extremely complex design pattern) to solve a specific element of a new problem. All design patterns can be described by specifying four pieces of information [GAM95]:

- the name of the pattern
- the problem to which the pattern is generally applied
- the characteristics of the design pattern
- the consequences of applying the design pattern

The design pattern name is an abstraction that conveys significant meaning about its applicability and intent. The problem description indicates the environment and conditions that must exist to make the design pattern applicable. The pattern characteristics indicate the attributes of the design that may be adjusted to enable the pattern to accommodate a variety of problems. These attributes represent characteristics of the design that can be searched (e.g., via a database) so that an appropriate pattern can be found. Finally, the consequences associated with the use of a design pattern provide an indication of the ramifications of design decisions.

The names of objects and subsystems (potential design patterns) should be chosen with care. As we discuss in Chapter 26, one of the key technical problems in software reuse is simply the inability to find existing reusable patterns when hundreds or thousands of candidate patterns exist. The search for the "right" pattern is aided immeasurably by a meaningful pattern name along with a set of characteristics that help in classifying the object [PRE95].

21.5.2 Using Patterns in Design

In an object-oriented system, design patterns[12] can be used by applying two different mechanisms: inheritance and composition. Inheritance is a fundamental OO concept and was described in detail in Chapter 19. Using inheritance, an existing design pattern becomes a template for a new subclass. The attributes and operations that exist in the pattern become part of the subclass.

Composition is a concept that leads to aggregate objects. That is, a problem may require objects that have complex functionality (in the extreme, a subsystem accomplishes this). The complex object can be assembled by selected a set of design patterns and composing the appropriate object (or subsystem). Each design pattern is treated as a black box, and communication among the patterns occurs only via well-defined interfaces.

Gamma and his colleagues [GAM95] suggest that object composition should be favored over inheritance when both options exist. Rather than creating large and sometimes unmanageable class hierarchies (the consequence of the overuse of inheritance), composition favors small class hierarchies and objects that remain focused on one objective. Composition uses existing design patterns (reusable components) in unaltered form.

21.6   OBJECT-ORIENTED PROGRAMMING

Although all areas of object technologies have received significant attention within the software community, no subject has produced more books, more discussion, and more debate than *object-oriented programming (OOP)*. There have been well over 100 books written on C++ programming, dozens dedicated to Smalltalk, a growing number dedicated to Ada95, and many books dedicated to less widely used OO languages.

The software engineering viewpoint stresses OOA and OOD, and considers OOP (coding) an important but secondary activity that is an outgrowth of analysis and design. The reason for this is simple. As the complexity of systems increases, the design architecture of the end product has a significantly stronger influence on its success than the programming language that has been used. And yet, "language wars" continue to rage.

The details of OOP are best left to books that are dedicated to the subject. The interested reader should refer to one or more of the OOP books noted in "Further Readings and Other Information Sources" at the end of this chapter.

21.7   SUMMARY

Object-oriented design translates the OOA model of the real world into an implementation-specific model that can be realized in software. The OOD process

---

[12]Gamma and his colleagues [GAM95] have published a catalog of 23 design patterns for use in OO systems.

can be described as a pyramid composed of four layers. The foundation layer focuses on the design of subsystems that implement major system functions; the class layer specifies the overall object architecture and the hierarchy of classes required to implement a system; the message layer indicates how collaboration between objects will be realized; and the responsibilities layer identifies the attributes and operations that characterize each class.

Like OOA, the are many different OOD methods. Although each differs from its counterparts, all conform to the design pyramid and all approach the design process through two levels of abstraction—design of the system and subsystems, and design of individual objects.

During subsystem design, four components are addressed: the problem domain component, the human interaction component, a task management component, and a data management component. The problem domain component implements the customer requirements for an OO application. The other components provide a design infrastructure that enables the application to operate effectively. The object design process focuses on the description of data structures that implement class attributes, algorithms that implement operations, and messages that enable collaborations and object relationships.

Object-oriented programming extends the design model into the executable domain. An OO programming language is used to translate the classes, attributes, operations, and messages into a form that can be executed by a machine.

Object-oriented design represents a unique approach for software engineers. To quote Tom Love [LOV85]:

> The roots of software problems may lie in the most traditional terms for describing our industry—data processing. We have been taught that data and processing are two distinct "things" which are somehow fundamental to our business. That partitioning may be far more detrimental than we realize.

OOD provides us with a means for breaking down the "partitions" between data and process. In doing so, software quality can be improved.

REFERENCES

[BIH92]   Bihari, T., and P. Gopinath, "Object-Oriented Real-Time Systems: Concepts and Examples," *Computer,* vol. 25, no. 12, December 1992, pp. 25–32.

[BOO94]   Booch, G., *Object-Oriented Analysis and Design,* 2nd edition, Benjamin Cummings, 1994.

[BOO96]   Booch, G., and J. Rambaugh, *Unified Method for Object-Oriented Development,* Rational Software Corp., 1996.

[BRO91]   Brown, A.W., *Object-Oriented Databases,* McGraw-Hill, 1991.

[COA91]   Coad, P., and E. Yourdon, *Object-Oriented Design,* Prentice-Hall, 1991.

[COX85]   Cox, B., "Software ICs and Objective-C," *UnixWorld,* Spring, 1985.

[DAV95]   Davis, A., "Object-Oriented Requirements to Object-Oriented Design: An Easy Transition?" *J. Systems Software,* vol. 30, 1995, pp. 151–159.

[DEC93]   de Champeaux, D., D. Lea, and P. Faure, *Object-Oriented System Development,* Addison-Wesley, 1993.

[FIC92]   Fichman, R. and C. Kemerer, "Object-Oriented and Conceptual Design Methodologies," *Computer,* vol. 25, no. 10, October 1992, pp. 22–39.

[GAM95]   Gamma, E. et al., *Design Patterns,* Addison-Wesley, 1995.

[GOL83]   Goldberg, A., and D. Robson, *Smalltalk-80: The Language and Its Implementation,* Addison-Wesley, 1983.

[JAC92]   Jacobson, I., *Object-Oriented Software Engineering,* Addison-Wesley, 1992.

[LOC96]   *Succeeding with the Booch and OMT Methods,* Lockheed-Martin and Rational Software Corporation, Addison-Wesley, 1996.

[LOV85]   Love, T., "Message Object Programming: Experiences with Commercial Systems," Productivity Products International, Sandy Hook, CT, 1985.

[MEY90]   Meyer, Bertrand, *Object-Oriented Software Construction,* 2nd edition, Prentice-Hall, 1988.

[PRE95]   Pree, W., *Design Patterns for Object-Oriented Software Development,* Addison-Wesley, 1995.

[RAM91]   Rambaugh, J. et al., *Object-Oriented Modeling and Design,* Prentice-Hall, 1991.

[RAO94]   Rao. B.A., *Object-Oriented Databases: Technology, Applications and Products,* McGraw-Hill, 1994.

[TAY92]   Taylor, D.A., *Object-Oriented Information Systems,* Wiley, 1992.

[WIR90]   Wirfs-Brock, R., B. Wilkerson, and L. Weiner, *Designing Object-Oriented Software,* Prentice-Hall, 1990.

PROBLEMS AND POINTS TO PONDER

21.1. The design pyramid for OOD differs somewhat from the pyramid described for conventional software design (Chapter 13). Discuss the differences and similarities of the two pyramids.

21.2. How do OOD and structured design differ? What aspects of these two design methods are the same?

21.3. Review the five criteria for effective modularity discussed in Section 21.1.2. Using the design approach described later in the chapter, demonstrate how these five criteria are achieved.

21.4. Select one of the OOD methods presented in Section 21.1.3 and prepare a one hour tutorial for your class. Be sure to show all graphical modeling conventions that the authors suggest.

21.5. Select an OOD method *not* presented in Section 21.1.3 (e.g., HOOD), and prepare a one hour tutorial for your class. Be sure to show all graphical modeling conventions that the authors suggest.

21.6. Discuss how the *use case* can serve as an important source of information for design.

21.7. Research a GUI development environment and show how the human–computer interaction component is implemented in the real world. What design patterns are offered and how are they used?

21.8. Task management for OO systems can be quite complex. Do some research on OOD methods for real-time systems (e.g., [BIH92]) and determine how task management is achieved in that context.

21.9. Discuss how the data management component is implemented in a typical OO development environment.

21.10. Write a two or three page paper on object-oriented databases and discuss how they might be used to develop the data management component.

21.11. How does a designer recognize tasks that must be concurrent?

21.12. Apply the OOD approach discussed in this chapter to flesh out the design for the SafeHome system. Define all relevant subsystems and develop object designs for important classes.

21.13. Apply the OOD approach discussed in this chapter to the PHTRS system described in problem 12.13.

21.14. Describe a video game and apply the OOD approach discussed in this chapter to represent its design.

21.15. You are responsible for the development of an electronic mail (e-mail) system to be implemented on a PC network. The e-mail system will enable users to create letters to be mailed to another user or to a specific address list. Letters can be read, copied, stored, etc. The e-mail system will make use of existing word-processing capability to create letters. Using this description as a starting point, derive a set of requirements and apply OOD techniques to create a top-level design of the e-mail system.

21.16. A small island nation has decided to build an air traffic control (ATC) system for its one airport. The system is specified as follows:

All aircraft landing at the airport must have a transponder that transmits aircraft type and flight data in high-density packed format to the ATC ground station. The ATC ground station can query an aircraft for specific information. When the ATC ground station receives data, it is unpacked and stored in an aircraft database. A computer graphics display is created from the stored information and displayed for an air traffic controller. The display is updated every 10 seconds. All information is analyzed to determine if "dangerous situations" are present. The air traffic controller can query the database for specific information about any plane displayed on the screen.

Using OOD, create a design for the ATC system. Do not attempt to implement it!

FURTHER READINGS AND OTHER INFORMATION SOURCES

The object-oriented design literature is expanding rapidly. Books by Reil (*Object-Oriented Design Through Heuristics,* Addison-Wesley, 1996), Gamma et al. [GAM95], Booch [BOO94], Jacobson [JAC92], Rambaugh et al. [RAM91], Coad and Yourdon [COA91], and Wirfs-Brock, Wilkerson, and Weiner [WIR90] provide excellent insight into this important area. In addition, the following books are worth reviewing:

Berard, E.V., *Essays on Object-Oriented Software Engineering,* Addison-Wesley, 1993.

de Champeaux, D., D. Lea, and P. Faure, *Object-Oriented System Development,* Addison-Wesley, 1993.

Coad, P., D. North, and M. Mayfield, *Object Models: Strategies, Patterns, and Applications,* Prentice-Hall, 1995.

Coleman, D. et al., *Object-Oriented Development: The FUSION Method,* Prentice-Hall, 1994.

Hutt, T.F. (ed.), *Object Analysis and Design: Description of Methods,* Wiley, 1994.

Meyer, B., *Reusable Software,* Prentice-Hall, 1995.

Page-Jones, M., *What Every Programmer Should Know about Object-Oriented Design,* Dorset House, 1995.

Schlaer, S., and Mellor, S., *Object Life Cycles: Modeling the World in States,* Prentice-Hall, 1992).

Wilkie, G., *Object-Oriented Software Engineering,* Addison-Wesley, 1993.

Yourdon, E., *Object-Oriented Systems Design: An Integrated Approach,* Prentice-Hall, 1994.

Yourdon, E. et al., *Mainstream Objects,* Prentice-Hall, 1995.

Buschmann and Meunier (*Pattern-Oriented Software Architecture,* Wiley, 1996) shows how design patterns can help in the development of large-scale applications. Hutt (*Object Analysis and Design,* Wiley, 1994) has edited a collection that presents and compares 16 different object-oriented analysis and design methods.

Literally hundreds of books have been published on object-oriented programming (OOP). A sampling of OOP language–specific books follows:

Ada95:	Barnes, J., *Programming in Ada95,* Addison-Wesley, 1995.
C++:	Eckel, B., *C++ Inside and Out,* McGraw-Hill, 1993.
	Lakos, J., *Large-Scale C++ Software Design,* 1996.
Eiffel:	Rist, R.S., and R. Terwillinger, *Object-Oriented Programming in Eiffel,* 1995
	Meyer, B, *Object-Oriented Software Construction,* 2nd edition, Prentice-Hall, 1995.
Java:	Arnold, K., and J. Gosling, *The Java Programming Language,* Addison-Wesley, 1996.
	Manger, J., *Essential Java,* McGraw-Hill, 1996.
SmallTalk:	LaLonde, W.R., and J.R. Pugh, *Programming in Smalltalk,* Prentice-Hall, 1995.
	Klimas, E. et al., *Smalltalk with Style,* Prentice-Hall, 1995.

The special requirements of real-time systems are covered by Selek and his colleagues (*Real-Time Object-Oriented Modeling,* Wiley, 1995). The use of "application frameworks" as a mechanism for design is considered by Lewis (editor) and his colleagues (*Object-Oriented Application Frameworks,* IEEE Computer Society Press, 1995).

The same Internet sources noted for Chapters 19 and 20 are also applicable for OOD. The Internet newsgroup **comp.object** and newsgroups dedicated to OO programming languages (e.g., **comp.lang.C++** and **comp.lang.**

smalltalk) are useful sources for information, discussion, and debate on OOD methods, programming techniques, and tools.

The following resources (listed without further comment) contain useful information on OOD and OOP, including additional references, articles, and information:

http://www.omg.org/

http://osm7.cs.byu.edu

http://www.mcs.com/ ~ woodsman/otek.html

http://wwwtrese.cs.utwente.nl/index.html

An up-to-date list of World Wide Web references for object-oriented design can be found at: **http://www.rspa.com**

OBJECT-ORIENTED TESTING

In Chapter 16 we learned that the objective of testing, stated simply, is to find the greatest possible number of errors with a manageable amount of effort applied over a realistic time span. Although this fundamental objective remains unchanged for object-oriented software, the nature of OO programs changes both testing strategy and testing tactics.

It might be argued that as OOA and OOD mature, greater reuse of design patterns will mitigate the need for heavy testing of OO systems. Exactly the opposite is true. Binder [BIN94b] discusses this when he states:

> [E]ach reuse is a new context of usage and retesting is prudent. It seems likely that more, not less testing will be needed to obtain high reliability in object-oriented systems.

To adequately test OO systems, three things must be done: (1) the definition of testing must be broadened to include error discovery techniques applied to OOA and OOD models; (2) the strategy for unit and integration testing must change significantly; and (3) the design of test cases must account for the unique characteristics of OO software.

22.1   BROADENING THE VIEW OF TESTING

The construction of object-oriented software begins with the creation of analysis and design models (Chapters 20 and 21). Because of the evolutionary nature of the OO software engineering paradigm, these models begin as relatively informal representations of system requirements and evolve into detailed models of classes, class connections and relationships, system design and allocation, and object design (incorporating a model of object connectivity via messaging). At each stage, the models can be testing in an attempt to uncover errors prior to their propagation to the next iteration.

It can be argued that the review of OO analysis and design models is especially useful because the same semantic constructs (e.g., classes, attributes, operations, messages) appear at the analysis, design, and code levels. Therefore, a problem in the definition of class attributes that is uncovered during analysis will circumvent side effects that might occur if the problem were not discovered until design or coding (or even the next iteration of analysis).

For example, consider a class in which a number of attributes are defined during the first iteration of OOA. An extraneous attribute is appended to the class (due to a misunderstanding of the problem domain). Two operations are then specified to manipulate the attribute. A review is conducted and a domain expert points out the problem. By eliminating the extraneous attribute at this stage, the following problems and unnecessary effort may be avoided during analysis:

1. Special subclasses may have been generated to accommodate the unnecessary attribute or exceptions to it. Work involved in the creation of unnecessary subclasses has been avoided.
2. A misinterpretation of the class definition may lead to incorrect or extraneous class relationships.
3. The behavior of the system or its classes may be improperly characterized to accommodate the extraneous attribute.

If the problem is not uncovered during analysis and propagated further, the following problems could occur (and will have been avoided because of the earlier review) during design:

1. Improper allocation of the class to a subsystem and/or tasks may occur during system design.
2. Unnecessary design work may be expended to create the procedural design for the operations that address the extraneous attribute.
3. The messaging model will be incorrect (because messages must be designed for the operations that are extraneous).

If the problem remains undetected during design and passes into the coding activity, considerable effort and energy will be expended to generate code that implements an unnecessary attribute, two unnecessary operations, messages that drive inter-object communication, and many other related issues. In addition, testing of the class will absorb more time than necessary. Once the problem is finally uncovered, modification to the system must be carried out with the ever-present potential for side effects that are caused by change.

During latter stages of their development, OOA and OOD models provide substantial information about the structure and behavior of the system. For this reason, these models should be subjected to rigorous review prior to the generation of code.

All object-oriented models should be tested (in this context, the term "testing" is used to incorporate formal technical reviews) for correctness, completeness, and consistency [MCG94] within the context of the model's syntax, semantics, and pragmatics [LIN94].

22.2　TESTING OOA AND OOD MODELS

Analysis and design models cannot be tested in the conventional sense, because they cannot be executed. However, formal technical reviews (Chapter 8) can be used to examine the correctness and consistency of both analysis and design models.

22.2.1　Correctness of OOA and OOD Models

The notation and syntax used to represent analysis and design models will be tied to the specific analysis and design method that is chosen for the project. Hence, syntactic correctness is judged on proper use of the symbology, and each model is reviewed to ensure that proper modeling conventions have been maintained.

During analysis and design, semantic correctness must be judged based on the model's conformance to the real world problem domain. If the model accurately reflects the real world (to a level of detail that is appropriate to the stage of development at which the model is reviewed) then it is semantically correct. To determine whether the model does, in fact, reflect the real world, it should be presented to problem domain experts, who will examine the class definitions and hierarchy for omissions and ambiguity. Class relationships (instance connections) are evaluated to determine whether they accurately reflect real world object connections.[1]

22.2.2　Consistency of OOA and OOD Models

The consistency of OOA and OOD models may be judged by "considering the relationships among entities in the model. An inconsistent model has representations in one part that are not correctly reflected in other portions of the model" [MCG94].

To assess consistency, each class and its connections to other classes should be examined. The class–responsibility–collaboration (CRC) model and an object-relationship diagram can be used to facilitate this activity. As we noted in Chapter 20, the CRC model is composed on CRC index cards. Each CRC card lists the class name, its responsibilities (operations), and its collaborators (other classes to which it sends messages and on which it depends for the accom-

---

[1]Use cases can be invaluable in tracking analysis and design models against real world usage scenarios for the OO system.

plishment of its responsibilities). The collaborations imply a series of relationships (i.e., connections) between classes of the OO system. The object relationship model provides a graphic representation of the connections between classes. All of this information can be obtained from the OOA model (Chapter 20).

To evaluate the class model the following steps have been recommended [MCG94]:

1. Revisit the CRC model and the object-relationship model. Cross check to ensure that all collaborations implied by the OOA model are properly reflected in both.

2. Inspect the description of each CRC index card to determine if a delegated responsibility is part of the collaborator's definition. For example, consider a class defined for a point-of-sale check-out system and called **credit sale**. This class has a CRC index card illustrated in Figure 22.1.

    For this collection of classes and collaborations, we ask whether a responsibility (e.g., *read credit card*) is accomplished if delegated to the named collaborator (**credit card**); that is, does the class **credit card** have an operation that enables it to be read? In this case the answer is "yes." The object relationship is traversed to ensure that all such connections are valid.

3. Invert the connection to ensure that each collaborator that is asked for service is receiving requests from a reasonable source. For example, if the **credit card** class receives a request for *purchase amount* from the **credit sale** class, there would be a problem. **Credit card** does not know the purchase amount.

class name: **credit sale**	
class type: transaction event	
class characteristics: nontangible, atomic, sequential, permanent, guarded	
responsibilities:	collaborators:
read credit card	credit card
get authorization	credit authority
post purchase amount	product ticket
	sales ledger
	audit file
generate bill	bill

FIGURE 22.1. A example CRC index card used for review

4. Using the inverted connections examined in step 3, determine whether other classes might be required or whether responsibilities are properly grouped among the classes.

5. Determine whether widely requested responsibilities might be combined into a single responsibility. For example, *read credit card* and *get authorization* occur in every situation. They might be combined into a *validate credit request* responsibility that incorporates getting the credit card number and gaining authorization

6. Steps 1 to 5 are applied iteratively to each class and through each evolution of the OOA model.

Once design models (Chapter 21) have been created, reviews of the system design and the object design should also be conducted. The system design depicts the subsystems that compose the product, the manner in which subsystems are allocated to processors, and the allocation of classes to subsystems. The object model presents the details of each class and the messaging activities that are necessary to implement collaborations between classes.

The system design is reviewed by examining the object-behavior model developed during OOA and mapping required system behavior against the subsystems designed to accomplish this behavior. Concurrency and task allocation are also reviewed within the context of system behavior. The behavioral states of the system are evaluated to determine which exist concurrently.

The object model should be tested against the object-relationship network to ensure that all design objects contain the necessary attributes and operations to implement the collaborations defined for each CRC index card. In addition, the detailed specification of operation details (i.e., the algorithms that implement the operations) are reviewed using conventional inspection techniques.

22.3   OBJECT-ORIENTED TESTING STRATEGIES

The classical strategy for testing computer software begins with "testing in the small" and works outward toward "testing in the large." Stated in the jargon of software testing (Chapter 17), we begin with *unit testing,* then progress toward *integration testing,* and culminate with *validation and system testing*. In conventional applications, unit testing focuses on the smallest compilable program unit—the subprogram (e.g., module, subroutine, procedure). Once each of these units has been testing individually, it is integrated into a program structure while a series of regression tests are run to uncover errors due to interfacing the modules and side effects that are caused by the addition of new units. Finally, the system as a whole is tested to ensure that errors in requirements are uncovered.

22.3.1   Unit Testing in the OO Context

When object-oriented software is considered, the concept of the unit changes. Encapsulation drives the definition of classes and objects. This means that each class and each instance of a class (object) packages attributes (data) and the operations (also known as methods or services) that manipulate these data. Rather than the individual module, the smallest testable unit is the encapsulated class or object. A class can contain a number of different operations, and a particular operation may exist as part of a number of different classes. Therefore, the meaning of unit testing changes dramatically.

We can no longer test a single operation in isolation (the conventional view of unit testing) but rather, as part of a class. To illustrate, consider a class hierarchy in which an operation X is defined for the superclass and is inherited by a number of subclasses. Each subclass uses operation X, but it is applied within the context of the private attributes and operations that have been defined for each subclass. Because the context in which operation X is used varies in subtle ways, it is necessary to test operation X in the context of each of the subclasses. This means that testing operation X in a vacuum (the traditional unit testing approach) is ineffective in the object-oriented context.

Class testing for OO software is the equivalent of unit testing for conventional software.[2] Unlike unit testing of conventional software, which tends to focus on the algorithmic detail of a module and the data that flow across the module interface, class testing for OO software is driven by the operations encapsulated by the class and the state behavior of the class.

22.3.2 Integration Testing in the OO Context

Because object-oriented software does not have a hierarchical control structure, conventional top-down and bottom-up integration strategies have little meaning. In addition, integrating operations one at a time into a class (the conventional incremental integration approach) is often impossible because of the "direct and indirect interactions of the components that make up the class" [BER93].

There are two different strategies for integration testing of OO systems [BIN94a]. The first, *thread-based testing,* integrates the set of classes required to respond to one input or event for the system. Each thread is integrated and tested individually. Regression testing is applied to ensure that no side effects occur. The second integration approach, *use-based testing,* begins the construction of the system by testing those classes (called *independent classes*) that use very few (if any) of server classes. After the independent classes are tested, the next layer of classes, called *dependent classes,* that use the independent classes are tested. This sequence of testing layers of dependent classes continues until the entire system is constructed. Unlike conventional integration, the use of drivers and stubs (Chapter 16) as replacement operations is to be avoided when possible.

Cluster testing [MCG94] is one step in the integration testing of OO software. Here, a cluster of collaborating classes (determined by examining the CRC and object-relationship model) is exercised by designing test cases that attempt to uncover errors in the collaborations.

---

[2]Test case design methods for OO classes are discussed in Sections 22.4 through 22.6.

22.3.3 Validation Testing in an OO Context

At the validation or system level, the details of class connections disappear. Like conventional validation, the validation of OO software focuses on user visible actions and user recognizable outputs from the system. To assist in the derivation of validation tests, the tester should draw upon use cases (Chapter 20) that are part of the analysis model. The use case provides a scenario that has a high likelihood of uncovered errors in user interaction requirements.

Conventional black-box testing methods (Chapter 16) can be used to drive validation tests. In addition, test cases may be derived from the object-behavior model and from the event flow diagram created as part of OOA.

22.4   TEST CASE DESIGN FOR OO SOFTWARE

Test case design methods for OO software are in their formative stages. However, an overall approach to OO test case design has been suggested by Berard [BER93]:

1.   Each test case should be uniquely identified and should be explicitly associated with the class to be tested.
2.   The purpose of the test should be stated.
3.   A list of testing steps should be developed for each test and should contain [BER93]:
     a. a list of specified states for the object that is to be tested
     b. a list of messages and operations that will be exercised as a consequence of the test
     c. a list of exceptions that may occur as the object is tested
     d. a list of external conditions (i.e., changes in the environment external to the software that must exist in order to properly conduct the test)
     e. supplementary information that will aid in understanding or implementing the test

Unlike conventional test case design, which is driven by an input–process–output view of software or the algorithmic detail of individual modules, object-oriented testing focuses on designing appropriate sequences of operations to exercise the states of a class.

22.4.1 The Test Case Design Implications of OO Concepts

As we have already seen, the OO class is the target for test case design. Because attributes and operations are encapsulated, the testing of operations outside of the class is generally unproductive. Although encapsulation is an essential design concept for OO, it can create a minor obstacle when testing. As Binder [BIN94a] notes, "[t]esting requires reporting on the concrete and abstract state of an object." Yet, encapsulation can make this information somewhat difficult to obtain. Unless built-in operations are provided to report the values for class attributes, a snapshot of the state of an object may be difficult to acquire.

Inheritance also leads to additional challenges for the test case designer. We have already noted that each new context of usage requires retesting, even though reuse has been achieved. In addition, multiple inheritance[3] complicates testing further by increasing the number of contexts for which testing is required [BIN94a]. If subclasses instantiated from a superclass are used within the same problem domain, it is likely that the set of test cases derived for the superclass can be used when testing the subclass. However, if the subclass is used in an entirely different context, the superclass test cases will have little applicability and a new set of tests must be designed.

22.4.2 Applicability of Conventional Test Case Design Methods

The white-box testing methods described in Chapter 16 can be applied to the operations defined for a class. Basis path, loop testing, or data flow techniques can help to ensure that every statement in an operation has been tested. However, the concise structure of many class operations causes some to argue that the effort applied to white-box testing might be better redirected to tests at a class level.

Black-box testing methods are as appropriate for OO systems as they are for systems developed using conventional software engineering methods. As we noted earlier in this chapter, use cases can provide useful input in the design of black-box and state-based tests [AMB95].

22.4.3 Fault-Based Testing[4]

The object of fault-based testing within an OO system is to design tests that have a high likelihood of uncovering plausible faults. Because the product or system must conform to customer requirements, the preliminary planning required to perform fault-based testing begins with the analysis model. The tester looks for plausible faults (i.e., aspects of the implementation of the system that may result in defects). To determine whether these faults exist, test cases are designed to exercise the design or code.

Consider a simple example.[5] Software engineers often make errors at the boundaries of a problem. For example, when testing a SQRT operation that returns errors for negative numbers, we know to try the boundaries: a negative number close to zero, and zero itself. "Zero itself" checks whether the programmer made a mistake like:

---

[3]An OO design concept that should be used with extreme care.

[4]Sections 22.4.3 through 22.4.7 have been adapted from an article by Brian Marick posted on the Internet newsgroup **comp.testing**. This adaptation is included with the permission of the author. For further discussion of these topics, see [MAR94].

[5]The code presented in this and the following sections uses C++ syntax. For further information, see any good book on C++.

```
if (x > 0) calculate_the_square_root();
```

instead of the correct:

```
if (x >= 0) calculate_the_square_root();
```

As another example, consider a Boolean expression:

```
if (a && !b || c)
```

Multicondition testing and related techniques probe for certain plausible faults in this expression, such as:

"&&" should be an " || "

"!" was left out where it was needed

There should be parentheses around "!b || "

For each plausible fault, we design test cases that will force the incorrect expression to fail. In the expression above, (a = 0, b = 0, c = 0) will make the expression as given evaluate false. If the "&&" should have been a "||", the code has done the wrong thing and might branch to the wrong path.

Of course, the effectiveness of these techniques depends on how testers perceive a "plausible fault." If real faults in an OO system are perceived to be "implausible," then this approach is really no better than any random testing technique. However, if the analysis and design models can provide insight into what is likely to go wrong, then fault-based testing can find significant numbers of errors with relatively low expenditures of effort.

Integration testing looks for plausible faults in message connections. Three types of faults are encountered in this context: unexpected result, wrong operation/message used, incorrect invocation. To determine plausible faults as functions (operations) are invoked, the behavior of the operation must be examined.

Integration testing applies to attributes as well as to operations. The "behaviors" of an object are defined by the values that its attributes are assigned. Testing should exercise the attributes to determine whether proper values occur for distinct types of object behavior.

It is important to note that integration testing attempts to find errors in the client object, not the server. Stated in conventional terms, the focus of integration testing is to determine whether errors exist in the calling code, not the called code. The operation call is used as a clue, a way to find test requirements that exercise the calling code.

22.4.4 The Impact of OO Programming on Testing

There are several ways object-oriented programming can have an impact on testing. Depending on the approach to OOP,

- some types of faults become less plausible (not worth testing for)
- some types of faults become more plausible (worth testing now)
- some new types of faults appear

When an operation is invoked, it may be hard to tell exactly what code gets exercised. That is, the operation may belong to one of many classes. Also, it can be hard to determine the exact type/class of a parameter. When the code accesses the parameter, it may get an unexpected value.

The difference can be understood by considering a conventional function call:

```
x = func (y);
```

For conventional software, the tester need consider all behaviors attributed to func and nothing more. In an OO context, the tester must consider the behaviors of base::func(), of derived::func(), and so on. Each time func is invoked, the tester must consider the union of all distinct behaviors. This is easier if good OO design practices are followed and the difference between superclasses and subclasses (in C++ jargon, these are called *base* and *derived classes*) are limited. The testing approach for base and derived classes is essentially the same. The difference is one of bookkeeping.

Testing OO class operations is analogous to testing code that takes a function parameter and then invokes it. Inheritance is a convenient way of producing polymorphic operations. At the call site, what matters is not the inheritance, but the polymorphism. Inheritance does make the search for test requirements more straightforward.

By virtue of the architecture and construction of OO systems, are some types of faults more plausible and others less plausible? The answer is "yes" for OO systems. For example, because OO operations are generally smaller, there tends to be a more integration required and more opportunities for integration faults. Therefore, integration faults become more plausible.

22.4.5 Test Cases and the Class Hierarchy

As noted earlier in this chapter, inheritance does not obviate the need for thorough testing of all derived classes. In fact, it can actually complicate the testing process.

Consider the following situation. A class **base** contains operations *inherited* and *redefined*. A class **derived** redefines *redefined* to serve in a local context. There is little doubt that derived::redefined() has to be tested because it represents a new design and new code. But does derived::inherited() have to be retested?

If derived::inherited() calls *redefined,* and the behavior of *redefined* has changed, derived::inherited() may mishandle the new behavior. Therefore, it needs new tests even though the design and code have not changed. It is important to note, however, that only a subset of all tests for derived::inherited() may have to be conducted. If part of the design and code for *inherited* does not depend on *redefined* (i.e., does not call it or any code that indirectly calls it), that code need not be retested in the **derived** class.

`Base::redefined()` and `derived::redefined()` are two different operations with different specifications and implementations. They would each have a set of test requirements derived from the specification and implementation. Those test requirements probe for plausible faults: integration faults, condition faults, boundary faults, and so forth. But the operations are likely to be similar. Their sets of test requirements will overlap. The better the OO design, the greater the overlap. New tests need to be derived only for those `derived::redefined()` requirements that are not satisfied by the `base::redefined()` tests.

To summarize, the `base::redefined()` tests are applied to objects of class **derived**. Test inputs may be appropriate for both **base** and **derived** classes, but the expected results may differ in the **derived** class.

22.4.6 Scenario-Based Test Design

Fault-based testing misses two main types of errors: (1) incorrect specifications and (2) interactions among subsystems. When errors associated with incorrect specification occur, the product doesn't do what the customer wants. It might do the wrong thing, or it might omit important functionality. In either circumstance, quality (conformance to requirements) suffers. Errors associated with subsystem interaction occur when the behavior of one subsystem creates circumstances (e.g., events, data flow) that cause another subsystem to fail.

Scenario-based testing concentrates on what the user does, not what the product does. It means capturing the tasks (via use cases) that the user has to perform, then applying them and their variants as tests.

Scenarios uncover interaction errors. To accomplish this, test cases must be more complex and more realistic than fault-based tests. Scenario-based testing tends to exercise multiple subsystems in a single test (users do not limit themselves to the use of one subsystem at a time).

As an example, consider the design of scenario-based tests for a text editor. Use cases follow:

Use Case: *Fix the Final Draft*
Background: It's not unusual to print the "final" draft, read it, and discover some annoying errors that weren't obvious from the on-screen image. This use case describes the sequence of events that occurs when this happens.
1. Print the entire document.
2. Move around in the document, changing certain pages.
3. As each page is changed, it's printed.
4. Sometimes a series of pages is printed.

This scenario describes two things: a test and specific user needs. The user needs are obvious: (1) a method for printing single pages and (2) a method for printing a range of pages. As far as testing goes, there is a need to test editing after printing (as well as the reverse). The tester hopes to discover that the printing function causes errors in the editing function; that is, that the two software functions are not properly independent.

Use Case: *Print a New Copy*
Background: Someone asks the user for a fresh copy of the document. It must be printed.
1. Open the document.
2. Print it.
3. Close the document.

Again, the testing approach is relatively obvious. Except that this document didn't appear out of nowhere. It was created in an earlier task. Does that task affect this one?

In many modern editors, documents remember how they were last printed. By default, they print the same way next time. After the *Fix the Final Draft* scenario, just selecting "Print" in the menu and clicking the "Print" button in the dialog box will cause the last corrected page to print again. So, according to the editor, the correct scenario should look like this:

Use Case: *Print a New Copy*
1. Open the document.
2. Select "Print" in the menu.
3. Check if you're printing a page range; if so, click to print the entire document.
4. Click on the "Print" button.
5. Close the document.

But this scenario indicates a potential specification error. The editor does not do what the user reasonably expects it to do. Customers will often overlook the check noted in step 3 above. They will then be annoyed when they trot off to the printer and find one page when they wanted 100. Annoyed customers signal specification bugs.

A test case designer might miss this dependency in test design, but it is likely that the problem would surface during testing. The tester would then have to contend with the probable response, "That's the way it's supposed to work!"

22.4.7 Testing Surface Structure and Deep Structure

Surface structure refers to the externally observable structure of an OO program. That is, the structure that is immediately obvious to an end user. Rather than performing functions, the users of many OO systems may be given objects to manipulate in some way. But whatever the interface, tests are still based on user tasks. Capturing these tasks involves understanding, watching, and talking with the representative user (and as many nonrepresentative users as are worth considering).

There will surely be some difference in detail. For example, in a conventional system with a command-oriented interface, the user might use the list of all commands as a testing checklist. If no test scenarios existed to exercise a command, testing has likely overlooked some user tasks (or the interface has useless commands). In a object-based interface, the tester might use the list of all objects as a testing checklist.

The best tests are derived when the designer looks at the system in a new or unconventional way. For example, if the system or product has a command-based interface, more thorough tests will be derived if the test case designer pretends that operations are independent of objects. Ask questions like, "Might the user want to use this operation—which applies only to the scanner object—while working with the printer?" Whatever the interface style, test case design that exercises the surface structure should use both objects and operations as clues leading to overlooked tasks.

Deep structure refers to the internal technical details of an OO program. That is, the structure that is understood by examining the design and/or code. Deep structure testing is designed to exercise dependencies, behaviors, and communication mechanisms that have been established as part of the subsystem and object design (Chapter 21) of OO software.

The analysis and design models are used as the basis for deep structure testing. For example, the object-relationship diagram or the subsystem collaboration graph depicts collaborations between objects and subsystems that may not be externally visible. The test case designer then asks: "Have we captured (as a test) some task that exercises the collaboration noted on the object-relationship diagram or the subsystem collaboration graph? If not, why not?"

Design representations of class hierarchy provide insight into inheritance structure. Inheritance structure is used in fault-based testing. Consider a situation in which an operation named *caller* has only one argument and that argument is a reference to a base class. What might happen when *caller* is passed a derived class? What are the differences in behavior that could affect *caller*? The answers to these questions might lead to the design of specialized tests.

22.5   TESTING METHODS APPLICABLE AT THE CLASS LEVEL

In Chapter 16, we noted that software testing begins "in-the-small" and slowly progresses toward testing "in-the-large." Testing in-the-small for OO systems focuses on a single class and the methods that are encapsulated by the class. *Random testing* and *partitioning* are methods that can be used to exercise a class during OO testing [KIR94].

22.5.1 Random Testing for OO Classes

To provide brief illustrations of these methods, consider a banking application in which an **account** class has the following operations: *open, setup, deposit, withdraw balance, summarize, creditLimit,* and *close* [KIR94]. Each of these operations may be applied for **account,** but certain constraints (e.g., the account must be opened before other operations can be applied and closed after all operations are completed) are implied by the nature of the problem. Even with these constraints, there are many permutations of the operations. The minimum behavioral life history of an instance of **account** includes the following operations:

```
open•setup•deposit•withdraw•close
```

This represents the *minimum test sequence* for **account**. However, a wide variety of other behaviors may occur within this sequence:

open•setup•deposit•[deposit | withdraw | balance | summarize | creditLimit]^n•withdraw•close

A variety of different operation sequences can be generated randomly. For example:

Test case #r_1:   open•setup•deposit•deposit•balance•summarize
•withdraw•close

Test case #r_2:   open•setup•deposit•withdraw•deposit•balance•
creditLimit•withdraw•close

These and other random order tests are conducted to exercise different class instance life histories.

22.5.2   Partition Testing at the Class Level

Partition testing reduces the number of test cases required to exercise the class in much the same manner as equivalence partitioning (Chapter 16) does for conventional software. Input and output are categorized, and test cases are designed to exercise each category. But how are the partitioning categories derived?

State-based partitioning categorizes class operations based on their ability to change the state of the class. Again considering the account class, state operations include *deposit* and *withdraw,* whereas non-state operations include *balance, summarize,* and *creditLimit*. Tests are designed in a way that exercises operations that change state and those that do not change state separately. Therefore,

Test case #p_1:   open•setup•deposit•deposit•withdraw•withdraw
•close

Test case #p_2:   open•setup•deposit•summarize•creditLimit•
withdraw•close

Test case #p_1 changes state, while test case #p_2 exercises operations that do not change state (other than those in the minimum test sequence).

Attribute-based partitioning categorizes class operations based on the attributes that they use. For the **account** class, the attributes *balance* and *credit limit* can be used to define partitions. Operations are divided into three partitions: (1) operations that use *credit limit,* (2) operations that modify *credit limit,* and operations that do not use or modify *credit limit*. Test sequences are then designed for each partition.

Category-based partitioning categorizes class operations based on the generic function that each performs. For example, operations in the **account** class can be categorized in initialization operations (*open, setup*), computational operations (*deposit, withdraw*), queries (*balance, summarize, creditLimit*), and termination operations (*close*).

22.6   ## INTERCLASS TEST CASE DESIGN

Test case design becomes more complicated as integration of the OO system begins. It is at this stage that testing of collaborations between classes must begin. To illustrate *inter-class test case generation* [KIR94], we expand the banking example introduced in Section 22.5 to include the classes and collaborations noted in Figure 22.2. The direction of the arrows in the figure indicates the direction of messages, and the labeling indicates the operations that are invoked as a consequence of the collaborations implied by the messages.

Like the testing of individual classes, class collaboration testing can be accomplished by applying random and partitioning methods as well as scenario-based testing and behavioral testing.

22.6.1   Multiple Class Testing

Kirani and Tsai [KIR94] suggest the following sequence of steps to generate multiple class random test cases:

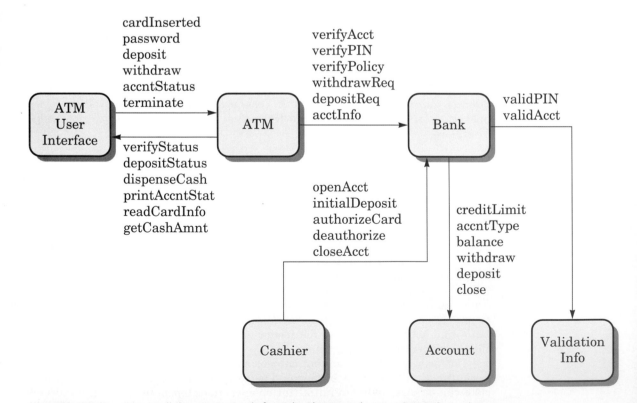

FIGURE 22.2.   Class-collaboration graph for a banking application [KIR94]

1. For each client class, use the list of class operators to generate a series of random test sequences. The operators will send messages to other server classes.

2. For each message that is generated, determine the collaborator class and the corresponding operator in the server object.

3. For each operator in the server object (that has been invoked by messages sent from the client object), determine the messages that it transmits.

4. For each of the messages, determine the next level of operators that are invoked and incorporate these into the test sequence.

To illustrate [KIR94], consider a sequence of operations for the **bank** class relative to an **ATM** class (Figure 22.2):

verifyAcct•verifyPIN•[[verifyPolicy•withdrawReq] | depositReq | acctInfoREQ]^n

A random test case for the **bank** class might be

Test case #r_3:   verifyAcct•verifyPIN•depositReq

In order to consider the collaborators involved in this test, the messages associated with each of the operations noted in test case r_3 are considered. **Bank** must collaborate with **ValidationInfo** to execute the *verifyAcct* and *verifyPIN*. **Bank** must collaborate with **account** to execute *depositReq*. Hence, a new test case that exercises the collaborations noted above is:

Test case #r_4:   verifyAcct$_{Bank}$[validAcct$_{ValidationInfo}$]•verify
PIN$_{Bank}$ •[validPin$_{ValidationInfo}$•depositReq•[deposit$_{account}$]

The approach for *multiple class partition testing* is similar to the approach used for partition testing of individual classes. A single class is partitioned as discussed in Section 22.5.2. However, the test sequence is expanded to include those operations that are invoked via messages to collaborating classes. An alternative approach partitions tests based on the interfaces to a particular class. As shown in Figure 22.1, the **bank** class receives messages from the **ATM** and **cashier** classes. The methods within **bank** can therefore be tested by partitioning them into those that serve **ATM** and those that serve **cashier**. State-based partitioning (Section 22.5.2) can be used to refine the partitions further.

22.6.2   Tests Derived from Behavior Models

In Chapter 20, we discussed the use of the state-transition diagram (STD) as a model that represents the dynamic behavior of a class. The STD for a class can be used to help derive a sequence of tests that will exercise the dynamic be-

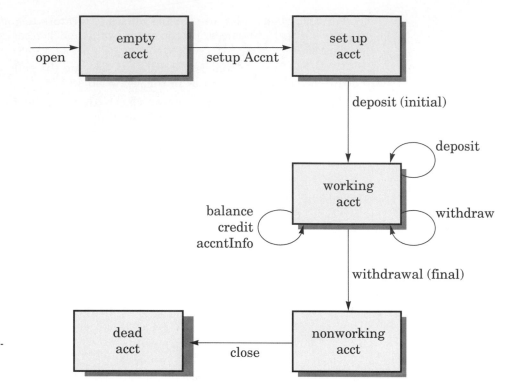

FIGURE 22.3.
State-transition diagram for account class [KIR94]

havior of the class (and those classes that collaborate with it). Figure 22.3 [KIR94] illustrates a STD for the **account** class discussed earlier. Referring to the figure, initial transitions move through the *empty acct* and *setup acct* states. The majority of all behavior for instances of the class occurs while in the *working acct* state. A final withdrawal and close cause the account class to make transitions to the *non-working acct* and *dead acct* states, respectively.

The tests to be designed should achieve *all state coverage* [KIR94]. That is, the operation sequences should cause the **account** class to make transition through all allowable states:

test case #s_1:   open•setupAccnt•deposit(initial)•withdraw(final)•close

It should be noted that this sequence is identical to the minimum test sequence discussed in Section 22.5.1. Adding addition test sequences to the minimum sequence:

test case #s_2:   open•setupAccnt•deposit(initial)•deposit•bal-
ance•credit•withdraw(final)•close

test case #s_3:   open•setupAccnt•deposit(initial)•deposit•
withdraw•accntInfo•withdraw(final)•close

Still more test cases could be derived to ensure that all behaviors for the class have been adequately exercised. In situations in which the class behavior results in a collaboration with one or more classes, multiple STDs are used to track the behavioral flow of the system.

The state model can be traversed in a "breadth first" [MCG94] manner. In this context, *breadth first* implies that a test case exercises a single transition and that when a new transition is to be tested only previously tested transitions are used.

Consider the **credit card** object discussed in Section 22.2.2. The initial state of **credit card** is *undefined* (i.e., no credit card number has been provided). Upon reading the credit card during a sale, the object takes on a *defined* state, that is, the attributes **card number** and **expiration date** along with bank-specific identifiers are defined. The credit card is *submitted* when it is sent for authorization, and it is *approved* when authorization is received. The transition of **credit card** from one state to another can be tested by deriving test cases that cause the transition to occur. A breadth first approach to this type of testing would *not* exercise *submitted* before it exercised *undefined* and *defined*. If it did, it would make use of transitions that had not been previously tested and would therefore violate the breadth first criterion.

22.7 SUMMARY

The overall objective of object-oriented testing—to find the maximum number of errors with a minimum amount effort—is identical to the objective of conventional software testing. But the strategy and tactics for OO testing differ significantly. The view of testing broadens to include the review of both the analysis and design model. In addition, the focus of testing moves away from the procedural component (the module) and toward the class.

Because the OO analysis and design models and the resulting source code are semantically coupled, testing (in the form of formal technical reviews) begins during these engineering activities. For this reason, a review of CRC, object-relationship, and object-behavior models can be viewed as first stage testing.

Once OOP has been accomplished, unit testing is applied for each class. Class testing uses a variety of methods: fault-based testing, random testing, and partition testing. Each of these methods exercises the operations encapsulated by the class. Test sequences are designed to ensure that relevant operations are exercised. The state of the class, represented by the values of its attributes, is examined to determine if errors exist.

Integration testing can be accomplished using a thread-based or use-based strategy. Thread-based testing integrates the set of classes that collaborate to respond to one input or event. Use-based testing constructs the system in layers, beginning with those classes that do not make use of server classes. Integration test case design methods can also make use of random and partition tests. In addition, scenario-based testing and tests derived from behavioral models can be used to test a class and its collaborators. A test sequence tracks the flow of operations across class collaborations.

OO system validation testing is black-box oriented and can be accomplished by applying the same black-box methods discussed for conventional software. However, scenario-based testing dominates the validation of OO systems, making the use case a primary driver for validation testing.

REFERENCES

[AMB95]   Ambler, S., "Using Use Cases," *Software Development,* July 1995, pp. 53–61.
[BER93]   Berard, E.V., *Essays on Object-Oriented Software Engineering,* Volume 1, Addison-Wesley, 1993.
[BIN94a] Binder, R.V., "Testing Object-Oriented Systems: A Status Report," *American Programmer,* vol. 7, no. 4, April 1994, pp. 23–28.
[BIN94b] Binder, R.V., "Object-Oriented Software Testing," *Communications of the ACM,* vol. 37, no. 9, September 1994, p. 29.
[KIR94]   Kirani, S., and W.T. Tsai, "Specification and Verification of Object-Oriented Programs," Technical Report TR 94-64, Computer Science Department, University of Minnesota, December, 1994.
[LIN94]   Lindland, O.I., et al. "Understanding Quality in Conceptual Modeling," *IEEE Software,* vol. 11, no. 4, July 1994, pp. 42–49.
[MAR94]   Marick, B., *The Craft of Software Testing,* Prentice-Hall, 1994.
[MCG94]   McGregor, J.D., and T.D. Korson, "Integrated Object-Oriented Testing and Development Processes," *Communications of the ACM,* vol. 37, no. 9, September 1994, pp. 59–77.

PROBLEMS AND POINTS TO PONDER

22.1. In your own words, describe why the class is the smallest reasonable unit for testing within an OO system.

22.2. Why do we have to retest subclasses that are instantiated from an existing class, if the existing class has already been thoroughly tested? Can we use the test cases designed for the existing class?

22.3. Why should "testing" begin with the OOA and OOD activities?

22.4. Derive a set of CRC index cards for SafeHome and conduct the steps noted in Section 22.2.2 to determine if inconsistencies exist.

22.5. What is the difference between thread-based and use-based strategies for integration testing? How does cluster testing fit in?

22.6. Apply random testing and partitioning to three classes defined in the design for the SafeHome system that you produced for problem 21.12. Produce test cases that indicate the operation sequences that will be invoked.

22.7. Apply multiple class testing and tests derived from the behavioral model to the SafeHome design.

22.8. Derive tests using methods noted in problems 22.6 and 22.7 for the PHTRS system described in problem 12.13.

22.9. Derive tests using methods noted in Problems 22.6 and 22.7 for the video game considered in problem 21.14.

22.10. Derive tests using methods noted in problems 22.6 and 22.7 for the e-mail system considered in problem 21.15.

22.11. Derive tests using methods noted in problems 22.6 and 22.7 for the ATC system considered in problem 21.16.

22.12. Derive four additional tests using each of the methods noted in problems 22.6 and 22.7 for the banking application presented in Sections 22.5 and 22.6.

FURTHER READINGS AND OTHER INFORMATION SOURCES

The literature for object-oriented testing is only beginning to evolve. Jorgensen (*Software Testing: A Craftsman's Approach,* CRC Press, 1995) and McGregor and Sykes (*Object-Oriented Software Development,* Van Nostrand Reinhold, 1992) present chapters dedicated to the topic. Beizer (*Black-Box Testing,* Wiley, 1995) discusses a variety of test case design methods that are appropriate in an OO context. Binder (*Testing Object-Oriented Systems,* Addison-Wesley, 1996) and Marick [MAR94] present detailed treatments of OO Testing. In addition, many of the sources noted for Chapter 16 are generally applicable to OO testing.

The September 1994 issue of *Communications of the ACM* is dedicated to OO testing. It presents a number of worthwhile a papers and a combined bibliography that covers a broad spectrum of research on OO testing.

The Internet newsgroup **comp.object** has an occasional posting on OO testing. Unfortunately, the FAQ for this newsgroup (although comprehensive in many respects) does not currently address OO testing. Further discussion of OO testing issues can sometimes be found in **comp.software-eng** and **comp.testing**.

The following Web sites contain bibliographies and other information on OO testing:

http://www.rbsc.com/pages/ootbib.html

http://donkey.cs.arizona.edu:1994/bib/Object

The following sites contain discussions of OO testing:

http://www.cs.washington.edu/homes/gmurphy/testSTApp.html

http://www.stlabs.com/marick/root.htm

http://www.toa.com

An up-to-date list of World Wide Web references for object-oriented testing can be found at: **http://www.rspa.com**

TECHNICAL METRICS FOR OBJECT-ORIENTED SYSTEMS

Early in this book we noted that measurement and metrics are key components of any engineering discipline—and object-oriented software engineering is no exception. Sadly, the use of metrics for OO systems has progressed much more slowly than the use of other OO methods. Ed Berard [BER95] notes the irony of measurement when he states:

> Software people seem to have a love-hate relationship with metrics. On one hand, they despise and distrust anything that sounds or looks like a measurement. They are quick to point out the "flaws" in the arguments of anyone who talks about measuring software products, software processes, and (especially) software people. On the other hand, these same people seem to have no problems identifying which programming language is the best, the stupid things that managers do to "ruin" projects, and whose methodology works in what situations.

The "love-hate relationship" that Berard notes is real. And yet, as OO systems become more pervasive, it is essential that software engineers have quantitative mechanisms for assessing the quality of designs and the effectiveness of OO programs.

23.1   THE INTENT OF OBJECT-ORIENTED METRICS

The primary objectives for object-oriented metrics are the same as those for metrics derived for conventional software:

- to better understand the quality of the product
- to assess the effectiveness of the process
- to improve the quality of work performed at a project level

Each of these objectives is important, but for the software engineer, product quality must be paramount. But how do we measure the quality of an OO system? What characteristics of the design model can be assessed to determine whether the system will be easy to implement, amenable to test, simple to modify, and most important, acceptable to end users? These questions are addressed throughout the remainder of this chapter.

23.2   THE DISTINGUISHING CHARACTERISTICS

Metrics for any engineered product are governed by the unique characteristics of the product. For example, it would be meaningless to compute miles per gallon for an electric automobile. The metric is sound for conventional (i.e., gasoline powered) cars, but it does not apply when the mode of propulsion changes radically. Object-oriented software is fundamentally different from software developed using conventional methods. For this reason, technical metrics for OO systems must be tuned to the characteristics that distinguish OO from conventional software.

Berard [BER95] defines five characteristics that lead to specialized metrics: localization, encapsulation, information hiding, inheritance, and object abstraction techniques. Each of these characteristics is discussed briefly in the sections that follow.[1]

23.2.1   Localization

Localization is a characteristic of software that indicates the manner in which information is concentrated within a program. For example, conventional methods for functional decomposition localize information around functions, which are typically implemented as procedural modules. Data driven methods localize information around specific data structures. In the OO context, information is concentrated by encapsulating both data and process within the bounds of a class or object.

Because conventional software emphasizes function as a localization mechanism, software metrics have focused on the internal structure or complexity of functions (e.g., module length, cohesion, or cyclomatic complexity) or the manner in which functions connect to one another (e.g., module coupling).

Since the class is the basic unit of an OO system, localization is based on objects. Therefore, metrics should apply to the class (object) as a complete en-

---

[1]This discussion has been adapted from [BER95].

tity. In addition, the relationship between operations (functions) and classes is not necessarily one-to-one. Therefore, metrics that reflect the manner in which classes collaborate must be capable of accommodating one-to-many and many-to-one relationships.

23.2.2 Encapsulation

Berard [BER95] defines encapsulation as "the packaging (or binding together) of a collection of items. Low-level examples of encapsulation [for conventional software] include records and arrays, [and] subprograms (e.g., procedures, functions, subroutines, and paragraphs) are mid-level mechanisms for encapsulation."

For OO systems, encapsulation encompasses the responsibilities of a class, including its attributes (and other classes for aggregate objects) and operations, and the states of the class, as defined by specific attribute values.

Encapsulation influences metrics by changing the focus of measurement from a single module to a package of data (attributes) and processing modules (operations). In addition, encapsulation encourages measurement at a higher level of abstraction. For example, later in this chapter metrics associated with the number of operations per class will be introduced. Contrast this level of abstraction to conventional metrics, which focus on counts of Boolean conditions (cyclomatic complexity) or lines of code.

23.2.3 Information hiding

Information hiding suppresses (or hides) the operational details of a program component. Only the information necessary to access the component is provided to those other components that wish to access it.

A well-designed OO system should encourage information hiding. Therefore, metrics that provide an indication of the degree to which hiding has been achieved should provide an indication of the quality of the OO design.

23.2.4 Inheritance

Inheritance is a mechanism that enables the responsibilities of one object to be propagated to other objects. Inheritance occurs throughout all levels of a class hierarchy. In general, conventional software does not support this characteristic.

Because inheritance is a pivotal characteristic in many OO systems, many OO metrics focus on it. Examples (discussed later in this chapter) include number of children (number of immediate instances of a class), number of parents (number of immediate generalizations), and class hierarchy nesting level (depth of a class in an inheritance hierarchy).

23.2.5 Abstraction

Abstraction is a mechanism that enables the designer to focus on the essential details of a program component (either data or process) without concern for lower-level details. As Berard states: "Abstraction is a relative concept. As we move to higher levels of abstraction we ignore more and more details, i.e., we provide a more general view of a concept or item. As we move to lower levels of abstraction, we introduce more details, i.e., we provide a more specific view of a concept or item."

Because a class is an abstraction that can be viewed at many different levels of detail and in a number of different ways (e.g., as a list of operations, as a sequence of states, as a series of collaborations), OO metrics represent abstractions in terms of measures of a class (e.g., number of instances per class per application, number of parameterized classes per application, and ratio of parameterized classes to nonparameterized classes).

23.3   METRICS FOR THE OO DESIGN MODEL

There is much about object-oriented design that is subjective—an experienced designer "knows" how to characterize an OO system so that it will effectively implement customer requirements. But as OO design models grow in size and complexity, a more objective view of the characteristics of the design can benefit both the experienced designer (who gains additional insight) and the novice (who obtains an indication of quality that would otherwise be unavailable).

An objective view of design should have a quantitative component—and that leads to OO metrics. In reality, technical metrics for OO systems can be applied not only to the design model, but also to the analysis model. In the sections that follow, we explore metrics that provide an indication of quality at the OO class level and the operation level as well as metrics that are applicable for project management and testing.

23.4   CLASS-ORIENTED METRICS

The class is the fundamental unit of an OO system. Therefore, measures and metrics for an individual class, the class hierarchy, and class collaborations will be invaluable to a software engineer who must assess design quality. In earlier chapters we have seen that the class encapsulates operations (processing) and attributes (data). The class is often the "parent" for subclasses (sometimes called "children") that inherit its attributes and operations. The class often collaborates with other classes. Each of these characteristics can be used as the basis for measurement.

23.4.1 The CK Metrics Suite

One of the most widely referenced sets of OO software metrics has been proposed by Chidamber and Kemerer [CHI94]. The authors have proposed six class-based design metrics (often referred to as the *CK metrics suite*) for OO systems.[2]

Weighted Methods per Class (WMC)   Assume that n methods of complexity c_1, $c_2, \ldots, c_n$ are defined for a class **C**. The specific complexity metric that is chosen (e.g., cyclomatic complexity) should be normalized so that nominal complexity for a method takes on a value of 1.0.

$$\text{WMC} = \sum c_i$$

for $i = 1$ to n.

The number of methods and their complexity is a reasonable indicator of the amount of effort required to implement and test a class. In addition, the larger the number of methods, the more complex the inheritance tree (all subclasses inherit the methods of their parents). Finally, as the number of methods grows for a given class, it is likely to become more and more application specific, thereby limiting potential reuse. For all of these reasons, WMC should be kept as low as is reasonable.

Although it would seem relatively straightforward to develop a count for the number of methods in a class, the problem is actually more complex than it seems. Churcher and Shepperd [CHU95] discuss this issue when they write:

> In order to count methods, we must answer the fundamental question "Does a method belong only to the class which defines it, or does it also belong to every class which inherits it directly or indirectly?" Questions such as this may seem trivial since the run-time system will ultimately resolve them. However, the implications for metrics may be significant.
>
> One possibility is to restrict counting to the current class, ignoring inherited members. The motivation for this would be that inherited members have already been counted in the classes where they are defined, so the class increment is the best measure of its functionality—what it does reflects its reason for existing. In order to understand what a class does, the most important source of information is its own operations. If a class cannot respond to a message (i.e., it lacks a corresponding method of its own) then it will pass the message on to its parent(s).
>
> At the other extreme, counting could include all methods defined in the current class, together with all inherited methods. This approach emphasizes the importance of the state space, rather than the class increment, in understanding a class.
>
> Between these extremes lie a number of other possibilities. For example, one could restrict counting to the current class and members inherited directly from parent(s). This approach would be based on the argument that the specialization of parent classes is the most directly relevant to the behavior of a child class.

---

[2]Chidamber and Kemerer use the term "methods" rather than "operations." Their usage of the term is reflected in this section.

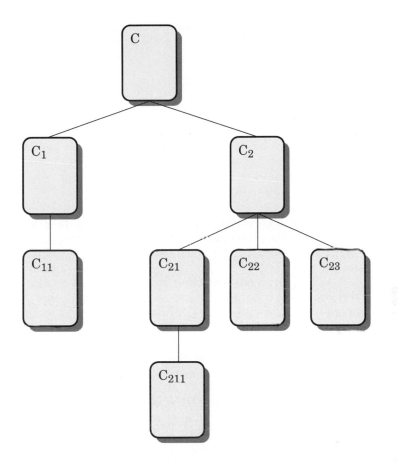

FIGURE 23.1. A
class hierarchy

Like most counting conventions in software metrics, any of the approaches outlined above are acceptable, as long as the counting approach is applied consistently whenever metrics are collected.

Depth of the Inheritance Tree (DIT)   This metric is defined as "the maximum length from the node to the root of the tree." [CHI94] In Figure 23.1, the value of DIT for the class hierarchy shown is 4.

   As DIT grows, it is likely that lower-level classes will inherit many methods. This leads to potential difficulties when attempting to predict the behavior of a class. A deep class hierarchy (DIT is large) also leads to greater design complexity. On the positive side, large DIT values imply that many methods may be reused.

Number of Children (NOC)   The subclasses that are immediately subordinate to a class in the class hierarchy are termed its *children*. In Figure 23.1, class C_2 has three children—subclasses C_{21}, C_{22}, and C_{23}.

   As the number of children grows, reuse increases, but it is also true that as NOC increases, the abstraction represented by the parent class can be diluted. That is, there is a possibility that some of the children are not really appropriate members of the parent class. As NOC increases, the amount of testing (required to exercise each child in its operational context) will also increase).

Coupling Between Object Classes (CBO)   The CRC model (Chapter 20) may be used to determine the value for CBO. In essence, CBO is the number of collaborations listed for a class on its CRC index card.

As CBO increases, it is likely that the reusability of a class will decrease. High values of CBO also complicate modifications and the testing that ensues when modifications are made. In general, the CBO values for each class should be kept as low as is reasonable. This is consistent with the general guideline to reduce coupling in conventional software.

Response for a Class (RFC)   The *response set* of a class is "a set of methods that can potentially be executed in response to a message received by an object of that class" [CHI94]. RFC is defined as the number of methods in the response set.

As RFC increases, the effort required for testing also increases because the test sequence (Chapter 22) grows. It also follows that as RFC increases, the overall design complexity of the class increases.

Lack of Cohesion in Methods (LCOM)   Each method within a class, **C**, accesses one or more attributes (also called *instance variables*) LCOM is the number of methods that access one or more of the same attributes.[3] If no methods access the same attributes, then LCOM is 0.

To illustrate the case where LCOM ≠ 0, consider a class with 6 methods. Four of the methods have one or more attributes in common (i.e., they access common attributes). Therefore, LCOM = 4.

If LCOM is high, methods may be coupled to one another via attributes. This increases the complexity of the class design. In general, high values for LCOM imply that the class might be better designed by breaking it into two or more separate classes. Although there are cases in which a high value for LCOM is justifiable, it is desirable to keep cohesion high, i.e., keep LCOM low.

23.4.2 Metrics Proposed by Lorenz and Kidd

In their book on OO metrics, Lorenz and Kidd [LOR94] divide class-based metrics into four broad categories: size, inheritance, internals, and externals. Size-oriented metrics for the OO class focus on counts of attributes and operations for an individual class and average values for the OO system as a whole. Inheritance-based metrics focus on the manner in which operations are reused throughout the class hierarchy. Metrics for class internals look at cohesion (Section 23.4.1) and code-oriented issues, and external metrics ex-

---

[3]The formal definition is a bit more complex. See [CHI94] for details.

amine coupling and reuse. A sampling of metrics proposed by Lorenz and Kidd follows:[4]

Class Size (CS)   The overall size of a class can be determined using the following measures:

- the total number of operations (both inherited and private instance operations) that are encapsulated within the class
- the number of attributes (both inherited and private instance attributes) that are encapsulated by the class

The WMC metric proposed by Chidamber and Kemerer (Section 23.4.1) is also a weighted measure of class size.

As we noted earlier, large values for CS indicate that a class may have too much responsibility, which will reduce the reusability of the class and complicate implementation and testing. In general, inherited or public operations and attributes should be weighted more heavily in determining class size [LOR94]. Private operations and attributes enable specialization and are more localized in the design.

Averages for the number of class attributes and operations may also be computed. The lower the average value for size, the more likely that classes within the system can be reused widely.

Number of Operations Overridden by a Subclass (NOO)   There are instances when a subclass replaces an operation inherited from its superclass with a specialized version for its own use, this is called *overriding*. Large values for NOO generally indicate a design problem. As Lorenz and Kidd point out:

> Since a subclass should be a specialization of its superclasses, it should primarily extend the services [operations] of the superclasses. This should result in unique new method names.

If NOO is large, the designer has violated the abstraction implied by the superclass. This results in a weak class hierarchy and OO software that can be difficult to test and modify.

Number of Operations Added by a Subclass (NOA)   Subclasses are specialized by adding private operations and attributes. As the value for NOA increases, the subclass drifts away from the abstraction implied by the superclass. In general, as the depth of the class hierarchy increases (DIT becomes large), the value for NOA at lower levels in the hierarchy should go down.

Specialization Index (SI)   The specialization index provides a rough indication of the degree of specialization for each of the subclasses in an OO system.

---

[4]For a complete discussion, see [LOR94].

Specialization can be achieved by adding or deleting operations or by overriding.

$$\text{SI} = [\text{NOO} \times level]/M_{\text{total}}$$

where *level* is the level in the class hierarchy at which the class resides and M_{total} is the total number of methods for the class. The higher the value of SI, the more likely that the class hierarchy has classes that do not conform to the superclass abstraction.

23.5   OPERATION-ORIENTED METRICS

Because the class is the dominant unit in OO systems, there have been fewer metrics proposed for class operations. Churcher and Shepperd [CHU95] discuss this when they state:

> Results of recent studies indicate that methods tend to be small, both in terms of number of statements and in logical complexity [WIL92], suggesting that connectivity structure of a system may be more important than the content of individual modules.

There are, however, some insights that can be gained by examining average characteristics for class operations. Three simple metrics, proposed by Lorenz and Kidd [LOR94], are noted below:

Average operation size (OS$_{avg}$)   Although lines of code could be used as an indicator for operation size, the LOC measure suffers from all of the problems discussed in Chapter 4. For this reason, the *number of messages sent by the operation* provides an alternative for operation size. As the number of messages sent by a single operation increases, it is likely that responsibilities have not been well allocated within a class.

Operation complexity (OC)   The complexity of an operation can be computed using any of the complexity metrics (Chapter 18) proposed for conventional software [ZUS90]. Because operations should be limited to a specific responsibility, the designer should strive to keep OC as low as possible.

Average number of parameters per operation (NP$_{avg}$)   The larger the number of operation parameters, the more complex the collaboration between objects. In general, NP$_{avg}$ should be kept as low as possible.

23.6   METRICS FOR OBJECT-ORIENTED TESTING

The design metrics noted in Sections 23.4 and 23.5 provide an indication of design quality. They also provide a general indication of the amount of testing effort required to exercise an OO system.

Binder [BIN94] suggests a broad array of design metrics that have a direct influence on the "testability" of an OO system. The metrics are organized into categories that reflect important design characteristics:

Encapsulation

Lack of cohesion in methods (LCOM)[5]   The higher the value of LCOM, the more states must be tested to ensure that methods do not generate side effects.

Percent public and protected (PAP)   Public attributes are inherited from other classes and are therefore visible to those classes. Protected attributes are a specialization and are private to a specific subclass. This metric indicates the percentage of class attributes that are public. High values for PAP increase the likelihood of side affects among classes. Tests must be designed to ensure that such side effects are uncovered.

Public access to data members (PAD)   This metric indicates the number of classes (or methods) that can access another class's attributes, a violation of encapsulation. High values for PAD lead to the potential for side effects among classes. Tests must be designed to ensure that such side effects are uncovered.

Inheritance

Number of root classes (NOR)   This metric is a count of the distinct class hierarchies that are described in the design model. Test suites for each root class and the corresponding class hierarchy must be developed. As NOR increases, testing effort also increases.

Fan in (FIN)   When used in the OO context, fan-in is an indication of multiple inheritance. FIN > 1 indicates that a class inherits its attributes and operations from more than one root class. FIN > 1 should be avoided when possible.

Number of children (NOC) and depth of the inheritance tree (DIT)[6]   As we discussed in Chapter 22, superclass methods will have to be retested for each subclass.

In addition to the above metrics, Binder [BIN94] also defines metrics for class complexity and polymorphism. The metrics defined for class complexity include three CK metrics (Section 23.4.1): weighted methods per class (WMC), coupling between object classes (CBO), and response for a class (RFC). In addition, metrics associated with method counts are also defined. The metrics associated with polymorphism are highly specialized. A discussion of them is best left to Binder.

23.7   METRICS FOR OBJECT-ORIENTED PROJECTS

As we discovered in Part Two of this book, the job of the project manager is to plan, coordinate, track, and control a software project. In Chapter 19 we dis-

---

[5]See Section 23.4.1 for a description of LCOM.

[6]See Section 23.4.1 for a description of NOC and DIT.

cussed some of the special issues associated with project management for OO projects. But what about measurement? Are there specialized OO metrics that can be used by the project manager to provide additional insight into progress? The answer, of course, is "yes."

The first activity performed by the project manager is planning, and one of the early planning tasks is estimation. Recall the evolutionary process model,[7] where planning is revisited after each iteration of the software. Therefore, the plan and its project estimates are revisited after each iteration of OOA, OOD, and even OOP.

One of the key issues facing a project manager during planning is an estimate of the implemented size of the software. Size is directly proportional to effort and duration. The following OO metrics [LOR94] can provide insight into software size:

Number of scenario scripts (NSS)   The number of scenario scripts or use cases (Chapter 20) is directly proportional to the number of classes required to meet requirements, the number of states for each class, and the number of methods, attributes, and collaborations. NSS is a strong indicator for program size.

Number of key classes (NKC)   A *key class* focuses directly on the business domain for the problem and will have a lower probability of being implemented via reuse.[8] For this reason, high values for NKC indicate substantial development work lies ahead. Lorenz and Kidd [LOR94] suggest that between 20 and 40 percent of all classes in a typical OO system are key classes. The remainder support infrastructure (GUI, communications, databases, etc.).

Number of subsystems (NSUB)   The number of subsystems provides insight into resource allocation, scheduling (with particular emphasis on parallel development), and overall integration effort.

The metrics NSS, NKC, and NSUB can be collected for past OO proj-ects and related to the effort expended on the project as a whole and on individual process activities (e.g., OOA, OOD, OOP, and OOT). These data can also be used along with design metrics discussed earlier in this chapter to compute "productivity metrics" such as average number of classes per developer or average methods per person-month. Collectively, these metrics can be used to estimate effort, duration, staffing, and other project information for the current project.

23.8   SUMMARY

Object-oriented software is fundamentally different from software developed using conventional methods. Therefore, the metrics for OO systems focus on metrics that can be applied to the class and the design characteristics—

---

[7]The evolutionary process model is most appropriate for OO systems (see Chapters 2 and 19).

[8]This will only be true until a robust library of reusable components is developed for a particular domain.

localization, encapsulation, information hiding, inheritance, and object abstraction techniques—that make the class unique.

The CK metrics suite defines six class-oriented software metrics that focus on the class and the class hierarchy. The metrics suite also develops metrics to assess the collaborations between classes and the cohesion of methods that reside within a class. At a class-oriented level, the CK metrics suite can be augmented with metrics proposed by Lorenz and Kidd. These include measures of class "size" and metrics that provide insight into the degree of specialization for subclasses.

Operation-oriented metrics focus on the size and complexity of individual operations. It is important to note, however, that the primary thrust for OO design metrics is at the class level.

A wide variety of OO metrics have been proposed to assess the testability of an OO system. These metrics focus on encapsulation, inheritance, class complexity, and polymorphism.

Measurable characteristics of the analysis and design model can assist the project manager for an OO system in planning and tracking activities. The number of scenario scripts (use cases), key classes, and subsystems all provide information about the level of effort required to implement a system.

REFERENCES

[BER95]   Berard, E., "Metrics for Object-Oriented Software Engineering," an Internet posting on **comp.software-eng,** January 28, 1995.

[BIN94]   Binder, R., "Testing Object-oriented Systems: A Status Report," *American Programmer,* vol. 7, no. 4, April 1994, pp. 22–29.

[CHI94]   Chidamber, S.R., and C.F. Kemerer, "A Metrics Suite for Object-Oriented Design," *IEEE Trans. Software Engineering,* vol. 20, no. 6, June 1994, pp. 476–493.

[CHU95]   Churcher, N.I., and M.J. Shepperd, "Towards a Conceptual Framework for Object-Oriented Metrics," *ACM Software Engineering Notes,* vol. 20, no. 2, April 1995, pp. 69–76.

[LOR94]   Lorenz, M., and J. Kidd, *Object-Oriented Software Metrics,* Prentice-Hall, 1994.

[WIL92]   Wilde, N., and R. Huitt, "Maintaining Object-Oriented Software," *IEEE Software,* January 1993, pp. 75–80.

[ZUS90]   Zuse, H., *Software Complexity: Measures and Methods,* DeGruyter, New York, 1990.

PROBLEMS AND POINTS TO PONDER

23.1.   Review the metrics presented in this chapter and in Chapter 18. How would you characterize the syntactic and semantic differences between metrics for conventional and OO software?

23.2.   How does localization affect metrics developed for conventional and OO software?

23.3. Why isn't more emphasis given to OO metrics that address the specific characteristics of operations within a class?

23.4. Review the metrics discussed in this chapter and suggest a few that directly or indirectly address information hiding.

23.5. Review the metrics discussed in this chapter and suggest a few that directly or indirectly address abstraction.

23.6. A class, **X**, has 12 operations. Cyclomatic complexity has been computed for all operations in the OO system, and the average value of module complexity is 4. For class **X** the complexity for operations 1 to 12 is 5, 4, 3, 3, 6, 8, 2, 2, 5, 5, 4, 4, respectively. Compute WMC.

23.7. Referring to Figure 19.8a and b, compute the value of DIT for each inheritance tree. What is the value of NOC for the class **X2** for both trees?

23.8. Refer to [CHI94] and present a one page discussion for the formal definition of the LCOM metric.

23.9. In Figure 19.8*b*, what is the value of NOA for classes **X3** and **X4**.

23.10. Referring to Figure 19.8*b*, assume that four operations have been overridden in the inheritance tree (class hierarchy), what is the value of SI for the hierarchy?

23.11. A software team has completed five projects to date. The following data have been collected for all size projects:

Project #	NSS	NKC	NSUB	Effort (days)
1	34	60	3	900
2	55	75	6	1575
3	122	260	8	4420
4	45	66	2	990
5	80	124	6	2480

A new project is in the early stages of OOA. It is estimated that 95 use cases will be developed for the project. Estimate:
a. the total number of classes that will be required to implement the system;
b. the total amount of effort required to implement the system.

23.12. Your instructor will provide you with a list of OO metrics from this chapter. Compute the values of these metrics for one or more of the problems noted below:
a. the design model for the SafeHome design.
b. the design model for the for the PHTRS system described in problem 12.13.
c. the design model for the video game considered in problem 21.14.
d. the design model for the e-mail considered in problem 21.15.
e. the design model for the ATC system considered in problem 21.16.

FURTHER READINGS AND OTHER INFORMATION SOURCES

A variety of books on OOA, OOD, and OOT (see "Further Readings and Other Information Sources" in Chapters 20, 21, and 22) make passing reference to OO metrics, but few address the subject in any detail. Books by Jacobson (*Object-Oriented Software Engineering,* Addison-Wesley, 1994) and Graham (*Object-Oriented Methods,* Addison-Wesley, 2nd edition, 1993) provide more treatment than most.

Lorenz and Kidd [LOR94] and Hendersen-Sellers (*Object-Oriented Metrics: Measures of Complexity,* Prentice-Hall, 1996) offer the only books dedicated to OO metrics published to date. Whitmire (*Encyclopedia of Software Engineering,* J. Marciniak (ed.), Wiley, 1994) has contributed a chapter on OO metrics. Other books dedicated to conventional software metrics (see "Further Readings and Other Information Sources" for Chapters 4 and 18) contain limited discussions of OO metrics.

The majority of information on OO metrics must be obtained from papers and articles published in the technical literature. Whitty (*Object-Oriented Metrics: People and Publications,* 1995) has compiled one of the most comprehensive object-oriented metrics bibliographies published to date. An electronic version may be obtained from:

http://www.sbu.ac.uk/ ~ csse/publications/OOMetrics.html

The Internet sources noted throughout Part Four of this book are worth investigating for discussions of OO metrics. In addition, occasional discussions of OO metrics are found in the Internet newsgroups **comp.object, comp.software-eng, comp.specification,** and **comp.testing.**

Additional information on OO metrics can be found at the following sites:

http://www.sbu.ac.uk/ ~ csse/metkit.html

http://louis.ecs.soton.ac.uk/dsse/moops.html

ftp://ftp.sbu.ac.uk/pub/Metrics

An up-to-date list of World Wide Web references for object-oriented metrics can be found at: **http://www.rspa.com**

PART FIVE

ADVANCED TOPICS IN SOFTWARE ENGINEERING

In this part of *Software Engineering: A Practitioner's Approach* we consider a number of advanced topics that will extend your understanding of software engineering. In the chapters that follow, we address the following questions:

- What are 'formal methods' and how are they used to specify software?
- What notation and mathematical preliminaries are required to formally describe software?
- How does the cleanroom software engineering approach differ from conventional approaches?
- What are the key technical activities that are conducted during the cleanroom process?
- How is domain engineering used as a precursor to building libraries of reusable components?
- What technical issues must be considered when a reuse process is initiated?
- What are the economic arguments that favor reuse?
- What is business process reengineering and how does it set the stage for software reengineering?
- What are the key technical activities required for software reengineering?
- How does the client/server architecture impact the way in which software is engineered?
- What are the architectural options for establishing a CASE tools environment?
- What are the future directions of software engineering?

Once these questions are answered, you'll understand topics that may have a profound impact on software engineering over the next decade.

FORMAL METHODS

Software engineering methods can be categorized on a "formality" spectrum. The analysis and design methods discussed earlier in this book would be placed at the informal to moderately rigorous end of the spectrum. A combination of diagrams, text, tables, and simple notation is used to create analysis and design models.

We now consider the other end of the formality spectrum. Here, a specification and design are described using a formal syntax and semantics that specify system function and behavior. A formal specification is mathematical in form (e.g., predicate calculus can be used as the basis for a formal specification language).

In his introductory discussion of formal methods, Anthony Hall [HAL90] states:

> Formal methods are controversial. Their advocates claim that they can revolutionize [software] development. Their detractors think they are impossibly difficult. Meanwhile, for most people, formal methods are so unfamiliar that it is difficult to judge the competing claims.

In this chapter, we explore formal methods and examine their potential impact on software engineering in the years to come.

24.1   BASIC CONCEPTS

The Encyclopedia of Software Engineering [MAR94] defines formal methods in the following manner:

Formal methods used in developing computer systems are mathematically based techniques for describing system properties. Such formal methods provide frameworks within which people can specify, develop, and verify systems in a systematic, rather than ad hoc manner.

A method is formal if it has a sound mathematical basis, typically given by a formal specification language. This basis provides a means of precisely defining notions like consistency and completeness, and, more relevant, specification, implementation, and correctness.

The desired properties of a formal specification—lack of ambiguity, consistency, and completeness—are the objectives of all specification methods. However, the use of formal methods results in a much higher likelihood of achieving these ideals. The formal syntax of a specification language (Section 24.4) enables requirements or design to be interpreted in only one way, eliminating ambiguity that often occurs when a natural language (e.g., English) or a graphical notation must be interpreted by a reader. The descriptive facilities of set theory and logic notation (Section 24.2) enable a clear statement of facts (requirements). To be consistent, facts stated in one place in a specification should not be contradicted in another place. Consistency is ensured by mathematically proving that initial facts can be formally mapped (using inference rules) into later statements within the specification.

Completeness is difficult to achieve, even when formal methods are used. Some aspects of a system may be left undefined as the specification is being created; other characteristics may be purposely omitted to allow designers some freedom in choosing an implementation approach; and it is impossible to consider every operational scenario in a large, complex system. Things may simply be omitted by mistake.

Although the formalism provided by mathematics has an appeal to some software engineers, others (some would say, the majority) look askance at a mathematical view of software development. To understand why a formal approach has merit, we must first consider the deficiencies associated with less formal approaches.

24.1.1 Deficiencies of Less Formal Approaches[1]

The methods discussed for analysis and design in Parts Three and Four of this book made heavy use of natural language and a variety of graphical notations. Although careful application of analysis and design methods coupled with thorough review can and does lead to high-quality software, sloppiness in the application of these methods can create a variety of problems. A system specification can contain contradictions, ambiguities, vagueness, incomplete statements, and mixed levels of abstraction.

---

[1]This section and others in the first part of this chapter have been adapted from work contributed by Darrel Ince for the European version of the third edition of *Software Engineering: A Practitioner's Approach.*

Contradictions are sets of statements that are at variance with each other. For example, one part of a system specification may state that the system must monitor all the temperatures in a chemical reactor while another part, perhaps written by another staff member, may state that only temperatures occurring within a certain range are to be monitored. Normally contradictions that occur on the same page of a system specification can be detected easily. However, contradictions are often separated by a large number of pages.

Ambiguities are statements that can be interpreted in a number of ways. For example, the following statement is ambiguous:

> The operator identity consists of the operator name and password; the password consists of six digits. It should be displayed on the security VDU and deposited in the login file when an operator logs into the system.

In this extract, does the word "it" refer to the password or the operator identity?

Vagueness often occurs because a system specification is a very bulky document. Achieving a high level of precision consistently is an almost impossible task. It can lead to statements such as "the interface to the system used by radar operators should be user friendly," or "the virtual interface shall be based on simple overall concepts which are straightforward to understand and use and which are few in number." A casual perusal of these statements might not detect the underlying lack of any useful information.

Incompleteness is probably one of the most frequently occurring problems with system specifications. For example, consider the functional requirement

> The system should maintain the hourly level of the reservoir from depth sensors situated in the reservoir. These values should be stored for the past six months.

This describes the main data storage part of a system. Suppose one of the commands for the system is

> The function of the AVERAGE command is to display on a PC the average water level for a particular sensor between two dates.

Assuming that no more detail was presented for this command, the details of the command would be seriously incomplete. For example, the description of the command does not include what should happen if a user of a system specifies a date that was more than six months before the current one.

Mixed levels of abstraction occur when very abstract statements are intermixed randomly with statements that are at a much lower level of detail. For example, statements such as

> The purpose of the system is to track the stock in a warehouse.

might be intermixed with

> When the loading clerk types in the *withdraw* command he or she will communicate the order number, the identity of the item to be removed, and the

quantity removed. The system will respond with a confirmation that the removal is allowable.

Although such statements are important in a system specification, specifiers often manage to intermix them to such an extent that it becomes very difficult to see the overall functional architecture of a system.

Each of these problems is more common that we would like to believe. And each represents a potential deficiency in conventional and object-oriented methods for specification.

24.1.2 Mathematics in Software Development

Mathematics has many useful properties for the developers of large systems. One of its most useful properties is that it is capable of succinctly and exactly describing a physical situation, an object, or the outcome of an action. When an applied mathematician states that the solution to a particular equation is given by the integral

$$\int \tan [x^2 + \exp(\cos (x))]$$

there is no argument about semantics. The person who solves the integral knows exactly *what* is required, although *how* to solve the integral may take a large amount of effort. For example, the integral may be amenable to an analytical solution, or it may require simulation or another numerical approach if the upper and lower limits to the integral are known. Ideally, the software developer should be in the same position as the applied mathematician. A mathematical specification of a system should be presented to him or her, and a solution developed in terms of a software architecture that implements the specification should be produced.[2]

Another advantage of using mathematics in the software process is that it provides a smooth transition between software engineering activities. Not only functional specifications but also system designs can be expressed in mathematics, and, of course, the program code is a mathematical notation—albeit a rather long-winded one.

The major property of mathematics is that it supports abstraction and is an excellent medium for modeling. Because it is an exact medium there is little possibility of ambiguity, specifications can be mathematically validated to uncover contradictions and incompleteness, and vagueness disappears completely. In addition mathematics can be used to represent levels of abstraction in a system specification in an organized way.

Mathematics is an ideal tool for modeling. It enables the bare bones of a specification to be exhibited and helps the analyst and system specifier to validate a specification for functionality without such issues as response time, de-

---

[2]A word of caution is appropriate at this point. The mathematical system specifications that are presented in this chapter will not be as succinct as the integral. Software systems are notoriously complex, and it would be unrealistic to expect that they could be specified in one line of mathematics.

sign directives, implementation directives, and project constraints intruding. It also helps the designer, because the system design specification exhibits the properties of a model, providing only sufficient details to enable the task in hand to be carried out.

The final point to make about mathematics as a software development medium is that it provides a high level of validation. It is possible to use a mathematical proof to demonstrate that a design matches a specification, and that some program code is a correct reflection of a design.

24.1.3   Formal Methods Concepts

The aim of this section is to present the main concepts involved in the mathematical specification of software systems, without encumbering the reader with too much mathematical detail. To accomplish this, we use a few simple examples:

Example 1: A Symbol Table   A program is used to maintain a symbol table. Such a table is used frequently in many different types of applications. It consists of a collection of items without any duplication. An example of a typical symbol table is shown in Figure 24.1. It represents the table used by an operating system to hold the names of the users of the system. Other examples of tables include the collection of names of staff in a payroll system, the collection of names of computers in a network communications system, and the collection of destinations in a system for producing railway timetables.

Assume that the table presented in this example consists of no more than *MaxIds* members of staff. This statement, which places a constraint on the table, is a component of a condition known as a *data invariant*—an important idea which we shall return to throughout this chapter.

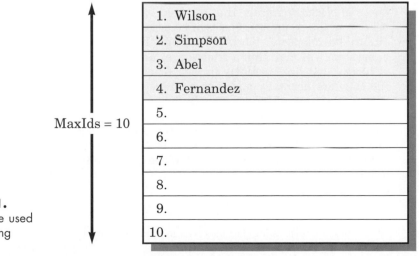

FIGURE 24.1.
A symbol table used for an operating system

MaxIds = 10

1. Wilson
2. Simpson
3. Abel
4. Fernandez
5.
6.
7.
8.
9.
10.

A *data invariant* is a condition that is true throughout the execution of the system that contains a collection of data. The data invariant that holds for the symbol table discussed above has two components: (1) that the table will contain no more than *MaxIds* names and (2) that there will be no duplicate names in the table. In the case of the symbol table program described above, this means that, no matter when the symbol table is examined during execution of the system, it will always contain no more than *MaxIds* staff identifiers and will contain no duplicates.

Another concept that is important is that of a *state*. In the context of formal methods,[3] a state is the stored data which a system accesses and alters. In the example of the symbol table program, the state is the symbol table.

The final concept is that of an *operation*. This is an action that takes place in a system and reads or writes data to a state. If the symbol table program is concerned with adding and removing staff names from the symbol table, then it will be associated with two operations: an operation to add a specified name to the symbol table and an operation to remove an existing name from the table. If the program provides the facility to check whether a specific name was contained in the table, then there would be an operation that would return some indication of whether the name was in the table.

An operation is associated with two conditions: a precondition and a postcondition. A *precondition* defines the circumstances in which a particular operation is valid. For example, the precondition for an operation that adds a name to the staff identifier symbol table is valid only if the name that is to be added is not contained in the table and there are fewer than *MaxIds* staff identifiers in the table. The *postcondition* of an operation defines what happens when an operation has completed its action. This is defined by its effect on the state. In the example of an operation that adds an identifier to the staff identifier symbol table, the postcondition would specify mathematically that the table has been augmented with the new identifier.

Example 2: A Block Handler   One of the more important parts of an operating system is the subsystem that maintains files that have been created by users. Part of the filing subsystem is the *block handler*. Files in the file store are composed of blocks of storage that are held on a file storage device. During the operation of the computer, files will be created and deleted, requiring the acquisition and release of blocks of storage. In order to cope with this, the filing subsystem will maintain a reservoir of unused blocks and will also keep track of blocks that are currently in use. When blocks are released from a deleted file they are normally added to a queue of blocks waiting to be added to the reservoir of unused blocks. This is shown in Figure 24.2. In this figure a number of components are shown: the reservoir of unused blocks, the blocks that currently make up the files administered by the operating system, and those blocks that are waiting to be added to the reservoir. The waiting blocks are held in a queue, with each element of the queue containing a set of blocks from a deleted file.

---

[3]Recall that the term "state" has also been used in Chapters 12 and 20 as a representation of the behavior of a system or objects.

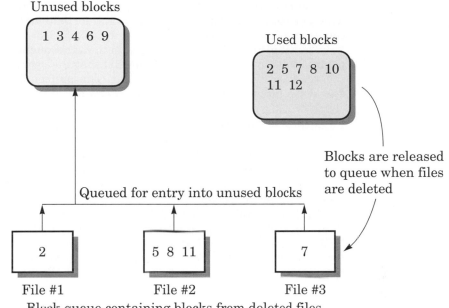

FIGURE 24.2.
A block handler

Block queue containing blocks from deleted files

For this subsystem the state is the collection of free blocks, the collection of used blocks, and the queue of returned blocks. The data invariant, expressed in natural language, is:

- No block will be marked as both unused and used.
- All the sets of blocks held in the queue will be subsets of the collection of currently used blocks.
- There will be no elements of the queue that will contain the same block numbers.
- The collection of used blocks and blocks that are unused will be the total collection of blocks that make up files.
- There will be no duplicate block numbers in the collection of unused blocks.
- There will be no duplicate block numbers in the collection of used blocks.

Some of the operations associated with this subsystem are:

- An operation that adds a collection of blocks to the end of the queue
- An operation that removes a collection of used blocks from the front of the queue and places them in the collection of unused blocks
- An operation that checks whether the queue of blocks is empty

The precondition of the first operation is that the blocks to be added must be in the collection of used blocks. The postcondition is that the collection of blocks must be added to the end of the queue.

The precondition of the second operation is that the queue must have at least one item in it. The postcondition is that the blocks must be added to the collection of unused blocks.

The final operation—checking whether the queue of returned blocks is empty—has no precondition. This means that the operation is always defined, regardless of what value the state has. The postcondition delivers the value *true* if the queue is empty and *false* otherwise.

Example 3: A Print Spooler   In multitasking operating systems, a number of tasks make requests to print files. Often, there are not enough printing devices to satisfy all current print requests simultaneously. Any print request that cannot be immediately satisfied is placed in a queue awaiting printing. The part of an operating system that deals with the administration of such queues is known as a *print spooler*.

In this example we assume that the operating system can employ no more than *MaxDevs* output devices and that each device has a queue associated with it. We will also assume that each device is associated with a limit of lines in a file which it will print. For example, an output device that has a limit of 1000 lines of printing will be associated with a queue that contains only files having no more than 1000 lines of text. Print spoolers sometimes impose this constraint in order to forbid large printing jobs, which may occupy slow printing devices for exceptionally long periods. A schematic representation of a print spooler is shown in Figure 24.3.

As shown in the figure, the spooler state consists of four components: the queues of files waiting to be printed, each queue being associated with a particular output device; the collection of output devices controlled by the spooler; the relationship between the output devices and the maximum file size that each can print; and the relationship between the files awaiting printing and their size in lines. For example, Figure 24.3 shows that the output device

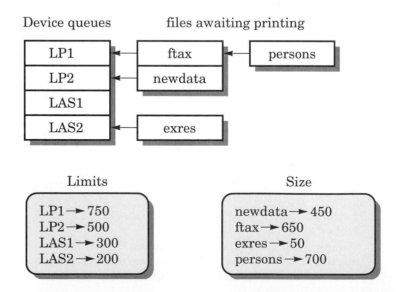

FIGURE 24.3.
A print spooler

LP1, which has a print limit of 750 lines, has two files, *ftax* and *persons,* awaiting printing, and that the size of the files are 650 lines and 700 lines, respectively.

The state of the spooler is represented by the four components *Queues, OutputDevices, Limits,* and *Sizes.* The data invariant has five components:

- Each output device is associated with an upper limit of print lines.
- Each output device is associated with a possibly nonempty queue of files awaiting printing.
- Each file is associated with a size.
- Each queue associated with an output device contains files that have a size smaller than the upper limit of the output device.
- There will be no more than *MaxDevs* output devices administered by the spooler.

A number of operations can be associated with the spooler. For example:

- An operation which adds a new output device to the spooler together with its associated print limit
- An operation which removes a file from the queue associated with a particular output device
- An operation which adds a file to the queue associated with a particular output device
- An operation which alters the upper limit of print lines for a particular output device
- An operation which moves a file from a queue associated with an output device to another queue associated with a second output device

Each of these operations corresponds to a function of the spooler. For example, the first operation would correspond to the spooler being notified of a new device.

As before, each operation is associated with a precondition and a postcondition. For example, the precondition for the first operation is that the output device name does not already exist and that there are currently less than *MaxDevs* output devices known to the spooler. The postcondition is that the name of the new device is added to the collection of existing device names, a new entry is formed for the device with no files being associated with its queue, and the device is associated with its print limit.

The precondition for the second operation (removing a file from a queue associated with a particular output device) is that the device is known to the spooler and that there is at least one entry in the queue associated with the device. The postcondition is that the head of the queue associated with the output device is removed and its entry in the part of the spooler that keeps tracks of file sizes is deleted.

The precondition for the fifth operation described above (moving a file from a queue associated with an output device to another queue associated with a second output device) is:

- The first output device is known to the spooler.
- The second output device is known to the spooler.
- The queue associated with the first device contains the file to be moved.
- The size of the file is less or equal to the print limit associated with the second output device.

The postcondition is that the file is removed from one queue and added to another queue.

In each of the examples noted in this section, we have introduced the key concepts of formal specification. This has been done without emphasizing the mathematics that are required to make the specification formal. In the next section we consider these mathematics.

24.2   MATHEMATICAL PRELIMINARIES

To apply formal methods effectively, the software engineer must have an working knowledge of the mathematical notation associated with sets and sequences and the logical notation used in predicate calculus. The intent of the section is to provide an introduction. For a more detailed discussion the reader is urged to examine books dedicated to these subjects (e.g., [WIL87], [GRI93], and [ROS95]).

24.2.1   Sets and Constructive Specification

A *set* is a collection of objects or elements. Sets are used as a cornerstone of formal methods. The elements contained within a set are unique (i.e., no duplicates are allowed). Sets with a small number of elements are written within braces ({,}) with the elements separated by commas. For example, the set

$$\{7, 14, 3, 12\}$$

is a collection of natural numbers and contains four elements. The set

$$\{C++, Pascal, Ada, COBOL, C\}$$

contains the names of five programming languages. The collection of numbers

$$\{13, 2, 9, 11, 12, 88, 2\}$$

is *not* a set because of the repeating element 2.

The order in which the elements appear within a set is immaterial. The number of items in a set is known as its *cardinality*. The # operator returns a set's cardinality. For example, the expression

$$\#\{A, B, C, D\} = 4$$

implies that the cardinality operator has been applied to the set shown, with a result indicating the number of items in the set.

There are two ways of defining a set. A set may be defined by enumerating its elements (this is how the sets noted above have been defined). The second approach is to create a *constructive set specification*. The general form of the members of a set is specified using a Boolean expression. Constructive set specification is preferable to enumeration because it enables a succinct definition of large sets. It also explicitly defines the rule that was used in constructing the set.

Consider the following constructive specification example:

$$\{n : \mathbb{N} \mid n < 3 \cdot n\}$$

This specification has three components, a signature, $n : \mathbb{N}$, a predicate, $n < 3$, and a term, n. The *signature* specifies the range of values that will be considered when forming the set, the *predicate* (a Boolean expression) defines how the set is to be constructed, and, finally, the *term* gives the general form of the item of the set. In the example above, $\mathbb{N}$ stands for the natural numbers; thus, natural numbers are to be considered, the predicate indicates that only natural numbers less than 3 are to be included, and the terms specifies that each element of the set will be of the form n. Thus, the specification above defines the set:

$$\{0, 1, 2\}$$

When the form of the elements of a set is obvious, the term can be omitted. For example, the set above could be specified as

$$(n : \mathbb{N} \mid n < 3\}$$

The sets that have been described above have all had elements that are single items. Sets can be made from elements that are pairs, triples, and so on. For example, the set specification

$$\{x, y : \mathbb{N} \mid x + y = 10 \cdot (x, y^2)\}$$

describes the set of pairs of natural numbers that have the form (x, y^2) and where the sum of x and y is 10. This is the set

$$\{(1, 81), (2, 64), (3, 49), \ldots\}$$

Another example of a constructive set specification is the set of pairs of natural numbers where the second element is 3 more than the first element and where the first element is greater than 120. The specification is

$$\{n : \mathbb{N} \mid n > 120 \cdot (n, n + 3)\}$$

In the example above, it is tempting to use two variables. However, there is no need to do this because the second element of the pair can be expressed solely in terms of the first element.

Obviously, a constructive set specification required to represent some component of computer software can be considerably more complex than those noted above. However, the basic form and structure remain the same.

24.2.2 Set Operators

A specialized set of symbology is used to represent set and logic operations. These symbols must be understood by the software engineer who intends to apply formal methods.

The ϵ operator is used to indicate membership in a set. For example, the expression

$$x \in X$$

has the value *true* if x is a member of the set X and the value *false* otherwise. For example, the predicate

$$12 \in \{6, 1, 12, 22\}$$

has the value *true* since 12 is a member of the set.

The opposite of the ϵ operator is the $\notin$ operator. The expression

$$x \notin X$$

has the value *true* if x is not a member of the set X and *false* otherwise. For example, the predicate

$$13 \notin \{13, 1, 124, 22\}$$

has the value *false*.

The operators $\subset$ and $\subseteq$ take sets as their operands. The predicate

$$A \subset B$$

has the value *true* if the members of the set A are contained in the set B and has the value *false* otherwise. Thus, the predicate

$$\{1, 2\} \subset \{4, 3, 1, 2\}$$

has the value *true*. However, the predicate

$$\{HD1, LP4, RC5\} \subset \{HD1, RC2, HD3, LP1, LP4, LP6\}$$

has a value of *false* because the element RC5 is not contained in the set to the right of the operator.

The operator $\subseteq$ is similar to $\subset$. However, if its operands are equal it has the value *false*. Thus, the value of the predicate

$$\{HD1, LP4, RC5\} \subseteq \{HD1, RC2, HD3, LP1, LP4, LP6\}$$

is *true,* and the predicate

$$\{HD1, LP4, RC5\} \subseteq \{HD1, LP4, RC5\}$$

is *false.*

A special set is the empty set $\varnothing$. This corresponds to zero in normal mathematics. The empty set has the property that it is a subset of every other set. Two useful identities involving the empty set are

$$\varnothing \cup A = A$$

and

$$\varnothing \cap A = \varnothing$$

for any set A. These identities follow directly from the definition of $\cup$ and $\cap$, presented below.

A number of binary operators take sets as their operands and have sets as their results. The three most common operators are the union operator $\cup$, sometimes known as "cup"; the intersection operator $\cap$, sometimes known as "cap"; and the set difference operator $\backslash$.

The *intersection operator* takes two sets and forms a set that contains all the elements in the set with duplicates eliminated. Thus, the result of the expression

$$\{File1, File2, Tax, Compiler\} \cup \{NewTax, D2, D3, File2\}$$

is the set

$$\{File1, File2, Tax, Compiler, NewTax, D2, D3\}$$

The *intersection operator* takes two sets and forms a set consisting of the common elements in each set. Thus, the expression

$$\{12, 4, 99, 1\} \cap \{1, 13, 12, 77\}$$

results in the set

$$\{12, 1\}$$

The *set difference operator,* as the name suggests, forms a set by removing the elements of its second operand from the elements of its first operand. Thus, the value of the expression

$$\{New, Old, TaxFile, Sysparam\} \backslash \{Old, SysParam\}$$

results in the set

$$\{New, TaxFile\}$$

The value of the expression

$$\{a, b, c, d\} \cap \{x, y\}$$

will be the empty set $\varnothing$. The operator always delivers a set; however, in this case there are no common elements between its operands so the resulting set will have no elements.

The final operator is the *cross product* $\times$, sometimes known as the *cartesian product.* This has two operands which are sets of pairs. The result is a set of pairs where each pair consists of an element taken from the first operand combined with an element from the second operand. An example of an expression involving the cross product is

$$\{1, 2\} \times \{4, 5, 6\}$$

The result of this expression is

$$\{(1, 4), (1, 5), (1, 6), (2, 4), (2, 5), (2, 6)\}$$

Notice that *every* element of the first operand is combined with every element of the second operand.

A concept that is important for formal methods is that of a *powerset.* A powerset of a set is the collection of subsets of that set. The symbol used for the powerset operator in this chapter is $\mathbb{P}$. It is a unary operator which, when applied to a set, returns the set of subsets of its operand. For example,

$$\mathbb{P}\{1, 2, 3\}$$

will be

$$\{\varnothing, \{1\}, \{2\}, \{3\}, \{1, 2\}, \{1, 3\}, \{2, 3\}, \{1, 2, 3\}\}.$$

since all the sets are subsets of $\{1, 2, 3\}$.

24.2.3 Logic Operators

Another important component of a formal method is logic: the algebra of true and false expressions. The meaning of common logical operators is well understood by every software engineer. However, the logic operators that are associated with common programming languages are written using readily available keyboard symbols. The equivalent mathematical operators to these are shown in Table 24.1. The only logic operator that is often missing in programming language notation is the *implies* operator, $\Rightarrow$. It has two operands and is read as "the first operand implies the second operand." For example,

$$x > 10 \Rightarrow x > 8$$

is read as "x is greater than 10 implies that x is greater than 8."

   Universal quantification is a way of making a statement about the elements of a set which is true for every member of the set. Universal quantification uses the symbol $\forall$. An example of its use is

$$\forall i, j : \mathbb{N} \cdot i > j \Rightarrow i^2 > j^2$$

which states that, for every pair of values in the set of natural numbers, if i is greater than j, then i^2 is greater than j^2.

24.2.4 Sequences

A *sequence* is a mathematical structure which models the fact that its elements are ordered. A sequence s is a set of pairs whose elements range from 1 to the highest number element. For example,

$$\{(1, Jones), (2, Wilson), (3, Shapiro), (4, Estavez)\}$$

TABLE 24.1

COMMON LOGIC OPERATORS

and	$\wedge$
or	$\vee$
not	$\neg$
implies	$\Rightarrow$

is a sequence. The items that form the first elements of the pairs are collectively known as the *domain* of the sequence, and the collection of second elements is known as the *range* of the sequence. In this book sequences will be designated using angle brackets. For example, the sequence above would normally be written as

$$< Jones, Wilson, Shapiro, Estavez >.$$

Unlike sets, duplication in a sequence is allowed and the ordering of a sequence is important. Thus,

$$< Jones, Wilson, Shapiro > \neq < Jones, Shapiro, Wilson >$$

and

$$< Jones, Wilson, Wilson > \neq < Jones, Wilson >.$$

The empty sequence is represented as $< >$.

A number of sequence operators are used in formal specifications. *Catenation,* $\frown$, is a binary operator which forms a sequence that is constructed by adding its second operand to the end of its first operand. For example,

$$< 2, 3, 34, 1 > \frown < 12, 33, 34, 200 >$$

results in the sequence

$$< 2, 3, 34, 1, 12, 33, 34, 200 >.$$

Other operators that can be applied to sequences are *head, tail, front,* and *last.* The operator *head* extracts the first element of a sequence; *tail* returns with the last $n - 1$ elements in a sequence of length n; *last* extracts the final element in a sequence; and *front* returns with the first $n - 1$ elements in a sequence of length n. For example,

$$head < 2, 3, 34, 1, 99, 101 > = 2$$

$$tail < 2, 3, 34, 1, 99, 101 > = < 3, 34, 1, 99, 101 >$$

$$last < 2, 3, 34, 1, 99, 101 > = 101$$

$$front < 2, 3, 34, 1, 99, 101 > = < 2, 3, 34, 1, 99 >$$

Since a sequence is a set of pairs, all set operators described in Section 24.2.2 are applicable. When a sequence is used in a state, it should be designated as such by using the keyword *seq*. For example,

$$FileList : seq\ FILES$$

$$NoUsers : \mathbb{N}$$

describes a state with two components: a sequence of files and a natural number.

24.3   APPLYING MATHEMATICAL NOTATION FOR FORMAL SPECIFICATION

To illustrate the use of mathematical notation in the formal specification of a software component, we revisit the block handler example presented in Section 24.1.3. To review, an important component of a computer's operating system maintains files that have been created by users. Part of this component is the block handler. The block handler maintains a reservoir of unused blocks and will also keep track of blocks that are currently in use. When blocks are released from a deleted file they are normally added to a queue of blocks waiting to be added to the reservoir of unused blocks. This has been depicted schematically in Figure 24.2. In this figure a number of components are shown: the reservoir of free (unused) blocks, the blocks that currently make up the files administered by the operating system, and those used blocks that are waiting to be added to the reservoir. The waiting blocks are held in a queue, with each element of the queue containing a set of blocks from a deleted file. The invariant that describes the block handler has a number of conditions:

- No block will be marked as both unused and used.
- All the sets of blocks held in the queue will be subsets of the collection of currently used blocks.
- There will be no duplicate block numbers in the collection of unused blocks.
- There will be no elements of the queue that will contain the same block numbers.
- The collection of used blocks and blocks that are unused will be the total collection of blocks that make up files.
- There will be no duplicate block numbers in the collection of used blocks.

There will be an assumed set *BLOCKS,* which will consist of a set of every block number, and a set *AllBlocks,* which is a set of blocks that lie between 1 and *MaxBlocks*. The state will be modeled by two sets and a sequence. The two sets are *used* and *free*. Both contain blocks—the *used* set contains the blocks that are currently used in files and the *free* set contains blocks that are available for new files. The sequence will contain sets of blocks that are ready to be released from files that have been deleted. The state can be described as

$$used, free : \mathbb{P}\ BLOCKS$$

$$BlockQueue : seq\ \mathbb{P}\ BLOCKS$$

This is very much like the declaration of program variables. It states that *used* and *free* will be sets of blocks and that *BlockQueue* will be a sequence, each element of which will be a set of blocks. The data invariant can be written as

$$used \cap free = \varnothing \wedge$$

$$used \cup free = AllBlocks \wedge$$

$$\forall\, i : \mathrm{dom}\ BlockQueue \cdot BlockQueue\ i \subseteq used \wedge$$

$$\forall\, i,j : \mathrm{dom}\ BlockQueue \cdot i \neq j \Rightarrow BlockQueue\ i \cap BlockQueue\ j = \varnothing$$

The mathematical components of the data invariant match four of the bulleted, natural-language components described earlier. The first line of the data invariant states that there will be no common blocks in the *used* collection of blocks and the *free* collection of blocks. The second line states that the collection of *used* blocks and *free* blocks will always be equal to the whole collection of blocks in the system. The third line indicates that the ith element in the block queue will always be a subset of the *used* blocks. The final line states that if any two elements of the block queue are not the same, there will be no common blocks in these two elements. The final two natural-language components of the data invariant are implemented by virtue of the fact that *used* and *free* are sets and therefore will not contain duplicates.

The first operation that we shall define is one that removes an element from the head of the block queue. The precondition is that there must be at least one item in the queue:

$$\#BlockQueue > 0$$

The postcondition is that the head of the queue must be removed and placed in the collection of free blocks and the queue adjusted to show the removal:

$$used' = used \setminus head\ BlockQueue \land$$

$$free' = free \cup head\ BlockQueue \land$$

$$BlockQueue' = tail\ BlockQueue$$

A convention used in many formal methods is that the value of a variable after an operation is primed. Thus, the first component of the expression above states that the new *used* blocks ($used'$) will be equal to the old *used* blocks minus the blocks that have been removed. The second component states that the new *free* blocks ($free'$) will be the old *free* blocks with the head of the block queue added. The third component states that the new block queue will be equal to the tail of the old value of the block queue, that is, all elements in the queue apart from the first one. A second operation is one that adds a collection of blocks *Ablocks* to the block queue. The precondition is that *Ablocks* is currently a set of used blocks:

$$Ablocks \subseteq used$$

The postcondition is that the set of blocks is added to the end of the block queue and the set of used and free blocks remains unchanged:

$$BlockQueue' = BlockQueue \frown < Ablocks > \land$$

$$used' = used \land$$

$$free' = free$$

There is no question that the mathematical specification of the block queue is considerably more rigorous than a natural language narrative or a graphical model. The additional rigor requires effort, but the benefits gained from improved consistency and completeness can be justified for many types of applications.

24.4 FORMAL SPECIFICATION LANGUAGES

A formal specification language is usually composed of three primary components: (1) a *syntax* that defines the specific notation with which the specification is represented, (2) a *semantics* that helps to define a "universe of objects" [WIN90] that will be used to describe the system, and (3) a set of *relations* that define the rules that indicate which objects properly satisfy the specification.

The *syntactic domain* of a formal specification language is often based on a syntax that is derived from standard set theory notation and predicate calculus. For example, *variables* such as x, y, and z describe a set of objects that relate to a problem (sometimes called the *domain of discourse*) and are used in conjunction with the operators described in Section 24.2. Although the syntax is usually symbolic, icons (e.g., graphical symbols such as boxes, arrows, and circles) can also be used if they are unambiguous.

The *semantic domain* of a specification language indicates how the language represents system requirements. For example, a programming language has a set of formal semantics that enables the software developer to specify algorithms that transform input to output. A formal grammar (such as BNF) can be used to describe the syntax of the programming language. However, a programming language does not make a good specification language because it can represent only computable functions. A specification language must have a semantic domain that is broader; that is, the semantic domain of a specification language must be capable of expressing ideas such as "For all x in an infinite set A, there exists a y in an infinite set B such that the property P holds for x and y" [WIN90]. Other specification languages apply a semantics that enables the specification of system behavior. For example, a syntax and semantics can be developed to specify states and state transitions, events and their effects on state transition, or synchronization and timing.

It is possible to use different semantic abstractions to describe the same system in different ways. We did this in a less formal fashion in Chapters 12 and 20. Data flow and corresponding processing was described using the data flow diagram, and system behavior was depicted with the state-transition diagram. Analogous notation was used to describe object-oriented systems. Different modeling notation can be used to represent the same system. The semantics of each representation provide complementary views of the system. To illustrate this approach when formal methods are used, assume that a formal specification language is used to describe the set of events that cause a particular state to occur in a system. Another formal relation depicts all functions that occur within a given state. The intersection of these two relations provides an indication of the events that will cause specific functions to occur.

A variety of formal specification languages are in use today—CSP [HIN95, HOR85], LARCH [GUT93], VDM [JON91], and Z [SPI88, SPI92] are representative formal specification languages that exhibit the characteristics noted above. In this chapter, the Z specification language is used for illustrative purposes. Z is coupled with an automated tool called a "proof assistant" that stores axioms, rules of inference, and application oriented theorems that lead to mathematical *proof of correctness* of the specification [WOO89].

24.5   USING Z TO REPRESENT AN EXAMPLE SOFTWARE COMPONENT

Z specifications are structured as a set of *schemas*—boxlike structures that introduce variables and specify the relationship between these variables. A schema is essentially the formal specification analog of the programming language subroutine or procedure. In the same way that procedures and subroutines are used to structure a system, schemas are used to structure a formal specification.

In this section, we use the Z specification language to model the block handler example, introduced in Section 24.1.3 and discussed further in Section 24.3. A summary of Z language notation is presented in Table 24.2. The following example of a schema describes the state of the block handler and the data invariant:

$_____$ *BlockHandler* $_____$
$used, free : \mathbb{P} \; BLOCKS$
$BlockQueue : \text{seq} \; \mathbb{P} \; BLOCKS$

$used \cap free = \varnothing \wedge$
$used \cup free = AllBlocks \; \wedge$
$\forall \, i : \text{dom} \; BlockQueue \cdot BlockQueue \; i \subseteq used \; \wedge$
$\forall \, i, j : \text{dom} \; BlockQueue \cdot i \neq j \Rightarrow$
$BlockQueue \; i \cap BlockQueue \; j = \varnothing$

The schema consists of two parts. The part above the central line represents the variables of the state, while the part below the central line describes the data invariant. Whenever the schema representing the invariant and the state is used in another schema, it is preceded by the Δ symbol. Thus, if the above schema is used in a schema which, for example, describes an operation, then it would be written as Δ *BlockHandler*. As the last sentence implies, schemas can be used to describe operations. The following example of a schema describes the operation that removes an element from the block queue:

$_____$ *RemoveBlock* $_____$
$\Delta BlockHandler$

$\#BlockQueue > 0$
$used' = used \setminus head \; BlockQueue \; \wedge$
$free' = free \cup head \; BlockQueue \; \wedge$
$BlockQueue' = tail \; BlockQueue$

The inclusion of Δ *BlockHandler* results in all the variables that make up the state being available for the *RemoveBlock* schema and ensures that the data invariant will hold before and after the operation has been executed.

The second operation, which adds a collection of blocks to the end of the queue, is represented as

---

TABLE 24.2

SUMMARY OF Z NOTATION

Z notation is based on typed set theory and first-order logic. Z provides a construct, called a *schema*, to describe a specification's state space and operations. A schema groups variable declarations with a list of predicates that constrain the possible values of a variable. In Z, the schema X is defined by the form

$$
\begin{array}{|l}
\hline
— X \;\rule[0.5ex]{18em}{0.4pt} \\
\quad \text{declarations} \\
\hline
\quad \text{predicates} \\
\hline
\end{array}
$$

Global functions and constants are defined by the form

$$
\begin{array}{l}
\quad \text{declarations} \\
\hline
\quad \text{predicates}
\end{array}
$$

The declaration gives the type of the function or constant, while the predicate gives its value. Only an abbreviated set of Z symbols is presented in this table.

Sets:

$S : \mathbb{P}\, X$	S is declared as a set of X's.
$x \in S$	x is a member of S.
$x \notin S$	x is not a member of S.
$S \subseteq T$	S is a subset of T: Every member of S is also in T.
$S \cup T$	The union of S and T: It contains every member of S or T or both.
$S \cap T$	The intersection of S and T: It contains every member of both S and T.
$S \setminus T$	The difference of S and T: It contains every member of S except those also in T.
$\varnothing$	Empty set: It contains no members.
$\{x\}$	Singleton set: It contains just x.
$\mathbb{N}$	The set of natural numbers 0, 1, 2, ...
$S : \mathbb{F}\, X$	S is declared as a finite set of X's.
$\max(S)$	The maximum of the nonempty set of numbers S.

Functions:

$f : X \rightarrowtail Y$	f is declared as a partial injection from X to Y
dom f	The domain of f: the set of values x for which $f(x)$ is defined.
ran f	The range of f: the set of values taken by $f(x)$ as x varies over the domain of f.
$f \oplus \{x \mapsto y\}$	A function that agrees with f except that x is mapped to y.
$\{x\} \vartriangleleft f$	A function like f, except that x is removed from its domain.

Logic:

$P \wedge Q$	P and Q: It is true if both P and Q are true.
$P \Rightarrow Q$	P implies Q: It is true if either Q is true or P is false.
$\theta S' = \theta S$	No components of schema S change in an operation.

```
┌──────────── AddBlock ─────────────────────
│ Δ BlockHandler
│ Ablocks?: ℙ BLOCKS
├────────────────────────────────────────────
│ Ablocks? ⊆ used
│ BlockQueue' = BlockQueue ⌢ < Ablocks? >
│ used' = used ∧
│ free' = free
└────────────────────────────────────────────
```

By convention in Z, an input variable that is read from and does not form part of the state is terminated by a question mark. Thus, *Ablocks?*, which acts as an input parameter, is terminated by a question mark.

24.6   THE TEN COMMANDMENTS OF FORMAL METHODS

The decision to make use of formal methods in the real world is not one that is taken lightly. Bowen and Hinchley [BOW94] have coined "the ten commandments of formal methods" as a guide for those who are about to apply this important software engineering approach.[4]

I.   **Thou shalt choose the appropriate notation.** In order to choose effectively from the wide array of formal specification languages, a software engineer should consider language vocabulary, application type to be specified, and breadth of usage of the language.

II. **Thou shalt formalize, but not overformalize.** It is generally not necessary to apply formal methods to every aspect of a major system. Those components that are safety critical are first choices, followed by components whose failure cannot be tolerated (for business reasons).

III. **Thou shalt estimate costs.** Formal methods have high start-up costs. Training of staff, acquisition of support tools, and use of contract consultants result in high first-time costs. These costs must be considered when examining the return on investment associated with formal methods.

IV. **Thou shalt have a formal methods guru on call.** Expert training and ongoing consulting are essential for success when formal methods are used for the first time.

V.   **Thou shalt not abandon thy traditional development methods.** It is possible, and in many case desirable, to integrate formal methods with conventional and/or object-oriented methods (Chapters 12 and 20). Each

---

[4]This treatment is a much abbreviated version of [BOW94]. The complete text and other useful information on formal methods can be obtained via the Internet at:

http://www.cl.cam.ac.uk/users/mgh1001

has strengths and weaknesses. A combination, if properly applied, can produce excellent results.[5]

VI. **Thou shalt document sufficiently.** Formal methods provide a concise, unambiguous, and consistent method for documenting system requirements. However, it is recommended that a natural-language commentary accompany the formal specification to serve as a mechanism for reinforcing the readers understanding of the system.

VII. **Thou shalt not compromise thy quality standards.** "There is nothing magical about formal methods" [BOW94], and for this reason, other SQA activities (Chapter 8) must continue to be applied as systems are developed.

VIII. **Thou shalt not be dogmatic.** A software engineer must recognize that formal methods are *not* a guarantee of correctness. It is possible (some would say, likely) that the final system, even when developed using formal methods, may have small omissions, minor bugs, and other attributes that do not meet expectations.

IX. **Thou shalt test, test, and test again.** The importance of software testing has been discussed in Chapters 16, 17, and 22. Formal methods do not absolve the software engineer from the need to conduct well-planned, thorough tests.

X. **Thou shalt reuse.** Over the long term, the only rational way to reduce software costs and increase software quality is through reuse (Chapter 26). Formal methods do not change this reality. In fact, it may be that formal methods are an appropriate approach when components for reuse libraries are to be created.

24.7   FORMAL METHODS—THE ROAD AHEAD

Although formal, mathematically based specification techniques are not as yet used widely in the industry, they do offer substantial advantages over less formal techniques. Liskov and Bersins [LIS86] summarize these in the following way:

> Formal specifications can be studied mathematically while informal specifications cannot. For example, a correct program can be proved to meet its specifications, or two alternative sets of specifications can be proved equivalent. . . . Certain forms of incompleteness or inconsistency can be detected automatically.

In addition, formal specification removes ambiguity and encourages greater rigor in the early stages of the software engineering process.

But problems remain. Formal specification focuses primarily on function and data. Timing, control, and behavioral aspects of a problem are more diffi-

---

[5]Cleanroom software engineering (Chapter 25) is an example of an integrated approach that uses formal methods and more conventional development notation.

cult to represent. In addition, there are elements of a problem (e.g., human–machine interfaces) that are better specified using graphical techniques. Finally, specification using formal methods is more difficult to learn than other analysis methods presented in this book and represents a significant "culture shock" for some software practitioners. For this reason, it is likely that formal, mathematical specification techniques will form the foundation for a future generation of CASE tools. When this occurs, mathematically based specification may be adopted by a wider segment of the software engineering community.[6]

24.8   SUMMARY

Formal methods provide a foundation for specification environments that lead to analysis models that are more complete, consistent, and unambiguous than those produced using conventional or object-oriented methods. The descriptive facilities of set theory and logic notation enable a software engineer to create a clear statement of facts (requirements).

The underlying concepts that govern formal methods are (1) the data invariant—a condition that is true throughout the execution of the system that contains a collection of data; (2) the state—the stored data which a system accesses and alters; and (3) the operation—an action that takes place in a system and reads or writes data to a state. An operation is associated with two conditions: a precondition and a postcondition.

Discrete mathematics—the notation and heuristics associated with sets and constructive specification, set operators, logic operators, and sequences—forms the basis of formal methods. These mathematics are implemented in the context of a formal specification language, such as Z.

Z, like all formal specification languages, has both a syntactic and semantic domain. The syntactic domain uses a symbology that is closely aligned with the notation of sets and predicate calculus. The semantic domain enables the language to express requirements in a concise manner. The structure of Z incorporates schemas—boxlike structures that introduce variables and specify the relationship between these variables.

A decision to use formal methods must consider start-up costs as well as the cultural changes associated with a radically different technology. In most instances, formal methods have highest payoff for safety-critical and business-critical systems.

REFERENCES

[BOW94] Bowan, J.P., and M.G. Hinchley, *Ten Commandments of Formal Methods*, Technical Report No. 350, University of Cambridge Computer Laboratory, Cambridge, UK, September 1994.

[GRI93] Gries, D., and F.B. Schneider, *A Logical Approach to Discrete Math*, Springer-Verlag, 1993.

---

[6]It is important to note that others disagree. See [YOU94].

[GUT93]   Guttag, J.V., and J.J. Horning, *Larch: Languages and Tools for Formal Specification,* Springer-Verlag, 1993.

[HAL90]   Hall, A., "Seven Myths of Formal Methods," *IEEE Software,* September 1990, pp. 11–20.

[HOR85]   Hoare, C.A.R., *Communicating Sequential Processes,* Prentice-Hall International, 1985.

[HIN95]   Hinchley, M.G., and S.A. Jarvis, *Concurrent Systems: Formal Development in CSP,* McGraw-Hill, 1995.

[JON91]   Jones, C.B., *Systematic Software Development Using VDM,* 2nd edition, Prentice-Hall, 1991.

[LIS86]   Liskov, B.H., and V. Berzins, "An Appraisal of Program Specifications," in *Software Specification Techniques,* N. Gehani and A.T. McKittrick (eds.), Addison-Wesley, 1986, p. 3.

[MAR94]   Marciniak, J.J. (ed.), *Encyclopedia of Software Engineering,* Wiley, 1994.

[ROS95]   Rosen, K.H., *Discrete Mathematics and Its Applications,* 3rd edition, McGraw-Hill, 1995.

[SPI88]   Spivey, J.M., *Understanding Z: A Specification Language and Its Formal Semantics,* Cambridge University Press, 1988.

[SPI92]   Spivey, J.M., *The Z Notation: A Reference Manual,* Prentice-Hall, 1992.

[WIL87]   Wiltala, S.A., *Discrete Mathematics: A Unified Approach,* McGraw-Hill, 1987.

[WIN90]   Wing, J.M., "A Specifier's Introduction to Formal Methods," *IEEE Computer,* vol. 23, no. 9, September 1990, pp. 8–24.

[WOO89]   Woodcock, J.C., "Calculating Properties of Z Specifications, *ACM Software Engineering Notes,* vol. 14, no. 5, July 1989, pp. 43–54.

[YOU94]   Yourdon, E., "Formal Methods," *Guerrilla Programmer,* Cutter Information Corp., October 1994.

PROBLEMS AND POINTS TO PONDER

24.1. Review the types of deficiencies associated with less formal approaches to software engineering in Section 24.1.1. Provide three examples of each from your own experience.

24.2. The benefits of mathematics as a specification mechanism have been discussed at length in this chapter. Is there a downside?

24.3. You have been assigned to a software team that is developing software for a fax modem. Your job is to develop the "phone book" portion of the application. The phone book function enables up to *MaxNames* names of addresses to be stored along with associated company names, fax numbers, and other related information. Using natural language define:
a. the data invariant
b. the state
c. the operations that are likely

24.4. You have been assigned to a software team that is developing software, called *MemoryDoubler,* that provides greater apparent memory for a PC than physical memory. This is accomplished by identifying, collecting, and reassigning blocks of memory that have been assigned to an existing application but are not being used. The unused blocks are reassigned to applications that require additional memory. Making appropriate assumptions and using natural language define:

a. the data invariant

b. the state

c. the operations that are likely for a phone book function

24.5. Develop a constructive specification for a set that contains tuples of natural numbers of the form (x, y, z^2) such that the sum of x and y equals z.

24.6. The installer for a PC-based application first determines whether an acceptable set of hardware and system resources are present. It checks the hardware configuration to determine whether various devices (of many possible devices) are present and determines whether specific versions of system software and drivers are already installed. What set operator could be used to accomplish this? Provide an example in this context.

24.7. Attempt to develop a expression using logic and set operators for the following statement: "For all x and y, if x is the parent of y and y is the parent of z, then x is the grandparent of z. Everyone has a parent." [Hint: Use the functions $P(x, y)$ and $G(x, z)$ to represent parent and grandparent functions, respectively.]

24.8. Develop a constructive set specification of the set of pairs where the first element of each pair is the sum of two nonzero natural numbers and the second element is the difference of the same two numbers. Both numbers should be between 100 and 200 inclusive.

24.9. Develop a mathematical description for the state and data invariant for problem 24.3. Refine this description in the Z specification language.

24.10. Develop a mathematical description for the state and data invariant for problem 24.4. Refine this description in the Z specification language.

24.11. Using the Z notation presented in Table 24.2, select some part of the SafeHome security system described earlier in this book and attempt to specify it with Z.

24.12. Using one or more of the information sources noted in the references to this chapter or "Further Readings, and Other Information Sources," develop a half-hour presentation on the basic syntax and semantics of a formal specification language other than Z.

FURTHER READINGS AND OTHER INFORMATION SOURCES

In addition to the books used as references in this chapter, a fairly large number of books on formal methods topics has been published over the past few years. A listing of some of the more useful offerings is presented below:

Barden, R., S. Stepney, and D.Cooper, *Z in Practice,* Prentice-Hall, 1994.

Bowen, J., *Formal Specification and Documentation using Z: A Case Study Approach,* International Thomson Computer Press, 1996.

Cooper, D., and R. Barden, *Z in Practice,* Prentice-Hall, 1995.

Craigen, D., S. Gerhart, and T. Ralston, *Industrial Application of Formal Methods to Model, Design and Analyze Computer Systems,* Noyes Data Corp., Park Ridge, NJ, 1995.

Diller, A., *Z: An introduction to Formal Methods,* 2nd edition, Wiley, 1994.

Hinchey, M., and J. Bowen, *Applications of Formal Methods,* Prentice-Hall, 1996.

Lano, J., and H. Haughton (eds.), *Object-Oriented Specification Case Studies,* Prentice-Hall, 1993.

Rann, D., J. Turner, and J. Whitworth, *Z: A Beginner's Guide,* Chapman & Hall, 1994.

Ratcliff, B., *Introducing Specification Using Z: A Practical Case Study Approach,* McGraw-Hill, 1994.

D. Sheppard, *An Introduction to Formal Specification with Z and VDM,* McGraw-Hill, 1995.

The September 1990 issues of *IEEE Transactions on Software Engineering, IEEE Software, and IEEE Computer* were all dedicated to formal methods. They remain an excellent source of useful information.

Schuman has edited a book that addresses formal methods and object technologies (*Formal Object-Oriented Development,* Springer-Verlag, 1996). The book provides guidelines on the selective use of formal methods and how such methods can be used in conjunction with OO approaches.

A wealth of formal methods information, including pointers to extensive bibliographies, technical reports, specification languages, tools, and many other useful pointers can be found at the NASA formal methods site and the Virtual Library on Formal Methods:

http://atb-www.larc.nasa.gov/cgi-bin/fm.cgi

http://www.comlab.ox.ac.uk /archive/formal-methods/

Additional discussion can be found in the newsgroups **comp.specification. misc** and **comp.specification.z**.

Comprehensive information on VDM (another formal specification language) can be obtained at:

gopher://nisp.ncl.ac.uk/11/lists-u-z/vdm-forum/files

General information on formal methods, as well as research and position papers and Web pointers can be obtained at:

http://www.research.att.com/orgs/ssr/areas.html

An up-to-date list of World Wide Web references for formal methods can be found at: **http://www.rspa.com**

CLEANROOM SOFTWARE ENGINEERING

The integrated use of conventional software engineering modeling, formal methods, program verification (correctness proofs), and statistical SQA have been combined into a technique that can lead to extremely high-quality software. *Cleanroom software engineering* is an approach that emphasizes the need to build correctness into software as it is being developed. Instead of the classic analyze, design, code, test, and debug cycle, the cleanroom approach suggests a different point of view [LIN94]:

> The philosophy behind cleanroom software engineering is to avoid dependence on costly defect removal processes by writing code increments right the first time and verifying their correctness before testing. Its process model incorporates the statistical quality certification of code increments as they accumulate into a system.

In many ways, the cleanroom approach elevates software engineering to another level. Like the formal methods techniques presented in Chapter 24, the cleanroom process emphasizes rigor in specification and design, and formal verification of each element of the resultant design model using correctness proofs that are mathematically based. Extending the approach taken in formal methods, the cleanroom approach also emphasizes techniques for statistical quality control, including testing that is based on the anticipated use of the software by customers.

When software fails in the real world, immediate and long-term hazards abound. The hazards can be related to human safety, economic loss, or effective operation of business and societal infrastructure. Cleanroom software engineering is a process model that removes defects before they can precipitate serious hazards.

25.1 THE CLEANROOM APPROACH

The philosophy of the "cleanroom" in hardware fabrication technologies is really quite simple: It is cost effective and time effective to establish a fabrication approach that precludes the introduction of product defects. Rather than fabricating a product and then working to remove defects, the cleanroom approach demands the discipline required to eliminate errors in specification and design and then fabricate in a "clean" manner.

The cleanroom philosophy was first proposed for software engineering by Mills and his colleagues [MIL87] during the 1980s. Although early experiences with this disciplined approach to software work showed significant promise [HAU94], it has not gained widespread usage. Henderson [HEN95] suggests three possible reasons:

1. A belief that the cleanroom methodology is too theoretical, too mathematical, and too radical for use in real software development.

2. It advocates no unit testing by developers but instead replaces it with correctness verification and statistical quality control—concepts that represent a major departure from the way most software developed today.

3. The maturity of the software development industry. The use of cleanroom processes requires rigorous application of defined processes in all life cycle phases. Since most of the industry is still operating at the ad hoc level (as defined by the Software Engineering Institute Capability Maturity Model), the industry has not been ready to apply those techniques.

Although there are elements of truth in each of the concerns noted above, the potential benefits of cleanroom software engineering far outweigh the investment required to overcome the cultural resistance that is at the core of these concerns.

25.1.1 The Cleanroom Strategy

The cleanroom approach makes use of a specialized version of the incremental software model (Chapter 2). A "pipeline of software increments" [LIN94] is developed by small, independent software engineering teams. As each increment is certified, it is integrated into the whole. Hence, functionality of the system grows with time.

The sequence of cleanroom tasks for each increment is illustrated in Figure 25.1. Overall system or product requirements are developed using the system engineering methods discussed in Chapter 10. Once functionality has been allocated to the software element of the system, the pipeline of cleanroom increments is initiated. The following tasks occur:

Increment Planning. A project plan that adopts the incremental strategy is developed. The functionality of each increment, its projected size, and a cleanroom development schedule are established. Special care must be taken to ensure that certified increments will be integrated in a timely manner.

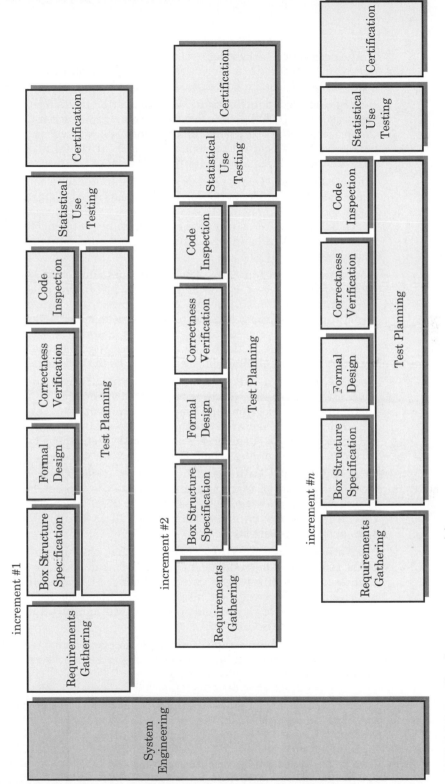

FIGURE 25.1. The cleanroom process model

Requirements Gathering. Using techniques similar to those introduced in Chapter 11, a more detailed description of customer-level requirements (for each increment) is developed.

Box Structure Specification. A specification method that makes use of *box structures* [HEV93] is used to describe the functional specification. Conforming to the operational analysis principles discussed in Chapter 11, box structures "isolate and separate the creative definition of behavior, data, and procedures at each level of refinement."

Formal Design. Using the box structure approach, cleanroom design is a natural and seamless extension of specification. Although it is possible to make a clear distinction between the two activities, Specifications (called "black boxes") are iteratively refined (within an increment) to become analogous to architectural and procedural designs (called "state boxes" and "clear boxes," respectively).

Correctness Verification. The cleanroom team conducts a series of rigorous correctness verification activities on the design and then the code. Verification (Sections 25.3 and 25.4) begins with the highest-level box structure (specification) and moves toward design detail and code. The first level of correctness verification occurs by applying a set of "correctness questions" [LIN88]. If these do not demonstrate that the specification is correct, more formal (mathematical) methods for verification are used.

Code Generation, Inspection, and Verification. The box structure specifications, represented in a specialized language, are translated into the appropriate programming language. Standard walkthrough or inspection techniques (Chapter 8) are then used to ensure semantic conformance of the code and box structures, and syntactic correctness of the code. Then correctness verification is conducted for the source code.

Statistical Test Planning. The projected usage of the software is analyzed and a suite of test cases that exercise the "probability distribution" of usage are planned and designed (Section 25.4). As shown in Figure 25.1, this cleanroom activity is conducted in parallel with specification, verification, and code generation.

Statistical Usage Testing. Recalling that exhaustive testing of computer software is impossible (Chapter 16), it is always necessary to design a finite number of test cases. *Statistical usage techniques* [POO88] execute a series of tests derived from a statistical sample (the probability distribution noted above) of all possible program executions by all users from a targeted population (Section 25.4).

Certification. Once verification, inspection, and usage testing have been completed (and all errors are corrected) the increment is certified as ready for integration.

Like other software process models discussed elsewhere in this book, the cleanroom process relies heavily on the need to produce high-quality analysis and design models. As we will see later in this chapter, box structure notation is simply another way for a software engineer to represent requirements and design. The real distinction of the cleanroom approach is that formal verification is applied to engineering models.

25.1.2 What Makes Cleanroom Different?

Dyer [DYE92] alludes to the differences of the cleanroom approach when he defines the process:

> Cleanroom represents the first practical attempt at putting the software development process under statistical quality control with a well-defined strategy for continuous process improvement. To reach this goal, a unique cleanroom life cycle was defined which focused on mathematics-based software engineering for correct software designs and on statistics-based software for certification of software reliability.

Cleanroom software engineering differs from the conventional and object-oriented views presented in Parts Three and Four of this book because:

1. It makes explicit use of statistical quality control.
2. It verifies design specification using a mathematically based proof of correctness.
3. It relies heavily on statistical usage testing to uncover high-impact errors.

Obviously, the cleanroom approach applies most, if not all, of the basic software engineering principles and concepts presented throughout this book. Good analysis and design procedures are essential if high quality is to result. But cleanroom engineering diverges from conventional software practices by deemphasizing (some would say, eliminating) the role of unit testing and debugging, and dramatically reducing (or eliminating) the amount of testing performed by the developer of the software.[1]

In conventional software development, errors are accepted as a fact of life. Because errors are deemed to be inevitable, each program module must be unit tested (to uncover errors) and then debugged (to remove errors). When the software is finally released, field use uncovers still more defects, and another test and debug cycle begins. The rework associated with these activities is costly and time-consuming. Worse, it can be degenerative—error correction can (inadvertently) lead to the introduction of still more errors.

In cleanroom software engineering, unit testing and debugging are replaced by correctness verification and statistically based testing. These activities, coupled with the record keeping necessary for continuous improvement, make the cleanroom approach unique.

25.2　　FUNCTIONAL SPECIFICATION

Regardless of the analysis method that is chosen, the operational principles presented in Chapter 11 always apply. Data, function, and behavior are modeled. The resultant models must be partitioned (refined) to provide increasingly

---

[1]Testing is conducted, but by an independent testing team.

greater detail. The overall objective is to move from a specification that captures the essence of a problem to a specification that provides substantial implementation detail.

Cleanroom software engineering complies with the operational analysis principles by using a method called *box structure specification*. A "box" encapsulates the system (or some aspect of the system) at some level of detail. Through a process of stepwise refinement, boxes are refined into a hierarchy in which each box has *referential transparency*—"the information content of each box specification is sufficient to define its refinement, without depending on the implementation of any other box" [LIN94]. This enables the analyst to partition a system hierarchically, moving from essential representation at the top to implementation-specific detail at the bottom. Three types of boxes are used:

Black Box. This box specifies the behavior of a system or a part of a system. The system (or part) responds to specific stimuli (events) by applying a set of transition rules that map the stimulus into a response.

State Box. This box encapsulates state data and services (operations) in a manner that is analogous to objects.[2] In this specification view, inputs to the state box (stimuli) and outputs (responses) are represented. The state box also represents the "stimulus history" of the black box, that is, the data encapsulated in the state box that must be retained between the transitions implied.

Clear Box. The transition functions that are implied by the state box are defined in the clear box. Stated simply, a clear box contains the procedural design for the state box.

Figure 25.2 illustrates the refinement approach using box structure specification. A black box (BB_1) defines responses for a complete set of stimuli. BB_1 can be refined into a set of black boxes. $BB_{1.1}$ to $BB_{1.n}$, which each address a class of behavior. Refinement continues until a cohesive class of behavior is identified (e.g. $BB_{1.1.1}$). A state box ($SB_{1.1.1}$) is then defined for the black box ($BB_{1.1.1}$). In this case $SB_{1.1.1}$ contains all data and services required to implement the behavior defined by $BB_{1.1.1}$. Finally, $SB_{1.1.1}$ is refined into a set of clear boxes ($CB_{1.1.1.n}$) and procedure design details are specified.

As each of these refinement steps occur, verification of correctness also occurs. State-box specifications are verified to ensure that each conforms to the behavior defined by the parent black-box specification. Similarly, clear-box specifications are verified against the parent state box.

It should be noted that specification methods based on formal methods (Chapter 24) can be used in lieu of the box structure specification approach. The only requirement is that each level of specification can be formally verified.

25.2.1 Black-Box Specification

A *black-box specification* is an abstraction that describes how a system responds to stimuli using the notation shown in Figure 25.3 [MIL88]. The func-

---

[2]See Part Four of this book.

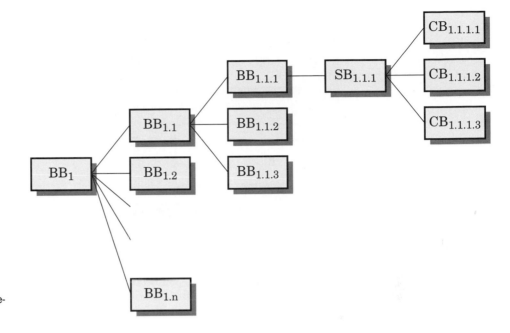

FIGURE 25.2.
Box structure refinement

tion f is applied to a sequence, S^*, of inputs (stimuli), S, and transforms them into an output (response), R. For simple software components, f may be a mathematical function, but in general, f is described using natural language (or a formal specification language).

Many of the concepts introduced for object-oriented systems (Chapter 19) are also applicable for the black box. Data abstractions and the operations that manipulate those abstractions are encapsulated by the black box. Like a class hierarchy, the black-box specification can exhibit usage hierarchies in which low-level boxes inherit the properties of those boxes higher in the tree structure.

25.2.2 State-Box Specification

The state box is "a simple generalization of a state machine" [MIL88]. A state is some observable mode of system behavior (recall the discussion of behavioral modeling and state-transition diagrams in Chapter 12). As processing occurs, a system responds to events (stimuli) by making a transition from the current state to some new state. As the transition is made, an action may occur. The

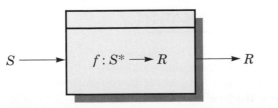

FIGURE 25.3.
A black-box specification [MIL88]

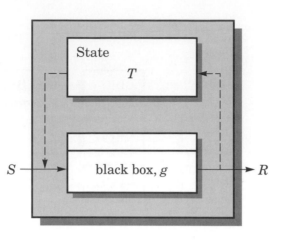

FIGURE 25.4.
A state-box specification [MIL88]

state box uses a data abstraction to determine the transition to the next state and the action (response) that will occur as a consequence of the transition.

As shown in Figure 25.4, the state box incorporates a black box. The stimulus, S, that is input to the black box arrives from some external source and a set of internal system states, T. Mills provides a mathematical description of the function, f, of the black box contained within the state box:

$$g : S^* \times T^* \to R \times T$$

where g is a subfunction that is tied to a specific state t. When considered collectively, the state–subfunction pairs (t, g) define the black-box function f.

25.2.3   Clear-Box Specification

The clear-box specification is closely aligned with procedural design and structured programming. In essence, the subfunction g within the state box is replaced by the structured programming constructs that implement g.

As an example, consider the clear box shown in Figure 25.5. The black box, g, shown in Figure 25.4 is replaced by a sequence construct that incorporates a conditional. These, in turn, can be refined into lower-level clear boxes as stepwise refinement proceeds.

It is important to note that the procedural specification described in the clear-box hierarchy can be proved to be correct. This topic is considered in the next section.

25.3   DESIGN REFINEMENT AND VERIFICATION

The design approach used in cleanroom software engineering makes heavy use of the structured programming philosophy (Chapter 14). But in this case, structured programming is applied far more rigorously.

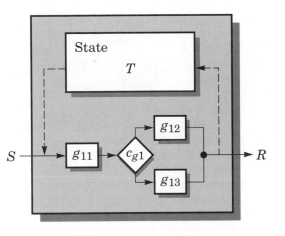

FIGURE 25.5.
A clear-box specification

Basic processing functions (described during earlier refinements of the specification) are refined using a "stepwise expansion of mathematical functions into structures of *logical connectives* [e.g., if-then-else] and subfunctions, where the expansion [is] carried out until all identified subfunctions could be directly stated in the programming language used for implementation" [DYE92].

The structured programming approach can be used effectively to refine function, but what about data design? Here a number of fundamental design concepts (Chapter 13) come into play. Program data are encapsulated as a set of abstractions that are serviced by subfunctions. The concepts of data encapsulation, information hiding, and data typing are used to create the data design.

25.3.1 Design Refinement and Verification

Each clear-box specification represents the design of a procedure (subfunction) required to accomplish a state-box transition. With the clear box, the structured programming constructs and stepwise refinement are used as illustrated in Figure 25.6. A program function, f, is refined into a sequence[3] of subfunctions g and h. These in turn are refined into conditional constructs (*if-then-else* and *do-while*). Further refinement illustrates continuing logical elaboration.

At each level of refinement, the cleanroom team[4] performs a formal correctness verification. To accomplish this, a set of generic correctness conditions are attached to the structured programming constructs. If a function f is expanded into a sequence g and h (as shown in Figure 25.6), the correctness condition for all input to f is:

---

[3]See Chapter 14 for a discussion of basic structured programming constructs.

[4]Because the entire team is involved in the verification process, it is less likely that an error will be made in conducting the verification itself.

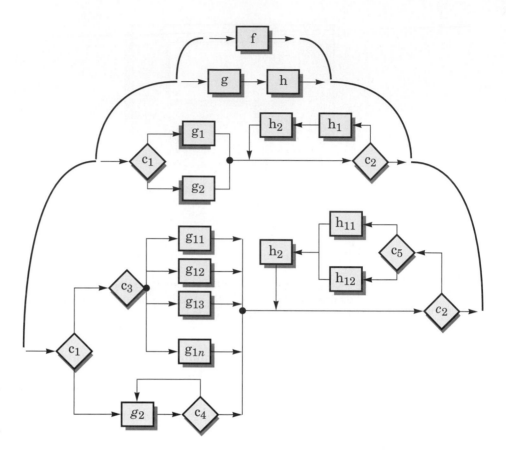

FIGURE 25.6.
Stepwise refinement

- Does g followed by h do f?

If a function p is refined into a conditional of the form, if (c) then q, else r, the correctness condition for all input to p is:

- Whenever condition $< c >$ is true does q do p and whenever $< c >$ is false, does r do p?

If a function m is refined as a loop, the correctness conditions for all input to m are:

- Is termination guaranteed?
- Whenever $< c >$ is true does n followed by m do m, and whenever $< c >$ is false, does skipping the loop still do m?

Each time a clear box is refined to the next level of detail, the correctness conditions noted above are applied.

It is important to note that the use of the structured programming constructs constrains the number of correctness tests that must be conducted. A

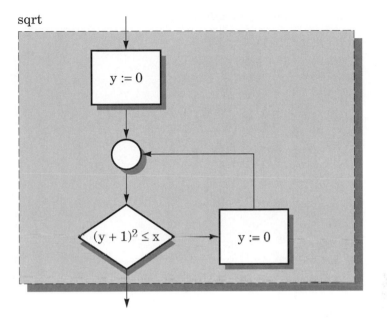

FIGURE 25.7.
Computing the integer part of a square root [LIN79]

single condition is checked for sequences; two conditions are tested for if-then-else; and three conditions are verified for loops.

To illustrate correctness verification for a procedural design, we use a simple example first introduced by Linger and his colleagues [LIN79]. The intent is to design and verify a small program that finds the integer part, y, of a square root of a given integer, x. The procedural design is represented using the flowchart in Figure 25.7.

To verify the correctness of this design, we must define *entry* and *exit* conditions as noted in Figure 25.8. The entry condition notes that x must be greater than or equal to 0. The *exit* condition requires that x remain unchanged and take on a value within the range noted in the figure. To prove the design to be correct, it is necessary to prove the conditions *init, loop, cont, yes,* and *exit* shown in Figure 25.8 are true in all cases. These are sometimes called *subproofs*.

1. The condition *init* demands that $[x \geq 0$ and $y = 0]$. Based on the requirements of the problem, the entry condition is assumed correct.[5] Therefore, the first part of the *init* condition, $x \geq 0$ is satisfied. In the flowchart, the statement immediately preceding the *init* condition sets $y = 0$. Therefore, the second part of the init condition is also satisfied. Hence, *init* is true.

2. The *loop* condition may be encountered in one of two ways: (1) directly from *init* (in this case, the loop condition is satisfied directly) or (2) via control flow that passes through the condition *cont*. Since the *cont* condition is

---

[5]A negative value for a square root has no meaning in this context.

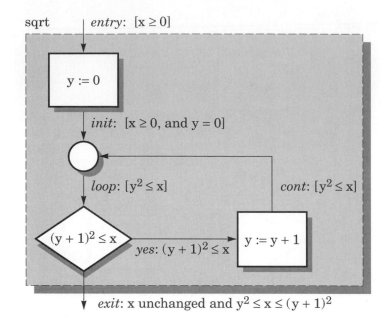

FIGURE 25.8.
Proving the design
correct [LIN79]

identical to the *loop* condition, *loop* is true regardless of the flow path that leads to it.

3.   The *cont* condition is encountered only after the value of y is incremented by 1. In addition, the control flow path that leads to *cont* can only be invoked if the *yes* condition is also true. Hence if $(y + 1)^2 \leq x$, it follows that $y^2 \leq x$. The *cont* condition is satisfied.

4.   The *yes* condition is tested in the conditional logic shown. Hence, the *yes* condition must be true when control flow moves along the path shown.

5.   The *exit* condition first demands that x remain unchanged. An examination of the design indicates that x appears nowhere to the left of an assignment operator. There are no function calls that use x. Hence it is unchanged. Since the conditional test $(y + 1)^2 \leq x$ must fail to reach the *exit* condition, it follows that $(y + 1)^2 > x$. In addition, the *loop* condition must still be true (i.e., $y^2 \leq x$). Therefore, $(y + 1)^2 > x$ and $y^2 \leq x$ can be combined to satisfy the exit condition.

We must further ensure that the loop terminates. An examination of the loop condition indicates that because y is incremented and $x \geq 0$, the loop must eventually terminate.

   The five steps noted above are a proof of the correctness of the design of the algorithm noted in Figure 25.7. We are now certain that the design will, in fact, compute the integer part of a square root.

   A more rigorous mathematical approach to design verification is possible. However, a discussion of this topic is beyond the scope of this book. Interested readers should refer to [LIN79].

Subproofs:

[f1]   f1 = [DO g1; g2; [f2] END] ?
  DO
    g1
    g2
    [f2]   f2 = [WHILE p1 DO [f3] END] ?
     WHILE
     p1
    DO [f3]   f3 = [DO g3; [f4]; g8 END] ?
     g3
     [f4]   f4 = [IF p2; THEN [f5] ELSE [f6] END] ?
     IF
      p2
     THEN [f5]   f5 = [DO g4; g5 END] ?
      g4
      g5
     ELSE [f6]   f6 = [DO g6; g7 END] ?
      g6
      g7
     END
     g8
    END
  END
END

FIGURE 25.9.
A design with sub-proofs [LIN94]

25.3.2 Advantages of Design Verification[6]

Rigorous correctness verification of each refinement of the clear-box design has a number of distinct advantages. Linger [LIN94] describes these in the following manner:

- *It reduces verification to a finite process.* The nested, sequential way in which control structures are organized in a clear box naturally defines a hierarchy that reveals the correctness conditions that must be verified. An *axiom of replacement* [LIN79] lets us substitute intended functions by their control structure refinements in the hierarchy of subproofs. For example, the subproof for the intended function f1 in Figure 25.9 requires proving that the composition of the operations g1 and g2 with the intended function f2 has the same effect on data as f1. Note that f2 substitutes for all the details of its refinement in the proof. This substitution localizes the proof argument to the control structure at hand. In fact, it lets the software engineer carry out the proofs in any order.

---

[6]This section and Figures 25.7 through 25.9 have been adapted from [LIN94]. Used with permission.

It is impossible to overemphasize the positive effect that reducing verification to a finite process has on quality. Even though all but the most trivial programs exhibit an essentially infinite number of execution paths, they can be verified in a finite number of steps.

- *It lets cleanroom teams verify every line of design and code.* Teams can carry out the verification through group analysis and discussion on the basis of the correctness theorem, and they can produce written proofs when extra confidence in a life- or mission-critical system is required.

- *It results in a near zero defect level.* During a team review, every correctness condition of every control structure is verified in turn. Every team member must agree that each condition is correct, so an error is possible only if every team member incorrectly verifies a condition. The requirement for unanimous agreement based on individual verifications results in software that has few or no defects before first execution.

- *It scales up.* Every software system, no matter how large, has top-level, clear-box procedures composed of sequence, alternation, and iteration structures. Each of these typically invokes a large subsystem with thousands of lines of code—and each of those subsystems has its own top-level intended functions and procedures. So the correctness conditions for these high-level control structures are verified in the same way as are those of low-level structures. Verification at high levels may take, and well be worth, more time, but it does not take more theory.

- *It produces better code than unit testing.* Unit testing checks only the effects of executing selected test paths out of many possible paths. By basing verification on function theory, the cleanroom approach can verify every possible effect on all data, because although a program may have many execution paths, it has only one function. Verification is also more efficient than unit testing. Most verification conditions can be checked in a few minutes, but unit tests take substantial time to prepare, execute, and check.

It is important to note that design verification must ultimately be applied to the source code itself. In this context, it is often called correctness verification.

25.4　　CLEANROOM TESTING

The strategy and tactics of cleanroom testing are fundamentally different from conventional testing approaches. Conventional methods derive a set of test cases to uncover design and coding errors. The goal of cleanroom testing is to validate software requirements by demonstrating that a statistical sample of use cases (Chapter 19) have been executed successfully.

25.4.1　Statistical Use Testing

The user of a computer program rarely needs to understand the technical details of the design. The user visible behavior of the program is driven by inputs and events that are often produced by the user. But in complex systems, the possible spectrum of input and events (i.e., the use cases) can be extremely wide. What is the subset of use cases that will adequately verify the behavior of the program? This is the first question that is addressed by statistical use testing.

Statistical use testing "amounts to testing software the way users intend to use it" [LIN94]. To accomplish this, cleanroom testing teams[7] must determine a *usage probability distribution* for the software. The specification (black box) for each increment of the software is analyzed to define a set of stimuli (inputs or events) that cause the software to change its behavior. Based on interviews with potential users, the creation of usage scenarios, and a general understanding of the application domain, a probability of use is assigned to each stimuli.

Test cases are generated for each stimulus[8] according to the usage probability distribution. To illustrate, consider the SafeHome security system discussed earlier in this book. Cleanroom software engineering is being used to develop a software increment that manages user interaction with the security system keypad. Five stimuli, listed in Table 25.1, have been identified for this increment. Analysis indicates the percent probability of each stimuli. To make selection of test cases easier, these probabilities are mapped into intervals numbered between 1 and 99 [LIN94].

To generate a sequence of usage test cases that conform to the usage probability distribution, a series of random numbers are generated between 1 and 99. The random number corresponds to the interval on the probability distribution (Table 25.1). Hence, the sequence of usage cases is defined randomly but corresponds to the appropriate probability of stimuli occurrence. For example, assume the following random number sequences are generated

```
13-94-22-24-45-56
81-19-31-69-45-9
38-21-52-84-86-97
```

Selecting the appropriate stimuli based on the distribution interval shown in Table 25.1, the following use cases are derived:

```
AD–T–AD–AD–AD–ZS
T–AD–AD–AD–Q–AD–AD
AD–AD–ZS–T–T–PA
```

The testing team executes the use cases noted above (and others) and verifies software behavior against the specification for the system. Timing for tests is recorded so that *interval times* may be determined. Using interval time, the certification team can compute *mean-time-to-failure*. If a long sequence of tests is

---

[7]Also called "certification teams."

[8]Automated tools are used to accomplish this. For further information, see [DYE92].

TABLE 25.1

PROGRAM STIMULI AND PROBABILITY DISTRIBUTION

Program stimulus	Distribution	Interval
Arm/disarm (AD)	50%	1–49
Zone set (ZS)	15%	50–63
Query (Q)	15%	64–78
Test (T)	15%	79–94
Panic alarm (PA)	5%	95–99

conducted without failure, the MTTF is low and software reliability may be assumed high.

25.4.2 Certification

The verification and testing techniques discussed earlier in this chapter lead to software components (and entire increments) that can be certified. Within the context of the cleanroom software engineering approach, *certification* implies that the reliability (measured by mean-time-to-failure, MTTF) can be specified for each component.

The potential impact of certifiable software components goes far beyond a single cleanroom project. Reusable software components can be stored along with their usage scenarios, program stimuli, and probability distributions. Each component would have a certified reliability under the usage scenario and testing regime described. This information is invaluable to others who intend to use the components.

The certification approach involves five steps [WOH94]:

1. Usage scenarios must be created.
2. A usage profile is specified.
3. Test cases are generated from the profile.
4. Tests are executed and failure data are recorded and analyzed.
5. Reliability is computed and certified.

Steps 1 through 4 have been discussed in earlier sections. In this section, we concentrate on reliability certification.

Certification for cleanroom software engineering requires the creation of three models [POO93]:

Sampling model. Software testing executes m random test cases and is certified if no failures or less than a specified number of failures occur. The value of m is derived mathematically to ensure that required reliability is achieved.

Component model. A system composed of n components is to be certified. The component model enables the analyst to determine the probability that component i will fail prior to completion.

Certification model. The overall reliability of the system is projected and certified.

At the completion of statistical usage testing, the certification team has the information required to deliver software that has a certified MTTF that is computed using the each of these models.

A detailed discussion of the computation of the sampling, component, and certification models is beyond the scope of this book. The interested reader should see [MUS87], [CUR86], and [POO93] for additional detail.

25.5   SUMMARY

Cleanroom software engineering is a formal approach to software development that can lead to software that has remarkably high quality. It uses box structure specification (or formal methods) for analysis and design modeling, and emphasizes correctness verification, rather than testing, as the primary mechanism for finding and removing errors. Statistical usage testing is applied to develop the failure rate information necessary to certify the reliability of delivered software.

The cleanroom approach begins with analysis and design models that use a box structure representation. A "box" encapsulates the system (or some aspect of the system) at a specific level of abstraction. Black boxes are used to represent the externally observable behavior of a system. State boxes encapsulate state data and operations. A clear box is used to model the procedural design that is implied by the data and operations of a state box.

Correctness verification is applied once the box structure design is complete. The procedural design for a software component is partitioned into a series of subfunctions. To prove the correctness of each of the subfunctions, exit conditions are defined for each of the subfunctions and a set of subproofs are applied. If each exit condition is satisfied, the design must be correct.

Once correctness verification is complete, statistical usage testing commences. Unlike conventional testing, cleanroom software engineering does not emphasize unit or integration testing. Rather, the software is tested by defining a set of usage scenarios, determining the probability of use for each scenario, and then defining random tests that conform to the probabilities. The error records that result are combined with sampling, component, and certification models to enable mathematical computation of projected reliability for the software component.

The cleanroom philosophy is a rigorous approach to software engineering. It is a software process model that emphasizes mathematical verification of correctness and certification of software reliability. The bottom line is extremely low failure rates, which would be difficult or impossible to achieve using less formal methods.

REFERENCES

[CUR86]   Curritt, P.A., M. Dyer, and H.D. Mills, "Certifying the Reliability of Software," *IEEE Trans, Software Engineering,* vol. SE-12, no. 1, January 1994.

[DYE92]   Dyer, M., *The Cleanroom Approach to Quality Software Development,* Wiley, 1992.

[HAU94]   Hausler, P.A., R. Linger, and C. Trammel, "Adopting Cleanroom Software Engineering with a Phased Approach," *IBM Systems Journal,* vol. 33, no. 1, January 1994, pp. 89–109.

[HEN95]   Henderson, J., "Why Isn't Cleanroom the Universal Software development Methodology?" *Crosstalk,* vol. 8, no. 5, May 1995, pp. 11–14.

[HEV93]   Hevner, A.R., and H.D. Mills, "Box Structure Methods for System Development with Objects," *IBM Systems Journal,* vol. 31, no. 2, February 1993, pp. 232–251.

[LIN79]   Linger, R.M., H.D. Mills, and B.I. Witt, *Structured Programming: Theory and Practice,* Addison-Wesley, 1979.

[LIN88]   Linger, R.M., and H.D. Mills, "A Case Study in Cleanroom Software Engineering: The IBM COBOL Structuring Facility," *Proc. COMPSAC '88,* Chicago, October 1988.

[LIN94]   Linger, R., "Cleanroom Process Model," *IEEE Software,* March 1994, pp. 50–58.

[MIL87]   Mills, H.D., M. Dyer, and R. Linger, "Cleanroom Software Engineering," *IEEE Software,* September 1987, pp. 19–24.

[MIL88]   Mills, H.D., "Stepwise Refinement and Verification in Box Structured Systems," *IEEE Computer,* June 1988, pp. 23–35.

[MUS87]   Musa, J.D., A. Iannino, and K. Okumoto, *Engineering and Managing Software with Reliability Measures,* McGraw-Hill, 1987.

[POO88]   Poore, J.H., and H.D. Mills, "Bringing Software Under Statistical Quality Control, *Quality Progress,* November 1988, pp. 52–55.

[POO93]   Poore, J.H., H.D. Mills, and D. Mutchler, "Planning and Certifying Software System Reliability," *IEEE Software,* vol. 10, no. 1, January 1993, pp. 88–99.

[WOH94]   Wohlin, C., and P. Runeson, "Certification of Software Components," *IEEE Trans, Software Engineering,* vol. 20, no. 6, June 1994, pp. 494–499.

PROBLEMS AND POINTS TO PONDER

25.1. If you had to pick one aspect of cleanroom software engineering that makes it radically different from conventional or object-oriented software engineering approaches, what would it be?

25.2. How do an incremental process model and certification work together to produce high-quality software?

25.3. Using box structure specification, develop "first-pass" analysis and design models for the SafeHome system.

25.4. Develop a box structure specification for a portion of the PHTRS system introduced in problem 12.13.

25.5. Develop a box structure specification for the e-mail system presented in problem 21.15.

25.6. A bubble sort algorithm is defined in the following manner:

```
procedure bubblesort;
    var i, t, integer;
    begin
    repeat until t = a[1]
        t: = a[1];
        for j: =  2 to n do
            if a[j-1] } a[j] then begin
                t: = a[j-1];
                a[j-1]: = a[j];
                a[j]: = t;
                end
    endrep
end
```

Partition the design into subfunctions and define a set of conditions that would enable you to prove that this algorithm is correct.

25.7. Document a correctness verification proof for the bubble sort discussed in problem 25.6.

25.8. Select a program component that you have designed in another context (or one assigned by your instructor) and develop a complete proof of correctness for it.

25.9. Select a program that you use regularly (e.g., an e-mail handler, a word processor, a spreadsheet program). Create a set of usage scenarios for the program. Define the probability of use for each scenario and then develop a program stimuli and probability distribution table similar to the one shown in Table 25.1.

25.10. For the program stimuli and probability distribution table developed in problem 25.9, use a random number generator to develop a set of test cases for use in statistical use testing.

25.11. In your own words, describe the intent of certification in the cleanroom software engineering context.

25.12. Write a short paper that describes the mathematics used to define the certification models described briefly in Section 25.4.2. Use [MUS87], [CUR86], and [POO93] as a starting point.

FURTHER READINGS AND OTHER INFORMATION SOURCES

The only readily available book on cleanroom software engineering is Dyer [DYE92]. The *Cleanroom Pamphlet* (Software Technology Support Center, Hill AF Base, UT, April 1995) contains reprints of a number of important articles. Linger [LIN94] is one of the better introductions to the subject. Asset Source for Software Engineering Technology, ASSET, (United States Department of Defense) offers an excellent six volume set of *Cleanroom Engineering Handbooks*. ASSET can be contacted at **info@source.asset.com.**

Michael Deck of Cleanroom Software Engineering, Inc. has prepared a bibliography on cleanroom topics. Among the references are the following:

General and introductory:

Cobb, R.H., and H.D. Mills, "Engineering Software under Statistical Quality Control," *IEEE Software,* November 1990, pp. 44–54.

Coffee, P., "Can Mass Testing Fix Windows' Quality Woes?" *PC Week,* September 19, 1994, p. 28. Responses in PC *Week,* October 10, 1994, pp. 73, 78.

Deck, M.D., "Cleanroom Software Engineering: Quality Improvement and Cost Reduction," *Proc. Pacific Northwest Software Quality Conference,* October 1994, pp. 243–258.

Hevner, A.R., S.A. Becker, and L.B. Pedowitz, "Integrated CASE for Cleanroom Development," *IEEE Software,* March 1992, pp. 69–76.

Keuffel, W., "Clean Your Room: Formal Methods for the '90s," *Computer Language,* July 1992, pp. 39–46.

Linger, Richard C., "Cleanroom Software Engineering for Zero-Defect Software", *Proc. 15th Intl. Conf. on Software Engineering,* May 1993.

Lokan, C.J., "The Cleanroom Process for Software Development," *The Australian Computer Journal,* vol. 25, no. 4, November 1993.

Management practices:

Deck, M.D., and P.A. Hausler, "Cleanroom Software Engineering: Theory and Practice," *Proc. Software Engineering and Knowledge Engineering 90,* June 1990, pp.71–77.

Linger, R.C., and Spangler, R.A., "The IBM Cleanroom Software Engineering Technology Transfer Program," *Sixth SEI Conf. on Software Engineering Education,* San Diego, CA, October 1992.

Specification, design, and review:

Deck, M.D., "Using Box Structures to Link Cleanroom and Object-Oriented Software Engineering," Technical Report 94.01b, Cleanroom Software Engineering, Inc., Boulder, CO, 1994.

Dyer, M., "Designing Software for Provable Correctness: The Direction for Quality Software," *Information and Software Technology,* vol. 30, no. 6, July/August 1988, pp. 331–340.

Testing and certification:

Dyer, M., "An Approach to Software Reliability Measurement," *Information and Software Technology,* vol. 29, no. 8, October 1987, pp. 415–420.

Whittaker, J.A., and Thomason, M.G., "A Markov Chain Model for Statistical Software Testing," *IEEE Trans. on Software Engineering,* October 1994, pp. 812–824.

Case studies and experience reports:

Green, S.E., A. Kouchakdjian, and V.R. Basili, "Evaluation of the Cleanroom Methodology in the Software Engineering Laboratory," *Proc. 14th Annual Software Engineering Workshop,* NASA Goddard Space Flight Center, November 1989.

Hausler, P.A., "A Recent Cleanroom Success Story: The Redwing Project," *Proc. 17th Annual Software Engineering Workshop,* NASA Goddard Space Flight Center, December 1992.

Head, G.E., "Six-Sigma Software Using Cleanroom Software Engineering Techniques," *Hewlett-Packard Journal,* June 1994, pp. 40–50.

Tann, L-G., "OS32 and Cleanroom," *Proc. 1st Annual European Industrial Symposium on Cleanroom Software Engineering,* Copenhagen, Denmark, 1993, pp. 1–40.

Trammel, C.J., Binder, L.H., and Snyder, C.E., "The Automated Production Control Documentation System: A Case Study in Cleanroom Software Engineering," *ACM Trans. on Software Engineering and Methodology,* vol. 1, no. 1, January 1992, pp. 81–94.

Wohlin, C., "Engineering Reliable Software," Proc. 4th *Intl. Symposium on Software Reliability Engineering,* November 1993, pp. 36–44.

Occasional discussions of cleanroom software engineering can be found in the Internet newsgroup **comp.software-eng**. A detailed discussion of cleanroom technologies including descriptions of courses offered in the subject area can be found at the IBM Cleanroom Software Technology Center:

http://www.clearlake.ibm.com/MFG/solutions/cstc.html

An extensive bibliography and articles for FTP have been prepared by Cleanroom Engineering, Inc., and can be obtained at:

http://www.csn.net/ ~ deckm/

An electronic mailing list and discussion group has been established for cleanroom methods. Information can be obtained at:

http://www.quality.org/qc/lists/sw-cleanroom.info.txt

An up-to-date list of World Wide Web references for cleanroom software engineering can be found at: **http://www.rspa.com**

CHAPTER 26

SOFTWARE REUSE

As human beings we learn the benefits of reuse as soon as we begin to perceive our world in a rational manner. We reuse almost everything—ideas, objects, arguments, abstractions, processes—that makes up the fabric of everyday life. The well-worn phrase "reinventing the wheel" says it all. It makes little sense—economically, intellectually, or pragmatically—to reinvent what has already been invented. Reinventing the wheel has plagued the software community for almost half a century.

Peter Freeman [FRE87] discusses reuse in the following manner:

> Reu se is an activity, not an object. It is such a common activity, in general, that most dictionaries don't even list it; it is assumed that the intelligent reader will understand that "reuse" means to "use something again." We are familiar with . . . recycling . . . , and the general maxim of making something "do double duty."
>
> In the context of creating software intensive systems, *reuse is very simply any procedure that produces (or helps produce) a system by reusing something from a previous development effort.* The only question then is *what* gets reused and what is the *procedure* that if followed will result in successful reuse.

In the software engineering context, reuse is both an old and a new idea. Programmers have reused ideas, objects, arguments, abstractions, and processes since the earliest days of computing, but our approach to reuse has been ad hoc. Today, complex, high-quality computer-based systems must be built in very short time periods. This demands a more organized approach to reuse.

But a number of questions arise. Is it possible to construct complex systems by assembling them from a catalog of reusable components? Can this be accomplished in a cost- and time-effective manner? Can appropriate incentives be established to encourage software engineers to reuse, rather than reinvent? Is management willing to incur the added expense associated with creating reusable software components? Can the library of components necessary to accomplish reuse be created in a way that makes it accessible to those who need it? Can components that do exist be found by those who need them?

These and many other questions continue to haunt the community of researchers and industry professionals who are striving to make software component reuse a mainstream approach to software engineering. We look at some of the answers in this chapter.

26.1   MANAGEMENT ISSUES[1]

A quick study of the possible benefits of reusing software reveals that there is much more to be gained than a simple cost saving during the development of a software product. For example, the reuse of a software component which is known to be reliable introduces less risk than redesigning and recoding the same component for each new application. Efficiency issues can also be more effectively addressed if one can focus attention on optimizing a set of reusable components rather than having to continually re-optimize new versions of previously existing modules.

However, the obvious benefits of reuse are often outweighed by organizational roadblocks, a lack of understanding of the true nature of software reuse, and a weak or nonexistent strategy for encouraging and implementing reuse technology. We consider each of these topics in the sections that follow.

26.1.1   Roadblocks to Reuse

There remains confusion about what an increased emphasis on software reusability might mean. Although many industry observers acknowledge that some existing software development practices will have to change, they seem unaware of which specific items will be different. There are a number of roadblocks to software reuse. In order to develop an effective reuse strategy, managers (and technologists) must understand what these roadblocks are.

1. *Few companies and organizations have anything that even slightly resembles a comprehensive software reusability plan.* Although many companies and organizations have someone somewhere who is "researching" the idea, few have any intention of implementing such a plan in the near future. Software reuse is hardly a "top-priority item" for many software firms.

2. *Although an increasing number of software vendors currently sell tools or components that provide direct assistance for software reuse, the majority*

---

[1]This section contains an edited and reorganized version of a series of articles written by Edward Berard posted on the Internet newsgroup **comp.software-eng** in 1994. This material is used with his permission.

of software developers do not use them. Software products that assist in achieving reuse include those that provide infrastructure support (e.g., repositories for reusable components, browsers), tools that help create reusable components, and entire software reusability systems—tools and software components specifically designed to aid and foster the reuse of software.

3. *Relatively little training is available to help software engineers and managers understand and apply reuse.* Not only do few training vehicles target reuse, but the topic is mentioned only briefly in most training that addresses software engineering.

4. *Many software practitioners continue to believe that reuse is "more trouble than it's worth."* It is not uncommon to hear technical personnel recite long lists of the "disadvantages of reusing software." Managers seem equally committed to maintaining the status quo. Even when managers purchase the tools and training necessary for rudimentary software reuse, staff resistance to the concept can still be high.

5. *Many companies continue to encourage software development methodologies which do not facilitate reuse* (e.g., functional decomposition), while discouraging others that seem to encourage reuse (e.g., object-oriented approaches).

6. *Few companies provide incentives to produce reusable program components.* In fact, there are disincentives. The customer for the current project will be hesitant to fund the extra expense required to develop reusable components. As a result, project managers push to get the job done with program components that are as specific as possible.

In addition to the technical problems which must be addressed, many other connected issues have an impact on reuse. Political, managerial, legal, cultural, financial, marketing, and productization issues must also be considered.

26.1.2   A Hardware Analogy

In the computer hardware industry, reuse is the norm. For example, there are standard CPU chips, standard RAM, mathematical coprocessors, and ROM chips. These and other integrated circuits are used in a wide variety of applications. A long time ago, electronics engineers discovered that one of the most important axioms of reusability was generality.

Unlike their software counterparts, electronics engineers do not have to verify, for example, that every "op-code" supported by a particular CPU is executed in a specific application. Nor do they have to demonstrate that every last byte of RAM is utilized. Electronics engineers have data that provide a quantitative indication of the reliability of the chip.

How does one apply the above analogy to reusable software? Consider the design of a reusable software component. To be truly reusable, a software component must be usable in some place other than its current specific application (or part of an application). To increase the chances of this happening, the software engineer must make the component more general. In fact, there are well-known ways of increasing the generality of a software component to a very high level.

Of course, there are trade-offs. Increasing the generality may decrease the efficiency, or even increase the complexity. These and other considerations must be balanced against such factors as the potential increased reliability resulting from using a known verified component and the cost and time savings resulting from software reuse.

Over the years, much has been learned about software reuse. Although debate continues about specific issues, the following points are generally accepted:

- Much more than source code can be reused. In fact, designs, plans, test data, and documentation (among other items in the software configuration) can be reused. Code reuse provides the smallest gains in productivity and reliability. Significantly greater benefit is achieved by reusing designs and the documentation associated with "reusable source code." Therefore, reusability is not a concept that is limited to coding.
- Research seems to indicate, and practice seems to show, that the majority of many software products can be assembled from reusable components.
- There are any number of metrics associated with software reuse. They range from metrics which measure the sheer bulk of source code and documentation reused in an application to metrics which measure the affects of software reusability (e.g., software productivity metrics).

Software reusability technology is indeed a collection of things. These things include reusable components, taxonomies, reusability systems, composition concepts, methodologies, and others. This technology is more coupled with the size of the software product than it is with the scale at which the reuse is to take place.

Software design methods (Chapters 14 and 21) do play an important part in software reuse. Some methods enhance software reuse; others discourage it. We have known for some time that software designs should be constructed so that they can easily be modified. We are only now beginning to understand that by bringing software reusability issues to the first phases of the software process, we can greatly enhance the impact of software reuse. Finally, by studying the designs of many systems within a particular application domain, candidate components for reuse can be isolated and developed.

26.1.3 Some Suggestions for Establishing an Approach to Reuse

The following steps will assist an organization in making the changes necessary to fully exploit the concept of software reusability:

1. Establish an internal software reuse plan. Such a plan can help an organization control both the quality and costs associated with software.
2. Require that software reusability be an integral part of any technical and managerial training. This should be especially true for object-oriented training.

3. In accordance with an in-house software reusability plan, acquire the tools and libraries that will most positively contribute to the reuse of software.

4. Encourage the use of methods and tools which have been demonstrated to enhance the reuse of software.

5. Track and measure both the reuse of software and the impact of software reuse. Policy decisions should be made on "hard data," not on guesswork.

6. Management must let it be known that it actively encourages the reuse of software.

7. Recognize that more than just "modules" can be reused. Tools, test data, designs, plans, environments, and other software items can be reused.

8. Above all, recognize that software reuse is not "business as usual." A commitment to software reuse will require some changes. These changes should be introduced in an effective manner. Remember that the concept of software reuse is alien to most technical and managerial personnel.

26.2   THE REUSE PROCESS

Reuse should be an integral part of every software process. In Chapter 2, a "component assembly model" (Figure 26.1) was used to illustrate how a library of reusable components can be integrated into a typical evolutionary process model. Later in this section, we explore a process model that emphasizes the activities that must occur to make reuse happen. But first, it is necessary to understand the "artifacts" that are reused when software engineering occurs.

26.2.1   Reusable Artifacts

We have already noted that software reuse encompasses more than just source code. But how much more? Capers Jones [JON94] defines 10 software artifacts that are candidates for reuse:

Project plans.   The basic structure and much of the content (e.g., the SQA plan) of a software project plan (see Part Two of this book) can be reused from project to project. This reduces the time required to develop the plan and the uncertainty associated with establishing schedules, risk analysis, and other features.

Cost estimates.   Because similar function is often implemented in different projects, it may be possible to reuse estimates (Chapter 5) for that function with little or no modification.

Architecture.   There are relatively few distinct program and data architectures (Chapter 13), even when different application domains are considered. It is possible to create a set of generic architectural templates (e.g., a transaction processing architecture) and establish those templates as a reusable framework for design.

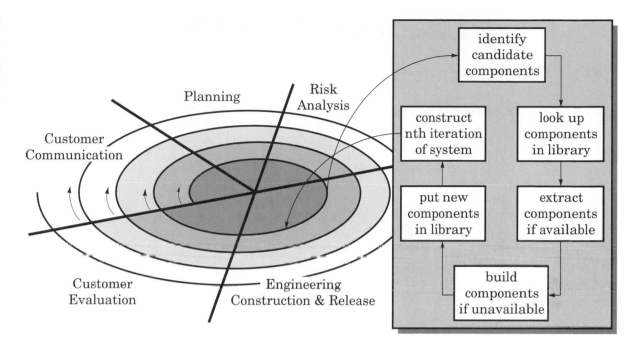

FIGURE 26.1. The component assembly model

Requirements models and specifications. Models and specifications for classes and objects (Chapter 20) are obvious candidates for reuse. In addition, analysis models (e.g., data flow diagrams) developed using conventional software engineering approaches (Chapter 12) can also be reused.

Designs. Architectural, data, interface, and procedural designs developed using conventional methods (Chapter 14) are candidates for reuse. More commonly, system and object designs (Chapter 21) are reused.

Source code. Verified program components written in compatible programming languages are candidates for reuse.

User and technical documentation. It is often possible to reuse large portions of user and technical documentation, even though the specific applications differ.

Human interfaces. Probably the most widely reused software artifact, GUI software is commonly reused. Because it can account for 60 percent of the code volume of an application, the benefits of reuse are significant.

Data. Among the most commonly reused artifacts, data encompasses internal tables, lists, and record structures, as well as files and complete databases.

Test cases. Whenever a design or code component is to be reused, the relevant test case should be "attached" to it.

Table 26.1 [JON94] presents anecdotal data (from military and system projects) that indicate the return on a $1.00 investment after four years and 24

TABLE 26.1

VALUE OF SOFTWARE REUSE OVER FOUR YEARS [JON94]

Reusable Artifact	Four-year Return
Project plans	$2.00
Cost estimates	3.00
Architecture	1.50
Requirements models/specs	3.00
Designs	5.00
Source code	6.00
User/technical documentation	1.50
Human interfaces	1.00
Data	3.50
Test cases	3.50

uses for each of the artifacts noted above. The overall impact is described by Jones [JON94]: "[T]he aggregate value of reusing all 10 artifacts generates what is probably the best return of any known software technology."

It is important to note that reuse extends beyond the deliverable artifacts discussed above and also includes elements of the software engineering process. Specific analysis modeling methods, inspection techniques, test case design techniques, quality assurance procedures, and many other software engineering practices can be "reused." For example, if a software team applies cleanroom software engineering (Chapter 25) effectively, the approach may have relevance to another project. To make this determination, it is necessary to define a set of characterization functions (Section 26.3.2) that enable potential users of cleanroom to make an appropriate determination on its applicability.

26.2.2 A Process Model

A variety of process models have been proposed for reuse. Each emphasizes parallel tracks in which domain engineering (Section 26.3) occurs concurrently with software engineering. Domain engineering performs the work required to establish a set of software artifacts that can be reused by the software engineer. These artifacts are then transported across a "boundary" that separates domain engineering from software engineering.

Figure 26.2 illustrates a typical process model that explicitly accommodates reuse [CHR95]. Domain engineering creates a model of the application domain that is used as a basis for analyzing user requirements in the software engineering flow. The software architecture (and corresponding structure points, see Section 26.3.3) provide input for the design of the application. Finally, after reusable components have been constructed (as part of domain engineering), they are made available to the software engineers during the software construction activity.

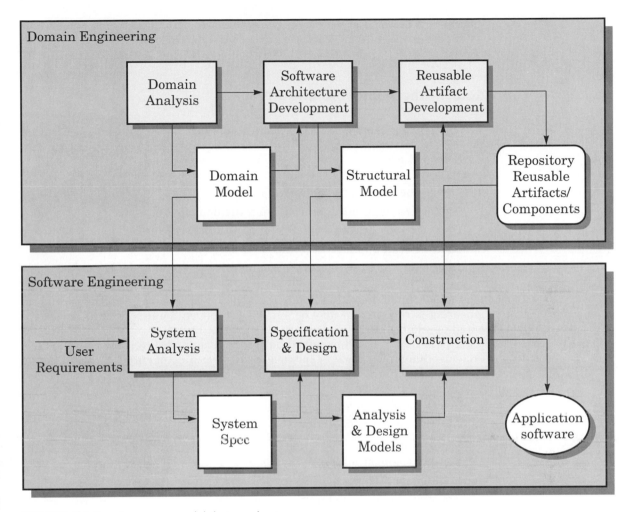

FIGURE 26.2. A process model that emphasizes reuse

26.3   DOMAIN ENGINEERING

The intent of *domain engineering* is to identify, construct, catalog, and disseminate a set of software artifacts that have applicability to existing and future software in a particular application domain. The overall goal is to establish mechanisms that enable software engineers to share these artifacts—to reuse them—during work on new and existing systems.

Domain engineering includes three major activities—analysis, construction, and dissemination. An overview of domain analysis was presented in Chapter 20. However, the topic is revisited in the sections that follow. Domain construction and dissemination are considered in later sections in this chapter.

It can be argued that "reuse will disappear, not by elimination, but by integration" into the fabric of software engineering practice [TRA95]. As greater emphasis is placed on reuse, some believe that domain engineering will become as important as software engineering over the next decade.

26.3.1 The Domain Analysis Process

In Chapter 20, we discussed the overall approach to domain analysis within the context of object-oriented software engineering. The steps in the process were defined as:

1. Define the domain to be investigated.
2. Categorize the items extracted from the domain
3. Collect a representative sample of applications in the domain
4. Analyze each application in the sample
5. Develop an analysis model for the objects

It is important to note that domain analysis is applicable to any software engineering paradigm and may be applied for conventional as well as object-oriented development.

Prieto-Diaz [PRI87] expands the second domain analysis step noted above and suggests an eight-step approach to the identification and categorization of reusable artifacts:

1. Select specific functions/objects.
2. Abstract functions/objects.
3. Define a taxonomy.
4. Identify common features.
5. Identify specific relationships.
6. Abstract the relationships.
7. Derive a functional model.
8. Define a domain language.

A domain language enables the specification and later construction of applications within the domain.

Although the steps noted above provide a useful model for domain analysis, they do not provide any guidance for deciding which software artifacts are candidates for reuse. Hutchinson and Hindley [HUT88] suggest the following set of pragmatic questions as a guide for identifying reusable software components:

- Is component functionality required on future implementations?
- How common is the component's function within the domain?
- Is there duplication of the component's function within the domain?
- Is the component hardware-dependent?

- Does the hardware remain unchanged between implementations?
- Can the hardware specifics be removed to another component?
- Is the design optimized enough for the next implementation?
- Can we parameterize a nonreusable component so that it becomes reusable?
- Is the component reusable in many implementations with only minor changes?
- Is reuse through modification feasible?
- Can a nonreusable component be decomposed to yield reusable components?
- How valid is component decomposition for reuse?

An in-depth discussion of domain analysis methods is beyond the scope of this book. For additional information on domain analysis, see [PRI93].

26.3.2 Characterization Functions

It is sometimes difficult to determine whether a potentially reusable artifact is in fact applicable in a particular situation. To make this determination, it is necessary to define a set of *domain characteristics* that are shared by all software within a domain. A domain characteristic defines some generic attribute of all products that exist within the domain. For example, generic characteristics might include the importance of safety/reliability, programming language, concurrency in processing, and many others.

A set of domain characteristics for a reusable artifact can be represented as $\{D_p\}$ where each item, D_{pi}, in the set represents a specific domain characteristic. The value assigned to D_{pi} represents an ordinal scale that is an indication of the relevance of the characteristic for artifact p. A typical scale [BAS94] might be:

1:     not relevant to whether reuse is appropriate

2:     relevant only under unusual circumstances

3:     relevant; the artifact can be modified so that it can be used, despite differences

4:     clearly relevant, and if the new software does not have this characteristic, reuse will be inefficient; reuse may still be possible

5:     clearly relevant, and if the new software does not have this characteristic, reuse will be ineffective; reuse is not recommended

When new software, w, is to be built within the application domain, a set of domain characteristics is derived for it. A comparison is then made between D_{pi} and D_{wi} to determine whether the existing artifact p can be effectively reused in application w.

Table 26.2 [BAS94] lists typical domain characteristics that can have an impact on software reuse. These domain characteristics must be taken into account in order to reuse an artifact effectively.

TABLE 26.2

DOMAIN CHARACTERISTICS AFFECTING REUSE [BAS94]

Product	Process	Personnel
Requirements stability	Process model	Motivation
Concurrent software	Process conformance	Education
Memory constraints	Project environment	Experience/training
Application size	Schedule constraints	• application domain
User interface complexity	Budget constraints	• process
Programming language(s)	Productivity	• platform
Safety/reliability		• language
Lifetime requirements		Development team
Product quality		productivity
Product reliability		

Even when software to be engineered clearly exists within an application domain, the reusable artifacts within that domain must be analyzed to determine their applicability. In some cases (hopefully, a limited number), "reinventing the wheel" may still be the most cost-effective choice.

26.3.3   Structural Modeling and Structure Points

When domain analysis is applied, the analyst looks for repeating patterns in the applications that reside within a domain. *Structural modeling* is a pattern-based domain engineering approach that works under the assumption that every application domain has repeating patterns (of function, data, and behavior) that have reuse potential.

Pollak and Rissman [POL94] describe structural models in the following way:

> Structural models consist of a small number of structural elements manifesting clear patterns of interaction. The architectures of systems using structural models are characterized by multiple ensembles that are composed from these model elements. Thus, the complex interactions among the systems many architectural units emerge from simple patterns of interaction among this small number of elements.

Each application domain can be characterized by a structural model (e.g., aircraft avionics differ greatly in specifics, but all modern software in this domain has the same structural model). Therefore, the structural model is an architectural artifact that can and should be reused across applications within the domain.

McMahon [MCM95] describes a *structure point* as "a distinct construct within a structural model." Structure points have three distinct characteristics:

1. A structure point is an abstraction that should have a limited number of instances. Restating this in object-oriented jargon (Chapter 19), the size of the class hierarchy should be small. In addition, the abstraction should recur throughout applications in the domain. Otherwise, the effort required to verify, document, and disseminate the structure point cannot be cost-justified.

2. The rules that govern the use of the structure point should be easily understood. In addition, the interface to the structure point should be relatively simple.

3. The structure point should implement information hiding by hiding all complexity contained within the structure point itself. This reduces the perceived complexity of the overall system.

As an example of structure points as architectural patterns for a system, consider the domain of software for alarm systems. This domain might encompass systems as simple as SafeHome[2] or as complex as the alarm system for an industrial process. In every case, however, a set of predictable structural patterns are encountered:

- an *interface* that enables the user to interact with the system
- a *bounds setting mechanism* that allows the user to establish bounds on the parameters to be measured
- a *sensor management mechanism* that communicates with all monitoring sensors
- a *response mechanism* that reacts to the input provided by the sensor management system
- a *control mechanism* that enables the user to control the manner in which monitoring is carried out.

Each of these structure points is integrated into a domain architecture.

It is possible to define generic structure points that transcend a number of different application domains [STA94]:

Application front end. The GUI, including all menus, panels, input, and command editing facilities

Database. The repository for all objects relevant to the application domain

Computational engine. The numerical and nonnumerical models that manipulate data

Reporting facility. The function that produces output of all kinds

Application editor. The mechanism for customizing the application to the needs of specific users

---

[2]The SafeHome security system has been used as an example in earlier chapters.

Structure points have been suggested as an alternative to lines of code and function points for software cost estimation [MCM95]. A brief discussion of costing using structure points is presented in Section 26.6.2.

26.4   BUILDING REUSABLE COMPONENTS

There is nothing magical about creating software that can be reused. Design concepts such as abstraction, hiding, functional independence, refinement, and structured programming, along with object-oriented methods, testing, SQA, and correctness verification methods—all contribute to the creation of software components that are reusable.[3] In this section we will not revisit these topics. Rather, we consider the reuse-specific issues that are complementary to solid software engineering practices.

26.4.1   Analysis and Design for Reuse

The components of the analysis model were discussed in detail in Parts Three and Four of this book. Data, functional, and behavioral models (represented in a variety of different notations) can be created to describe what a particular application must accomplish. Written specifications are then used to describe these models and result in a complete description of requirements.

Ideally, the analysis model is analyzed to determine those elements of the model that point to existing reusable artifacts. The problem is extracting information from the requirements model in a form that can lead to "specification matching." Bellinzoni and his colleagues [BEL95] describe one approach for object-oriented systems:

> Components are defined and stored as specification, design, and implementation classes at various levels of abstraction—with each class being an engineered description of a product from previous applications. The specification knowledge—development knowledge—is stored in the form of *reuse-suggestion* classes, which contain directions for retrieving reusable components on the basis of their description and for composing and tailoring them after retrieval.

Automated tools are used to browse a repository in an attempt to match the requirement noted in the current specification with those described for existing reusable components (classes). Characterization functions (Section 26.3.2) and keywords are used to help find potentially reusable components.

If specification matching yields components that fit the needs of the current application, the designer can extract these components from a reuse library (repository) and use them in the design of the new system. If design components cannot be found, the software engineer must apply conventional or OO design methods to create them. It is at this point—when the designer begins

---

[3]To learn more about these topics, see Chapters 13, 14, 16, 17, 21, and 25.

to create a new component—that *design for reuse (DFR)* should be considered.

As we have already noted, design for reuse requires the software engineer to apply solid software design concepts and principles (Chapter 13). But the characteristics of the application domain must also be considered. Binder [BIN93] suggests a number of key issues that should be considered[4] as a basis for design for reuse:

> **Standard data.** The application domain should be investigated, and standard global data structures (e.g., file structures or a complete database) should be identified. All design components can then be characterized to make use of these standard data structures.

> **Standard interface protocols.** Three levels of interface protocol should be established: the nature of intramodular interfaces, the design of external technical (nonhuman) interfaces, and the human–machine interface.

> **Program templates.** The structure model (Section 26.3.3) can serve as a template for the architectural design of a new program.

Once standard data, interfaces, and program templates have been established, the designer has a framework in which to create the design. New components that conform to this framework have a higher probability for subsequent reuse.

26.4.2 Construction Methods

Like design, the construction of reusable artifacts draws on software engineering methods that have been discussed elsewhere in this book. Construction can be accomplished using conventional third generation programming languages, fourth generation languages and code generators, visual programming techniques, or more advanced tools.

A representative example of more advanced construction techniques has been developed by Netron, Inc. [BAS94b]. Called *frame technology,* the Netron approach defines a set of adaptable, generic components called *frames.* Like objects, frames encapsulate data and operations, but they extend the definition of an object by incorporating mechanisms that enable a software engineer to adapt the frame by selecting, deleting, modifying, or iterating any of the subcomponents that make up the frame.

An application is constructed by assembling components from a frame hierarchy. Frames at the bottom of the hierarchy are analogous to worker modules in a factored architecture (Chapter 13). That is, they contain data structures and operations that perform low-level system functions (e.g., operating system interaction, interface construction, database interaction). Frames that reside in the middle of the hierarchy focus on functions that are relevant to specific information systems domains (e.g., transaction processing, banking, customer service). At the top of the hierarchy is a "specification frame" that acts

---

[4]In general, the preparations noted for design for reuse should be undertaken as part of domain engineering (Section 27.3).

as "the master blueprint for the system and the only frame that the developer creates to define the system" [YOU94].

26.4.3 Component-Based Development

When reuse predominates during the development of an application, the construction approach is sometimes referred to as *component-based development* or *component software*. As we have already seen, domain engineering provides the library of reusable components that are required for component-based development. Some of these reusable components are developed in-house, others can be extracted from existing applications, and still others may be acquired from third parties.

But how do we create a library of components that have a consistent structure—that can be acquired from a variety of different internal and external sources and still be integrated into any system within an application domain? The answer lies in the adoption of a standard for such components. A set of four "architectural ingredients" [ADL95] should be present to implement component-based development:

Data exchange model. Mechanisms that enable users and applications to interact and transfer data (e.g., drag and drop, cut and paste) should be defined for all reusable components. The data exchange mechanisms not only allow human-to-software and component-to-component data transfer, but also enable transfer among system resources (e.g., dragging a file to a printer icon for output.)

Automation. A variety of tools, macros, and scripts should be implemented to facilitate interaction between reusable components.

Structured storage. Heterogeneous data (e.g., graphical data, voice, text, and numerical data) contained in a "compound document" should be organized and accessed as a single data structure rather than a collection of separate files. "Structured data maintains a descriptive index of nesting structures that applications can freely navigate to locate, create, or edit individual data contents as directed by the end user" [ADL95].

Underlying object model. The object model ensures that components developed in different programming languages that reside on different platforms can be interoperable. That is, objects must be capable of communicating across a network. To achieve this, the object model defines a standard for component interoperability. The standard is language independent and is defined using an *interface definition language (IDL)*.

Because the potential impact of reuse on the software industry is enormous, a number of major companies and industry consortia[5] have proposed standards for component software:

---

[5]An excellent discussion of the "distributed objects" standards that are discussed briefly here is presented in [ORF96].

OpenDoc. A consortium of major technology companies (including IBM, Apple, and Novell) have proposed the OpenDoc standard for compound documents and component software. The standard defines the services, control infrastructure, and architecture that must be implemented to enable components provided by one developer to interoperate with components provided by another developer.

OMG/CORBA. The Object Management Group has published a *common object request broker architecture (OMG/CORBA)*. An *object request broker (ORB)* provides a variety of services that enable reusable components (objects) to communicate with other components, regardless of their location within a system. When components are built using the OMG/CORBA standard, integration of those components (without modification) within a system is assured.[6]

To use a client/server metaphor, objects within the client application request one or more services from the ORB server. Requests are made via IDL or dynamically at run-time. An interface repository contains all necessary information about the service requests and response formats. CORBA is discussed further in Chapter 28.

OLE 2.0. Microsoft has developed a component object model (COM) that provides a specification for using objects produced by various vendors within a single application. *Object linking and embedding (OLE)* is part of COM and defines a standard structure for reusable components. OLE is used as part of Microsoft's operating systems (e.g., Windows 95, Windows NT).

Which of these standards will dominate the industry? There is no easy answer at this time. Currently OLE is used more widely (due to widespread use in Windows-based applications). But many OMG/CORBA tools and development environments are being introduced. For further discussion of component standards and the tools that support them see [ADL95] and [LIN95].

26.5   CLASSIFYING AND RETRIEVING COMPONENTS

Consider a large university library. Tens of thousands of books, periodicals, and other information resources are available for use. But to access these resources, a categorization scheme must be developed. To navigate this large volume of information, librarians have defined a classification scheme that includes a library of congress classification code, keywords, author names, and other index entries. All enable the user to find the needed resource quickly and easily.

Now, consider a large component repository. Tens of thousands of reusable software components reside in it. But how does a software engineer find the one she needs? To answer this question, another question arises: How do we describe software components in unambiguous, classifiable terms? These are difficult questions, and no definitive answer has yet been developed. In this section we explore current directions that will enable future software engineers to navigate reuse libraries.

---

[6]OMG documents can be obtained at **http://www.omg.org/**.

26.5.1 Describing Reusable Components

A reusable software component can be described in many ways, but an ideal description encompasses what Tracz [TRA90] has called the *3C Model*—concept, content, and context.

The *concept* of a software component is "a description of what the component does" [WHI95]. The interface to the component is fully described and the semantics—represented within the context of pre- and postconditions—is identified. The concept should communicate the intent of the component.

The *content* of a component describes how the concept is realized. In essence, the content is information that is hidden from casual users and need be known only to those who intend to modify the component.

The *context* places a reusable software component within its domain of applicability. That is, by specifying conceptual, operational, and implementation features, the context enables a software engineer to find the appropriate component to meet application requirements.

To be of use in a pragmatic setting, concept, content, and context must be translated into a concrete specification scheme. There have been dozens of papers and articles written about classification schemes for reusable software components.[7] The methods proposed can be categorized into three major areas: library and information science methods, artificial intelligence methods, and hypertext systems. The vast majority of work done to date suggests the use of library science methods for component classification.

Figure 26.3 presents a taxonomy of library science indexing methods. *Controlled indexing vocabularies* limit the terms or syntax that can be used to classify an object (component). Uncontrolled indexing vocabularies place no restrictions on the nature of the description. The majority of classification schemes for software components fall into three categories:

Enumerated Classification Components are described by defining a hierarchical structure in which classes and varying levels of subclasses of software components are defined. Actual components are listed at the lowest level of any path in the enumerated hierarchy. For example, an enumerated hierarchy for window operations[8] might be

```
window operations
    display
        open
            menu-based
                openWindow
            system-based
                sysWindow
        close
            via pointer
                . . . .
```

---

[7][WHI95] contains an extensive bibliography.

[8]Only a small subset of all possible operations is noted.

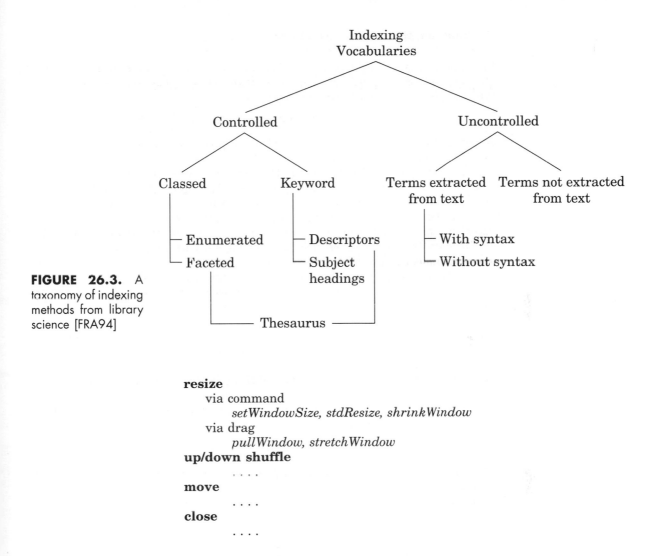

FIGURE 26.3. A taxonomy of indexing methods from library science [FRA94]

resize
    via command
        setWindowSize, stdResize, shrinkWindow
    via drag
        pullWindow, stretchWindow
up/down shuffle
    . . . .
move
    . . . .
close
    . . . .

The hierarchical structure of an enumerated classification scheme makes it easy to understand and to use. However, before a hierarchy can be built, domain engineering must be conducted so that sufficient knowledge of the proper entries in the hierarchy is available.

Faceted Classification   A domain area is analyzed, and a set of basic descriptive features are identified. These features, called *facets,* are then prioritized by importance and connected to a component. A facet can describe the function that the component performs, the data that are manipulated, the context in which they are applied, or any other feature. The set of facets that describe a component is called the *facet descriptor.* Generally, the facet description is limited to no more than seven or eight facets.

As a simple illustration of the use of facets in component classification, consider a scheme [LIA93] that makes use of the following facet descriptor:

{function, object type, system type}

Each facet in the facet descriptor takes on one or more values that are generally descriptive keywords. For example, if *function* is a facet of a component, typical values assigned to this facet might be:

$$function = (copy, from) \quad \text{or} \quad (copy, replace, all)$$

The use of multiple facet values enables the primitive function *copy* to be refined more fully.

Keywords (values) are assigned to the set of facets for each component in a reuse library. When a software engineer wants to query the library for possible components for a design, a list of values is specified and the library is searched for matches. Automated tools can be used to incorporate a *thesaurus function*. This enables the search to encompass not only the keyword specified by the software engineer, but also technical synonyms for those keywords.

A faceted classification scheme gives the domain engineer greater flexibility in specifying complex descriptors for components [FRA94]. Because new facet values can be added easily, the faceted classification scheme is easier to extend and adapt that the enumeration approach.

Attribute-Value Classification   A set of attributes are defined for all components in a domain area. Values are then assigned to these attributes in much the same way as faceted classification. In fact, attribute value classification is similar to faceted classification with the following exceptions: (1) There is no limit on the number of attributes that can be used; (2) attributes are not assigned priorities; and (3) the thesaurus function is not used.

Based on an empirical study of each of the above classification techniques, Frakes and Pole [FRA94] indicate that there is no clear "best" technique and that "no method did more than moderately well in search effectiveness. . . ." It would appear that further work remains to be done in the development of effective classification schemes for reuse libraries.

26.5.2 The Reuse Environment

Software component reuse must be supported by an environment that encompasses the following elements:

- a *component database* capable of storing software components and the classification information necessary to retrieve them
- a *library management system* that provides access to the database
- a *software component retrieval system* (e.g., an object request broker) that allows a client application to retrieve components and services from the library server
- *CASE tools* that support the integration of reused components into a new design or implementation.

Each of these functions interacts with or is embodied within the confines of a reuse library.

The *reuse library* is one element of a larger CASE repository (Chapter 29) and provides facilities for the storage of a wide variety of reusable artifacts (e.g., specifications, designs, code, test cases, user guides). The library encompasses a database and the tools that are necessary to query the database and retrieve components from it. A component classification scheme (Section 26.5.1) serves as the basis for library queries.

Queries are often characterized using the *context* element of the 3C Model described earlier. If an initial query results in a voluminous list of candidate components, the query is refined to narrow the list. *Concept* and *content* information are then extracted (after candidate components are found) to assist the developer in selecting the proper component.

A detailed discussion of the structure of reuse libraries and the tools that manage them is beyond the scope of this book. The interested reader should see [HOO91] and [LIN95] for additional information.

26.6   ECONOMICS OF SOFTWARE REUSE

Software reuse has an intuitive appeal. In theory, it should provide a software organization with advantages in quality and timeliness. And these should translate into cost savings. But are there hard data that support our intuition?

To answer this question we must first understand what it is that can be reused in a software engineering context and then what the costs associated with reuse really are. As a consequence, it is possible to develop a cost–benefit analysis for reuse.

26.6.1 Impact on Quality, Productivity, and Cost

Over the past few years, considerable evidence from industry case studies (e.g., [HEN95], [MCM95], [LIM94]) indicates that substantial business benefits can be derived from aggressive software reuse. Product quality, development productivity, and overall cost are all improved.

Quality In an ideal setting, a software component that is developed for reuse would be verified to be correct (see Chapter 25) and would contain no defects. In reality, formal verification is not carried out routinely, and defects can and do occur. However, with each reuse, defects are found and eliminated, and a component's quality improves as a result. Over time, the component becomes virtually defect free.

In a study conducted at Hewlett-Packard, Lim [LIM94] reports that the defect rate for reused code is 0.9 defects per KLOC, while the rate for newly developed software is 4.1 defects per KLOC. For an application that was composed of 68 percent reused code, the defect rate was 2.0 defects per KLOC—a 51 percent improvement from the expected rate, had the application been developed without reuse. Henry and Faller [HEN95] report a 35 percent improvement in quality. Although anecdotal reports span a reasonably wide spectrum of quality improvement percentages, it is fair to state that reuse provides a nontrivial benefit in terms of the quality and reliability for delivered software.

Productivity When reusable artifacts are applied throughout the software process, less time is spent creating the plans, models, documents, code, and data that are required to create a deliverable system. It follows that the same level of functionality is delivered to the customer with less input effort. Hence, productivity is improved. Although percentage productivity improvement reports are notoriously difficult to interpret,[9] it appears that 30 to 50 percent reuse can result in productivity improvements in the 25 to 40 percent range.

Cost The net cost savings for reuse are estimated by projecting the cost of the project if it were developed from scratch, C_s, and then subtracting the sum of the costs associated with reuse, C_r, and the actual cost of the software as delivered, C_d.

C_s can be determined by applying one or more of the estimation techniques discussed in Chapter 5. The costs associated with reuse, C_r, include [CHR95]:

- Domain analysis and modeling
- Domain architecture development
- Increased documentation to facilitate reuse
- Maintenance and enhancement of reuse artifacts
- Royalties and licenses for externally acquired components
- Creation or acquisition and operation of a reuse repository
- Training of personnel in design and construction for reuse

Although costs associated with domain analysis (Section 26.4) and the operation of a reuse repository can be substantial, they can be amortized across many projects. Many of the other costs noted above address issues that are part of good software engineering practice, whether or not reuse is a priority.

26.6.2 Cost Analysis Using Structure Points

In Section 26.3.3, we defined a structure point as an architectural pattern that recurs through a particular application domain. A software designer (or system engineer) can develop an architecture for a new application, system, or product by defining a domain architecture and then populating it with structure points.

---

[9]There are many extenuating circumstances (e.g., application area, problem complexity, team structure and size, project duration, technology applied) that can have an impact on the productivity of a project team.

These structure points are either individual reusable components or packages of reusable components.

Even though structure points are reusable, their adaptation, integration, and maintenance costs are not trivial. Before proceeding with reuse, the project manager must understand the costs associated with the use of structure points.

Since all structure points (and reusable components in general) have a past history, cost data can be collected for each. In an ideal setting, the adaptation, integration, and maintenance costs associated with each component in a reuse library are maintained from each instance of usage. These data can then be analyzed to develop projected costs for the next instance of reuse.

As an example, consider a new application, X, that requires 60 percent new code and the reuse of three structure points, SP_1, SP_2 and SP_3. Each of these reusable components has been used in a number of other applications, and average costs for adaptation, integration, and maintenance are available.

To estimate the effort required to deliver X, the following must be determined:

$$\text{overall effort} = E_{new} + E_{adapt} + E_{int}$$

where E_{new} is the effort required to engineer and construct new software components (determined using techniques described in Chapter 5)

E_{adapt} is the effort required to adapt SP_1, SP_2, and SP_3

E_{int} is the effort required to integrate SP_1, SP_2, and SP_3

The effort required to adapt and integrate SP_1, SP_2, and SP_3 is determined by taking the average of historical data collected for adaptation and integration of the reusable components in other applications.

26.6.3 Reuse Metrics

A variety of software metrics have been developed in an attempt to measure the benefits of reuse within a computer-based system. The benefit associated with reuse within a system S can be expressed as a ratio

$$R_b(S) = [C_{noreuse} - C_{reuse}]/C_{noreuse} \qquad (26.1)$$

where $C_{noreuse}$ is the cost of developing S with no reuse

C_{reuse} is the cost of developing S with reuse

It follows that $R_b(S)$ can be expressed as a nondimensional value in the range

$$0 \le R_b(S) \le 1 \qquad (26.2)$$

Devanbu and his colleagues [DEV95] suggest that (1) R_b will be affected by the design of the system; (2) since R_b is effected by the design, it is important to make R_b a part of an assessment of design alternatives; and (3) the benefits associated with reuse are closely aligned to the cost benefit of each individual reusable component. The higher the value of $R_b(S)$, the more attractive reuse becomes.

A general measure of reuse in object-oriented systems, termed *reuse leverage* [BAS94a] is defined as:

$$R_{\text{lev}} = \text{OBJ}_{\text{reused}}/\text{OBJ}_{\text{built}} \qquad (26.3)$$

where $\text{OBJ}_{\text{reused}}$ is the number of objects reused in a system

$\text{OBJ}_{\text{built}}$ is the number of objects built for a system

It follows that as R_{lev} increases, R_b also increases.

26.7   SUMMARY

Component reuse offers inherent benefits in software quality, developer productivity, and overall system cost. And yet, many roadblocks must be overcome before the reuse process model is widely used throughout the industry.

A variety of reusable artifacts can be acquired by a software engineer. These include technical representations of the software (e.g., specifications, architectural models, design, and code), documents, test data, and even process-related tasks (e.g., inspection techniques).

The reuse process encompasses two concurrent subprocesses—domain engineering and software engineering. The intent of domain engineering is to identify, construct, catalog, and disseminate a set of software artifacts in a particular application domain. Software engineering then extracts these artifacts for reuse during the development of a new system.

Analysis and design techniques for reusable components draw on the same principles and concepts that are part of good software engineering practice. Reusable components should be designed within an environment that establishes standard data structures, interface protocols, and program architectures for each application domain.

Component-based development uses a data exchange model, tools, structured storage, and an underlying object model to construct applications from pre-existing components. The object model generally conforms to one or more component standards (e.g., OMG/CORBA) that define the manner in which an application can access reusable objects. Classification schemes enable a developer to find and retrieve reusable components and conform to a model that identifies concept, content, and context. Enumerated classification, faceted classification, and attribute-value classification are representative of many component classification schemes.

The economics of software reuse are addressed by a single question: Is it cost effective to build less and reuse more? In general, the answer is "yes," but a software project planner must consider the nontrivial costs associated with the adaptation and integration of reusable components.

REFERENCES

[ADL95]   Adler, R.M., "Emerging Standards for Component Software, *IEEE Computer,* vol. 28, no. 3, March 1995, pp. 68–77.

[BAS94a] Basili, V.R., L.C. Briand, and W.M. Thomas, "Domain Analysis for the Reuse of Software Development Experiences," *Proc. 19th Annual Software Engineering Workshop,* NASA/GSFC, Greenbelt, MD, December 1994.

[BAS94b] Bassett, P.G., *What Is Frame Technology?* Netron, Inc., Toronto, Canada, October 1994.

[BEL95]   Bellinzona R., M.G. Gugini, and B. Pernici, "Reusing Specifications in OO Applications," *IEEE Software,* March 1995, pp. 65–75.

[BIN93]   Binder, R., "Design for Reuse is for Real," *American Programmer,* vol. 6, no. 8, August 1993, pp. 30–37.

[CHR95]   Christensen, S.R., "Software Reuse Initiatives at Lockheed," *CrossTalk,* vol. 8, no. 5, May 1995, pp. 26–31.

[DEV95]   Devanbu, P. et al., "Analytical and Empirical Evaluation of Software Reuse Metrics," Technical Report, Computer Science Department, University of Maryland, August 1995.

[FRA94]   Frakes, W.B., and T.P. Pole, "An Empirical Study of Representation Methods for Reusable Software Components," *IEEE Trans. Software Engineering,* vol. 20, no. 8, August 1994, pp. 617–630.

[FRE87]   Freeman, P., "A Perspective on Reusability," in *Software Reusability,* P. Freeman (ed.), IEEE Computer Society Press, 1987, pp. 2–3.

[HEN95]   Henry, E., and B. Faller, "Large Scale Industrial Reuse to Reduce Cost and Cycle Time, *IEEE Software,* September 1995, pp. 47–53.

[HOO91]   Hooper, J.W., and R.O. Chester, *Software Reuse: Guidelines and Methods,* Plenum Press, 1991.

[HUT88]   Hutchinson, J.W., and P.G. Hindley, "A Preliminary Study of Large Scale Software Reuse," *Software Engineering Journal,* vol. 3, no. 5, 1988, pp. 208–212.

[JON94]   Jones, C., "The Economics of Object-Oriented Software," *American Programmer,* vol. 7, no. 10, October 1994, pp. 28–35.

[LIA93]   Liao, H., and Wang, F., "Software Reuse Based on a Large Object-Oriented Library," *Software Engineering Notes,* vol. 18, no. 1, January 1993, pp. 74–80.

[LIM94]   Lim, W.C., "Effects of Reuse on Quality, Productivity, and Economics, *IEEE Software,* September 1994, pp. 23–30.

[LIN95]   Linthicum, D.S., "Component Development (a special feature), *Application Development Trends,* June 1995, pp. 57–78.

[MCM95] McMahon, P.E., "Pattern-Based Architecture: Bridging Software Reuse and Cost Management, *Crosstalk,* vol. 8, no. 3, March 1995, pp. 10–16.

[ORF96]   Orfali, R., D. Harkey, and J. Edwards, *The Essential Distributed Objects Survival Guide,* Wiley, 1996.

[POL94]   Pollak, W., and M. Rissman, "Structural Models and Patterned Architectures," *IEEE Computer,* vol. 27, no. 8, August 1994, pp. 67–68.

[PRI87]   Prieto-Diaz, R., "Domain Analysis for Reusability," *Proc. COMPSAC `87,* Tokyo, October 1987, pp. 23–29.

[PRI93] Prieto-Diaz, R., "Issues and Experiences in Software Reuse," *American Programmer,* vol. 6, no. 8, August 1993, pp. 10–18.

[STA94] Staringer, W., "Constructing Applications from Reusable Components," *IEEE Software,* September 1994, pp. 61–68.

[TRA90] Tracz, W., "Where Does Reuse Start?" *Proc. Realities of Reuse Workshop,* Syracuse University CASE Center, January 1990.

[TRA95] Tracz, W., "Third International Conference on Software Reuse— Summary," *Software Engineering Notes,* vol. 20, no. 2, April 1995, pp. 21–22.

[WHI95] Whittle, B., "Models and Languages for Component Description and Reuse," *Software Engineering Notes,* vol. 20, no. 2, April 1995, pp. 76–89.

[YOU94] Yourdon, E., "Software Reuse," *Application Development Strategies,* Cutter Information Corp., vol. VI, no. 12, December 1994, p. 11.

PROBLEMS AND POINTS TO PONDER

26.1. One of the key roadblocks to reuse is getting software developers to consider reusing existing components, rather than reinventing new ones. (After all, building things is fun!) Suggest three or four different ways in which a software organization can provide incentives for software engineers to reuse. What technologies should be in place to support the reuse effort?

26.2. Among the "reuse artifacts" discussed in this chapter were project plans and cost estimates. How can these be reused and what are the benefits of doing so?

26.3. Do a bit of research on domain engineering and flesh out the process model outlined in Figure 26.2. Identify the tasks that are required for domain analysis and software architecture development.

26.4. How are characterization functions for application domains and component classification schemes the same? How are they different?

26.5. Develop a set of domain characteristics for information systems that are relevant to a university's student data processing.

26.6. Develop a set of domain characteristics that are relevant for word-processing/desk-top publishing software.

26.7. Develop a simple structural model for an application domain assigned by your instructor or one with which you are familiar.

26.8. What is a structure point?

26.9. Acquire a copy of the most recent OMG/CORBA standard and prepare a three to five page paper that discusses its major highlights. Get information on an object-request broker tool and illustrate how the tool achieves the standard.

26.10. Develop an enumerated classification for an application domain assigned by your instructor or one with which you are familiar.

26.11. Develop a faceted classification scheme for an application domain assigned by your instructor or one with which you are familiar.

26.12. Research the literature to acquire recent quality and productivity data that support the use of reuse. Present the data to your class.

26.13. An object-oriented system is estimated to require 320 objects when complete. It is further estimated that 190 objects can be acquired from an existing repository. What is the reuse leverage? Assume that new objects cost $1000, and that it costs $600 to adapt an object and $400 to integrate an object. What is the estimated cost of the system? What is the value for R_b?

FURTHER READINGS AND OTHER INFORMATION SOURCES

The literature on reuse is growing rapidly. Lim (*Managing Software Reuse*, Prentice-Hall, 1996) discusses management issues such as cost justification and strategies to implement and deploy reuse in a corporate environment. Bassett (*Framing Software Reuse: Lessons from the Real World*, Yourdon Press, 1996) describes an industry implementation of automated tools for achieving reuse of large scale information systems projects. A more technical approach to reuse has been written by Karlsson (*Software Reuse: A Holistic Approach*, Wiley, 1995).

Tutorials by Freeman (*Software Reusability*, IEEE Computer Society Press, 1987) and Tracz (*Software Reuse: Emerging Technology*, IEEE Computer Society Press, 1988) are excellent anthologies of early papers. Hooper and Chester [HOO91] cover all important subtopics and present a comprehensive bibliography. Tracz (*Confessions of a Used Program Salesman: Institutionalizing Software Reuse*, Addison-Wesley, 1995) presents a sometimes lighthearted, but meaningful, discussion of the issues associated with creating a reuse culture. Nierstrasz and Tsichritzis (*Object-Oriented Software Composition*, Prentice-Hall, 1996) have edited a book that presents the results of a series of research projects related to object-oriented software composition and reuse.

Collections edited by Biggerstaff and Perlis (*Software Reusability*, Volumes. 1 and 2, ACM Press, 1989) and Schaefer, Prieto-Diaz, and Matsumoto (*Software Reusability*, Ellis Horwood, New York, 1994) contain useful insight into ongoing research and opinion. The September 1994 issue of *IEEE Software* is dedicated to reuse and contains a number of useful articles.

Books on the prevailing standards for object reuse have been written by Orfali (*The Essential Distributed Objects Survival Guide*, Wiley, 1995), Mowbray and Zahavi (*The Essential CORBA*, Wiley, 1994), and Denning (*OLE Controls: Inside and Out*, Microsoft Press, 1995). Each of these books provides detailed technical descriptions of the object model.

The electronic newsletter "Reuse News" is published regularly and can be found posted on a number of software related newsgroups including **comp.object** and **comp.software-eng.** A wide array of information sources on reuse are available on the World Wide Web. Many contain pointers to other sites. The following Web sites provide FTP for a wide variety of interesting papers on reuse, including a discussion of reuse metrics and other related topics:

http://rbse.jsc.nasa.gov/eichmann/wisr/wisr.html
http://www.cs.umd.edu/projects/SoftEng/tame/

The following Web sites contain general information on reuse, technical papers, and/or pointers to sources of information on reuse and related topics:

ARPS STARS Reuse Paper	**http://www.stars.ballston.paramax.com/Papers/ReusePapers.html**
ASSET	**http://source.asset.com/**
Courseware in Software Reuse	**http://ricis.cl.uh.edu/virt-lib/reuse_courses.html**
European SER Consortium	**http://www.sema.es/projects/SER**
Loral (Unisys) Domain Engineering	**http://www.stars.reston.unisy gsg.com/process/domain_engineering/DE_guidebook.html**
Object Management Group	**http://www.omg.org/**
Pacific Software Research Center	**http://www.cse.ogi.edu/PacSoft**
SEI SE Information	**http://www.sei.cmu.edu/**
Software Design by Reuse	**http://www-ksl.stanford.edu/KSL_Abstracts/KSL-92-38.html**

SPC Reuse Adoption Guidebook **http://software.software.org/vcoe/products/reuse_adoption_gb.html**

U. Leipzig—Reuse/Reengineering	**http://rzaix340.rz.uni-leipzig.de/ ~ siebert/reuse.html**

Information on using the WWW to maintain a reuse library can be found at:

http://www.ncsa.uiuc.edu/SDG/IT94/Proceedings/DDay/werkman/www94.html

Reusable software libraries in a number of different application domains can be accessed by exploring the following Web sites:

Defense Software Repository	**http://ssed1.ims.disa.mil/srp/dsrs page.html**
Electronic Library Services (ELSA)	**http://rbse.mountain.net/ELSA/**
Guide to Mathematical Software	**http://gams.nist.gov/**
HPCC National Software Exchange	**http://www.netlib.org/nse/**
Public Software Archives	**http://wuarchive.wustl.edu**
Public Ada Library	**http://wuarchive.wustl.edu/languages/ada/**

Reusable DoD Software (CARDS)   **http://dealer.cards.com/**
Reuse Based on OO Technology   **http://www.sema.es/projects/**
                                    SER/reboot.html

An up-to-date list of World Wide Web references for software reuse can be found at: **http://www.rspa.com**

REENGINEERING

In a seminal article written for the *Harvard Business Review,* Michael Hammer [HAM90] laid the foundation for a revolution in management thinking about business processes and computing:

> It is time to stop paving the cow paths. Instead of embedding outdated processes in silicon and software, we should obliterate them and start over. We should "reengineer" our businesses: use the power of modern information technology to radically redesign our business processes in order to achieve dramatic improvements in their performance.
>
> Every company operates according to a great many unarticulated rules. . . . Reengineering strives to break away from the old rules about how we organize and conduct our business.

Like all revolutions, Hammer's call to arms[1] has resulted in both positive and negative changes. Some companies have made a legitimate effort to reengineer, and the results have led to improved competitiveness. Others have relied solely on downsizing and outsourcing (instead of reengineering) to improve their bottom line. Too often, "mean" organizations with little potential for future growth have resulted [DEM95].

But what is the nexus between business reengineering and software engineering? The answer lies in a "system view."

---

[1]Hammer's notoriety and influence grew dramatically when he co-authored the best-selling book, *Reengineering the Corporation* [HAM93].

Software is often the realization of the business rules that Hammer discusses. As these rules change, software must also change. Today, major companies have tens of thousands of computer programs that support the "old business rules." As managers work to modify the rules to achieve greater effectiveness and competitiveness, software must keep pace. In some cases, this means the creation of major new computer-based systems, but in many others, it means the modification and/or rebuilding of existing applications so that they will be competent to meet the business needs of the twenty-first century.

In this chapter we examine reengineering in a top-down manner, beginning with an overview of business process reengineering and proceeding to a more detailed discussion of the technical activities that occur when software is reengineered.

27.1   BUSINESS PROCESS REENGINEERING

Business process reengineering (BPR) extends far beyond the scope of information technologies and software engineering. Among the many definitions (most somewhat abstract) that have been suggested for BPR is one published in *Fortune* magazine [STE93]: "the search for, and the implementation of, radical change in business process to achieve breakthrough results." But how is the search conducted, and how is the implementation achieved? More important, how can we ensure that the "radical change" that is suggested will in fact lead to "breakthrough results" instead of organizational chaos?

During the early 1990s, there was much hype associated with BPR. Today, the mood has mellowed. In fact, many of the early proponents of BPR have moderated their view considerably. However, no one questions the need to make business more competitive. Information technology is the means to this end. Whether BPR has a role is a continuing topic of debate.

An overview of business process reengineering is presented in this section. Our intent is to establish a context into which software reengineering can be placed.

27.1.1   Business Processes

A business process is "a set of logically related tasks performed to achieve a defined business outcome" [DAV90]. Within the business process, people, equipment, material resources, and business procedures are combined to produce a specified result. Examples of business processes include:

- designing a new product
- purchasing services and supplies
- hiring a new employee
- paying suppliers

Each demands a set of tasks, and each draws on diverse resources within the business.

Every business process has a defined customer—a person or group that receives the outcome (e.g., an idea, a report, a design, a product). In addition, business processes cross organizational boundaries. They require that different organization groups participate in the "logically related tasks" that define the process.

In Chapter 10, we noted that every system is actually a hierarchy of subsystems. A business is no exception. Figure 27.1 illustrates the hierarchy in which BPR operates. The overall business is segmented into a number of business systems (also called business functions). Each business system is composed of one or more business processes, and each business process is defined by a set of subprocesses.

BPR can be applied at any level of the hierarchy shown in Figure 27.1, but as the scope of BPR broadens (i.e., as we move upward in the hierarchy), the risks associated with BPR grow dramatically. For this reason most BPR efforts focus on individual processes or subprocesses.

There is a strong cyclical relationship between the capabilities of information technologies (IT) and the process reengineering that takes place within a business. As IT capabilities grow, they can drive changes in business processes. Figure 27.2 illustrates this relationship.

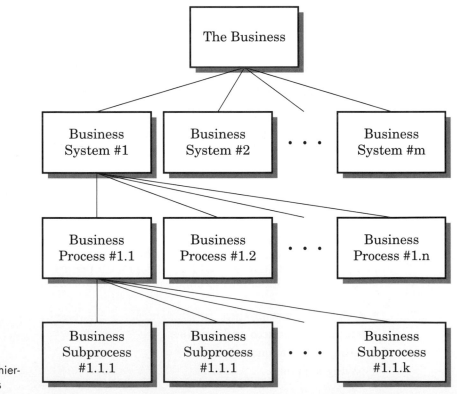

FIGURE 27.1.
The business—a hierarchy of systems

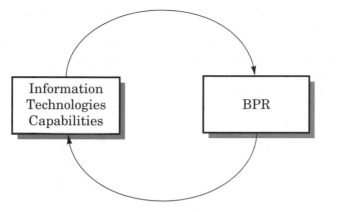

FIGURE 27.2.
The relationship between IT and BPR

As an example, consider the notebook computer. As this technology became widespread, it spurred changes in many business processes. Salespeople could provide instant price quotes for even the most complex job or product. Product catalogs disappeared and were replaced by CD-ROMs or diskettes, which could be accessed on the spot. As the sales process changed, people in the field saw additional opportunity. Communication with the home office was a must, they said. IT responded with new notebook computers (and appropriate software) that provided cellular communication capabilities. The cycle continues.

27.1.2 Principles of Business Process Reengineering

In many ways, BPR is identical in focus and scope to the information engineering process discussed in Chapter 10. In an ideal setting, BPR should occur in a top-down manner, beginning with the identification of major business objectives and goals, and culminating with a much more detailed specification of the tasks that define a specific business process.

Hammer [HAM90] suggests a number of principles that guide BPR activities when they begin at the top (business) level:

Organize around outcomes, not tasks. Many companies have compartmentalized business activities so that no single person (or organization) has responsibility (or control) of a business outcome. It such cases, it is difficult to determine the status of work and even more difficult to debug process problems if they do occur. BPR should design processes that avoid this problem.

Have those who use the output of the process perform the process. The intent of this recommendation is to allow those who need business output to control all of the variables that allow them to get the output in a timely manner. The fewer separate constituencies that are involved in a process, the smoother the road to an rapid outcome.

Incorporate information processing work into the real work that produces the raw information. As IT becomes more distributed, it is possible to locate most information processing within the organization that produces the raw data. This localizes control, reduces communication time, and puts computing power in the hands of those who have a vested interest in the information that is produced.

Treat geographically dispersed resources as though they were centralized. Computer-based communications have become so sophisticated that geographically diverse groups can be placed in the same "virtual office." For example, instead of running three engineering shifts at a single location, a global company can run the one shift in Europe, a second shift in North America, and a third shift in Asia. In each case, engineers will work during daylight hours and communicate via high-bandwidth networks.

Link parallel activities instead of integrating their results. When different constituencies are performing work in parallel, it is essential to design a process that demands continuing communication and coordination. Otherwise, integration problems are sure to result.

Put the decision point where the work is performed, and build control into the process. Using software design jargon, this principle suggests a flatter organizational architecture with reduced factoring.

Capture data once, at its source. Data should be stored on-line so that once collected it need never be re-entered.

Each of the above principles represents a "big picture" view of BPR. Guided by these principles, business planners and process designers must begin process redesign. In the next section, we examine the process of BPR in a bit more detail.

27.1.3 A BPR Model

Like most engineering activities, business process reengineering is iterative. Business goals and the processes that achieve them must be adapted to a changing business environment. For this reason, there is no start and end to BPR—it is an evolutionary process. A model for business process reengineering is depicted in Figure 27.3. The model defines six activities:

Business definition. Business goals are identified within the context of four key drivers: cost reduction, time reduction, quality improvement, and personnel development and empowerment. Goals may be defined at the business level or for a specific component of the business.

Process identification. Processes that are critical to achieving the goals defined in business definition are identified. They may then be prioritized by importance, by need for change, or in any other way that is appropriate for the reengineering activity.

Process evaluation. The existing process is thoroughly analyzed and measured. Process tasks are identified; the costs and time consumed by process tasks are noted; and quality/performance problems are isolated.

Process specification and design. Based on information obtained during the first three BPR activities, use cases (Chapter 20) are prepared for

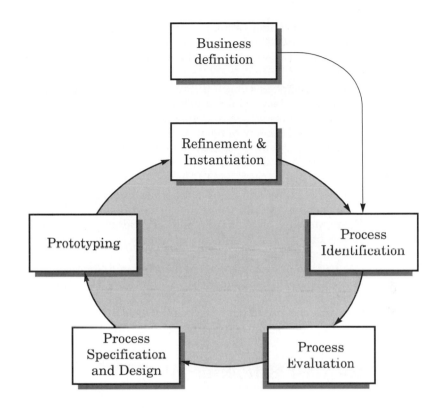

FIGURE 27.3.
A BPR model

each process that is to be redesigned. Within the context of BPR, use cases identify a scenario that delivers some outcome to a customer. With the use case as the specification of the process, a new set of tasks (that conform to the principles noted in Section 27.2.1) are designed for the process.

Prototyping. A redesigned business process must be prototyped before it is fully integrated into the business. This activity "tests" the process so that refinements can be made.

Refinement and instantiation. Based on feedback from the prototype, the business process is refined and then instantiated within a business system.

The BPR activities described above are sometimes used in conjunction with *workflow analysis tools*. The intent of these tools is to build a model of existing workflow in a effort to better analyze existing processes. In addition the modeling techniques commonly associated with information engineering activities such as information strategy planning and business area analysis (Chapter 10) can be used to implement the first four activities described in the process model.

27.1.4 Words of Warning

It is not uncommon that a new business approach—in this case BPR—is at first hyped as a panacea, and then criticized so severely that it becomes a pariah.

Over the past few years, a debate has raged about the efficacy of BPR (e.g., [BLE93], [DIC95]). In an excellent summary of the case for and against BPR, Weisz [WEI95] summarizes the argument in the following way:

> It is tempting to bash BPR as another silver-bullet fad. From several points of view—systems thinking, peopleware, simple history—you'd have to predict high failure rates for the concept, rates which seem to be borne out by empirical evidence. For many companies, the silver bullet has apparently missed.
>
> For others, though, the reengineering effort has evidently been fruitful . . . .

BPR can work, if it is applied by motivated, trained people who recognize that process reengineering is a continuous activity. If BPR is conducted effectively, information systems are better integrated into the business process. Reengineering older applications can be examined in the context of a broad-based business strategy, and priorities for software reengineering can be established intelligently.

But even if business reengineering is a strategy that is rejected by a company, software reengineering is something that must be done. Tens of thousands of *legacy systems*—applications that are crucial to the success of businesses large and small—are in dire need of refurbishing or rebuilding.

27.2   SOFTWARE REENGINEERING

The scenario is all too common: An application has served the business needs of a company for 10 or 15 years. During that time it has been corrected, adapted, and enhanced many times. People approached this work with the best intentions, but good software engineering practices were always shunted to the side (the press of other matters). Now the application is unstable. It still works, but every time a change is attempted, unexpected and serious side effects occur. Yet the application must continue to evolve. What to do?

Unmaintainable software is not a new problem. In fact, the broadening emphasis on software reengineering has been spawned by a software maintenance "iceberg" that has been building for more than three decades.

27.2.1 Software Maintenance

Almost 30 years ago, *software maintenance* was characterized [CAN72] as an "iceberg." we hoped that what was immediately visible was all there was to it but we knew that an enormous mass of potential problems and cost lay under the surface. In the early 1970s the maintenance iceberg was big enough to sink an aircraft carrier. Today, it could easily sink the entire Navy!

The maintenance of existing software can account for over 60 percent of all effort expended by a development organization, and the percentage continues to rise as more software is produced [HAN93]. On the horizon we can foresee "maintenance-bound" software development organizations that can no longer produce new software because all available resources are expended maintaining old software.

Uninitiated readers may ask why so much maintenance is required and why so much effort is expended. Osborne and Chikofsky [OSB90] provide a partial answer:

> Much of the software we depend on today is on average 10 to 15 years old. Even when these programs were created using the best design and coding techniques known at the time [and most were not], they were created when program size and storage space were principal concerns. They were then migrated to new platforms, adjusted for changes in machine and operating system technology and enhanced to meet new user needs—all without enough regard to overall architecture.
>
> The result is the poorly designed structures, poor coding, poor logic, and poor documentation of the software systems we are now called on to keep running . . .

The ubiquitous nature of change underlies all software work. Change is inevitable when computer-based systems are built; therefore, we must develop mechanisms for evaluating, controlling and making modifications.

Upon reading the paragraphs above, a reader may protest: "but I don't spend 60 percent of my time fixing mistakes in the programs I develop." Software maintenance is, of course, far more than "fixing mistakes." We may define maintenance by describing four activities [SWA76] that are undertaken after a program is released for use:

- corrective maintenance
- adaptive maintenance
- perfective maintenance or enhancement
- preventive maintenance or reengineering

Only about 20 percent of all maintenance work is spent "fixing mistakes." The remaining 80 percent is spent adapting existing systems to changes in their external environment, making enhancements requested by users, and reengineering an application for future use. When maintenance is considered to encompass all of these activities, it is relatively easy to see why it absorbs so much effort.

27.2.2 A Software Reengineering Process Model

Reengineering takes time; it costs significant amounts of money, and absorbs resources that might be otherwise occupied on immediate concerns. For all of these reasons, reengineering is not accomplished in a few months or even a few years. Reengineering of information systems is an activity that will absorb information technology resources for many years. That's why every organization needs a pragmatic strategy for software reengineering.

A workable strategy is encompassed in a reengineering process model. We'll discuss the model later in this section, but first, some basic principles.

Reengineering is a rebuilding activity, and we can better understand the reengineering of information systems if we consider an analogous activity: rebuilding a house. Consider the following situation:

> Let's assume that you've purchased a house in another state. You've never actually seen the property, but you acquired it at an amazingly low price, with the warning that it might have to be completely rebuilt. How would you proceed?

- Before you can start rebuilding, it would seem reasonable to inspect the house. To determine whether it is in need of rebuilding, you (or a professional inspector) would create a list of criteria so that your inspection would be systematic.

- Before you tear down and rebuild the entire house, be sure that the structure is weak. If the house is structurally sound, it may be possible to "remodel" without rebuilding (at much lower cost and in much less time).

- Before you start rebuilding, be sure you understand how the original was built. Take a peek behind the walls. Understand the wiring, the plumbing, and the structural internals. Even if you trash them all, the insight you'll gain will serve you well when you start construction.

- If you begin to rebuild, use only the most modern, long-lasting materials. This may cost a bit more now, but it will help you to avoid expensive and time-consuming maintenance later.

- If you decide to rebuild, be disciplined about it. Use practices that will result in high quality—today and in the future.

Although the above principles focus on the rebuilding of a house, they apply equally well to the reengineering of computer-based systems and applications.

To implement these principles, we apply a software reengineering process model that defines six activities shown in Figure 27.4. In some situations, these activities occur in a linear sequence, but this is not always the case. For example, it may be that reverse engineering (understanding the internal working of a program) may have to occur before document restructuring can commence.

The reengineering paradigm shown in the figure is a cyclical model. This means that each of the activities presented as a part of the paradigm may be revisited. For any particular cycle, the process can terminate after any one of these activities.

Inventory Analysis   Every software organization should have an inventory of all applications. The inventory can be nothing more than a spreadsheet model that contains the following information:

- name of the application
- year it was originally created
- number of substantive changes made to it

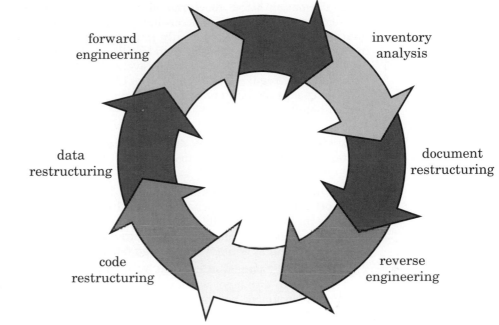

FIGURE 27.4.
A software reengineering process model

- total effort applied to make these changes
- date of last substantive change
- effort applied to make the last change
- system(s) in which it resides
- applications with which it interfaces
- database(s) that it accesses
- errors reported over the past 18 months
- number of users
- number of machines on which it is installed
- complexity of:
  - program architecture
  - code
  - documentation
- quality of documentation
- overall maintainability (scale value)
- projected longevity (in years)
- projected number of changes over the next 36 months
- annual cost of maintenance
- annual cost of operation
- annual business value
- business criticality

The information listed above should be collected for every active application. By sorting this information according to business criticality, longevity, current maintainability, and other locally important criteria, candidates for reengineering appear. Resources can then be allocated intelligently.

It is important to note that the inventory table described above should be revisited on a regular cycle. The status of applications (e.g., business criticality) can change as a function of time, and as a result, priorities for reengineering will shift.

Document Restructuring   Weak documentation is the trademark of many legacy systems. But what do we do about it?

> *Option #1:* Creating documentation is far too time-consuming. The system works, we'll live with what we have. In some cases, this is the correct approach. It is not possible to re-create documentation for hundreds of computer programs. If a program is relatively static, is coming to the end of its useful life, and is likely to undergo few changes, let it be!
>
> *Option #2:* Documentation must be updated, but we have limited resources. We'll use a "document when touched" approach. It may not be necessary to fully redocument an application. Rather, those portions of the system that are currently undergoing change are fully documented. Over time, a collection of useful and relevant documentation will evolve.
>
> *Option #3:* The system is business critical and must be fully redocumented. Even in this case, an intelligent approach is to pare documentation to an essential minimum.

Each of these options is viable. A software organization must choose the one that is most appropriate for each case.

Reverse Engineering   The term "reverse engineering" has its origins in the hardware world. A company disassembles a competitive hardware product in an effort to understand its competitor's design and manufacturing "secrets." These secrets could be easily understood if the competitor's design and manufacturing specifications were obtained. But these documents are proprietary and are not available to the company doing the reverse engineering. In essence, successful reverse engineering derives one or more design and manufacturing specifications for a product by examining actual specimens of the product.

Reverse engineering for software is quite similar. In most cases, however, the program to be reverse engineered is not a competitor's. Rather, it is the company's own work (often done many years earlier). The "secrets" to be understood are obscure because no specification was ever developed. Therefore, reverse engineering for software is the process of analyzing a program in an effort to create a representation of the program at a higher level of abstraction than source code. Reverse engineering is a process of design recovery. Reverse engineering tools extract data, architectural, and procedural design information from an existing program.

Code Restructuring   The most common type of reengineering (actually, the use of the term "reengineering" is questionable in this case) is code restructuring. Some legacy systems have a relatively solid program architecture, but individual modules were coded in a way that makes them difficult to understand, test, and maintain. In such cases, the code within the suspect modules can be restructured.

To accomplish this activity, the source code is analyzed using a restructuring tool. Violations of structured programming constructs are noted and code is then restructured (this can be done automatically). The resultant restructured code is reviewed and tested to ensure that no anomalies have been introduced. Internal code documentation is updated.

Data Restructuring   A program with weak data architecture will be difficult to adapt and enhance. In fact, for many applications, data architecture has more to do with the long-term viability of a program than the source code itself.

Unlike code restructuring, which occurs at a relatively low level of abstraction, data structuring is a full scale reengineering activity. In most cases, data restructuring begins with a reverse engineering activity. Current data architecture is dissected. When necessary, data models are defined (Chapter 12), data objects and attributes are identified, and existing data structures are reviewed for quality.

When data structure is weak (e.g., flat files are currently implemented, when a relational approach would greatly simplify processing), the data are reengineered.

Because data architecture has a strong influence on program architecture and the algorithms that populate it, changes to the data will invariably result in either architectural or code-level changes.

Forward Engineering   In an ideal world, applications would be rebuilt using a automated "reengineering engine." The old program would be fed into the engine, analyzed, restructured, and then regenerated in a form that exhibited the best aspects of software quality. In the short term, it is unlikely that such an "engine" will appear, but CASE vendors have introduced tools that provide a limited subset of these capabilities that address specific application domains (e.g., applications that are implemented using a specific database system). More important, these reengineering tools are becoming increasingly more sophisticated.

Forward engineering, also called *renovation* or *reclamation* [CHI90], not only recovers design information from existing software, but uses this information to alter or reconstitute the existing system in an effort to improve its overall quality. In most cases, reengineered software re-implements the function of the existing system and also adds new functions and/or improves overall performance.

27.3   REVERSE ENGINEERING

Reverse engineering conjures up an image of the "magic slot." We feed an unstructured, undocumented source listing into the slot and out the other end comes full documentation for the computer program. Unfortunately, the magic slot doesn't exist. Reverse engineering can extract design information from source code, but the abstraction level, the completeness of the documentation, the degree to which tools and a human analyst work together, and the directionality of the process are highly variable [CAS88].

The *abstraction level* of a reverse engineering process and the tools that are used to effect it refers to the sophistication of the design information that can be extracted from source code. Ideally, the abstraction level should be as high as possible. That is, the reverse engineering process should be capable of deriving procedural design representations (a low level of abstraction); program and data structure information (a somewhat higher level of abstraction); data and control flow models (a relatively high level of abstraction); and entity-relationship models (a high level of abstraction). As the abstraction level increases, the software engineer is provided with information that will allow easier understanding of the program.

The *completeness* of a reverse engineering process refers to the level of detail that is provided at an abstraction level. In most cases, the completeness decreases as the abstraction level increases. For example, given a source code listing, it is relatively easy to develop a complete procedural design representation. Simple data flow representations may also be derived, but it is far more difficult to develop a complete set of data flow diagrams or a state-transition diagram.

Completeness improves in direct proportion to the amount of analysis performed by the person doing reverse engineering. *Interactivity* refers to the degree to which the human is "integrated" with automated tools to create an effective reverse engineering process. In most cases, as the abstraction level increases, interactivity must increase or completeness will suffer.

If the *directionality* of the reverse engineering process is one-way, all information extracted from the source code is provided to the software engineer who can then use it during any maintenance activity. If directionality is two-way, the information is fed to a reengineering tool that attempts to restructure or regenerate the old program.

The reverse engineering process is represented in Figure 27.5. Before reverse engineering activities can commence, unstructured ("dirty") source code is restructured (Section 27.4.1) so that it contains only the structured programming constructs.[2] This makes the source code easier to read and provides the basis for all subsequent reverse engineering activities.

The core of reverse engineering is an activity called *extract abstractions*. The engineer must evaluate the old program and from the (often undocumented) source code, extract a meaningful specification of the processing that is performed, the user interface that is applied, and the program data structures or database that is used.

27.3.1 Reverse Engineering to Understand Processing

The first real reverse engineering activity begins with an attempt to understand and then extract procedural abstractions represented by the source code. To understand procedural abstractions, the code is analyzed at varying levels of abstraction: system, program, module, pattern, and statement.

---

[2]Code can be restructured automatically using a "restructuring engine"—a CASE tool that restructures source code.

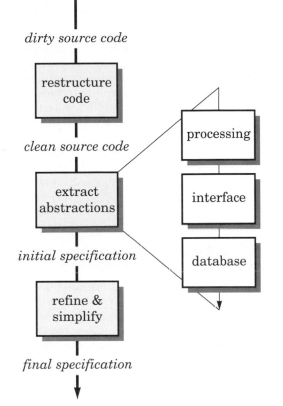

dirty source code

clean source code

initial specification

final specification

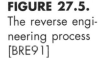

FIGURE 27.5.
The reverse engineering process [BRE91]

The overall functionality of the entire system must be understood before more detailed reverse engineering work occurs. This establishes a context for further analysis and provides insight into interoperability issues among applications within the system. Each of the programs that comprise the application system represents a functional abstraction at a high level of detail. A block diagram, representing the interaction between these functional abstractions, is created. Modules each perform some subfunction and represent a defined procedural abstraction. Processing narratives for each model are created. In some cases, system, program, and module specifications already exist. When this is the case, the specifications are reviewed for conformance to existing code.[3]

Things become more complex when the code inside a module is considered. The engineer looks for sections of code that represent generic procedural patterns. In almost every module, a section of code prepares data for processing (within the module), a different section of code does the processing, and another section of code prepares the results of processing for export from the module. Within each of these sections, we can encounter smaller patterns (e.g., data val-

---

[3]Often, specifications written early in the life history of a program are never updated. As changes are made, the code no longer conforms to the specification.

idation and bounds checking often occurs within the section of code that prepares data for processing).

A technique called *program segmentation* [NIN94] has been suggested as one way to identify procedural patterns with a model and then repackage these patterns into a meaningful function. Using an automated browsing tool, the software engineer isolates *focusing operations*—noncontiguous segments of code that are functionally (semantically) related. Once focusing operations have been isolated, factoring operations are applied. Focused code segments are extracted from existing code and repackaged into a new module.

For large systems, reverse engineering is generally accomplished using a semi-automated approach. CASE tools (e.g., [MAR94]) are used to "parse" the semantics of existing code. The output of this process is then passed to restructuring and forward engineering tools to complete the reengineering process.

27.3.2   Reverse Engineering to Understand Data

Reverse engineering of data occurs at different levels of abstraction. At the program level, internal program data structures must often be reverse engineered as part of an overall reengineering effort. At the system level, global data structures (e.g., files, databases) are often reengineered to accommodate new database management paradigms (e.g., the move from flat file to relational or object-oriented database systems). Reverse engineering of the current global data structures sets the stage for the introduction of a new system wide database.

Internal Data Structures   Reverse engineering techniques for internal program data focus on the definition of classes of objects.[4] This is accomplished by examining the program code with the intent of grouping related program variables. In many cases, the data organization within the code identifies abstract data types. For example, record structures, files, lists, and other data structures often provide an initial indicator of classes.

Breuer and Lano [BRE91] suggest the following approach for reverse engineering classes:

1.   Identify flags and local data structures within the program that record important information about global data structures (e.g., a file or database).

2.   Define the relationship between flags and local data structures and the global data structures. For example, a flag may be set when a file is empty, or a local data structure may serve as a buffer that contains the last 100 records acquired from a central database.

3.   For every variable (within the program) that represents an array or file, list all other variables that have a logical connection to it.

---

[4]For a complete discussion of these object-oriented concepts, see Chapter 19.

These steps enable a software engineer to identify classes within the program that interact with the global data structures.

Database structure   Regardless of its logical organization and physical structure, a database allows the definition of data objects and supports some method for establishing relationships among the objects. Therefore, reengineering one database schema into another requires an understanding of existing objects and their relationships.

The following steps [PRE94] may be used to define the existing data model as a precursor to reengineering a new database model:

1. *Build an initial object model*. The classes defined as part of the model may be acquired by reviewing records in a flat file database or tables in a relational schema. The items contained in records or tables become attributes of a class.

2. *Determine candidate keys*. The attributes are examined to determine whether they are used to point to another record or table. Those that serve as pointers become candidate keys.

3. *Refine the tentative classes*. Determine whether similar classes can be combined into a single class.

4. *Define generalizations*. Examine classes that have many similar attributes to determine whether a class hierarchy should be constructed with a generalization class at its head.

5. *Discover associations*. Use techniques that are analogous to the CRC approach (Chapter 20) to establish associations among classes.

Once information defined in the above steps is known, a series of transformations [PRE94] can be applied to map the old database structure into a new database structure.

27.3.3   Reverse Engineering User Interfaces

As sophisticated GUIs become *de rigueur* for computer-based products and systems of every type, the redevelopment of user interfaces has become one of the most common types of reengineering activities. But before a user interface can be rebuilt, a reverse engineering activity should occur.

For us to fully understand an existing user interface (UI), the structure and behavior of the interface must be specified. Merlo and his colleagues [MER93] suggest three basic questions that must be answered as reverse engineering of the UI commences:

• What are the basic actions that the interface must process—for example, keystrokes and mouse clicks?

• What is a compact description of the behavioral response of the system to these actions?

- What is meant by a "replacement," or more precisely, what concept of equivalence of interfaces is relevant here?

Behavioral modeling notation (Chapter 12) can provide a means for representing the answers to the first two questions noted above. Much of the information necessary to create a behavioral model can be obtained by observing the external manifestation of the existing interface. But additional information necessary to create the behavioral model must extracted from the code.

Process algebra may be used to represent the behavior of an interface in a formal manner. Merlo and his colleagues [MER93] put process algebra into content when they state:

> In describing processes that occur in interfaces, a key novelty is that certain objects must be ready to respond to user inputs, which cannot be controlled, but only rejected. Thus, one needs to capture the idea that there are at least two concurrent active entities: the system and the user. Second, one must be able to express certain "external" choices that are not under user control. These ingredients, reactivity, concurrency, and external choice are basic to process algebra.

The description of the interface makes use of *agents* and *actions*. An agent is something that accomplishes some aspect of the system. Actions allow agents to communicate with one another. In essence, process algebra is a shorthand notation for representing how agents and actions achieve the function of a UI. The basic syntax is illustrated in Figure 27.6.

As an example, consider an modern interface that has a printer icon in a tool bar. The printer icon P, is an agent. Printing can also be accomplished by a print command (action c) passed through the keyboard to a print driver

Name	Notation	Meaning
An inactive agent	0	
Constant	A	the agent A
Prefix	$a.E$	do action a and behave like agent E
Summation	$E_1 + E_2$	agent E_1 composed with agent E_2
Composition	$E_1 \mid E_2$	behave like agent E_1 or agent E_2
Restriction	$E_1 \setminus L$	agent E restricted to actions in the set L
Relabeling	$E[f]$	renaming of agent E according to function f
Substitution	E/X	replace agent X by agent E
Recursion	$\text{fax}(X = E)$	the agent X such that $X = E$

FIGURE 27.6. Process algebra notation [MER93]

agent, *D*. Alternatively, a mouse click (action *m*) can be initiated via a pull-down menu agent, *M*, which interfaces directly with the print driver. Using the summation operator defined for process algebra notation and indicated in Figure 27.6, we can represent the print behavior as:

$$P = c.D + m.M$$

This states that agent *P* behaves in a manner that is identical to action *c* and the resultant behavior of agent *D* or action *m* and the resultant behavior of agent *M*.

A detailed discussion of process algebra and its use in interface reengineering is beyond the scope of this book. The interested reader should see [MER93] or [MIL89] for more detail.

27.4   RESTRUCTURING

Software restructuring modifies source code and/or data in an effort to make it amenable to future changes. In general, restructuring does not modify the overall program architecture. It tends to focus on the design details of individual modules and on local data structures defined within modules. If the restructuring effort extends beyond module boundaries and encompasses the software architecture, restructuring becomes forward engineering (Section 27.5).

Arnold [ARN89] defines a number of benefits that can be achieved when software is restructured:

- Leads to programs that have higher quality—better documentation and less complexity; conformance to modern software engineering practices and standards
- Reduces frustration among software engineers who must work on the program, thereby improving productivity and making learning easier
- Reduces the effort required to perform maintenance activities
- Makes software easier to test and debug

Restructuring occurs when the basic architecture of an application is solid, even though technical internals need work. It is initiated when major parts of the software are serviceable and only a subset of all modules and data need extensive modification.[5]

27.4.1   Code Restructuring

Code restructuring is performed to yield a design that produces the same function but with higher quality than the original program. In general, code re-

---

[5]It is sometimes difficult to make a distinction between extensive restructuring and redevelopment. Both are *reengineering*.

structuring techniques (e.g., Warnier's logical simplification techniques [WAR74]) model program logic using Boolean algebra and then apply a series of transformation rules that yield restructured logic. The objective is to take "spaghetti-bowl" code and derive a procedural design that conforms to the structured programming philosophy (Chapter 14).

27.4.2 Data Restructuring

Before data restructuring can begin, a reverse engineering activity, analysis of source code, must be conducted. All programming language statements that contain data definitions, file descriptions, I/O, and interface descriptions are evaluated. The intent is to extract data items and objects, to get information on data flow, and to understand the existing data structures that have been implemented. This activity is sometimes called *data analysis* [RIC89].

Once data analysis has been completed, *data redesign* commences. In its simplest form, a *data record standardization* step clarifies data definitions to achieve consistency among data item names or physical record formats within an existing data structure or file format. Another form of redesign, called *data name rationalization,* ensures that all data naming conventions conform to local standards and that aliases are eliminated as data flow through the system.

When restructuring moves beyond standardization and rationalization, physical modifications to existing data structures are made to make the data design more effective. This may mean a translation from one file format to another, or in some cases, a translation from one type of database to another.

27.5   FORWARD ENGINEERING

A program with control flow that is the graphical equivalent of a bowl of spaghetti with "modules" that are 2000 statements long, with few meaningful comment lines in 290,000 source statements, and with no other documentation must be modified to accommodate changing user requirements. We have the following options:

1. We can struggle through modification after modification, "fighting" the implicit design and source code to implement the necessary changes.
2. We can attempt to understand the broader inner workings of the program in an effort to make modifications more effectively.
3. We can redesign, recode, and test those portions of the software that require modification, applying a software engineering approach to all revised segments.
4. We can completely redesign, recode, and test the program, using CASE tools (reengineering tools) to assist us in understanding the current design.

There is no single "correct" option. Circumstances may dictate the first option even if the others are more desirable.

Rather than waiting until a maintenance request is received, the development or maintenance organization selects a program (1) that will remain in use for a preselected number of years, (2) that is currently being used successfully, and (3) that is likely to undergo major modification or enhancement in the near future. Then, option 2, 3, or 4 above is applied.[6]

This preventive maintenance approach was pioneered by Miller [MIL81] under the title "structured retrofit." He defined this concept as "the application of today's methodologies to yesterday's systems to support tomorrow's requirements."

At first glance, the suggestion that we redevelop a large program when a working version already exists may seem quite extravagant. Before passing judgment, consider the following points:

1. The cost to maintain one line of source code may be 20 to 40 times the cost of initial development of that line.

2. Redesign of the software architecture (program and/or data structure) using modern design concepts can greatly facilitate future maintenance.

3. Because a prototype of the software already exists, development productivity should be much higher than average.

4. The user now has experience with the software. Therefore, new requirements and the direction of change can be ascertained with greater ease.

5. CASE tools for reengineering will automate some parts of the job.

6. A complete software configuration (documents, programs, and data) will exist upon completion of preventive maintenance.

When a software development organization sells software as a product, preventive maintenance is seen in "new releases" of a program. A large in-house software developer (e.g., a business systems software development group for a large consumer products company) may have 500 to 2000 production programs within its domain of responsibility. These programs can be prioritized by importance and then reviewed as candidates for preventive maintenance.

The forward engineering process applies software engineering principles, concepts, and methods to re-create an existing application. In most cases forward engineering does not simply create a modern equivalent of an older program. Rather, new user and technology requirements are integrated into the reengineering effort. The redeveloped program extends the capabilities of the older application.

27.5.1 Forward Engineering for Client/Server Architectures

Over the past decade many mainframe applications have been reengineered to accommodate client/server (C/S) architectures (Chapter 28). In essence, cen-

---

[6]Before continuing, review Chapter 1. As management correctly responds to the specter of an "aging software plant," redevelopment has become mandatory in many companies.

tralized computing resources (including software) are distributed among many client platforms. Although a variety of different distributed environments can be designed, the typical mainframe application that is reengineered into a client/server architecture has the following features:

- application functionality migrates to each client computer;
- new GUI interfaces are implemented at the client sites;
- database functions are allocated to the server;
- specialized functionality (e.g., computation-intensive analysis) may remain at the server site; and
- new communications, security, archiving, and control requirements must be established at both the client and server sites.

It is important to note that the migration from mainframe to C/S computing requires both business and software reengineering. In addition an "enterprise network infrastructure" [JAY94] must be established.

Reengineering for C/S applications begins with a thorough analysis of the business environment that encompasses the existing mainframe. Three layers of abstraction (Figure 27.7) can be identified. The database sits at the foundation of a client/server architecture and manages transactions and queries. Yet these transactions and queries must be controlled within the context of a set of busi-

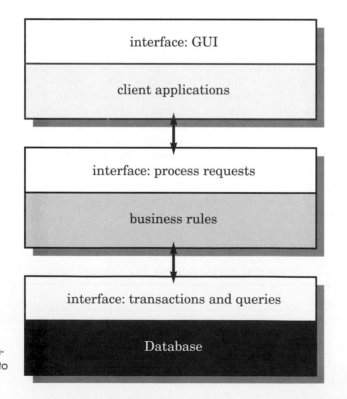

FIGURE 27.7.
Reengineering main-frame applications to client/server

ness rules (defined by an existing or reengineered business process). Client applications provide targeted functionality to the user community.

The functions of the existing database management system and the data architecture of the existing database must be reverse-engineered as a precursor to the redesign of the database foundation layer. In some cases a new data model (Chapter 12) is created. In every case, the C/S database is reengineered to ensure that transactions are executed in a consistent manner; that all updates are performed only by authorized users; that core business rules are enforced (e.g., before a vendor record is deleted, the server ensures that no related accounts payable, contracts, or communications exist for that vendor); that queries can be accommodated efficiently; and that full archiving capability has been established.

The business rules layer represents software that is resident at both the client and the server. This software performs control and coordination tasks to ensure that transactions and queries between the client application and the database conform to the established business process.

The client applications layer implements business functions that are required by specific groups of end users. In many instances, a mainframe application is segmented into a number of smaller, reengineered desk-top applications. Communication among the desk-top applications (when necessary) is controlled by the business rules layer.

27.5.2 Forward Engineering for Object-Oriented Architectures

Object-oriented software engineering is rapidly becoming the development paradigm of choice for many software organizations. But what about existing applications that were developed using conventional methods? In some cases, the answer is to leave such applications "as is." But in others, older applications must be reengineered so that they can be easily integrated into large, object-oriented systems.

Reengineering conventional software into an object-oriented implementation uses many of the same techniques discussed in Part Four of this book. First, the existing software is reverse engineered so that appropriate data, functional, and behavioral models can be created. If the reengineered system extends the functionality or behavior of the original application, use cases (Chapter 20) are created. The data models created during reverse engineering are then used in conjunction with CRC modeling (Chapter 20) to establish the basis for the definition of classes. Class hierarchies, object-relationship models, object-behavior models, and subsystems are defined, and object-oriented design commences.

As object-oriented forward engineering progresses from analysis to design, the reuse process model (Chapter 26) can be invoked. If the existing application has a domain that is already populated by many object-oriented applications, it is likely that a robust reuse library exists and can be used during forward engineering.

For those classes that must be engineered from scratch, it may be possible to reuse algorithms and data structures from the existing conventional application. However, these must be redesigned to conform to the object-oriented architecture.

27.5.3 Forward Engineering User Interfaces

As applications migrate from the mainframe to the desk-top, users are no longer willing to tolerate arcane, character-based user interfaces. In fact, a significant portion of all effort expended in the transition from mainframe to client/server computing can be spent in the reengineering of client application user interfaces.

Merlo and his colleagues [MER95] suggest the following model for reengineering user interfaces:

1. *Understand the original interface and the data that move between it and the remainder of the application.* The intent is to understand how other elements of a program interact with existing code that implements the interface. If a new GUI is to be developed, the data that flow between the GUI and the remaining program must be consistent with the data that currently flow between the character-based interface and the program.

2. *Remodel the behavior implied by the existing interface into a series of abstractions that have meaning in the context of a GUI.* Although the mode of interaction may be radically different, the business behavior exhibited by users of the old and new interface (when considered in terms of a usage scenario) must remain the same. A redesigned interface must still allow a user to exhibit the appropriate business behavior. For example, when a database query is to be made, the old interface may require a long series of text-based commands to specify the query. The reengineered GUI may streamline the query to a small sequence of mouse picks, but the intent and content of the query remain unchanged.

3. *Introduce improvements that make the mode of interaction more efficient.* The ergonomic failings of the existing interface are studied and corrected in the design of the new GUI.

4. *Build and integrate the new GUI.* The existence of class libraries and fourth generation tools can reduce the effort required to build the GUI significantly. However, integration with existing application software can be more time-consuming. Care must be taken to ensure that the GUI does not propagate adverse side effects into the remainder of the application.

27.6   THE ECONOMICS OF REENGINEERING

In a perfect world, every unmaintainable program would be retired immediately, to be replaced by high-quality, reengineered applications developed using modern software engineering practices. But we live in a world of limited resources. Reengineering drains resources that can be used for other business purposes. Therefore, before an organization attempts to reengineer an existing application, it should perform a cost–benefit analysis.

A cost–benefit analysis model for reengineering has been proposed by Sneed [SNE95]. Nine parameters are defined:

P_1 = current annual maintenance cost for an application

P_2 = current annual operation cost of an application

P_3 = current annual business value of an application

P_4 = predicted annual maintenance cost after reengineering

P_5 = predicted annual operations cost after reengineering

P_6 = predicted annual business value after reengineering

P_7 = estimated reengineering costs

P_8 = estimated reengineering calendar time

P_9 = reengineering risk factor (P_9 = 1.0 is nominal)

L = expected life of the system (in years)

The cost associated with continuing maintenance of a candidate application (i.e., reengineering is not performed) can be defined as:

$$C_{\text{maint}} = [P_3 - (P_1 + P_2)] \times L \qquad (27.1)$$

The costs associated with reengineering are defined using the following relationship:

$$C_{\text{reeng}} = [P_6 - (P_4 + P_5) \times (L - P_8) - (P_7 \times P_9)] \qquad (27.2)$$

Using the costs presented in equations (27.1) and (27.2), the overall benefit of reengineering can be computed as:

$$\text{Cost benefit} = C_{\text{reeng}} - C_{\text{maint}} \qquad (27.3)$$

The cost–benefit analysis presented in the above equations can be performed for all high-priority applications identified during inventory analysis (Section 27.2.2). Those applications that show the highest cost benefit can be targeted for reengineering, while work on others can be postponed until resources are available.

27.7   SUMMARY

Reengineering occurs at two different levels of abstraction. At the business level, reengineering focuses on the business process with the intent of making changes to improve competitiveness in some area of the business. At the software level, reengineering examines information systems and applications with the intent of restructuring or reconstructing them so that they exhibit higher quality.

Business process reengineering (BPR) defines business goals, identifies and evaluates existing business processes (in the context of defined goals), specifies and designs revised processes, and prototypes, refines, and instantiates them within a business. Like information engineering, BPR has a focus that extends beyond software. The result of BPR is often the definition of ways in which information technologies can better support the business.

Software reengineering encompasses a series of activities that include inventory analysis, document restructuring, reverse engineering, program and data restructuring, and forward engineering. The intent of these activities is to create versions of existing programs that exhibit higher quality and better maintainability—programs that will be viable well into the twenty-first century.

Inventory analysis enables an organization to assess each application systematically, with the intent of determining which are candidates for reengineering. Document restructuring creates a framework of documentation that is necessary for the long-term support of an application. Reverse engineering is the process of analyzing a program in an effort to extract data, architectural, and procedural design information. Finally, forward engineering reconstructs a program using modern software engineering practices and information learned during reverse engineering.

The costs and benefits of reengineering can be determined quantitatively. The cost of the *status quo,* that is, the costs associated with ongoing maintenance of an existing application) are compared to the projected costs of the reengineering and the resultant reduction in maintenance costs. In almost every case in which a program has a long life and currently exhibits poor maintainability, reengineering represents a cost-effective business strategy.

REFERENCES

[ARN89]   Arnold, R.S., "Software Restructuring," *Proc. IEEE,* vol. 77, no. 4, April 1989, pp. 607–617.

[BLE93]   Bleakley, F.R., "The Best Laid Plans: Many Companies Try Management Fads, Only to See Them Flop," *The Wall Street Journal,* July 6, 1993.

[BRE91]   Breuer, P.T., and K. Lano, "Creating Specification From Code: Reverse-Engineering Techniques," *Journal of Software Maintenance: Research and Practice,* Volume 3, Wiley, 1991, pp. 145–162.

[CAN72]   Canning, R., "The Maintenance 'Iceberg'," *EDP Analyzer,* vol. 10, no. 10, October 1972.

[CAS88]   "Case Tools for Reverse Engineering," *CASE Outlook,* CASE Consulting Group, Lake Oswego, OR, vol. 2, no. 2, 1988, pp. 1–15.

[CHI90]   Chikofsky, E.J., and J.H. Cross, II, "Reverse Engineering and Design Recovery: A Taxonomy," *IEEE Software,* January 1990, pp. 13–17.

[DAV90]   Davenport, T.H., and J.E. Young, "The New Industrial Engineering: Information Technology and Business Process Redesign," *Sloan Management Review,* Summer 1990, pp. 11–27.

[DEM95]   DeMarco, T., "Lean and Mean," *IEEE Software,* November 1995, pp. 101–102.

[DIC95]   Dickinson, B., *Strategic Business Reengineering,* LCI Press, 1995.

[HAM90]   Hammer, M., "Reengineer Work: Don't Automate, Obliterate," *Harvard Business Review,* July/August 1990, pp. 104–112.

[HAM93]   Hammer, M., and J. Champy, *Reengineering the Corporation,* HarperCollins, 1993.

[HAN93]   Hanna, M., "Maintenance Burden Begging for a Remedy," *Datamation,* April 1993, pp. 53–63.

[JAY94]   Jaychandra, Y., *Re-engineering the Networked Enterprise,* McGraw-Hill, 1994.

[MAR94]   Markosian, L. et al., "Using an Enabling Technology to Reengineer Legacy Systems," *Communications of the ACM,* vol. 37, no. 5, May 1994, pp. 58–70.

[MER93]   Merlo, E. et al., "Reverse Engineering of User Interfaces," *Proc. Working Conference on Reverse Engineering,* IEEE, Baltimore, MD, May 1993, pp. 171–178.

[MER95]   Merlo, E., et al., "Reengineering User Interfaces," *IEEE Software,* January 1995, pp. 64–73.

[MIL81]   Miller, J., in *Techniques of Program and System Maintenance,* G. Parikh (ed.), Winthrop Publishers, 1981.

[MIL89]   Milner, R., *Communication and Concurrency,* Prentice-Hall, 1989.

[NIN94]   Ning, J.Q., A. Engberts, and W. Kozaczynski, "Automated Support for Legacy Code Understanding," *Communications of the ACM,* vol. 37, no. 5, May 1994, pp. 50–57.

[OSB90]   Osborne, W.M., and E.J. Chikofsky, "Fitting Pieces to the Maintenance Puzzle," *IEEE Software,* January 1990, pp. 10–11.

[PRE94]   Premerlani, W.J., and M.R. Blaha, "An Approach for Reverse Engineering of Relational Databases," *Communications of the ACM,* vol. 37, no. 5, May 1994, pp. 42–49.

[RIC89]   Ricketts, J.A., J.C. DelMonaco, and M.W. Weeks, "Data Reengineering for Application Systems," *Proc. Conf. Software Maintenance—1989,* IEEE, 1989, pp. 174–179.

[SNE95]   Sneed, H. "Planning the Reengineering of Legacy Systems," *IEEE Software,* January 1995, pp.24–25.

[STE93]   Stewart, T.A., "Reengineering: The Hot New Managing Tool," *Fortune,* August 23, 1993, pp. 41–48.

[SWA76]   Swanson, E.B., "The Dimensions of Maintenance," *Proc. 2nd Intl. Conf. on Software Engineering,* IEEE, October 1976, pp. 492–497.

[WAR74]   Warnier, J.D., *Logical Construction of Programs,* Van Nostrand Reinhold, 1974.

[WEI95]   Weisz, M., "BPR is Like Teenage Sex," *American Programmer,* vol. 8, no. 6, June 1995, pp. 9–15.

PROBLEMS AND POINTS TO PONDER

27.1.   Consider any job that you've held in the last five years. Describe the business process in which you played a part. Use the BPR model described in Section 27.1.3 to recommend changes to the process in an effort to make it more efficient.

27.2.   Do some research on the efficacy of business process reengineering. Present pro and con arguments for this approach.

27.3.   Your instructor will select one of the programs that everyone in the class has developed during this course. Exchange your program randomly with someone else in the class. *Do not* explain or walk through the program. Now, implement an enhancement (specified by your instructor) in the program you have received.

      a. Perform all software engineering tasks including a brief walkthrough (but not with the author of the program).

      b. Keep careful track of all errors encountered during testing.

      c. Discuss your experiences in class.

27.4. Using some or all of the criteria for inventory analysis described in Section 27.2.2, attempt to develop a quantitative software rating system that could be applied to existing programs in an effort to pick candidate programs for reengineering.

27.5. Suggest alternatives to paper and ink or conventional electronic documentation that could serve as the basis for document restructuring. [Hint: Think of new descriptive technologies that could be used to communicate the intent of the software.]

27.6. Some people believe that artificial intelligence techniques will increase the abstraction level of the reverse engineering process. Do some research on this subject (i.e., the use of AI for reverse engineering) and write a brief paper that takes a stand on this point.

27.7. Why is completeness more difficult to achieve as abstraction level increases?

27.8. Why must interactivity increase if completeness is to increase?

27.9. Get product literature on three reverse engineering tools and present their characteristics in class.

27.10. Do some research on process algebra and develop a simple specification of a process using the notation described in Figure 27.6.

27.11. There is a subtle difference between restructuring and forward engineering. What is it?

27.12. Research the literature to find one or two papers that discuss case studies of mainframe to client/server reengineering. Present a summary.

27.13. How would you determine P_4 through P_7 in the cost–benefit model presented in Section 27.6?

FURTHER READINGS AND OTHER INFORMATION SOURCES

Reengineering is a "hot" topic in the software engineering community. Because the technology that encompasses reengineering continues to evolve, technical periodicals are the best sources of information. The June 1995 edition of *American Programmer,* the January 1995 edition of *IEEE Computer,* and the May 1994 edition of *Communications of the ACM* are representative of many periodicals that contain special features on reengineering topics.

    Relatively few books have been dedicated to software reengineering. A good starting point (dedicated to business process reengineering) is Hammer and Champy's best-selling book [HAM93]. Arnold (*Software Reengineering,* IEEE Computer Society Press, 1993) has published an excellent anthology of important papers that focus on software reengineering technologies. Berztiss (*Software Methods for Business Reengineering,* Springer-Verlag, 1996) and Spurr and her colleagues (*Software Assistance for Business Reengineering,* Wiley, 1994) discuss tools and techniques that facilitate BPR. Aiken (*Data Reverse Engineering,* McGraw-Hill, 1996) discusses how to reclaim, reorganize, and reuse organizational data.

Extensive information about reengineering and a comprehensive bibliography can be found at the Software Reengineering Web page:

http://www.erg.abdn.ac.uk/users/brant/sre/

The following sites provide additional reengineering information and pointers:

The Asset Repository	**http://source.asset.com**
ESEG at UMCP	**http://www.cs.umd.edu/ projects/SoftEng/tame**
REDO Project Archive (Esprit)	**http://www.comlab.ox.ac.uk/ archive/redo.html**
Reverse Engineering—Georgia Tech	**http://www.cc.gatech.edu/ reverse/**
UCSD Software Evolution Group	**http://www-cse.ucsd.edu/ users/wgg/swevolution.html**
WWW Virtual Library—SE	**http://ricis.cl.uh.edu/virt-lib/ software-eng.html**

Reasoning Systems, Inc. has created an "On-Line Bibliography of Reengineering Papers" that is based on their Software Refinery product:

http://www.reasoning.com/papers.html

An up-to-date list of World Wide Web references for software reengineering can be found at: **http://www.rspa.com**

CLIENT/SERVER
SOFTWARE
ENGINEERING

When a new computer-based system is to be developed, an engineer is constrained by the limitations of existing technology and empowered when new technologies provide capabilities that were unavailable to earlier engineers. At the turn of the century, the development of a new generation of machine tools capable of holding very tight tolerances empowered the engineers who designed a new factory process called mass production. Before the advent of the new machine tool technology, machines could not hold tight tolerances. Without tight tolerances, easily assembled interchangeable parts—the cornerstone of mass production—could not have been built.

The evolution of distributed computer architectures has enabled system and software engineers to develop new approaches to how work is structured and how information is processed within an organization. New organizational structures and new information processing approaches (e.g., decision support systems, groupware, and imaging) represent a radical departure from the earlier mainframe- and minicomputer-based technologies. New computing architectures have provided the technology that has enabled organizations to reengineer their business processes (Chapter 27).

In this chapter,[1] we examine a dominant new architecture for information processing—*client/server (C/S)* systems. Client/server systems have evolved in conjunction with advances in desk-top computing, new storage technologies, improved network communications, and enhanced database technology. The objective of this chapter is to present a brief overview of client/server systems

---

[1]Portions of this chapter have been adapted from course material developed by John Porter for the Client/Server Curriculum offered at The BEI Engineering School of Fairfield University. Used with permission.

with an emphasis on the special software engineering issues that must be addressed when such C/S systems are analyzed, designed, tested, and supported.

28.1   THE STRUCTURE OF CLIENT/SERVER SYSTEMS

Hardware, software, database, and network communications technologies all contribute to distributed and cooperative computer architectures. In its most general form, a distributed and cooperative computer architecture is illustrated in Figure 28.1. A root system, typically a mainframe, serves as the repository for corporate data. The root system is connected to servers (typically powerful workstations or PCs) that have a dual role. The servers act to update and request corporate data maintained by the root system. They also maintain local departmental systems and play a key role in networking user-level PCs via a local area network (LAN).

In a C/S structure, the computer that resides above another computer (in Figure 28.1) is called the *server*, and computers at the level below are called *clients*. The client requests services,[2] and the server provides them. However, within the context of the architecture represented in Figure 28.2, a number of different implementations can be achieved [ORF94]:

---

[2]In this context, "services" can be broadly interpreted to mean data, processing, or a combination of the two.

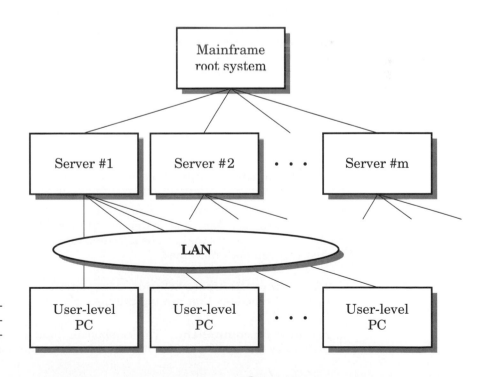

FIGURE 28.1.
Distributed, cooperative computer architectures in a corporate setting

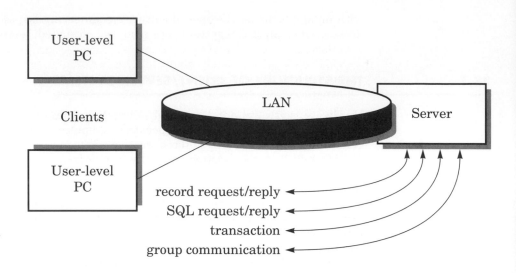

FIGURE 28.2.
Client/server archi-
tecture options

File servers.   The client requests specific records from a file. The server transmits these records to the client across the network.

Database servers.   The client sends *structured query language (SQL)* requests to the server. These are transmitted as messages across the network. The server processes the SQL request and finds the requested information, passing only the results back to the client.

Transaction servers.   The client sends a request that invokes remote procedures at the server site. The *remote procedures* can be a set of SQL statements. A transaction occurs when a request results in the execution of the remote procedure and transmission of the result back to the client.

Groupware servers.   When the server provides a set of applications that enable communication among clients (and the people using them) using text, images, bulletin boards, video, and other representations, a groupware architecture exists.

28.1.1   Software Components for C/S Systems

Instead of viewing software as a monolithic application to be implemented on one machine, the software that is appropriate for a C/S architecture has several distinct components that can be allocated to the client or the server, or distributed between both machines:

User interaction/presentation component.   This component implements all functions that are typically associated with a graphical user interface (GUI).

Application component.   This component implements the requirements defined by the application within the context of the domain in which the application operates. For example, a business application might produce a variety of printed reports based on numeric input, calculations, database information, and other considerations. A groupware application might provide the facilities for enabling bulletin board communication or e-mail. In both cases, the application software may be partitioned so that some components reside on the client and others reside on the server.

Database management. This component performs the data manipulation and management required by an application. Data manipulation and management may be as simple as the transfer of a record or as complex as the processing of sophisticated SQL transactions.

In addition to these components, another software building block, often called *middleware,* exists in all C/S systems. Middleware is comprised of software elements that exist on both the client and the server, and includes elements of network operating systems as well as specialized application software that supports database-specific applications, object-request broker standards (Section 28.1.5), groupware technologies, communication management, and other features that facilitate the client/server connection. Orfali [ORF94] and his colleagues have referred to middleware as "the nervous system of a client/server system."

28.1.2 The Distribution of Software Components

Once the basic requirements for a client/server application have been determined, the software engineer must decide how to distribute the software components discussed in Section 28.1.1 between the client and the server. When most of the functionality associated with each of the three components is allocated to the server, a *fat server* design has been created. Conversely, when the client implements most of the user interaction/presentation, application, and database components, a *fat client* design results.

Fat clients are commonly encountered when file server and database server architectures are implemented. In this case, the server provides data management support, but all application and GUI software resides at the client. Fat servers are often designed when transaction and groupware systems are implemented. The server provides application support required to respond to transactions and communication from clients. The client software focuses on GUI and communication management.

Fat clients and fat servers can be used to illustrate the general approach for the allocation of client/server software components. However, a more granular approach to software component allocation defines five different configurations:

Distributed presentation. In this rudimentary client/server approach, database logic and the application logic remain on the server, typically a mainframe. The server also contains the logic for preparing screen information, using software such as CICS. Special PC-based software is used to convert character-based screen information transmitted from the server into a GUI presentation on a PC.

Remote presentation. In this extension of the distributed presentation approach, primary database and application logic remain on the server, and data sent by the server are used by the client to prepare the user presentation.

Distributed logic. The client is assigned all user presentation tasks and the processes associated with data entry such as field-level validation, server query formulation, and server update information and requests. The server is assigned database management tasks and the processes for client queries, server file updates, client version control, and enterprise-wide applications.

Remote data management. Applications on the server create a new data source by formatting data that have been extracted from elsewhere (e.g., from a corporate-level source). Applications allocated to the client are used to exploit the new data that have been formatted by the server. Decision support systems are included in this category.

Distributed databases. The data comprising the database are spread across multiple servers and clients. Therefore, the client must support data management software components as well as application and GUI components.

28.1.3 Guidelines for Distributing Application Components

While there are no absolute rules covering the distribution of application components between the client and server, the following guidelines are generally followed:

The presentation/interaction component is generally placed on the client. The availability of windows-based environments and the computing power required for a graphical user interface makes this approach cost effective.

If the database is to be shared by multiple users connected by the LAN, the database is typically located on the server. The database management system and the database access capability are also located on the server, together with the physical database.

Static data that are used for reference should be allocated to the client. This places the data closer to the users that require them and minimizes unnecessary network traffic and loading on the server.

The balance of the application component is distributed between the client and server based on the distribution that optimizes the server and client configurations and the network that connects them. For example, the implementation of a mutually exclusive relationship typically involves a search of the database to determine if there is a record that matches the parameters for a search pattern. If no match is found, an alternate search pattern is used. If the application that controls this search pattern is entirely contained on the server, network traffic is minimized. The first network transmission from the client to the server would contain the parameters for both the primary and the secondary search pattern. Application logic on the server would determine if the secondary search is required. The response message to the client would contain the record found as a result of either the primary or the secondary search. The alternate approach (the client implements the logic to determine if a second search is required) would involve a message for the first record retrieval, a response over the network if the record is not found, a second message containing the parameters for the second search, and a final response with the retrieved record. If the second search is required 50 percent of the time, placing the logic on the server to evaluate the first search and initiate the second search if necessary would reduce network traffic significantly.

The final decision on component distribution should be based not only on the individual application, but on the mix of applications operating on the system. For example, an installation might contain some applications that require extensive GUI processing and little central database processing. This would lead to the use of powerful workstations on the client side and a bare bones server. With this configuration in place, other applications would favor the fat client approach so that the capabilities of the server would not need to be upgraded.

It should be noted that as the use of the client/server architecture matures, the trend is to place volatile application logic on the server. This simplifies deployment of software updates as changes are made to the application logic [PAU95].

28.1.4 Linking C/S Software Components

A number of different mechanisms are used to link the various components of the client/server architecture. These mechanisms are incorporated into the network and operating system structure, and are transparent to the end user at the client site. The most common types of linking mechanisms are:

- *Pipes*—widely used in UNIX-based systems, pipes permit messaging between different machines running on different operating systems.
- *Remote procedure calls*—permit one process to invoke the execution of another process or module which resides on a different machine.
- *Client/server SQL interaction*—used to pass SQL requests and associated data from one component (typically on the client) to another component (typically the DBMS on the server). This mechanism is limited to RDBMS applications only.

In addition, object-oriented implementation of the C/S software components results in "linkage" using an object request broker. This approach is discussed in the following section.

28.1.5 Middleware and Object Request Broker Architectures

The C/S software components discussed in the preceding sections are implemented by objects that must be capable of interacting with one another within a single machine (either client or server) or across the network. An *object request broker (ORB)* is a middleware component that enables an object that resides on a client to send a message to a method that is encapsulated by an object that resides on a server. In essence, the ORB intercepts the message and handles all of the communication and coordination activities required to find the object to which the message was addressed, invoke its method, pass appropriate data to the object, and transfer the resulting data back to the object that generated the message in the first place.

A widely used standard for object-request brokers, called CORBA, has been developed by the Object Management Group (OMG). The CORBA standard [MOW95] was discussed briefly in Chapter 26. The basic structure of a CORBA architecture is illustrated in Figure 28.3.

When CORBA is implemented in a client/server system, objects and object classes (Chapter 19) on both the client and the server are defined using an *interface description language (IDL)*, a declarative language that allows a software engineer to define objects, attributes, methods, and the messages that are required to invoke them. In order to accommodate a request for a server-resident method by a client-resident object, client and server IDL stubs are created. The stubs provide the gateway through which requests for objects across the C/S system are accommodated.

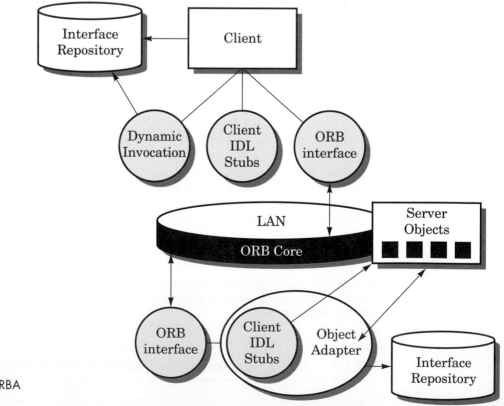

FIGURE 28.3.
The basic CORBA architecture

Because requests for objects across the network occur at run-time, a mechanism for storing the object description must be established so that pertinent information about the object and its location are available when needed. The interface repository accomplishes this.

When a client application must invoke a method contained within an object elsewhere in the system, CORBA uses dynamic invocation to (1) obtain pertinent information about the desired method from the interface repository; (2) create a data structure with parameters to be passed to the object; (3) create a request for the object; and (4) invoke the request. The request is then passed to the *ORB Core*—an implementation-specific part of the network operating system that manages requests—and the request is fulfilled.

The request is passed through the core and is processed by the server. At the server site, an *object adapter* stores class and object information in a server resident interface repository, accepts and manages incoming requests from the client, and performs a variety of other object management functions [ORF94]. At the server, IDL stubs that are similar to those defined at the client machine are used as the interface to the actual object implementation resident at the server site.

Software development for modern C/S systems is object-oriented. Using the CORBA architecture described briefly in this section, software developers can create an environment in which objects can be reused throughout a large network. For further information on CORBA and its overall impact on software engineering for C/S systems, the interested reader should refer to [ORF96] and [MOW95].

28.2   SOFTWARE ENGINEERING FOR C/S SYSTEMS

A number of different software process models were introduced in Chapter 2. Although any of them could be adapted for use during the development of software for C/S systems, an evolutionary paradigm that makes use of event-based and/or object-oriented software engineering appears to work most effectively.

Client/server systems are developed using the classic software engineering activities—analysis, design, construction, and testing—as the system evolves from a set of general business requirements to a collection of validated software components that have been implemented on client and server machines.

28.3   ANALYSIS MODELING ISSUES

The requirements activity for C/S systems differs little from the analysis modeling methods applied for more conventional computer architectures. Therefore, the basic analysis principles discussed in Chapter 11 and the analysis modeling methods presented in Chapters 12 and 20 apply equally well to C/S software.

Because analysis modeling avoids the specification of implementation detail, it is only as the transition is made to design that issues associated with the allocation of software components to client and server are considered.[3]

---

[3]For example, a CORBA-compliant C/S architecture (Section 28.1.5) will have a profound impact on design and implementation decisions.

However, because an evolutionary approach to software engineering is applied for C/S systems, implementation decisions on the overall C/S approach (e.g., fat client vs. fat server) may be made during early analysis and design iterations.

28.4   DESIGN FOR C/S SYSTEMS

When software is being developed for implementation using a specific computer architecture, the design approach must consider the specific construction environment. In essence, design should be customized to accommodate the hardware architecture.

When software is designed for implementation using client/server architecture, the design approach must be "customized" to accommodate the following issues:

- Data design (Chapter 14) dominates the design process. To effectively use the capabilities of a relational database management system (RDBMS) or object-oriented database management system (OODBMS)[4] the design of the data becomes even more significant than in conventional applications.
- When the event-driven paradigm is chosen, behavioral modeling (an analysis activity, Chapter 12) should be conducted and the control-oriented aspects implied by the behavioral model should be translated into the design model.
- The user interaction/presentation component of a C/S system implements all functions that are typically associated with a graphical user interface (GUI). Therefore, interface design (Chapter 14) is elevated in importance.
- An object-oriented view of design (Chapter 21) is often chosen. Instead of the sequential structure that is provided by a procedural language, an object structure is provided by the linkage between an event initiated at the GUI and an event handling function within the client-based software.

Although debate continues on the best analysis and design approach for C/S systems, object-oriented methods (Chapters 20 and 21) appear to have the best combination of features. However, conventional methods (Chapters 12 and 14) can also be adopted. Conventional notation for analysis and design includes the data flow diagram (DFD), the entity-relationship diagram (ERD), and the structure chart.[5]

---

[4]RDBMS and object-oriented database management systems are used heavily in C/S architectures.

[5]This notation is discussed in detail in Chapter 12.

28.4.1 Conventional Design Approaches

In client/server systems, the DFD can be used to establish the scope of a system, identify the high-level functions and subject data areas (data stores), and permit the decomposition of the high-level functions. In a departure from the traditional DFD approach, however, decomposition stops at the level of an elementary business process rather than continuing to the level of an atomic process.

In the C/S context, an *elementary business process (EBP)* can be defined as a set of tasks performed without a break by one user at the client sites. The tasks are either performed fully or not at all.

The ERD also assumes an expanded role. It continues to be used to decompose the subject data areas (data stores) of the DFD in order to establish a high-level view of a database which is to be implemented using a RDBMS. Its new role is to provide the structure for defining high-level business objects (Section 28.4.2).

Instead of serving as a tool for functional decomposition, the structure chart is now used as an assembly diagram to show the components involved in the solution for an elementary business process. These components, consisting of interface objects, application objects, and database objects, establish how the data are to be processed.

28.4.2 Database Design

Database design is used to define and then specify the structure of business objects used in the client/server system. The analysis required to identify business objects is accomplished using information engineering methods discussed in Chapter 10. Conventional analysis modeling notation (Chapter 12), such as the ERD, can be used to define business objects, but a database repository should be established to capture the additional information that cannot be fully documented using a graphical notation such as an ERD.

In this repository, a business object is defined as information that is visible to the purchasers and users of the system, not its implementors. Each object (entity) identified in the ERD is expanded during design into: a data structure (e.g., a file and its related fields); all definitions governing files; relationships among data items in the records of the file; validation rules for these relationships; and business rules that specify the external view of the processing that is to occur for the data.

A wide array of design information must be developed during database design. This information, implemented using a relational database, can be maintained in a design repository modeled in Figure 28.4 [POR94]. Individual tables (the left side of the diagram) are used to define the following design information for the client/server database:

- *Entities*—are identified on the ERD for the new system.
- *Files*—which implement the entities identified on the ERD.
- *File-to-field relationship*—establishes the layout for the files by identifying which fields are included in which files.

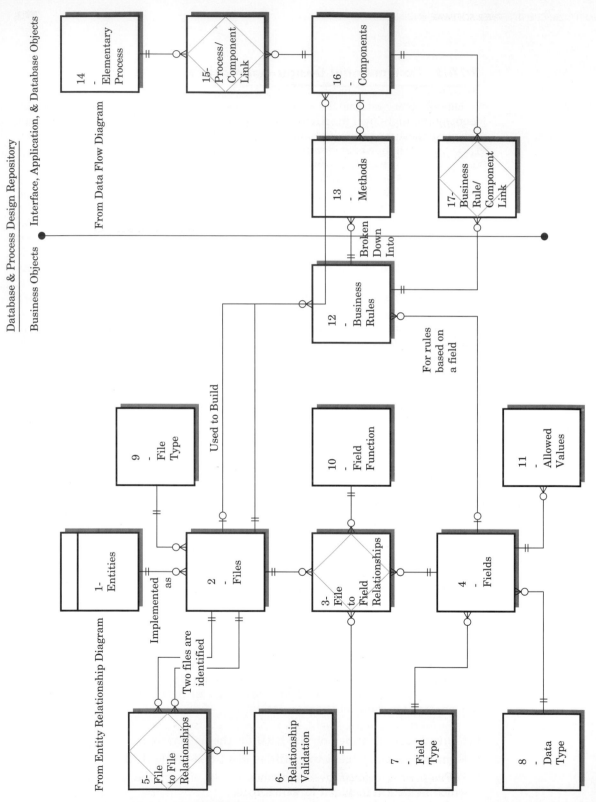

FIGURE 28.4. ERD for C/S design repository [POR94]

- *Fields*—defines the fields in the design (the data dictionary).
- *File-to-file relationships*—identify related files that can *be joined* to create logical views or queries.
- *Relationship validation*—identifies the type of file-to-file or file-to-field relationships used for validation.
- *Field type*—is used to permit inheritance of field characteristics from field superclasses (e.g., date, text, number, value, price).
- *Data type*—the characteristics of the data contained in a field.
- *File type*—is used to identify either the location of the file.
- *Field function*—key, foreign key, attribute, virtual field, derived field, etc.
- *Allowed values*—identifies allowed values for status-type fields.
- *Business rules*—rules for editing, calculating derived fields, etc.

As C/S architectures have become more pervasive, the trend toward distributed data management has accelerated. In C/S systems that implement this approach, the data management component resides on both the client and the server. Within the context of database design, a key issue is *data distribution*. That is, how is data distributed between the client and server and how is it dispersed across the nodes of a network?

A relational database system (RDBMS) enables easy access to distributed data through the use of *structured query language (SQL)*. The advantage of SQL in a C/S architecture is that it is "non-navigational" [BER92]. In an RDBMS, the type of data are specified using SQL, but no navigational information is required. Of course, the implication of this is that the RDBMS must be sophisticated enough to maintain the location of all data and be capable of defining the best path to it. In less sophisticated database systems, a request for data must indicate what is to be accessed and where it is. If application software must maintain navigational information, data management becomes much more complicated for C/S systems.

It should be noted that other data distribution and management techniques are also available to the designer [BER92]:

Manual extract. The user is allowed to manually copy appropriate data from a server to a client. This approach is useful when static data is required by a user and the control of the extract can be left in the user's hands.

Snapshot. This technique automates the manual extract by specifying a "snapshot" of data that should be transferred from a server to a client at predefined intervals. This approach is useful for distributing relatively static data that require only infrequent update.

Replication. This technique can be used when multiple copies of data must be maintained at different sites (e.g., different servers or clients and servers). Here, the level of complexity escalates because data consistency, updates, security, and processing must all be coordinated at multiple sites.

Fragmentation. In this approach, the system database is fragmented across multiple machines. Although intriguing in theory, fragmentation is exceptionally difficult to implement and is not, as yet, encountered frequently.

Database design, and more specifically, database design for C/S systems, are topics that are beyond the scope of this book. The interested reader should see [BRO91], [BER92], [VAS93], and [ORF94] for additional discussion.

28.4.3   An Overview of a Design Approach

Porter [POR95] suggests a set of steps for designing an elementary business process that combine elements of conventional design with elements of object-oriented design. It is assumed that a requirements model which defines business objects has been developed and refined prior to the start of the design of elementary business processes. The following steps are then used to derive the design:

1. For each elementary business process, identify the files that are created, updated, referenced, or deleted.
2. Use the files identified in step 1 as the basis for defining components or objects.
3. For each component, retrieve the business rules and other business object information that has been established for the relevant file.
4. Determine which rules are relevant to the process, and decompose the rules down to a method level.
5. As required, define any additional components that are needed to implement the methods.

Porter [POR95] suggests a specialized structure chart notation (Figure 28.5) for representing the component structure of an elementary business process. However, a different symbology is used so that the chart will conform to the object-oriented nature of C/S software. In the figure, five different symbols are encountered:

Interface Object. This type of component, also called the user interaction/presentation component, is typically built over a single file or a single file and related files that have been joined through a query. It includes methods for formatting the GUI interface and the client-resident application logic associated with the controls on the interface. It also includes embedded SQL statements, which specify the database processing performed on the primary file over which the interface is built. If application logic normally associated with an interface object is implemented on a server instead, typically through the use of the middleware tools, the application logic operating on the server should be identified as a separate application object.

Database Object. This type of component is used to identify database processing such as record creation or selection that is based on a file other

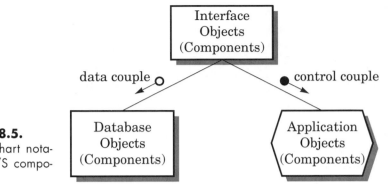

FIGURE 28.5.
Structure chart nota-
tion for C/S compo-
nents

than the primary file over which an interface object is built. It should be
noted that if the primary file over which an interface object is built is
processed in a different manner, a second set of SQL statements may be
used to retrieve a file in an alternate sequence. The second file processing
technique should be identified separately on the structure chart as a separate database object.

Application Object.   Used by either a interface object or a database object, this component is invoked by either a database trigger or a remote
procedure call. It can also be used to identify business logic normally associated with interface processing that has been moved to the server for operation.

Data Couple.   When one object invokes another independent object, a
message (Chapter 19) is passed between the two objects. The data couple
symbol (Figure 28.5) is used to denote this occurrence.

Control Couple.   When one object invokes another independent object
and no data are passed between the two objects, a control couple symbol is
used.

28.4.4   Process Design Iteration

The design repository (Section 28.4.2) used to represent business objects is also
used to represent interface, application, and database objects (see the right
hand side of Figure 28.4). Referring to Figure 28.4, note that the following entities are identified:

- *Methods*—describes *how* a business rule is to be implemented.
- *Elementary processes*—defines the elementary business processes identified
  in the analysis model.
- *Process/component link*—Similar to a bill of materials in manufacturing, this
  table identifies the components that make up the solution for an elementary
  business process. It is important to note that this linkage technique permits
  a given component to be included in the solution for multiple elementary
  business processes.

- *Components*—describes the components shown on the structure chart.
- *Business rule/component link*—identifies the components that are significant to the implementation of a given business rule.

If a repository of the type described in Figure 28.4 is implemented using an RDBMS, the designer will have access to a useful design tool that provides reporting to aid both construction and future maintenance of a C/S system.

28.5   TESTING ISSUES[6]

The distributed nature of client/server systems poses a set of unique problems for software testers. Binder [BIN92] suggests the following areas of focus:

- Client GUI considerations
- Target environment and platform diversity considerations
- Distributed database considerations (including replicated data)
- Distributed processing considerations (including replicated processes)
- Nonrobust target environment
- Nonlinear performance relationships

The strategy and tactics associated with C/S testing must be designed in a manner that allows each of the above issues to be addressed.

28.5.1   Overall C/S Testing Strategy

In general, the testing of client/server software occurs at three different levels: (1) individual client applications are tested in "disconnected" mode—the operation of the server and the underlying network are not considered; (2) the client software and associated server applications are tested in concert, but network operations are not explicitly exercised; (3) the complete C/S architecture, including network operation and performance, is tested.

Although many different types of tests are conducted at each of the above levels of detail, the following testing approaches are commonly encountered for C/S applications:

Application function tests.   The functionality of client applications is tested using the methods discussed earlier in this book. In essence, the application is tested in standalone fashion in an attempt to uncover errors in its operation.

---

[6]This section is a much abbreviated and adapted version of a paper written by Daniel Mosley [MOS96]. It is used with the author's permission.

Server tests.   The coordination and data management functions of the server are tested. Server performance (overall response time and data throughput) is also considered.

Database tests.   The accuracy and integrity of data stored by the server is tested. Transactions posted by client applications are examined to ensure that data are properly stored, updated, and retrieved. Archiving is also tested.

Transaction testing.   A series of tests are created to ensure that each class of transactions is processed according to requirements. Tests focus on the correctness of processing and also on performance issues (e.g., transaction processing times and transaction volume testing).

Network communication testing.   These tests verify that communication among the nodes of the network occurs correctly and that message passing, transactions, and related network traffic occur without error. Network security tests may also be conducted as part of this testing activity.

To accomplish these testing approaches, Musa [MUS93] recommends the development of operational profiles derived from client/server user scenarios. An *operational profile* indicates how different types of users interoperate with the C/S system. That is, the profiles provide a "pattern of usage" that can be applied when tests are designed and executed. For example, for a particular type of user, what percentage of transactions will be inquiries? updates? orders?

To develop the operational profile, it is necessary to derive a set of *user scenarios* [BIN95]. Each scenario addresses who, where, what, and why. That is, who the user is, where (in the physical C/S architecture) the system interaction occurs, what the transaction is, and why it has occurred. Scenarios can be derived during FAST meetings (Chapter 11) or through less formal discussions with end users. The result, however, should be the same. Each scenario should provide an indication of the system functions that will be required to service a particular user, the order in which those functions are required, the timing and response that is expected, and the frequency with which each function is used. These data are then combined (for all users) to create the operational profile.

The strategy for testing C/S architectures is analogous to the testing strategy for software-based systems described in Chapter 17. Testing begins with testing in-the-small. That is, a single client application is tested. Integration of the clients, the server, and the network is tested progressively. Finally, the entire system is tested as an operational entity.

Traditional testing views module/subsystem/system integration and testing (Chapter 17) as top-down, bottom-up, or some variation of the two. Module integration in C/S development may have some top-down or bottom-up aspects, but integration in C/S projects tends more toward parallel development and integration of modules across all design levels. Thus, integration testing in C/S projects is sometimes best accomplished using a nonincremental or "big bang" approach.

The fact that the system is not being built to use prespecified hardware and software impacts system testing. The networked cross-platform nature of C/S systems requires that we pay considerably more attention to configuration testing and compatibility testing.

1.0 Windows (Graphical User Interface) Testing
1.1   Business Scenario Identification
1.2   Test Case Creation
1.3   Verification
1.4   Test Tools

2.0 Server
21.   Test Data Creation
2.2   Volume/Stress Testing
2.3   Verification
2.4   Test Tools

3.0 Connectivity
3.1   Performance
3.2   Volume/Stress Testing
3.3   Verification
3.4   Test Tools

4.0 Technical Quality
4.1   Definitions
4.2   Defect Identification
4.3   Metrics
4.4   Code Quality
4.5   Test Tools

5.0 Functional Testing
5.1   Definitions
5.2   Test Data Creation
5.3   Verification
5.4   Test Tools

6.0 System Testing
6.1   Definition
6.2   Usability Testing
6.3   User Satisfaction Surveys
6.4   Verification
6.6   Test Tools

7.0 Testing Management
7.1   Test Team
7.2   Testing Schedule
7.3   Required Resources
7.4   Test Analysis, Reporting, and Tracking Mechanisms

FIGURE 28.6.
A revised client/server test plan based on GartnerGroup recommendations

Configuration testing doctrine forces testing of the system in all of the known hardware and software environments in which it will operate. *Compatibility testing* ensures a functionally consistent interface across hardware and software platforms. For example, the windows-type interface may be visually different depending on the implementation environment, but the same basic user behaviors should produce the same results regardless of whether the client interface is IBM's OS/2 Presentation Manager, Microsoft's Windows, Apple's Macintosh, or Open Software Foundation's Motif. The GartnerGroup [GAR93] suggests a *client/server* test plan outlined in Figure 28.6.

28.5.2 C/S Testing Tactics

Even if the C/S system has not been implemented using object-technology, object-oriented testing techniques (Chapter 22) make good sense because the replicated data and processes can be organized into classes of objects that share the same set of properties. Once test cases have been derived for a class of objects (or their equivalent in a conventionally developed system), those test cases should be broadly applicable for all instances of the class.

The OO point of view is particularly valuable when the graphical user interface of modern C/S systems is considered. The GUI is inherently object-oriented and departs from traditional interfaces because it must operate on many platforms. In addition, testing must explore a large number of logic paths because the GUI creates, manipulates, and modifies a broad range of graphical objects. Testing is further complicated because the objects can be present or absent, they may exist for a length of time, and they can appear anywhere on the desk-top.

What this means is that the traditional *capture/playback* approach for testing conventional character-based interfaces must he modified in order to handle the complexities of the GUI environment. A functional variation of the capture/playback paradigm called *structured capture/playback* [FAR93] has evolved for GUI testing.

Traditional capture/playback records input as keystrokes and output as screen images which are saved to compare against inputs and output images of subsequent tests. Structured capture/playback is based on an internal (logical) view of external activities. The application program's interactions with the GUI are recorded as internal events which can be saved as "scripts" written in Microsoft's Visual Basic, in one of the C variants, or in the vendor's proprietary language. A variety of useful tools (e.g., [HAY93], [QUI93], and [FAR93]) have been developed to accommodate this testing approach.

Tools that exercise GUIs do not address traditional data validation or path testing needs. The black-box and white-box testing methods discussed in Chapter 16 are applicable in many instances, and the special object-oriented strategies presented in Chapter 22 are appropriate for both client and server software.

28.6   SUMMARY

Although client/server systems can adopt one or more of the software process models and many of the analysis, design, and testing methods described earlier in this book, the special architectural features of C/S require customization of the software engineering approach. In general, the software process model applied for C/S systems is evolutionary in nature, and the technical methods often gravitate toward object-oriented approaches. The developer must describe objects that result in the implementation of user interaction/presentation, database, and application components. The objects defined for these components must be allocated to either the client or server machines, and can be linked via an object request broker.

Object request broker architectures support C/S designs in which client objects send messages to server objects. The CORBA standard makes use of interface definition language, and interface repositories manage requests for objects regardless of their location on the network.

Analysis and design for client/server systems make use of data flow and entity-relationship diagrams, modified structure charts, and other notation that is encountered in the development of conventional applications. Testing strategies must be modified to accommodate tests that examine network communication and the interplay between software that resides on client and server.

REFERENCES

[BER92]   Berson, A., *Client/Server Architecture,* McGraw-Hill, 1992.

[BIN92]   Binder, R., "A CASE-Based Systems Engineering Approach to Client-Server Development," *CASE Trends,* 1992.

[BIN95]   Binder, R., "Scenario-Based Testing for Client Server Systems," *Software Development,* vol. 3, no. 8, August 1995, pp. 43–49.

[BRO91]   Brown, A.W., *Object-Oriented Databases,* McGraw-Hill, 1991.

[FAR93]   Farley, K.J., "Software Testing For Windows Developers," *Data Based Advisor,* November 1993, pp. 45–46, 50–52.

[GAR93]   The GartnerGroup, conference presentation, 1993.

[HAY93]   Hayes, L.G., "Automated Testing For Everyone," *OS/2 Professional,* November 1993, p. 51.

[MOS96]   Mosley, D., "Managing Software Testing in the Client/Server Milieu," (in press).

[MOW95]   Mowbray and Zahavi, *The Essential CORBA,* Wiley, 1995.

[MUS93]   Musa, J., "Operational Profiles in Software Reliability Engineering," *IEEE Software,* March 1993, pp. 14–32.

[ORF94]   Orfali, R., D. Harkey, and J. Edwards, *Essential Client/Server Survival Guide,* Wiley, 1994.

[ORF96]   Orfali, R., D. Harkey, and J. Edwards, *The Essential Distributed Objects Survival Guide,* Wiley, 1996.

[PAU95]   Paul, L.G., "Client/Server Deployment," *Computerworld,* December 18, 1995.

[POR94]   Porter, J., *O-DES Design Manual,* Fairfield University, 1994.

[POR95]   Porter, J., *Synon Developer's Guide,* McGraw-Hill, 1995.

[QUI93]   Quinn, S.R., J.C. Ware, and J. Spragens, "Tireless Testers; Automated Tools Can Help Iron Out the Kinks in Your Custom GUI Applications," *Infoworld,* September 1993, pp. 78–79, 82–83, 85.

[VAS93]   Vaskevitch, D., *Client/Server Strategies,* IDG Books, 1993.

PROBLEMS AND POINTS TO PONDER

28.1. Using trade publications or Internet resources for background information, define a set of criteria for evaluating tools for C/S software engineering.

28.2. Suggest five applications in which a fat server would seem to be an appropriate design strategy.

28.3. Suggest five applications in which a fat client would seem to be an appropriate design strategy.

28.4. Do some additional research on the CORBA standard and determine how the latest release of the standard addresses interoperability among different ORBs provided by different vendors.

28.5. Research a structured query language (SQL) and provide a brief example of how a transaction might be characterized using the language.

28.6. Research the latest advances in groupware and develop a brief presentation for your class. Your instructor may assign a specific function to different presenters.

28.7. A company is establishing a new catalog sales division to sell casual apparel and outdoor merchandise. The catalog will be published on the World Wide Web, and orders can be placed by e-mail, via the Web site, or via telephone, or fax. A client/server system will be built to support order processing at the company site. Define a set of high-level objects that would be required for the order-processing system and organize these objects into three component categories: the user interaction/presentation, database, and application.

28.8. Formulate business rules to establish when shipment can be made if payment is by credit card for the system described in problem 28.7. Add additional rules if payment is by check.

28.9. Develop a state-transition diagram (Chapter 12) that defines the events and states that would be visible to an order entry clerk working at a client PC within the catalog sales division (problem 28.7).

28.10. Provide examples of three or four messages that might result in a request from a client for a method maintained on the server.

FURTHER READINGS AND OTHER INFORMATION SOURCES

Although the basic methods for analysis and design of client/server architectures are quite similar to more conventional systems, C/S-specific knowledge must be introduced. Orfali and his colleagues [ORF94] have written one of the more readable introductions to the technology. Watterson (*Client/Server Technology for Managers*, Addison-Wesley, 1995) provides an introductory overview of the technologies involved and the application focus of early systems. On a more detailed level, Nance (*Introduction to Networking*, Que Corporation, 1994) and Dewire (*Client/Server Computing*, McGraw-Hill, 1993) provide a thorough discussion of technology issues.

Tech-Ease (*Client-Server Computing*, Prentice-Hall, 1996) has published a general introduction to C/S systems and architectures. The following books are also worth examining:

Berson, A., *Client / Server Architecture,* 2nd edition, McGraw-Hill, 1996.

Goglia, P. A., *Testing Client / Server Applications,* Wiley, 1993.

Inmon, W.H., *Developing Client / Server Applications,* Wiley, 1994

Koelmel, R. L., *Implementing Application Solutions in a Client / Server Environment,* Wiley, 1995

Spohn, D.L., *Data Network Design,* 2nd edition, McGraw-Hill, 1996.

Because client/server technology is evolving so rapidly, industry periodicals and electronic information resources may be the best source of current information. The FAQ for the newsgroup **comp.client-server** can be found at:

http://www.abs.net/~lloyd/csfaq.txt

or

ftp://rtfm.mit.edu/pub/usenet/news.answers/client-server-faq

Information on the latest CORBA standards can be obtained at:

http://www.omg.org

A discussion of testing for C/S systems can be found at:

http://www.icon-stl.net/~djmosley

The Client/Server Coffeehouse provides a forum for Q&A among professionals who are trying to implement C/S technologies:

http://www.onr.com/oz/house.html

An up-to-date list of World Wide Web references for client/server software engineering can be found at: **http://www.rspa.com**

COMPUTER-AIDED SOFTWARE ENGINEERING

Everyone has heard the saying about the shoemaker's children: The shoemaker is so busy making shoes for others that his children don't have shoes of their own. Over the past 20 years, many software engineers have been the "shoemaker's children." Although these technical professionals have built complex systems that automate the work of others, they have used very little automation themselves. In fact, until recently software engineering was fundamentally a manual activity in which tools[1] were used only at latter stages of the process.

Today, software engineers have finally been given their first new pair of shoes—*computer-aided software engineering (CASE)*. The shoes don't come in as many varieties as they would like, are often a bit stiff and sometimes uncomfortable, don't provide enough sophistication for those who are stylish, and don't always match other garments that software developers use. But they provide an absolutely essential piece of apparel for the software developer's wardrobe, and will, over time, become more comfortable, more usable, and more adaptable to the needs of individual practitioners.

In earlier chapters of this book we have attempted to provide a reasonable understanding of the underpinnings of software engineering technology. In this chapter, the focus shifts to the tools and environments that will help to automate the software process.

---

[1] In many cases, the only tools available to the software engineer were compilers and text editors. These tools address only coding—an activity that should take no more than 20 percent of the overall software process.

29.1 WHAT IS CASE?

The best workshop for any craftsperson—a mechanic, a carpenter, or a software engineer—has three primary characteristics: (1) a collection of useful tools that will help in every step of building a product; (2) an organized layout that enables tools to be found quickly and used efficiently; and (3) a skilled craftsman who understands how to use the tools in an effective manner. Software engineers now recognize that they need more and varied tools (hand tools alone just won't meet the demands of modern computer-based systems), and they need an organized and efficient workshop in which to place the tools.

The workshop for software engineering is called an *integrated project support environment* (discussed later in this chapter), and the tool set that fills the work shop is called *computer-aided software engineering (CASE)*.

CASE tools add to the software engineer's tool box. CASE provides the engineer with the ability to automate manual activities and to improve engineering insight. Like computer-aided engineering and design tools that are used by engineers in other disciplines, CASE tools help to ensure that quality is designed in before the product is built.

29.2 BUILDING BLOCKS FOR CASE

Computer-aided software engineering can be as simple as a single tool that supports a specific software engineering activity or as complex as a complete environment that encompasses tools, a database, people, hardware, a network, operating systems, standards, and myriad other components. The building blocks for CASE are illustrated in Figure 29.1. Each building block forms a foundation for the next, with tools sitting at the top of the heap. It is interesting to note that the foundation for effective CASE environments has relatively little to do with software engineering tools themselves. Rather, successful en-

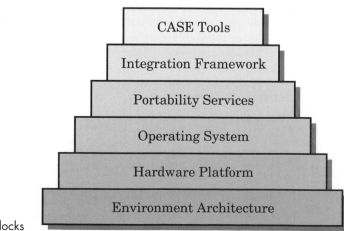

FIGURE 29.1.
Case building blocks

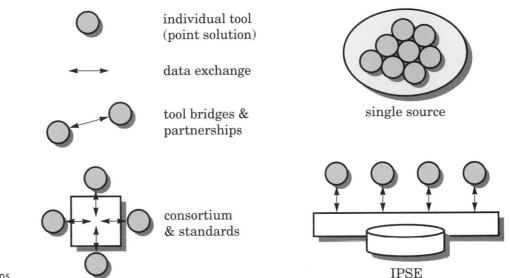

FIGURE 29.2.
Integration options

vironments for software engineering are built on an *environment architecture* that encompasses appropriate hardware and systems software. In addition, the environment architecture must consider the human work patterns that are applied during the software engineering process.

The environment architecture, composed of the hardware platform and operating system support (including networking and database management software), lays the ground work for CASE. But the CASE environment itself demands other building blocks. A set of *portability services* provides a bridge between CASE tools and their *integration framework* and the environment architecture. The integration framework is a collection of specialized programs that enables individual CASE tools to communicate with one another, to create a project database, and to exhibit the same look and feel to the end user (the software engineer). Portability services allow CASE tools and their integration framework to migrate across different hardware platforms and operating systems without significant adaptive maintenance.

The building blocks depicted in Figure 29.1 represent a comprehensive foundation for the integration of CASE tools. However, most CASE tools in use today have not been constructed using all of the building blocks discussed above. In fact, some CASE tools remain "point solutions." That is, a tool is used to assist in a particular software engineering activity (e.g., analysis modeling), but does not directly communicate with other tools, is not tied into a project database, and is not part of an *integrated CASE environment (I-CASE)*. Although this situation is not ideal, a CASE tool can be used quite effectively, even if it is a point solution.

The relative levels of CASE integration are shown in Figure 29.2. At the low end of the integration spectrum is the *individual* (point solution) *tool*. When individual tools provide facilities for *data exchange* (most do), the integration level is improved slightly. Such tools produce output in a standard format that should be compatible with other tools that can read the format. In some cases, the builders of complementary CASE tools work together to form a *bridge* between the tools (e.g., an analysis and design tool that is coupled with a code generator). Using this approach, the synergy between the tools can produce end products that would be difficult to create using either tool separately. *Single source integration* occurs when a single CASE tools vendor integrates a number of different tools and sells them as a package. Although this approach is quite effective, the closed architecture of most single source environments precludes easy addition of tools from other vendors.

At the high end of the integration spectrum is the *integrated project support environment (IPSE)*. Standards for each of the building blocks described above are created. CASE tools vendors use these IPSE standards to build tools that will be compatible with the IPSE and therefore compatible with one another.

29.3   A TAXONOMY OF CASE TOOLS[2]

A number of risks are inherent whenever we attempt to categorize CASE tools. There is a subtle implication that to create an effective CASE environment one must implement all categories of tools—this is simply not true. Confusion (or antagonism) can be created by placing a specific tool within one category when others might believe it belongs in another category. Some readers may feel that an entire category has been omitted—thereby eliminating an entire set of tools for inclusion in the overall CASE environment. In addition, simple categorization tends to be flat—that is, we do not show the hierarchical interaction of tools or the relationships among them. Even with these risks, it is necessary to create a taxonomy of CASE tools—to better understand the breadth of CASE and to better appreciate where such tools can be applied in the software process.

CASE tools can be classified by function, by their role as instruments for managers or technical people, by their use in the various steps of the software engineering process, by the environment architecture (hardware and software) that supports them, or even by their origin or cost [QED89]. The taxonomy presented below uses function as a primary criteria.

Information Engineering Tools. By modeling the strategic information requirements of an organization, *information engineering tools* provide a "metamodel" from which specific information systems are derived. Rather then focusing on the requirements of a specific application, these CASE tools model business information as it moves between various organizational entities within a company. The primary objective for tools in this category is to represent business data objects, their relationships, and how these data objects flow between different business areas within a company.

---

[2]Sources for vendors who offer representative tools for each category presented in the sections that follow have been listed in "Further Readings and Other Information Sources" at the end of this chapter.

Process Modeling and Management Tools. If an organization works to improve a business (or software) process, it must first understand it. Process modeling tools (also called "process technology" tools) are used to represent the key elements of a process so that it can be better understood. Such tools can also provide links to process descriptions that help those involved in the process to understand the work tasks that are required to perform the process. In addition, process management tools can provide links to other tools that provide support to defined process activities.

Project Planning Tools. Tools in this category focus on two primary areas: software project effort and cost estimation, and project scheduling. Estimation tools compute estimated effort, project duration, and recommended number of people using one or more of the techniques introduced in Chapter 5. Project scheduling tools enable the manager to define all project tasks (the work breakdown structure), create a task network (usually using graphical input), represent task interdependencies, and model the amount of parallelism possible for the project (Chapter 7).

Risk Analysis Tools. Identifying potential risks and developing a plan to mitigate, monitor, and manage them is of paramount importance on large projects. Risk analysis tools enable a project manager to build a risk table (Chapter 6) by providing detailed guidance in the identification and analysis of risks.

Project Management Tools. The project schedule and project plan must be tracked and monitored on a continuing basis. In addition, a manager should use tools to collect metrics that will ultimately provide an indication of software product quality. Tools in the category are often extensions to project planning tools.

Requirements Tracing Tools. When large systems are developed, the delivered system often fails to meet customer specified requirements. The objective of requirements tracing tools is to provide a systematic approach to the isolation of requirements, beginning with the customer request for proposal (RFP) or specification. The typical requirements tracing tool combines human-interactive text evaluation, with a database management system that stores and categorizes each system requirement that is "parsed" from the original RFP or specification.

Metrics and Management Tools. Software metrics improve a manager's ability to control and coordinate the software process and a practitioner's ability to improve the quality of the software that is produced. Today's metrics and measurement tools focus on process, project, and product characteristics. Management-oriented tools capture project-specific metrics (e.g., LOC/person-month, defects per function point) that provide an overall indication of productivity or quality. Technically oriented tools determine technical metrics (Chapters 18 and 23) that provide greater insight into the quality of design or code. Many of the more advanced metrics tools maintain a database of "industry average" measures. Based on project and product characteristics provided by the user, such tools "rate" local numbers against industry averages (and past local performance) and suggest strategies for improvement.

Documentation Tools. Document production and desk-top publishing tools support nearly every aspect of software engineering and represent a substantial "leverage" opportunity for all software developers. Most software development organizations spend a substantial amount of time developing documents, and in many cases the documentation process itself is quite inefficient. It is not unusual for a software development organization to spend as much as 20 or 30 percent of all software development effort on documentation. For this reason, documentation tools provide an important opportunity to improve productivity.

System Software Tools. CASE is a workstation technology. Therefore, the CASE environment must accommodate high-quality network system software, electronic mail, bulletin boards, and other communication capabilities.

Quality Assurance Tools. The majority of CASE tools that claim to focus on quality assurance are actually metrics tools that audit source code to determine compliance with language standards. Other tools extract technical metrics (Chapter 18) in an effort to project the quality of the software that is being built.

Database Management Tools. Database management software serves as a foundation for the establishment of a CASE database (repository), which we have also called the project database (Chapter 9). Given the emphasis on configuration objects, database management tools for CASE may evolve from relational database management systems (RDMS) to object-oriented database management systems (OODMS).

Software Configuration Management Tools. Software configuration management (SCM) lies at the kernel of every CASE environment. Tools can assist in all five major SCM tasks—identification, version control, change control, auditing, and status accounting. The CASE database provides a mechanism for identifying each configuration item and relating it to other items; the control process discussed in Chapter 9 can be implemented with the aid of specialized tools; easy access to individual configuration items facilitates the auditing process; and CASE communication tools can greatly improve status accounting (reporting information about changes to all who need to know).

Analysis and Design Tools. Analysis and design tools enable a software engineer to create models of the system to be built. The models contain a representation of data, function, and behavior (at the analysis level), and characterizations of data, architectural, procedural, and interface design. By performing consistency and validity checking on the model, analysis and design tools provide a software engineer with some degree of insight into the analysis representation and help to eliminate errors before they propagate into the design, or worse, into implementation itself.

PRO/SIM Tools. PRO/SIM (prototyping and simulation) tools [NIC90] provide the software engineer with the ability to predict the behavior of a real-time system prior to the time that it is built. In addition, they enable the software engineer to develop mock-ups of the real-time system that allow the customer to gain insight into its function, operation, and response prior to actual implementation.

Interface Design and Development Tools. Interface design and development tools are actually a tool kit of program components such as menus, buttons, window structures, icons, scrolling mechanisms, device drivers and so forth. However, these tool kits are being replaced by interface prototyping tools that enable rapid on-screen creation of sophisticated user interfaces that conform to the interfacing standard that has been adopted for the software.

Prototyping Tools. A variety of different prototyping tools can be used. *Screen painters* enable a software engineer to define screen layout rapidly for interactive applications. More sophisticated CASE prototyping tools enable the creation of a data design, coupled with both screen and report layouts. Many analysis and design tools have extensions that provide a prototyping option. PRO/SIM tools generate skeleton Ada and C source code for engineering (real-time) applications. Finally, a variety of fourth generation tools have prototyping features.

Programming Tools. The programming tools category encompasses compilers, editors, and debuggers that are available to support most conventional programming languages. In addition, object-oriented (OO) programming environments, fourth generation languages, graphical programming environments, application generators, and database query languages also reside within this category.

Integration and Testing Tools. In their directory of software testing tools, Software Quality Engineering [SQE95] defines the following testing tools categories:

- *data acquisition*—tools that acquire data to be used during testing
- *static measurement*—tools that analyze source code without executing test cases
- *dynamic measurement*—tools that analyze source code during execution
- *simulation*—tools that simulate functions of hardware or other externals
- *test management*—tools that assist in the planning, development, and control of testing
- *cross-functional tools*—tools that cross the bounds of the above categories.

It should be noted that many testing tools have features that span two or more of the above categories.

Static Analysis Tools. Static testing tools assist the software engineer in deriving test cases. Three different types of static testing tools are used in the industry: code-based testing tools, specialized testing languages, and requirements-based testing tools. *Code-based testing tools* accept source code (or PDL) as input and perform a number of analyses that result in the generation of test cases. *Specialized testing languages* (e.g., ATLAS) enable a software engineer to write detailed test specifications that describe each test case and the logistics for its execution. Requirements-based testing tools isolate specific user requirements and suggest test cases (or classes of tests) that will exercise the requirements.

Dynamic Analysis Tools. Dynamic testing tools interact with an executing program, checking path coverage, testing assertions about the value of specific variables, and otherwise instrumenting the execution flow of the program. Dynamic tools can be either intrusive or nonintrusive. An *intrusive tool* changes the software to be tested by inserted probes (extra instructions) that perform the activities mentioned above. *Nonintrusive testing tools* use a separate hardware processor that runs in parallel with the processor containing the program that is being tested.

Test Management Tools. Test management tools are used to control and coordinate software testing for each of the major testing steps (Chapter 17). Tools in this category manage and coordinate regression testing, perform comparisons that ascertain differences between actual and expected output, and conduct batch testing of programs with interactive human–computer interfaces. In addition to the functions noted above, many test management tools also serve as generic test drivers. A test driver reads one or more test cases from a testing file, formats the test data to conform to the needs of the software under test, and then invokes the software to be tested.

Client/Server Testing Tools. The C/S environment demands specialized testing tools that exercise the graphical user interface and the network communications requirements for client and server.

Reengineering Tools. The reengineering tools category can be subdivided into the following functions:

- *reverse engineering to specification tools*—take source code as input and generate graphical structured analysis and design models, where-used lists, and other design information;

- *code restructuring and analysis tools*—analyze program syntax, generate a control flow graph, and automatically generate a structured program; and

- *on-line system reengineering tools*—used to modify on-line database systems (e.g., convert IDMS or DB2 files into entity-relationship format).

Many of the above tools are limited to specific programming languages (although most major languages are addressed) and require some degree of interaction with the software engineer.

Next generation reverse and forward engineering tools will make much stronger use of artificial intelligence techniques, applying a knowledge base that is application domain specific (i.e., a set of decomposition rules that would apply to all programs in a particular application area such as manufacturing control or aircraft avionics). The AI component will assist in system decomposition and reconstruction, but will still require interaction with a software engineer throughout the reengineering cycle.

29.4 INTEGRATED CASE ENVIRONMENTS

Although benefits can be derived from individual CASE tools that address separate software engineering activities, the real power of CASE can only be achieved through integration. The benefits of *integrated CASE (I-CASE)* include (1) smooth transfer of information (models, programs, documents, data) from one tool to another and one software engineering step to the next; (2) a reduction in the effort required to perform umbrella activities such as software configuration management, quality assurance, and document production; (3) an increase in project control that is achieved through better planning, monitoring, and communication; and (4) improved coordination among staff members who are working on a large software project.

But I-CASE also poses significant challenges. Integration demands consistent representations of software engineering information, standardized interfaces between tools, a homogeneous mechanism for communication between the software engineer and each tool, and an effective approach that will enable I-CASE to move among various hardware platforms and operating systems. Although solutions to the problems implied by these challenges have been proposed, comprehensive I-CASE environments are only beginning to emerge.

The term "integration" implies both "combination" and "closure." I-CASE combines a variety of different tools and different information in a way that enables closure of communication among tools, between people, and across the software process. Tools are integrated so that software engineering information is available to each tool that needs it; usage is integrated so that a common look and feel is provided for all tools; and a development philosophy is integrated, implying a standardized software engineering approach that applies modern practice and proven methods.

To define *integration* in the context of the software process, it is necessary to establish a set of requirements for I-CASE: An integrated CASE environment should [FOR89a]:

- provide a mechanism for sharing software engineering information among all tools contained in the environment;
- enable a change to one item of information to be tracked to other related information items;
- provide version control and overall configuration management for all software engineering information;
- allow direct, nonsequential access to any tool contained in the environment;
- establish automated support for a procedural context for software engineering work that integrates the tools and data into a standard work breakdown structure (Chapter 7);
- enable the users of each tool to experience a consistent look and feel at the human–computer interface;
- support communication among software engineers; and
- collect both management and technical metrics that can be used to improve the process and the product.

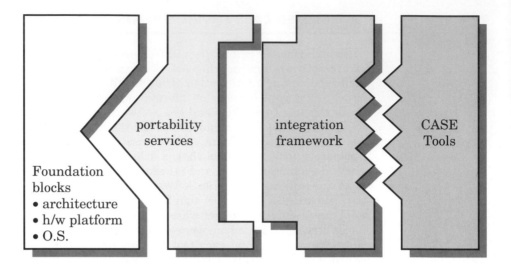

FIGURE 29.3.
Elements of I-CASE

To achieve these requirements, each of the building blocks of a CASE architecture (Figure 29.1) must fit together in a seamless fashion. As shown in Figure 29.3, the foundation building blocks—environment architecture, hardware platform, and operating system—must be "joined" through a set of portability services to an *integration framework* that achieves the requirements noted above.

29.5   THE INTEGRATION ARCHITECTURE

A software engineering team uses CASE tools, corresponding methods, and a process framework to create a pool of software engineering information. The integration framework facilitates transfer of information into and out of the pool. To accomplish this, the following architectural components must exist: a database to store the information, an object management system to manage changes to the information, a tools control mechanism to coordinate the use of CASE tools, and a user interface to provide a consistent pathway between actions made by the user and the tools contained in the environment. Most models (e.g., [FOR90], [SHA95]) of the integration framework represent these components as *layers*. A simple model of the framework depicting only the components noted above is shown in Figure 29.4.

The *user interface layer* (Figure 29.4) incorporates a standardized interface tool kit with a common presentation protocol. The *interface tool kit* contains software for human–computer interface management and a library of display objects. Both provide a consistent mechanism for communication between the interface and individual CASE tools. The *presentation protocol* is the set of guidelines that gives all CASE tools the same look and feel. Screen layout conventions, menu names and organization, icons, object names, the use of the keyboard and mouse, and the mechanism for tools access are all defined as part of the presentation protocol.

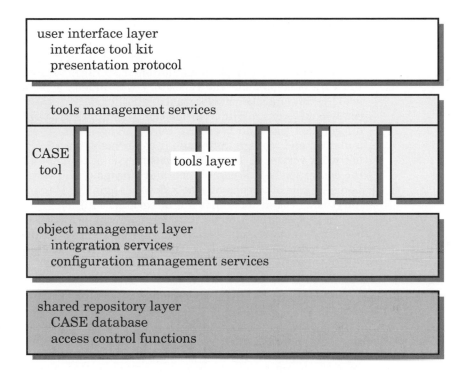

FIGURE 29.4.
Architectural model for the integration framework

The *tools layer* incorporates a set of tools management services with the CASE tools themselves. *Tools management services (TMS)* control the behavior of tools within the environment. If multitasking is used during the execution of one or more tools, TMS performs multitask synchronization and communication, coordinates the flow of information from the repository and object management system into the tools, accomplishes security and auditing functions, and collects metrics on tool usage.

The *object management layer (OML)* performs the configuration management functions described in Chapter 8. In essence, software in this layer of the framework architecture provides the mechanism for tools integration. Every CASE tool is "plugged into" the object management layer. Working in conjunction with the CASE repository, the OML provides *integration services*—a set of standard modules that couple tools with the repository. In addition, the OML provides configuration management services by enabling the identification of all configuration objects, performing version control, and providing support for change control, audits, and status accounting.

The *shared repository layer* is the CASE database[3] and the access control functions that enable the object management layer to interact with the database. Data integration is achieved by the object management and shared repository layers.

---

[3]In Chapter 9 we referred to the repository as the project database.

29.6   THE CASE REPOSITORY

Webster's Dictionary defines the word "repository" as "any thing or person thought of as a center of accumulation or storage."[4] During the early history of software development, the repository was indeed a person—the programmer who had to remember the location of all information relevant to a software project, who had to recall information that was never written down and reconstruct information that had been lost. Sadly, using a person as "the center for accumulation and storage" (although it conforms to the dictionary definition), does not work very well. Today, the repository is a "thing"—a database that acts as the center for both accumulation and storage of software engineering information. The role of the person (the software engineer) is to interact with the repository using CASE tools that are integrated with it.

In this book, a number of different terms are used to refer to the storage place for software engineering information: CASE database, project database, integrated project support environment (IPSE) database, data dictionary (a limited database), and repository. Although there are subtle differences between some of these terms, all refer to the thing—the center for accumulation and storage.

29.6.1   The Role of the Repository in I-CASE

The repository for an I-CASE environment is the set of mechanisms and data structures that achieve data–tool and data–data integration. It provides the obvious functions of a database management system,[5] but in addition, the repository performs or precipitates the following functions [FOR89b]:

- *data integrity*—includes functions to validate entries to the repository, ensure consistency among related objects, and automatically perform "cascading" modifications when a change to one object demands some change to objects that are related to it;

- *information sharing*—provides a mechanism for sharing information among multiple developers and between multiple tools, manages and controls multiuser access to data and locks/unlocks objects so that changes are not inadvertently overlaid on one another;

- *data–tool integration*—establishes a data model that can be accessed by all tools in the I-CASE environment, controls access to the data, and performs appropriate configuration management functions;

---

[4]Some of the other definitions of this word are equally intriguing when we consider the current state of software engineering practice: "(1) a room where things are placed for safekeeping; (2) a building for exhibiting objects; (3) a burial vault."

[5]Although many investigators feel that an object-oriented database management system is the correct approach, others believe that a relational DBMS can do the job adequately.

- *data–data integration*—the database management system relates data objects so that other functions can be achieved;

- *methodology enforcement*—the E-R model of data stored in the repository can imply a specific paradigm for software engineering—at a minimum, the relationships and objects define a set of steps that must be conducted to build the contents of the repository; and

- *document standardization*—the definition of objects in the database leads directly to a standard approach for the creation of software engineering documents.

To achieve these functions, the repository is defined in terms of a *metamodel*. The metamodel determines how information is stored in the repository, how data can be accessed by tools and viewed by software engineers, how well data security and integrity can be maintained, and how easily the existing model can be extended to accommodate new needs [WEL89].

The metamodel is the template into which software engineering information is placed. An entity-relationship metamodel can be created, but other, more sophisticated models are also under consideration. A detailed discussion of these models is beyond the scope of this book. For further information, the interested reader should see [WEL89], [SHA95], and [GRI95].

29.6.2 Features and Content[6]

The features and content of the repository are best understood by looking at it from two perspectives: What is to be stored in the repository and what specific services are provided by the repository? In general, the types of things to be stored in the repository include:

- the problem to be solved
- information about the problem domain
- the system solution as it emerges
- rules and instructions pertaining to the software process (methodology) being followed
- the project plan, resources, and history
- information about the organizational context

A detailed list of types of representations, documents, and deliverables that are stored in the CASE repository is included in Table 29.1.

A robust CASE repository provides two different classes of services: (1) the types of services that might be expected from any sophisticated database management system, and (2) services that are specific to the CASE environment.

---

[6]This section has been adapted from [FOR89b] with permission of CASE Consulting Group.

TABLE 29.1

CASE REPOSITORY CONTENTS [FOR89B]

Enterprise information 　　Organizational structure 　　Business area analyses 　　Business functions 　　Business rules 　　Process models (scenarios) 　　Information architecture	**Construction** 　　Source code; Object code 　　System build instructions 　　Binary images 　　Configuration dependencies 　　Change information
Application design 　　Methodology rules 　　Graphical representations 　　System diagrams 　　Naming standards 　　Referential integrity rules 　　Data structures 　　Process definitions 　　Class definitions 　　Menu trees 　　Performance criteria 　　Timing constraints 　　Screen definitions 　　Report definitions 　　Logic definitions 　　Behavioral logic 　　Algorithms 　　Transformation rules	**Validation and verification** 　　Test plan; Test data cases 　　Regression test scripts 　　Test results 　　Statistical analyses 　　Software quality metrics **Project management information** 　　Project plans 　　Work breakdown structure 　　Estimates; Schedules 　　Resource loading; Problem reports 　　Change requests; Status reports 　　Audit information **System documentation** 　　Requirements documents 　　External/internal designs 　　User manuals

Many repository requirements are the same as those of typical applications built on a commercial database management system (DBMS). In fact, most of today's CASE repositories employ a DBMS (usually relational or object-oriented) as the basic data management technology. The standard DBMS features of a CASE repository supporting the management of software development information include:

Nonredundant data storage. The CASE repository provides a single place for the storage of all information pertinent to the development of software systems, eliminating wasteful and potentially error-prone duplication.

High-level access. The repository provides a common data access mechanism so that data handling facilities do not have to be duplicated in each CASE tool.

Data independence. CASE tools and the target applications are isolated from physical storage so that they are not affected when the configuration is changed.

Transaction control. The repository manages multipart interactions in a manner that maintains the integrity of the data when there are concurrent users and in the event of a system failure. This usually implies record locking, two-stage commits, transaction logging, and recovery procedures.

Security. The repository provides mechanisms to control who can view and modify information contained within it. At a minimum, the repository should enforce multilevel passwords and permission levels assigned by individual users. The repository should also provide assistance for automatic backup and restore, and archiving of selected groups of information—for example, by project or application.

Ad hoc data queries and reports. The repository allows direct access to its contents through a convenient user interface such as SQL or a forms-oriented "browser," enabling user-defined analysis beyond the standard reports provided with the CASE tool set.

Openness. Repositories usually provide a simple import/export mechanism to enable bulk loading or transfer. The interfaces are usually a flat ASCII file transfer or a standard SQL interface. Some repositories have higher-level interfaces that reflect the structure of their metamodels.

Multiuser support. A robust repository must permit multiple developers to work on an application at the same time. It must manage concurrent access to the database by multiple tools and users with access arbitration and locking at the file or record level. For environments based on networking, multiuser support also implies that the repository can interface with common networking protocols and facilities.

The CASE environment also makes special demands on the repository that go beyond what is directly available in a commercial DBMS. The special features of CASE repositories include:

Storage of sophisticated data structures. The repository must accommodate complex data types such as diagrams, documents and files, as well as simple data elements. A repository also includes an information model (or metamodel) describing the structure, relationships, and semantics of the data stored in it. The metamodel must be extensible so that new representations and unique organizational information can be accommodated. The repository not only stores models and descriptions of the systems under development, but also associated metadata (i.e., additional information describing the software engineering information itself, such as when a particular design component was created, what its current status is, and what other components it depends upon).

Integrity enforcement. The repository information model also contains rules, or policies, describing valid business rules and other constraints and requirements on information being entered into the repository (directly or via a CASE tool). A facility called a *trigger* may be employed to activate the rules associated with an object whenever it is modified, making it possible to check the validity of design models in real time.

Semantic-rich tool interface. The repository information model (meta-model) contains semantics that enable a variety of tools to interpret the meaning of the data stored in the repository. For example, a data flow diagram created by a CASE tool is stored in the repository in a form based on the information model and independent of any internal representations used by the tool itself. Another CASE tool can then interpret the contents of the repository and use the information as needed for its task. Thus, the semantics stored in the repository permit data sharing among a variety of tools, as opposed to specific tool-to-tool conversions or "bridges."

Process/project management. A repository contains information not only about the software application itself, but also about the characteristics of each particular project and the organization's general process for software engineering (phases, tasks, and deliverables). This opens up possibilities for automated coordination of technical development activity with the project management activity. For example, updating the status of project tasks could be done automatically or as a by-product of using the CASE tools. Status updating could be made very easy for developers to perform without having to leave the normal development environment. Task assignment and queries can also be handled by electronic mail. Problem reports, maintenance tasks, change authorization, and repair status can be coordinated and monitored via tools accessing the repository.

The following repository features are all encompassed by software configuration management (Chapter 9). They are re-examined here to emphasize their interrelationship to I-CASE environments.

Versioning   As a project progresses, many versions of individual work products will be created. The repository must be able to save all of these versions to enable effective management of product releases and to permit developers to go back to previous versions during testing and debugging. Versioning is done with a compression algorithm to minimize storage allocation, and permits regeneration of any previous version with some processing overhead.

Dependency Tracking and Change Management   The repository manages a wide variety of relationships among the data elements stored in it. These include relationships between enterprise entities and processes, among the parts of an application design, between design components and the enterprise information architecture, between design elements and deliverables, and so on. Some of these relationships are merely associations, and some are dependencies or mandatory relationships. Maintaining these relationships among development objects is called *link management*.

The ability to keep track of all of these relationships is crucial to the integrity of the information stored in the repository and to the generation of deliverables based on it, and it is one of the most important contributions of the repository concept to the improvement of the software development process. Among the many functions that link management supports is the ability to identify and assess the effects of change. As designs evolve to meet new requirements, the ability to identify all objects that might be affected enables more accurate assessment of cost, downtime, and degree of difficulty. It also helps prevent unexpected side effects that would otherwise lead to defects and system failures.

Requirements Tracing   A special function depending on link management is *requirements tracing*. This is the ability to track all the design components and deliverables that result from a specific requirement specification (forward tracking), as well as the ability to identify which requirement generated any given deliverable (backward tracking).

Configuration Management   Another function depending on link management is configuration management. A configuration management facility works closely with the link management and versioning facilities to keep track of a series of configurations representing specific project milestones or production releases. Version management provides the needed versions, and link management keeps track of interdependencies. For example, configuration management often provides a *build* facility to automate the process of transforming design components into executable deliverables.

Audit Trails   Related to change management is the need for an audit trail that establishes additional information about when, why, and by whom changes are made. Actually, this is not a difficult requirement for a repository that has a robust information model. Information about the source of changes can be entered as attributes of specific objects in the repository. A repository trigger mechanism is helpful for prompting the developer or the tool he or she is using to initiate entry of audit information (such as the reason for a change) whenever a design element is modified.

29.7   SUMMARY

Computer-aided software engineering tools span every step in the software process and those umbrella activities that are applied throughout the process. CASE combines a set of building blocks that begin at the hardware and operating system software level and end with individual tools.

In this chapter we have considered a taxonomy of CASE tools. Categories encompass both management and technical activities and span most software application areas. Each category of tool has been considered as a "point solution."

The I-CASE environment combines integration mechanisms for data, tools, and human–computer interaction. Data integration can be achieved through direct exchange of information, through common file structures, by data sharing or interoperability, or through the use of a full I-CASE repository. Tools integration can be custom-designed by vendors who work together or can be achieved through management software provided as part of the repository.

Human–computer integration is achieved through interface standards that are becoming increasingly common throughout the industry. An integration architecture is designed to facilitate the integration of users with tools, tools with tools, tools with data, and data with data.

The CASE repository has been referred to as a "software bus." Information moves through it, passing from tool to tool as the software process progresses. But the repository is much more than a "bus." It is also a storage place that combines sophisticated mechanisms for integrating CASE tools and thereby improving the process through which software is developed. The repository is a relational or object-oriented database that is "the center of accumulation and storage" for software engineering information.

REFERENCES

[FOR89a]   Forte, G., "In Search of the Integrated Environment," *CASE Outlook,* March/April 1989, pp. 5–12.

[FOR89b]   Forte, G., "Rally Round the Repository," *CASE Outlook,* December 1989, pp. 5–27.

[FOR90]   Forte, G., "Integrated CASE: A Definition," *Proc. 3rd Annual TEAM-WORKERS Intl. User's Group Conference,* Cadre Technologies, Providence, RI, March 1990.

[GRI95]   Griffen, J., "Repositories: Data Dictionary Descendant Can Extend Legacy Code Investment," *Application Development Trends,* April 1995, pp. 65–71.

[NIC90]   Nichols, K.M., "Performance Tools," *IEEE Software,* May 1990, pp. 21–23.

[QED89]   *CASE: The Potential and the Pitfalls,* QED Information Sciences, Inc., Wellsley, MA, 1989.

[SHA95]   Sharon, D., and R. Bell, "Tools that Bind: Creating Integrated Environments," *IEEE Software,* March 1995, pp. 76–85.

[SQE95]   *Testing Tools Reference Guide,* Software Quality Engineering, Jacksonville, FL, 1995.

[WEL89]   Welke, R.J., "Meta Systems on Meta Models," *CASE Outlook,* December 1989, pp. 35–45.

PROBLEMS AND POINTS TO PONDER

29.1.   Make a list of all software development tools that you use. Organize them according to the taxonomy presented in this chapter.

29.2.   What are the strengths of the "old-fashioned" software development environment architecture that made use of a mainframe and terminals? What are the disadvantages?

29.3.   Using the ideas introduced in Chapter 14 and/or 19, how would you suggest that portability services be built?

29.4.   Build a paper prototype for a project management tool that encompasses the categories noted in Section 29.3. Use Part Two of this book for additional guidance.

29.5. Do some research on object-oriented database management systems. Discuss why OODMS would be ideal for SCM tools.

29.6. Gather product information on at least three analysis and design tools. Develop a matrix that compares features.

29.7. Gather product information on two PRO/SIM tools. Develop a matrix that compares features.

29.8. Gather product information on at least three fourth generation coding tools. Develop a matrix that compares features.

29.9. Are there situations in which dynamic testing tools are "the only way to go." If so, what are they?

29.10. Discuss other human activities in which the integration of a set of tools has provided substantially more benefit than the use of each of the tools individually. Do not use examples from computing.

29.11. Describe what is meant by data-tool integration in your own words.

29.12. In a number of places in this chapter, the terms "metamodel" and "metadata" are used. Describe what these terms mean in your own words.

29.13. Can you think of additional configuration items that might be included in the repository contents shown in Table 29.1? Make a list.

FURTHER READINGS AND OTHER INFORMATION SOURCES

A number of books on CASE were published in the 1980s in an effort to capitalize on the high degree of interest in the industry at that time. Subsequently, relatively few books on the subject have appeared. Of the books that have been published, many suffer from one or more of the following failings: (1) the book only focuses on a narrow band of tools (e.g., analysis and design) while claiming to cover a wider categorization; (2) the book spends relatively little time on CASE and more time surveying (often poorly) the underlying methods that the tools deliver; (3) the book spends little time discussing integration issues; and (4) the presentation is outdated because of an emphasis on specific CASE products. The books that follow have avoided at least some of these failings:

Braithwaite, K.S., *Application Development Using CASE Tools,* Academic Press, 1990.

Fisher, C., *CASE: Using Software Development Tools,* Wiley, 1988.

Gane, C., *Computer-Aided Software Engineering: The Methodologies, the Products and the Future,* Prentice-Hall, 1990.

Lewis, T.G., *Computer-Aided Software Engineering,* Van Nostrand Reinhold, 1990.

McClure, C., *CASE is Software Automation,* Prentice-Hall, 1988.

Schindler, M., *Computer-Aided Software Design,* Wiley, 1990.

Towner, L.E, *CASE: Concepts and Implementation,* McGraw-Hill, 1989.

An anthology by Chikofsky (*Computer-Aided Software Engineering,* IEEE Computer Society Press, 1988) contains a useful collection of early papers on CASE and software development environments. The best sources of current information on CASE tools are technical periodicals and industry newsletters.

Although there is great interest in I-CASE environments and the CASE repository, relatively few books treat these subjects in detail. Garg and Jazayeri (*Process Centered Software Engineering Environments,* IEEE Computer Society Press, 1995) consider development environments that are driven by process models. Books by Brereton (*Software Engineering Environments,* Wiley, 1988), Charette (*Software Engineering Environments,* McGraw-Hill, 1986), and Barstow, Shrobe, and Sandewall (*Interactive Programming Environments,* McGraw-Hill, 1984) present different views of the "ideal" CASE environment and provide an historical supplement to the information presented in this chapter.

IEEE Standard 1209 (*Evaluation and Selection of CASE Tools*) presents a set of guidelines for evaluating CASE tools for "project management processes, predevelopment processes, development processes, postdevelopment processes, and integral processes." *Automated Software Engineering* (Kluwer Academic Publishers, URL: **http://www.wkap.nl**) is a journal that discusses new advances in software tools.

A wide array of CASE tools information is available on the World Wide Web. Every major CASE vendor maintains its own site, and many compendiums of tools have been developed. An extensive CASE tools index has been developed and can be found at:

http://www.cern.ch/PTTOOL/SoftKnow.html

Many major CASE vendors provide Web sites. A comprehensive set of pointers, organized by tool category, can be obtained at:

http://www.qucis.queensu.ca/Software-Engineering/toolcat.html

Direct access to freeware and shareware CASE tools and a directory of CASE Vendor Web sites can be obtained at the CASE Tools page:

http://osiris.sunderland.ac.uk/sst/casehome.html

Electronic copies of various tools integration standards (including PCTE) can be obtained at The MIT Microsystems Lab:

http://www-mtl.mit.edu/CFI/Whole_server.html

Many of the electronic references contained in earlier chapters contain pointers to specific CASE tools.

An up-to-date list of World Wide Web references for software reengineering can be found at: **http://www.rspa.com**

THE ROAD AHEAD

In the 29 chapters that have preceded this one, we have explored a process for software engineering. We have presented management procedures and technical methods, basic principles and specialized techniques, people-oriented activities and tasks that are amenable to automation, paper and pencil notation and CASE tools. We have argued that measurement, discipline, and an overriding focus on quality will result in software that meets the customer's needs, software that is reliable, software that is maintainable, software that is *better*. Yet, we have never promised that software engineering is a panacea.

As we move toward the dawn of a new century, software and systems technologies remain a challenge for every software professional and every company that builds computer-based systems. Max Hopper [HOP90] suggests the current state of affairs when he states:

> Because changes in information technology are becoming so rapid and unforgiving, and the consequences of falling behind are so irreversible, companies will either master the technology or die. . . . Think of it as a technology treadmill. Companies will have to run harder and harder just to stay in place.

Changes in software engineering technology are indeed "rapid and unforgiving," but at the same time progress is often quite slow. By the time a decision is made to adopt a new method (or a new tool), conduct the training necessary to understand its application, and introduce the technology into the software development culture, something new (and even better) has come along, and the process begins anew.

In this chapter, we examine the road ahead. Our intent is not to explore every area of research that holds promise. Nor is it to gaze into a "crystal ball" and prognosticate about the future. Rather, we will explore the scope of change and how change itself will affect the software process in the years ahead.

30.1   THE IMPORTANCE OF SOFTWARE—REVISITED

The importance of computer software can be stated in many ways. In Chapter 1, software was characterized as a differentiator. The function delivered by software differentiates products, systems, and services, and provides competitive advantage in the marketplace. But software is more than a differentiator. The programs, documents, and data that are software help to generate the most important commodity that any individual, business, or government can acquire—information. Pressman and Herron [PRE91] describe software in the following way:

> Computer software is one of only a few key technologies that will have a significant impact on nearly every aspect of modern society during the 1990s. It is a mechanism for automating business, industry, and government, a medium for transferring new technology, a method of capturing valuable expertise for use by others, a means for differentiating one company's products from its competitors, and a window into a corporation's collective knowledge. Software is pivotal to nearly every aspect of business. But in many ways, software is also a hidden technology. We encounter software (often without realizing it) when we travel to work, make any retail purchase, stop at the bank, make a phone call, visit the doctor, or perform any of the hundreds of day-to-day activities that reflect modern life.
>
> Software is pervasive, and yet, many people in positions of responsibility have little or no real understanding of what it really is, how it's built, or what it means to the institutions that they (and it) control. More important, they have little appreciation of the dangers and opportunities that software offers.

The pervasiveness of software leads us to a simple conclusion: Whenever a technology has broad impact—impact that can save lives or endanger them, build businesses or destroy them, inform government leaders or mislead them, it must be "handled with care."

30.2   THE SCOPE OF CHANGE

Change in the technologies that have an impact on computing seems to take on a progression that can be called the *5-5-5 rule*.[1] A fundamentally new concept seems to move from initial idea to a mass market product in about 15 years.[2] During the first 5 years a new idea is formulated and evolves into a prototype that is used to demonstrate basic concepts. The experimental prototype is refined by scientists and engineers over the next 5 years, and the first prod-

---

[1] The ideas for this discussion were first suggested in a presentation [HOR90] by Michael Horner of the Digital Equipment Corporation.

[2] We assume, of course, that the idea is a good one and that sufficient resources are available to nurture it.

ucts (reflecting the new idea) are introduced during this time. The final 5 years are spent introducing the product (and its descendants) to the marketplace. By the end of 15 years (5-5-5), a new idea with technological merit can grow to encompass a multibillion-dollar market (Figure 30.1).[3] Although the 5-5-5 rule is only an approximation, the 15 year time-span from initial idea to major market seems to be a reasonable scale with which we can measure the evolutionary change in the computer business.

The changes in computing over the past four decades have been driven by advances in the "hard sciences"—physics, chemistry, materials science, and engineering. The 5-5-5 rule seems to work reasonably well when new technologies are derived from a basis in the hard sciences. However, during the next few decades, revolutionary advances in computing may well be driven by "soft sciences"—human psychology, neurophysiology, sociology, philosophy, and others. The gestation period for technologies derived from these disciplines is very difficult to predict.

For example, the study of human intelligence has been conducted for centuries and has resulted in only fragmentary understanding of the psychology of thought and the neurophysiology of the brain. However, significant progress has been made over the past 30 years. Information derived from the soft sci-

---

[3]The gestation period for new computing hardware is considerably faster and has been juxtaposed on Figure 30.1. The life of a new processor chip, from inception until obsolescence, is now less than 4 years!

Year in which a new technology can be
expected to reach the product stage:

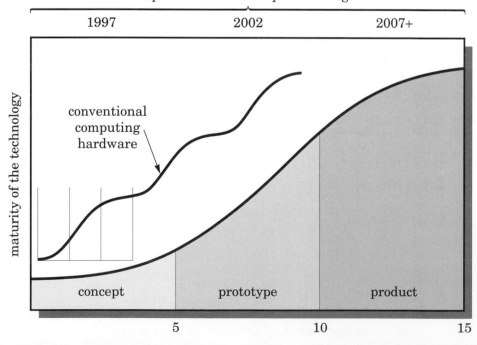

FIGURE 30.1.
The 5-5-5 rule

ences is being used to create a new approach to software—artificial neural networks [WAS89]—that may lead to machine learning and the solution of "fuzzy" problems that have heretofore been impossible to solve using conventional computer-based systems.

The influence of the soft sciences may help mold the direction of computing research in the hard sciences. For example, the design of "future computers" may be guided more by an understanding of brain physiology than by an understanding of conventional microelectronics.

The changes that will affect software engineering over the next decade will be influenced from four simultaneous directions: (1) the people who do the work; (2) the process that they apply; (3) the nature of information; and (4) the underlying computing technology. In the sections that follow, each of these components—people, process, information, and technology—is examined in more detail.

30.3   PEOPLE AND HOW THEY BUILD SYSTEMS

A dilemma faces every company that must build modern computer-based systems. The software required for high-technology systems becomes more and more complex, and the size of resultant programs increases proportionally. There was a time when a program that required 100,000 lines of code was considered to be a large application. Today, the average program for a personal computer application (e.g., word processors, spreadsheets, graphics programs) is often many times that size. Programs built for use in industrial control, computer-aided design, information systems, electronic instrumentation, factory automation, and nearly every other "industry capable" application often exceed 1,000,000 lines of code.[4]

The rapid growth in the size of the "average" program would present us with few problems if it wasn't for one simple fact: As program size increases, the number of people who must work on the program also increases. Experience indicates that as the number of people on a software project team increases, the overall productivity of the group may suffer. One way around this problem is to create a number of software engineering teams (Chapter 3), thereby compartmentalizing people into individual working groups. However, as the number of software engineering teams grows, communication between them becomes as difficult and time-consuming as communication between individuals. Worse, communication (between individuals or teams) tends to be inefficient—that is, too much time is spent transferring too little information content, and all too often, important information "falls into the cracks."

If the software engineering community is to deal effectively with the communication dilemma, the road ahead for software engineers must include radical changes in how individuals and teams communicate with one another. Electronic mail, bulletin boards, and centralized video-conferencing are now

---

[4]With the advent of object-oriented technologies and increased reuse of program components, it is likely that the number of lines of code that must be built "from scratch" will decrease considerably over time. However, there is every indication that the overall size of programs (including reusable components) will continue to grow.

commonplace as mechanisms for connecting a large number of people to an information network. The importance of these tools in the context of software engineering work cannot be overemphasized. With an effective electronic mail or bulletin board system, the problem encountered by a software engineer in New York City may be solved with the help of a colleague in Tokyo. In a very real sense, bulletin boards and Web sites become knowledge repositories that allow the collective wisdom of a large group of technologists to be brought to bear on a technical problem or management issue.

Video personalizes the communication. At its best, it enables colleagues at different locations (or on different continents) to "meet" on a regular basis. But video also provides another benefit. It can be used as a repository for knowledge about the software and to train newcomers on a project.

As hardware and software technologies advance, the very nature of the workplace will change. The following scenario, adapted from Pressman and Herron [PRE91], provides one vision of a software engineer's work environment during the first decade of the twenty-first century:

> "Good morning," you say as you enter the office.
>
> Your workstation screen brightens, a window appears on the screen, an androgynous face appears, and a very human voice says, "Good morning. You have six voice mail messages, two facsimile transmissions and a list of daily action items. Five development tasks are listed." The face and the voice belong to your "agent," an interface program that performs a variety of sophisticated clerical duties. It has been customized to anticipate your needs, recognizes your voice, and can do many things at once—like answer your phone around the clock, look up information, communicate directly with you, and perform other data processing functions. Communication with the agent can be verbal or written, but most people prefer to speak to their agents.
>
> "Show me the action items and development tasks," you say.
>
> Immediately the list of action items appears on the display and the agent begins to read the list aloud, highlighting each item as it is read.
>
> "Silence please, and hold the list," you interrupt. "While you're holding, check any of the voice mail or fax transmissions for key words."
>
> You have just asked the agent to perform an analysis of each incoming message to determine whether it contains any of a set of key words (these could be people's names, places, phone numbers or topics that you deem especially important). As you scan the list of action items on the screen, you see two appointments, a few telephone calls to be made, and an anniversary present to be purchased.
>
> By the time you have scanned the list of action items the agent's face has reappeared on the screen.
>
> It's early and you're not tuned into the work day as yet. Embarrassed (but why should you be, you're communicating with a machine!), you ask, "What did I ask you to do?"
>
> "You asked me to check any of the voice mail or fax transmissions for key words. Would you like a list?

"Yes, but only those with reference to *changes.*" A list of messages appears on your screen. You fix on one item from the list and say "open." In less than a second, a video camera built into the workstation has tracked your eye movement at the time you said "open" and the system has calculated which item you were looking at. You begin to read for a few moments and then stop.

"Please find all modules in the Factory Automation System that have been changed in the last month. Store the names of the modules, the sources of the changes, and the date, and generate an action item for me to review them."

"What version of the system would you like to use?" asks the agent as a scrolling window appears.

"All," you reply.

"O.K." says the agent.

While you're going through your mail the agent will have an "apprentice" perform the task you requested. That is, the agent "spawns" a task to perform configuration management functions. Within seconds, the agent returns to do your bidding. Simultaneously, the first apprentice is searching the CASE repository looking for module names.

"Can I have a word processor?" you ask the agent. A word-processing program, not unlike the best that you see today, appears on the screen. You begin dictating a letter (the keyboard or a handwriting tablet can also be used). The text appears on the screen as you speak each word. While you are dictating, you think of something for the agent to do. Using a pointing device, you click on the agent's window.

"I need a source listing for module **find.inventory.item.** Insert it at the marker I'll note in the text of the document I was working on. Also, call Emily Harrison in system engineering and tell her that I'll be transmitting the document later today."

"O.K." responds the agent. Apprentices are spawned to generate the table and make the call while you return to your dictation.

The environment implied by the above "conversation" will change the work patterns of a software engineer. Instead of a workstation used as a tool, hardware and software become an assistant, performing menial tasks, coordinating human-to-human communication, and in some cases, applying domain-specific knowledge to enhance the engineer's ability.

The acquisition of knowledge is changing in profound ways. On the Internet, a software engineer can subscribe to newsgroups that focus on technology areas of immediate concern. A question posted within a newsgroup precipitates answers from other interested parties around the globe. The World Wide Web provides a software engineer with the world's largest library of research papers and reports, tutorials, commentary, and references in software engineering.[5]

---

[5]See "Further Readings and Other Information Sources" throughout this book for starting points.

If past history is any indication, it is fair to say that people themselves will not change. However, how they communicate, the environment in which they work, how they acquire knowledge, the methods they use, the discipline that they apply—and therefore, the overall culture for software development—will change in significant and even profound ways. Some of the changes that will affect the people who do software engineering work are noted in Figure 30.2.

30.4   THE "NEW" SOFTWARE PROCESS

It is reasonable to characterize the first two decades of software engineering practice as the era of "linear thinking." Fostered by the classic life cycle model, software engineering was approached as a linear activity in which a series of sequential steps could be applied in an effort to solve complex problems. Yet, linear approaches to software development run counter to the way in which most systems are actually built. In reality, complex systems evolve iteratively, even incrementally. It is for this reason that a large segment of the software engineering community is moving toward evolutionary models for software development.

Evolutionary process models recognize that uncertainty dominates most projects; that time lines are often impossibly short; and that iteration provides the ability to deliver an incremental solution, even when a complete product is not possible within the time allotted. Evolutionary models emphasize the need

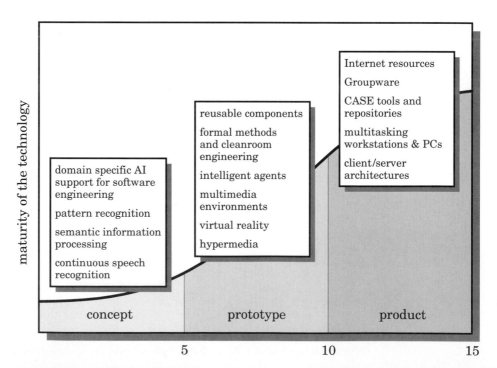

FIGURE 30.2.
Influences on software engineers and their work

for incremental work products, risk analysis, planning and then plan revision, and customer feedback.

But what activities must populate the evolutionary process? Over the past decade, the *Capability Maturity Model (CMM)* developed by the Software Engineering Institute [PAU93] has had a substantial impact on efforts to improve software engineering practices. The CMM has generated much debate (e.g., [BOL91], [GIL96]), and yet, it provides a good indicator of the attributes that must exist when solid software engineering is practiced.

The use of object technologies (Part Four of this book) is a natural outgrowth of the trend toward evolutionary process models. Component-based assembly (if it can be achieved widely) will have a profound impact on software development productivity and product quality. The derivation of reusable program components is a natural consequence of the object-oriented paradigm.

Component reuse provides immediate and compelling benefits (Chapter 26). When reuse is coupled with CASE tools for application prototyping, program increments can be built far more rapidly than through the use of conventional approaches. Prototyping draws the customer into the process. Therefore, it is likely that customers and users will become much more involved in the development of software. This, in turn, may lead to higher end-user satisfaction and better software quality overall.

30.5 NEW MODES FOR REPRESENTING INFORMATION

Over the past two decades, a subtle transition has occurred in the terminology that is used to describe software development work performed for the business community. Twenty years ago, the term "data processing" was the operative phrase for describing the use of computers in a business context. Today, data processing has given way to another phrase—"information technology"—that implies the same thing but presents a subtle shift in focus. The emphasis is not merely to process large quantities of data, but rather to extract meaningful information from this data. Obviously, this was always the intent, but the shift in terminology reflects a far more important shift in management philosophy.

When software applications are discussed today, the words "data" and "information" occur repeatedly. We encounter the word "knowledge" in some artificial intelligence applications, but its use is relatively rare. Virtually no one discusses *wisdom* in the context of computer software applications.

Data is raw information—a collection of facts that must be processed to be meaningful. Information is derived by associating facts within a given context. Knowledge associates information obtained in one context with other information obtained in a different context. Finally, wisdom occurs when generalized principles are derived from disparate knowledge. Each of these four views of "information" is represented schematically in Figure 30.3.

To date, the vast majority of all software has been built to process data or information. Software engineers of the twenty-first century will be equally concerned with systems that process knowledge. Knowledge is two-dimensional. Information collected on a variety of related and unrelated topics is connected

data:
no associativity

information:
associativity within
one context

knowledge:
associativity within
multiple contexts

wisdom:
creation of generalized
principles based on
existing knowledge
from different sources

FIGURE 30.3.
An "information"
spectrum

to form a body of fact that we call knowledge. The key is our ability to associate information from a variety of different sources that may not have any obvious connection to one another and combine it in a way that provides us with some distinct benefit.

To illustrate the progression from data to knowledge, consider census data indicating that the number of births in 1991 in the United States was 4.1 million. This number represents a data value. Relating this piece of data with births for the preceding forty years we can derive a useful piece of information—aging "baby boomers" of the 1950s were making a last gasp effort to have children prior to the end of their childbearing years. This piece of information can then be connected to other seemingly unrelated pieces of information—for example, the current number of elementary school teachers who will retire during the next decade; the number of college students graduating with degrees in primary and secondary education; or the pressure on politicians to hold down taxes and therefore limit pay increases for teachers.

Each of these pieces of information can be combined to formulate a representation of knowledge—there will be significant pressure on the education system in the United States in the late 1990s, and this pressure will continue for over a decade. Using this knowledge, a business opportunity may emerge. There may be significant opportunities to develop new modes of learning that are more effective and less costly than current approaches.

We have been processing data for almost forty years and extracting information for over two decades. One of the most significant challenges facing the software engineering community is to build systems that take the next step along the spectrum—systems that extract knowledge from data and information in a way that is practical and beneficial.

30.6   TECHNOLOGY AS A DRIVER

The people who build and use software, the software engineering process that is applied, and the information that is produced are all affected by advances in hardware and software technology. Historically, hardware has served as the technology driver in computing. A new hardware technology provides potential. Software builders then react to customer demands in an attempt to tap the potential. Figure 30.4 applies the 5-5-5 rule in an attempt to place various hardware technologies in the overall evolutionary cycle. Placing a particular technology on the 5-5-5 curve can be difficult. For example, mobile computing technology has currently evolved to the product stage, but it is not yet a mature market. Hence, it has been placed in the "prototype" stage of technology maturity.

The road ahead for hardware technology is likely to progress along two parallel paths. Along one path, hardware technologies will continue to evolve at a rapid pace. With greater capacity provided by traditional hardware technologies, the demands on software engineers will continue to grow.

But the real changes in hardware technology may occur along another path. The development of nontraditional hardware architectures (e.g., massively parallel machines, optical processors, neural network machines) may cause radical changes in kind of software that we build and fundamental changes in our approach to the software engineering. Since these nontraditional approaches remain in the first segment of the 15 year cycle, it is diffi-

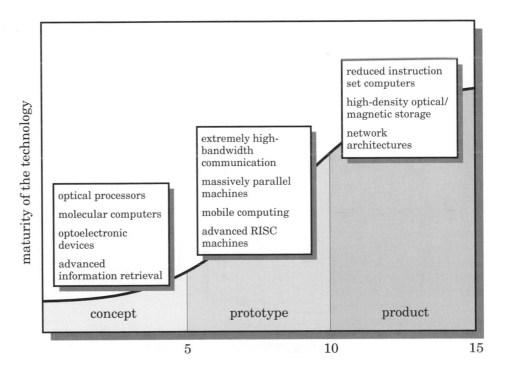

FIGURE 30.4.
Changes in hardware technology

(Chart axis label: maturity of the technology)

reduced instruction set computers

high-density optical/magnetic storage

network architectures

extremely high-bandwidth communication

massively parallel machines

mobile computing

advanced RISC machines

optical processors

molecular computers

optoelectronic devices

advanced information retrieval

concept   prototype   product

5   10   15

cult to determine which will survive to maturity and even more difficult to predict how the world of software will change to accommodate them.

We have already noted that software technology tends to react to changes in hardware technology. Applying the 5-5-5 rule to software technology (Figure 30.5), we find that the software products of today will be joined and possibly displaced by software technologies in the first and second stages of maturity. There is little doubt that the technologies shown in the prototype stage of Figure 30.5 will become extremely important as the twenty-first century dawns. In fact, reuse- and component-based software engineering may offer the best opportunity for order of magnitude improvements in system quality and time to market.

The road ahead for software engineering will be driven by software technologies. As software moves more forcefully into the realm of fuzzy problems (AI, artificial neural networks, expert systems), it is likely that an evolutionary approach to software development will dominate all other paradigms. As object-oriented approaches move to dominate the software community, evolutionary paradigms for software engineering will be modified to accommodate component reuse. "Foundries" that build "software ICs" may become a major new software business. In fact, as time passes, the software business may begin to look very much like the hardware business of today. There may be vendors that build discrete devices (reusable software components), other vendors that build system components (e.g., a set of tools for human–computer interaction), and system integrators that provide solutions for the end user.

Software engineering will change—of that we can be certain. But regardless of how radical the changes are, we can be assured that quality will

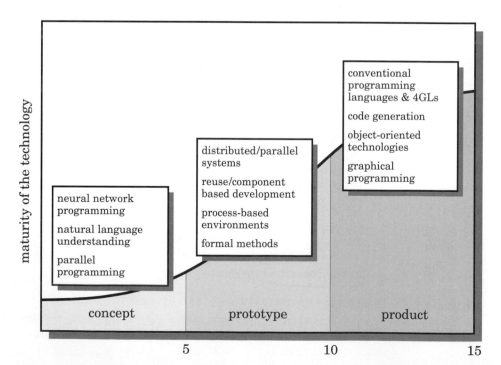

FIGURE 30.5.
Changes in software technology

never lose its importance and that effective analysis and design and competent testing will always have a place in the development of computer-based systems.

30.7   A CONCLUDING COMMENT

It is interesting, and not altogether coincidental, that the fourth edition of this book completes a 5-5-5 rule. The preliminary "concept" (the first edition) was published in 1982; a more refined "prototype" (the second edition) was released in 1987; the not-so-final "product" (the third edition) was introduced in 1992. Now, the fourth edition completes the last 5 year cycle. Over the past 15 years, this book has changed dramatically—in scope, in size, and in content. Like software engineering, it has grown and (hopefully) matured over the years.

An engineering approach to the development of computer software is a philosophy whose time has come. Although debate continues on the right paradigm, the degree of automation, and the most effective methods, the underlying principles of software engineering are now accepted throughout the industry. Why, then, are we only recently seeing their broad adoption?

The answer, I think, lies in the difficulty of technology transition and the cultural change that accompanies it. Even though most of us appreciate the need for an engineering discipline for software, we struggle against the inertia of past practice.

To ease the transition we need many things—a more mature software process, effective methods, powerful tools, acceptance by practitioners and support from managers, and no small dose of education and "advertising." Software engineering has not had the benefit of massive advertising, but as time passes the concept sells itself. In a way, this book is an "advertisement" for the technology.

You may not agree with every approach described in this book. Some of the techniques and opinions are controversial; others must be tuned to work well in different software development environments. It is my sincere hope, however, that *Software Engineering: A Practitioner's Approach* has delineated the problems we face, demonstrated the strength of software engineering concepts, and provided a framework of methods and tools.

As we begin our march into the new millennium, software has become the most important product and the most important industry on the world stage. Its impact and importance have come a long, long way. And yet, a new generation of software developers must meet many of the same challenges that faced earlier generations. Let us hope that the people who meet the challenge—software engineers—will have the wisdom to develop systems that improve the human condition.

REFERENCES

[BOL91]   Bollinger, T., and McGowen, C., "A Critical Look at Software Capability Evaluations," *IEEE Software,* July 1991, pp. 25–41.

[GIL96]   Gilb, T., "What is Level Six?" *IEEE Software,* January 1996, pp. 97–98, 103.

[HOP90]   Hopper, M.D., "Rattling SABRE, New Ways to Compete on Information," *Harvard Business Review,* May/June 1990.

[HOR90]   Horner, M., "Future Directions in CASE," Le Rendez-vous du Génie Logicial, Centre International de Communication Avancée (CICA), Sophia Antipolis, France, May 29, 1990.

[PAU93]   Paulk, M. et al., *Capability Maturity Model for Software,* Software Engineering Institute, Carnegie Mellon University, Pittsburgh, PA, 1993.

[PRE91]   Pressman, R.S., and S.R. Herron, *Software Shock,* Dorset House, 1991.

[WAS89]   Wasserman, P.D., *Neural Computing: Theory and Practice,* Van Nostrand Reinhold, 1989.

PROBLEMS AND POINTS TO PONDER

30.1. Get a copy of this week's major business and news magazines (e.g., *Newsweek, Time, Business Week*). List every article or news item that can be used to illustrate the importance of software.

30.2. Select three "fundamentally new ideas" that have lead to major products. Draw a timeline and determine whether the 5-5-5 rule is too conservative, too optimistic, or right on target.

30.3. Add additional features to the software engineer's environment described in Section 30.3. Draw an annotated sketch that illustrates a software engineer's office in the year 2005.

30.4. Review the discussion of the evolutionary process models in Chapter 2. Do some research and collect recent papers on the subject. Summarize the strengths and weakness of evolutionary paradigms based on experiences outlined in the papers.

30.5. Attempt to develop an example that begins with the collection of raw data and leads to acquisition of information, then knowledge, and finally, wisdom.

30.6. Select any one of the hardware technologies represented at the concept level in Figure 30.4 and write a two or three page paper that presents an overview of the technology. Present the paper to your class.

30.7. Select any one of the software technologies represented at the concept level in Figure 30.5 and write a two or three page paper that presents an overview of the technology. Present the paper to your class.

FURTHER READINGS AND OTHER INFORMATION SOURCES

Books that discuss the road ahead for software and computing span a vast array of technical, scientific, economic, political and social issues. Negroponte's best-selling book (*Being Digital,* Alfred A. Knopf, Inc., 1995) provides a view of computing and its overall impact in the twenty-first century. Naisbitt and Aburdene (*Megatrends 2000,* William Morrow & Co., 1990) provide an intriguing picture of changes that are already well underway. Rich and Waters (*The Programmer's Apprentice,* Addison-Wesley, 1990) present one view of "what to expect in the future of software development." Bowyer (*Ethics and Computing,* IEEE Computer Society Press, 1995) considers the need for software "professionals to act in a socially responsible manner."

Within the more narrow context of computing and software, Allman (*Apprentices of Wonder,* Bantam Books, 1989) describes the potential impact of artificial neural networks—a book that suggests radical changes in what we will mean when the word "software" is used. Stoll (*The Cuckoo's Egg,* Doubleday, 1989) presents a fascinating look into the world of computer networks, hackers, and computer security—topics that are of significant importance as we become an integrated "electronic community." Yourdon (*The Rise and Resurrection of the American Programmer,* Prentice-Hall, 1996) predicts the continuing dominance of the software industry in the United States.

For historical interest, Alvin Toffler (*Powershift,* Bantam Publishers, 1990) completed a trilogy that began with *Future Shock* by discussing the disintegration of well-established power structures that is occurring throughout the world—a shift in power that he attributes directly to software and the information that it produces. Many of his predictions are now reality.

The GartnerGroup publishes detailed reports that project future trends in many areas of computing technologies. Some of these can be obtained at:

http://www.gartner.com/default.html

Byte Magazine is always a good source for information on current and future trends in software and computing in general. Its site can be visited at:

http://www.byte.com

Somewhat more radical views can be obtained by visiting *Hotwired* and *Trajectories* at:

http://www.hotwired.com/login/
http://www.nets.com/site/raw/trajectories.html

An in-depth treatment of technology trends for the twenty-first century can be found at:

http://www.nml.org/resources/misc/nasa_technology_directions/ tablecontents.html

The Institute for Learning Sciences has assembled an intriguing look at the future impact of computing and software on education. It can be found at:

http://www.ils.nwu.edu/ ~ e_for_e/nodes/NODE-269-pg.html

Other discussions of current and future trends in computing can be obtained using the standard search engines on the World Wide Web.